AF323723

ADVANCES IN IMAGE PROCESSING AND UNDERSTANDING

Series in Machine Perception and Artificial Intelligence – Vol. 52

ADVANCES IN IMAGE PROCESSING AND UNDERSTANDING

A Festschrift for Thomas S. Huang

Editors

Alan C. Bovik
University of Texas, Austin, USA

Chang Wen Chen
University of Missouri, Columbia, USA

Dmitry Goldgof
University of South Florida, Tampa, USA

World Scientific
New Jersey • London • Singapore • Hong Kong

Published by

World Scientific Publishing Co. Pte. Ltd.

P O Box 128, Farrer Road, Singapore 912805

USA office: Suite 202, 1060 Main Street, River Edge, NJ 07661

UK office: 57 Shelton Street, Covent Garden, London WC2H 9HE

British Library Cataloguing-in-Publication Data
A catalogue record for this book is available from the British Library.

ADVANCES IN IMAGE PROCESSING AND UNDERSTANDING

ISBN 981-238-091-4

Printed in Singapore by **World Scientific** Printers (S) Pte Ltd

Contents

Developmental Vision, Audition, Robots and Beyond

Juyang Weng, Wey-Shiuan Hwang, and Yilu Zhang
Department of Computer Science and Engineering
Michigan state University
East Lansing, MI 48824

Abstract

It is well recognized that hand programming for vision, audition, and autonomous robots is extremely challenging, especially in partially unknown or complex environments. Although machine learning techniques have been widely used in these fields, fundamental limits remain. Here, we discuss some fundamental problems of the current task-specific paradigm to building complex systems and contrast it with some recent studies in neuroscience that indicates the power of developmental mechanisms in animals that enable autonomous development of cognitive and behavioral capabilities in humans and animals. What do we mean by development? Does it lead us to a more tractable and more systematic approach to vision, audition, robotics and beyond? Motivated by human mental development from infancy to adulthood, the work presented here aims to enable robots to develop their mental skills automatically, through online, real time interactions with its environment. The SAIL developmental robot that has been built at MSU is an early prototype of such a new kind of robots. Our experiments indicated that it appears feasible to develop vision, audition and other cognitive capabilities as well as cognition based behaviors through online interactions by an autonomous robot.

1.1 Introduction

In order to understand the motive of the work, we need to first examine **the** established engineering paradigm. The new approach requires that we **ret**hink the paradigm that we all are used to.

1.1.1 *The traditional manual development paradigm*

The process for developing an artificial system (e.g., an image analysis system) is not automatic — the human designer is in the loop. It follows a traditional, well established paradigm for making a man-made device:

(1) Start with a task: Given a task to be executed by a machine, it is the human engineer who understands the task (not the machine).

(2) Design a task-specific representation: The human engineer translates his understanding into a representation (e.g., giving some symbols or rules that represent particular concepts for the task and the correspondence between the symbols and physical concepts). The representation reflects how the human engineer understands the task.

(3) Programming for the specific task: The human engineer then writes a program (or designs a mechanism) that controls the machine to perform the task using the representation.

(4) Run the program on the machine. If machine learning is used, sensory data are then used to modify the parameters of the task-specific representation. However, since the representation is designed for the specific task only, the machine cannot do anything beyond the pre-designed representation. In fact, it does not even know what it is doing. All it does is run the program.

Although the above manual developmental paradigm is very effective for clean tasks, it has met tremendous difficulties for tasks that cannot be clearly formulated and thus include a large number of unknowns in task specification. If the task performer is a human adult, these unknowns in task specification are dealt with by his cognitive and behavioral capabilities that have been developed since infancy. However, the situation **is** **very** different with a machine that is programmed following the traditional **paradigm**. The machine is not able to automatically generate new representation for environments or tasks that its programmer has not considered at the programming stage.

1.1.2 *Is human vision system totally genetically predetermined?*

One may think that the human brain has an innate representation for the tasks that humans generally do. For example, one may believe that the human vision system and audition system are very much determined by the human genes. However, recent studies of brain plasticity have shown that our brain is not as task-specific as commonly believed. There exist rich studies of brain plasticity in neuroscience, from varying extent of sensory input, to redirecting input, to transplanting cortex, to lesion studies, to sensitive periods. Redirecting input seems illuminating in explaining how much task-specific our brain really is. For example, Mriganka Sur and his coworkers rewired visual input to primate auditory cortex early in life. The target tissue in the auditory cortex, which is supposed to take auditory representation, was found to take on *visual* representation instead [M. Sur et. al. (1986)]. Furthermore, they have successfully trained the animals to form visual tasks using the rewired auditory cortex [S. L. Pallas et. al. (2000)]. Why are the self-organization schemes that guide development in our brain so general that they can deal with either speech or vision, depending on what input it takes through the development? Why are vision systems, audition systems and robots that are programmed using human designed, task-specific representation do not do well in complex, changing, partially unknown environments? What is the fundamental limitation of programming a single-modality system (e.g., vision or speech) without developing a multimodal agent*? What are the self-organization schemes that robots can use to automatically develop mental skills through interactions with the environment? Is it more advantageous to enable robots to automatically develop its mental skills than to program robots using human-specified, task-specific representation? Therefore, it is useful to rethink the traditional engineering paradigm.

---

*By definition, an agent is something that senses and acts.

1.1.3 *The new autonomous development paradigm*

In order to overcome fundamental difficulties that face the computer vision researchers, we have been investigating a new paradigm — the autonomous development paradigm, which is motivated by human mental development from infancy to adulthood. The new paradigm is as follows:

(1) Design body: According to the general ecological condition in which the robot will work (e.g., on-land or underwater), human designers determine the sensors, the effectors and the computational resources that the robot needs and then design a sensor-rich robot body.

(2) Design developmental program: A human programmer designs a developmental program for the robot.

(3) Birth: A human operator turns on the robot whose computer then runs the developmental program.

(4) Develop mind: Humans mentally "raise" the developmental robot by interacting with it. The robot develops its cognitive skills through real-time, online interactions with the environment which includes humans (e.g., let them attend special lessons). Human trainers teach robots through verbal, gestural or written commands in much the same way as parents teach their children. New skills and concepts are autonomously learned by the robots everyday. The software (brain) can be downloaded from robots of different mental ages to be run by millions of other computers, e.g., desktop computers.

A robot that runs a developmental program is called a developmental robot. Such a robot is not simply an incremental learning system that can grow from small to big in terms of its occupied memory size. Such systems have already existed (e.g., some systems that use neural network techniques). Traditional machine learning systems still operate in the manual development mode outlined above but cognitive development requires the new autonomous development mode.

What is the most basic difference between a traditional learning algorithm and a developmental algorithm? Autonomous development does require a capability of learning but it requires something more fundamental. A developmental algorithm must be able to learn tasks that its programmer does not know or even cannot predict. This is because a developmental algorithm, once being designed before robot's"birth," must be able to learn new tasks and new skills without requiring re-programming. The representation of a traditional learning algorithm is designed by a human for a given task; but that for a developmental algorithm must be automatically generated based on its own experience. This basic capability enables humans to learn more and more new tasks and skills using the same developmental program in the human genes.

1.1.4 *The developmental approach*

Since 1996 [J. Weng (1996)], we have been working on a robotic project called SAIL (short for Self-organizing, Autonomous, Incremental Learner) and SHOSLIF is its predecessor [J. Weng (1998)]. The goal of the SAIL project is to *automate* the process of mental *development* for robots, following the new autonomous development paradigm.

An important issue with a developmental robot is what should be programed and what should be learned. The nervous system of a primate may operate at several levels:

(1) Knowledge level (e.g., symbolic skills, thinking skills, general understanding of the world around us, learned part of emotions, and rich consciousness).
(2) Inborn behavior level (e.g., sucking, breathing, pain avoidance and some primitive emotions in neonates). In neurons, they are related to synapses at the birth time.
(3) Representation level (e.g., how neurons grow based on sensory stimuli).
(4) Architecture level (corresponding to anatomy of an organism. E.g., a cortex area is prepared for eyes, if everything is developed normally).
(5) Timing level (the time schedule of neural growth of each area of the nervous system during development).

Studies in neuroscience seem to show that all of the above 5 levels are experience-dependent[†]. In fact, experience can shape all these levels to a very great extent. But it seems that our gened have specified a lot for

---

[†]The literature about this subject is very rich. A good start is "Rethinking innateness" [J. L. Elman et. al. (1997)] (pages 270-314).

6

Levers 2 through 5. The level 1 is made possible by levels 2 through 5 plus experience; but level 1 is not wired in. Thus, levels 2 through 5 seem what a programmer for a developmental algorithm may want to design — but not rigidly — they should be experience dependent. The designer of a developmental robot may have some information about the ecological condition of the environment in which the robots will operate, very much in a way that we know the ecological condition of typical human environment. Such known ecological conditions are very useful for designing a robot body. However, the designer does not known what particular tasks that the robot will end up learning.

According to the above view, our SAIL developmental algorithm has some "innate" reflexive behaviors built-in. At the "birth" time of the SAIL robot, its developmental algorithm starts to run. It runs in real time, through the entire "life span" of the robot. In other words, the design of the developmental program cannot be changed once the robot is "born," no matter what tasks it ends up learning. The robot learns while performing simultaneously. Its innate reflexive behaviors enable it to explore the environment while improving its skills. The human trainer trains the robot by interacting with it, very much like the way a human parent interacts with her infant, letting it seeing around, demonstrating how to reaching objects, teaching commands with the required responses, delivering reward or punishment (pressing "good" or "bad" buttons on the robot), etc. The SAIL developmental algorithm updates the robot memory in real-time according to what was sensed by the sensors, what it did, and what it received as feedback from the human trainer.

1.1.5 *Comparison of approaches*

The new developmental approach is fundamentally different from all the existing approaches. Table 1.1 outlines the major characteristics of existing approaches to constructing an artificial system and the new developmental approach. The developmental approach relieves humans from explicit design of (a) any task-specific representation and knowledge and (b) task-specific behavior representation, behavior modules and their interactions. Some innate behaviors are programmed into a developmental program, but they are not task specific. In other words, that are generally applicable and can be overridden by new, learned behaviors. As indicated by the above table, the developmental approach is the first approach that is not task

Table 1.1   Comparison of Approaches

Approach	Species architecture	World knowledge	System behavior	Task specific
Knowledge-based	programming	manual modeling	manual modeling	Yes
Behavior-based	programming	avoid modeling	manual modeling	Yes
Learning-based	programming	model with parameters	model with parameters	Yes
Evolutionary	genetic search	model with parameters	model with parameters	Yes
Developmental	programming	avoid modeling	avoid modeling	No

specific[‡].

1.1.6 *More tractable*

Is it true that the developmental approach makes system development more difficult? Not really, if the tasks to be executed by the system is very muddy. The task nonspecific nature of a developmental program is a blessing. It relieves human programmer from the daunting tasks of programming task-specific visual recognition, speech recognition, autonomous navigation, object manipulation, etc, for unknown environments. The programming task for a developmental algorithm concentrates on self-organization schemes, which are more manageable by human programmers than the above task-specific programming tasks.

Although the concept of developmental program for a robot is very new [J. Weng (1996)], a lot of well-known self-organization tools can be used in designing a developmental program. In this paper, we informally describe the theory, method and experimental results of our SAIL-2 developmental algorithm tested on the SAIL robot. In the experiments presented here, our SAIL-2 developmental algorithm was able to automatically develop low-level vision and touch-guided motor behaviors.

[‡]In engineering application of the evolutional appoarch, the representation of chromosomes is task specific.

1.2 The SAIL-2 developmental program

We first describe the operation mode of a developmental program: AA-learning mode.

1.2.1 *Mode of operation: AA-learning*

A robot agent M may have several sensors. By definition, the *extroceptive,* *proprioceptive* and *interoceptive* sensors are, respectively, those that sense stimuli from external environment (e.g., visual), relative position of internal control (e.g., arm position), and internal events (e.g., internal clock).

The operational mode of automated development can be termed AA-learning (named after *automated, animal*-like learning *without claiming to be complete*) for a robot agent.

Definition 1.1 A robot agent M conducts AA-learning at discrete time instances, $t = 0, 1, 2, ...$, if the following conditions are met: (I) M has a number of sensors, whose signal at time t is collectively denoted by $x(t)$. (II) M has a number of effectors, whose control signal at time t is collectively denoted by $a(t)$. (III) M has a "brain" denoted by $b(t)$ at time t. (IV) At each time t, the time-varying state-update function f_t updates the "brain" based on sensory input $x(t)$ and the current "brain" $b(t)$:

$$b(t + 1) = f_t(x(t), b(t)) \tag{1.1}$$

and the action-generation function g_t generates the effector control signal based on the updated "brain" $b(t + 1)$:

$$a(t + 1) = g_t(b(t + 1)) \tag{1.2}$$

where $a(t + 1)$ can be a part of the next sensory input $x(t + 1)$. (V) The "brain" of M is closed in that after the birth (the first operation), $b(t)$ cannot be altered directly by human teachers for teaching purposes. It can only be updated according to Eq. (1.1).

As can be seen, AA-learning requires that a system should not have two separate phases for learning and performance. An AA-learning agent learns while performing.

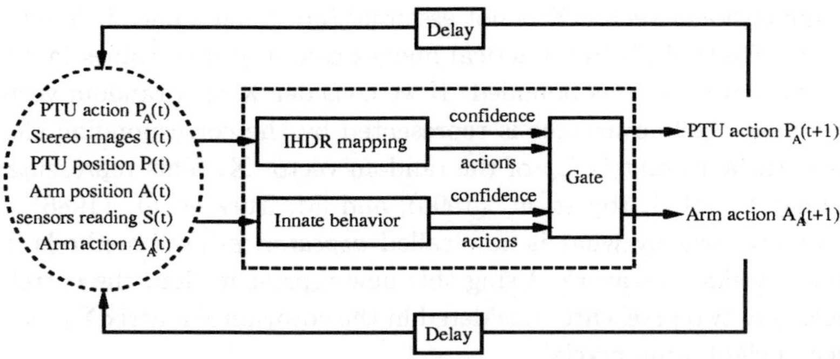

Fig. 1.1 A schematic illustration of the architecture of SAIL-2 robot. The sensory inputs of the current implementation include stereo images, position of the pan-tilt unit (PTU) for each camera, touch/switch sensors, and the position of arm joints, as well as the action of every effector. The gate is to select an appropriate action from either cognitive mapping (learned) or innate behaviors (programmed in) according to the confidence values.

1.2.2 *SAIL-2 developmental architecture*

Fig. 1.1 gives a schematic illustration of the implemented architecture of SAIL-2 robot. The current implementation of the SAIL-2 system includes extroceptive sensors and proprioceptive sensors.

In the SAIL robot, the color stereo images come from two CCD cameras with wide-angle lens. 32 touch/switch sensors are equipped for the robot. Each eye can pan and tilt independently and the neck can turn. A six-joint robot arm is the robot's manipulator.

1.2.3 *Sensory vector representation*

A developmental program may preprocess the sensory signal but human programmer should not directly program feature detectors into the program, since these predefined features are not sufficient to deal with unknown environment. Thus, we must use a very general vector representation that keeps almost all the essential information in the raw sensory signal.

A digital image with r pixel rows and c pixel columns can be represented by a vector in (rc)-dimensional space S without loss of any information. For example, the set of image pixels $\{I(i,j) \mid 0 \leq i < r, 0 \leq j < c\}$ can be written as a vector $\mathbf{X} = (x_1, x_2, \cdots, x_d)^t$ where $x_{ri+j+1} = I(i,j)$ and $d = rc$. The actual mapping from the 2-D position of every pixel to a component in the d-dimensional vector $\mathbf{X}$ is not essential but is fixed once it is selected. Since the pixels of all the practical images can only take values in a finite range, we can view S as bounded. If we consider $\mathbf{X}$ as a random vector in S, the cross-pixel covariance is represented by the corresponding element of the covariance matrix Σ_x of the random vector $\mathbf{X}$. This representation, used early by [M. Kirby et. al. (1990)] and [M. Turk et. al. (1986)], have been widely used by what is now called *appearance-based* methods in the computer vision literature. Using this new representation, the correlation between any two pixels are considered in the covariance matrix Σ_x, not just between neighboring pixels.

1.2.4 *Working memory and long-term memory*

In the SAIL-2 system, the "brain" contains a working memory called state $w(t)$ and long-term memory as a tree. The state keeps information about the previous actions (context). If $x(t)$ is the vector of all sensory inputs and action outputs at time t, the state is a long vector $w(t) = (x(t-1), x(t-2), ..., x(t-k))$, where k is the temporal extent of the state. Typically, to save space, we make k small for sensory input but large for action so that action keeps more context. This gives a way of updating the working memory of the brain by function f_t. The updating of long-term memory (part of f_t) as well as the generation of action (what g_t does) are realized by the IHDR mapping in Fig. 1.1. The IHDR mapping accepts $(x(t), w(t))$ as input and it generates $a(t+1)$ as the output, as well as updating the long term memory of $b(t+1)$, for each time t. The IHDR is a general mapping approximator and will be discussed in the following section.

1.2.5 *Innate and learned behaviors*

The innate behavior is programmed before the machine is "born." The current implemented built-in innate behavior is the motion detection and tracking mechanism for vision. When an object is moving in the scene, the absolute difference of each pixel between two consecutive image frame gives another image called intensity-change image, which is directly mapped to the control of PTU of each eye, using also the IHDR mapping technique but this mapping was generated in a "prenatal" offline learning process. In other words, this offline learning generates innate behaviors in the newborns. Our experience indicated that it is much computationally faster and more reliable to generate innate behavior this way than explicitly finding the regions of moved objects through explicit programming.

The online learned IHDR mapping and the innate behavior may generate PTU motion signal at the same time. The resolution of such conflict is performed by the gate system. In the current implementation, the gate system performs subsumption. Namely, the learned behavior takes the higher priority. Only when the learned behavior does not produce actions, can the innate behavior be executed. A more resilient way of conducting subsumption is to use the confidence of each action source, but this subject is beyond the scope of this article.

1.3 The Mapping Engine: IHDR

One of the most challenging components of a developmental program is the mapping engine, one that maps from sensory input and state (for context) to the effector control signal. Existing neural networks are not applicable due to the following reasons:

(1) The mapping engine must perform one-instance learning. An event represented by only one input sensory frame needs to be learned and recalled. Thus, iterative learning methods such as back-propagation learning or iterative pulling in self-organizing maps are not applicable.

(2) It must adapt to increasing complexity dynamically. It cannot have a fixed number of parameters, like a traditional neural network, since a developmental program must dynamically create system parameters to adapt to regions where an increased complexity behaviors are needed due to, e.g., increased practice for some tasks.

(3) It must deal with the local minima problem. In methods that use traditional feed-forward neural networks with back-propagation learning, typically many instances of neural networks are created in the development stage, each with a different random initial guess. The best performing network is chosen as the final system. However, the mapping engine of the developmental program cannot use this kind of method, due to the real-time requirement. The system must perform on the fly in real time and thus does not allow a separate off-line system evaluation stage. Further, the system that

performs the best now may not necessarily perform best later. We use a coarse-to-fine local fitting scheme.

(4) It must be incremental. The input must be discarded as soon as it is used for updating the memory. It is not possible to keep all the training samples during open-ended incremental development.

(5) It must be able to retain information of some old memory. The effect of old samples used to train an artificial network is lost if these old samples do not appear repeatedly in the stream of training samples.

(6) It must have a very low time complexity so that the response time is within a fraction of second even if the memory size has grown very large. Thus, any slow learning algorithm is not applicable here. Although the entire developmental process of a robot can extend to a long time period, the response time for each sensory input must be very short, e.g., a fraction of a second.

These considerations have been taken into account in our IHDR mapping engine described below.

1.3.1 *Regression*

Therefore, a major technical challenge is to incrementally generate the IHDR mapping. In the work reported here, online training is done by supplying desired action at the right time. When action is not supplied, the system generates its own actions using the IHDR mapping updated so far. In other words, the robot runs in real time. When the trainer likes to teach the robot, he pushes the effector, through the corresponding touch sensor that directly drives the corresponding motor. Otherwise, the robot runs on its own, performing.

Thus, the major problem is to approximate a mapping $h : \mathcal{X} \mapsto \mathcal{Y}$ from a set of training samples $\{(x_i, y_i) \mid x_i \in \mathcal{X}, \ y_i \in \mathcal{Y}, \ i = 1, 2, \ldots, n\}$, that arrives one pair (x_i, y_i) at a time, where $y_i = *$ if y_i is not given (in this case, the approximator will produce estimated y_i corresponding to x_i). The mapping must be updated for each (x_i, y_i). If y_i was a class label, we could use linear discriminant analysis (LDA) [K. Fukunaga (1990)] since the within-class scatter and between-class scatter matrices are all defined. However, if y_i is a numerical output, which can take any value for each input component, it is a challenge to figure out an effective discriminant analysis

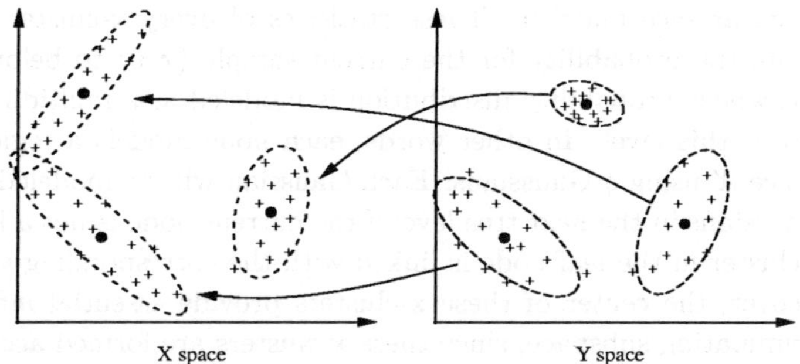

Fig. 1.2 Y-clusters in space $\mathcal{Y}$ and the corresponding x-clusters in space $\mathcal{X}$. The first and the second order statistics are updated for each cluster.

procedure that can disregard input components that are either irrelevant to output or contribute little to the output. We introduce a new hierarchical statistical modeling method. Consider the mapping $h : \mathcal{X} \mapsto \mathcal{Y}$, which is to be approximated by a regression tree, called incremental hierarchical discriminating regression (IHDR) tree, for the high dimensional space $\mathcal{X}$. Our goal is to automatically derive discriminating features although no class label is available (other than the numerical vectors in space $\mathcal{Y}$). In addition, for real-time requirement, we must process each sample (x_i, y_i) to update the IHDR tree using only a minimal amount of computation (e.g., in 0.05 second).

1.3.2 *Clustering in both input and output space*

Two types of clusters are incrementally updated at each node of the IHDR tree — y-clusters and x-clusters, as shown in Fig. 1.2. The y-clusters are clusters in the output space $\mathcal{Y}$ and x-clusters are those in the input space $\mathcal{X}$. There are a maximum of q (e.g., $q = 10$) clusters of each type at each node. The q y-clusters determine the virtual class label of each arriving sample (x, y) based on its y part. Each x-cluster approximates the sample population in $\mathcal{X}$ space for the samples that belong to it. It may spawn a child node from the current node if a finer approximation is required. At each node, y in (x, y) finds the nearest y-cluster in Euclidean distance and updates (pulling) the center of the y-cluster. This y-cluster indicates which corresponding x-cluster the input (x, y) belongs to. Then, the x part of (x, y) is used to update the statistics of the x-cluster (the mean vector and the covariance matrix). These statistics of every x-cluster are used to estimate the probability for the current sample (x, y) to belong to the x-cluster, whose probability distribution is modeled as a multidimensional Gaussian at this level. In other words, each node models a region of the input space $\mathcal{X}$ using q Gaussians. Each Gaussian will be modeled by more small Gaussians in the next tree level if the current node is not a leaf node. Each x-cluster in the leaf node is linked with the corresponding y-cluster.

Moreover, the center of these x-clusters provide essential information for discriminating subspace, since these x-clusters are formed according to virtual labels in $\mathcal{Y}$ space. We define a discriminating subspace as the linear space that passes through the centers of these x-clusters. A total of q centers of the q x-clusters give $q - 1$ discriminating features which span $(q - 1)$-dimensional discriminating space. A probability-based distance called size-dependent negative-log-likelihood (SNLL) [W. Hwang et. al. (1999)] is computed from x to each of the q x-clusters to determine which x-cluster should be further searched. If the probability is high enough, the sample (x, y) should further search the corresponding child (maybe more than one but with an upper bound k) recursively, until the corresponding terminal nodes are found.

The algorithm incrementally builds an IHDR tree from a sequence of training samples. The deeper a node is in the tree, the smaller the variances of its x-clusters are. When the number of samples in a node is too small to give a good estimate of the statistics of q x-clusters, this node is a leaf node. If y is not given in the input, the x part is used to search the tree, until the nearest x-cluster in a leaf node is find. The center of the corresponding y-cluster is the produced estimated y output[§].

Why do we use a tree? Two major reasons: (1) automatically deriving features (instead of human defining features) and (2) fast search. The number of x-clusters in the tree is a very large number. The y-clusters allow the search to disregard input components that are not related to the output. For example, if some sensors are not related to the action of the humanoid, under a context, these sensors are disregarded automatically by the IHDR mapping, since each node partition the samples in $q - 1$ dimensional discriminating subspace, instead of in the original input space. This subspace is the automatically derived feature space for the samples in

---

[§]In each leaf node, we allow more than q clusters to fully use the samples available at each leaf node.

the subtree. Further, the tree allows a large portion of far-away clusters to disregarded from consideration. This results in the well-known logarithmic time complex for tree retrieval: $O(\log m)$ where m is the number of leaf nodes in the tree.

1.3.3 *IHDR procedure*

The algorithm incrementally builds a tree from a sequence of training samples. The deeper a node is in the tree, the smaller the variances of its x-clusters are. When the number of samples in a node is too small to give a good estimate of the statistics of q x-clusters, this node is a leaf node. The following is the outline of the incremental algorithm for tree building (also tree retrieval when y is not given).

Procedure 1 `Update-node`: Given a node N and (x, y) where y is either given or not given, update the node N using (x, y) recursively. Output: top matched terminal nodes. The parameters include: k which specifies the upper bound in the width of parallel tree search; δ_x the sensitivity of the IHDR in $\mathcal{X}$ space as a threshold to further explore a branch; and c representing if a node is on the central search path. Each returned node has a flag c. If $c = 1$, the node is a central cluster and $c = 0$ otherwise.

(1) Find the top matched x-cluster in the following way. If $c = 0$ skip to step (2). If y is given, do (a) and (b); otherwise do (b).

    (a) Update the mean of the y-cluster nearest y in Euclidean distance by using amnesic averages. Update the mean and the covariance matrix of the x-cluster corresponding to the y-cluster by using amnesic average.

    (b) Find the x-cluster nearest x according to the probability-based distances. The central x-cluster is this x-cluster. Update the central x-cluster if it has not been updated in (a). Mark this central x-cluster as active.

(2) For all the x-clusters of the node N, compute the probability-based distances for x to belong to each x-cluster.

(3) Rank the distances in increasing order.

(4) In addition to the central x-cluster, choose peripheral x-clusters according to increasing distances until the distance is larger than δ_x or a total of k x-clusters have been chosen.

(5) Return the chosen x-clusters as active clusters.

From the above procedure, we can observe the following points. (a) When y is given, the corresponding x-cluster is updated, although this x-cluster is not necessarily the one on the central path from which the tree is explored. Thus, we may update two x-clusters, one corresponding to the given y, the other being the one used for tree exploration. The update for the former is an attempt to pull it to the right location. The update for the latter is an attempt to record the fact that the central x-cluster has hit this x-cluster once. (b) No matter y is given or not, the x-cluster along the central path is always updated. (c) Only the x-clusters along the central path are updated, other peripheral x-clusters are not. We would like to avoid, as much as possible, storing the same sample in different brother nodes.

Procedure 2 Update-tree: Given the root of the tree and sample (x, y), update the tree using (x, y). If y is not given, estimate y and the corresponding confidence. The parameters include: k which specifies the upper bound in the width of parallel tree search.

(1) From the root of the tree, update the node by calling Update-node using (x,y).
(2) For every active cluster received, check if it points to a child node. If it does, mark it inactive and explore the child node by calling Update-node. At most q^2 active x-clusters can be returned this way if each node has at most q children.
(3) The new central x-cluster is marked as active.
(4) Mark additional active x-clusters according to the smallest probability-based distance d, up to k total if there are that many x-clusters with $d \leq \delta_x$.
(5) Do the above steps 2 through 4 recursively until all the resulting active x-clusters are all terminal.
(6) Each leaf node keeps samples (or sample means) $(\hat{x}_i, \hat{y}_i)$ that belong to it. If y is not given, the output is $\hat{y}_i$ if $\hat{x}_i$ is the nearest neighbor among these samples. If y is given, do the following: If $\|y - \hat{y}_i\|$ is smaller than an error tolerance, (x, y) updates $(\hat{x}_i, \hat{y}_i)$ only. Otherwise, (x, y) is a new sample to keep in the leaf.
(7) If the current situation satisfies the spawn rule, i.e. the number of samples exceeds the number required for estimating statistics in new child, the top-matched x-cluster in the leaf node along the

central path spawns a child which has q new x-clusters. All the internal nodes are fixed in that their clusters do not further update using future samples so that their children do not get temporarily inconsistent assignment of samples.

The above incrementally constructed tree gives a coarse-to-fine probability model. If we use Gaussian distribution to model each x-cluster, this is a *hierarchical version* of the well-known mixture-of-Gaussian distribution models: the deeper the tree is, the more Gaussians are used and the finer are these Gaussians. At shallow levels, the sample distribution is approximated by a mixture of large Gaussians (with large variances). At deep levels, the sample distribution is approximated by a mixture of many small Gaussians (with small variances). The multiple search paths guided by probability allow a sample x that falls in-between two or more Gaussians at each shallow level to explore the tree branches that contain its neighboring x-clusters. Those x-clusters to which the sample (x, y) has little chance to belong are excluded for further exploration. This results in the well-known logarithmic time complex for tree retrieval: $O(\log m)$ where m is the number of leaf nodes in the tree, assuming that the number of samples in each leaf node is bounded above by a constant.

1.3.4 *Amnesic average*

In incremental learning, the initial centers of each state clusters are largely determined by early input data. When more data are available, these centers move to more appropriate locations. If these new locations of the cluster centers are used to judge the boundary of each cluster, the initial input data were typically incorrectly classified. In other words, the center of each cluster contains some earlier data that do not belong to this cluster. To reduce the effect of these earlier data, the amnesic average can be used to compute the center of each cluster. The amnesic average can also track dynamic change of the input environment better than a conventional average.

The average of n input data $x_1, x_2, ..., x_n$ can be recursively computed from the current input data x_n and the previous average $\bar{x}^{(n-1)}$ by equation (1.3):

$$\bar{x}^{(n)} = \frac{(n-1)\bar{x}^{(n-1)} + x_n}{n} = \frac{n-1}{n}\bar{x}^{(n-1)} + \frac{1}{n}x_n. \qquad (1.3)$$

In other words, the previous average $\bar{x}^{(n)}$ gets a weight $n/(n+1)$ and the new input x_{n+1} gets a weight $1/(n+1)$. These two weights sum to one. The recursive equation Eq. (1.3) gives an equally weighted average. In amnesic average, the new input gets more weight than old inputs as given in the following expression: $\bar{x}^{(n+1)} = \frac{n-l}{n+1}\bar{x}^{(n)} + \frac{1+l}{n+1}x_{n+1}$, where l is a parameter.

The amnesic average can also be applied to the recursive computation of a covariance matrix Γ_x from incrementally arriving samples: $x_1, x_2, ..., x_n, ...$ where x_i is a column vector for $i = 1, 2, ...$ The unbiased estimate of the covariance matrix from these n samples $x_1, x_2, ..., x_n$ is given in a batch form as

$$\frac{1}{n-1}\sum_{i=1}^{n}(x_i - \bar{x})(x_i - \bar{x})^T \tag{1.4}$$

with $n > 1$, where $\bar{x}$ is the mean vector of the n samples. Using the amnesic average, $\bar{x}^{(n+1)}$, up to the $(n+1)$-th sample, we can compute the amnesic covariance matrix up to the $(n+1)$-th sample as

$$\Gamma_x^{(n+1)} = \frac{n-1-l}{n}\Gamma_x^{(n)} + \frac{1+l}{n}(x_{n+1} - \bar{x}^{(n+1)})(x_{n+1} - \bar{x}^{(n+1)})^T \tag{1.5}$$

for $n > l + 1$. When $n \leq l + 1$, we may use the batch version as in expression (1.4). Even with a single sample x_1, the corresponding covariance matrix should not be estimated as a zero vector, since x_1 is never exact if it is measured from a physical event. For example, the initial variance matrix $\Gamma_x^{(1)}$ can be estimated as $\sigma^2 I$, where σ^2 is the expected digitization noise in each component and I is the identity matrix of the appropriate dimensionality.

1.3.5 *Discriminating subspace*

Due to a very high input dimensionality (typically at least a few thousands), for computational efficiency, we should not represent data in the original input space $\mathcal{X}$. Further, for better generalization characteristics, we should use discriminating subspaces in which input components that are irrelevant to output are disregarded.

We first consider x-clusters. Each x-cluster is represented by its mean as its center and the covariance matrix as its size. However, since the dimensionality of the space $\mathcal{X}$ is typically very high, it is not practical to directly keep the covariance matrix. If the dimensionality of $\mathcal{X}$ is 3000, for example, each covariance matrix requires $3000 \times 3000 = 9,000,000$ numbers! We adopt a more efficient method that uses subspace representation.

As explained in Section 1.3.1, each internal node keeps up to q x-clusters. The centers of these q x-clusters are denoted by

$$C = \{c_1, c_2, ..., c_q \mid c_i \in \mathcal{X}, i = 1, 2, ..., q\}. \tag{1.6}$$

The locations of these q centers tell us the subspace $\mathcal{D}$ in which these q centers lie. $\mathcal{D}$ is a discriminating space since the clusters are formed based on the clusters in output space $\mathcal{Y}$.

The discriminating subspace $\mathcal{D}$ can be computed as follow. Suppose that the number of samples in cluster i is n_i and thus the grand total of samples is $n = \sum_{i=1}^{q} n_i$. Let $\bar{C}$ be the mean of all the q x-cluster centers. $\bar{C} = \frac{1}{n} \sum_{i=1}^{q} n_i c_i$ The set of scatter vectors from their center then can be defined as $s_i = c_i - \bar{C}$, $i = 1, 2, ..., q$. These q scatter vectors are not linearly independent because their sum is equal to a zero vector. Let S be the set that contains these scatter vectors: $S = \{s_i \mid i = 1, 2, ..., q\}$. The subspace spanned by S, denoted by span(S), consists of all the possible linear combinations from the vectors in S, as shown in Fig. 1.3.5.

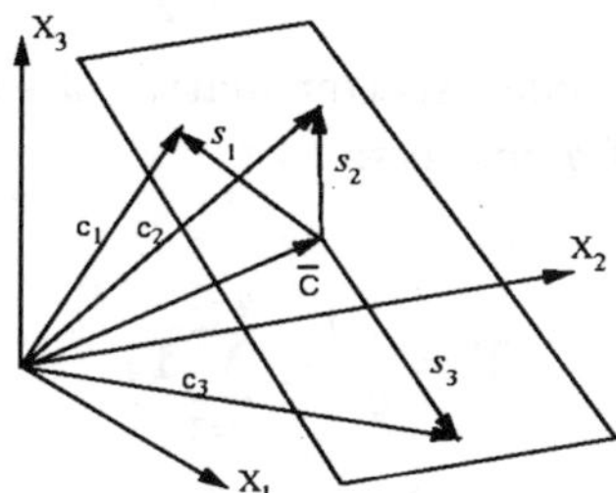

Fig. 1.3 The linear manifold represented by $\bar{C} + \text{span}(S)$, the spanned space from scatter vectors translated by the center vector $\bar{C}$.

The orthonormal basis $a_1, a_2, ..., a_{q-1}$ of the subspace span(S) can be constructed from the radial vectors $s_1, s_2, ..., s_q$ using the *Gram-Schmidt Orthogonalization* (GSO) procedure. The number of basis vectors that can be computed by the GSO procedure is the number of linearly independent radial vectors in S.

Given a vector $x \in \mathcal{X}$, we can compute its scatter part $s = x - \bar{C}$. Then compute the projection of x onto the linear manifold by $f = M^T s$, where $M = [a_1, a_2, \ldots, a_{q-1}]$. We call the vector f the discriminating features of

x in the linear manifold S. The mean and the covariance of the clusters then are computed on the discriminating subspace.

1.3.6 *The probability-based metric*

Let us consider the negative-log-likelihood (NLL) defined from Gaussian density of dimensionality $q - 1$:

$$G(x, c_i) = \frac{1}{2}(x - c_i)^T \Gamma_i^{-1}(x - c_i) + \frac{q-1}{2}\ln(2\pi) + \frac{1}{2}\ln(|\Gamma_i|). \qquad (1.7)$$

We call it Gaussian NLL for x to belong to the cluster i. c_i and Γ_i are the cluster sample mean and sample covariance matrix, respectively, computed using the amnesic average in Section 1.3.4. Similarly, we define Mahalanobis NLL and Euclidean NLL as:

$$M(x, c_i) = \frac{1}{2}(x - c_i)^T \Gamma^{-1}(x - c_i) + \frac{q-1}{2}\ln(2\pi) + \frac{1}{2}\ln(|\Gamma|), \qquad (1.8)$$

$$E(x, c_i) = \frac{1}{2}(x - c_i)^T \rho^2 I^{-1}(x - c_i) + \frac{q-1}{2}\ln(2\pi) + \frac{1}{2}\ln(|\rho^2 I|). \qquad (1.9)$$

where Γ is the within-class scatter matrix of each node — the average of covariance matrices of q clusters:

$$\Gamma = \frac{1}{q-1}\sum_{i=1}^{q-1}\Gamma_i \qquad (1.10)$$

computed using the same technique of the amnesic average.

Suppose that the input space is $\mathcal{X}$ and the discriminating subspace for an internal node is $\mathcal{D}$. The Euclidean NLL treats all the dimensions in the discriminating subspace $\mathcal{D}$ the same way, although some dimensionalities can be more important than others. It has only one parameter ρ to estimate. Thus it is the least demanding among the three NLL in the richness of observation required. When very few samples are available for all the clusters, the Euclidean likelihood is the suited likelihood.

The Mahalanobis NLL uses within-class scatter matrix Γ computed from all the samples in all the q x-clusters. Using Mahalanobis NLL as the weight for subspace $\mathcal{D}$ is equivalent to using Euclidean NLL in the basis computed from Fisher's LDA procedure [K. Fukunaga (1990)] [D. L. Swet et. al. (1986)]. It decorrelates all dimensions and weights each dimension using a different weight. The number of parameters in Γ is $q(q-1)/2$, and thus, the Mahalanobis NLL requires more samples than the Euclidean NLL.

The Mahalanobis NLL does not treat different x-lusters differently because it uses a single within-class scatter matrix Γ for all the q x-clusters in each internal node. For Gaussian NLL, $L(x, c_i)$ in Eq.(1.7) uses the covariance matrix Γ_i of x-cluster i. In other words, Gaussian NLL not only decorrelates the correlations but also applied a different weight at different location along each rotated basis. However, it requires that each x-cluster has enough samples to estimate the $(q-1) \times (q-1)$ covariance matrix. It thus is the most demanding on the number of observations. Note that the decision boundary of the Euclidean NLL and the Mahalanobis NLL is linear but that by the Gaussian NLL is quadratic.

1.3.7 *The transition among different likelihoods*

We would like to use the Euclidean NLL when the number of samples in the node is small. Gradually, as the number of samples increases, the within-class scatter matrix of q x-clusters are better estimated. Then, we would like to use the Mahalanobis NLL. When a cluster has very rich observations, we would like to use the full Gaussian NLL for it. We would like to make an automatic transition when the number of samples increases. We define the number of samples n_i as the measurement of maturity for each cluster i. $n = \sum_{i=1}^{q} n_i$ is the total number of samples in a node.

For the three types of NLLs, we have three matrices, $\rho^2 I$, Γ, and Γ_i. Since the reliability of estimates are well indicated by the number of samples, we consider the number of scales received to estimate each parameter, called the number of scales per parameter (NSPP), in the matrices. The NSPP for $\rho^2 I$ is $(n-1)(q-1)$, since the first sample does not give any estimate of the variance and each independent vector contains $q-1$ scales. For the Mahalanobis NLL, there are $(q-1)q/2$ parameters to be estimated in the (symmetric) matrix Γ. The number of independent vectors received is $n - q$ because each of the q x-cluster requires a vector to form its mean vector. Thus, there are $(n-q)(q-1)$ independent scalars. The NSPP for the matrix Γ is $\frac{(n-q)(q-1)}{(q-1)q/2} = \frac{2(n-q)}{q}$. To avoid the value to be negative when $n < q$, we take NSPP for Γ to be $\max\left\{\frac{2(n-q)}{q}, 0\right\}$. Similarly, the NSPP for

Γ_i for the Gaussian NLL is $\frac{1}{q} \sum_{i=1}^{q} \frac{2(n_i-1)}{q} = \frac{2(n-q)}{q^2}$. Table 1.2 summarizes the result of the NSPP values of the above derivation.

Table 1.2   Characteristics of three types of scatter matrices

Type	Euclidean $\rho^2 I$	Mahalanobis Γ	Gaussian Γ_i
NSPP	$(n-1)(q-1)$	$\frac{2(n-q)}{q}$	$\frac{2(n-q)}{q^2}$

A bounded NSPP is defined to limit the growth of NSPP so that other matrices that contain more scalars can take over when there are a sufficient number of samples for them. Thus, the bounded NSPP for $\rho^2 I$ is $b_e = \min\{(n-1)(q-1), n_s\}$, where n_s denotes the soft switch point for the next more complete matrix to take over. To estimate n_s, we consider a serious of random variables drawn independently from a distribution with a variance σ^2, the expected sample mean of n random variables has a expected variance $\sigma^2/(n-1)$. We can choose a switch confidence value α for $1/(n-1)$. When $1/(n-1) = \alpha$, we consider that the estimate can take about a 50% weight. Thus, $n = 1/\alpha + 1$. As an example, let $\alpha = 0.05$ meaning that we trust the estimate with 50% weight when the expected variance of the estimate is reduced to about 5% of that of a single random variable. This is like a confidence value in hypothesis testing except that we do not need an absolute confidence, relative one suffices. We get then $n = 21$, which leads to $n_s = 21$.

The same principle applies to Mahalanobis NLL and its bounded NSPP for Γ is $b_m = \min\left\{\max\left\{\frac{2(n-q)}{q}, 0\right\}, n_s\right\}$. It is worth noting that the NSPP for the Gaussian NLL does not need to be bounded, since among our models it is the best estimate with increasing number of samples beyond. Thus the bounded NSPP for Gaussian NLL is $b_g = \frac{2(n-q)}{q^2}$.

How do we realize automatic transition? We define a *size-dependent scatter matrix* (SDSM) W_i as a weighted sum of three matrices:

$$W_i = w_e \rho^2 I + w_m \Gamma + w_g \Gamma_i \tag{1.11}$$

where $w_e = b_e/b$, $w_m = b_m/b$, $w_g = b_g/b$ and b is a normalization factor so that these three weights sum to 1: $b = b_e + b_m + b_g$. Using this size-dependent scatter matrix W_i, the *size-dependent negative log likelihood*

(SDNLL) for x to belong to the x-cluster with center c_i is defined as

$$L(x, c_i) = \frac{1}{2}(x - c_i)^T W_i^{-1}(x - c_i) + \frac{q-1}{2}\ln(2\pi) + \frac{1}{2}\ln(|W_i|). \qquad (1.12)$$

With b_e, b_m, and b_g change automatically, $(L(x, c_i)$ transit smoothly through the three NLLs. It is worth noting the relation between LDA and SDNLL metric. LDA in space $\mathcal{D}$ with original basis η gives a basis ϵ for a subspace $\mathcal{D}' \subseteq \mathcal{D}$. This basis ϵ is a properly oriented and scaled version for $\mathcal{D}$ so that the within-cluster scatter in $\mathcal{D}'$ is a unit matrix [K. Fukunaga (1990)] (Sections 2.3 and 10.2). In other words, all the basis vectors in ϵ for D' are already weighted according to the within-cluster scatter matrix Γ of $\mathcal{D}$. If $\mathcal{D}'$ has the same dimensionality as $\mathcal{D}$, the Euclidean distance in $\mathcal{D}'$ on ϵ is equivalent to the Mahalanobis distance in $\mathcal{D}$ on η, up to a global scale factor. However, if the covariance matrices are very different across different x-clusters and each of them has enough samples to allow a good estimate of individual covariance matrix, LDA in space $\mathcal{D}$ is not as good as Gaussian likelihood because covariance matrices of all X-clusters are treated as the same in LDA while Gaussian likelihood takes into account of such differences. The SDNLL in (1.12) allows automatic and smooth transition between three different types of likelihood, Euclidean, Mahalanobis and Gaussian, according to the predicted effectiveness of each likelihood.

1.3.8 *Computational considerations*

The matrix weighted squared distance from a vector $x \in \mathcal{X}$ to each X-cluster with center c_i is defined by

$$d^2(x, c_i) = (x - c_i)^T W_i^{-1}(x - c_i) \qquad (1.13)$$

which is the first term of Eq.(1.12).

This distance is computed only in $(q-1)$-dimensional space using the basis M. The SDSM W_i for each x-cluster in then only a $(q-1) \times (q-1)$ square symmetric matrix, of which only $q(q-1)/2$ parameters need to be estimated. When $q = 6$, for example, this number is 15.

Given a column vector v represented in the discriminating subspace with an orthonormal basis whose vectors are the columns of matrix M, the representation of v in the original space $\mathcal{X}$ is $x = Mv$.

To compute the matrix weighted squared distance in Eq.(1.13), we use a numerically efficient method, Cholesky factorization [G. H. Golub et. al.

24

(1989)] (Sec. 4.2). The Cholesky decomposition algorithm computes a lower triangular matrix L from W so that W is represented by $W = LL^T$. With the lower triangular matrix L, we first compute the difference vector from the input vector x and each x-cluster center c_i: $v = x - c_i$. The matrix weighted squared distance is given by

$$d^2(x, c_i) = v^T W_i^{-1} v = v^T (LL^T)^{-1} v = (L^{-1}v)^T(L^{-1}v). \qquad (1.14)$$

We solve for y in the linear equation $Ly = v$ and then $y = L^{-1}v$ and $d^2(x, c_i) = (L^{-1}v)^T(L^{-1}v) = \|y\|^2$. Since L is a lower triangular matrix, the solution for y in $Ly = v$ is trivial since we simply use the backsubtitution method as described in [W. H. Press et. al. (1986)] (page 42).

1.4 Experiments

1.4.1 *SAIL robot*

Fig. 1.4 **The SAIL robot built at the Pattern Recognition and Image Processing Laboratory at Michigan State University.**

A human-size robot called SAIL was assembled at MSU, as shown in Fig. 1.4. SAIL robot's "neck" can turn. Each of its two "eyes" is controlled by a fast pan-tilt head. Its torso has 4 pressure sensors to sense push actions and force. It has 28 touch sensors on its arm, neck, head, and bumper to allow human to teach how to act by direct touch. Its drive-base is adapted from a wheelchair and thus the SAIL robot can operate both indoor

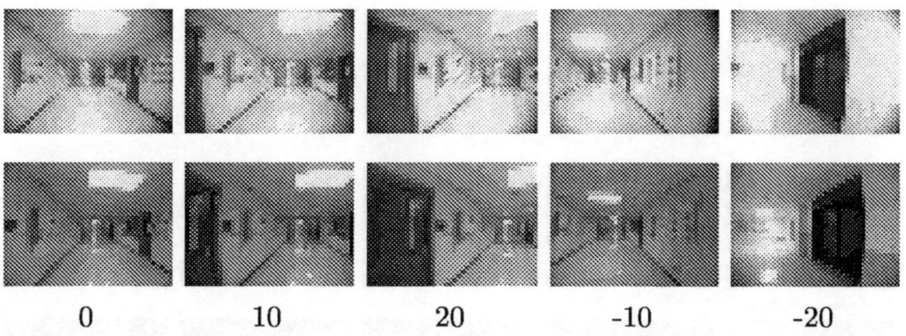

Fig. 1.5   A subset of images used in autonomous navigation. The number right below the image shows the needed heading direction (in degrees) associated with that image.   The first row shows the images from the right camera while the second row shows those from the left camera.

and outdoor. Its main computer is a high-end dual-processor dual-bus PC workstation with 512MB RAM and an internal 27GB three-drive disk array for real-time sensory information processing, real-time memory recall and update as well as real-time effector controls. This platform is being used to test the architecture and the developmental algorithm outlined here.

1.4.2   *Autonomous navigation*

At each time instance, the vision-based navigation system accepts a pair of stereo images, updates its states which contains past sensory inputs and actions, and then outputs the control signal C to update the heading direction of the vehicle. In the current implementation, the state transition function f_t in Eq. 1.1 is programmed so that the current state includes a vector that contains the sensory input and past heading direction of last T cycles. The key issue then is to approximate the action generation function g_t in Eq. 1.2.   This is a very challenging approximation task since the function to be approximated is for a very high dimensional input space and the real application requires the navigator to perform in real time.

We applied our IHDR algorithm to this challenging problem. Some of the example input images are shown in Fig 1.5. We first applied the IHDR algorithm to simulate the actual vision-based navigation problem. Totally 2106 color stereo images with the corresponding heading directions were used for training. The resolution of each image is 30 by 40. The input dimensionality of the IHDR algorithm is $30 \times 40 \times 3 \times 2 = 7200$, where 3 is

Fig. 1.6   A subset of images which were inputs to guide the robot turn. Row one and three show the images from left camera. The second and fourth rows show the images taken from right camera.

the length of history in state. We used the other 2313 stereo images to test the performance of the trained system. Fig 1.7 shows the error rate versus the number of training epochs, where each epoch corresponds to the feeding of the entire training sensory sequence once. As shown even after the first epoch, the performance of the IHDR tree is already reasonably good. With the increase of the number of epochs, we observed the improvements of the error rate. The error rate for the test set is 9.4% after 16 epochs.

The IHDR algorithm then was applied on the real training/testing experiment. The SAIL robot was trained interactively by a human trainer using the force sensors equipped on the body of the robot. The forces sensed by the sensors are translated to the robot heading direction and speed. The training is on-line in real time. The trainer pushed just two force sensors to guide the robot to navigate through the corridor of about 3.5 meter wide in the Engineering building of Michigan State University. The navigation site includes a turn, two straight sections which include a corridor door. Then trips were found sufficient to reach a reliable behavior. During the training, the IHDR algorithm receives both the color stereo images as input and

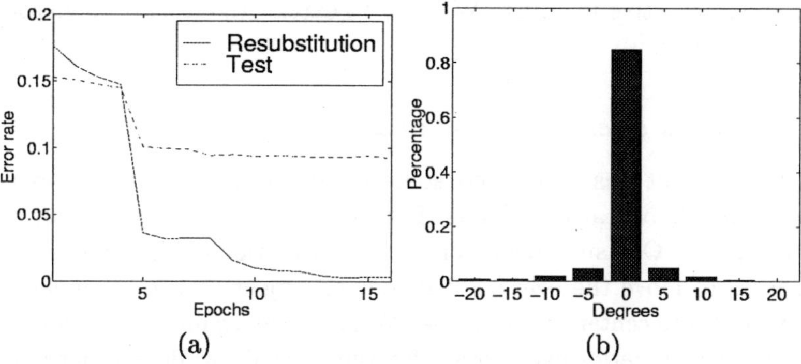

(a)   (b)

Fig. 1.7   The performance for autonomous navigation. (a) The plot for the error rates vs. epochs. The solid line represents the error rates for resubstitution test. The dash line represents the error rates for the testing set. (b) The error histogram of the testing set after 16 epochs.

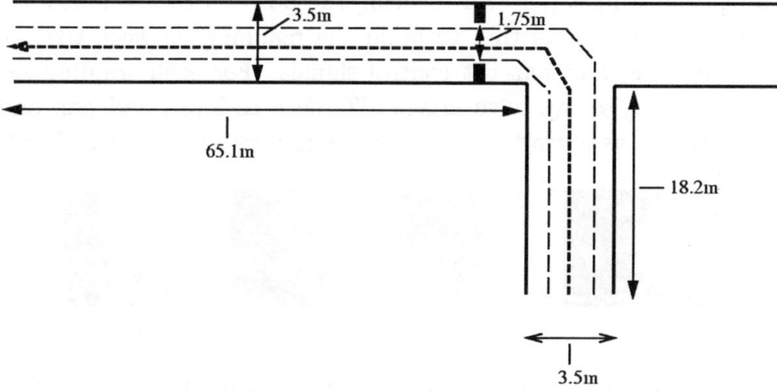

Fig. 1.8   The navigation path. The blue line is the desired navigation path and the tan lines are the navigation bounds. During the test, the SAIL robot navigated within the boundaries.

heading direction as output. It rejects samples (not used for learning) if the input images are too similar to samples already learned. We tested the performance by letting the robot go through the corridor 10 times. All the tests were successful. The closest distance between the SAIL robot and the wall is about 40 cm among the 10 tests. The test showed the SAIL robot can successfully navigate in the indoor environment as shown in Fig 1.8

after the interactive training. We plan to extend the area of navigation in the future work.

1.4.3 *Visual attention using motion*

The SAIL robot has embedded some innate behaviors, behaviors either programmed-in or learned off-line. For this behavior we used off-line supervised learning. One such behavior is vision attention driven by the motion. Its goal is to move the eyes so that moving object of interest is moved to the "fovea", the center of the image. With this mechanism, perception and measurement is performed mainly for the "fovea", while the periphery of image frame is used only to find the object of interest.

To implement this mechanism, we first collect a sequence of images with moving objects. The input to the IHDR mapping is an image in which each pixel is the absolute difference of pixels in consecutive images. For training, we acquired the center of moving object and the amount of motion that the pan-tilt unit must perform to bring the position to the image center. We used the IHDR algorithm to build the mapping between the motion (image difference) and pan-tilt control signals. For each training sample point i, $i = 1, \ldots, n$, we have image difference as input and pan and tilt angle increments as output. Some example images are shown in Fig 1.9.

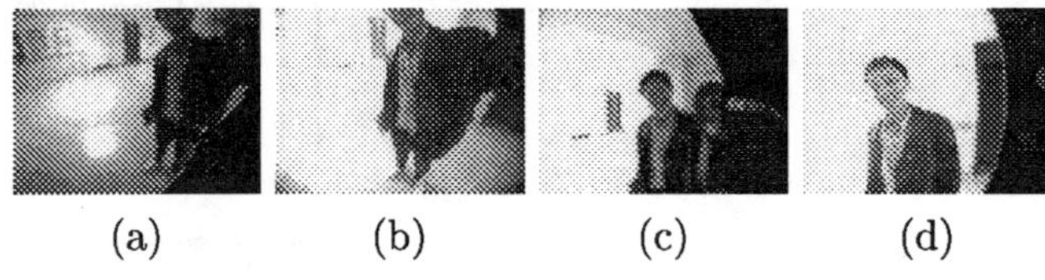

(a)   (b)   (c)   (d)

Fig. 1.9 An example of motion tracking, or motion guided visual attention. (a) and (b) are the left and right images when an object moves in. (c) and (d) are the images after desired pan and tilt of the eyes.

1.4.4 *Test for the developmental algorithm SAIL-2*

We ran the developmental algorithm on the SAIL robot. Since tracking objects and reaching objects are sensorimotor behaviors first developed in early infants, we trained our SAIL robot for two tasks. In the first task, called finding-ball task, we trained the SAIL robot to find a nearby ball and then turn eyes to it so that the ball is located on the center of sensed image. In the second task, called pre-reaching task, we trained the SAIL robot to reach for the object once it has been located and the eyes fixate on it.

Existing studies on visual attention selection are typically based on low-level saliency measures, such as edges and texture. [M. Bichsel (1991)] In Birnbaum's work [L. Birnbaum et. al. (1993)], the visual attention is based on the need to explore geometrical structure in the scene. In our case, the visual attention selection is a result of past learning experience. Thus, we do not need to define any task-specific saliency features. It is the SAIL robot that automatically derives the most discriminating features for the tasks being learned. At the time of learning, the ball was presented in the region of interest (ROI) inside the stereo images. The human trainer interactively pulls the robot's eyes toward the ball (through the touch sensors for the pan-tilt heads) so that the ball is located on the center of the region of ROI (fixating the eyes on the ball)[¶]. The inputs to the developmental algorithm are the continuous sequence of stereo images and the sequence of the pan-tilt head control signal. Three actions are defined for the pan-tilt head in pan direction: 0 (stop), 1 (move to the left), or -1 (move to the right). The size of ROI we chose for this experiment is defined as 120×320. In the mind of trainer, the ROI is divided into five regions so that each region is of size 120×64. The goal of the finding-ball task, is to turn the pan-tilt head so that the ball is at the center region. Fig. 1.10 shows some example images for the tracking task.

The transitions during the training session are described below:

(1) The task input is initiated by pushing a pressure sensor of the robot (or typing in a letter via keyboard) before imposing action to pan the camera. The action of the pan is zero at this time since no action is imposed.

(2) The action of the pan is imposed at time t. The initialization flag is on at the same time. The main program issues a control signal to pan the camera.

(3) The PTU starts to pan. The pan position as well as the image changes. Note that at time $t + 1$ the previous pan action is zero.

[¶]This is not typically done with human infants, since we cannot pull infant's eye. However, this makes robot learning much faster than what a human baby can. This is in fact an advantage of robot over humans in that the robot can be built to fascinate training.

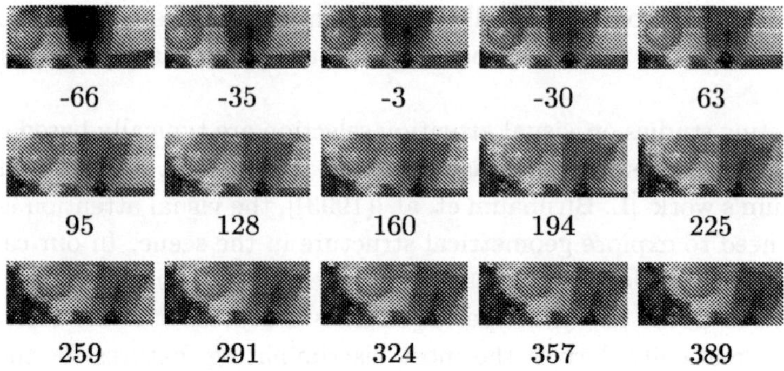

Fig. 1.10   A subset of images used in the tracking problem. The number right below the image shows the PTU position associated with that image. From left to right, one image sequence of ball-tracking is shown.

(4) When the ball is at the fixation of the view at time T, we stops the imposition of action of pan, and the initialization flag is off.

(5) At time $T + 1$, the PTU stopped moving and the image does not change any more. It is worth noting that the pan action is all zero after time $T - 1$.

Similarly, the testing session can be explained as follows:

(1) The human tester pushes a pressure sensor to simulate a task command and the initialization flag is on at time t.

(2) The action of the pan is automatically generated by the IHDR tree. A non-zero action is expected according to the training process.

(3) The PTU starts to move automatically and the image changes.

(4) When the ball is at the fixation of the view at time T, the query result of the IHDR is a zero action. This zero action (stop) is sent to the PTU and the initialization flag is off.

(5) At time $T + 1$, the PTU stops moving and the image does not change any more.

Why is the state important here? If the state, which keeps the previous pan action is not used, as input to the IHDR tree, the image and the pan position will be very similar at the point where the action should stop. This will make the PTU stop and go in a random fashion at this boundary point. The context (direction from which the arm is from) resolves the ambiguity.

The online training and testing were performed successfully and the robot can perform finding-ball task and pre-reaching task successfully, after interactive training, although the developmental algorithm was not written particularly for these two tasks.

To quantitatively evaluate the performance of the online learning and performance, we recorded recorded the sensory data and studied the performance off-line. Since the developmental algorithm runs indefinitely, does its memory grow without bound? Fig. 1.11(a) shows the memory usage of the program. In the first stage, the tree grows since the samples are accumulated in the shallow nodes. When the performance of the updated tree is consistent to the desired action, the tree does not grow and thus the memory curve becomes flat. The tree will grow only when the imposed action is significantly different from what the tree comes up with. Otherwise, the new inputs only participate in the average of the corresponding cluster, simulating sensorimotor refinement of repeated practice, but there is not need for additional memory. This is a kind of forgetting — without remembering every detail of repeated practice. How fast the developmental algorithm learn? Fig. 1.11(b) shows the accuracy of the PTU action in terms of the percentage of field of view. After the 3-rd epoch (repeated training), the systems can reliably move the eye so that the ball is at the center of ROI. Does the developmental algorithm slow down when it has learned more? Fig. 1.11(c) gives the plot of the average CPU time for each sensory-action update. The average CPU time for update is within 100 millisecond, meaning that the system runs at about 10 Hertz, 10 refresh of sensory input and 10 updated actions per second. Since the IHDR tree is dynamically updated, all the updating and forgetting are performed in each cycle. This relatively stable time profile is due to the use of the tree structure. The depth of the tree is stable.

1.4.5 *Speech recognition*

Speech recognition has achieved significant progress in the past ten years. It still faces, however, many difficulties, one of which is the training mode. Before training any acoustic models, such as HMM, the human trainer must do data transcription, a procedure of translating a speech waveform into a string of symbols representing the acoustic unit, like phonemes. In other words, the training data must be organized manually according to the acoustic characteristics. This procedure requires the expertise of linguistics

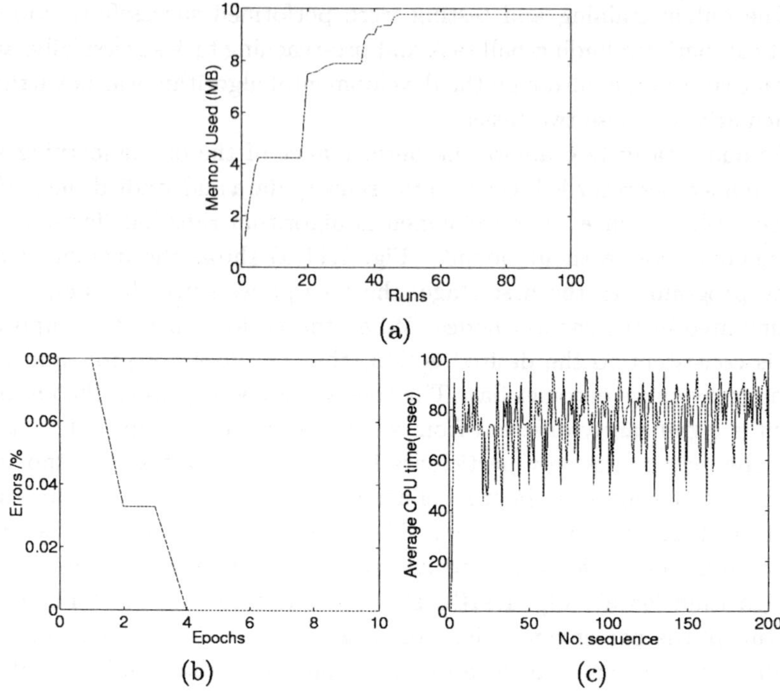

Fig. 1.11 (a) The memory usage for the off-line simulation of finding-ball task. (b) The accuracy of finding-ball task versus the number of training cases. (c) The CPU time for each update.

and is very labor-intensive. Moreover, inherently, this training can only be done off-line, making on-line experience learning not possible. We used our SAIL-2 developmental algorithm to realize online learning based on supervised learning.

Once SAIL starts running, the microphone keeps collecting the environment sound. A SoundBlast card digitizes the signals from microphone at 10 kHz. For every segment of 256 speech data points, which is roughly 25 ms of data, cepstrum analysis gives a 16-dimensional Mel-Cepstrum feature vector. There are 56-point overlap between two consecutive segments.

When teaching SAIL, the trainer says the word first and then imposes actions through the touch sensors to generate control signal vectors.

The control signal sequence together with the 16 cepstrum feature vector stream goes into the IHDR mapping engine. As speech patterns are temporal patterns, a piece of 20 ms segment does not include much pattern information. In other words, we need longer working memory or state. In effect, the designed speech state covers 32 time steps which amounts to 640 ms, while the control signal state covers 16 time steps which is of 320 ms long.

After training, the trainer can test it by saying the word again and see whether SAIL repeats the action. Each sound corresponds to a verbal command of a different action.

To evaluate the performance more conveniently, we first did the experiment in simulation. We recorded the voice of 141 persons with a variety of nationalities, including American, Chinese, French, India, Malaysian and Spanish, and ages, from 18 to 50. Each person made 5 utterances for each of the 5 vowels, a, e, i, o, u. There is silence of 0.5s between two consecutive utterances. Thus, we got a one-hour speech dataset of isolated vowel utterances. There are totally 3525 utterances. The control signal vectors sequence is generated so that there are different control signals after different vowels.

We used, in training session, 4 out of 5 utterances of each of the 5 vowels of each person and the remaining utterance of each vowel was used for test. The data were fed to the developmental algorithm in the way described above.

The performance is evaluated as followings. Within 10 time steps (200ms) before and after the position the system is supposed to react, if there is one wrong reaction or if the system keeps quiet by doing nothing, we mark it as doing wrong. If the system reacts correctly once or more than once within the time window we are interested, we mark it as doing correct. The whole experiment was done with a 5-fold cross-validation. The average error rate was 0.99%.

We also ran the experiment on SAIL robot. Its performance varied, very much depending on the trainer. In the simulation mode, the time of the imposed actions can be given pretty consistently for different utterances. In real test, however, it is not easy for a trainer to impose the action precisely at the same time instant after each utterance. If he/she is not consistent, SAIL will be confused and in many cases keeps doing nothing. We are currently working on two ways to resolve this issue, one is attention selection, the other is reinforcement learning.

1.5 Conclusions

We have introduced here a new kind of robot: robots that can develop their mental skills autonomously through real-time interactions with the environment. The representation of the system is automatically generated through online interaction between the developmental program and the experience. This new kind of robot opens an array of new research problems, from computer vision, to speech recognition, to robotics. From the perspective of mental development, the work here raised the need for rethinking the traditional static ways of programing and teaching a system, either for vision, speech or an autonomous robot.

A technical challenge for the developmental algorithm is that the mapping engine must be scalable — keeping real-time speed and a stable performance for a very large number of high dimensional sensory and effector data. In our IHDR mapping engine, the developmental algorithm operates in real time. The SAIL-2 developmental algorithm has successfully run on the SAIL robot for real-time interactive training and real-time testing for two sensorimotor tasks: finding ball and reaching the centered ball, two early tasks that infants learn to perform. These two tasks do not seem very difficult judged by a human layman, but they mark a significant technical advance since the program has little to do the task. First, the same developmental program can be continuously used to train other tasks. This marks a significant paradigm change. Second, if a task-specific program was used for the two tasks that the SAIL robot infant has learned, it cannot run in real-time without special image process hardware, due to the extensive computation required for image analysis. Apart from the appearance-based methods, almost no other image analysis methods can run in real time without special-purpose image processing hardware. Third, detecting an arbitrary object from arbitrary background is one of the most challenge tasks for a robot. The main reason that our developmental algorithm can learn to do this challenging task is that it does not rely on human to pre-define representation. The same is true for our autonomous navigation experiment — the amount of scene variation along the hallways of our engineering building is beyond hand programming.

The automatically generated representation is able to use context very intimately. Every action is tightly dependent on the rich information available in the sensory input and the state. In other words, every action is context dependent. The complexity of the rules of such context dependence is beyond human programming. A human defined representation is not be able to keep such rich information, without making the hand-designed representation too complicated to design any effective rules.

Since the developmental algorithm is not task specific, we plan to train the SAIL robot for other more tasks to study the limitation of the current SAIL-2 developmental algorithm as well as the SAIL robot design. The future research directions include using longer context, attention selection, incorporating reinforcement learning mechanisms, and the value system. As pointed out by a recent article[J. Weng (2001)] in *Science*, computational studies of mental development may set a common ground for understanding both machine and human intelligences.

Acknowledgements

The authors would like to thank Yilu Zhang for producing the speech related experimental result briefly mentioned in Section1.4.5, Changjiang Yang for writing a preprocessing program for the touch sensors of the SAIL robot, and Rebecca Smith and Matthew Ebrom for assistance in conducting experiments. The work is supported in part by National Science Foundation under grant No. IIS 9815191, DARPA ETO under contract No. DAAN02-98-C-4025, DARPA ITO under grant No. DABT63-99-1-0014 and research gifts from Siemens Corporate Research and Zyvex.

Bibliography

Martin Bichsel. *Strategies of Robust Object Recognition for the Automatic Identification of Human Faces.* Swiss Federal Institute of Technology, Zurich, Switzerland, 1991.

Lawernce Birnbaum, Matthew Brand, and Paul Cooper. Looking for Trouble: Using Causal Semantics to Direct Focus of Attention. In *Proc of the IEEE Int'l Conf on Computer Vision*, pages 49–56, Berlin, Germany, May 1993. IEEE Computer Press.

J.L. Elman, E. A. Bates, M. H. Johnson, A. Karmiloff-Smith, D. Parisi, and K. Plunkett. *Rethinking Innateness: A connectionist perspective on development.* MIT Press, Cambridge, MA, 1997.

K. Fukunaga. *Introduction to Statistical Pattern Recognition.* Academic Press, New York, NY, second edition, 1990.

G. H. Golub and C. F. van Loan. *Matrix Computations.* The Johns Hopkins University Press, Baltimore, MD, 1989.

W. Hwang, J. Weng, M. Fang, and J. Qian. A fast image retrieval algorithm with automatically extracted discriminant features. In *Proc. IEEE Workshop on Content-based Access of Image and Video Libraries*, pages 8–15, Fort Collins, Colorado, June 1999.

M. Kirby and L. Sirovich. Application of the karhunen-loève procedure for the characterization of human faces. *IEEE Trans. Pattern Analysis and Machine Intelligence*, 12(1):103–108, Jan. 1990.

S. L. Pallas L. von Melchner and M. Sur. Visual behavior mediated by retinal projections directed to the auditory pathway. *Nature*, 404:871–876, 2000.

W.H. Press, B.P. Flannery, S.A. Teukolsky, and W.T. Vetterling. *Numerical Recipes.* Cambridge University Press, New York, 1986.

M. Sur, A. Angelucci, and J. Sharm. Rewiring cortex: The role of patterned activity in development and plasticity of neocortical circuits. *Journal of Neurobiology*, 41:33–43, 1999.

D. L. Swets and J. Weng. Hierarchical discriminant analysis for image retrieval.

IEEE Trans. Pattern Analysis and Machine Intelligence, 21(5):386–401, 1999.

M. Turk and A. Pentland. Eigenfaces for recognition. *Journal of Cognitive Neuroscience*, 3(1):71–86, 1991.

J. Weng. The living machine initiative. Technical Report CPS 96-60, Department of Computer Science, Michigan State University, East Lansing, MI, Dec. 1996. A revised version appeared in J. Weng, "Learning in Computer Vision and Beyond: Development," in C. W. Chen and Y. Q. Zhang (eds.), Visual Communication and Image Processing, Marcel Dekker Publisher, New York, NY, 1999.

J. Weng and S. Chen. Vision-guided navigation using SHOSLIF. *Neural Networks*, 11:1511–1529, 1998.

J. Weng, J. McClelland, A. Pentland, O. Sporns, I. Stockman, M. Sur, E. Thelen, "Autonomous Mental Development by Robots and Animals," *Science*, 291:599–600, 2001.

A PIECEWISE BÉZIER VOLUME DEFORMATION MODEL AND ITS APPLICATIONS IN FACIAL MOTION CAPTURE

HAI TAO

Sarnoff Corporation, 201 Washington Rd, Princeton, NJ 08543, USA
E-mail: htao@sarnoff.com

THOMAS S. HUANG

Image Processing and Formation Laboratory, Beckman Institute, University of Illinois at Urbana-Champaign, Urbana, IL 61801, USA
E-mail: huang@ifp.uiuc.edu

Capturing real facial motions from videos enables automatic creation of dynamic models for facial animation. In this paper, we propose an explanation-based facial motion tracking algorithm based on a piecewise Bézier volume deformation model (PBVD). The PBVD is a suitable model both for synthesis and analysis of facial images. With this model, basic facial movements, or action units, are first interactively defined. Then, by linearly combining these action units, various facial movements are synthesized. The magnitudes of these action units can be estimated from real videos using a model-based tracking algorithm. The predefined PBVD action units may also be adaptively modified to customize the dynamic model for a particular face. In this paper, we first briefly introduce the PBVD model and its application in computer facial animation. Then a coarse-to-fine PBVD-based motion tracking algorithm is presented. We also describe an explanation-based tracking algorithm that takes a collection of predefined action units as the initial dynamic model and adaptively improves this model during the tracking process. Experimental results on PBVD-based animation, model-based tracking, and explanation-based tracking are demonstrated.

1 Introduction

Recently, great efforts have been made to combine computer vision and computer graphics techniques in the research areas of human computer interaction, model-based video conferencing, visually guided animation, and image-based rendering. A key element in these vision-based graphics systems is the object model. An object model provides the information regarding the geometry, the dynamics, and many other attributes of an object. It usually represents the *a priori* knowledge of a particular type of objects and imposes a set of constraints in the process of visual computing [1]. Among many applications, the analysis and synthesis of facial images is a good example that demonstrates the close relationships between the technologies in computer graphics and computer vision. As shown in Figure 1, a model-based facial image communication system usually consists of three main components: (a) a analyzer or a motion generator, (b) a synthesizer that renders the facial images, and (c) a transmission channel that efficiently communicates between (a) and (b). All these components are based on an underlying face model.

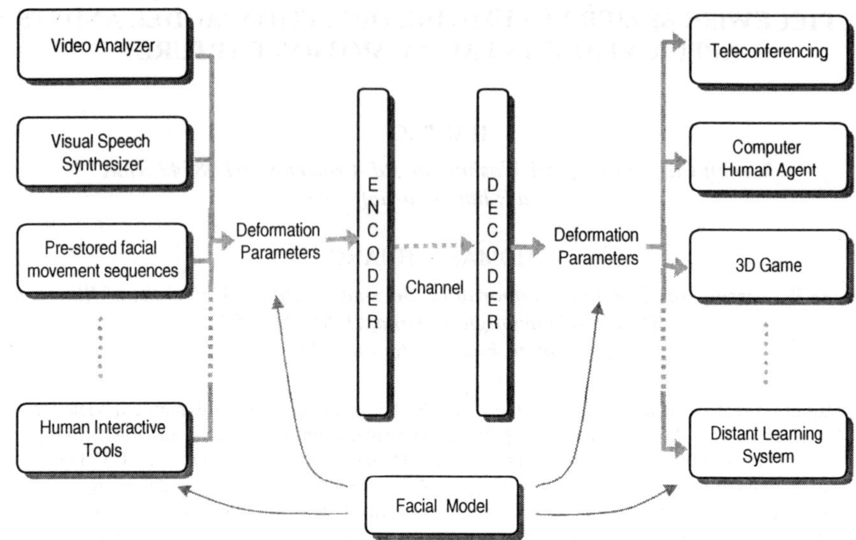

Figure 1. A facial image communication system.

Both geometric and deformation representations are equally important components in face modeling. We have developed a system to obtain 3D mesh model of a face from 3D CyberWare scanner (Figure 2). In this paper, however, our focus is the face deformation model, which represents the dynamics of a face. Four categories of face deformation models have been proposed in the past. They are parameterized models [2], physics-based muscle models [3], free-form deformation models[4], and performance-driven animation models [5]. In analysis, these models are applied as constraints that regulate the facial movements.

In this paper, a new free-form face deformation model called *piecewise Bézier volume deformation* (PBVD) is proposed. Some of its properties such as the linearity and being independent of the underlying mesh structure make it a suitable model for both realistic computer facial animation and robust facial motion analysis. The difference between this approach and Kalra's method [4] is twofold. By using nonparallel volumes, 3D manifolds of arbitrary shapes can be formed. As a result, fewer deformation volumes are needed and the number of control points is reduced. This is a desired property for tracking algorithms. In addition, based on facial feature points, this model is mesh independent and can be easily adopted to articulate any face model.

By using the PBVD model, a computer facial animation system, a model-based facial motion tracking algorithm, and an explanation-based tracking algorithm are presented. These algorithms have been successfully implemented in several applications including video-driven facial animation, lip motion tracking, and real-time facial motion tracking. The remaining sections are organized as following: Section 2 introduces the PBVD model and the PBVD-based animation system. Section 3 describes a PBVD model-based tracking algorithm. Explanation-based tracking is then described in Section 4. Some experimental results are demonstrated in Section 5, followed by discussions and concluding remarks in Section 6.

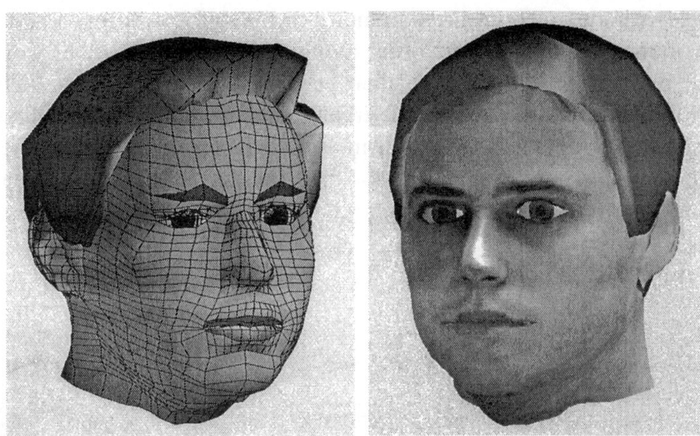

Figure 2. A facial mesh model derived from the CyberWare scanner data. Left: the mesh model. Right: the texture-mapped model.

2 The PBVD model

2.1 PBVD – formulation and properties

A 3D Bézier volume [10] is defined as

$$\mathbf{x}(u,v,w) = \sum_{i=0}^{n}\sum_{j=0}^{m}\sum_{k=0}^{l}\mathbf{b}_{i,j,k}B_i^n(u)B_j^m(v)B_k^l(w),\tag{1}$$

where $\mathbf{x}(u,v,w)$ is a point inside the volume, which, in our case, is a facial mesh point. Variables (u,v,w) are the parameters ranging from 0 to 1, $\mathbf{b}_{i,j,k}$ are the control points, and $B_i^n(u)$, $B_j^m(v)$, and $B_k^l(w)$ are the Bernstein polynomials. By moving each control point $\mathbf{b}_{i,j,k}$ with an amount of $\mathbf{d}_{i,j,k}$, the resulting displacement of the facial mesh point $\mathbf{x}(u,v,w)$ is

$$\mathbf{v}(u,v,w) = \sum_{i=0}^{n}\sum_{j=0}^{m}\sum_{k=0}^{l}\mathbf{d}_{i,j,k}B_i^n(u)B_j^m(v)B_k^l(w).\tag{2}$$

Figure 3 shows the deformation of a Bézier volume that contains a part of the facial mesh. In order to deform the face, multiple Bézier volumes are formed to embed all the deformable parts. These volumes are formed based on the facial feature points such as eye corners, mouth corners, etc. Each Bézier volume consists of two layers: the external layer and the internal layer. They form the volume that contains the facial mesh. Normal vectors of each facial feature points are used to form these volumes. To ensure continuity in the deformation process, neighboring Bézier volumes are of the same order along the borders. In other words, there are the same number of control points on each side of a boundary. The piecewise Bézier volume structure used in our implementation is shown in Figure 4. Using this model, facial regions with similar motions are controlled by a single volume and different volumes are connected so that the smoothness between regions is maintained.

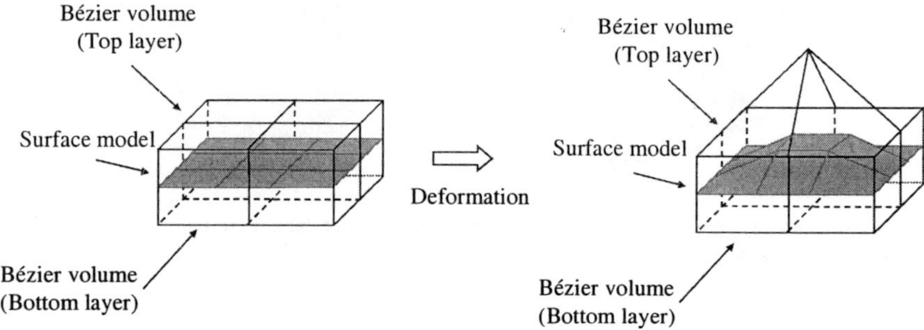

Figure 3. A Bézier volume and the embedded facial mesh.

Once the PBVD model is constructed, for each mesh point on the face model, its corresponding Bernstein polynomials are computed. Then the deformation can be written in a matrix form as

$$\mathbf{V} = B\mathbf{D},\qquad(3)$$

where $\mathbf{V}$ is the nodal displacements of the mesh points, $\mathbf{D}$ represents the displacement vectors of Bézier volume control nodes. The matrix B describes the mapping function composed of Bernstein polynomials. Manipulating the control points through an interactive tool may derive various desired expressions, visual speech, or action units. In Figure 5, the real control mesh and the rendered expression smile is illustrated. At each time instant, the nonrigid motion of a face is modeled as a linear combination of different expressions or visemes (*visual phonemes*), or

$$\mathbf{V} = B[\mathbf{D}_0\mathbf{D}_1 \ldots \mathbf{D}_m][p_0 p_1 \ldots p_m]^t = BDP = LP\qquad(4)$$

where $\mathbf{D}_i$ is an expression or a viseme, and p_i is its corresponding intensity. The overall motion is

$$R(\mathbf{V}_0 + LP) + T \qquad (5)$$

where $\mathbf{V}_0$ is the neutral facial mesh, R is the rotation decided by the three rotation angles $(\omega_x, \omega_y, \omega_z)^t = \Omega$, and T is the 3D translation.

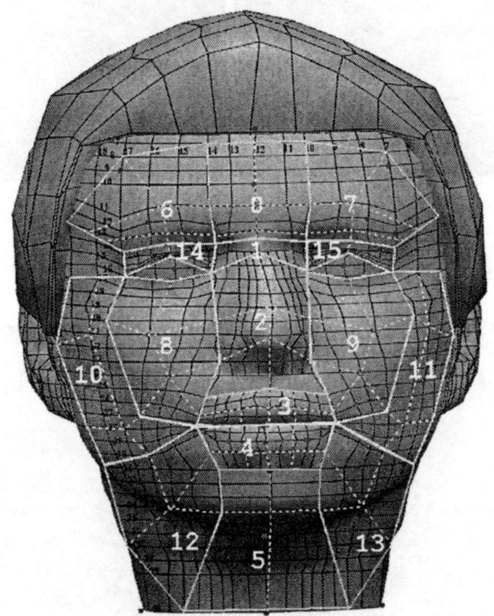

Figure 4. The facial mesh and the associated 16 Bézier volumes.

2.2 *PBVD-based facial animation*

Based on the PBVD model, facial action units are constructed using an interactive tool. Then various expressions and visemes are created either from combining these action units or from manually moving some control nodes. We have created 23 visemes manually to implement a talking head system. Six of them are shown in Figure 6. In addition, six universal expressions have also been created.

Once visemes and expressions are created, animation sequences can be generated by assigning appropriate values to the magnitudes of these visemes and expressions at each time instant. In our implementation, a human subject speaks to a microphone according to a script. The phoneme segmentation is then obtained using a speech recognition tool. Based on the phoneme segmentation results, mouth shapes and expressions are computed using a coarticulation model similar to [11]. Audio and animation results are then synchronized to generate realistic talking head sequences. Figure 7 shows some frames from a synthetic visual speech sequence.

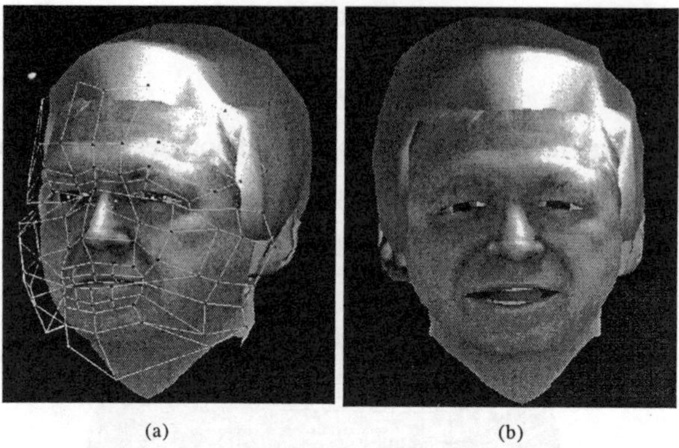

(a)   (b)

Figure 5. (a) The PBVD volumes and (b) the expression *smile*.

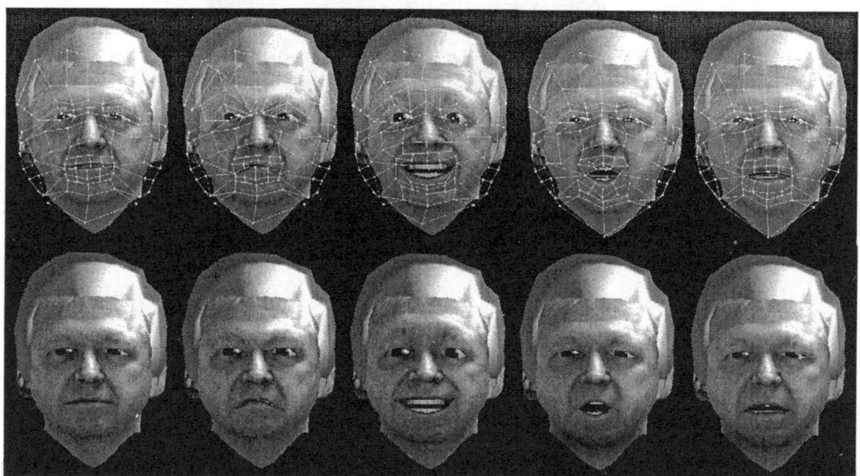

Figure 6. Expressions and visemes created using the PBVD model. The expressions and visemes (bottom row) and their corresponding control meshes (top row). The facial movements are, from left to right, *neutral*, *anger*, *smile*, *vowel_or*, and *vowel_met*.

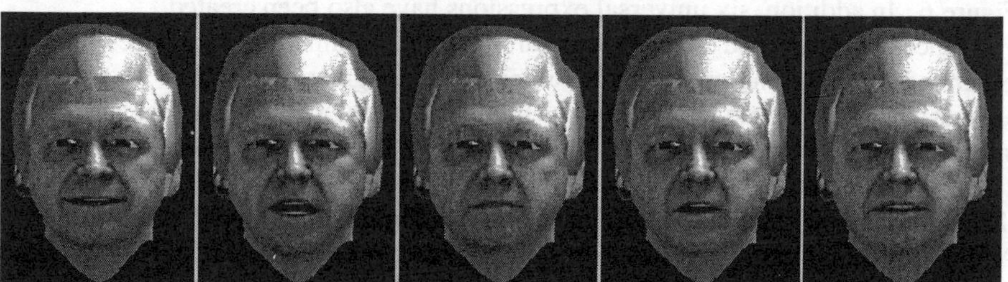

Figure 7. An animation sequence with *smile* and speech *I am George McConkie*.

3 PBVD model-based tracking algorithm

3.1 Video analysis of the facial movements

Several algorithms for extracting face motion information from video sequences have been proposed [6,7,8,9]. Most of these methods are designed to detect action-unit level animation parameters. The assumption is that the basic deformation model is already given and will not change. In this section, we propose a tracking algorithm in the same flavor but using the PBVD model. The algorithm adopts a coarse-to-fine framework to integrate the low-level motion field information with the high-level deformation constraints. Since the PBVD model is linear, an efficient optimization process using lease squares estimator is formulated to incrementally track the head poses and the facial movements. The derived motion parameters can be used for facial animation, expression recognition, and bimodal speech recognition.

3.2 Model-based tracking using the PBVD model

The changes of the motion parameters between two consecutive video frames are computed based on the motion field. The algorithm is shown in Figure 8. We assume that the camera is stationary. At the initialization stage, the face needs to be approximately frontal view so that the generic 3D model can be fitted. The inputs to the fitting algorithms are the positions of facial feature points, which are manually picked. All motion parameters are set to zeroes (i.e., $(\hat{T}_0, \hat{\Omega}_0, \hat{P}_0) = 0$), which means a neutral face is assumed. The intrinsic camera parameters are known in our implementation. Otherwise, a small segment of the video sequence should be used to estimate these parameter using photogrammetry techniques.

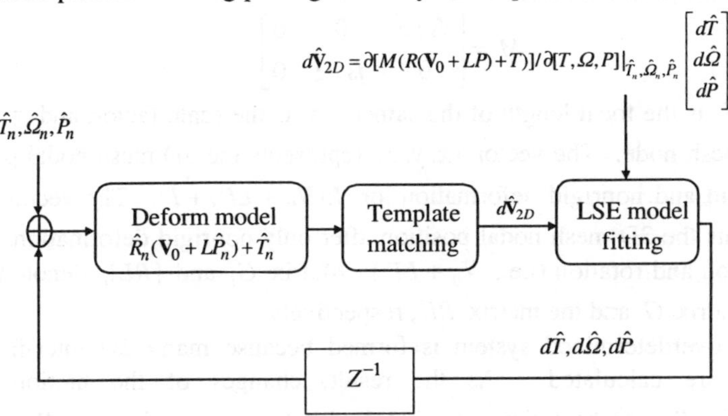

Figure 8. Block diagram of the model-based PBVD tracking system.

From the video frames n and $n+1$, the 2D motion vectors of many mesh nodal points are estimated using the template matching method. In our implementation, the template for each node consists of 11×11 pixels and the searching region is 17×17 pixels. To deal with the drifting problem, both the templates from the previous frame and the templates from the initial frame are used: the even nodes of a patch are tracked using the templates from the previous frame and the odd nodes are tracked using those of the initial frame. Our experiments showed that this approach is very effective.

From the resulting motion vectors, 3D rigid motions and nonrigid motions (intensities of expressions/visemes or action units) are computed simultaneously using a least squares estimator. Since the PBVD model is linear, only the perspective projection and the rotation introduce non-linearity. This property makes the algorithm simpler and more robust. The 2D interframe motion for each node is

$$
d\hat{\mathbf{V}}_{2D} \approx \frac{\partial[M(R(\mathbf{V}_0 + LP) + T)]}{\partial[T, \Omega, P]}\bigg|_{\hat{T}_{n+1}, \hat{\Omega}_{n+1}, \hat{P}_{n+1}} \begin{bmatrix} d\hat{T} \\ d\hat{\Omega} \\ d\hat{P} \end{bmatrix}
$$

$$
= M\left(\begin{bmatrix} 1 & 0 & -x/z \\ 0 & 1 & -y/z \end{bmatrix}\begin{bmatrix} G_0 - x/zG_2 \\ G_1 - y/zG_2 \end{bmatrix}\begin{bmatrix} [RL]_0 - x/z[RL]_2 \\ [RL]_1 - y/z[RL]_2 \end{bmatrix}\right)\begin{bmatrix} d\hat{T} \\ d\hat{\Omega} \\ d\hat{P} \end{bmatrix}
$$

$$(6)$$

where $d\hat{\mathbf{V}}_{2D}$ is the 2D interframe motion, and

$$
G = \begin{bmatrix} 0 & z_1 & -y_1 \\ -z_1 & 0 & x_1 \\ y_1 & -x_1 & 0 \end{bmatrix}. \tag{7}
$$

The projection matrix M is

$$
M = \begin{bmatrix} fs/z & 0 & 0 \\ 0 & fs/z & 0 \end{bmatrix} \tag{8}
$$

where f is the focal length of the camera, s is the scale factor, and z is the depth of the mesh node. The vector (x, y, z) represents the 3D mesh nodal position after both rigid and nonrigid deformation, or $R(\mathbf{V}_0 + LP) + T$. The vector (x_1, y_1, z_1) represents the 3D mesh nodal position after only nonrigid deformation, but without translation and rotation (i.e., $\mathbf{V}_0 + LP$). Matrix G_i and $[RL]_i$ denote the i th row of the matrix G and the matrix RL, respectively.

An overdetermined system is formed because many 2D inter-frame motion vectors are calculated. As the result, changes of the motion parameters $(d\hat{T}, d\hat{\Omega}, d\hat{P})$ can be estimated using the least squares estimator. By adding these changes to the previously estimated motion parameters $(\hat{T}_n, \hat{\Omega}_n, \hat{P}_n)$, new motion parameters $(\hat{T}_{n+1}, \hat{\Omega}_{n+1}, \hat{P}_{n+1})$ are derived.

3.3 Coarse-to-fine framework

Two problems with the above algorithm are the computationally expensive template matching and the noisy motion estimation. The first problem is obvious because the computational complexity for each motion vector is approximately $(17 \times 17) \times (11 \times 11) \times 3 = 104{,}907$ integer multiplication. The second problem is partially caused by the fact that in the above algorithm, the computation of the motion field is totally independent of the motion constraints, which makes it vulnerable to various noises. If the lower-level motion field measurements are very noisy, good estimation of motion parameters can never be achieved, even with the correct constraints.

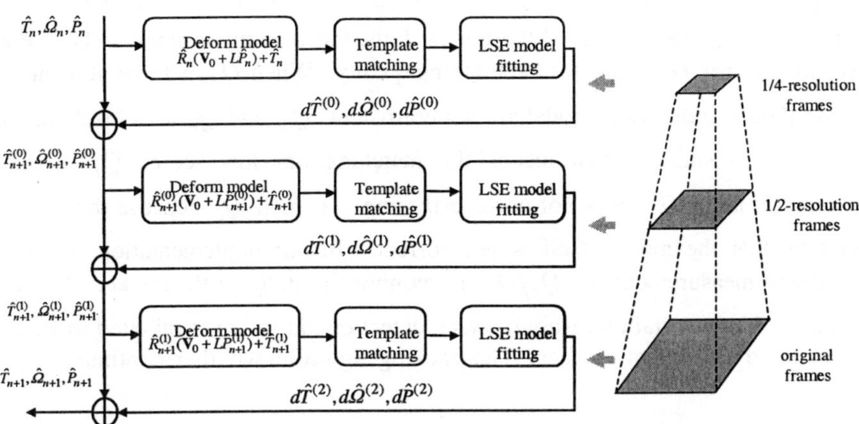

Figure 9. The coarse-to-fine PBVD tracking algorithm.

A coarse-to-fine framework is proposed in this section to partially solve the above problems. The block diagram of this new algorithm is illustrated in Figure 9. An image pyramid is formed for each video frame. The algorithm proposed in the previous section is then applied to the consecutive frames sequentially from lowest resolution to the original resolution. For the diagram depicted in Figure 9, changes of motion parameters are computed in quarter-resolution images as $(d\hat{T}^{(0)}, d\hat{\Omega}^{(0)}, d\hat{P}^{(0)})$. By adding these changes to $(\hat{T}_n, \hat{\Omega}_n, \hat{P}_n)$, the estimated new motion parameters are derived as $(\hat{T}_{n+1}^{(0)}, \hat{\Omega}_{n+1}^{(0)}, \hat{P}_{n+1}^{(0)})$. Similarly, changes of motion parameters are computed in the half-resolution images as

$(d\hat{T}^{(1)}, d\hat{\Omega}^{(1)}, d\hat{P}^{(1)})$ based on the previous motion parameter estimation $(\hat{T}^{(0)}_{n+1}, \hat{\Omega}^{(0)}_{n+1}, \hat{P}^{(0)}_{n+1})$. This process continues until the original resolution is reached.

In this coarse-to-fine algorithm, motion vector computation can be achieved with smaller searching regions and smaller templates. In our implementation, for each motion vector, the number of multiplication is $[(5\times 5)\times(7\times 7)\times 3]\times 4 = 14,700$, which is about seven times fewer than the model-based scheme. A more important property of this method is that, to certain extent, this coarse-to-fine framework integrates motion vector computation with high-level constraints. The computation of the motion parameter changes is based on the approximated motion parameters at low-resolution images. As the result, more robust tracking results are obtained.

3.4   Confidence measurements

Two quantities are computed for each frame as the confidence measurements. The average normalized correlation Q_c is computed based on nodes using the templates from the initial video frame. If the tracker fails, this quantity is small. The average LSE fitting error Q_f indicates the tracking quality. When Q_f is large, it means the motion field and the fitted model are not consistent. Q_f and Q_c are closely related. When Q_c is small, which means the matching has low score, Q_f is large. However, a large Q_f does not necessarily imply a small Q_c because the situation could be that the model itself is not correct. In our implementation, we use a confidence measurement $J = Q_c/Q_f$ to monitor the status of the tracker. When J is smaller than a certain threshold, a face detection algorithm is initiated to find the approximate location of the face. The tracking algorithm will then continue.

4   Explanation-based motion tracking

The model-based approach is powerful because it dramatically reduces the solution space by imposing domain knowledge as constraints. However, if the model is oversimplified, or is not consistent with the actual dynamics, correct results can not be obtained. To be able to learn new facial motion patterns without loosing the benefits of model-based approach, a new tracking algorithm called explanation-based method is proposed in this section.

4.1 Approach

We use the term explanation-based to describe the strategy that starts from a rough representation of the domain knowledge and then incrementally elaborates this representation through learning new events. The existing domain knowledge representation provides the initial explanation of each new event; the learning algorithm exploits the information provided by the data to adjust the knowledge representation. For a PBVD tracking algorithm, the predefined action units provide an explanation for the estimated motion vectors. The fitting error, which is the combination of the noise and the error of the deformation model, is then analyzed to modify the model. A block diagram is shown in Figure 10. It is basically the same as the block diagram for the model-based PBVD method except that an additional block is added to adjust the nonrigid motion model L. The model L consists of two parts: B and D. Both of them can be adjusted. Changing D means changing the displacement vector or control nodes for each action unit so that the model fits the data better. Modifying B means modifying Bézier volumes so that descriptive power of the model is enhanced. In this paper, we discuss the learning of D.

$$d\hat{\mathbf{V}}_{2D} = \partial[M(R(\mathbf{V}_0 + LP) + T)]/\partial[T,\Omega,P]\Big|_{\hat{T}_n,\hat{\Omega}_n,\hat{P}_n} \begin{bmatrix} d\hat{T} \\ d\hat{\Omega} \\ d\hat{P} \end{bmatrix}$$

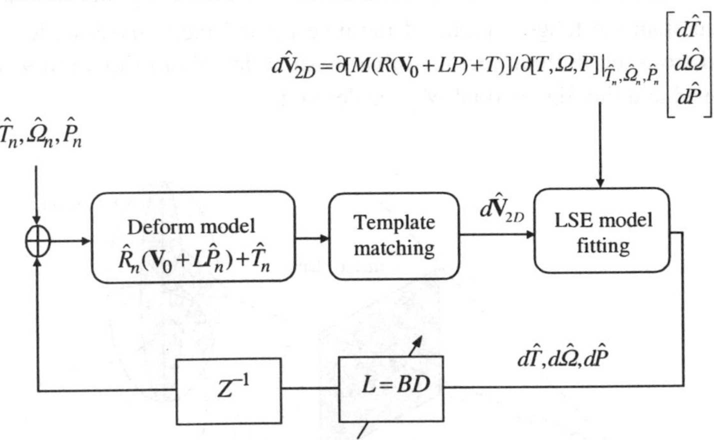

Figure 10. The block diagram for the explanation-based tracking algorithm.

4.2 Learning expressions/visemes or action units

The learning of D is based on the model-based analysis of a video segment. As shown in Figure 11, the predefined action units D are first used in a model-based method to track n frames, then the tracking error is analyzed and the deformation D is modified. The new D is then used as the model in the next segment. This process is performed during the entire tracking process.

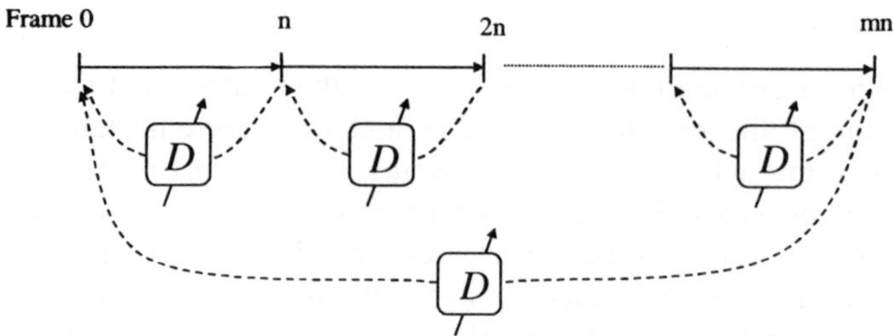

Figure 11. Learning of the expressions/visemes or action units (D) in a video sequence.

To adjust D, for each frame, 2D motion residuals are projected back to 3D nonrigid motion according to the 3D model and the in-surface motion assumption (see Figure 12). The fitting error for any mesh nodes can be written as

$$\mathbf{V}_{res2D} = M\hat{R}\mathbf{V}_{res} = M\hat{R}(a\mathbf{u}_1 + b\mathbf{u}_2) \tag{9}$$

where $\mathbf{V}_{res2D}$ is the 2D fitting error in the LSE equation, M is the perspective projection matrix, and R is the rotation matrix. Vectors $\mathbf{u}_1$ and $\mathbf{u}_2$ are the 3D vectors that span the tangent plane of the investigated facial mesh node. They can be decided from the normal vector of that mesh node. From Equation 9, a and b can be solved and the 3D residual $\mathbf{V}_{res}$ is derived.

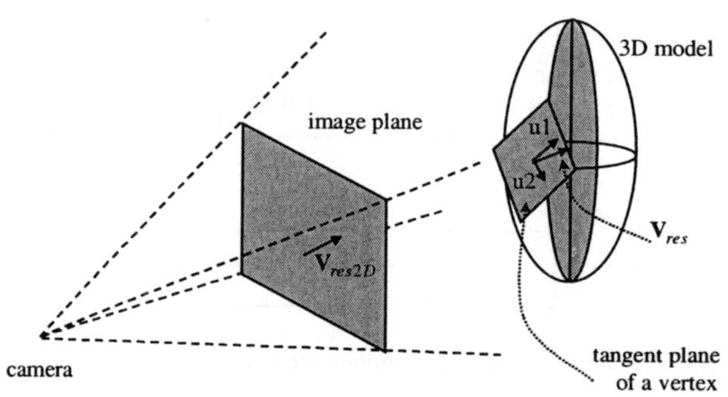

Figure 12. Project a 2D motion fitting residual vector back to 3D space.

For each frame, the projected 3D motion is

$$\mathbf{V}_{mes} = L\hat{P} + \alpha\mathbf{V}_{res} \tag{10}$$

where L is the previous PBVD model, $\hat{P}$ is the vector representing the nonrigid motion magnitudes, and α is the learning rate. The term $L\hat{P}$ means the fitted part of the motion. The vector $\mathbf{V}_{mes}$ is collected for each frame in a video segment. At the end of that segment, adjustment of D is performed.

Adjusting D is equivalent to adjusting $\mathbf{D}_i$ (Equation 4). An iterative algorithm is proposed in this paper. In each iteration, only one $\mathbf{D}_i$ is modified, with the others fixed. For example, in the first iteration, only $\mathbf{D}_0$ is adjusted. For each frame, we derive the 3D-motion vector that equals

$$\mathbf{V}_{r0} = \mathbf{V}_{mes} - B[\mathbf{0}\,\mathbf{D}_1\ldots\mathbf{D}_m]\hat{P}. \tag{11}$$

The PCA analysis of $\mathbf{V}_{r0}$ in a video segment is performed to extract the major motion patterns such as $\mathbf{V}_{e00}$, $\mathbf{V}_{e01}$, etc. The number of these patterns is decided by the energy distribution indicated by eigenvalues. The maximum number of these patterns can also be imposed to avoid over-fitting. We assume these motions are due to some $\mathbf{D}_{0i}$.

To find the deformation units that cause each eigenvector, the following LSE problem is solved

$$\begin{bmatrix} \mathbf{V}_{e0k} \\ 0 \end{bmatrix} = \begin{bmatrix} B \\ C \end{bmatrix} \mathbf{D}_{0k} \tag{12}$$

where C is the smoothness constraint that regulates $\mathbf{D}_{0k}$ so that the motions of PBVD control nodes are smooth.

5 Implementation and experimental results

The PBVD model has been implemented on a SGI ONYX machine with a VTX graphics engine. Real-time tracking at 10 frame/s has been achieved using the coarse-to-fine framework. It has also been used for bimodal speech recognition and bimodal emotion recognition. Explanation-based method has been implemented to improve the facial image synthesis.

5.1 Face model initialization

The face in the first video frame needs to be approximately frontal view and with a neutral expression. From this frame, facial feature points are extracted manually. Based on these feature points, the 3D fitting algorithm is then applied to warp the generic model. However, since we only have 2D information, the whole warping process is performed in 2D except the initial scaling. Once the geometric face model is fitted, a PBVD model is automatically derived from some facial feature points and their corresponding normal vectors.

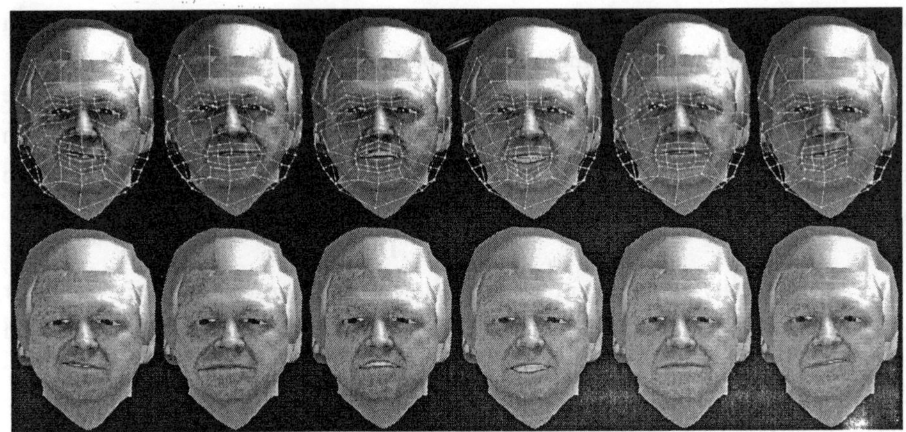

Figure 13. Action units in bimodal speech recognition. Top: the control nodes. Bottom: the action units.

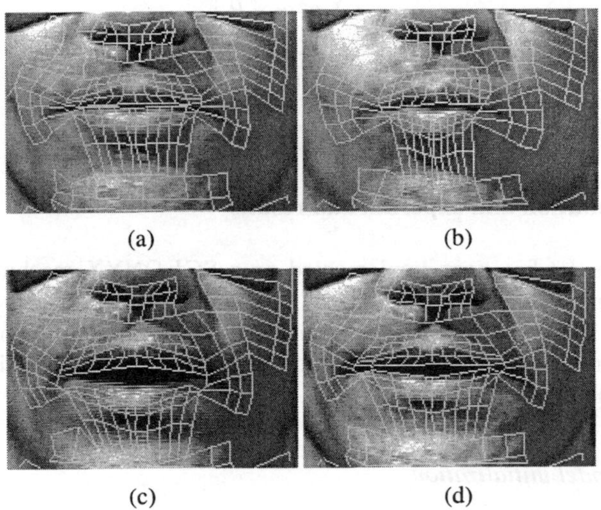

(a)   (b)

(c)   (d)

Figure 14. Lip tracking for bimodal speech recognition.

5.2   *PBVD model-based tracking*

In PBVD tracking algorithm, the choice of deformation units $\mathbf{D}_i$ depends on the application. In a bimodal speech recognition application, 6 action units are used to describe the motions around the mouth. These action units are illustrated in Figure

13. The tracking result for each frame is twelve parameters including the rotation, the translation, and the intensities of these action units.

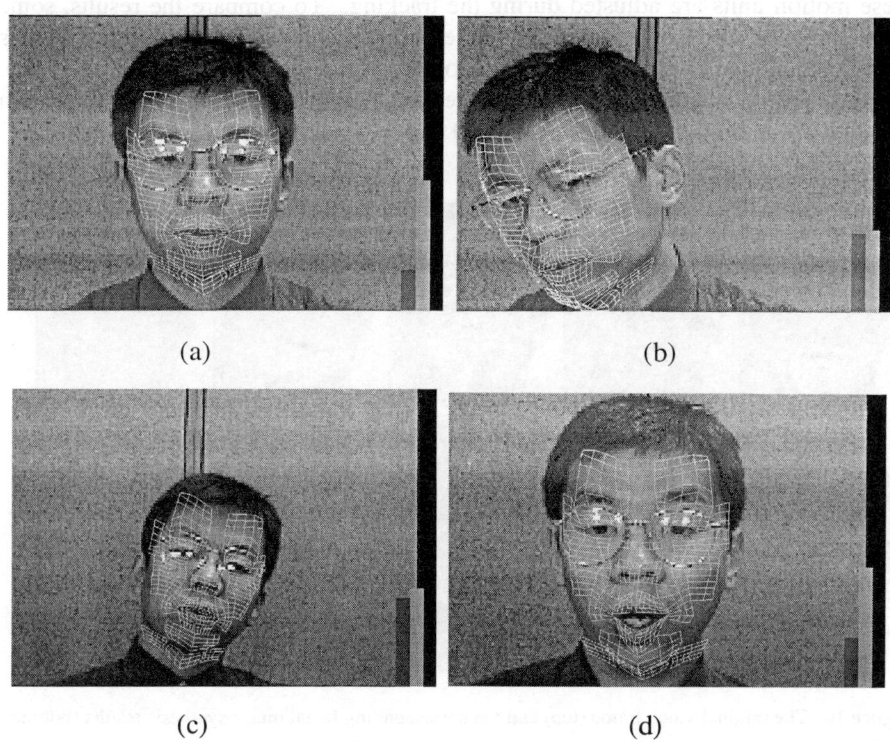

(a)   (b)

(c)   (d)

Figure 15. Results of the real-time tracking system. The two color bars on the right side of the image are Q_c (left) and Q_f (right), respectively.

For the bimodal emotion recognition and the real-time tracking system, 12 action units are used. Users can design any set of deformation units for the tracking algorithm. These deformations can be either at expression level or at action unit level. Lip tracking results are shown in Figure 14. Figure 15 shows the results of the real-time tracker.

Facial animation sequences are generated from the detected motion parameters. Figure 16 shows the original video frame and the synthesized results. The synthesized face model uses the initial video frame as the texture. The texture-mapped model is then deformed according to the motion parameters.

5.3 *Explanation-based tracking*

A set of predefined motion units is used as the initial deformation model. Then, these motion units are adjusted during the tracking. To compare the results, some generic motion units are used in the model-based method. The resulting synthesis does not agree well with the original video around the mouth region (Figure 17(b)). In Figure 17(c), the improved result of the explanation-based method is shown. In our implementation, the segment size is 20 frames, and the learning rate is $\alpha = 0.4$.

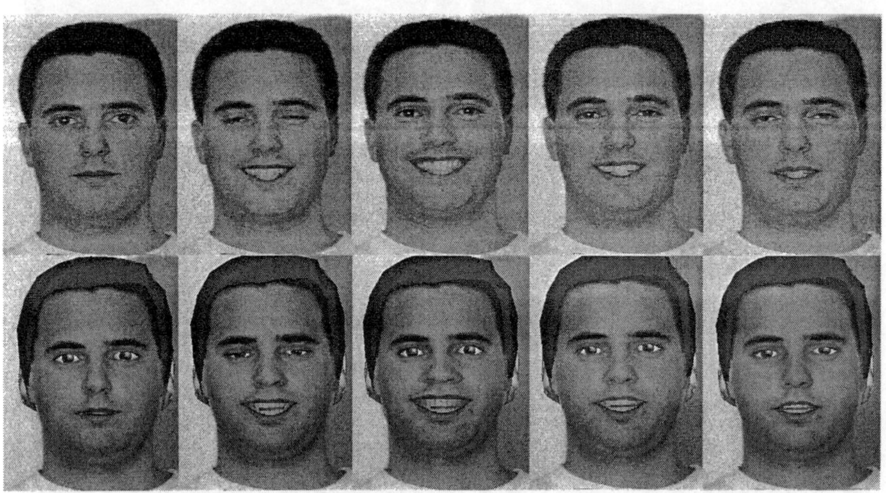

Figure 16. The original video frame (top) and the corresponding facial image synthesis results (bottom).

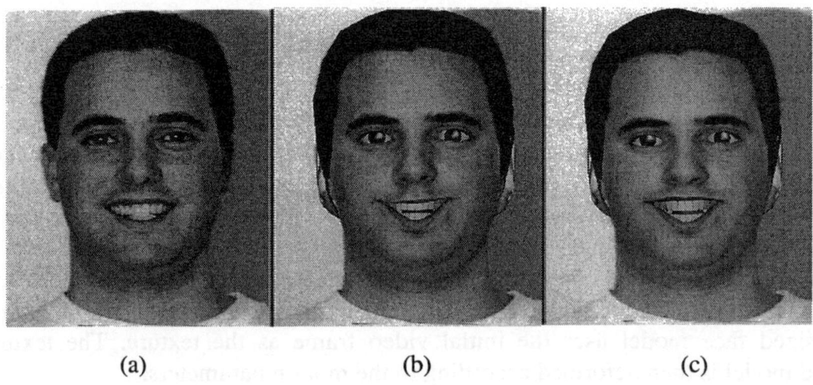

(a)   (b)   (c)

Figure 17. The synthesis results: (a) original frame, (b) model-based, and (c) explanation–based .

6 Discussion

In this paper, issues on generating face articulation models from real videos are addressed. Three major contributions are the new PBVD facial animation model, the PBVD model-based tracking algorithm, and the explanation-based tracking algorithm. For future research, the emphasis will be on improving low-level motion estimation, combining the explanation-based approach with the coarse-to-fine framework, and recognizing spatial-temporal patterns from the resulting facial motion parameters.

7 Acknowledgements

This work was supported in part by the Army Research Laboratory Cooperative Agreement No. DAAL01-96-0003.

References

1. C. Kambhamettu, D. B. Goldgof, D. Terzopoulos, and T. S. Huang, "Nonrigid motion analysis," in *Handbook of PRIP: Computer Vision*, vol. 2. San Diego, CA: Academic Press, 1994, pp. 405-430.
2. F. I. Parke, "Parameterized models for facial animation," *IEEE Comput. Graph. and Appl.*, vol. 2, no. 9, pp. 61-68, Nov. 1982.
3. Y. Lee, D. Terzopoulos, and K. Waters, "Realistic modeling for facial animation," in *Proc. SIGGRAPH 95*, 1995, pp. 55-62.
4. P. Kalra, A. Mangili, N. M. Thalmann, and D. Thalmann, "Simulation of facial muscle actions based on rational free form deformations," in *Proc. EUROGRAPHICS'92*, Sept. 1992, pp. 59-69.
5. L. Williams, "Performance-driven facial animation," in *Proc. SIGGRAPH 90*, Aug. 1990, pp. 235-242.
6. H. Li, P. Roivainen, and R. Forchheimer, "3-D motion estimation in model-based facial image coding," *IEEE Trans. Pattern Analysis and Machine Intelligence*, vol. 15, no. 6, pp. 545-555, June 1993.
7. C. S. Choi, K. Aizawa, H. Harashima, and T. Takebe, "Analysis and synthesis of facial image sequences in model-based image coding," *IEEE Trans. Circuit Sys. Video Technol.*, vol. 4, no. 3, pp. 257-275, June 1994.
8. I. Essa and A. Pentland, "Coding, analysis, interpretation and recognition of facial expressions," *IEEE Trans. Pattern Analysis and Machine Intelligence*, vol. 19, no. 7, pp. 757-763, July 1997.
9. D. DeCarlo and D. Metaxas, "The integration of optical flow and deformable models with applications to human face shape and motion estimation," in *Proc. CVPR '96*, 1996, pp. 231-238.

10. T. W. Sederberg and S. R. Parry, "Free-form deformation of solid geometric models," in *Proc. SIGGRAPH 86*, 1986, pp. 151-160.
11. D. W. Massaro and M. M. Cohen, "Modeling coarticulation in synthetic visual speech," in N. M. Thalmann & D. Thalmann (Eds.) *Models and Techniques in Computer Animation*, Tokyo: Springer-Verlag, 1993, pp. 139-156.

NONRIGID MOTION AND STRUCTURE ANALYSIS FROM 2D WITH APPLICATION TOWARDS 3D CLOUD TRACKING

Lin Zhou and Chandra Kambhamettu

Video/Image Modeling and Synthesis (VIMS) Lab
Department of Computer and Information Sciences
University of Delaware
Newark, Delaware, 19716
E-mail: {lzhou, chandra}@cis.udel.edu

Dmitry B. Goldgof

Deparment of Computer Science and Engineering
University of South Florida
Tampa, Florida, 33620
E-mail: goldgof@csee.usf.edu

1. Introduction

Over the past decade, significant advances were seen in both nonrigid motion modeling and visualization [21,25,2], and extensive applications of nonrigid motion analysis have been investigated and presented. For example, [49] deals with heart motion, [14] with face motion, and [42] with cloud motion. In this chapter, we present a methodology for the recovery of structure and motion from 2D image sequences when the object of interest is undergoing a nonrigid motion. In the literature of computer vision, many studies have been conducted on structure recovery from rigid motion [61,64,8] or multi-view stereo matching [7,1]. The problem of structure and nonrigid motion recovery is quite challenging as it is under-constrained in terms of the number of unknowns that need to be estimated. Yet it is very important problem, and is applicable in various fields. For example, since it is very expensive to have stereoscopic satellite images of clouds in a super rapid scan mode (i.e, data every minute) for analysis of depth and motion, structure and non-rigid motion tracking using monocular image sequences is very beneficial for use in weather prediction models. Accurate structure and nonrigid motion estimates would also be helpful in human face, hand, and body gesture interfaces.

Several efforts have been made to solve the dual problem of structure and nonrigid motion recovery. In general, the existing methods can be classified into two categories: the local patch based methods and the model based methods. The local patch based methods simply abandon the idea of recovering a whole body description of the motion, and recover structure on a patch-by-patch basis in order to cope with nonrigidity [51,62]. Unfortunately, using a local description limits the methods themselves to using only noise-sensitive local measurements. Consequently, such patch-by-patch recovery of structure is not likely to be either very meaningful or robust. On the contrary, the model based methods utilize predefined 3D active shape models to recover a global description of nonrigid motion. Essentially, the predefined shape models provide extra constraints which incorporate prior knowledge about a shape's smoothness and its resistance to deformation. A number of different 3D deformable model formulations have been proposed and actually used for the task of structure and nonrigid motion recovery [56,44,22,37,38,35,57]. Terzopoulos *et al.* [56] proposed a physically based modeling framework and recovered limited global descriptions (e.g., symmetry axis shape) from nonrigid motion. Pentland *et al.* [44] used finite element method (FEM) models which incorporate elastic properties of real materials for the recovery of structure and nonrigid motion. Huang and Goldgof [22] proposed the adaptive-size physically-based models for nonrigid shape and motion analysis. Many applications of model-based structure and nonrigid motion recovery were also presented [30,55,33,24,5,12,52]. For example, Kakadiaris and Metaxas [24] discussed the human body tracking; DeCarlo and Metaxas [12] estimated the shape and motion of human faces with a deformable model. However, the major limitation of such methods is that only over-constrained global shape descriptions of nonrigid motion are recovered. With the absence of local measurements, it would be very hard to obtain dense and accurate structure information and 3D correspondences. In addition, there exist a large amount of applications, such as clouds, terrains and water flows, whose nonrigid motion cannot be described well by any global shape models.

In this chapter, we present a novel algorithm to estimate both dense structure and nonrigid motion from a sequence of 2D images. The 2D images are first segmented into small regions and local analysis is performed for each region, assuming that similar nonrigid motion is present within each region. Then, a recursive algorithm is used to integrate local analysis with appropriate global constraints. A system called SMAS has been implemented based on our algorithm. Experiments on Hurricane Luis satellite image sequences are performed to generate the complete hurricane structure and 3D motion correspondences, along with extensive error analysis. The remainder of this chapter is organized as follows. Section 2 motivates our work and discusses previous work on cloud motion analysis. Section 3 explains data acquisition of cloud image sequences. Section 4 presents an outline of our structure and motion analysis system. Local analysis of 2D cloud image sequences is described in Sections 5 and 6. Section 7 discusses the global analysis. Section 8 presents the experimental results on satellite images of Hurricane Luis. Section 9 validates and evaluates our results. Finally, conclusions and future work are presented in Section 10.

2. Motivation and Previous Work

Cloud motion analysis is a very important application area in computer vision, especially in nonrigid motion analysis. Accurate cloud heights and winds are significant for a number of meteorological and climate applications [18], such as cloud model verification, physically-based numerical weather prediction and data assimilation, cloud-wind height assignment [17,19,39,18], convective intensity estimation [47,48], naval aviation, and radiation balance estimation for Mission to Planet Earth type climate baseline studies.

During the past decade, vision algorithms were proposed and employed to address the problem of cloud motion analysis. Initially, automatic cloud tracking algorithms were based on 2D cross-correlation, which were pioneered by Leese *et al.* [32] and improved by Smith *et al.* [50] and Phillips *et al.* [46]. The underlying assumption of correlation-based methods is that the feature or object being tracked undergoes rigid motion without deformation. However, this assumption fails in tracking mesoscale atmospheric phenomena such as hurricane and severe convective storms [20]. Automatic cloud motion analysis under nonrigid deformations has been developed by Kambhamettu *et al.* [28], Palaniappan *et al.* [42,41], and Hasler *et al.* [20]. Kambhamettu *et al.* [28] used a *continuous motion model*, where individual cloud elements are assumed to undergo locally continuous deformation (i.e., the cloud surface patch can be smoothly stretched with local elements maintaining their neighborhood relationships) while Palaniappan *et al.* [42,41] used a *semi-fluid model* which allows cloud surface patches to merge, split or cross over. In particular, [20] presented very accurate tracking results on a large amount of satellite cloud data. However, their methods were based on 3D cloud data since they utilized the changes in differential geometric properties of 3D cloud surfaces in motion in order to perform cloud tracking. The 3D cloud data were obtained from stereo analysis, and/or by approximating 2D intensity images for depth information. Kambhamettu *et al.* [26] also coupled stereo and motion analysis of clouds using a simple-to-complex multiresolution approach. Recently, multispectral satellite information such as moisture data and infrared data has been incorporated into the automatic cloud analysis algorithms by Velden et al. [58,59,60]. They discussed the impact of multispectral satellite information on both tropical cyclone tracking and cloud intensity analysis. In all the previous work so far, none had recovered both dense structure and nonrigid motion of clouds simultaneously from the satellite cloud image sequences.

In this chapter, we present a novel algorithm in order to estimate both the structure and nonrigid motion at the same time from 2D views with application towards cloud images acquired by meteorological satellites [68,69]. Main challenges are posed not only by the complex dynamics of the imaging instruments and the underlying non-linear phenomena of cloud formation and weather, but also by the scaled orthographic projection of cloud images, which makes the structure estimation problem even more difficult.

3. GOES Cloud Image Sequences

The current generation of Geostationary Operational Environmental Satellite (NOAA GOES 8, 9, 10) has an Imager instrument with five multispectral channels of high spatial resolution, and very high dynamic range radiance measurements with 10-bit precision. Some characteristics of the five channels of the GOES Imager instrument are shown in Table 1. In our work, we only consider the visible channel – the Imager instrument can image with high spatial, temporal, radiometric and spectral resolution, which makes it possible for automatic cloud-tracking algorithms to track mesoscale atmospheric phenomena such as hurricane and severe convective storms [20].

Table 1. Channel characteristics of GOES.

Channel No.	Wavelength	Resolution
1. visible	0.52 to 0.72	28
2. shortwave	3.78 to 4.03	112
3. water vapor	6.47 to 7.02	224
4. long wave	10.20 to 11.20	112
5. IR	11.50 to 12.50	112

As shown in Fig. 1, two satellites, GOES-8 and GOES-9 are focused during the data acquisition. During Hurricane Luis, GOES-9 collected data in Super Rapid Scan Operation mode (SRSO), in which the GOES Imager collects imagery of a fixed sector approximately once every minute, and GOES-8 collected data in routine mode, which includes four U.S. views per hour. GOES-8 was in routine mode to provide mandatory operational hemispheric coverage for other weather events that would otherwise conflict with SRSO. The sub-satellite point of GOES-8 (GOES-East) is 75° W longitude, which has been re-mapped in our experiments to GOES-9 (GOES-West) having a sub-satellite point of 135° W longitude using geolocation latitude-longitude information. Stereo analysis of these two image sequences has been done on a Maspar parallel machine, using a coarse-to-fine, hierarchical algorithm which was previously developed at NASA-Goddard [42,20,43]. This gives us a sequence of disparities every 15 minutes. In this work, we utilized a GOES-9 image sequence (1 frame/minute) and the available disparities (1 frame/15 minutes) to estimate dense structure, nonrigid motion, and 3D correspondences of clouds for every frame (every minute).

4. System Outline

The main component of our system is the nonrigid motion model. However, due to the varying nature of nonrigid motion, it is unlikely that one can find a single perfect nonrigid motion model which can be applied to estimate 3D motion and structure for an entire nonrigid object. For example, we found that in facial motion, the motion of cheeks, lips, and so on, correspond to different kinds of nonrigid motion [10]. Cloud motion is even more complex due to its fluid dynamics. Ideally, one would like to segment the nonrigid objects appropriately and fit different nonrigid motion models

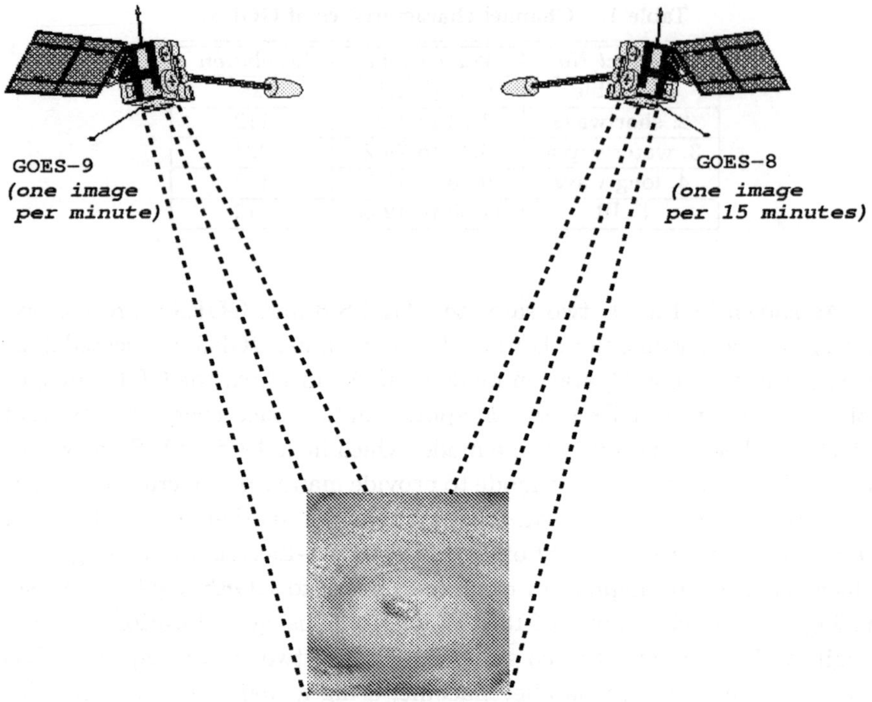

Fig. 1.   GOES Cloud Image Sequences.

to the corresponding segmented regions. In order to avoid the difficulty in cloud segmentation, we segment the cloud images evenly into several small regions. For each small region, if the area is small enough, say 3×3 pixels, we can assume that this small region is undergoing nonrigid motion according to the same nonrigid motion model. Our earlier observation of cloud motion has suggested that this is a valid assumption [20]. We fit nonrigid motion model subject to global constraints for each small region in order to get both the structure and nonrigid motion. The architecture of the system is illustrated in Fig. 2. Local analysis tries to recover small details and finds the best results for each small region independently, but may be overfitted. Then, global analysis regularizes the local results and limits possible nonrigid behaviors according to appropriate global constraints.

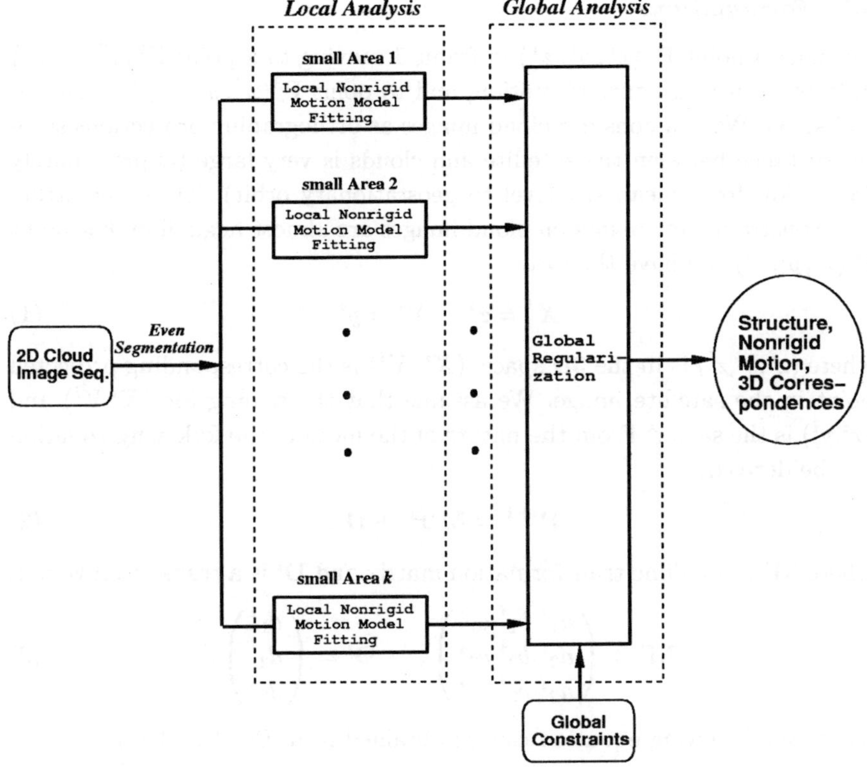

Fig. 2.   System Architecture.

5. Local Nonrigid Motion Model

In the local analysis, the most important step is to define a good nonrigid motion model for each small cloud region. In our work, affine motion model is chosen because it is a general nonrigid motion model and is more powerful in describing nonrigid motion than other restricted nonrigid motion models. In addition, affine motion model has been experimentally proven to be a suitable model for small local cloud motion [20]. We also derive the relationship between the affine motion model and fluid dynamics in order to evaluate and present affine's physical meaning for cloud fluid motion [67]. Let us first examine the algebraic formulations to derive structure and nonrigid motion from cloud images.

5.1. *Formulations*

Consider a point $\mathbf{P}^1(x^1, y^1, z^1)$ in frame 1 moving to a point $\mathbf{P}^2(x^2, y^2, z^2)$ in frame 2 after a nonrigid motion, and to point $\mathbf{P}^3(x^3, y^3, z^3)$ in frame 3, and so on. We can consider cloud images as orthographic projections since the distance between the satellite and clouds is very large (approximately 35,787 km from mean sea level to geostationary orbit). Thus, the structure constraints for points on cloud images are almost negligible. For point $\mathbf{P}^i(x^i, y^i, z^i)$, we have the form

$$X^i = x^i, \quad Y^i = y^i, \tag{1}$$

where (x^i, y^i, z^i) is in the 3D space, (X^i, Y^i) is the corresponding projected point in the satellite image. We assume that the scaling for (X^i, Y^i) and (x^i, y^i) is the same.[a] From the nature of the motion, the following equation can be derived,

$$\mathbf{P}^{i+1} = \mathbf{M}^i \mathbf{P}^i + \mathbf{D}^i, \tag{2}$$

where $\mathbf{M}^i$ is an affine transformation matrix and $\mathbf{D}^i$ is a translation vector,

$$\mathbf{M}^i = \begin{pmatrix} a_1{}^i & b_1{}^i & c_1{}^i \\ a_2{}^i & b_2{}^i & c_2{}^i \\ a_3{}^i & b_3{}^i & c_3{}^i \end{pmatrix}, \quad \mathbf{D}^i = \begin{pmatrix} d_1{}^i \\ d_2{}^i \\ d_3{}^i \end{pmatrix}. \tag{3}$$

Then, the following equation can be obtained from Eq. 1 and Eq. 2,

$$\begin{pmatrix} X^{i+1} \\ Y^{i+1} \\ z^{i+1} \end{pmatrix} = \mathbf{M}^i \begin{pmatrix} X^i \\ Y^i \\ z^i \end{pmatrix} + \mathbf{D}^i. \tag{4}$$

We assume that the motion between successive frames is under the same motion model, as the cloud regions move smoothly during a short time interval [20]. Thus, we have

$$\mathbf{M}^i = \mathbf{M} = \begin{pmatrix} a_1 & b_1 & c_1 \\ a_2 & b_2 & c_2 \\ a_3 & b_3 & c_3 \end{pmatrix}, \quad \mathbf{D}^i = \mathbf{D} = \begin{pmatrix} d_1 \\ d_2 \\ d_3 \end{pmatrix}. \tag{5}$$

However, the time gaps between successive cloud images are not always one-minute. Thus, an additional scaling factor δ_i is added to Eq. 4 in order

---

[a]Note that this will not affect the local motion optimization because the scaling factor can be actually incorporated into the local affine coefficients.

to compensate for possible data taken at irregular times (e.g., three-minute, four-minute time gaps),

$$\begin{pmatrix} X^{i+1} \\ Y^{i+1} \\ z^{i+1} \end{pmatrix} = \delta_i \mathbf{M} \begin{pmatrix} X^i \\ Y^i \\ z^i \end{pmatrix} + \delta_i \mathbf{D}. \tag{6}$$

Eq. 6 represents constraint equation for tracking a point across a sequence of images using the affine motion model.

5.2. *The Affine Motion Model and Cloud Fluid dynamics*

For fluid flows which are incompressible[b] and flows for which the variation of fluid viscosity can be considered negligible, the Navier-Stokes equations describe the flow fluid dynamics,

$$\rho \frac{Dv_x}{Dt} = -\frac{\partial p}{\partial x} + \mu \left(\frac{\partial^2 v_x}{\partial x^2} + \frac{\partial^2 v_x}{\partial y^2} + \frac{\partial^2 v_x}{\partial z^2} \right) + \rho g_x, \tag{7}$$

$$\rho \frac{Dv_y}{Dt} = -\frac{\partial p}{\partial y} + \mu \left(\frac{\partial^2 v_y}{\partial x^2} + \frac{\partial^2 v_y}{\partial y^2} + \frac{\partial^2 v_y}{\partial z^2} \right) + \rho g_y, \tag{8}$$

$$\rho \frac{Dv_z}{Dt} = -\frac{\partial p}{\partial z} + \mu \left(\frac{\partial^2 v_z}{\partial x^2} + \frac{\partial^2 v_z}{\partial y^2} + \frac{\partial^2 v_z}{\partial z^2} \right) + \rho g_z. \tag{9}$$

These equations can be easily written into a compact vector form as

$$\rho \frac{D\mathbf{v}}{Dt} = -\nabla \cdot p + \mu \nabla^2 \cdot \mathbf{v} + \rho \mathbf{g}, \tag{10}$$

where p is the pressure, ρ is the fluid density, μ is the viscosity of the fluid, $\mathbf{v}$ is the velocity vector, and $\mathbf{g}$ is the gravity vector.

Considering the affine motion model, let the time gap between two successive frames be the unit time, then the velocity vector can be easily obtained by

$$\mathbf{v} = \mathbf{MP} + \mathbf{D} - \mathbf{P} = (\mathbf{M} - \mathbf{I})\mathbf{P} + \mathbf{D}. \tag{11}$$

Hence, we have

$$\frac{D\mathbf{v}}{Dt} = \frac{D(\mathbf{M} - \mathbf{I})\mathbf{P}}{Dt} + \frac{D\mathbf{D}}{Dt} = (\mathbf{M} - \mathbf{I})\mathbf{v}, \tag{12}$$

---

[b]For the cloud application, since most parts of hurricanes consist thick water vapor with considerable high density, we assume that the incompressibility assumption holds.

66

and

$$\nabla^2 \cdot \mathbf{v} = \nabla^2 \cdot ((\mathbf{M} - \mathbf{I})\mathbf{P} + \mathbf{D}) = 0. \tag{13}$$

Substituting Eq. 12 and Eq. 13 into Eq. 10, we have

$$\rho(\mathbf{M} - \mathbf{I})\mathbf{v} = -\nabla \cdot p + \rho\mathbf{g}. \tag{14}$$

For cloud motion, since clouds are far away from the earth surface, gravity vector $\mathbf{g}$ is almost negligible. Thus, the following equation can be obtained,

$$\nabla \cdot p = -\rho(\mathbf{M} - \mathbf{I})\mathbf{v}. \tag{15}$$

Eq. 15 represents the relationship between the affine motion model and cloud fluid dynamics. From the fluid dynamics point of view, the use of the affine motion model to simulate cloud motion is just assuming that the divergence of pressure p in cloud motion is a linear combination of cloud velocity components.

6. Local Motion Model Fitting

6.1. *Minimization Method and Error-of-Fit Function*

Balasubramanian *et al.* discussed the minimum number of data points required for the analytical solution to Eq. 6 [3]. In our work, we intend to track more than the minimum number of points, rather, all the points in a small region. This, of course, produces more equations than unknowns. We use Levenberg-Marquardt method to find a least-square solution to Eq. 6 and fit a nonrigid motion model for each small region. To make the algorithm robust and be able to find a good solution, a good error-of-fit (EOF) function that measures the difference between a learned model and given data set is very important. However, with the absence of actual motion correspondences, it is almost impossible to define such an EOF function. In this work, several 2D correspondence candidates are estimated by cross-correlation method. Each point in the first frame is compared within a small neighborhood (3×3) of the second frame and the three points with highest correlation match scores are selected as the correspondence candidates. Since the satellite cloud images have a high resolution (10 bits), cross-correlation is found to yield good results.

Using the 2D correspondence candidates, we define the EOF function as the sum of the minimal distance between the 2D correspondence candidates and the orthographic projection of the hypothesized point obtained by Eq. 6:

$$EOF_{local1} = \sum_{i=1}^{m \text{ frames}} \sum_{j=1}^{n \text{ points}} \min\left(d_{i,j}{}^1, d_{i,j}{}^2, d_{i,j}{}^3\right), \qquad (16)$$

where

$$d_{i,j}{}^k = \left\| \left(\delta^i \left(\mathbf{MP}_{i,j} + \mathbf{D}\right)^T \mathbf{R}_{ort}\right)^T - \mathbf{C}_{i,j}{}^k \right\|, \quad k = 1, 2, 3. \qquad (17)$$

$\mathbf{C}_{i,j}{}^k$ are the three 2D correspondence candidates for point $\mathbf{P}_{i,j}$ and $\mathbf{R}_{ort}$ is the orthographic projection matrix,

$$\mathbf{R}_{ort} = \begin{pmatrix} 1 & 0 \\ 0 & 1 \\ 0 & 0 \end{pmatrix}. \qquad (18)$$

The reason for using multiple correspondence candidates is that it provides more flexibility to the minimization energy in tracking the highly complex and dynamic cloud motion. The three correspondence candidates together predict a small correspondence search area containing the actual correspondence. Fig. 3 shows this strategy.

6.2. *Initial Guesses and Initial Depth Assumption*

The initial guesses for all unknowns in Eq. 6 are required in the optimization, consisting of 9 affine motion parameters, three translational parameters, depth for every point in the first frame and δ_i for each pair of successive images. It is known that almost all non-linear system solvers are highly sensitive to initial guesses. For numerical simplicity and ensuring convergence, two eliminations of unknowns have been made in our method. First, since all correspondence candidates are obtained only based on 2D intensity information, the only depth constraint in Eq. 16 comes from the affine motion model (Eq. 6). Hence, when we minimize Eq. 16 in order to get both the depth and the affine motion model, this procedure may not converge to the optimal solution. Since the disparities of hurricane cloud images are available every 15 frames (beginning with the first frame), we eliminate the depth unknowns in the first frame by fixing them to these disparities. This is a very important step to ensure our algorithm's robustness and convergence. Due to the poor depth constraints in the monocular views, many

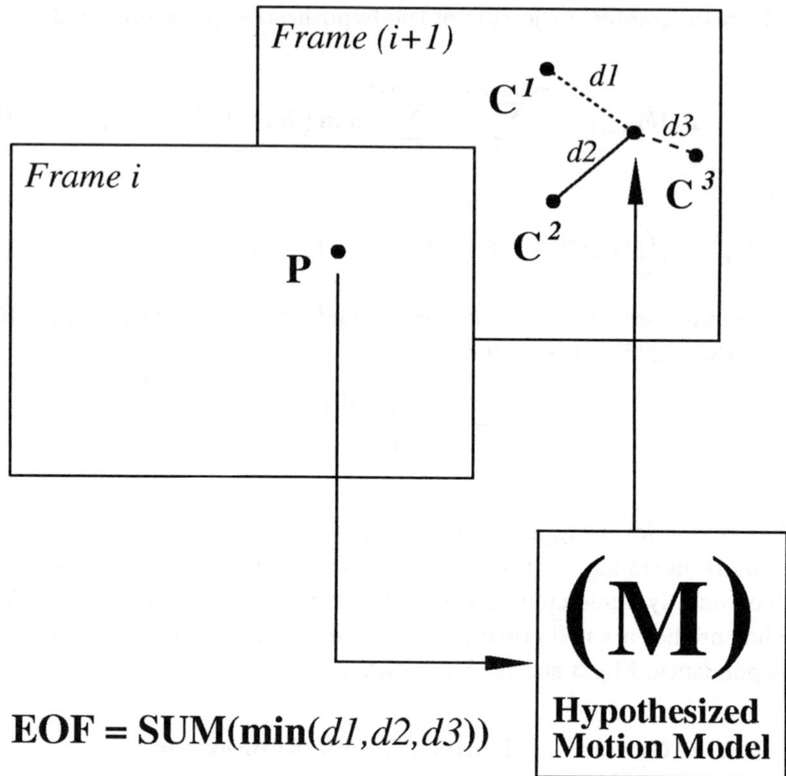

Fig. 3. Defining EOF function using correspondence candidates.

more constraints on depth are necessary. Stronger constraints will be discussed in the following subsection. Second, we eliminate the translational unknowns by setting the translation components, i.e., d_1, d_2, d_3, to small constants. This also makes sure that the trivial solution, all unknowns being zero, cannot be reached. For the other nine motion parameters and δ_i, initial values are chosen assuming the smallness of motion between two successive frames, i.e.,

$$\mathbf{M} = \begin{pmatrix} 1 & 0 & 0 \\ 0 & 1 & 0 \\ 0 & 0 & 1 \end{pmatrix}, \quad \delta_i = 1. \tag{19}$$

6.3. *Depth Constraints*

Although the depth unknowns in the first frame are eliminated by fixing them to disparities, the EOF function will still have infinite local minima because there is no information about the change of the cloud-top height in successive frames. Clearly, we need some more restrictions on the range of values the depth can take. For cloud motion, the cloud-top height will not change much in one minute, which means the depth difference between two successive frames has an upper bound. Based on this observation, we can specify a small range for the depth of each point. Thus, we have

$$z_{i-1,j} - a \leq z_{i,j} \leq z_{i-1,j} + a, \tag{20}$$

where $z_{i,j}$ is the depth of the jth point in the ith frame, and $z_{i-1,j}$ is the depth of the jth point in the $(i-1)$th frame. $2a$ is the range for the depth. In our experiments, a is set to 0.4 (in disparity units), as it is the upper bound of cloud motion between successive frames in our earlier observations [20]. In order to incorporate this depth constraint into the minimization process, a penalty method [34] is utilized in our algorithm.

Consider a minimization problem,

$$minimize \ f(\mathbf{x}) \quad subject \ to \ \mathbf{x} \in S, \tag{21}$$

where f is a continuous function on E^n and S is a constraint region. The penalty method replaces the above problem by an unconstrained problem of the form

$$minimize \ f(\mathbf{x}) + cP(\mathbf{x}), \tag{22}$$

where c is a positive constant and P is penalty function on E^n such that

1. *P is continuous;*
2. $P(\mathbf{x}) \geq 0 \ \forall \, \mathbf{x} \in E^n;$
3. $P(\mathbf{x}) = 0$ *if and only if* $\mathbf{x} \in S$.

Clearly, for large values of c, the minimum of the above problem will lie in a region where P is small. We expect that as c increases, the corresponding solution will approach the feasible region S and will minimize f. In other words, we expect the solution point of Eq. 22 to converge to the solution of Eq. 21 as $c \to \infty$.

With the cloud application, we can rewrite our original constrained minimization problem as an unconstrained minimization problem as follows,

$$EOF_{local2} = \sum_{i=1}^{m\ \text{frames}} \sum_{j=1}^{n\ \text{points}} \left(\min \left(d_{i,j}{}^1, d_{i,j}{}^2, d_{i,j}{}^3 \right) + cP_{i,j} \right), \qquad (23)$$

where

$$P_{i,j} = \left(\max \left[0, z_{i,j} - (z_{i-1,j} + a) \right] \right)^2 + \left(\max \left[0, (z_{i-1,j} - a) - z_{i,j} \right] \right)^2. \quad (24)$$

It is clear that the penalty function $P_{i,j}$ satisfies the depth constraints. Also, we experimentally found that it is sufficient to solve Eq. 22 with a single large value of c. In our experiments, c was set to 1000 and was found to yield good results. Fig. 4 illustrates the need for constraints. Although

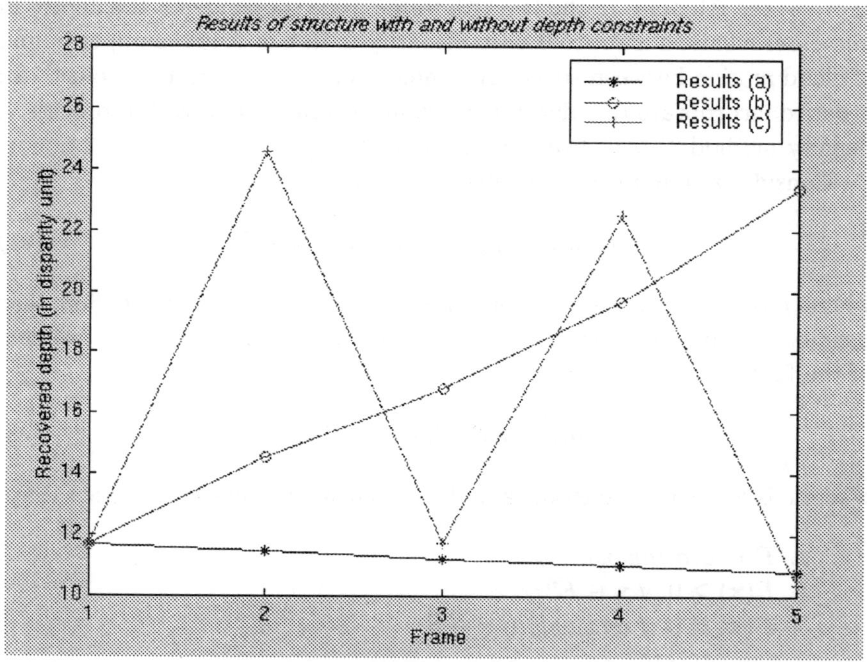

Fig. 4.   Results of structure for five cloud images with and without depth constraints. (a): results with constraints. (b), (c): two set of results of recovered depth without constraints.

the depth is fixed in the first frame, the values for the following frames can change dramatically without constraints. The result with constraints is smooth and all the recovered values satisfy the constraint conditions.

7. Global Constraints

Since the above optimization scheme performs motion analysis on each small region locally and independently, it suffers from discontinuities across borders, as the recovered structure and motion may change considerably from one small region to the other. Hence, appropriate global constraints are necessary in order to limit possible nonrigid behaviors and regularize the locally-recovered motion and structure. In the past, different shape models based on superquadrics [4,9], hyperquadrics [16,31], deformable superquadrics [54], extended superquadrics [66], finite element surface models [11,44], spherical-harmonics [40], polynomials [53,6], etc. have been proposed and actually used as global descriptions of nonrigid motion. However, it is very hard to find a suitable global shape model which is able to describe cloud motion adequately. With the absence of the global shape model, it is almost impossible to define global shape constraints such as in [44,14,52]. [27] used a hierarchical motion model with a global rigid motion to model the storm system translation and rotation. In our work, a set of novel global constraints are defined based on both the general motion smoothness assumption and specific fluid dynamics.

7.1. *Smooth Motion Assumption*

Since cloud motion is mostly smooth and has gradual variations in velocities in most parts [20], the smooth motion assumption can be utilized. This assumption was successfully utilized for nonrigid motion recovery from 3D data [29]. In our work, we assume that the fluid flow velocity components can be represented by a Taylor series expansion as

$$\mathbf{v}_t(\mathbf{P}) = (v_{tx}(\mathbf{P}), v_{ty}(\mathbf{P}), v_{tz}(\mathbf{P}))^T, \qquad (25)$$

where

$$v_{tx}(\mathbf{P}) = u_0 + u_1 x + u_2 y + u_3 z + u_4 x^2 + u_5 y^2 + u_6 z^2 + u_7 xy + u_8 xz + u_9 yz + \cdots,$$

$$v_{ty}(\mathbf{P}) = v_0 + v_1 x + v_2 y + v_3 z + v_4 x^2 + v_5 y^2 + v_6 z^2 + v_7 xy + v_8 xz + v_9 yz + \cdots,$$

$$v_{tz}(\mathbf{P}) = w_0 + w_1 x + w_2 y + w_3 z + w_4 x^2 + w_5 y^2 + w_6 z^2 + w_7 xy +$$

$$w_8 xz + w_9 yz + \cdots. \tag{26}$$

Essentially, Eq. 26 assumes that the velocity components are smoothly varying functions with continuous derivatives. Many researchers have used it in fluid flow modeling and visualization. Perry [45] used it to model stationary incompressible flow fields and Ford *et al.* [15] used it for fluid flow image visualization. In our algorithm, we found that second order Taylor series expansion is a good approximation of the cloud velocity field and a smoothness force can be defined as follows based on this observation,

$$E_{smoothness} = \sum_{i=1}^{m \text{ frames}} \sum_{j=1}^{n \text{ points}} \left\| \text{diag}\left(\left(\mathbf{v}_{i,j} - \mathbf{v}_t^i\left(\mathbf{P}_{i,j}\right)\right) \boldsymbol{\lambda}\right) \right\|, \tag{27}$$

where

$$\mathbf{v}_{i,j} = \delta^i(\mathbf{MP}_{i,j} + \mathbf{D}) - \mathbf{P}_{i,j}, \tag{28}$$

and $\mathbf{v}_t^i$ is the second order Taylor series expansions defined for the velocity field in frame i and $\boldsymbol{\lambda} = (\lambda_1, \lambda_2, \lambda_3)^T$ are positive weights. Clearly, Eq. 27 can serve as an internal force which will constrain and regularize the cloud motion flow and make the motion field smooth over the entire nonrigid object (cloud). However, all the coefficients in Eq. 26 are unknown initially. Methodology for obtaining these coefficients will be discussed later.

7.2. *Fluid Dynamics*

The dynamics of fluid flows are governed by three fundamental laws: the mass conservation law, Newton's second law of motion, commonly known as Navier-Stokes equations in fluid mechanics, and the energy conservation law. Several researchers have successfully employed them in recovering 2D flows from images [63,13,36]. In our work, since only kinematic information is available, we can use the mass conservation law to constrain the fluid cloud motion. The law of conservation of mass states that the net flux of mass entering an infinitesimal control volume is equal to rate of change of the mass of the element. For homogeneous incompressible fluid, it is the divergence-free condition,

$$\nabla \cdot \mathbf{v} = \frac{\partial v_x}{\partial x} + \frac{\partial v_y}{\partial y} + \frac{\partial v_z}{\partial z} = 0. \tag{29}$$

Since the cloud velocity components are represented by second order Taylor series expansion, the following constraint can be obtained after the mass conservation law is applied,

$$\nabla \cdot \mathbf{v}(\mathbf{P}) = u_1 + 2u_4 x + u_7 y + u_8 z + v_2 + 2v_5 y + v_7 x + v_9 z + w_3 + 2w_6 z + w_8 x + w_9 y$$

$$= (u_1 + v_2 + w_3) + (2u_4 + v_7 + w_8)x +$$

$$(2v_5 + u_7 + w_9)y + (2w_6 + u_8 + v_9)z = 0. \tag{30}$$

Eq. 30 provides an additional constraint when we solve the coefficients in Eq. 26.

7.3. *Incorporating the Global Constraints*

As mentioned before, all the coefficients in Eq. 26 are unknown initially. In order to incorporate the global constraints, a recursive algorithm is used.

First, we can get the initial point correspondences for each small region without global constraints by minimizing Eq. 23 locally. While the initial results may have a lot of noise, we can still use them to fit all the 30 coefficients in Eq. 26 (second order Taylor series expansion) for all the frames. The Levenberg-Marquardt method is employed. The EOF function to fit the velocity field function in frame i can be simply defined as

$$EOF^i_{global1} = \sum_{j=1}^{N \text{ points}} \left\| \mathbf{v}'_{i,j} - \mathbf{v}^i_t(\mathbf{P}_{i,j}) \right\|, \tag{31}$$

where $\mathbf{v}'_{i,j}$ is point j's velocity vector in frame i computed from the initial point correspondences. In addition, we want to include the fluid divergence-free condition (Eq. 29) in the fitting procedure, which can be done by rewriting Eq. 31 as the following,

$$EOF^i_{global2} = \sum_{j=1}^{N \text{ points}} \left(\left\| \mathbf{v}'_{i,j} - \mathbf{v}^i_t(\mathbf{P}_{i,j}) \right\| + \beta \left\| (\nabla \cdot \mathbf{v}^i_t(\mathbf{P}_{i,j}) \right\| \right), \tag{32}$$

where β is a positive constant.

Second, after all the coefficients in Eq. 26 are fitted, the global constraints can be easily incorporated into the local nonrigid motion model optimization by adding the smoothness force to Eq. 23,

$$EOF_{local3} = \sum_{i=1}^{m \text{ frames}} \sum_{j=1}^{n \text{ points}} \left(\min \left(d_{i,j}{}^1, d_{i,j}{}^2, d_{i,j}{}^3 \right) + cP_{i,j} \right) + E_{smoothness}.$$

$$(33)$$

Clearly, the new defined EOF function (Eq. 33) contains both local and global information. More regularized results can be obtained by performing optimization on each small cloud region by using the new EOF function. The above procedure is performed iteratively and the complete recursive algorithm is given in Algorithm 1.

Algorithm 1: A Recursive Algorithm for Structure and Nonrigid Motion Analysis

---

begin
    for $i := 1$ **to** n Regions **step** 1 **do**
        minimize Eq. 23 (without smoothness force) to get initial point
        correspondences for small cloud region i; **od**
    choose arbitrary initial **s** of large magnitude;
    while $\|s\|$ is greater than some threshold **do**
        compute **v**$'$ from the current point correspondences;
        for $i := 1$ **to** m Frames **step** 1 **do**
        minimize Eq. 32 to fit $\mathbf{v}_t^i(\mathbf{P}_{i,j})$ to $\mathbf{v}'$; **od**
        for $i := 1$ **to** n Regions **step** 1 **do**
        minimize Eq. 33 (with smoothness force) to get a new set
        of point correspondences for small cloud region i; **od**
        calculate the difference **s** between the current point
        correspondences and the previous point correspondences; **od**
end

The essence of this algorithm is to retrieve useful information under some proper constraints from current rough results and then use the information as global constraints for the next iteration's optimization. It is found that the algorithm works very well for the cloud application, and the desired convergence is achieved in our experiments. Fig. 5 presents the initial results (without global constraints) and the results after seven iterations. It is clear that the initial recovered depth can change dramatically from one small region to another and have a lot of noise while the results after incorporating global constraints are very smooth.

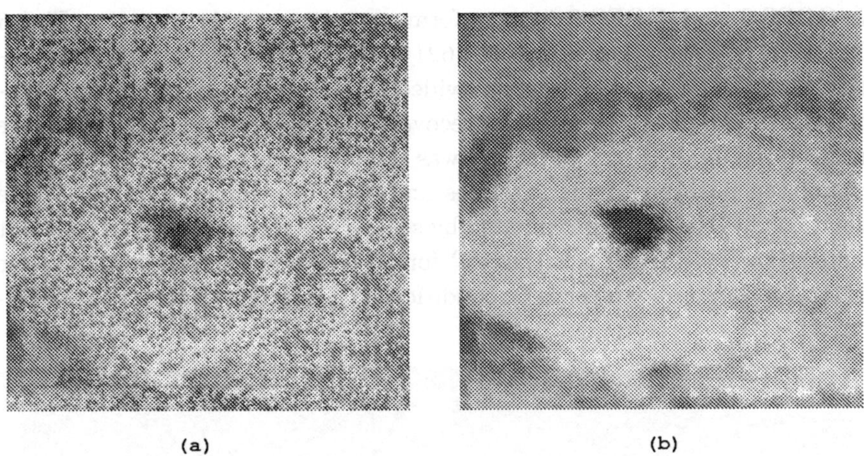

(a)   (b)

Fig. 5. Comparison of the results with and without global constraints: (a) initial results without global constraints; (b) results after seven iterations.

8. Experimental Results

Our system SMAS, implemented in C (on SGI platform), performs nonrigid motion and structure analysis on the cloud image sequences captured by GOES. To the best of our knowledge, this is the first reported system that automatically extracts dense cloud-top heights and winds from a sequence of cloud images.

We have conducted our experiments on hurricane Luis, which formed as tropical depression on Aug. 28, 1995. After 3.5 days as a tropical storm, it intensified to a Category 1 hurricane on Aug. 31 and later became a Category 4 hurricane on Sept. 1. The track of Luis covered the outer regions of Caribbean islands, Puerto Rico and some of the Virgin Islands. Luis did not make landfall in the U.S. but went back out to sea on Sept. 7 and by Sept. 11 was off the coast of Newfoundland where it had downgraded to a Category 1 hurricane.

We present the results for a sequence of 12 hurricane Luis images (from

1621 UTC to 1634 UTC). UTC (Coordinated Universal Time) formerly known as Greenwich Mean Time (GMT) refers to the time at zero degree meridian which crosses through Greenwich, England. 1621 UTC (Coordinated Universal Time) is used as the first frame in the experiments, as GOES-8 and GOES-9 images form a stereo at this instance. Fig. 6 shows the intensity images, from 1621 UTC to 1634 UTC (1-minute images from GOES-9), which are provided to our system. After seven iterations in SMAS, Fig. 7 shows the recovered dense cloud heights which are in disparity units (pixel shifts). It was found through mathematical analysis of the position of the satellites and viewing geometry that the true cloud heights can be approximated by scaling the disparity with a constant ($height(km) = 1.78097 \times disparity$) for midlatitude tropical storms under assumptions about atmospheric conditions [20]. In order to depict the recov-

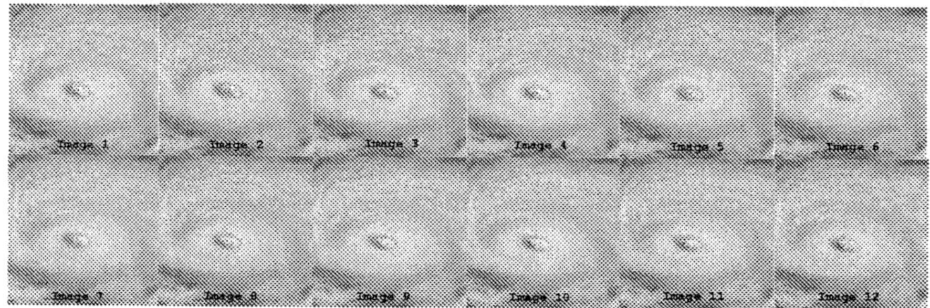

Fig. 6.   Input GOES images of Hurricane Luis (from 1621 UTC to 1634 UTC).

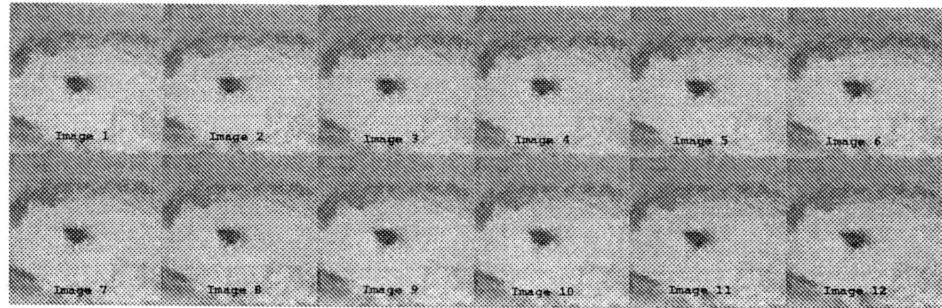

Fig. 7.   Recovered cloud-top heights of Hurricane Luis (from 1621 UTC to 1634 UTC).

ered cloud motion, we visualize the cloud motion in the $x - y$ plane and in the z axis separately. In fact, due to the scaled orthographic projection of the cloud images, the recovery of z motion becomes very important. Fig. 8 shows the recovered cloud motion which is projected on the $x - y$ plane and Fig. 9 illustrates the recovered z direction's motion (v_z) at every iteration step. As one may expect, the initially recovered z motion has a lot of noise. However, after the global constraints were applied, very good results are obtained at the seventh iteration step. It can be seen in Fig. 9 that the final recovered cloud motion has higher v_z in the hurricane eye and lower v_z in the hurricane body, which is a regular phenomenon for mature hurricanes [23]. In addition, when comparing the recovered 3D cloud motion with the original images visually through animations[c], the resulting tracking is accurate. Close examination showed that local analysis enables our algorithm to recover different kinds of nonrigid motions locally, including cloud surface expansion, contraction and also fluid phenomena such as cloud surface merging, splitting and crossing over. Quantitative validations are presented in the following section.

9. Validations

We explored various ways of validating our results, as it is almost impossible to get the ground truth of cloud top heights and motion. We found that our motion estimates are quite accurate when compared to manual analysis (within 1 pixel). In this section, we elaborate more on our structure estimation.

First, we compared SMAS estimated structure against the automatic stereo disparities in the last frame (UTC 1634) because UTC 1634 is the only frame (through UTC 1622 to UTC 1634) where the disparities are available. In this comparison, we found that our results are very close to the corresponding disparities for almost all the areas of the hurricane. Table 2 shows the mean errors for different parts of the hurricane. We also performed the same comparison at every iteration step at UTC 1634 in order to further evaluate the convergence and stability of our algorithm. Fig. 9 illustrates the change of the mean errors over successive iterations. Note that although the initial mean errors (at iteration 0) are very large (about

---

[c]For more results and animations, please refer to [65].

Fig. 8. 2D projection ($x - y$ plane) of the recovered cloud motion.

2.5), they decrease very quickly after the global constraints are applied. Stable mean errors are achieved at the seventh iteration.

Table 2. Comparison of the recovered structure and the stereo disparities at successive iterations.

	Hurricane Eye	*Hurricane Body*	*Hurricane Edge*
Mean Error	1.037744	0.707002	1.217665
$\dfrac{\text{Mean Error}}{\text{Overall Cloud Height}}$	6.92%	4.71%	8.12%

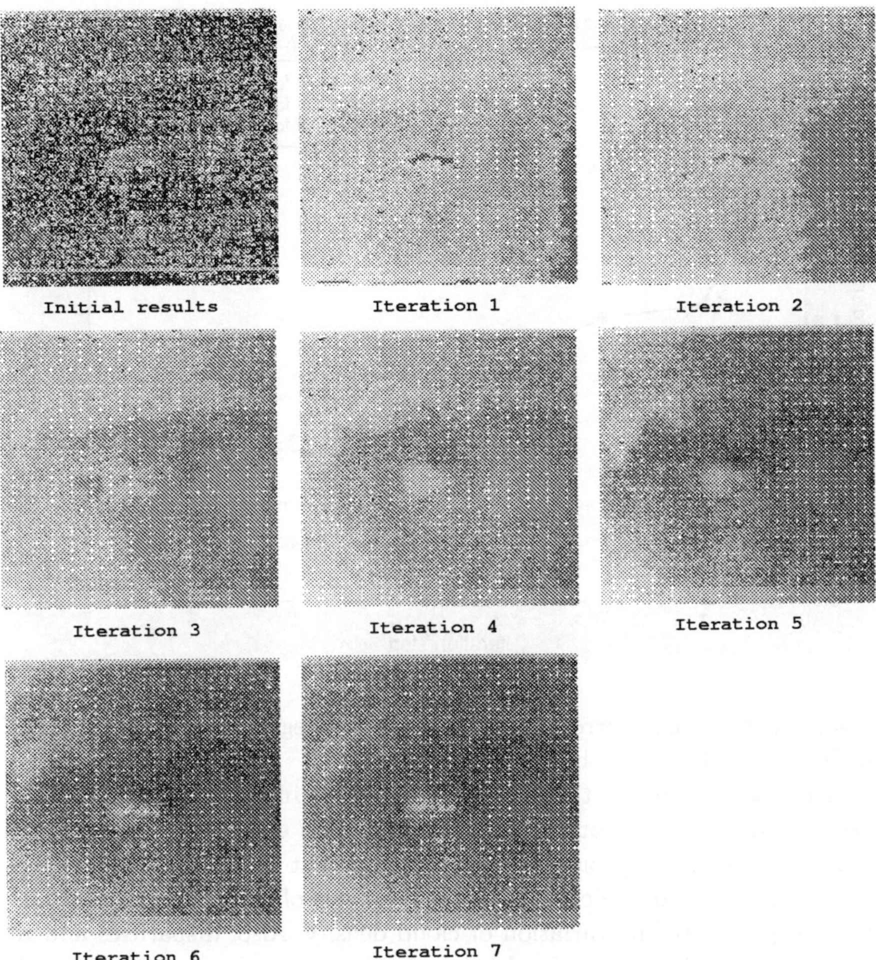

Initial results — Iteration 1 — Iteration 2

Iteration 3 — Iteration 4 — Iteration 5

Iteration 6 — Iteration 7

Fig. 9.   Recovered motion in the z direction (v_z) at every iteration step.

Another evaluation was made by comparing the recovered cloud-top heights against the IR (infrared) cloud-top heights, as IR is believed to be the closest to the ground-truth for cloud-top heights at the areas where the clouds are dense. Since IR heights are available at all the times, comparisons can be done for every frame (from UTC 1621 to UTC 1634). Fig. 10 shows the mean errors for different parts of the hurricane at every frame. It can

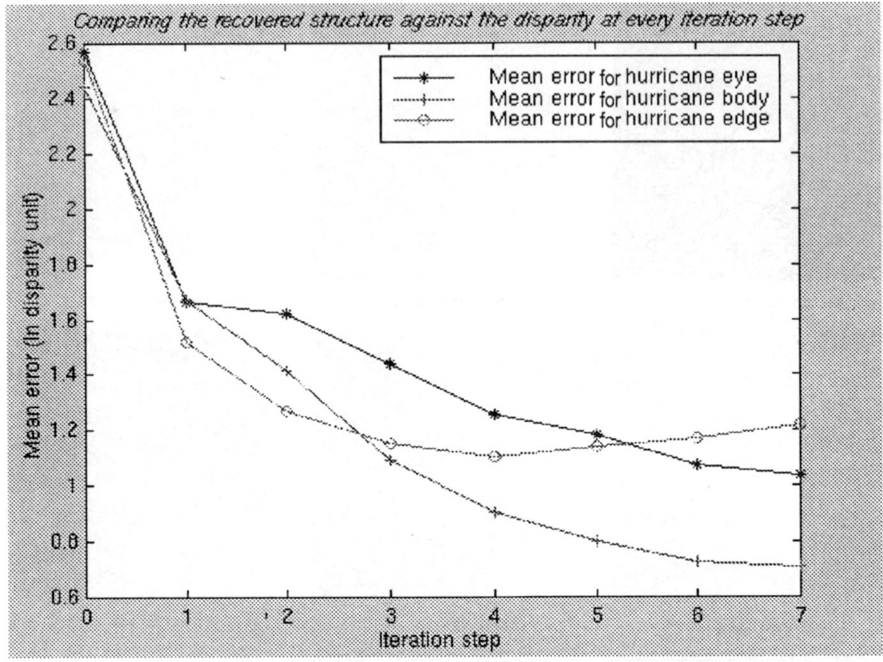

be seen that the mean errors are consistent and negligible for most parts of
the hurricane (hurricane body).

It can also be noted that larger errors occur in the hurricane eye and
the hurricane edge in both our evaluations. This error distribution stems
from the assumption in our global constraints that cloud is a homogeneous
incompressible fluid, which may fail in the areas of hurricane eye and hurricane edge due to the variation of cloud density. Also, disparities and IR
are not good estimates of cloud height in these areas since these areas do
not consist of thick clouds. However, for most parts of the clouds, the mean
errors are negligible (0.6 to 0.8 disparity units).

10. Conclusions and Future Work

This chapter presents the tracking of dense structure and nonrigid motion
from a sequence of 2D images with application towards 3D cloud tracking.
The main contribution of this work is that it not only deals with the problem of recovering structure from the scaled orthographic projection views

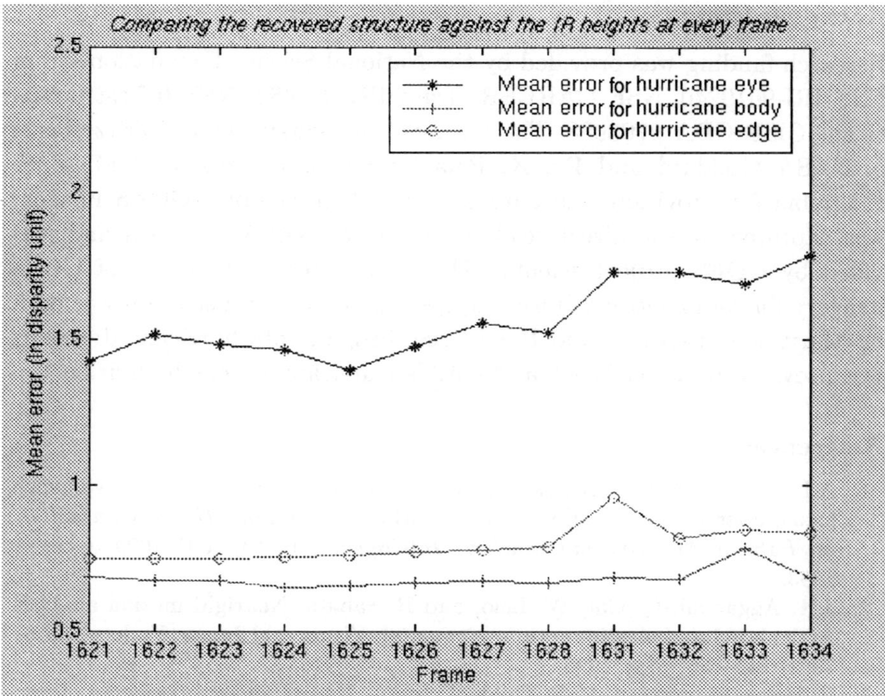

Fig. 10.   Comparison of the recovered structure and the IR heights at successive frames.

but also performs nonrigid motion estimation to obtain 3D correspondences by integrating local and global analysis. The results are very encouraging and have applications in earth and space sciences, especially in cloud models for weather prediction. This work can also be easily applied for data under perspective projections such as lip motion, human facial expressions, biomedical applications etc. Our ultimate goal is to have a set of techniques that can perform cloud motion classification and apply appropriate motion models in cloud tracking and nonrigid motion and structure analysis for climate studies.

Our specific future work includes: 1) Use of complex fluid models to capture the variation of fluid density in clouds; 2) Cloud motion segmentation; 3) Use of multispectral satellite images in cloud structure and nonrigid motion tracking; 4) Robust parallel implementation of the algorithms to improve the efficiency.

Acknowledgments

Research funding was provided by the National Science Foundation Grant NSF IRI-9619240, NSF CAREER Grant IRI 998482, NSF Infrastructure Grant CISE CDA 9703088. The authors are thankful to Dr. Fritz Hasler of NASA Goddard and Dr. K. Palaniappan of University of Missouri-Columbia for providing the data and useful discussions. GOES imagery was captured by the direct readout system at NASA Goddard and provided by GOES project scientist Dennis Chesters. Processing of GOES imagery for radiometric calibration, geolocation and registration was done by Marit Jentoft-Nilsen and Hal Pierce. Insights into hurricane dynamics was provided by Peter Black at NOAA's Hurricane Research Division.

References

1. A.L. Abbott and N. Ahuja. Active stereo: Integrating disparity, vergence, focus, aperture, and calibration for surface estimation. *IEEE Transactions on Pattern Analysis and Machine Intelligence*, 15(10):1007–1029, October 1993.
2. J.K. Aggarwal, Q. Cai, W. Liao, and B. Sabata. Nonrigid motion analysis: Articulated and elastic motion. *Computer Vision and Image Understanding*, 70(2):142–156, May 1998.
3. R. Balasubramanian, D. B. Goldgof, and C. Kambhamettu. Tracking of nonrigid motion and 3d structure from 2d image sequences without correspondences. *Proceedings of International Conference on Image Processing*, 1:933 – 937, October 1998.
4. A. H. Barr. Superquadrics and angle preserving transformations. *IEEE Computer Graphics and Applications*, 1:11–23, 1981.
5. M.J. Black and Y. Yacoob. Recognizing facial expressions in image sequences using local parameterized models of image motion. *International Journal of Computer Vision*, 25(1):23–48, October 1997.
6. R. M. Bolle and B. C. Vemuri. On three-dimensional surface reconstruction methods. *IEEE Transactions on Pattern Analysis and Machine Intelligence*, 13(1):1–13, 1991.
7. K.L. Boyer and A.C. Kak. Structural stereo for 3-d vision. *IEEE Transactions on Pattern Analysis and Machine Intelligence*, 10(2):144–166, March 1988.
8. R. Chellappa. Structure from motion: Light at the end of tunnel! In *Proceedings of International Conference on Image Processing*, page 26PS1, 1999.
9. C. W. Chen and T. S. Huang. Nonrigid object motion and deformation estimation from three-dimensional data. *International Journal of Imaging Systems and Technology*, 2:385–394, 1990.
10. K. Chen, C. Kambhamettu, and D. B. Goldgof. Extraction of mpeg-4 fap parameters from 3d face data sequences. *International Workshop on Very*

Low Bitrate Video Coding, pages 77–80, October 8-9, 1998.

11. S. S. Chen and A. Zhao. Image representation of moving nonrigid objects. *Journal of Visual Communication and Image Representation*, pages 199–207, 1991.

12. D. DeCarlo and D. Metaxas. Deformable model-based shape and motion analysis from images using motion residual error. In *Proceedings of IEEE Computer Society International Conference on Computer Vision*, pages 113–119, 1998.

13. E.M. Emin and P. Perez. Fluid motion recovery by coupling dense and parametric vector fields. In *Proceedings of IEEE Computer Society International Conference on Computer Vision*, pages 620–625, 1999.

14. I. A. Essa and A. P. Pentland. Coding, analysis, interpretation, and recognition of facial expressions. *IEEE Transactions on Pattern Analysis and Machine Intelligence*, 19, No. 7:757–763, 1997.

15. R.M. Ford and R.N. Strickland. Representing and visualizing fluid-flow images and velocimetry data by nonlinear dynamical-systems. *Graphical Models and Image Processing*, 57(6):462–482, November 1995.

16. A. J. Hanson. Hyperquadrics: Smoothly deformable shapes with convex polyhedral bounds. *Computer Vision, Graphics and Image Processing*, 44:191–210, 1988.

17. A. F. Hasler. Stereographic observations from satellites: An important new tool for the atmospheric sciences. *Bull. Amer. Meteor. Soc.*, 62:194–212, 1981.

18. A. F. Hasler. Stereoscopic measurements. In P. K. Rao, S. J. Holms, R. K. Anderson, J. Winston, and P. Lehr, editors, *Weather Satellites: Systems, Data and Environmental Applications, Section VII-3*, pages 231–239. Amer. Meteor. Soc., Boston, MA, 1990.

19. A. F. Hasler and K. R. Morris. Hurricane structure and wind fields from stereoscopic and infrared satellite observations and radar data. *J. Climate Appl. Meteor.*, 25:709–727, 1986.

20. A.F. Hasler, K. Palaniappan, C. Kambhamettu, P. Black, E. Uhlhorn, and D. Chesters. High-resolution wind fields within the inner core and eye of a mature tropical cyclone from GOES 1-min images. *Bulletin of the American Meteorological Society*, 79(11):2483–2496, November, 1998.

21. T. S. Huang. Modeling,analysis,and visualization of nonrigid object motion. *Proceedings of International Conference on Pattern Recognition*, pages 361–364, December 1990.

22. W. C. Huang and D. B. Goldgof. Adaptive-size meshes for rigid and nonrigid shape analysis and synthesis. *IEEE Transactions on Pattern Analysis and Machine Intelligence*, 15(6):611–616, June, 1993.

23. D.P. Jorgensen. Mesoscale and convective-scale characteristics of mature hurricanes: Part I. general observations by research aircraft. *Journal of the Atmospheric Sciences*, 41:1268–1285, 1984.

24. I.A. Kakadiaris and D. Metaxas. Model-based estimation of 3D human motion with occlusion based on active multi-viewpoint selection. In *Proceedings*

of IEEE conference on Computer Vision and Pattern Recognition, pages 81–87, 1996.

25. C. Kambhamettu, D. B. Goldgof, D. Terzopoulos, and T. S. Huang. Nonrigid motion analysis. In Tzay Young, editor, *Handbook of Pattern Recognition and Image Processing: Computer vision*, volume II, pages 405–430. Academic Press, San Diego, California, 1994.

26. C. Kambhamettu, K. Palaniappan, and A. F. Hasler. Coupled, multi-resolution stereo and motion analysis. *IEEE International Symposium on Computer Vision*, pages 43–48, November 1995.

27. C. Kambhamettu, K. Palaniappan, and A. F. Hasler. Hierarchical motion decomposition for cloud-tracking. In *AMS 17th Conference on Interactive Information and Processing Systems (IIPS) for Meteorology, Oceanography, and Hydrology*, pages 318–323, Albuquerque, New Mexico, 2001.

28. C. Kambhamettu, K. Palaniappan, and A. F. Hasler. Automated cloud-drift winds from GOES images. *SPIE Proceedings on GOES-8 and Beyond*, 2812:122–133, August, 1996.

29. ChandraSekhar Kambhamettu. *Nonrigid Motion Analysis Under Small Deformations*. PhD thesis, University of South Florida, December 1994. Department of Computer Science and Engineering.

30. R. Koch. Dynamic 3-D scene analysis through synthesis feedback control. *IEEE Transactions on Pattern Analysis and Machine Intelligence*, 15(6):556–568, June 1993.

31. S. Kumar, S. Han, D. Goldgof, and K. Bowyer. On recovering hyperquadrics from range data. *IEEE Transactions on Pattern Analysis and Machine Intelligence*, 17(11):1079–1083, November 1995.

32. J. A. Leese, C. S. Novak, and B. B. Clark. An automated technique for obtaining cloud motion from geosynchronous satellite data using cross-correlation. *Journal of Applied Meteorology*, 10:118–132, 1971.

33. H. Li, P. Roivainen, and R. Forchheimer. 3-D motion estimation in model-based facial image coding. *IEEE Transactions on Pattern Analysis and Machine Intelligence*, 15(6):545–555, June 1993.

34. D. G. Luenberger. In *Linear and Nonlinear Programming*. Addison-Wesley, 1984.

35. C. Mandal, B.C. Vemuri, and H. Qin. Shape recovery using dynamic subdivision surfaces. In *Proceedings of IEEE Computer Society International Conference on Computer Vision*, pages 805–810, 1998.

36. M. Maurizot, P. Bouthemy, and B. Delyon. 2D fluid motion analysis from a single image. In *Proceedings of IEEE conference on Computer Vision and Pattern Recognition*, pages 184–191, 1998.

37. T. McInerney and D. Terzopoulos. A finite element model for 3d shape reconstruction and nonrigid motion tracking. *Proceedings of IEEE Computer Society International Conference on Computer Vision*, 1993.

38. D. Metaxas and D. Terzopoulos. Shape and nonrigid motion estimation through physics-based synthesis. *IEEE Transactions on Pattern Analysis and*

Machine Intelligence, 15(6):580–591, June 1993. Also in Proceedings of IEEE Computer Vision and Pattern Recognition Conference (CVPR'91), pp. 337–343, Hawaii, June 1991.

39. P. Minnis, P. W. Heck, and E. F. Harrison. The 27-28 october 1986 fire ifo cirrus case study: Cloud parameter fields derived from satellite data. *Monthly Weather Review*, 118:2426–2447, 1990.

40. S. K. Mishra, D. B. Goldgof, and T. S. Huang. Non-rigid motion analysis and epicardial deformation estimation from angiography data. *Proceedings of IEEE conference on Computer Vision and Pattern Recognition*, pages 331–336, June 1991.

41. K. Palaniappan, M. Faisal, C. Kambhamettu, and A. F. Hasler. Implementation of an automatic semi-fluid motion analysis algorithm on a massively parallel computer. *IEEE International Parallel Processing Symposium*, pages 864–872, 1996.

42. K. Palaniappan, C. Kambhamettu, A. Frederick Hasler, and D. B. Goldgof. Structure and semi-fluid motion analysis of stereoscopic satellite images for cloud tracking. *Proceedings of the International Conference on Computer Vision*, pages 659–665, 1995.

43. K. Palaniappan, J. Vass, and X. Zhuang. Parallel robust relaxation algorithm for automatic stereo analysis. In *Proceedings of SPIE Parallel and Distributed Methods for Image Processing II*, pages 958–962, San Diego, CA, 1998.

44. A. Pentland and B. Horowitz. Recovery of nonrigid motion and structure. *IEEE Transactions on Pattern Analysis and Machine Intelligence*, pages 730–742, July 1991.

45. A. E. Perry and M. S. Chong. A description of eddying motions and flow patterns using critical point concepts. *Ann. Rev. Fluid Mech.*, 19:125–155, 1987.

46. D. R. Phillips, E. A. Smith, and V. E. Suomi. Comment on 'An automated technique for obtaining cloud motion from geosynchronous satellite data using cross-correlation'. *Journal of Applied Meteorology*, 11:752–754, 1972.

47. A. F. Hasler R. A. Mack and R. F. Adler. Thunderstorm cloud top observations using satellite stereoscopy. *Monthly Weather Review*, 111:1949–1964, 1983.

48. E. Rodgers, R. Mack, and A. F. Hasler. A satellite stereoscopic technique to estimate tropical cyclone intensity. *Monthly Weather Review*, 111:1599–1610, 1983.

49. P. Shi, A.J. Sinusas, R.T. Constable, and J.S. Duncan. Volumetric deformation analysis using mechanics-based data fusion: Applications in cardiac motion recovery. *International Journal of Computer Vision*, 35(1):87–107, November 1999.

50. E. A. Smith and D. R. Phillips. Automated cloud tracking using precisely aligned digital ATS pictures. *IEEE Transactions on Computers*, C-21:715–729, 1972.

51. M. Subbarao. Interpretation of image flow: A spatio-temporal approach.

IEEE Transactions on Pattern Analysis and Machine Intelligence, 11(3):266–278, March 1989.

52. H. Tao and T.S. Huang. Explanation-based facial motion tracking using a piecewised bezier volume deformation model. In *Proceedings of IEEE conference on Computer Vision and Pattern Recognition*, pages I:611–617, 1999.

53. G. Taubin. Estimation of planar curves, surfaces, and nonplanar curves defined by implicit equations with applications to edge and range image segmentation. *IEEE Transactions on Pattern Analysis and Machine Intelligence*, 13(11):1115–1138, Nov. 1991.

54. D. Terzopoulos and D. Metaxas. Dynamic 3D models with local and global deformations: Deformable superquadrics. *IEEE Transactions on Pattern Analysis and Machine Intelligence*, (13):703–714, July 1991.

55. D. Terzopoulos and K. Waters. Analysis and synthesis of facial image sequences using physical and anatomical models. *IEEE Transactions on Pattern Analysis and Machine Intelligence*, 15(6):569–579, 1993. Also *Proc. Third International Conf. on Computer Vision* Osaka, Japan, December, 1990, 727–732.

56. D. Terzopoulos, A. Witkin, and M. Kass. Constraints on deformable models: Recovering 3D shape and nonrigid motion. *Artificial Intelligence*, 36(1):91–123, 1988.

57. L.V. Tsap, D.B. Goldgof, S. Sarkar, and W.C. Huang. Efficient nonlinear finite element modeling of nonrigid objects via optimization of mesh models. *Computer Vision and Image Understanding*, 69(3):330–350, March 1998.

58. C.S. Velden. Winds derived from geostationary satellite moisture channel observations: Applications and impact on numerical weather prediction. *Meteorology and Atmospheric Physics*, 60:37–46, 1996.

59. C.S. Velden, C.M. Hayden, S. Nieman, W.P. Menzel, S. Wanzong, and J. Goerss. Upper-tropospheric winds derived from geostationary satellite water vapor observations. *American Meteorological Society*, 78:173–195, 1997.

60. C.S. Velden, T.L. Olander, and S. Wanzong. The impact of multispectral GOES-8 wind information on Atlantic tropical cyclone track forecasts in 1995. Part 1: Dataset methodology, description and case analysis. *Monthly Weather Review*, 1998.

61. J. Weng, T.S. Huang, and N. Ahuja. Motion and structure from line correspondences: Closed-form solution, uniqueness, and optimization. *IEEE Transactions on Pattern Analysis and Machine Intelligence*, 14(3):318–336, March 1992.

62. P. Werkhoveh, A. Toet, and J.J. Koenderink. Displacement estimates through adaptive affinities. *IEEE Transactions on Pattern Analysis and Machine Intelligence*, 12(7):658–663, July 1990.

63. R.P. Wildes, M.J. Amabile, A.M. Lanzillotto, and T.S. Leu. Recovering estimates of fluid flow from image sequence data. *Computer Vision and Image Understanding*, 80(2):246–266, November 2000.

64. T.H. Wu, R. Chellappa, and Q.F. Zheng. Experiments on estimating egomo-

tion and structure parameters using long monocular image sequences. *International Journal of Computer Vision*, 15(1-2):77–103, June 1995.

65. L. Zhou and C. Kambhamettu. *http://www.cis.udel.edu/~vims*.

66. L. Zhou and C. Kambhamettu. Extending superquadrics with exponent functions: Modeling and reconstruction. *Graphical Models*, 63(1):1–20, January 2001.

67. L. Zhou, C. Kambhamettu, and D. Goldgof. Fluid structure and motion analysis from multi-spectrum 2D cloud image sequences. In *Proceedings of IEEE conference on Computer Vision and Pattern Recognition*, pages II:744–751, 2000.

68. L. Zhou, C. Kambhamettu, D. B. Goldgof, K. Palaniappan, and Hasler A. F. Tracking nonrigid motion and structure from 2D satellite cloud images without correspondences. *IEEE Transactions on Pattern Analysis and Machine Intelligence*, 2001.

69. Lin Zhou. *3D Nonrigid Motion Analysis from 2D Images*. PhD thesis, University of Delaware, February 2001. Department of Computer and Information Sciences.

tion and structure parameters using long monocular image sequences. International Journal of Computer Vision, 18(1-2):77–103, June 1995.

55. L. Zhao and O. Kambhamettu. http://www.cis.udel.edu/~vims.

56. L. Zhou and C. Kambhamettu. Extending superquadrics with exponent functions: Modeling and reconstruction. Graphical Models 63(1):1–20, January 2001.

57. L. Zhou, C. Kambhamettu, and D. Goldgof. Fluid structure and motion analysis from multi-spectrum 2D cloud image sequences. In Proceedings of IEEE conference on Computer Vision and Pattern Recognition, pages II:744–751, 2000.

58. L. Zhou, C. Kambhamettu, D. B. Goldgof, K. Palaniappan, and Hasler A. F. tracking nonrigid motion and structure from 2D satellite cloud images without correspondences. IEEE Transactions on Pattern Analysis and Machine Intelligence, 2001.

59. Lin Zhou. 3D Nonrigid Motion Analysis from 2D Images. PhD thesis, University of Delaware, February 2001. Department of Computer and Information Sciences.

Map Structure Recognition and Automatic Map Data Acquisition

Yuncai Liu

Shanghai Jiao Tong University
1954 Hua Shan Road
Shanghai 20030, P. R. China

1. Introduction

With rapid development in technologies of Intelligent Transportation Systems (ITS), Global Position Systems (GPS) and computer science, digital map databases have become ever more important in many applications. Digital map databases play a core rule in the systems of vehicle location, vehicle navigation and land planning. In creation of map databases, presently, computer-interactive digitalization is popularly used. Since considerable time and a large number of manual operators are necessary in the map tracing process, it usually leads to high costs of map databases and slow updating of map information. Automatic methods, however, can solve the problems using techniques of computer vision and pattern recognition in creatting digital map databases. By employing automation in the operation of map database production, costs of map databases are reduced and the time for updating of map information is shortened.

Digital map databases have several layers, such as the administrative layer, the layers of road database, building/house block database, contour lines and other layers. In producing digital map databases from pictorial maps, generating vector road data and building/house block data are major tasks. We will concentrate ourselves on generations of road data and building block data in the following discussions. From the point of view of computer vision and image processing, the major technical issues are map structure segmentation, map structure recognition and map data vectorization.

Over past two decades, researchers made continuous efforts trying to understand geometric information from map images. Examples of those who worked on building/house structure recognition are Tavokili and Rosenfeld (1982), Mclone and Shufelt (1993) and Lin and Nevatia (1996). The researchers working on road map structure detection include Geman and Jedynak (1996) and Barzohar and Cooper (1996). Although they made significant work in map structure detection and recognition, the distances from their research achievements to the technical requirements of industrial applications are quite large. Toward actual industrial applications of automatic generation of digital map data, some researchers started to build real systems to create digital map data from pictorial images. The research in the field of generating digital map data from pictorial images is very significant presently since the resource of master maps are largely available in paper map forms. Map database companies are still using manual methods to collect map data from pictorial map resources.

The most significant researches in digital map database generation can be traced to early 1990s. In 1988, Musavi et al. (1988) proposed a digitizing method for efficient storage of maps. As it was developed only for map storage, map components were not recognized. In 1990, Suzuki and Yamada (1990) published a paper describing an actual system called MARIS. This system was used to generate databases of building blocks and contour lines from large-scale-reduced Japanese maps. Late, Boatto et al. (1992) developed a system of land map interpretation. This system aimed to abstract and recognize shaded regions, such as building blocks, and characters for land registration. Yamada et al. (1991) made discussions for map component separation. In Kasturi et al. (1990), line drawing interpretation is addressed, which technique can be used for map graph segmentation.

In this chapter, we present a prototype industrial system of digital map database generation. In the applications of vehicle navigation and vehicle location, a map database mainly consists of road data, building block data and contour lines. With the proposed system, each type of map data, in vector format, can be automatically generated from images of paper maps. In this chapter, we also introduce a new algorithm named "rolling ball", which works efficiently for road data generation.

The organization of this chapter is as follows. Section 2 describes the configuration of the system. Section 3 discusses pixel-level processes used in this system. Section 4 presents the presentations of map graphs. In Section 5, we discuss the method of map graph segmentations and re-linking. In section

6, we will mention the techniques of road data generation and introduce an algorithm of *rolling ball,* which can recognize and vectorize map data simultaneously. Section 7 gives the method of building/house data generation. In Section 8, we conclude this chapter with the results of digital map data generated from real map images.

2. System Framework

The purpose of the system of map structure recognition and map data generation is to convert binary map images obtained from pictorial maps to the vector data of digital maps. According to applications, the digital map data can be classified into two categories. One category of digital map data is road map data. Road map data are graphs of road central lines and road inter-junctions. Central line graphs of roads consist of road-central line nodes linked in sequences. The distances between two road nodes are about a half a road width. This kind of digital road map data is usually used for the purpose of land vehicle navigation.

Another category of digital map data is graphs of house data. House map data are often used in geographic positioning. For such an application, each house or building is required to have its independent graph structure. Even several houses or buildings are interconnected in original master maps, they should have individual structure in the digital map database to allow individually accessing in position applications. Digital house map data also require that the map data keep the shapes of original houses or buildings. Therefore, polygons are used in representation of house structures.

In our proposed system, the operations of map preprocessing, map image thinning and converting map images to map graphs are carried out in pixel image domains. All the remaining processes, including map graph segmentation, road structure and house structure recognitions and map data vectorizations are performed in graph domains. Processing in graph domains has advantages of flexible access and easy management.

The Figure 1 gives the diagram of the systemic concept of automatic digital map data generation. In this system, the operations of preprocessing and thinning are pixel-level processes. Graph conversion acts as a bridge to link pixel maps and graph maps, converting skeleton map images of thinning results to graphs. The map structure segmentation has two components, house structure segmentation and road structure segmentation. In house segmentation, houses or buildings are separated from roads, characters and map coordinated lines. Furthermore, interconnected draws of houses are decomposed to individual ones in this operation. In road structure segmentation, characters

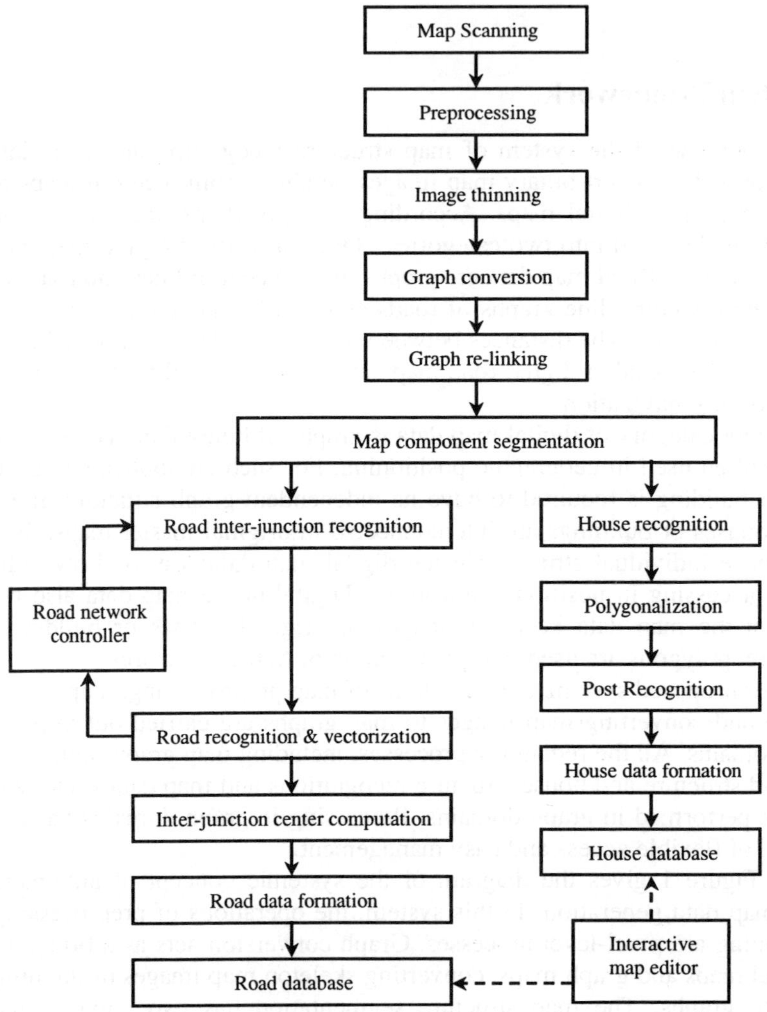

Figure 1. System configuration

and symbols including isolated ones and those lying on road lines are removed. The other map draws between a pair of road lines, such as road bridges, can also be removed in road structure segmentation, leading it "clean" between a pair of road boundaries.

Road data generation consists of several processes. They are road structure recognition and vectorization, road inter-junction recognition, road network exploration and road inter-junction computation. In road structure recognition and vectorization, we developed a process called rolling ball, which can simultaneously recognize and vectorize a road body. Here a road body is a piece of road between two road inter-junctions or road ends. The operation of road inter-junction recognition detects road inter-junction structures and branches of the inter-junctions. Road network exploration interweaves the operations of road body recognition and road inter-junction recognition to vectorize a whole road network from a single search-point. Road inter-junction computation mathematically computes the center of a road inter-junction, yielding an accurate position of a road inter-junction in the resultant road map database.

House data generation consists of polygonalization and related operations. To preserve the shapes and locations of original house structures, we first detect the breaking points of graphs of house. Then, polygonalization is applied to each piece of graphs. This kind process can generate very accurate polygon approximation of original house structures. Polygon beautification operation is not necessary in this system.

3. Pixel-Level Processing

The map images obtained from scanners are binary pixel images. In binary pixel images, each pixel has valued 0/1, or black/white. In acquisition of map images, binarization is performed in scanning process by properly selecting model of a scanner. The pixel-level operations in our system consist of preprocessing, binary image thinning and map graph conversion.

3.1. Preprocessing

The raw map images acquired from scanning usually contain noise that is from the imperfect of original master maps or generated in map scanning. The common type of the noise is salt-and-pepper noise. This noise appears as isolated white pixels or pixel regions within black image areas, or black pixels or pixel regions within white areas. This kind of noise is very harmful, especially when the noise appears in the map feature areas, since it can cause extraneous features in map graphs, leading to subsequent errors in recognitions and vectorizations.

Preprocessing is to reduce image noise. In our system, two kinds of filling methods are used in noise reduction. One is median filtering. The other is morphological closing operation. Morphological closing is made up with other two morphological operations: a binary dilation followed by binary erosion. In general cases, median filter works efficiently in noise reduction for almost all map images. However, in the case that graphical components of original map images are too thin, e.g., line draws of a single pixel width, the operation of a median filter intends to remove the graphical components. In this case, the number of on-pixels of the map image will be sharply reduced. The system can detect this phenomenon and then switch to use a morphological filter to redo the noise reducing operation.

3.2. Map Image Thinning

Thinning operation in our system is to reduce the contents of map images to curves that approximate to the central lines of the map components. The resultant central lines of map components are called map skeletons. Therefore, the operation of map image thinning is also called skeletoning in our system. We perform the thinning operation to change the images of map components to the curves of single pixel width so that the maps can be converted to map graphs. For maximum preservation of original shapes of map components in graph domain and minimum reduction of graph redundancy, the thinning operation should meet the following requirements: (1) resultant map skeletons from thinning operation must have strictly a single pixel width with eight-connection neighboring. (2) No disconnection should be created in thinning process. (3) Road inter-junctions of original map components should be well preserved. (4) Corner points of original map components should be maintained. Besides, the extraneous spurs created in map thinning operation should be minimized.

In general, thinning operation is an iterative process. It will take longer time to process since the operation needs to visit every pixel of a map image in all iterations. Seeking for a fast performance of a tinning operation is critical in our application. In selection of thinning algorithms, two requirements need to fit. First, the thinning algorithm should have a fast operation. Second, it can be easily implemented by hardware, since hardware thinner can provide very fast operation. It is suitable for industrial applications of automatic digital map generation.

As binary image thinning is a classic technique, there are many algorithms available. With the above technical requirements, we found that the method of Chen and Tsai (1990) suitable to our application even it needs some modifications. The method of Chen and Tsai is a one-pass parallel algorithm. In an iteration of thinning, only the immediately previous frame of image is examined, the operation speed is fast. The technique of thinning is a template-based process. The software implementation of the algorithm needs only logical operations at pixel level of images. Therefore, this tinning operation can be easily implemented by hardware. The method of Chen and Tsai involves 35 operational templates: 26 A-type templates and 9 B-type templates. In our testing, we find that templates of A_{11}, A_{12}, A_{13}, A_{14}, A_{15}, A_{16}, A_{16}, A_{17} and A_{18} intend to remove the skeleton lines of $\forall 45$ degrees. These templates originally were designed to remove image noise. Since image noise had been removed in the operation of preprocessing, the operations of A_{11} to A_{18} are not implemented in our system. Meantime, we find that the operational templates A_{19}, A_{20}, A_{21}, A_{22}, A_{23}, A_{24}, A_{25} and A_{26} are redundant, their operations have been involved in the other template operations. Thus, the template operations of A_{19} to A_{26} are omitted in our thinning operation. Since there are only 19 templates in thinning, the operation speed is improved. For a 2000H2000map image, one minute is enough to thin a map image with 12 iterations if the technique is implemented by software at a Sun 170E workstation.

4. Graph Representations of Maps

Original map images and thinned map skeletons are pixel-level images. Since pixel level images are difficult to handle in feature level processes, we encode the images of map skeleton into map graphs. In early graphical processes of the system, each graph node represents an on-pixel of a map skeleton. Late, super graph is introduced for feature level processes, such as map graph segmentation and map structure recognition. A super graph of map has two components: super nodes and super chains. A super graph fully describes geometrical and topological properties of a map and gives a whole picture of the original skeleton map image.

4.1. Graph Conversion

Map skeletons, the thinned map images, can be efficiently represented by map graph. In this stage, each on-pixel of map skeleton is converted to a graph node. In the graph representation, each connected component of map skeleton is represented by a graph. Because of the topological relations among graph nodes, it brings great convenient to feature level processes. Unlike pixel-level operations, the pixels outside a map skeleton do not need to be examined anymore.

In our definition, a graph node has six attributes to describe its geometric and topological properties. These attributes are node number, curve number, position, type, link-list and flag. The node number of a graph node is the serial number of the node in a node collection. The curve number of a node is the sequential number of the connected graphic component that the node belongs to. The position of a graph node gives the coordinates of the node in map image plane. The attribute "type" is the number of links that connect from the node to its neighboring nodes in a graph. Link-list describes the topological relations of the node with other neighbor nodes. A node flag is usually used only in graphic processing of maps.

Among the attributes of a graph node, "type" is especially useful. Since it gives the number of topological links of a node, the attribute can be used to classify the category of a node. For example, type valued zero of a node indicates that the node is an isolated node. Type equal to 1 indicates that the node is an end node. If a node has type 2, this node is a chin node inside a graph. When the type of a graph node is greater than 2, this node is then a

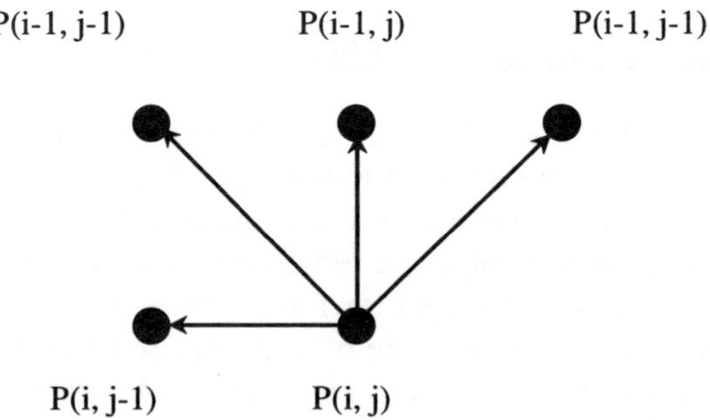

Figure 2. Pixel-labeling to convert skeleton to graph

junction node. Furthermore, the value of the type of a junction node clearly indicates how many branches the junction has. It can be efficiently used in many graph processes such as graph segmentation.

The graph representation of a skeleton map image can be obtained by labeling, as shown in Figure 2. Scanning a map skeleton image from top-left to bottom-right, when a skeleton on-pixel is met, we record the pixel as a node and initialize the type of the node to be zero. Then we check the left, up-left, up and up-right neighbors of the currently considered pixel. If any one of the neighbor pixels is a skeleton on-pixel, the value of type increases by one, and the node number of the neighboring on-pixel is added to the link list of the current node. Meantime, the on-pixel neighboring nodes also increase their type values and record the current node in their link lists to form a bi-directional graph. If no on-pixel is find in the neighboring examination, the node is then considered as a starting node to create a new graph. In this way, after going through all the pixels of a skeleton map image, the connected components in the map image are coded to topological graphs.

4.2. Graph Redundancy and Redundancy Elimination

In a well-defined graph structure, there should be only one path from a graph node to another if the distance between the two nodes is equal to or less than $\sqrt{2}$ pixel grids in eight-neighboring connections. Map graphs created by labeling method may have multiple paths between two neighbor nodes. This kind of multiple linkage between two nodes, so-called graph redundancy, can cause problems in feature level processes. To discuss the redundancy and redundancy elimination of graphs, we first make the definition of knot, and the definitions of dimension and rank of a knot.

Definition: in a map graph, a knot is a collection of graph nodes in which all the nodes have the link lists with at least two nodes that are neighboring nodes. The number of nodes in a knot is called the dimension of the knot.

Definition: the rank of a graph knot is an integer that equals to the number of the branch nodes of the knot. The branch nodes of a knot are the neighboring nodes outside the knot and directly link with the nodes inside of the knot. The branch nodes do not belong to nodes of the knot.

Figure 3 gives examples of graph knots. In the figures, graph (a) is a knot of dimension of 3 and rank of 1, the graph (b) dimension 3 and rank 2, graph (c) dimension 5 and rank 4, and graph (d) dimension 9 and rank 8. In a knot, graph nodes have multiple paths to reach its neighboring nodes. This is graphically redundant, and it can cause problems in graph processes. This graphical redundancy should be eliminated before any further processes.

Definition: a map graph is called redundant if it has one or more knots inside the graph. Redundancy of a map graph can be eliminated. The redundancy elimination can be don by reducing a knot of the graph to a graph node. If the rank of a graph knot is equal to or less than 8, it can be replaced a graph node with the type value of the node equal to the rank of the knot, the link-list of the node is the lists of the branch nodes of the knot.

With above definition, eliminating graph redundancy is easy. In real application, we also enforced three constraints to the operation of redundancy elimination to maintain the shapes of original skeleton images unchanged.

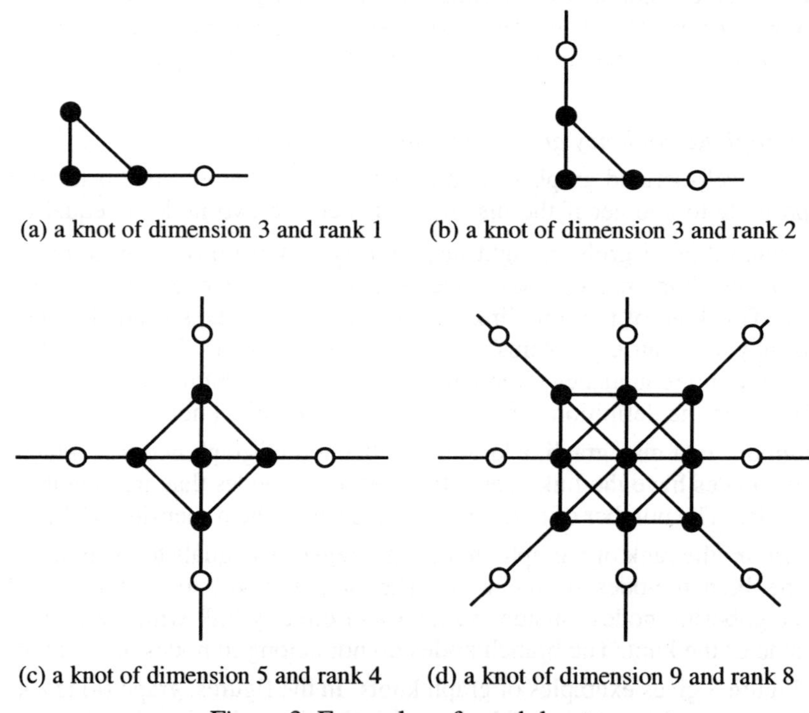

(a) a knot of dimension 3 and rank 1   (b) a knot of dimension 3 and rank 2

(c) a knot of dimension 5 and rank 4   (d) a knot of dimension 9 and rank 8

Figure 3. Examples of graph knots

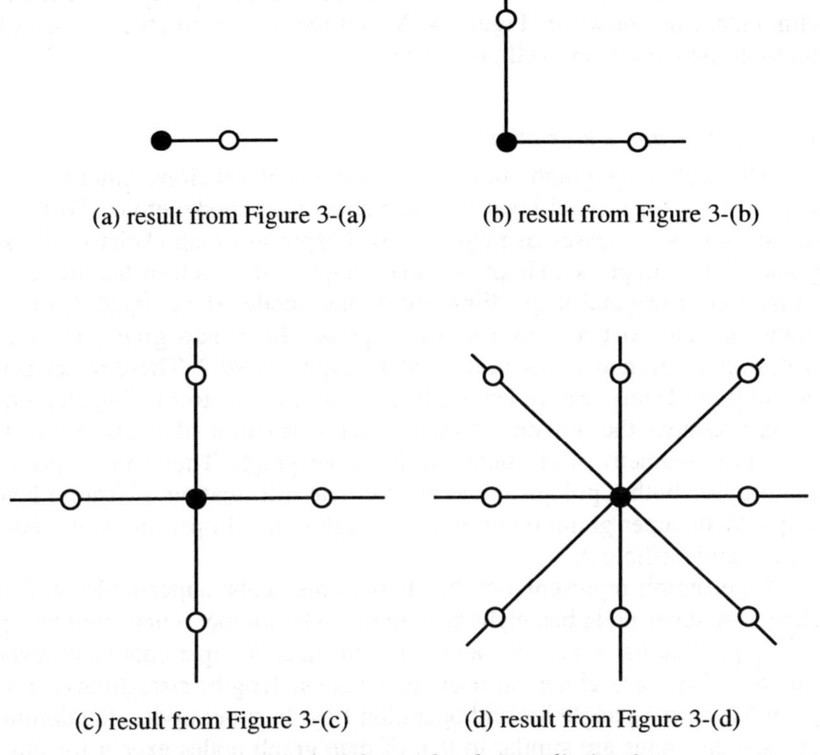

(a) result from Figure 3-(a)   (b) result from Figure 3-(b)

(c) result from Figure 3-(c)   (d) result from Figure 3-(d)

Figure 4. Graphs after redundancy elimination

(i) If a knot has dimension of 3 and rank of 1, in this knot a node that is nearest to the branch node of the knot is preserved and converted to a graph node. The other two nodes of the knot are removed.

(ii) If a knot has dimension 3 and rank greater than 1, in this knot a node from which a right angle is made to the other two nodes is preserved and converted to the graph node.

(iii) If the dimension of a graph knot is greater than 3, a new graph node is created at a pixel of the position nearest to the geometric center of the knot to replace the original knot of the graph.

By these constraints, the graph redundancies in Figure 3 are completely eliminated, as shown in Figure 4. Meantime, the geometric shapes of the original map graph are well preserved.

4.3. Super Graph Description

Although map graph introduces topological relations among skeleton pixels, it is still a pixel-level representation of map skeletons. To facilitate feature levels processes of maps, we will represent map skeletons by super graph. Super graph is a simplified map graph that is rich of feature level information of original maps. First, most chain nodes (type equal 2) of a map graph do not exist anymore in super graph. In a map graph, most graph nodes are chain nodes that have attribute type valued 2. These nodes usually do not provide any feature level information of maps. Removing chain nodes greatly reduces the amount of data in representation of maps. Second, we add more geometrical attributes to the super graph. Therefore, super graph can provide both topological and geometrical information of feature level of maps. With super graph representation, feature level operations will become significantly efficient.

Super graph representation has two components: super nodes and super chains. A super node has eight attributes: node number, curve number, position, type, link list, chain list, angle list and flag. A super chain has seven attributes. They are chain number, end nodes, length, straightness, turning point list, turning angle list and operation flag. In super nodes, the definitions of most attributes are similar to that of map graph nodes except for link list, chain list and angle list. A link list provides the nodes to which the current node topologically connects. Although the linking relation of super nodes is similar to that of map graph, the nodes in a linking list are not neighboring pixels of the current node. In general, current node and the nodes of its linking list are far away. As no type 2 nodes are used in the descriptions of a super graph, the node density of a map is greatly reduced from map graph, leading to further operations possible at a high speed. The attribute of chain list of a super node states all the supper chains that connected to this node. Supper chains provide important geometric information of original maps. When visiting a super graph from a super node to another, the information of super chain between the two super nodes is accessed through this attribute. The other attribute of super node is angle list. This attribute provides the orientations of super chains linking at a super node. The orientation of a super chain from a super node is defined as the tangent angle of the chain at the node counted from x-axis in counter-clock direction. If a super chain is straight, the "angle" of an angle list gives the orientation of the chain from the node. When a chain is curved, the "angle" describes the orientation of the line approximation of the first certain number of pixels of the curve from the super node. It can be seen that super graph description has provided some geographic information of original maps.

The chains of super graph give more detail geographic descriptions of map curves. Since a map curve usually is not straight, we use seven attributes to describe the properties of a super chain. These attributes are chain number, end nodes, length, straightness, turning point list, turning angle list, and flag. In these attributes, end nodes are the sequential numbers of the nodes ending at the super chain, from which the super chains and super nodes are related. The attribute length measures the length of the chain in a number of pixels. Straightness is an attribute describes the number of turning points of the chain after it is approximated by a polyline. If a map curve is straight, the straightness of the super chain is zero. Otherwise, the "straightness" is the number of the joint points of line segments when a map curve is approximated by a polyline. For example, if a map curve is polygonalized by a polyline of three line segments, the super chain has correspondingly straightness 2. The attribute of turning point list provides the information of all the turning point of the super chain in sequence, including positions and other related information of the nodes. Turning angle list records the values of all the turning angles in the supper chain at corresponding turning points. A turning angle measures the orientation change of super chain in a counter-

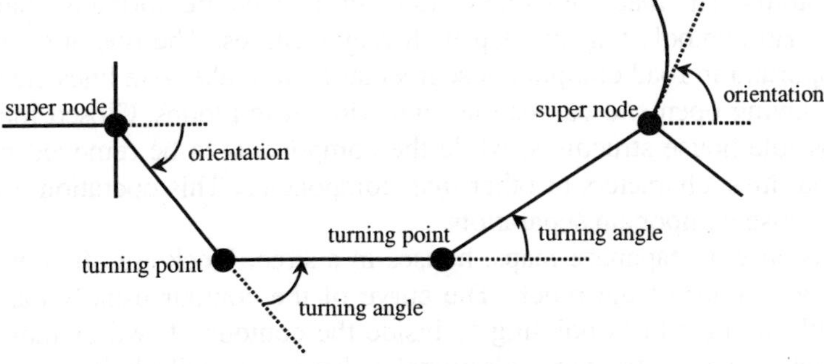

Figure 5. Super graph representation

clock direction at a turning point. The attributes chain number and flag just provide a serial number and operation status. Since turning points give more geometric properties about the map, the super graph provides a whole picture of original map including topological and geometric information. The concept of a super graph is given in Figure 5. The information that super graphs provide is very useful in map structure segmentation, re-linking, recognition and other feature level operations.

5. Map Graph Segmentation and Re-linking

Before map structure recognition and verctoriztion, obtaining "clean" map graphs is very important. In general cases, useful map structures often connect with other graph components such as characters of names of roads or buildings. House structures often link with road structures and other unrelated draws. Furthermore, several houses linked with sharing parts of house contours are commonly met in original map resources. These graphical phenomena must be removed. Using the super graph description of maps, the tasks of map structure segmentation become easier. In our system, the map graph segmentation needs to complete the following tasks.

(1) removing the map components which size are smaller than meaningful map structures. Usually, these map components are isolated characters or map symbols.

(2) eliminating small map components that lie on major curves. Major curves are long and smooth curves in a map, such as road curbs or house contours. The map components to be eliminated are normally characters or map symbols that overlap with major curves. The operation is very important in road component segmentation to make road lines clean.

(3) removing open end curves that link with closed loops. Closed loops are possible house structures, while the components to be removed may be road lines, characters or other map components. This operation is useful in house component separation.

(4) Specially, in Japanese maps, houses in a street block are often enclosed by a contour of the block. The curve of the contour usually has many teeth of short lines pointing to inside the contour. If two or more teeth touch a house structure, additional polygons, usually being rectangles, are formed. If not being removed, they may be recognized as houses in map recognition process. These short teeth are typically called "short-H"

in our system. The short-H must be properly removed before segmenting the house structures and polygonalizing them to vectors.

(5) separating inter-linked house structures into independent houses. For the land location purpose, houses or buildings need to register individually.

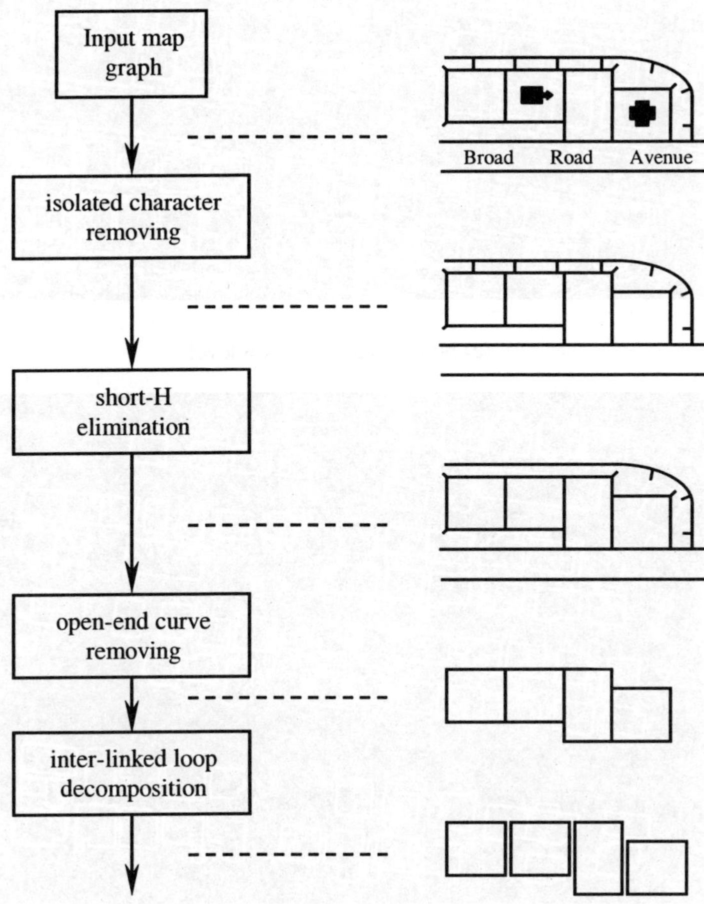

Figure 6. Flow chart of house structure segmentation

104

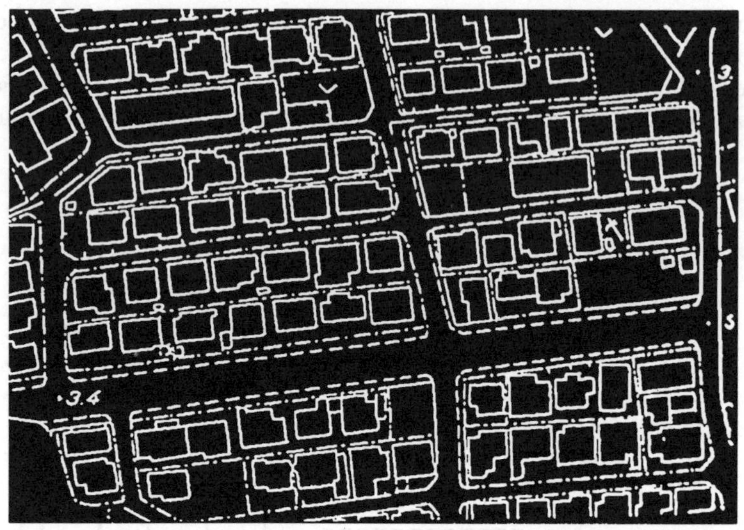

(a) house image of pixel level

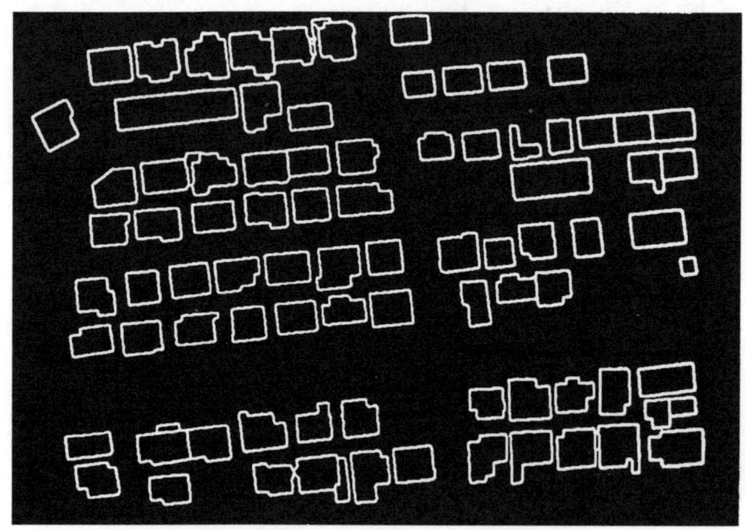

(b) map graph after house graph segmentation

Figure 7. Example of house graph segmentation

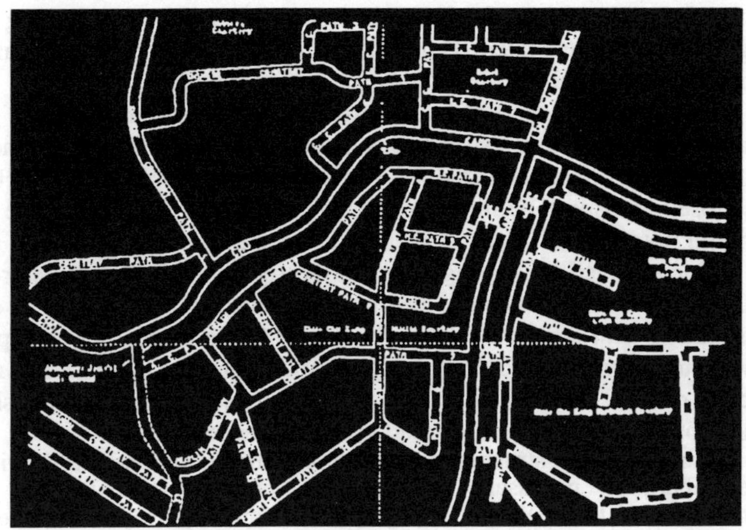

(a) road image of pixel level

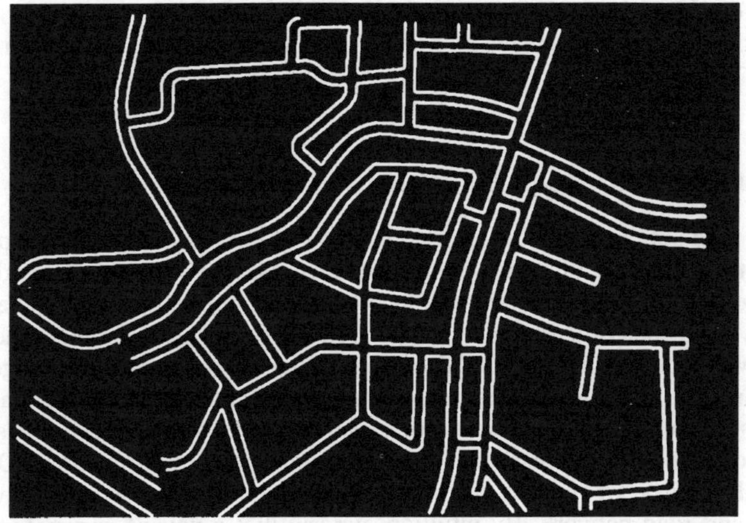

(b) map graph after road graph segmentation

Figure 8. Example of road graph segmentation

Therefore, in a digital map database, the houses inter-linked by sharing sides in original map are separated. Thus, data records of each house are available in a map database to allow positioning them individually.

Figure 6 is a flow chart of house structure segmentation. Figure 7 gives an example result of house structure segmentation. In the result, characters, symbols and road lines are removed, remaining only closed loop structures. These closed loops will be further recognized and vectorized for house data. We should note that all loops in the result are independent. Although some loops look connected by sharing edges in the figure, each loop structure has actually its own edge. They are displayed in overlap and look as if some houses shared with common edges. In Figure 8, we present an example of road structure segmentation. In the original map image of Figure 8-(a), many characters of road names badly stick at road curb lines. Figure 8-(b) shows the result of the road image after road graph segmentation.

In contract to map structure segmentation, map component re-linking is another operation necessary in automatic map data acquisition. This operation is used to repair the map graphs that are broken due to either the imperfect of original master map images, or that generated in image scanning processes. Linking two map lines is easy. The width of a gap and collinearity of the curves in both sides of the gap are criteria of curve linkage. However, we must be careful of over-link. Incorrectly joint two map components can also create problems for map component recognition and vectorization.

6. Rolling Ball: Road Structure Vectorization

A road structure in a binary map is a pair of curves that are almost parallel with a distance of certain range between the two curves. A road can change both in road direction and in road width, but width usually changes slowly. The ends of a road may be open, closed or linked with other roads. A road with a closed end is called dead-road. When several roads joint together, the part of a map for roads to joint is called road inter-junction. By road inter-junctions, jointed roads can form a road network. A road network has two types of map components: roads themselves and road inter-junctions. Often, we call a piece of road as road-body to distinguish the concepts between roads and road network. By intuition, we say that a pair of curves forms a road body if these two curves are long enough and almost parallel. By intuition, we also consider a pair of parallel lines linking at a road network as a road body. In our system of road data generation, we developed an algorithm named rolling-ball. This algorithm combines the operations of road structure recognition and road vectorization into one process. In vectorizing a road map, we first detect one or more open road ends from a road network. Then from a valid road open end, rolling ball operation is performed. This rolling ball operation goes only between road curb lines. Therefore, the process recognizes and vectorizes a road body simultaneously. The map structures outside road lines, such as house structures, do not affect the operation of road data recognition. When the operation goes to a road inter-junction, the process of road inter-junction detection becomes active, and the road branches at the road inter-junction are detected and registered. The rolling ball operation then restarts to process from the registered new road branches. In this way, a whole road network is vectorized. A road data generator consists of three major processes: rolling ball, road inter-junction detection and road network exploration. We next introduce the concept of rolling ball operation.

6.1. Rolling ball method

The rolling ball technique is used to produce vector data of road central lines of road bodies. Road body is a piece of road with open or closed road ends but not connects with road inter-junctions. Generating road central line data from road bodies is an essential step in road map data generation. The concept of rolling ball is simple. Since a road body in a map is a pair of almost parallel lines, we can imagine that two walls stand along curbs of a road. Let us further assume that we have a great ball on the road. The ball can automatically change its radius and the position of the center, so that the surface of the ball always is tangent to both of the walls of the road. Now, let us push the ball rolling along the road. When the ball gets a new location, the radius and the center position of the ball are adjusted so that the surface of

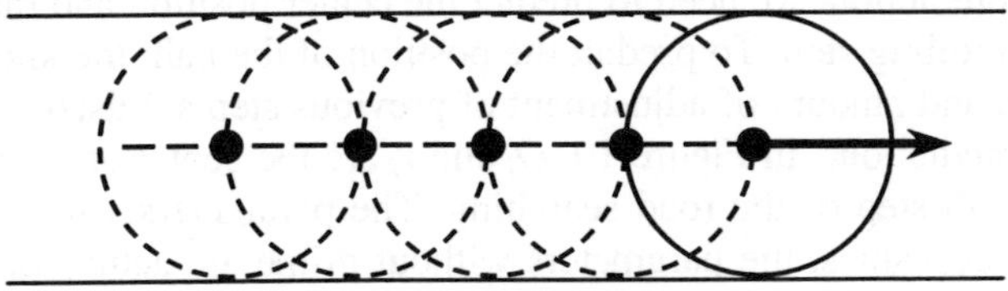

Figure 9. Concept of rolling ball

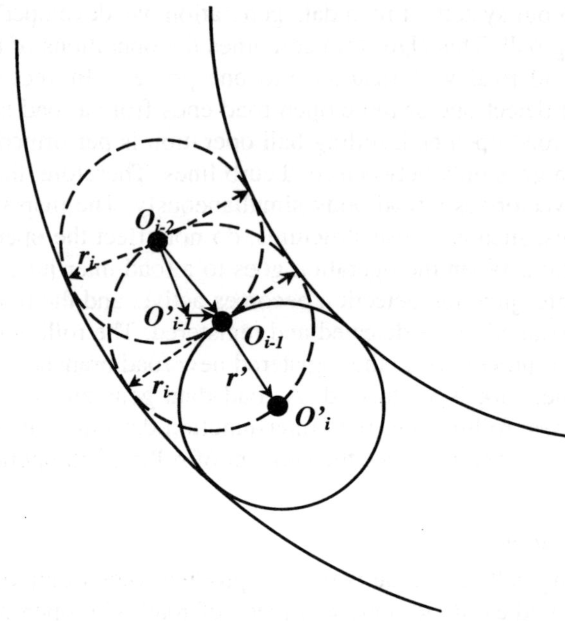

Figure 10. Prediction of the center of rolling ball

the ball is tangent to both of the walls. In this way, upon the completion of rolling the ball along the road, we obtain a trajectory of the ball center that defines the road central line. Figure 9 shows the concept of rolling ball.

In doing rolling ball process, two operations are essential. One operation is ball prediction. Another is ball adjustment. The second operations ensure that the surface of the ball always is tangent to the road curb lines so that the center of the ball is at the central line of a road.

In ball prediction, we need to predict the center position and radius of the ball in each rolling step. To predict the position of the ball, the knowledge of the position and amount of adjustment of previous step are used. It is similar for radius prediction. In Figure 10, O_i and r_i are the center and radius of the ball in the i-th step of the road searching. The parameters with a prime denote predicted values, the parameters without prime are actual values of the parameters after ball adjustment. The formula below gives the equations of predicting the center and radius of the ball.

$$\vec{O}_i = \vec{O}_{i-1} + \overrightarrow{O_{i-2}O_{i-1}} + \overrightarrow{O'_{i-1}O_{i-1}}$$

$$r'_i = r_{i-1} + (r_{i-1} - r_{i-2}) = 2r_{i-1} - r_{i-2}$$

6.2. Road Inter-Junction Detection

When a road ball goes to a road inter-junction, inter-junction detection is triggered. Detection of road inter-junctions has two purposes. First, detection of road inter-junction provides continuity to rolling ball, making it possible for the ball to roll from one road body to another, as at a road inter-junction, at least two road branches must joint. Second, road inter-junction detection generates nodes of road inter-junction centers with accurate positions. Nodes of road inter-junction centers are important data in road map databases.

Let us consider a ball rolling along a road that links at a road inter-junction. When the ball rolls into the road inter-junction, the rolling process cannot continue. Thus, the ball will expend its size by a factor η so that the

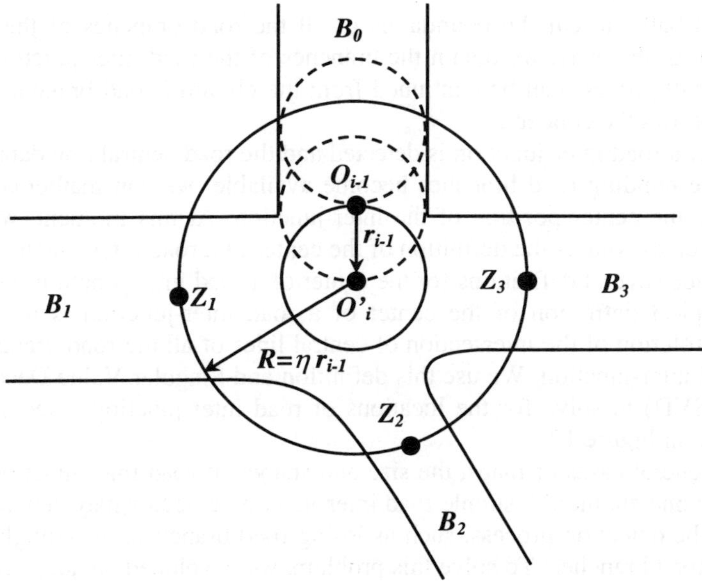

Figure 11. Concept of road inter-junction detection

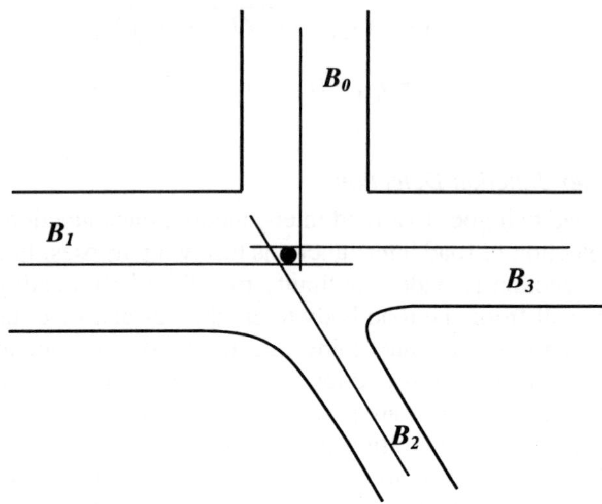

Figure 12. Definition of the center of road inter-junction

enlarged ball can cut the boundaries of all the road branches of the inter-junction. In this way, we obtain the branches of the road inter-junction, and rolling ball process can be continued from the obtained road branches. Figure 11 shows the concept.

After a road inter-junction is detected and the road central line data of all the corresponding road branches become available, we can mathematically compute the center position of the inter-junction. At this moment, we will ask ourselves what is the definition of the center of a road inter-junction? We have made several definitions for the center of a road inter-junction. Perhaps the simplest definition of the center of a road inter-junction is the Least Square solution of the intersection of central lines of all the road branches at the road inter-junction. We use this definition and Singular Value Decomposition (SVD) to solve for the locations of road inter-junctions. See the description in Figure 12.

In general cases of maps, the size and shapes of road inter-junctions differ from one another. A simple road inter-junction detector may generate errors in the detection process, such as losing road branches, or wrongly generating road branches. To solve this problem, we developed an adaptive road inter-junction detector, which can measure the size and shape of a road inter-junction and detect all road branches connecting to it. In our experiment, we found the technique worked very efficiently for road network exploration.

6.3. Road Network Exploration

The operation of road network exploration interweaves the processes of rolling ball and road inter-junction detection, making it possible to vectorize all the roads and inter-junctions of a road network from a single road entrance. In our system, a BFR strategy is used to explore road network.

In road network exploration, there are a few things needing to consider beforehand. The first is how to find an entrance to a road network. Namely, what is the first road to start a rolling ball process? The second is the termination conditions of rolling ball process for each road body. When the termination conditions of rolling ball for all the road are made, the termination condition of a network is automatically reached since there is no new road branch is found. Also, we need to consider the condition to joint roads at a broken road body or at a road inter-junction.

In most maps, even in small pieces of maps, more than one road network can exist. To digitize all road networks of a map, we start exploring road networks of the map from top, bottom, left and right of maps. The first step of road network exploration is to detect road entrances. We search for road entrances from the four sides of a map image and register the obtained road entrances in a bank. The road entrances are open ends of a pair of parallel lines with certain distance of separation. Of course, open parallel lines may not all be road entrances. They may come from a rectangular house structure or the contours of two neighboring houses. Valid road entrances can be verified by rolling ball operation. From a pair of lines of candidate road entrance, we start rolling ball into the direction of the lines pointing inside the map image. If the rolling ball operation can successfully perform for a predetermined number of rolling steps, it indicates that the pair of lines is a valid road line pair, and it is assigned as a valid road entrance. The line pairs that not qualifying for road entrances will be discarded. We can noticed that more than one road entrances may be created for a single road network but usually only one road entrance is actually used to go through a complete road network. Multiple road entrances do not affect the operation of road network exploration since the other road entrances will be automatically closed in network visiting process from a valid road entrance.

The terminal condition of rolling ball is simple. When the road ball cannot go further in a rolling ball process, it will trigger up the operation of inter-junction detection. If there is no new road branches are detected, the rolling ball operation in this road body is declared to terminate. The rolling ball termination usually occurs at open road ends, dead roads or the road ends reaching to image boards.

7. House Data Generation

House structure recognition and vectorization are major operations in house data generation. The tasks become simpler after house structures are separated from original maps. In the process of house structure segmentation, closed loops are segmented from other map structures and decomposed into individual loops. We only need to recognize houses by their geometric properties and vectorize them into polygonal vector data.

7.1. Recognize House Structures

Since closed loop structures have been obtained from the operation of house structure segmentation, the recognition work here becomes to select the loops of proper size and shape from the given. In actual map data productions, all the maps in a volume have the same scale. House structures have similar statistic properties. This allows us to estimate the ranges of the area and the perimeter of houses beforehand. Therefore, we can set thresholds for loop area and the ratio of loop's perimeter square to loop area. Using the preset thresholds, house structure can be selected. The ratio of loop's perimeter square to area measures the shapes of a loop structure. If a loop structure is a very elongated, the ratio of loop's perimeter perimeter square to area will become large and goes out the range of the threshold. The formulas of house structure selection are given as the follows.

$$A_{min} < A < A_{max}$$

$$\frac{P^2}{A} < R_{max}$$

Where A and P are area and perimeter of a graph loop structure. The loop structures which areas are lesser than A_{min} usually come from Japanese characters or map symbols. Those larger than A_{max} are often street blocks. The loops of very elongated shapes normally come from street structures that occasionally become closed graph loops.

7.2. House Data Vectorization

There are some existing methods to polygonalize an image contour to a polyline. In our system, we used the method of Wall, referring to Figure 13, which is a fast sequential method of polygonalization. In this method, we use the error measurement defined by the ratio of the area between a curve and its chord to the square of the chord as a criterion. Tracing the curve from a starting point and continuously computing the error measurement, if the measurement is greater than a preset threshold, a segmentation is made at the point, and the tracing processing is restarted from the point.

Although Wall's method works well to polygonalize irregular curves, we find problems in vectorizing house structures. In comparison with original map data, the resultant house polygons usually deform their shapes by "rotating" a small angle, see figure 14. This phenomenon is caused by the fact that error measurement must be greater than zero in the operation of polygonalization. In a map, most house structures are already in polygonal shapes: the sides of house are straight-line segments. Since polygonalization is a error measurement dependent operation, segmentation points are often created at the next tracing lines after corners, instead of at corner points.

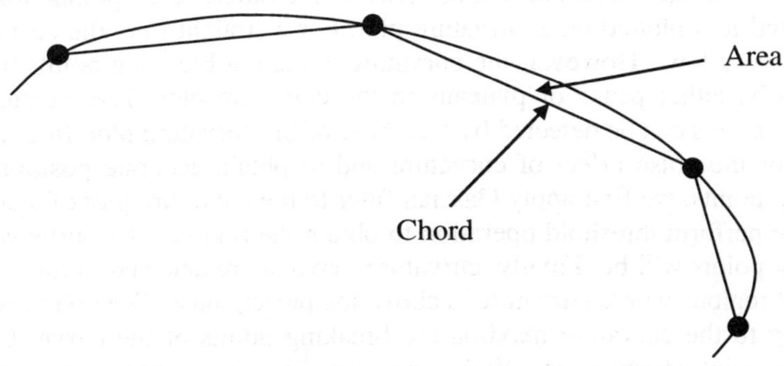

Figure 13. Wall's polygonalization method

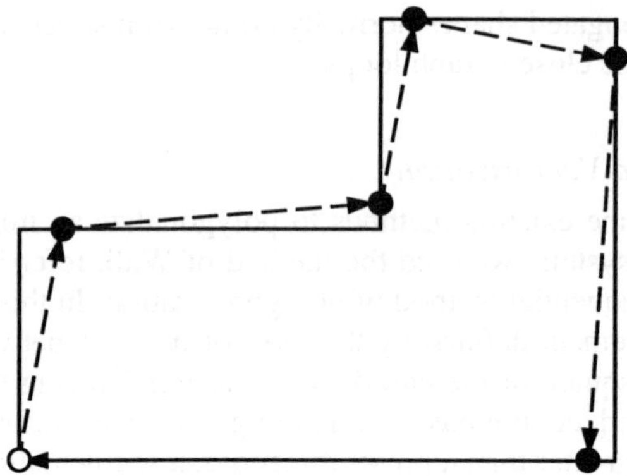

Figure 14. Simple polygonalization makes house data deformed

To improve the quality of house polygonalization, we vectorizing a house structure piecewise. In house structure vectorization, we first detect breaking points of a house structure. The breaking points, also called critical points or domain points of curves, are usually corners or joint point of a segment of straight line and a curve. After breaking points are found, a house structure is segmented to several pieces of curves. Then, we perform the operation of polygonalization with each curve segments.

In detecting breaking points of curves, k-curvature approach is used. In the method, curvature is measured as the angular difference between the slopes of two line segments fitting to the data around each curve point of distance k to the measured point. Curvature is measured at all points along a curve, and it is plotted on a curvature plot. For a straight line, the curvature value is very low. However, the curvature is high at breaking points, it appears to be either peaks or plateaus in the curvature plot. The location of breaking points can be detected by threshold of the curvature plot. In order to get rid of the noise affect of curvature and to obtain accurate positions of breaking points, we first apply Gassian filter to the curvature plot of a curve. Then we perform threshold operation to obtain the regions of a curve where breaking points will be. Finally, curvature maxima are detected in the curvature plot regions where curvature is above the preset value. The points corresponding to the curvature maxima are breaking points of the curve. Using breaking point detection and Wall's polygonalization in combination, position error in resultant map vector data can almost be eliminated. The data can well meet industrial standard.

8. Discussion

Our prototype system was implemented at a Sun 170 workstation. It consists of ten software modules capsulated in two packages: road data generator and house data generator. The resources of maps for system input come from real maps. The maps of Singapore Street Directory and the maps of the city of Osaka were used in our experiments. The reduction scale of the maps ranges from 1:2500 to 1:10000. In image scanning operation, binary model was chosen. Thus, the binarization of map images was performed in the process of image scanning. The resolution of 600 dpi was selected when we scan maps into the system. But the resolution of 300 dip sometime is used for the maps which contents are not very congested.

Figure 15 demonstrates an experimental result of house data generation. The map image was obtained from Singapore Street Directory. Figure 15-(a) is the original binary map image scanned at 300 dpi. Figure 15-(b) is the corresponding map graph image after graph re-linking. It can be seen that the gaps of house structures in the original map image do not exist in the map graph image. In Figure 15-(c), vectorized map data are given. Figure 15-(d) shows the map data displayed on the original map images in overlap.

In Figure 16, we show an experiment result of house data generation using Japanese maps that are used for actual map data production. Figure 16-(a) is a part of the Osaka map. It can be noticed that map contents are very congested. Many map structures are also inter-connected. Figure 16-(b) gives the vector data of house structures of the map. Figure 16-(c) displays the map data on the original map images in overlap.

The experiment results of road data generation are shown in figure 17, in which Figure 17-(a) is the original map image. Figure 17(b) is the graph representation of the map. As all the characters and map symbols between road lines have been removed, the graph of the road network becomes clean. The road seeds generated in the operation of road inter-junction detection are also shown in the picture. Figure 17-(c) gives the vector data of road: road central line data. The dots in the map data are the nodes of road central-lines. In Figure 17-(d), we provide the data of contours of street block that are created by house data generator. Figure 17-(e) shows the map data on the original map images in overlap.

The processing time of each operation of automatic map data generations is listed in Table 1 with typical sizes of maps. It can be seen that the most time-consuming operation is image thinning, which takes more than 70% time of processes. As the algorithm of image thinning can be implemented

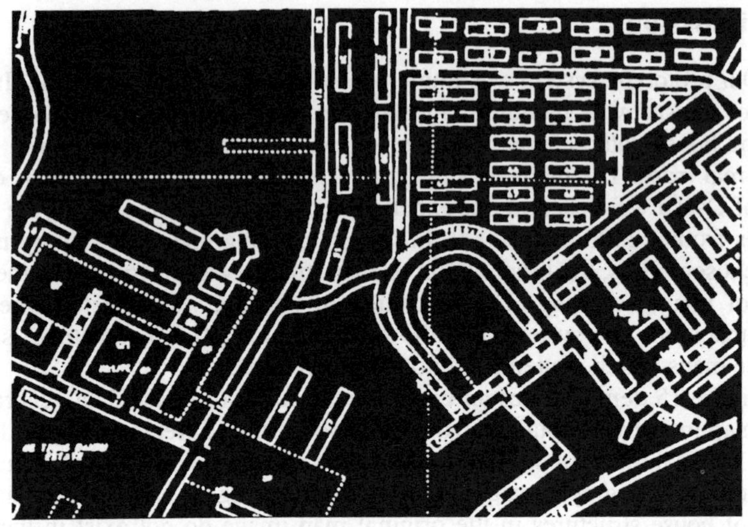

(a) original map image

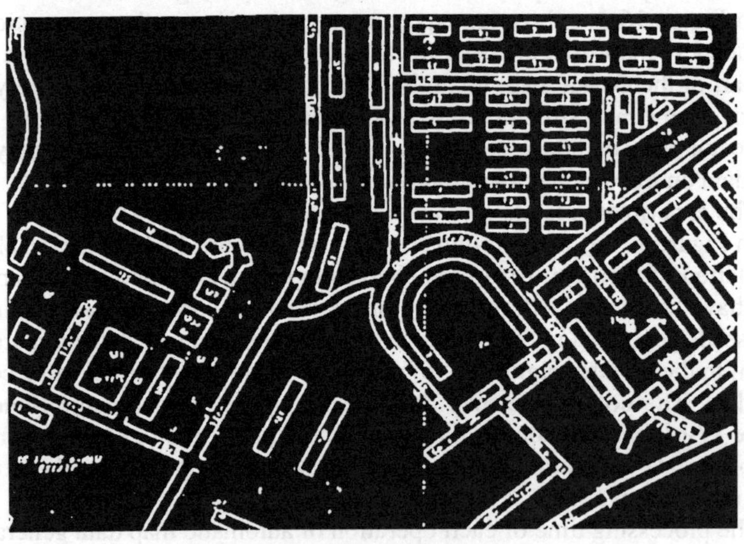

(b) map graph representation

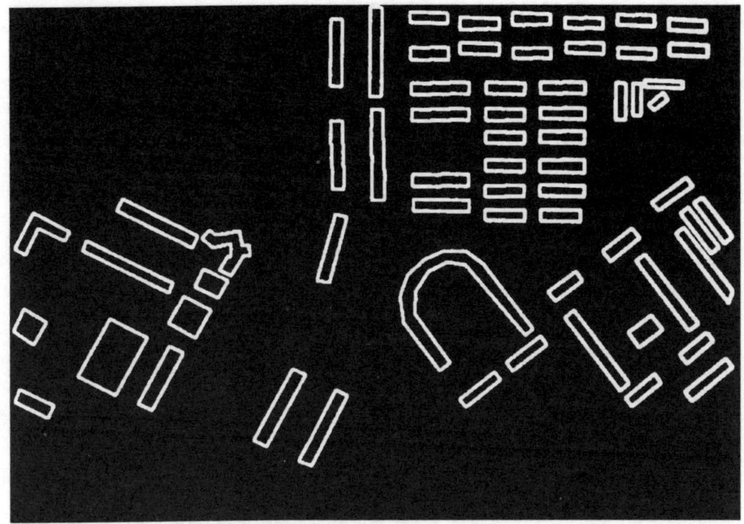

(c) vector data of houses

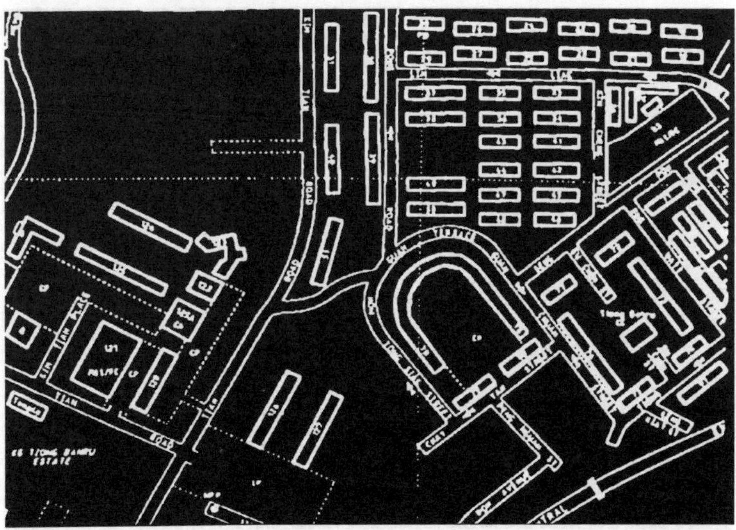

(b) house data and original map displayed in overlap

Figure 15. Results of house data generation

(a) original map image

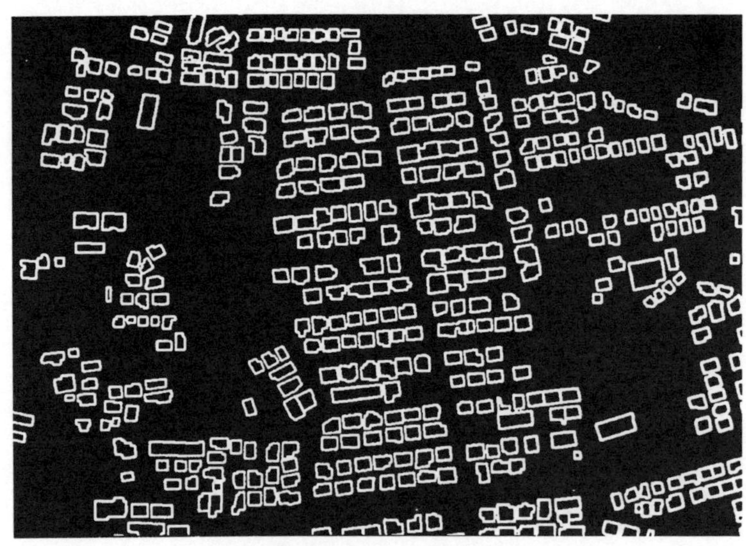

(b) vector data of houses

(c) house data and original map displayed in overlap

Figure 16. House generation of Osaka city

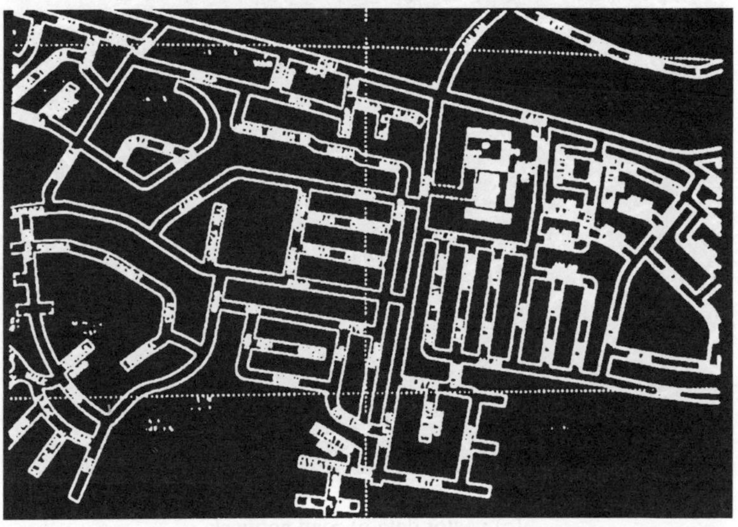

(a) original map image

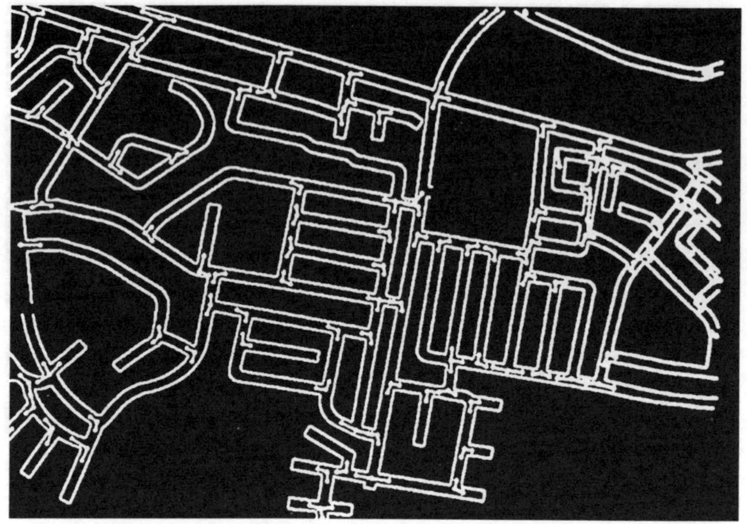

(b) map graph with road seeds

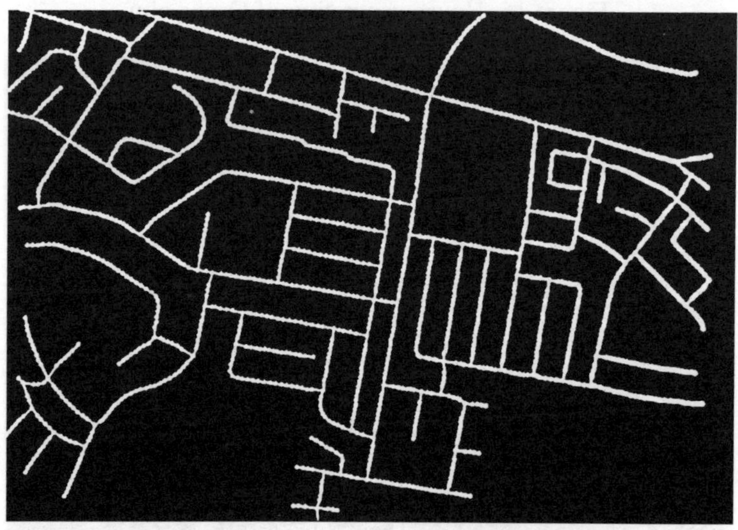

(c) vector data of road network

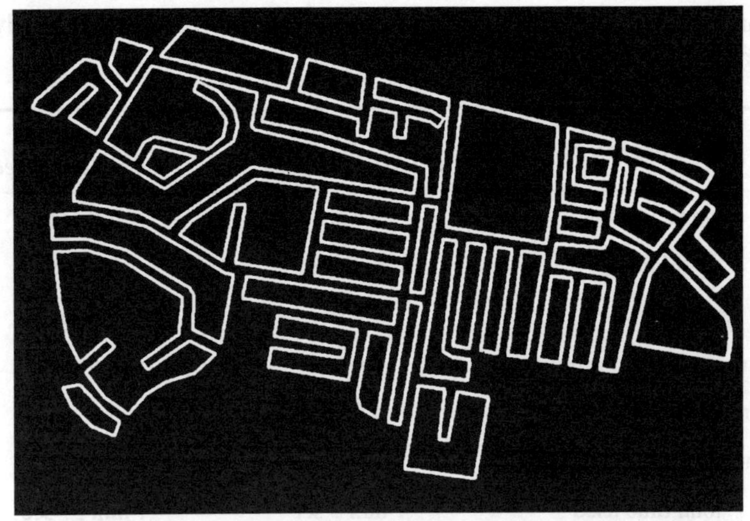

(d) data of street blocks

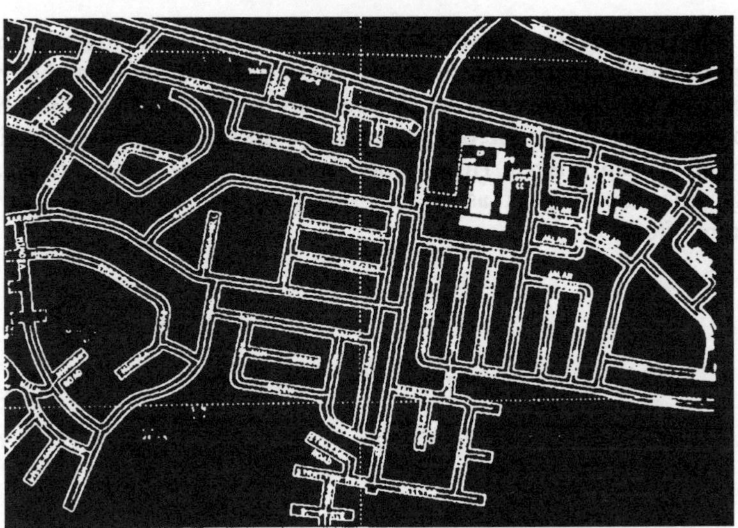

(e) map data and original map image displayed in overlap

Figure 17. Road data generation

by hardware, the processing time can be greatly reduced if hardware of image thinner is used.

name of process	map Fig 14 (1536H1136 pixel)	map Fig. 15 (2300H1632 pixel)
preprocessing	3.6 sec	7.8 sec
thinning	41.8 sec	74 sec
graph conversion	5.0 sec	7.5 sec
segmentation and re-linking	6.6 sec	4.5 sec
road data generation	4.9 sec	3.6 sec
house data generation	-	-
total time used	1 min 2 sec	1 min 37 sec

Table 1.Processing time of map data generation

In this Chapter, we described an automatic system of digital map data generation using pictorial map resources. This system has potential to be developed to a system taking aerial photographs of maps as input. The bridge links photographic maps and our system is the operation of edge detection of photographic map images. How to obtain quality edge images from aerial photographic maps as good as the map skeletons used for the system will be our future efforts.

Reference

Boatto L., et al, "An Interpretation System for Land Register Maps", *Computer*, Vol. 25, No 7, , pp. 25-33, July 1992.

Bro-Nielsen, M., "Building Detection in Aerial Images," Master's thesis, Inst. of Mathematical Statistics and Operations Research, Technical Univ. of Denmark, Aug. 1992.

Chen, C-S. and Tsai, W-H., "A New Fast One-Pass Thinning Algorithm and its Parallel Hardware Implementation," *Pattern Recognition Letters*, Vol. 11, No, 7, pp. 471-477, 1990.

Collins, R.T., Hanson, A.R., Riseman, EM., Jaynes, C., Stolle, F., Wang, X. and Cheng, Y-Q., "UMass Progress in 3D Building Model Acquisition," *Proc. ARPA Image Understanding Workshop*, Vol. 1, pp. 305-315, Palm Springs, Calif., Feb. 1996.

Conners, R.W., Trivedi, M.M. and Harlow, C.A., "Segmentation of a High-Resolution Urban Scene Using Texture Operators," *Computer Vision, Graphics, and Image Processing*, vol. 25, pp. 273-310, 1984.

Fua, P. and Hanson, A.J., "An Optimization Framework for Feature Extraction," *Machine Vision and Applications*, vol. 4, no. 2, pp. 5987,1991.

Harwood, D., Chang, S., and Davis, L., "Interpreting Aerial Photographs by Segmentation and Search," *Proc. DARPA Image Understanding Workshop*, pp. 507-520, Feb.1987.

Herman, M. and Kanade, T., "Incremental Reconstruction of 3D Scenes from Multiple, Complex Images," *Artificial Intelligence*, vol. 30, pp. 289-341, 1986.

Huertas, A. and Nevatia, R., "Detecting Buildings in Aerial Images," *Computer Vision, Graphics, and Image Processing*, vol. 41, pp. 131-152, Apr. 1988.

Irvin, R.B. and McKeown, D.M., "Methods for Exploiting the Relationship Between Buildings and Their Shadows in Aerial Imagery," *IEEE Trans. Systems, Man, and Cybernetics*, vol. 19, no. 6, pp. 1,564-1,575, Nov. 1989.

Jaynes, C., Stolle, F., and Collins, R., "Task Driven Perceptual Organization for Extraction of Rooftop Polygons," *Proc. ARPA Image Understanding Workshop*, vol. 1, pp. 359-365, Nov. 1994.

Kasturi, R., et. al, "A System for Interpretation of Line Drawings", *IEEE Trans. Pattern Analysis and Machine Intelligence*, Vol 12, No. 10, pp. 978-992, October 1990.

Lin, C., Huertas, A. and Nevatia, R., "Detection of Buildings Using Perceptual Grouping and Shadows," *Proc. IEEE Conf. Computer Vision and Pattern Recognition*, pp. 62-69, June 1994.

Lin, C. and Nevatia, R., "Buildings Detection and Description from Monocular Aerial Images," *Proc. ARPA Image Understanding Workshop*, pp. 461-468, Feb. 1996.

Liow, Y-T. and Pavlidis, T., "Use of Shadows for Extracting Buildings in Aerial Images, " *Computer Vision, Graphics, and Image Processing*, vol. 49, pp. 242-277, 1990.

McGlone, J.C. and Shufelt, J.A., "Projective and Object Space Geometry for Monocular Building Extraction," *Proc. IEEE Conf. Computer Vision and Pattern Recognition,* pp. 54-61, June 1994.

McKeown, D.M. and Denlinger, J.L., "Map-Guided Feature Extraction from Aerial Imagery," *Proc. IEEE Workshop Computer Vision: Representation and Control,* pp. 205-213, A-nnapolis, Md., 1984.

McKeown, D.M., "Toward Automatic Cartographic Feature Extraction, " *Mapping and Spatial Modelling for Navigation,* L.F. Pau, ed., NATO ASI series, vol. F65, pp. 149-180,1990.

Mohan, R. and Nevatia, R., "Using Perceptual Organization to Extract 3-D Structures, " *IEEE Trans. Pattern Analysis and Machine Intelligence, vol.* 11, no. 11, pp. 1,121-1,139, Nov. 1989.

Musavi, M.T., Shirvaikar, M.V., Ramanathan, E. and Nekovei, A.R., "A Vision Based Method to Automate Map Processing", *Pattern Recognition,* Vol. 21, No 4, pp. 319-236, 1988.

Nicolin, B. and Gabler, R., "A Knowledge-Based System for the Analysis of Aerial Images, " *IEEE Trans. Geoscience and Remote Sensing,* vol. 25, no. 3, pp. 317-329, May 1987.

O'Gorman, L., "Image and Document Processing Techniques for Right Pages Electronic Laboratory System", *Proc. Int'l Conf. Pattern Recognition,* pp. 260-263., IEEE CS Press, Los Alamitos, California, 1992.

Shufelt, J.A. and McKeown, D.M., "Fusion of Monocular Cues to Detect Man-Made Structures in Aerial Imagery," *Computer Vision, Graphics and Image Processing: Image Understanding,* vol. 57, no. 3, pp. 307-330, May 1993.

Suzuki, S., Yamada, T., "MARIS: Map Recognition Input System", *Pattern Recognition,* Vol. 23, No 8, pp. 919-933, 1990.

Tavakoli, M. and Rosenfeld, A., "Building and Road Extraction from Aerial Photographs," *IEEE Trans. Systems, Man, and Cybernetics,* vol. 12, no. 1, pp. 84-91, Jan. /Feb. 1982.

Venkateswar, V. and Chellappa, R., "A Framework for Interpretation of Aerial Images," *Proc. 10th Int'l Conf. Pattern Recognition,* pp. 204-206, 1990.

Wall, K. and Danielsson, P., "A Fast Sequential Method for Polygonal Approximation of Digital Curves", *Computer Vision, Graphics and Image Processing,* pp. 220-227, Vol. 28, 1984.

Wu, W. and Wang, M. J., "Detecting the Dominant Points by the Curvature-Based Polygonal Approximation", *Computer Vision, Graphics and Image Processing: Graphical Models and Image Processing,* Vol. 55, No. 2, pp. 79-88, March 1993.

Yamada, H., Yamamoto, K., Saito, T. and Matsui, S., "Map: Multi-angled Parallelism for Feature Extraction from Topographical Maps", *Pattern Recognition,* Vol. 24, No 6, pp. 479-488, 1991.

LEARNING VISUAL CONCEPTS FOR CONTENT BASED RETRIEVAL

Michael S. Lew

LIACS, Leiden University, Netherlands

1. Introduction

Recently there has been an explosion of visual multimedia information in the forms of images and video. Images are available from billions of WWW sites and in large CD-ROM and DVD collections. Video is generally considered to be the next major consumer media revolution due to the arrival and acceptance of digital video standards and inexpensive prosumer video devices.

There are several different ways of interacting with media, which include (but are not limited to) viewing, browsing, and searching. In this chapter we will be focussing on the aspect of searching for media. In the context of textual based media, there are many established methods for finding text documents. In its most primitive sense, text searching can be treated as string searching. However, text searching is much deeper because the ultimate goal is to find documents which are highly relevant to what the user wants, which may not necessarily be highly correlated with what the user types as a query.

A significant advantage to text based searching is that the text frequently corresponds to semantically meaningful human concepts since it is founded in the language in which we communicate. However, in other forms of media such as images and video, the fundamental representation is not obviously correlated with human language. If we are to endow computers with the ability to understand humans, then either the humans must learn how computers perceive media or the computers must learn how humans perceive media. If it is important for a visual search system to be usable by a wide set of people such as the users of the WWW, then it is crucial that computers learn how humans perceive visual media. Petkovic[1] has called this finding "simple semantics." From recent literature, this generally means finding computable image features which are correlated with visual concepts.

Regarding visual media, one interesting direction is to develop algorithms which can detect visual concepts corresponding to words in human language. Mapping visual media to human language would be a significant step forward, but it would not be the final solution. If we consider the analogous situation in text matching, then we see that we are precisely at the level of keyword matching. Completely understanding natural language queries is still beyond current text analysis methods.

Giving the computer the ability to understand how humans perceive visual media is not limited to mapping visual media to human language. Other content based retrieval paradigms exist such as similar image searches, abstraction based searches, and relevance feedback, which are discussed in the next section.

The most common method for finding visual media is by *similar image based search*. In this paradigm, the user clicks on an image, and then the search engine ranks the database images by similarity with respect to color, texture, and shape. For an overview, see Gudivada and Raghavan[2], Flickner, et al.[3], and especially Eakins[4].

In *abstraction based search methods*[5], the user supplies an abstract depiction of the desired image to the search system. For example, in sketch based search methods, the user draws a rough sketch of the goal image. The assumption is that the sketch corresponds to the object edges and contours. The database images which have the most similar shapes to the user sketch are returned. Sketches represent an abstract representation of the image. Another abstract method uses icons to represent visual concepts in the image. The user places the icons on a canvas in the position where they should appear in the goal image. In this context, the database images must have been preprocessed for the locations of the available visual concepts. The database images which are most similar by the content of the visual concepts to the iconic user query are returned.

In the typical database query situation, the user expects to find the correct set of results from a single query. In *relevance feedback techniques*[6,7], the expectation changes from finding the correct results from a single query to finding better results with successive queries. In a relevance feedback session, the user is shown a list of candidates. The user decides which candidates are relevant and which are irrelevant. The relevant candidates can be thought of as positive examples and the rest as negative examples. The relevance feedback system chooses the next list of candidates as the ones which are more similar to the positive examples and less similar to the negative examples.

In this work, our goal is to examine the state of the art in learning visual concepts in the context of content based retrieval. In the next section, we begin our journey by attempting to place visual learning into a precise framework.

2. Learning Visual Concepts

In this chapter we discuss learning visual concepts. For our purposes, a visual concept is anything which we can apply a label or recognize visually. These could be clearly defined objects like faces or more abstract concepts such as textures because most textures do not have corresponding labels in common language. This brings into mind the question "What is visual learning?" Such a general term could refer to anything involving artificial or human intelligence. Rather than a vague description, we seek to define it clearly at least within the boundaries of this work as either (1) feature tuning; (2) feature selection; or (3) feature construction. Feature tuning refers to determining the parameters which optimize the use of the feature. This is often called parameter estimation. Feature selection means choosing one or more features from a given initial set of features. The chosen features typically optimize the discriminatory power regarding the ground truth which consists of positive and negative examples. Feature construction is defined as creating or extracting new features.

2.1. *Feature Selection*

One of the long standing puzzles in artificial intelligence, psychology, computer vision, and biology is detecting and segmenting visual concepts from imagery. It is ironic that human visual understanding which is effortless and instantaneous would be perplexing and difficult to reproduce in computers. In fact, after decades of active research, it is arguable whether we are significantly closer to reproducing the speed, generality, and accuracy of the human visual system.

Suppose that we have a large set of candidate features and a classifier. We would like to select the feature subset which gives us the highest classification accuracy. One possibility is to try every possible feature subset. The problem is that the number of possibilities grows exponentially with the number of candidate features, which means that it is not computable in practice for a large set of candidate features.

It may also seem appealing to use all of the candidate features. In a statistical sense, it is well known that the classification error should decrease when additional measurements are used. However, this is true when the samples sets have infinite extent. In most practical applications, only sparse training sets are available which means there could be insufficient data to arrive at statistically representative values for the unknown parameters associated with the features. Specifically, the classifier would be well tuned for the training set, but would lack the ability to generalize to new instances, which is also called the curse of dimensionality. Therefore, we usually wish to minimize the size of the selected feature subset, which should minimize the number of unknown parameters, and require a smaller training set.

Classifying patterns requires an assumption that classes occupy distinct regions in the pattern space. When the classes have less overlap, the probability of correct classification increases. Therefore, the general approach is to select the feature subspace which has the maximum class separation. Formally, the problem of feature selection can be described as selecting the best subset U from the set V which contains D candidate feature classes. In the ideal case, the feature subset should maximize the probability of correct classification.

It has been argued that the execution time of a particular algorithm is less important than the classification accuracy because in practice, feature selection is typically done off-line. Although this may be true for feature sets of moderate size, there are important applications where the data sets have hundreds of features, and running a feature selection algorithm even once may be impractical.

There have been a wide variety of feature selection techniques in the research literature. A representative overview is given in Table 1.

In principle, we can either start with the empty set and then add features; or start with the entire feature set and delete features. Sequential Forward Search (SFS)[8] is a method where one feature class is added at a

Table 1. Search Methods for Finding Optimal and Suboptimal Feature Sets.

Branch and Bound	A top-down search procedure with backtracking, which allows all of the combinations to be implicitly searched without an exhaustive search
Sequential Forward Selection (SFS)	A bottom-up search procedure where the feature which will yield a maximum of the criterion function is added one at a time to the NULL set.
Generalized Sequential Forward Selection (GSFS)	Similar to SFS, but instead of adding one feature at a time, r features are added.
Sequential Backward Selection (SBS)	Starting from the complete set of features, we discard one feature until $D - d$ features have been deleted
Generalized Sequential Backward Selection (GSBS)	Similar to SBS, but instead of discarding one feature, multiple features are discarded.
Floating Methods	Similar to GLRS, but instead of having fixed l and r, the size of the feature set can increase and decrease
Stochastic Methods	Applying genetic algorithm based optimization to feature selection.
Direct Methods	Finding a feature subset without involving a search procedure

time to the current feature set. At each iteration, the feature class to be included in the feature set is selected from among the remaining feature classes such that the new feature set yields the greatest possible value of a criterion function, which should be correlated with the rate of correct classification. Sequential Backward Search (SBS)[9] is similar to SFS except that one feature class is deleted at a time. When multiple features are added or deleted, we arrive at the generalized versions of SFS and SBS called GSFS and GSBS[10]. One could also add L features and delete R features, which is called LRS[11], and the generalized version is called GLRS. Instead of adding and deleting fixed numbers of features, we could adjust L and R dynamically, which results in floating feature selection[12]. Stochastic search methods have been explored using genetic algorithms (GA)[13]. The search process can be computationally complex so methods which do not rely on search have also been explored and are called Direct Methods[14,15]. Kittler, et al.[16] showed that combining classifiers can improve performance.

In the field of mathematical feature selection, the pioneering work is usually associated with Sebestyen[17], Lewis[18], and Marill and Green[9]. Sebestyen[17] was the early proponent of the use of interclass distance. Marill and Green[9] advocated a probabilistic distance measure. Lewis[18] and Marill and Green[9] were also among the first to address the problem of feature set search. In optimal feature selection, the branch and bound algorithm was proposed by Narendra and Fukunaga[19]. The potential of any suboptimal feature selection algorithm to select the worst subset of features was discussed in Cover and Van Campenhout[20].

Which feature selection is best? In a classification test by Jain and Zongker[21], they evaluated 15 promising feature selection algorithms on a 20 dimensional, 2 class data set. They found that the SFS and SBS algorithms have comparable performance, but the SFS is faster because it starts with small subsets and enlarges them while the SBS starts with large subsets and reduces them. The explanation was that it is more efficient to evaluate small subsets than large subsets. Furthermore, the floating selection methods were generally faster than the branch and bound algorithm and also gave comparable results.

Regarding the stochastic methods, Ferri[22] showed that the performance of GA and SFS are comparable but GA degrades with increasing dimensionality. Jain and Zongker[21] conclude that the GA algorithm is promising but there are several parameters which do not have a clear mechanism for setting their values.

Picard[6] asks how people can identify classes of photos without taking time to look at the precise content of each photo. These are visual concepts which can be identified "at a glance." Her work seeks to create a "society of models" which consists of a set of texture descriptions. The goal was to develop a system which could select the best model when one is best, and figure out how to combine models when that is best. The system shold also be able to learn to recognize, remember, and refine best model choices and combinations by analysis of both the data features and user interaction.

Forsyth, et al.[23] discuss the importance of using several grouping strategies in combination with pixel and template based features such as color and texture. Promising results were found for fusing texture and spatial models to represent trees; and fusing color, texture, and spatial models to find people and animals.

One example of their system is designed to find unclothed people. It first locates areas which contain skin-colored regions. Within the skin-colored regions, it finds elongated regions and groups them into plausible skeletal possibilities of limbs and groups of limbs. More recent work by Carson, et al.[24] shows the potential of using an ensemble of "blobs" representing image regions which are roughly homogeneous regarding color and texture. Their system was able to find images containing tigers, cheetahs, zebras, and planes.

Vailaya, Jain, and Zhang[25] have reported success in classifying images as city vs. landscape by using edge direction features. Intuitively, the system was classifying images with high percentages of linear edges as cities.

Regarding object recognition, the recent surge of research toward face recognition has motivated robust methods for face detection in complex scenery. Representative results have been reported by Sung and Poggio[26], Rowley and Kanade[27], Lew and Huijsmans[28], and Lew and Huang[29]. These methods typically gave good results for frontal face images, but were relatively fragile to detecting side views.

Lew and Sebe[5] developed several strategies toward automatic visual concept learning. For each visual concept, they collected a large set of positive and negative examples. They measured a variety of texture, color, and shape features, and for each feature subset, measured the discriminatory power using the Kullback[30] discriminant. The candidate features for the system included the color, gradient, Laplacian, and texture information from every pixel as shown in Figure 1.

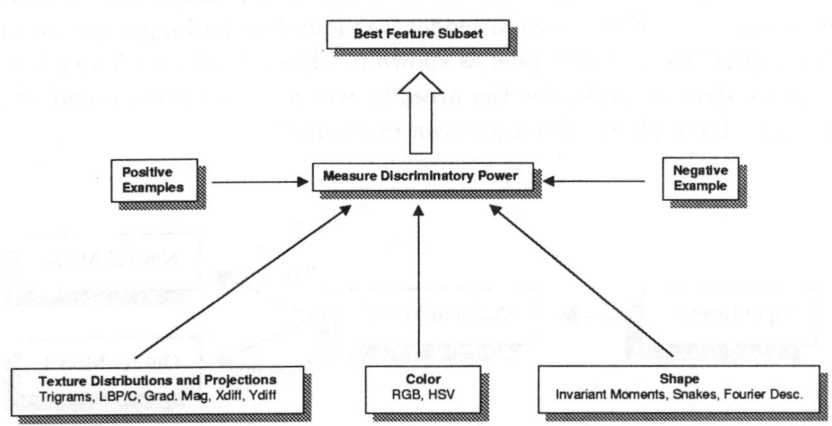

Fig. 1. Selecting the best feature subset of N features from texture, color, and shape features. (Trigrams[31], LBP[32], LBP/C, Grad. Mag., XDiff, YDiff[33], Snakes[34], invariant moments[35], and Fourier Descriptors[36])

132

2.2. *Dynamic Feature Sets*

The previous algorithm had the problem that it used a static feature set. Static feature sets may be inappropriate for specific classes of imagery. For example, using color to find skin is appropriate if the image is color, but inappropriate if the image is grayscale. This observation led to the use of dynamic feature sets.

Instead of using a single feature set for detecting the visual concept, dynamic feature sets apply a specific feature set depending on the content of the visual media. In normal feature selection, a small subset of features is typically chosen to avoid overfit. The resulting feature subset will typically misclassify part of the training set. The novel method introduced by Lew and Sebe[5] was to choose a feature set dynamically based on the content of the image. Specifically, they used floating feature selection to find the initial feature subset (Normal Model). Second, they reclassified the ground truth training set to determine in which images the misclassifications occured. In order to identify these images and classify them, they designed two more feature sets. The second feature set (Decision Model) was trained to discriminate between the correctly classified images and the misclassified images. Using this model, they attempted to determine the contexts when the initial model was inappropriate. The third feature set (Outlier Model) was trained to discriminate between the misclassified images and the nonobject images. So, if the normal model was found to be inappropriate then they applied the outlier model as shown in Figure 2. Figures 3 and 4 show representative examples for the areas in which their system found visual concepts. Example queries are shown in Figure 5.

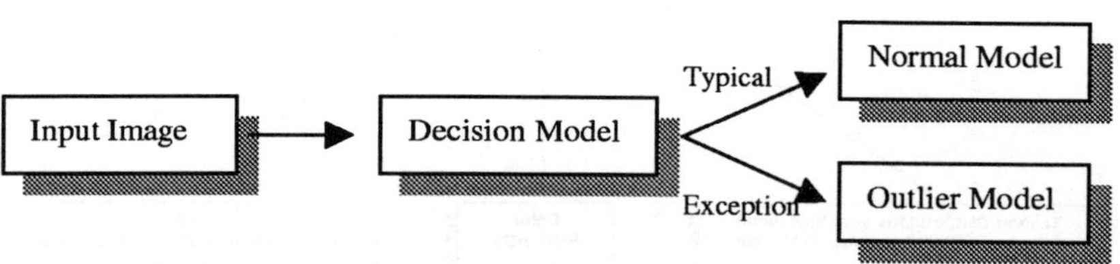

Fig. 2.   Dynamic feature set

Fig. 3.   Detecting the class of trees/grass in an image.

2.3. *Feature Construction*

Almost all visual concept learning methods have been based on feature selection. The critical disadvantage with feature selection techniques is that they are limited by the discriminative power of the set of candidate features, which are typically pre-chosen by the system designer. In principle, a system which can automatically construct features could have improved detection rates. Regarding automatic feature construction, Buijs[37] presented a rule based method for combining the atomic features of color, texture, and shape toward representing more sophisticated visual concepts. The atomic textural features were coarse, semi-coarse, semi fine, fine, nonlinear, semi-linear, linear, and texture features based on examples: marble, wood, water, herringbone, etc.

For the atomic shape features, he created a basic set of geometric primitives: circular, elliptical square, triangular, rectangular, and pentagonal. Concepts were represented as AND/OR expressions such as:

Fig. 4.   Detecting the class of sand/stone in an image.

> If ((color is yellow OR color is white)
>   AND (texture is fine)
>   AND (texture is nonlinear))
> Then object is sand

Rules were automatically generated from positive and negative example training sets using decision trees. The results were promising but by no means definitive. One of the main challenges in feature construction is that the complexity grows exponentially with the size of the rules. Consequently, the automatically discovered rules were not sufficiently complex to discriminate between a wide range of visual concepts.

3. Discussion

In many ways, feature selection is a mature field. For example, there are extensive test sets for benchmarking the effectiveness of various methods. Techniques exist for finding optimal and near optimal solutions. However, currently there are no broad scale content based retrieval systems which

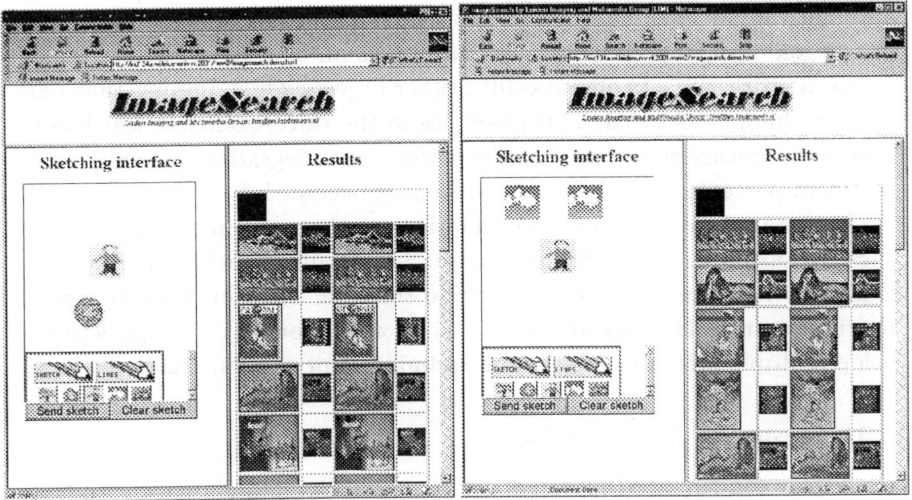

Fig. 5. Queries and results using semantic icons

can detect thousands of visual concepts automatically from images with complex backgrounds.

3.1. *Major Challenges*

In this section we discuss several major challenges in learning visual concepts. If we are to avoid overfit in feature selection, a large training set is required. However, in many applications it is impractical to gather large training sets. Furthermore, when the Mahalanobis distance is used to measure class separation, the error from estimating the covariance matrix can lead to inferior results even if the selected feature subset is optimal for the training data[38]. Therefore, the first challenge is to develop techniques performing feature selection using sparse training sets.

Suppose an optimal feature subset is found for the class of visual concepts which include frontal and side-views of human faces. Recent work by Sung and Poggio[26] and Buijs and Lew[39] indicate that better performance might be found from splitting the class of human faces into clusters: i.e. the frontal-view class and the side-view class, and then finding the appropriate feature subset for each class. Depending on how the visual concept is clustered, the classification rate may vary. Therefore, the second challenge is to automatically determine when to split the training examples into multiple classes and find feature subsets for each of them.

In practice, objects often occlude other objects which implies that partial matching is required. This gives rise to the third challenge which is to design the feature subset so that the performance degrades gracefully when a greater percentage of the visual concept is occluded.

In real applications, sparse information may be given in multiple modalities. For example in video, there may be text, audio, and visual imagery. Currently it is unclear how to combine these information sources toward maximizing the classification rate. Therefore, the fourth challenge is to develop multiple modality integration techniques for content based retrieval.

3.2. *Capability for Learning*

On a more controversial note, one might ask which methods show the greatest capability for learning new visual concepts. This is a difficult question to answer for several fundamental reasons. Relevance feedback methods such as the ones proposed by Picard[6] appear to be promising because they can adapt to the user's preference for a visual concept. Automatic visual learning methods such as the ones proposed by Lew and Sebe[5] are interesting since they take into account the pictorial features and spatial models. However, a closer look at their algorithm shows that the spatial models are represented by static instances of the shape of the object. In the case of humans, the limbs can be at a wide variety of poses, each of which would require a static instance of the shape.

If we consider the method advocated by Forsyth[23], we see that it involves both feature selection combined with spatial models. His system is effective at detecting unclothed people in images with complex backgrounds. Part of the attractiveness of his approach is that it involves spatial reasoning about the class of visual concepts. His work indicates that it is possible to manually construct features and models which can detect complex visual concepts, however, it is not clear how to automatically generate the features nor models for wide classes of visual concepts.

In the system by Buijs[37], both the feature selection process and the spatial model selection are automated. However, the complexity of the search process for finding the features and spatial models is exponential which means that in practice, the rules must be short. For his system, it is essential to find ways to prune large areas of the search tree.

If we are to detect wide classes of visual concepts automatically, it is important to add a higher degree of spatial model reasoning to the feature selection based methods or to find practical methods for reducing the complexity of the feature construction systems.

4. Summary

There have been a wide variety of visual concept learning algorithms proposed in the research literature such as relevance feedback, feature blobs, dynamic feature sets, and feature construction. These algorithms showed good results at detecting small sets of visual concepts. However, there are several major obstacles which include but are not limited to the following:

- How can we avoid overfit in feature selection when there is minimal training data?
- How can we determine when to split the training examples into multiple subclasses and find separate feature sets for each subclass?
- How can we detect partially occluded examples of visual concepts?
- How can we combine multiple modalities (text, audio, visual imagery) toward maximizing the classification rate?
- How can we add a deeper level of spatial reasoning to visual concept detection methods?

Visual concept learning holds the promise of bringing intuitive visual information retrieval to the nonexpert user. It is within the realm of possibility that in the not so far future, it will be accessible via a WWW browser near you.

References

1. D. Petkovic, Challenges and Opportunities for Pattern Recognition and Computer Vision Research in Year 2000 and Beyond, *Proc. of the Int. Conf. on Image Analysis and Processing*, Florence, vol. 2, pp. 1-5, (1997).
2. V. N. Gudivada and V. V. Raghavan, Finding the Right Image, Content-Based Image Retrieval Systems, *Computer*, IEEE Computer Society, pp. 18-62, (Sept. 1995).
3. M. Flickner, H. Sawhney, W. Niblack, J. Ashley, Q. Huang, B. Dom, M. Gorkani, J. Hafner, D. Lee, D. Petkovic, D. Steele, and P. Yanker, Query by Image and Video Content: The QBIC System, *Computer*, IEEE Computer Society, pp. 23-32, (Sept. 1995).

4. J. P. Eakins, Techniques for Image Retrieval, *Library and Information Briefings*, 85, British Library and South Bank University, London, (1998).

5. M. Lew and N. Sebe, Visual Websearching using Iconic Queries, *Proc. of the IEEE Conference on Computer Vision and Pattern Recognition*, Hilton Head Island, (2000).

6. R. Picard, A Society of Models for Video and Image Libraries, *IBM Systems Journal*, (1996).

7. L. Taycher, M. Cascia, and S. Sclaroff, Image Digestion and Relevance Feedback in the ImageRover WWW Search Engine, *VISUAL97*, San Diego, pp. 85-91, (1997).

8. A. Whitney, A Direct Method of Nonparametric Measurement Selection, *IEEE Transactions on Computing*, vol. 20, pp. 1100-1103, (1971).

9. T. Marill and D.M. Green, On the Effectiveness of Receptors in Recognition Systems, *IEEE Transactions on Information Theory*, vol. 9, pp. 11-17, (1963).

10. J. Kittler, Une generalisation de quelques algorithmes sous-optimaux de recherche d'ensembles d'attributs, *Reconnaissance des Formes et Traitement des Images*, Paris, pp. 678-686, (1978).

11. S. Stearns, On Selecting Features for Pattern Classifiers, *Proc. of the International Conference on Pattern Recognition*, pp. 71-75, (1976).

12. P. Pudil, J. Novovicova, and J. Kittler, Floating Search Methods in Feature Selection, *Pattern Recognition Letters*, pp. 1119-1125, (1994).

13. W. Siedlecki and J. Sklansky, A Note on Genetic Algorithms for Large-Scale Feature Selection, *Pattern Recognition Letters*, vol. 10, pp. 335-347, (1989).

14. P. Pudil, J. Novovicova, and J. Kittler, Automatic Machine Learning of Decision Rule for Classification Problems in Image Analysis, *Proc. 4th British Machine Vision Conference*, vol. 1, pp. 15-24, (1993).

15. J. Novovicova, P. Pudil, and J. Kittler, Divergence Based Feature Selection for Multimodal Class Densities, *IEEE Transactions on Pattern Analysis and Machine Intelligence*, vol. 18, no. 2, (1996).

16. J. Kittler, M. Hatef, R. Duin, and J. Matas, On Combining Classifiers, *IEEE Transactions on Pattern Analysis and Machine Intelligence*, vol. 20, no. 3, (1998).

17. G. Sebestyen, Decision Making Processes in Pattern Recognition, Macmillan, New York, (1962).

18. P. Lewis, The Characteristic Selection Problem in Recognition Systems, *IRE Transactions on Information Theory*, vol. 8, pp. 171-178, (1962).

19. P. M. Narendra and K. Fukunaga, A Branch and Bound Algorithm for Feature Subset Selection, *IEEE Transactions on Computing*, vol. 26, pp. 917-922, (1977).

20. T. Cover and J. Van Campenhout, On the Possible Orderings in the Measurement Selection Problem, *IEEE Trans. Systems Man Cybernetics*, vol. 7, pp. 657-661, (1977).

21. A. Jain and D. Zongker, Feature Selection: Evaluation, Application, and Small Sample Performance, *IEEE Transactions on Pattern Analysis and Machine Intelligence*, vol. 19, no. 2, pp. 153-158, (1997).

22. F. Ferri, P. Pudil, M. Hatef, and J. Kittler, Comparative Study of Techniques for Large Scale Feature Selection, *Pattern Recognition in Practice IV*, E. Gelsema and L. Kanal, eds., pp. 403-413, Elsevier Science, (1994).

23. D. Forsyth, J. Malik, M. Fleck, T. Leung, C. Bregler, C. Carson, and H. Greenspan, Finding Pictures of Objects in Large Collections of Images, *Proc. International Workshop on Object Recognition*, April, (1996).

24. C. Carson, M. Thomas, S. Belongie, J. Hellerstein, and J. Malik, Blobworld: A System for Region-Based Image Indexing and Retrieval, *Proc. VISUAL'99*, Amsterdam, pp. 509-516, (1999).

25. A. Vailaya, A. Jain and H. Zhang, On Image Classification: City vs. Landscape, *IEEE Workshop on Content-Based Access of Image and Video Libraries*, Santa Barbara, (1998).

26. K. K. Sung and T. Poggio, Example-Based Learning for View-Based Human Face Detection, *IEEE Transactions on Pattern Analysis and Machine Intelligence*, vol. 20, no. 1, pp. 39-51, (1998).

27. H. Rowley and T. Kanade, Neural Network Based Face Detection, *IEEE Transactions on Pattern Analysis and Machine Intelligence*, vol. 20, no. 1, pp. 23-38, (1998).

28. M. Lew and N. Huijsmans, Information Theory and Face Detection, *Proc. of the International Conference on Pattern Recognition*, Vienna, pp.601-605, (1996).

29. M. Lew and T. Huang, Optimal Supports for Image Matching, *Proc. of the IEEE Digital Signal Processing Workshop*, Loen, Norway, pp. 251-254, 1996.

30. S. Kullback, Information Theory and Statistics, Wiley, New York, 1959.

31. D. P. Huijsmans, M. Lew, and D. Denteneer, Quality Measures for Interactive Image Retrieval with a Performance Evaluation of Two 3x3 Texel-based Methods, *Proc. International Conference on Image Analysis and Processing*, Florence, (1997).

32. L. Wang and D. C. He, Texture Classification Using Texture Spectrum, *Pattern Recognition*, 23, pp. 905-910, (1990).

33. T. Ojala, M. Pietikainen and D. Harwood, A Comparative Study of Texture Measures with Classification Based on Feature Distributions, *Pattern Recognition*, 29, no. 1, pp. 51-59, (1996).

34. A. Del Bimbo and P. Pala, Visual Image Retrieval by Elastic Matching of User Sketches, *IEEE Trans. Pattern Analysis and Machine Intelligence*, pp. 121-132, (1997).

35. M. Hu, Visual Pattern Recognition by Moment Invariants, *IRA Trans. on Information Theory*, vol. 17-8, no. 2, pp. 179-187, (1962).

36. R. Gonzalez and R. E. Woods, Digital Image Processing, Addison Wesley, 1993.

37. J. M. Buijs, Toward Semantic Based Multimedia Search, Masters Thesis, Leiden Institute for Advanced Computer Science, (1998).

38. S. Raudys and A. Jain, Small Sample Size Effects in Statistical Pattern Recognition: Recommendations for Practitioners, *IEEE Transactions on Pattern Analysis and Machine Intelligence*, vol. 13, pp. 252-264, (1991).

39. J. M. Buijs and M. Lew, Learning Visual Concepts, *ACM Multimedia'99*, vol. 2, pp. 5-8, (1999).

AUTOMATED HUMAN FACIAL FEATURE EXTRACTION USING DOUBLE RESOLUTION PYRAMID

Li-an Tang

Intel Corporation

Introduction to Human Facial Feature Extraction

Facial feature extraction has become an important topic in both automated visual interpretation and human face recognition for many years. Facial features are the salient appearances on human faces, for example, eyes, eyebrows, nose and mouth. Usually the facial features are extracted from either the front or side profile view of the face image. A number of algorithms have been proposed for facial feature extraction. The Snakes method uses an energy-minimizing spline to find the boundary around a feature. The deformable templates method uses parameterized templates that are based on a priori knowledge about the expected shape of the facial feature to find facial features, mainly the eyes and mouth. Some extended versions of these methods have also been developed. However, most algorithms assume either uniform background so that the face area can be located by simple segmentation or known initialization of the features. Another disadvantage of these methods is that they only use localized information, for example, the edges, so that they could be easily trapped to local extrema in noisy images.

We strongly believe that the facial feature can be well-defined only when it is viewed as a whole. An image pattern is considered a mouth only when it satisfies the global arrangement of the mouth. It is this idea that motivates us to develop an automatic facial feature extraction algorithm based on template matching that utilizes both intensity and geometric information about the facial features.

Overview of Automated Facial Feature Extraction Algorithm

We have developed a robust facial feature extraction algorithm using the template matching technique. It can automatically detect the face area and locate individual facial features, *i.e.* eyebrows, eyes, nose, mouth and face outlines. All feature points shown in Figure 1 can be located using this algorithm. Each feature is first globally extracted using a template that encloses the entire feature. Then smaller templates around feature points are used to find them locally.

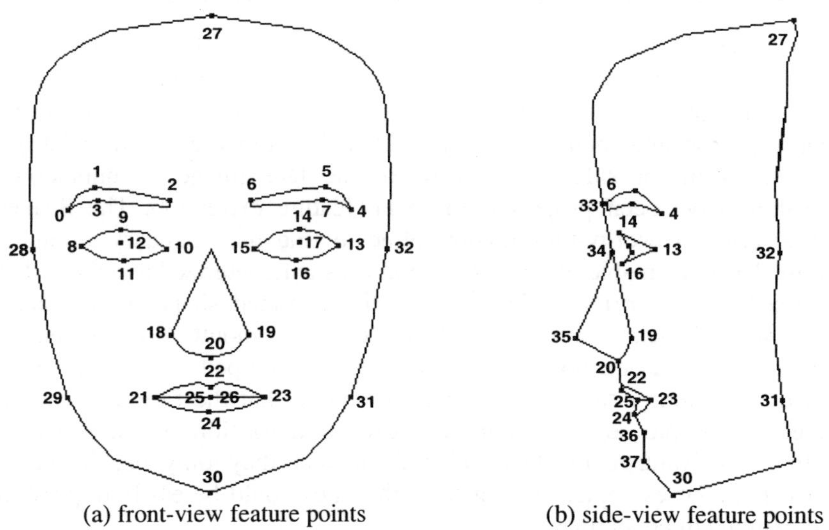

(a) front-view feature points   (b) side-view feature points

Figure 1. Human face feature points

Often faces can be more easily detected in images that have lower resolutions. There are two reasons for this. First, the computations are much faster due to the dimensionality reduction. Second, confusing details presented in higher resolution images may not appear at reduced resolution. Although the sizes and proportions among facial features differ significantly in high resolution images, all faces look almost the same at very low resolution. However, accurate extraction of facial features requires details which are only revealed in high resolution images. This naturally suggests a hierarchical template matching strategy as we shall describe in detail in this chapter.

The algorithm is an integration of "coarse-to-fine searching" (face detection) and "global-to-local matching" (feature extraction). A set of multi-resolution templates is built for the whole face and individual facial components. A resolution pyramid structure is also established for the input face image. This algorithm first tries to find a rough face location in the image at the lowest resolution by globally matching with the face templates. The higher resolution images and templates are used to refine the face location. Then each facial feature is located using a combination of techniques, including image processing, template matching and deformable templates. Finally, a feedback procedure is provided to verify extracted features using the anthropometry of human faces and, if necessary, the features will be re-matched.

The most significant part of this algorithm is that we have developed a technique which can be called "double resolution pyramid" that makes this algorithm scale-invariant and the computations much faster than for a single resolution pyramid. Figure 2 gives a systematic view of this algorithm.

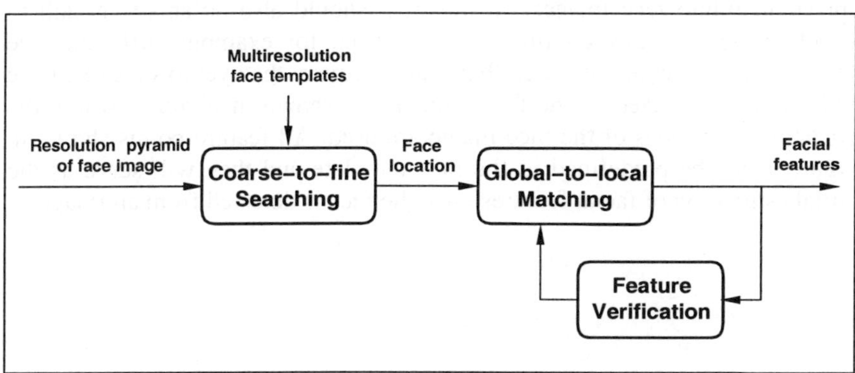

Figure 2. Automatic facial feature extraction system

We impose the following constraints to make this algorithm work well:
- We assume the face images have known orientations, either front-view or side profile view. However, we make no assumptions about the scale and location of face in the image.

- The facial features should not be occluded by other objects, *e.g.* long hairs, thick mustache and beard.
- The person should not be wearing eyeglasses.
- The face should have a neutral expression.
- As for the background, there is no necessary assumption of uniformity for detecting face area and extracting facial features. However, the algorithm does require that the background around the face boundary (in both front- and side-views) be in sharp contrast to the face area so that the feature points on the face boundary could be determined.

Multi-resolutional Face Templates

A set of templates with different resolutions are obtained from gradient magnitude of a face image.

Choosing face template

In choosing the template for the face area, two factors are considered. First, the area should be large enough to differ from any similar region which may appear in future face images. However, it should also be small enough to avoid introducing any confusing information, for example, different face shapes and hair styles. An area that mainly covers the eyebrows, eyes, nose and mouth is selected as the face template as shown in Figure 3 where the gradient magnitudes of the face image are used. All feature points shown in Figure 1 can be predefined in the face template and they will serve as the initial estimation of facial features once the face is detected from an image.

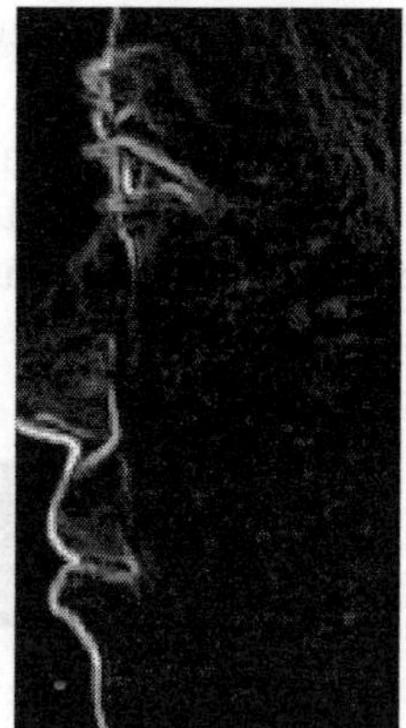

(a) front view face template   (b) left view face template

Figure 3. Face templates

Template consolidation

Pixel consolidation is used to average the original image over an $n \times n$ neighborhood followed by subsampling at every n pixels. The consolidation process has the ability to offset the aliasing which would be introduced by subsampling.

A set of multi-resolution face templates are generated by the pixel consolidation procedure as shown in Figure 4. More resolution levels can be created by interpolation followed by pixel consolidation.

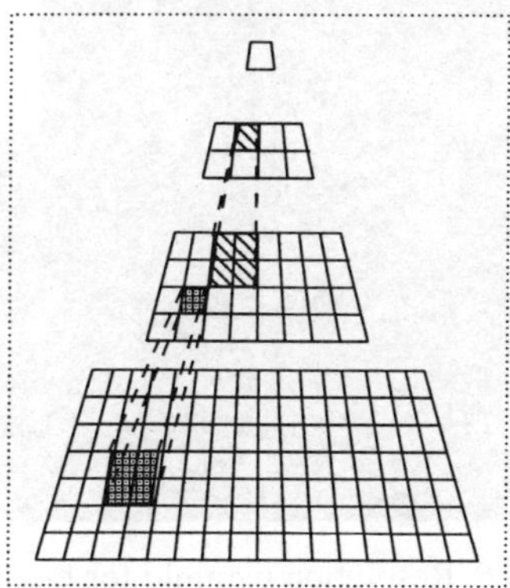

Figure 4. Pixel consolidation

146

Subtemplates for facial features

For facial features, areas around them are chosen as feature templates. Templates covering larger areas are used for globally locating facial features; Smaller templates are used to determine feature points. Figure 5 shows the subtemplates for whole mouth, upper lip and its two corners.

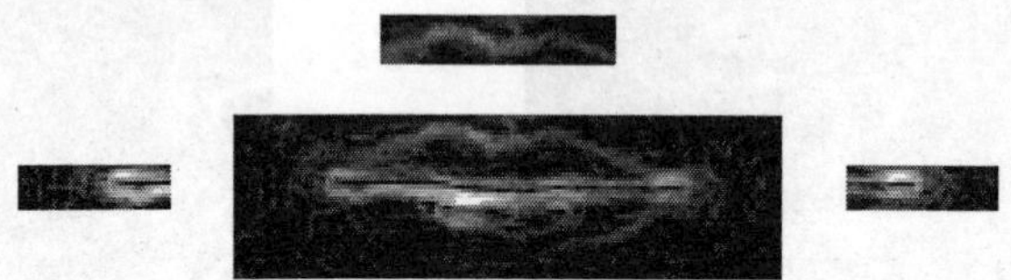

Figure 5. Subtemplates for the mouth

Resolution pyramid of face image

For the same reason, the face image in which all facial features have to be extracted also undergoes the consolidation process as do the face templates, except that the size of the neighborhood is fixed to be 2×2 pixels. Figure 6 shows an example of a four-level resolution pyramid of a face image.

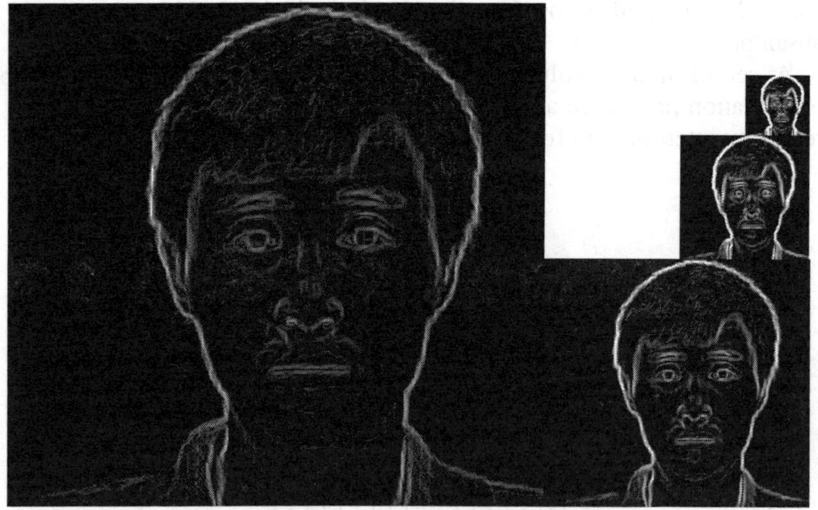

Figure 6. Resolution pyramid for face image

Similarity measures

Similarity measures provide quantitative means of determining the degree of match between a template T and a patch of the image I. The following are three typical similarity measures.

- traditional cross-correlation:

$$c(u,v) = \sum_x \sum_y T(x,y)I(x+u,y+v) \tag{Eq. 1}$$

- normalized correlation coefficient:

$$\rho(u,v) = \frac{\sum_x \sum_y (T(x,y) - \mu_T)(I(x+u,y+v) - \mu_I)}{\sqrt{\sum_x \sum_y (T(x,y) - \mu_T)^2 \sum_x \sum_y (I(x+u,y+v) - \mu_I)^2}} \tag{Eq. 2}$$

where μ_T is the average of the template and μ_I is the average of image region covered by the template,

- sum of absolute differences for efficient computation:

$$\varepsilon(u,v) = \sum_x \sum_y |T(x,y) - I(x+u,y+v)| \tag{Eq. 3}$$

Search strategies

Among many search strategies, two-stage template matching and sequential similarity detection algorithms are two commonly used methods.

The former method tries to first locate the possible candidates for a match without investing time on locations that show no evidence for a match. The best match position is found in the second stage. Usually, a sub-area of the template or a reduced resolution template is used at the first stage.

In sequential search strategy, Equation 3 is used as similarity measure. For each window of the test image, a number of random points are chosen as test points. Every ε (here, it should be considered the absolute difference between two corresponding pixels) is accumulated until some predefined threshold is exceeded. The window that tests the maximum number of points is assumed to be the best match.

Face Detection by Coarse-to-fine Multi-resolution Searching

As mentioned earlier, for a given face image, we know neither location nor size of the face. Therefore, simple two-stage template matching does not work. Instead, we introduce a two-stage multi-resolution template matching strategy to detect the best possible face candidate including location and size of the face. The method is sketched in Figure 7.

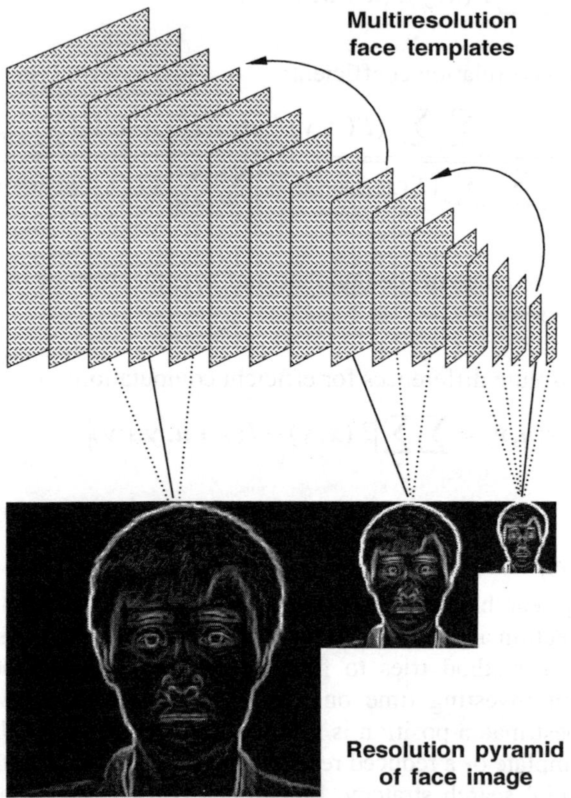

Figure 7. Coarse-to-fine search scheme

The search starts from the highest level (with the lowest resolution) of resolution pyramid of the face image. Every face template with the size smaller than that of the face image is matched within the whole image to get the maximum correlation coefficient, and its location is also recorded. The template possessing the largest correlation coefficient is the best match. In this way, the rough position and approximate size of the face can be found in the image. Since at the lowest resolution, both image and template are small, the search can be done quickly even though a full search along whole image is required at this stage. To speed up this procedure, a sequential search strategy can be adopted during the matching with every template.

Then the search is implemented at next level of the resolution pyramid, *i.e.* the image size is doubled. We also choose the template that has resolution roughly increased by a factor of 2 from the previous one. Together with two neighboring templates, three templates are again correlated with the higher resolution image. At this step, the correlations are only implemented in a small search area around estimated face location. The one with the maximum correlation coefficient is chosen to refine the face location and size. This procedure is repeated until the full resolution image has been processed. We can see that continuous refinement can be realized at each step of coarse-to-fine multi-resolution template matching. It is possible to find a nearly exact face scale provided the templates cover as many resolution levels as possible. However, we shall also see that this is usually not necessary for our purpose.

Next a global-to-local matching procedure will deal with the problem of finding facial features after location and size of the face are detected.

Feature Extraction by Global-to-local Matching

Just as the differences among various faces tend to disappear when the resolution of the face images is lowered, the differences exhibited by facial components on different faces are also diminished when we compare very small areas of these features. For example, from a global point of view, all mouths seem completely different. However, if we look closely at the mouth corners, they are almost the same. Since the local areas are usually very small, searching these kinds of templates along a relatively large area will result in many false alarms of possible locations. A possible location of the whole feature should be determined before its feature points can be extracted. This is main idea of the global-to-local matching strategy. Since local feature areas involve more details, this matching is usually implemented on the original face image.

After the face location has been detected, the initial position of all facial features can be estimated immediately according to the face template. The estimated facial features should not be far away from their actual positions. Therefore, for each facial feature, we first try to find its global location by matching a whole feature template with the face image in a designated search area around initial position. The search area for each feature is predefined based on the proportions among facial features. After some facial features have been determined, the search areas for the rest of the features can be more accurately decided. We have found that feature points on the mouth can always be more robustly located. Actually the vertical line passing the centroid of mouth feature points serves as the middle line of the face that is used later in symmetry verification.

We have also noticed that not all feature points can be accurately extracted using the template matching procedure alone. For example, point 24 in Figure 1 is not always recognizable since the bottom boundary of the lower lip often discontinues in the middle part due to image noise. Some other feature extraction techniques, in this case the deformable template method, are used to deal with these features. Another example is the edge detection, which is used to find the boundary points of the face.

Feedback Process

In describing the global-to-local matching procedure to find all facial features, we assumed that every feature point was determined correctly. However, this is usually not the case in real situations. The estimated best matching feature points may deviate from their actual position due to image noise and large variations between the templates and the real facial features. A feedback strategy is introduced to verify extracted feature points to ensure that they are all correctly identified. The following criteria have been used.

- Symmetry metric

In a front-view face image, most feature points are symmetric to the middle face line. The asymmetric measure of each pair of corresponding feature points should not exceed a threshold.

- Anthropometry metric

The proportions among the feature points should not exceed the statistical average from human face anthropometry.

The points for which the tests fail will undergo matching process again. A pairwise matching will be implemented at this time. The best match subject to the symmetry or proportion constraints will be chosen as the position of these features.

Let us take the eyes as an example to see how the symmetry verification works. Suppose that inner corner of the left eye is located at (X_l, Y_l) and that of the right eye at (X_r, Y_r) and the middle line of the front-view face is centered at $X=0$. The symmetry test checks both $|(|X_l|-|X_r|)|$ and $|(|Y_l|-|Y_r|)|$. If either of the two values exceeds the designated threshold, the symmetry of the eyes is violated. A new matching procedure will be carried out. From the previous matching, we have already known the correlation coefficients when both eyes are best matched, say, ρ_l for the left eye and ρ_r for the right eye.

- Assuming that the left eye is correctly located already, the right eye template is matched with the face image within a small area centered at $(-X_l, Y_l)$ to get the best match with correlation coefficient ρ_r';

- Next, assuming that the location of the right eye is originally correct, then the left eye template is matched with the face image within a small area centered at $(-X_r, Y_r)$ to get the best match giving correlation coefficient ρ_l';

- If $\rho_l + \rho_r' > \rho_l' + \rho_r$, the new location of the right eye is adopted;

- otherwise, the left eye is moved to its new location.

Usually testing the symmetry for eyes should guarantee their correct positions. We have found it rather rare that both eyes are initially estimated incorrectly.

The proportional verification of facial features is relatively difficult, since there is no guarantee which facial feature can be determined accurately. We mainly use this to verify nose and points on face boundary provided that the interior facial features are determined correctly.

Let us take nose as another example to see how the facial proportions are used. From our experience, the nose seems to be a less reliable feature on human face due to its large variations among different people. Often its vertical position is mislocated so that the symmetry check could easily pass. As a result, the ratio of vertical distance between eyes and nose and that between nose and mouth is verified. If the ratio exceeds 2 times of its statistic standard deviation, the nose will be re-matched around the statistic position. The best match will be chosen as the nose location.

Experiments

We have applied this algorithm to a set of face images of *30* different people at our laboratory. These images are taken with different background and various zooming factors. Every image is *512 × 480* pixels, and a four-level resolution pyramid is created using its gradient magnitude. Figure 8 shows one particular set of multi-resolution face templates, which are extended from the face template shown in Figure 3.

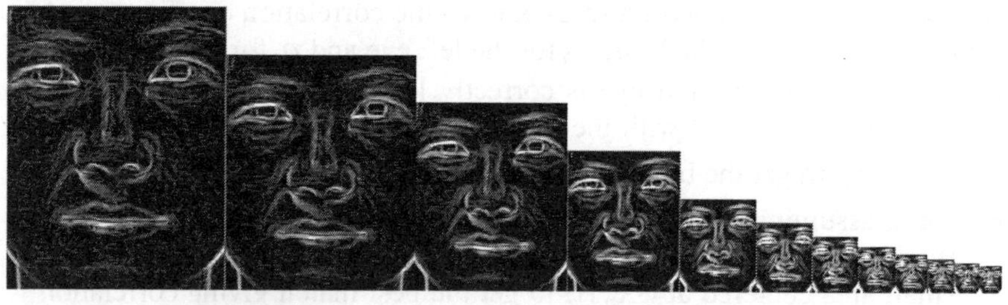

(a) front-view

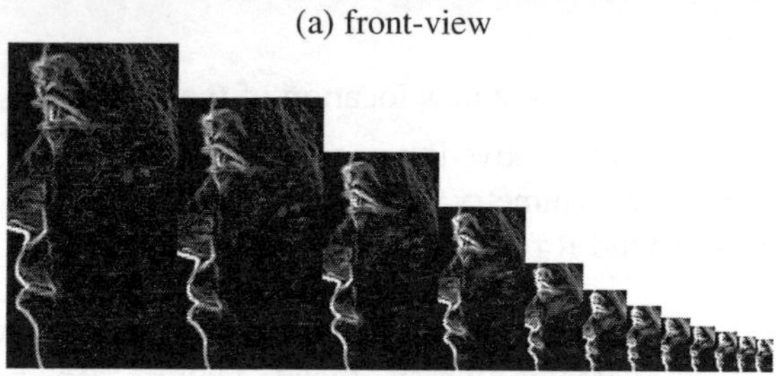

(b) left side-view

Figure 8. Multi-resolution face templates

The ratios of sizes between two consecutive templates range from *0.83–0.9*. The highest resolution template has size of *180 × 230* for front-view image and *120 × 230* for side-view image. The lowest resolution template has size of *18 × 23* for front-view image and *12 × 23* for side-view image. The size of the lowest resolution template roughly corresponds to Samal's suggestion that *32 $\times$ 32* be the smallest size of an image in which the face can be possibly detected. In much smaller images, there is little resemblance to a face. For another reason that will become clear in later section, we do not intend to use templates with very small sizes. This set of face templates is used to test all face images in our database.

Locating face area

The location of face is determined by the coarse-to-fine searching strategy. All face templates with size less than that of the lowest resolution image are completely matched with that image. A typical curve of correlation coefficient *vs.* size of the template is plotted in Figure 9.

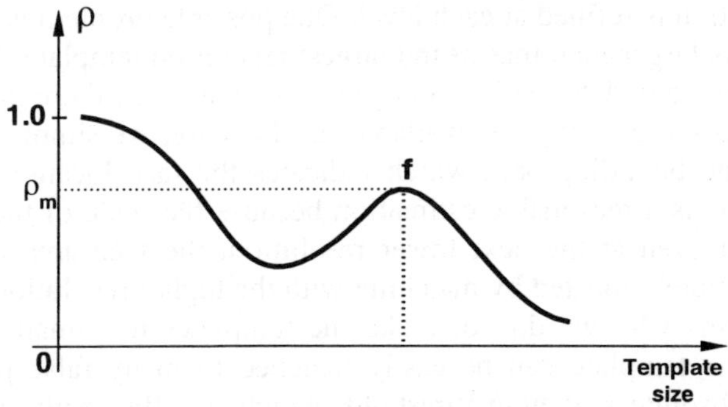

Figure 9. Relation between the correlation coefficient and the template size

When size of the template is much larger than that of the actual face area, the correlation coefficient is usually very small. As size of the template decreases, it becomes increasingly similar to face area and the correlation coefficient increases until a peak is reached where the scale of the template is almost equal to that of the face. Further reduction of template size will worsen the match. However, as size of the template continues to decrease, it becomes so small that it will easily match to any area in the image.

The folowing steps describe implementations of the algorithm.

1. Starting from the largest possible template, match every template with the image to obtain the peak point *f* shown in Figure 9.
2. If the peak value ρ_m exceeds the matching threshold, which is fixed to be *0.3* for front-view image and *0.5* for side-view image in all experiments,

this template is the best match. The match position will be the rough location of face area.

3. At any resolution of the template, if the correlation coefficient exceeds the absolute matching threshold, which is a fixed number of *0.4* for front-view image and *0.6* for side-view image in our experiments, this template determines the rough location of the face.

4. If the peak value is not larger than the matching threshold or the global maximum of correlation curve does not exceed the absolute matching threshold, the face area is thought to be too small to be matched even with the lowest resolution template. The image is updated to the next level of the resolution pyramid and steps 1--3 are repeated until rough location of the face is found.

5. Both template and image are updated to the next resolution level and the face location is refined at each level. One possible problem is that size of the face is larger than that of the largest resolution template. This means that when we update the face image to the next level, there may not be a higher resolution template available. In this case, we simply double the size of the bounding box, which indicates the face location at the last level. This is a reasonable estimation because the scale of the face is so large that even at the next lower resolution, the face area has already been accurately located by matching with the higher resolution template.

Step 3 explains why we do not make the templates too small. With very small size, the template can be easily matched to many false positions to exceed the absolute matching threshold, which usually results in a wrong estimation of face area.

Matching with facial features

Once the face area has been detected, a set of subtemplates around the facial features is used to determine exact positions of the facial features. Figure 10 shows the locations of these subtemplates along with the feature points. Template matching, image processing and deformable templates techniques are further combined to locate the exact feature points.

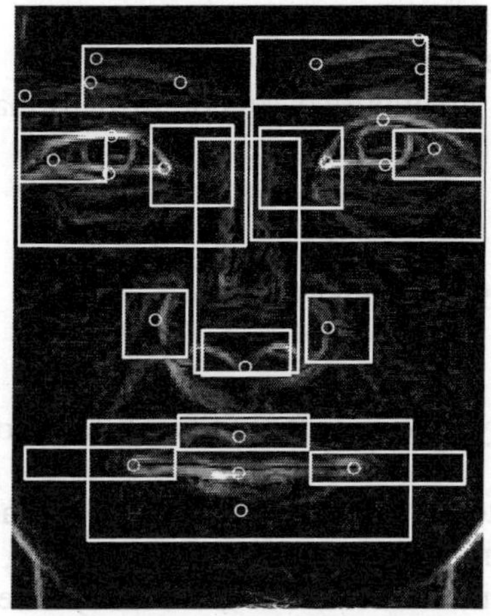

(a) front-view subtemplates.

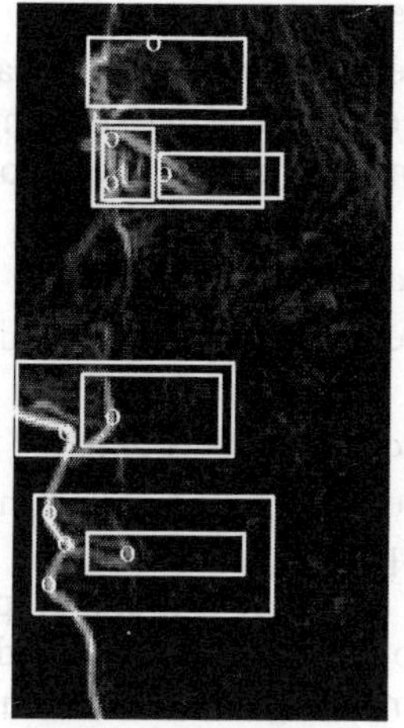

(b) left-view subtemplates

Figure 10. Locations of face subtemplates

Extracting features from front-view face image

Mouth

Although the mouth is the most deformable feature on the human face, it is also the most reliable feature that can be identified once the face area is detected. This is true for both the front- and side- face images. The rough location of the mouth can be determined by matching with the whole mouth template. Then the two corners and the upper-lip point are located using corresponding subtemplates. The lower-lip point is determined using a simplified deformable template of the mouth. Only the vertical position of that point has to be determined using the maximum gradient energy criterion.

After the mouth is located, the middle face line will be determined as the vertical line passing through the center of mouth.

Nose

The nose points are determined by template matching using different subtemplates.

Eyes

The eyes are first located using eye template. Then the corners are determined using subtemplates. Finally, a simplified version of deformable template method is employed to extract the rest of the points.

Eyebrows

The eyebrows are determined by template matching.

Face boundary points

There are six points on the face boundary. However, only five of them could be possibly determined.

Refer to Figure 1, point 27 is determined based on statistical facial proportion. Points 29 and 31 are two symmetric boundary points having the same height as the mouth corners. Points 28 and 32 are two symmetric boundary points having the same height as the eye corners. The chin point 30 is determined by a parabola that passes through points 29, 30 and 31 and possesses the maximum gradient energy. Finally, vertex point 27 is determined such that the eye points 10 and 15 are located vertically in the middle of points 27 and 30.

Feature verification

Symmetry is verified on the eyes, eyebrows and four boundary points 28, 29, 31 and 32. Proportion is tested on the nose and boundary points.

If necessary, these features will be re-matched as described in Section "Feedback Process".

Extracting features from side-view face image

Face boundary line

The boundary of middle face line is an important feature in the side-view face. Many facial feature points locate on this line. After the face is detected, this line is determined by edge detection. Since we assume the background is in high contrast with the face around the boundary, this line could be easily detected.

Mouth

We again start feature extraction from the mouth. It is first roughly located using mouth template. Then its visible corner is determined using mouth corner subtemplate. The rest of mouth points can be determined by finding the local extremes of horizontal distances on the face boundary line.

Nose

The nose is roughly located by template matching and its visible wing point is also determined by subtemplates. The rest of nose points are determined by finding local extremes on the face boundary line.

Eye

In side-view face, the eye is an unreliable feature due to its small size. Template matching around initial estimation often results in the wrong location. Instead, we re-initialize the eye position using the nose root point 34. Then the eye points can be determined by template matching.

Eyebrow

The eyebrow is also re-initialized according to point 33, which is the local extreme on face boundary line right above nose root. Then template matching is used to find the best match of eyebrow.

Chin

The chin points are determined from face boundary line as local extrema below mouth.

Combining features extracted from different face views

One goal of extracting facial features from different views is to obtain their 3-D locations. However, since the scales of faces in these images are not necessarily the same, we should normalize the results. In most applications, the front-view face is more important than the side-view face, so feature points on the side-view image are aligned to the front-view image by scaling. Since the corners of both eyes and mouth can be correctly determined from both face images, the scale factor will be the ratio of vertical distances between eye and mouth in two face images. After this procedure, the two sets of feature points can be combined to get their 3-D coordinates. For most points, the z coordinates of side-view features are appended to the (x, y) of front-view face features. However, for some feature points on the middle face line, *e.g.* the tip of nose and chin points, the y coordinates of front feature points should also be replaced by those of side-view features since they can be more accurately determined from side-view face images.

Results and Conclusions

Figure 11 and Figure 12 show the results of our automated facial feature extraction algorithm for both front and left side face images.

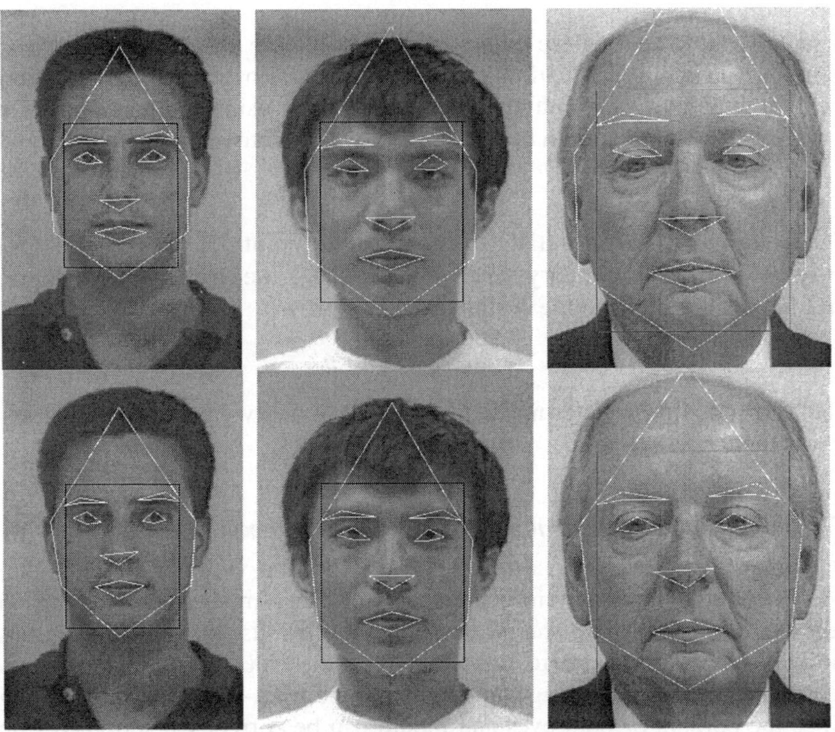

Figure 11. Results of front facial feature extraction

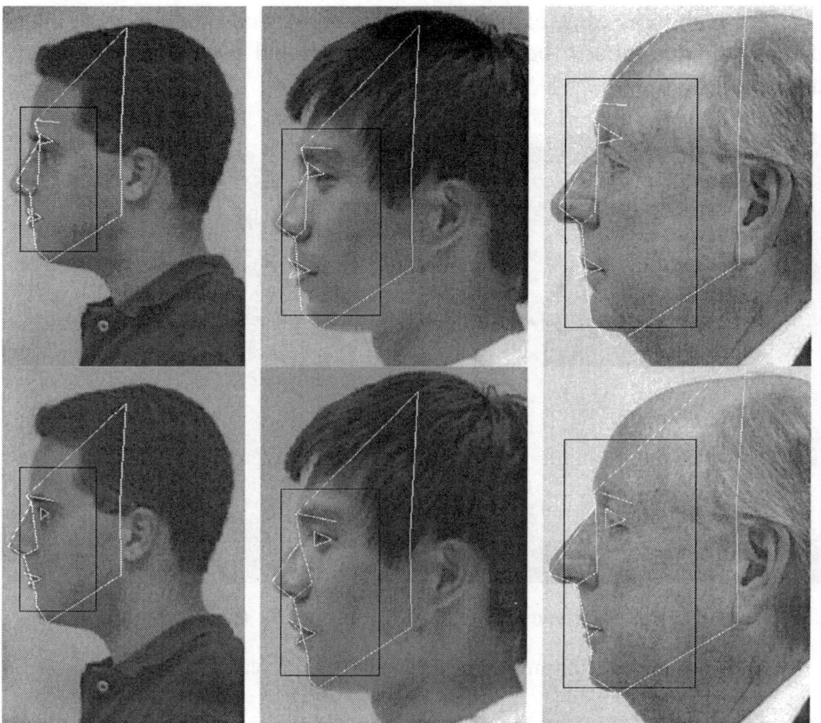

Figure 12. Results of side facial feature extraction

The top row shows initial estimation of the feature points right after the face location has been determined. The bottom row shows all feature points after local feature matching and feature verification procedure. The three original face images have quite different scales compared with the largest face template, but this algorithm performs very well. The average time for finding all facial features is *4* seconds on an SGI Crimson workstation.

While this algorithm works robustly for almost all images we have taken, it does fail in some circumstances, such as when the size of the face is too small compared with the image size. However, in such cases, probably even humans can not easily identify the facial feature points. Other examples of failure are due to great variations of shapes and size of facial features among different people.

Figure 13 shows some examples of missing facial features. We have found that the eyes tend to be more likely mislocated because more details are involved with eyes.

(a) missing the eyes   (b) missing the nose

Figure 13. Examples of mislocated facial features

One solution to this problem is to use multiperson templates which include people with different face shapes. Every face template is matched with the input image and the one with largest correlation coefficient is chosen as the best match. The same procedure can also be applied to the subtemplates of facial features to find the location of each feature. An alternative solution is to also use a coarse-to-fine search procedure to find size and location of the facial features. This means that the subtemplates for matching facial features may be taken from face templates different from the one with which the face area is detected. In addition to facial feature extraction, this algorithm can be used as a preprocessing step in some applications, for example, automatic face recognition where detecting face scale and location is an essential requirement. Another application of this algorithm is to build 3-D face model for a particular person using facial feature points extracted from different views of the face.

References

A. W. M. Kass and D. Terzopoulos, "Snakes: Active contour models," in *Proceedings of International Conference on Computer Vision*, pp.259--269, 1987.

A. L. Yuille, "Deformable templates for face recognition," *Journal of Cognitive Neuroscience*, Vol. 3, No. 1, pp. 59--70, 1991.

C. Huang and C. Chen, "Human facial feature extraction for face interpretation and recognition, *Pattern Recognition*, Vol. 25, No. 12, pp. 1435--1444, 1992.

X. Xie, R. Sudhakar, and H. Zhuang, "On improving eye feature extraction using deformable templates," *Pattern Recognition*, Vol. 27, No. 6, pp. 791--799, 1994.

G. Chow and X. Li, "Towards a system for automatic facial feature detection," *Pattern Recognition*, Vol. 26, No. 12, pp. 1739--1755, 1993.

L. G. Brown, "A survey of image registration techniques," *ACM Computing Surveys*, Vol. 24, pp. 325--376, December 1992.

D. H. Ballard and C. M. Brown, *Computer Vision*. New Jersey: Prentice-Hall, Inc., 1982

A. Samal, "Minimum resolution for human face detection," *Proceedings of SPIE/SPSE Symposium on Electronic Imaging*, January, 1991.

L. Tang, "Human face modeling, analysis and synthesis," Ph.D. Dissertation, University of Illinois at Urbana-Champaign, 1996.

References

A. W. M. Kass and D. Terzopoulos, "Snakes: Active contour models," in Proceedings of International Conference on Computer Vision, pp. 259-269. 1987.

A. L. Yuille, "Deformable templates for face recognition," Journal of Cognitive Neuroscience, Vol.3, No.1, pp. 59-70, 1991.

C. Huang and C. Chen, "Human facial feature extraction for face interpretation and recognition," Pattern Recognition Vol.25, No.12, pp. 1435-1444. 1992.

X. Xie, R. Sudhakar, and H. Zhuang, "On improving eye feature extraction using deformable templates," Pattern Recognition, Vol 27, No.6, pp. 791-799. 1994.

G. Chow and X. Li, "Towards a system for automatic facial feature detection," Pattern Recognition, Vol. 26, No.12, pp. 1739-1755. 1993.

L. G. Brown, "A survey of image registration techniques," ACM Computing Surveys, Vol. 24, pp. 325-376, December 1992.

D. H. Ballard and C. M. Brown, Computer Vision, New Jersey: Prentice-Hall, Inc. 1982.

A. Samal, "Minimum resolution for human face detection," Proceedings of SPIE-SPSE Symposium on Electronic Imaging, January, 1991.

L. Tang, "Human face modeling, analysis and synthesis," Ph.D. Dissertation, University of Illinois at Urbana-Champaign, 1996.

LEARNING BASED RELEVANCE FEEDBACK
IN IMAGE RETRIEVAL

Yong Rui

Microsoft Research
One Microsoft Way, Redmond, WA 98052
yongrui@microsoft.com

Thomas Huang

University of Illinois at Urbana-Champaign
405 N. Matthews Ave., Urbana, IL 61801
huang@ifp.uiuc.edu

Contents

1. Introduction

Low-level vision is concerned with extracting visual features such as color, texture and edges, among others. While low-level vision techniques continue to advance, researchers have realized the importance of integrating learning techniques into vision systems. Successful examples are numerous – HMM-based human tracking [1], face recognition using the EM algorithm [2], and human action recognition using statistical models [3].

Early research in image retrieval has been focused on low-level vision alone [4,5]. Unfortunately, after years of research, the retrieval performance is still far from users' expectations. Past efforts have made it clear that learning techniques need to be integrated into the retrieval system. Learning is a general concept. It can be from statistical models as in the above mentioned examples [1,2,?]. It can also be from humans who are part of the vision system. This paper focuses on the latter learning paradigm.

One of the interactive learning techniques is relevance feedback, originally developed in the information retrieval community [6]. In recent years, it has been brought to visual image retrieval [7,8,9]. During retrieval, the users interact with the system and rate the "relevance" of the images retrieved by the system according to their true information needs. Based on the feedback, the system dynamically learns and updates its query structure that best captures users' concepts.

There are two important components to be learned in the retrieval systems. One is an appropriate transformation that maps the original visual feature space into a space that better models user desired high-level concepts. As a special case, this transformation can be as simple as re-weighting different axes in the original feature space. The other important component is the "ideal" query in the user's mind. For example, a user may not initially have the query image at hand or the ideal query may evolve during the retrieval process.

By converting the retrieval process into a learning process of the above two components, we can avoid *ad hoc* solutions and can approach this problem in a principled way. There exist various techniques in learning the above two components. MARS [7] proposed two independent learning techniques for the two components based on intuitive heuristics. MindReader [10] developed a more vigorous formulation of the problem but failed to analyze the working conditions. To address these limitations, we will propose an optimization-based learning technique in this paper that not only works in all conditions but also has principled explicit solutions.

The rest of the paper is organized as follows. In Section 2, we introduce important concepts and notations used in the paper. In Section 3, we review related work in this research field and discuss their strength and weakness. Efforts towards resolving the limitations in the existing techniques lead to the global optimization approach proposed in Section 4. We will give detailed descriptions of the problem formulation, derivation of explicit optimal solutions, and computation complexity analysis. Evaluation of an image retrieval system's performance has been a weak spot in the past. In this paper, we have performed extensive experiments over a large heterogeneous image collection consisting of 17,000 real-world images. Various retrieval performance criteria, such as precision-recall curve and rank measure, have been used to validate the proposed algorithm. These experimental results are reported in Section 5. Discussions, conclusions and future work are given in Section 6.

2. Concepts and Notations

In this section, we describe important concepts and their notations that will be used throughout the paper. Let I be the number of features we are studying and let M be the total number of images in the database. We use $\vec{x}_{mi} = [x_{mi1}, \cdots, x_{mik}, \cdots x_{miK_i}]$ to denote the ith feature vector of the mth image, where K_i is the length of the feature vector i. For example, for a six-element color moment feature vector $K_i = 6$.

Let $\vec{q}_i = [q_{i1}, \cdots, q_{ik}, \cdots q_{iK_i}]$ be a query vector in feature i's feature space. To compute the distance g_{mi} between the two points $\vec{q}_i$ and $\vec{x}_{mi}$, we need to define a distance metric. The Norm-2 (Euclidean) metric is chosen because of its nice properties in quadratic optimization. There are several variants of the Euclidean distance: plain Euclidean, weighted Euclidean and generalized Euclidean.

- Plain Euclidean

$$g_{mi} = (\vec{q}_i - \vec{x}_{mi})^T (\vec{q}_i - \vec{x}_{mi}) \tag{1}$$

- Weighted Euclidean

$$g_{mi} = (\vec{q}_i - \vec{x}_{mi})^T \Lambda_i (\vec{q}_i - \vec{x}_{mi}) \tag{2}$$

where Λ_i is a diagonal matrix and its diagonal elements model the different importance of x_{mik}.

- Generalized Euclidean

$$g_{mi} = (\vec{q_i} - \vec{x_{mi}})^T \, W_i \, (\vec{q_i} - \vec{x_{mi}}) \tag{3}$$

where W_i is a real symmetric full matrix.

Plain Euclidean cannot model any transformation between different feature spaces. Weighted Euclidean can reweight the original feature space. Generalized Euclidean can both map the original space to a new space and reweight the transformed space.

[Theorem 1] For a real symmetric matrix W_i, it can be decomposed into the following form [11]:

$$W_i = P_i^T \, \Lambda_i \, P_i \tag{4}$$

where P_i is an orthonormal matrix consisting W_i's eigen vectors and Λ_i is a diagonal matrix whose diagonal elements are the eigen values of W_i.

Based on the theorem, the generalized Euclidean distance can be rewritten as:

$$\begin{aligned}
g_{mi} &= (\vec{q_i} - \vec{x_{mi}})^T \, W_i \, (\vec{q_i} - \vec{x_{mi}}) \\
&= (\vec{q_i} - \vec{x_{mi}})^T \, P_i^T \, \Lambda_i \, P_i \, (\vec{q_i} - \vec{x_{mi}}) \\
&= (P_i \, (\vec{q_i} - \vec{x_{mi}}))^T \, \Lambda_i \, (P_i \, (\vec{q_i} - \vec{x_{mi}}))
\end{aligned}$$

The above derivation says that the old feature space is first transformed into a new feature space by P_i and then the new feature space is re-weighted by Λ_i.

So far we have only discussed how to compute image distances based on an individual feature. As for the overall distance d_m based on multiple features, it can be computed in two ways. One way is to not differentiate the difference between a feature element and a feature and stack all the feature elements (from all the individual features) into a big overall feature vector and then use Equations 1 - 3 to compute d_m. This approach was used in most of the existing systems. Because this model has no hierarchy, we refer it as the "flat model" in this paper. Another way is to construct a hierarchical model, where the overall distance d_m is defined as:

$$d_m = U(g_{mi}) \tag{5}$$

where $U(.)$ is a function that combines the individual distances g_{mi} to form the overall distance d_m. We will refer this model as the "hierarchical model".

This model is a fundamental part of the proposed approach. We will show in Section 5 how this model significantly outperforms the flat model.

As stated in Section 1, there are two components that need to be learned by relevance feedback. One is the feature space transformation and the other is the optimal query vector. Following this section's notations, the former includes the learning of W_i and $U(.)$ and the latter is to learn $\vec{q_i}$.

3. Related Work

existing techniques have used the flat model and ignored $U(.)$. Even for learning the flat model (W_i and $\vec{q_i}$ only), there is still much room for improvements.

3.1. *The MARS approach*

The MARS system was among the first in the field that introduced relevance feedback into image retrieval [7]. It proposed two independent techniques for learning W_i and $\vec{q_i}$. For the former, the MARS system assumes W_i will take a diagonal form, thus using the weighted Euclidean metric. The heuristics for learning the weights (diagonal elements) were based on the following observation. If a particular feature element captures a user's query concept, that element's values x_{ik} will be consistent among all the positive examples given by the user. The standard deviation of all the x_{ik}'s will therefore be small. The inverse of the standard deviation thus furnishes a good estimate of the weight for feature element x_{ik}.

$$w_{i_{kk}} = \frac{1}{\sigma_{ik}} \tag{6}$$

where $w_{i_{kk}}$ is the kk^{th} element of matrix W_i and σ_{ik} is the standard deviation of the sequence of x_{ik}'s.

The MARS system also proposed a technique for learning the query vectors. The learned query vector should move towards the positive examples and away from negative examples:

$$\vec{q}\,'_i = \alpha \vec{q_i} + \beta(\frac{1}{N_{R'}} \sum_{n \in D'_R} \vec{x}_{ni}) - \gamma(\frac{1}{N_{N'}} \sum_{n \in D'_N} \vec{x}_{ni})$$
$$i = 1, \cdots, I$$

where $alpha, \beta$, and γ are suitable constants [6]; $N_{R'}$ and $N_{N'}$ are the numbers of images in the relevant set D'_R and non-relevant set D'_N; and $\vec{x}_{ni}$ is the nth training sample in the sets D'_R and D'_N.

Even though working reasonably well, the MARS techniques were based on *ad hoc* heuristics and did not have a solid theoretical foundation. Since its appearance, many improved versions have been proposed. One of the most elegant approaches is MindReader.

3.2. *The MindReader approach*

The MindReader system was developed by Ishikawa et al. [10]. This system integrated the two independent learning processes in MARS into a single algorithm and proposed a well-founded theoretical framework for the learning process.

Instead of being a diagonal matrix as in the MARS system, W_i is a full matrix in this algorithm to model the generalized Euclidean distance. By minimizing the distances between the query vector and all the positive fedback examples, MindReader system obtained the following optimal solutions to $\vec{q_i}$ and W_i [10]:

$$\vec{q_i}^{T^*} = \frac{\vec{\pi}^T X_i}{\sum_{n=1}^N \pi_n} \tag{7}$$

$$W_i^* = (det(C_i))^{\frac{1}{K_i}} C_i^{-1} \tag{8}$$

where N is the number of positive examples and π_n is the degree of relevance for image n given by the user. X_i is the example matrix obtained by stacking the N training vectors $(\vec{x}_{ni})$ into a matrix. It is therefore a $(N \times K_i)$ matrix. The term C_i is the weighted $(K_i \times K_i)$ covariance matrix of X_i. That is,

$$C_{i_{rs}} = \frac{\sum_{n=1}^N \pi_n (x_{nr} - q_r) (x_{ns} - q_s)}{\sum_{n=1}^N \pi_n}$$
$$r, s = 1, \cdots, K_i$$

A major *difference* between the MindReader approach (Equation 8) and the MARS approach (Equation 6) is that W_i is a full matrix in the former but a diagonal matrix in the latter. The advantages and disadvantages of these two methods will be demonstrated by experiments in Section 5.

The MindReader approach avoided *ad hoc* heuristics and developed a mathematical framework for learning W_i and $\vec{q_i}$. However, it failed to analyze the working conditions. In fact, even though elegant in theory, it faces many difficulties in reality.

3.2.1. *Discussions*

In order to obtain W_i (Equation (8)), we need to compute the inverse of the covariance matrix C_i. It is clear that, if $N < K_i$, then C_i is not invertible and we cannot obtain W_i. In MindReader, the authors proposed a solution to solve this by using a pseudo-inverse defined below [10].

The singular value decomposition (SVD) of C_i is

$$C_i = A \; \Lambda \; B^T \tag{9}$$

where Λ is a diagonal matrix: $diag(\lambda_1, \cdots, \lambda_k, \cdots, \lambda_{K_i})$. Those λ's are either positive or zero. Suppose there are L nonzero λ's, the pseudo-inverse of C_i is defined as

$$C_i^+ = A \; \Lambda^+ \; B^T$$
$$\Lambda^+ = diag(\frac{1}{\lambda_1}, \cdots, \frac{1}{\lambda_L}, 0, \cdots, 0).$$

where $+$ denotes the pseudo-inverse of a matrix. The approximation solution to W_i^* is then [10]

$$W_i^* = (\prod_{l=1}^{L} \lambda_l)^{\frac{1}{L}} \; C_i^+ \tag{10}$$

Even though, in theory, we can get around the *singular* problem by using the above procedure, in reality this solution does not give satisfactory results. This is especially true when N is far less than K_i. Remember, we need to use $(N-1) \times K_i$ numbers from the training samples to estimate $\frac{K_i(K_i+1)}{2}$ parameters in matrix C_i. In MindReader, the authors used a $K_i = 2$ example to show the performance of the algorithm. However, in real image retrieval systems, feature vectors' dimensions are much higher. For example, in HSV color histograms, the feature vector's dimension can be as high as $(8 \times 4 \times 1 = 32)$ [5]. During retrieval, in most situations, the condition $N > K_i$ will not be satisfied and this algorithm performs poorly (see Section 5).

4. The Proposed Approach

As reviewed above, there are three major difficulties in the existing systems: *ad hoc* heuristics, limited working conditions, and most importantly utilizing the flat model to compute the overall distance. To address these difficulties, in this section, we will propose an optimization-based learning algorithm that not only works in all conditions, but also has explicit optimal solutions for multiple visual features simultaneously.

4.1. *Problem formulation*

We model each individual feature's similarity as the generalized Euclidean distance because of its expressiveness and model the overall similarity as linear combinations of each individual feature's similarity because of its simplicity. That is, W_i takes the form of a matrix and $U(.)$ takes the form of a vector $\vec{u} = [u_1, \cdots, u_i, \cdots, u_I]$. The above choices are after careful considerations which, for clarity, will be presented in Section 6.

Let N be the number of retrieved relevant images (training samples). Let π_n be the degree of relevance for training sample n given by the user. The overall distance between a training sample and a query is defined as:

$$d_n = \vec{u}^T \vec{g}_n \tag{11}$$

$$\vec{g}_n = [g_{n1}, \cdots, g_{ni}, \cdots, g_{nI}]^T \tag{12}$$

$$g_{ni} = (\vec{x}_{ni} - \vec{q}_i)^T W_i (\vec{x}_{ni} - \vec{q}_i) \tag{13}$$

The above distance definition leads to the following optimization problem:

$$min \ J = \vec{\pi}^T \times \vec{d} \tag{14}$$

$$\vec{d} = [d_1, \cdots, d_n, \cdots, d_N]^T \tag{15}$$

$$d_n = \vec{u}^T \vec{g}_n \tag{16}$$

$$\vec{g}_n = [g_{n1}, \cdots, g_{ni}, \cdots, g_{nI}]^T \tag{17}$$

$$g_{ni} = (\vec{x}_{ni} - \vec{q}_i)^T W_i (\vec{x}_{ni} - \vec{q}_i) \tag{18}$$

$$s.t. \quad \sum_{i=1}^{I} \frac{1}{u_i} = 1 \tag{19}$$

$$det(W_i) = 1 \tag{20}$$

$$n = 1, \cdots, N \tag{21}$$

$$i = 1, \cdots, I \tag{22}$$

It is easy to see that if there are no constraints for $\vec{u}$ and W_i, this optimization problem will reduce to a trivial solution of all zeros. We therefore enforce Equations (19) and (20) as constraints for scaling purposes.

This problem formulation is a general framework which can include both MARS and MindReader. If we would disregard the overall distance (d_n) and only concentrate on each individual distance (g_{ni}), a diagonal matrix of W_i would reduce this formulation to the MARS algorithm and a full matrix of W_i would reduce this formulation to the MindReader approach.

The above objective function says that optimality will be achieved only if both the transformations ($\vec{u}$ and W_i) and query vectors $\vec{q_i}$ are optimally learned. This will be accomplished by minimizing the distances between the "ideal" query and all the positive fedback examples. The degree of relevance π_n of each example is given by the user according to his or her judgment. The objective function J is linear in $\vec{u}$ and W_i and quadratic in $\vec{q_i}$. We will first use Lagrange multipliers to reduce this constrained problem to an unconstrained one, and then de-couple the problem by first solving $\vec{q_i}$, and then W_i and $\vec{u}$. The following is the unconstrained problem:

$$L = \vec{\pi}^{\,T} \times \vec{d} - \lambda(\sum_{i=1}^{I} \frac{1}{u_i} - 1) - \sum_{i=1}^{I} \lambda_i (det(W_i) - 1) \tag{23}$$

4.2. *Optimal solution for $\vec{q_i}$*

$$\frac{\partial L}{\partial \vec{q_i}} = \vec{\pi}^{\,T} \times \begin{bmatrix} \frac{\partial d_1}{\partial \vec{q_i}} \\ \cdots \\ \frac{\partial d_n}{\partial \vec{q_i}} \\ \cdots \\ \frac{\partial d_N}{\partial \vec{q_i}} \end{bmatrix}$$

$$= \vec{\pi}^{\,T} \times \begin{bmatrix} -2\,u_i\,(\vec{x}_{1i} - \vec{q_i})^{\,T}\,W_i \\ \cdots \\ -2\,u_i\,(\vec{x}_{ni} - \vec{q_i})^{\,T}\,W_i \\ \cdots \\ -2\,u_i\,(\vec{x}_{Ni} - \vec{q_i})^{\,T}\,W_i \end{bmatrix}$$

By setting the above equation to zero, we can obtain the final solution to $\vec{q_i}$:

$$\vec{q_i}^{\,T*} = \frac{\vec{\pi}^{\,T} X_i}{\sum_{n=1}^{N} \pi_n} \tag{24}$$

where X_i is the training sample matrix for feature i, obtained by stacking the N training vectors $(\vec{x}_{ni})$ into a matrix. It is therefore an $(N \times K_i)$ matrix.

Equation (24) closely matches our intuition. That is, $\vec{q}_i^{T*}$ (the optimal query vector for feature i) is nothing but the weighted average of the training samples for feature i.

4.3. *Optimal solution for W_i*

$$\frac{\partial L}{\partial w_{i_{rs}}} = \vec{\pi}^{\;T} \times \begin{bmatrix} \vec{u}^T \; \frac{\partial \vec{g}_1}{\partial w_{i_{rs}}} \\ \cdots \\ \vec{u}^T \; \frac{\partial \vec{g}_n}{\partial w_{i_{rs}}} \\ \cdots \\ \vec{u}^T \; \frac{\partial \vec{g}_N}{\partial w_{i_{rs}}} \end{bmatrix} - \lambda_i \, (-1)^{r+s} det(W_{i_{rs}})$$

$$= \sum_{n=1}^{N} \pi_n \, (x_{nir} - q_{ir})(x_{1is} - q_{is})$$

$$- \lambda_i \, (-1)^{r+s} det(W_{i_{rs}})$$

After setting the above equation to zero, we get:

$$W_i^* = (det(C_i))^{\frac{1}{K_i}} \; C_i^{-1} \tag{25}$$

where the term C_i is the $(K_i \times K_i)$ weighted covariance matrix of X_i. That is, $C_{i_{rs}} = \sum_{n=1}^{N} \pi_n(x_{nir} - q_{ir})(x_{1is} - q_{is}) / \sum_{n=1}^{N} \pi_n, r, s = 1, \cdots, K_i$.

Note that in MARS, W_i is always a diagonal matrix. This limits its ability to modeling transformations between feature spaces. On the other hand, MindReader's W_i is always a full matrix. It cannot be reliably estimated when the number of training samples (N) is less than the length of the feature vector (K_i). Unlike these two algorithms, the proposed technique dynamically and intelligently switches between a diagonal matrix and a full matrix, depending on the relationship between N and K_i. When $N < K_i$, the proposed algorithm forms a diagonal matrix to ensure reliable estimation; and when $N > K_i$, it will form a full matrix to take full advantage of the training samples.

4.4. *Optimal Solution for $\vec{u}$*

To obtain u_i^*, set the partial derivative to zero. We then have

$$\frac{\partial L}{\partial u_i} = \sum_{n=1}^{N} \pi_n \, g_{ni} + \lambda \, u_i^{-2} = 0, \; \forall i \tag{26}$$

Multiply both sides by u_i and sum over i. We have

$$\sum_{i=1}^{I} u_i \left(\sum_{n=1}^{N} \pi_n \, g_{ni}\right) + \lambda\left(\sum_{i=1}^{I} \frac{1}{u_i}\right) = 0 \tag{27}$$

Since $\sum_{i=1}^{I} \frac{1}{u_i} = 1$, the optimal λ is

$$\lambda^* = -\sum_{i=1}^{I} u_i \, f_i \tag{28}$$

where $f_i = \sum_{n=1}^{N} \pi_n \, g_{ni}$. This will lead to the optimal solution for u_i:

$$u_i^* = \sum_{j=1}^{I} \sqrt{\frac{f_j}{f_i}} \tag{29}$$

This solution tells us, if the total distance (f_i) of feature i is small (meaning it is close to the ideal query), this feature should receive a higher weight and vice versa.

The solutions for $\vec{q}_i$ and W_i have been partially studied in MARS and MindReader. The solution for u_i, however, has not been investigated by either system. Both MARS and MindReader do not differentiate the difference between feature elements and features and use a flat image content model. This is not only computationally expensive, but also far less effective in retrieval performance. For computation complexity, take MindReader as an example. It needs $O((\sum_i^I K_i)^3 + 2N(\sum_i^I K_i)^2))$ multiplications or divisions while the proposed algorithm only needs $O(\sum_j^I ((K_i)^3 + 2N(K_i)^2))$ operations. Note that the different locations of $\sum_i^I$ in the two formulae result in *significantly* different computation counts.

5. Experiments, Results and Evaluations

5.1. *Data set*

In the experiments reported in this section, all the algorithms are tested on the Corel data set. This data set meets all the requirements to evaluate an image retrieval system. It is large, heterogeneous and has human annotated ground truth. This data set consists of 17,000 images, covering a wide variety of content ranging from animals and birds to Tibet and Czech Republic. Each category contains 100 images and these images are classified by domain professionals. In the experiments, images from the same category are considered **relevant**. Note that the ground truth we used in the experiments are based on high-level concepts. They are much more difficult to achieve than visual similarities. But they are the *ultimate* queries that users would like to ask. We therefore did not count an image as a correct answer even if it is visually similar to the query image but represents different high-level concepts.

The Corel data set was also used in other systems and relatively high retrieval performance was reported. However, those systems only used pre-selected categories with distinctive visual characteristics (e.g., cars vs. mountains). In our experiments, no pre-selection is made. We believe only in this manner can we obtain an objective evaluation of different retrieval techniques.

5.2. *Queries*

Some existing systems only used pre-selected images as the queries. It is arguable that those systems will perform equally well on other not-selected images. Other systems only tested on queries with unique answers. This is called "point queries" in database research community. This type of queries is used to model *exact* matches, e.g., name = "John Smith". On the other hand, "range queries" are used to accomplish similarity-based matches, e.g., find all students whose ages are between 10 and 20. It is therefore more appropriate to use range queries to evaluate image retrieval systems. For example, find all the images that contain animals. In our experiments reported here, there is no pre-selected query images and all the queries are range queries. We randomly generated 400 queries for each retrieval condition. The reported retrieval performance is then the average of all the 400 queries against ground truth as annotated by Corel professionals. We execute queries in this very careful manner to ensure meaningful evaluations.

5.3. *Visual features*

There are three features used in the system: color moments, wavelet based texture, and water-fill edge feature. The color space we use is HSV because of its decorrelated coordinates and its perceptual uniformity [5]. We extract the first two moments (mean and standard deviation) from the three color channels and therefore have a color feature vector of length $3 \times 2 = 6$.

For wavelet based texture, the original image is fed into a wavelet filter bank and is decomposed into 10 de-correlated sub-bands. Each sub-band captures the characteristics of a certain scale and orientation of the original image. For each sub-band, we extract the standard deviation of the wavelet coefficients and therefore have a texture feature vector of length 10.

For water-fill edge feature vector, we first pass the original images through an edge detector to generate their corresponding edge maps. We then extract eighteen (18) elements from the edge maps, including *max fill time*, *max fork count*, etc. For a complete description of this edge feature vector, interested readers are referred to [12].

5.4. *Performance measures*

The Precision-recall curve is the conventional information retrieval (IR) performance measure [6]. Precision (Pr) is defined as the number of retrieved relevant objects (i.e., N) over the number of total retrieved objects. Recall (Re) is defined as the number of retrieved relevant objects (i.e., N) over the total number of relevant object (in our case 99). The performance for an "ideal" system is to have both high Pr and Re. Unfortunately, they are conflicting entities and cannot be at high values at the same time. Because of this, instead of using a single value of Pr and Re, a $Pr(Re)$ curve is normally used to characterize the performance of an IR system.

Even though well suited for text-based IR, $Pr(Re)$ is less meaningful in image retrieval systems where recall is consistently low. More and more researchers are adopting precision-scope curve to evaluate image retrieval performance [13]. Scope (Sc) specifies the number of images returned to the user. For a particular scope Sc, e.g., top 20 images, $Pr(Sc)$ can be computed as:

$$Pr(Sc) = \frac{N}{Sc} \tag{30}$$

Huang et. al. proposed another performance measure: the rank (Ra) measure [13]. The rank measure is defined as the average rank of the retrieved relevant images. It is clear that the smaller the rank, the better the performance. While $Pr(Sc)$ only cares if a relevant image is retrieved or not, $Ra(Sc)$ also cares what's the rank of that image. Caution must be taken when using $Ra(Sc)$, though. If $Pr_A(Sc) > Pr_B(Sc)$ and $Ra_A(Sc) < Ra_B(Sc)$, it says A is definitely better than B, because not only A retrieves more relevant images than B, but also all those retrieved images are closer to top in A than in B. But if $Pr_A(Sc) > Pr_B(Sc)$ and $Ra_A(Sc) > Ra_B(Sc)$, no conclusion can be made based on Ra.

5.5. *System description*

We have constructed an image retrieval system based on the optimization algorithm developed in Section 4. Figure 1 is its interface.

Fig. 1.   **The interface of the system**

On the left are the query image and returned results (the top-left image is the query image). For each returned image, there is a degree-of-relevance slider. A user uses these sliders to give his or her relevance feedback to the system. On the right-hand side, there are progress controls displaying how W_i and $\vec{u}$ dynamically change during the retrieval.

5.6. *Results and observations*

The proposed approach (PP) differs from the MARS (MS) and MindReader (MR) approaches in two major ways. First, PP models image content hierarchically. It has a two-level feature transformation $\vec{u}$ and W_i. The learning via relevance feedback is also hierarchical. MS and MR, on the other hand, do not differentiate a feature element x_{nik} and a feature $\vec{x}_{ni}$ and use a flat image content model. The other major difference is the form of W_i. While MS uses a strict diagonal matrix and MR uses a strict full matrix, PP adaptively switches between the two forms depending on the relationship between N and K_i (Section 4.4). In addition to evaluate the above two differences, we will also study the working conditions for each of the approaches.

The experiments are configured into two cases. Case one uses only the color feature (referred as Case C) and case two uses all the three features (referred as Case CTE). Since the color feature has only 6 elements ($K_i = 6$), Case C simulates the condition that K_i is comparable to N. Note that we can not explicitly control the value of N, the number of relevant images, but we can implicitly control it by using different values of Sc. In general, a larger Sc implies a larger N, as illustrated in Figure 4 (N is proportional to recall Re given the total number of relevant images is a constant of 99). Since there is only a single feature in Case C, the flat model and the hierarchical model are the same in this case. The performance differences between the three approaches are coming from the form of W_i only. This gives us a concrete situation to quantify the amount of contribution from adaptive W_i switching alone(Section 4.3). Case CTE has multiple features. For the PP approach, $K_1 = 6$, $K_2 = 10$ and $K_3 = 18$. For MS and MR, $K_1 = 6+10+18 = 34$. This case gives us an ideal situation to study how the hierarchical content model affects retrieval performance and under which conditions each algorithm will work.

	0 rf	1 rf	2 rf	0 rf	1 rf	2rf
C(MS)	7.52	9.75	10.27	2.77	1.52	1.25
C(MR)	7.52	3.48	4.95	2.77	1.64	1.38
C(PP)	7.52	9.75	10.65	2.77	1.46	1.20
C(MS)	4.81	6.98	7.85	26.81	18.29	16.04
C(MR)	4.81	6.18	7.43	26.81	21.98	17.57
C(PP)	4.81	7.49	8.76	26.81	16.29	12.64
C(MS)	3.95	5.85	6.52	55.90	40.91	37.82
C(MR)	3.95	5.81	6.82	55.90	43.46	36.06
C(PP)	3.95	6.35	7.40	55.90	34.98	27.75

Table 1 is for case C and Table 2 is for case CTE. The top three rows in the tables are the results for $Sc = 20$, the middle three rows are for

$Sc = 100$, and the bottom three rows are for $Sc = 180$. The first three columns in the two tables are Pr (in percentage) for zero, one and two iterations of relevance feedback. The last three columns in the tables are Ra for zero, one and two iterations of relevance feedback. The following observations can be made based the results of the two tables:

- PP approach performs consistently better in all conditions than the other two approaches. Case C (Table 1) demonstrates the gain of PP over MS and MR based on the adaptive switch. By utilizing this technique, the gain is about 5-10% increase. Note that, in this case, not only is PP's Pr higher than those of MS and MR, but also its rank is lower than those of MS and MR. That is, not only PP retrieves more relevant images than MS or MR, but also all the retrieved images are closer to top in PP than in MS or MR. Case CTE (Table 2) has multiple features. The gain that PP has over MS and MR is from both adaptive switching and hierarchical relevance feedback. The gain can be as much as 20-40%. This significant increase demonstrates the effectiveness of hierarchical image content modeling.

- MR approach achieves reasonable performance when N is comparable to or larger than K_i. For example, in Table 1 when $Sc = 180$, MR's performance is better than that of MS and is next to that of PP. This is because when there are sufficient training samples compared with K_i, the covariance matrix C_i can be reliably learned. This allows the algorithm to take advantage of the generalized Euclidean distance measure (Equation 3). But in situations where N is smaller than K_i, the algorithm simply falls apart, as indicated in Table 2 where $K_i = 34$.

- Overall, MS's performance ranks second. Its performance is comparable to PP when there is a single feature (Case C). Where there are multiple features, because it uses a flat image content model, its performance is significantly worse than that of PP. Furthermore, since it only uses diagonal matrix for W_i, this limits its ability to modeling transformations between feature spaces. In the case $Sc = 180$ in Table 1, its performance is even worse than that of MR.

Figures 2, 3 and 4 compare the $Pr(Re)$ curves, $Pr(Sc)$ curves, and

	0 rf	1 rf	2 rf	0 rf	1 rf	2rf
MS	7.23	10.99	12.09	3.00	1.56	1.27
MR	7.23	0.58	0.29	3.00	0.83	0.22
PP	10.18	14.18	15.85	1.71	1.20	1.10
MS	4.36	7.60	8.82	27.50	16.32	13.70
MR	4.36	1.02	2.20	27.50	24.61	14.72
PP	5.75	9.47	11.60	39.24	27.31	23.45
MS	3.53	6.00	7.02	53.83	35.88	30.81
MR	3.53	1.06	1.77	53.83	52.53	53.81
PP	4.63	7.78	9.39	125.56	83.74	67.47

$Re(Sc)$ curves in cases C and CTE, after two feedback iterations. The solid curves, dashed curves and dashdot curves are for PP, MS and MR, respectively. The values of Sc range from 20 to 180 with an increment of 20. We have the following observations based on the figures:

- $Pr(Sc)$ curve and $Pr(Re)$ curve depict the similar information. But as also being observed by other researchers [13], for image retrieval systems where Re is consistently low, $Pr(Sc)$ curve is more expressive for comparison than $Pr(Re)$ curve.
- Figures 3 and 4 tell us if we increase Sc, more relevant images will be retrieved with the sacrifice of precision.
- Independent of the feature sets used (C vs. CTE) and the number of images returned ($Sc = 20$ vs. $Sc = 180$), PP is the best in all $Pr(Re)$, $Pr(Sc)$ and $Re(Sc)$.
- Even though elegant in theory, MR performs poorly in most cases because its working conditions are not satisfied. More attention should be paid on analyzing working conditions in future research.

6. Discussions and Conclusions

In Section 4, we used the generalized Euclidean distance for computing g_{ni} and linear combination for computing d_n. A natural thinking would be "how about choosing the generalized Euclidean distance to compute d_n as well?" That is, $d_n = \vec{g_n}^T U \vec{g_n}$, where U is an $(I \times I)$ matrix. Indeed this formulation is more powerful to model non-linear (quadratic) relations in $\vec{g_n}$. Unfortunately, the objective function J of this formulation would then be a function of q_{ik}^4 and no *explicit* solutions can be derived. Optimal

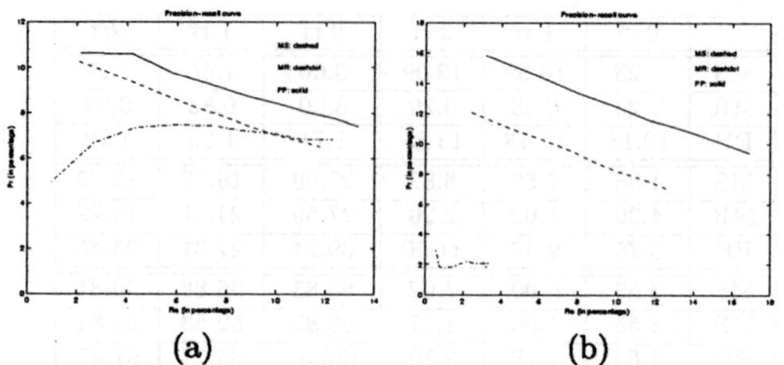

Fig. 2.   Precision-recall curve (a)Case C. (b)Case CTE.

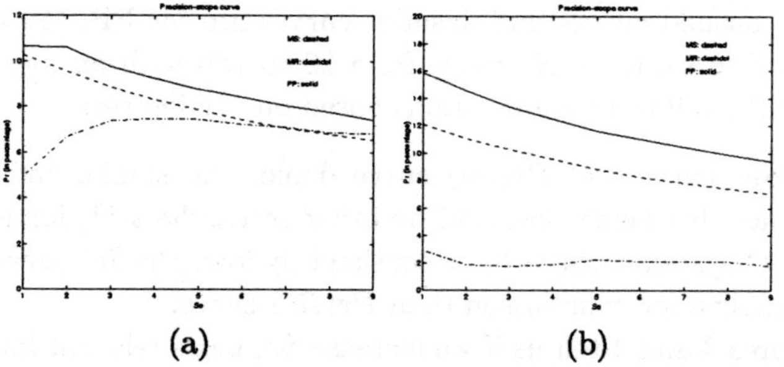

Fig. 3.   Precision-scope curve (a)Case C. (b)Case CTE.

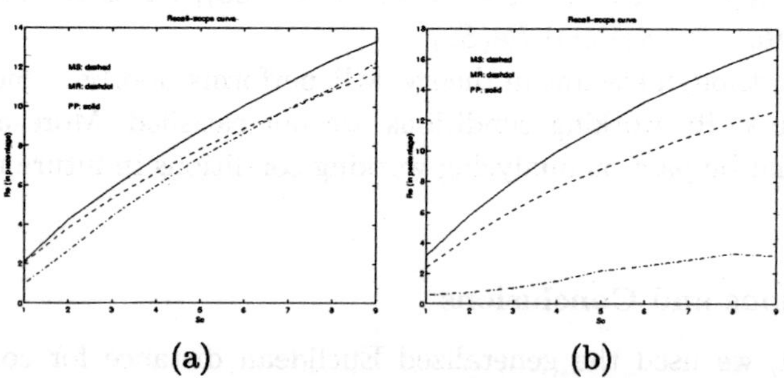

Fig. 4.   Recall-scope curve (a)Case C. (b)Case CTE.

solutions for $\vec{q}_i$, W_i and U would only be obtained *iteratively*. This is extremely undesirable for image retrieval systems, because users need to wait for minutes before the iterative algorithm can converge. Being quadratic in

g_{ni} and linear in d_n is the highest possible order for J to have *explicit* solutions. The flip side of the distance measure choices for g_{ni} and d_n is that for retrieval systems where "response time" is *not* a critical requirement, non-linear learning tools such as neural networks [14] and support vector machines [15] are worth exploring.

One thing worth pointing out is that the focus of this paper is not on finding the best visual features, but rather on exploring the best learning techniques. We are aware of sophisticated features including localized color and segmented shape [5]. We used less sophisticated features to obtain a bottom line for other systems to compare against. The proposed algorithm is an open framework and is ready to incorporate other more sophisticated features.

Vision and learning techniques are just some of the techniques that will make image retrieval successful. Other techniques, including information retrieval, database management and user interface, are also of crucial importance. However, these techniques, for example multi-dimensional indexing for faster search [5], are beyond the scope of this paper.

In conclusion, this paper developed a technique that gives optimized explicit solutions to hierarchical learning in image retrieval. Its image content model and adaptive W_i switching make it significantly outperform existing techniques. This has been demonstrated by the extensive experiments on a large heterogeneous image collection. However, there are still many dimensions to improve the current system. Both the low-level vision part (more sophisticated features [5]) and the learning part (more powerful tools [14,15]) should continue to advance to meet users' true information needs.

7. Acknowledgment

The Corel data set of images were obtained from the Corel collection and used in accordance with their copyright statement.

References

1. C. Bregler, "Learning and recognizing human dynamics in video sequences," in *Proc. IEEE Conf. on Comput. Vis. and Patt. Recog.*, July 1997.
2. B. Frey and N. Jojic, "Estimating mixture models of images and inferring spatial transformations using the em algorithm," in *Proc. IEEE Conf. on Comput. Vis. and Patt. Recog.*, July 1999.
3. M. Black, "Explaining optical flow events with parameterized spatio-

temporal models," in *Proc. IEEE Conf. on Comput. Vis. and Patt. Recog.*, July 1999.

4. W. Niblack, R. Barber, and et al., "The QBIC project: Querying images by content using color, texture and shape," in *Proc. SPIE Storage and Retrieval for Image and Video Databases*, Feb 1994.

5. Y. Rui, T. S. Huang, and S.-F. Chang, "Image retrieval: Current techniques, promising directions, and open issues," *Int. J. Vis. Commun. Image Rep.*, vol. 10, pp. 39–62.

6. G. Salton and M. J. McGill, *Introduction to Modern Information Retrieval*. New York: McGraw-Hill Book Company, 1982.

7. Y. Rui, T. S. Huang, and S. Mehrotra, "Content-based image retrieval with relevance feedback in MARS," in *Proc. IEEE Int. Conf. on Image Proc.*, 1997.

8. R. W. Picard, "Digital libraries: Meeting place for high-level and low-level vision," in *Proc. Asian Conf. on Comp. Vis.*, Dec. 1995.

9. I. J. Cox, M. L. Miller, S. M. Omohundro, and P. N. Yianilos, "Target testing and the pichunter bayesian multimedia retrieval system," in *Advanced Digital Libraries Forum*, (Washington D.C.), May 1996.

10. Y. Ishikawa, R. Subramanya, and C. Faloutsos, "Mindreader: Query databases through multiple examples," in *Proc. of the 24th VLDB Conference*, (New York), 1998.

11. H. Stark and J. W. Woods, *Probability, Random Processes, and Estimation Theory for Engineers*. Englewood Cliffs, NJ: Prentice-Hall, 1986.

12. S. X. Zhou, Y. Rui, and T. S. Huang, "Water-filling algorithm: A novel way for image feature extraction based on edge maps," in *Proc. IEEE Int. Conf. on Image Proc.*, 1999.

13. J. Huang, S. Kumar, M. Mitra, W.-J. Zhu, and R. Zabih, "Image indexing using color correlogram," in *Proc. IEEE Conf. on Comput. Vis. and Patt. Recog.*, 1997.

14. S. Haykin, *Neural Networks: A Comprehensive Foundation*. Upper Saddle River, NJ: Prentice-Hall, 1999.

15. J. Platt, "Fast training of support vector machines using sequential minimal optimization," *Advances in Kernel Methods - Support Vector Learning*, April 1999.

Object-Based Subband/Wavelet Video Compression

Soo-Chul Han

John W. Woods[1]

ABSTRACT This chapter presents a subband/wavelet video coder using an object-based spatiotemporal segmentation. The moving objects in a video are extracted by means of a joint motion estimation and segmentation algorithm based on a compound Markov random field (MRF) model. The two important features of our technique are the temporal linking of the objects, and the guidance of the motion segmentation with spatial color information. This results in spatiotemporal (3-D) objects that are stable in time, and leads to a new motion-compensated temporal updating and contour coding scheme that greatly reduces the bit-rate to transmit the object boundaries. The object interiors can be encoded by either 2-D or 3-D subband/wavelet coding. Simulations at very low bit-rates yield comparable performance in terms of reconstructed PSNR to the H.263 coder. The object-based coder produces visually more pleasing video with less blurriness and is devoid of block artifacts.

1 Introduction

Video compression to very low bit-rates has attracted considerable attention recently in the image processing community. This is due to the growing list of very low bit-rate applications such as video-conferencing, multimedia, video over telephone lines, wireless communications, and video over the internet.

However, it has been found that standard block-based video coders perform rather poorly at very low bit-rates due to the well-known blocking artifacts. A natural alternative to the block-based standards is object-based coding, first proposed by Musmann *et al* [1]. In the object-based approach, the moving objects in the video scene are extracted, and each object is represented by its shape, motion, and texture. Parameters representing the three components are encoded and transmitted, and the reconstruction is performed by synthesizing each object. Although a plethora of work on the extraction and coding of the moving objects has appeared since [1], few works carry out the entire analysis-coding process from start to finish.

---

[1]This work was supported in part by National Science Foundation grant MIP-9528312.

Thus, the widespread belief that object-based methods could outperform standard techniques at low bit-rates (or any rates) has yet to be firmly established. In this chapter, we attempt to take the step in that direction with new ideas in both motion analysis and the source encoding. Furthermore, the object-based scheme leads to increased functionalities such as scalability, content-based manipulation, and the combination of synthetic and natural images. This is evidenced by the MPEG-4 standard, which is adopting the object-based approach.

Up to now, several roadblocks have prevented object-based coding systems from outperforming standard block-based techniques. For one thing, extracting the moving objects, such as by means of segmentation, is a very difficult problem in itself due to its ill-posedness and complexity [2]. Next, the gain in improving the motion compensated prediction must outweigh the additional contour information inherent in an object-based scheme. Applying intraframe techniques to encode the contours at each frame has been shown to be inefficient. Finally, it is essential that some objects or regions be encoded in "Intra" mode at certain frames due to lack of information in the temporal direction. This includes uncovered regions due to object movement, new objects that appear in a scene, and objects which undergo complex motion that cannot be properly described by the adopted motion model.

An object-based coder addressing all of the above mentioned issues is presented in this chapter. Moreover, we need to make no *a priori* assumptions about the contents of the video scene (such as constant background, head-and-shoulders only, etc). The extraction of the moving objects is performed by a joint motion estimation and segmentation algorithm based on compound Markov random field (MRF) models. In our approach, the object motion and shape are guided by the spatial color intensity information. This not only improves the motion estimation/segmentation process itself by extracting meaningful objects true to the scene, but it also aids the process of coding the object intensities. The latter because a given object has a certain spatial cohesiveness. The MRF formulation also allows us to temporally link objects, thus creating object volumes in the space-time domain. This helps stabilize the object segmentation process in time, but more importantly, allows the object boundaries to be predicted temporally using the motion information, reducing the boundary coding overhead. With linked objects, uncovered regions and new objects are detected by utilizing both the motion and intensity information.

Object interiors are encoded by either 2-D or 3-D subband/wavelet coding. The 2-D hybrid coding allows objects to be encoded adaptively at each frame, meaning that objects well described by the motion parameters are encoded in "Inter" mode, while those that cannot be predicted in time are encoded in "Intra" mode. This is analogous to P-blocks and I-blocks in the MPEG coding structure, where we now have P-objects and I-objects. Alternatively, the spatiotemporal objects can be encoded

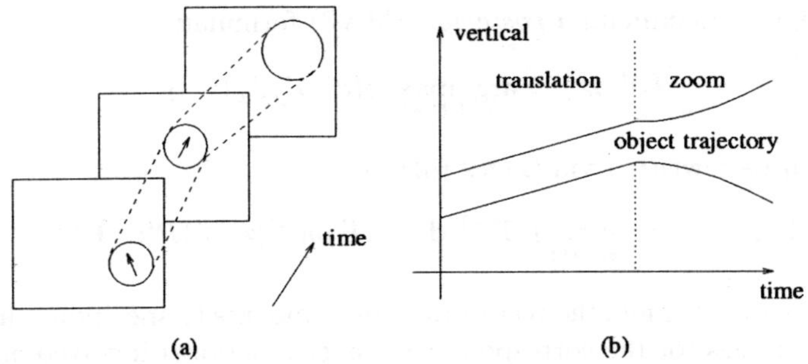

FIGURE 1. The trajectory of a moving ball.

by 3-D subband/wavelet coding, which leads to added advantages such as frame-rate scalability and improved rate control [3]. In either case, the sub-band/wavelet transform must be modified to account for arbitrarily-shaped objects.

2   Joint Motion Estimation and Segmentation

In this section, a novel motion estimation and segmentation scheme is presented. Although the algorithm was specifically designed to meet coding needs as described in the previous section, the end results could very well be applied to other image sequence processing applications. The main object-ive is to segment the video scene into objects that are undergoing distinct motion, along with finding the parameters that describe the motion. In Fig. 1(a), the video scene consists of a ball moving against a stationary back-ground. At each frame, we would like to segment the scene into two objects (the ball and background) and find the motion of each. Furthermore, if the objects are linked in time, we can create 3-D objects in space-time as shown in Fig. 1(b). We adopt a Bayesian formulation based on a Markov random field (MRF) model to solve this challenging problem. Our algorithm extends previously published works [4, 5, 6, 7, 8].

2.1   Problem formulation

Let $\mathbf{I}^t$ represent the frame at time t of the discretized image sequence. The motion field $\mathbf{d}^t$ represents the displacement between $\mathbf{I}^t$ and $\mathbf{I}^{t-1}$ for each pixel. The segmentation field $\mathbf{z}^t$, consists of numerical labels at every pixel with each label representing one moving object, i.e. $\mathbf{z}^t(\mathbf{x}) = n$ ($n = 1, 2, .., N$), for each pixel location $\mathbf{x}$ on the lattice Λ. Here, N refers to the total number of moving objects. Using this notation, the goal of motion estimation/segmentation is to find $\{\mathbf{d}^t, \mathbf{z}^t\}$ given $\mathbf{I}^t$ and $\mathbf{I}^{t-1}$.

We adopt a maximum *a posteriori* (MAP) formulation:

$$\{\hat{\mathbf{d}}^t, \hat{\mathbf{z}}^t\} = \arg \max_{\{\mathbf{d}^t, \mathbf{z}^t\}} p(\mathbf{d}^t, \mathbf{z}^t | \mathbf{I}^t, \mathbf{I}^{t-1}), \tag{1.1}$$

which can be rewritten via Bayes rule as

$$\{\hat{\mathbf{d}}^t, \hat{\mathbf{z}}^t\} = \arg \max_{\{\mathbf{d}^t, \mathbf{z}^t\}} p(\mathbf{I}^{t-1} | \mathbf{d}^t, \mathbf{z}^t, \mathbf{I}^t) p(\mathbf{d}^t | \mathbf{z}^t, \mathbf{I}^t) P(\mathbf{z}^t | \mathbf{I}^t). \tag{1.2}$$

Given this formulation, the rest of the work amounts to specifying the probability densities (or the corresponding energy functions) involved and solving.

2.2 *Probability models*

The first term on the right-hand side of (1.2) is the likelihood functional that describes how well the observed images match the motion field data. We model the likelihood functional by

$$p(\mathbf{I}^{t-1} | \mathbf{d}^t, \mathbf{z}^t, \mathbf{I}^t) = Q_l^{-1} exp\{-U_l(\mathbf{I}^{t-1} | \mathbf{d}^t, \mathbf{I}^t)\}, \tag{1.3}$$

which is also Gaussian. Here the energy function

$$U_l(\mathbf{I}^{t-1} | \mathbf{d}^t, \mathbf{I}^t) = \sum_{\mathbf{x} \in \Lambda} (\mathbf{I}^t(\mathbf{x}) - \mathbf{I}^{t-1}(\mathbf{x} - \mathbf{d}^t(\mathbf{x})))^2 / 2\sigma^2, \tag{1.4}$$

and Q_l is a normalization constant [5, 9].

The *a priori* density of the motion $p(\mathbf{d}^t | \mathbf{z}^t, \mathbf{I}^t)$, enforces prior constraints on the motion field. We adopt a coupled MRF model to govern the interaction between the motion field and the segmentation field, both spatially and temporally. The energy function is given as

$$U_d(\mathbf{d}^t | \mathbf{z}^t) =$$
$$\lambda_1 \sum_{\mathbf{x}} \sum_{\mathbf{y} \in N_{\mathbf{x}}} \| \mathbf{d}^t(\mathbf{x}) - \mathbf{d}^t(\mathbf{y}) \|^2 \delta(z^t(\mathbf{x}) - z^t(\mathbf{y}))$$
$$+ \lambda_2 \sum_{\mathbf{x}} \| \mathbf{d}^t(\mathbf{x}) - \mathbf{d}^{t-1}(\mathbf{x} - \mathbf{d}^t(\mathbf{x})) \|^2$$
$$- \lambda_3 \sum_{\mathbf{x}} \delta(z^t(\mathbf{x}) - z^{t-1}(\mathbf{x} - \mathbf{d}^t(\mathbf{x}))), \tag{1.5}$$

where $\delta(\cdot)$ refers to the usual Kronecker delta function, $\| \cdot \|$ is the Euclidean norm in $\mathbf{R}^2$, and $\mathcal{N}_{\mathbf{x}}$ indicates a spatial neighborhood system at location $\mathbf{x}$. The first two terms of (1.5) are similar to those in [7], while the third term was added to encourage consistency of the object labels along the motion trajectories. The first term enforces the constraint that the motion vectors be locally smooth on the spatial lattice, but only within the same object label. This allows motion discontinuities at object boundaries without introducing any extra variables such as line fields [10]. The second term accounts for causal temporal continuity, under the model restraints (ref. second factor in 1.2) that the motion vector changes slowly frame-to-frame along the motion trajectory. Finally, the third term in (1.5) encourages the object labels to be consistent along the motion trajectories. This constraint allows a framework for the object labels to be linked in time.

Lastly, the third term on the right hand side of (1.2) $P(\mathbf{z}^t|\mathbf{I}^t)$, models our *a priori* expectations about the nature of the object label field. In the temporal direction, we have already modeled the object labels to be consistent along the motion trajectories. Our model incorporates spatial intensity information ($\mathbf{I}^t$) based on the reasonable assumption that object discontinuities coincide with spatial intensity boundaries. The segmentation field is a discrete-valued MRF with the energy function given as

$$U_z(\mathbf{z}^t|\mathbf{I}^t) = \sum_{\mathbf{x}} \sum_{\mathbf{y} \in \mathcal{N}_{\mathbf{x}}} V_c(z(\mathbf{x}), z(\mathbf{y})|\mathbf{I}^t), \tag{1.6}$$

where we specify the clique function as

$$V_c(z(\mathbf{x}), z(\mathbf{y})|\mathbf{I}^t) = \begin{cases} -\gamma & \text{if } z(\mathbf{x}) = z(\mathbf{y}),\ s(\mathbf{x}) = s(\mathbf{y}) \\ 0 & \text{if } z(\mathbf{x}) = z(\mathbf{y}),\ s(\mathbf{x}) \neq s(\mathbf{y}) \\ +\gamma & \text{if } z(\mathbf{x}) \neq z(\mathbf{y}),\ s(\mathbf{x}) = s(\mathbf{y}) \\ 0 & \text{if } z(\mathbf{x}) \neq z(\mathbf{y}),\ s(\mathbf{x}) \neq s(\mathbf{y}). \end{cases} \tag{1.7}$$

Here, $\mathbf{s}$ refers to the spatial segmentation field that is pre-determined from $\mathbf{I}$. It is important to note that $\mathbf{s}$ is treated as *deterministic* in our Markov model. A simple region-growing method [11] was used in our experiments. According to (1.7), if the spatial neighbors $\mathbf{x}$ and $\mathbf{y}$ belong to the same *intensity-based* object ($s(\mathbf{x}) = s(\mathbf{y})$), then the two pixels are encouraged to belong to the same *motion-based* object. This is achieved by the $\pm\gamma$ terms. On the other hand, if $\mathbf{x}$ and $\mathbf{y}$ belong to *different* intensity-based objects ($s(\mathbf{x}) \neq s(\mathbf{y})$), we do not enforce z to be either way, and hence, the 0 terms in (1.7). This slightly more complex model ensures that the moving object segments we extract have some sort of spatial cohesiveness as well. This is a very important property for our adaptive coding strategy to be presented in Section 4. Furthermore, the above clique function allows the object segmentations to remain stable over time and adhere to what the human observer calls "objects."

2.3 Solution

Due to the equivalence of MRFs and Gibbs distributions [10], the MAP solution amounts to a minimization of the sum of potentials given by (1.4), (1.5), and (1.6). To ease the computation, a two-step iterative procedure [8] is implemented, where the motion and segmentation fields are found in an alternating fashion assuming the other is known. Mean field annealing [9] is

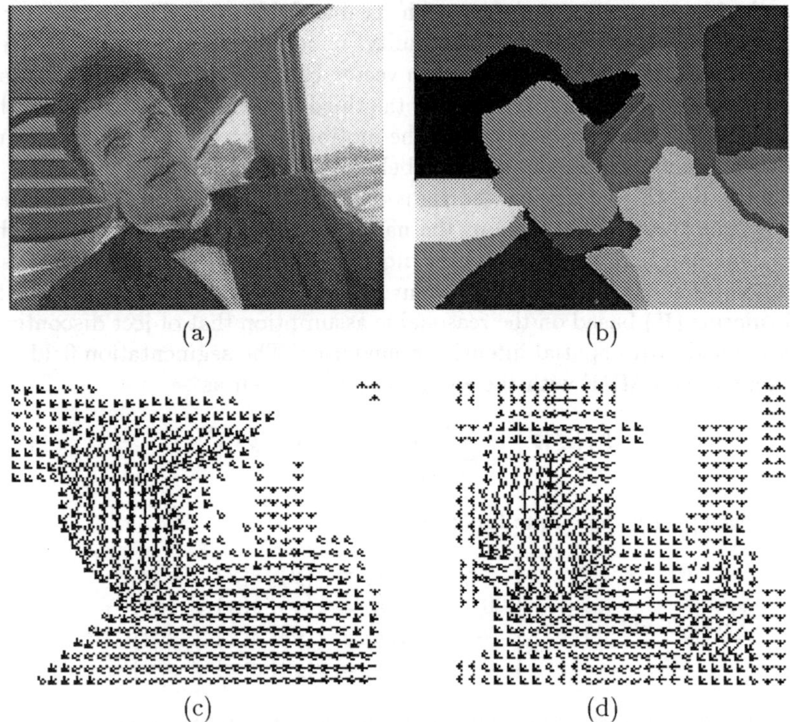

(a)   (b)

(c)   (d)

(a) *Carphone* frame no 88 (b) Motion segmentation
motion field by (c) proposed method (d) hierarchical block matching.

FIGURE 2. Motion estimation and segmentation for *Carphone*.

used for the motion field estimation, while the object label field is found by
the deterministic iterated conditional modes (ICM) algorithm [2]. Furthermore, the estimation is performed on a multiresolution pyramid structure.
Thus, crude estimates are first obtained at the top of the pyramid, with successive refinement as we traverse down the pyramid. This greatly reduces
the computational burden, making it possible to estimate relatively large
motion, and also allowing the motion and segmentation to be represented
in a scalable way.

2.4 Results

Simulations for the motion analysis and subsequent video coding were done
on three test sequences, *Miss America*, *Carphone*, and *Foreman*, all suitable
for low bit-rate applications.

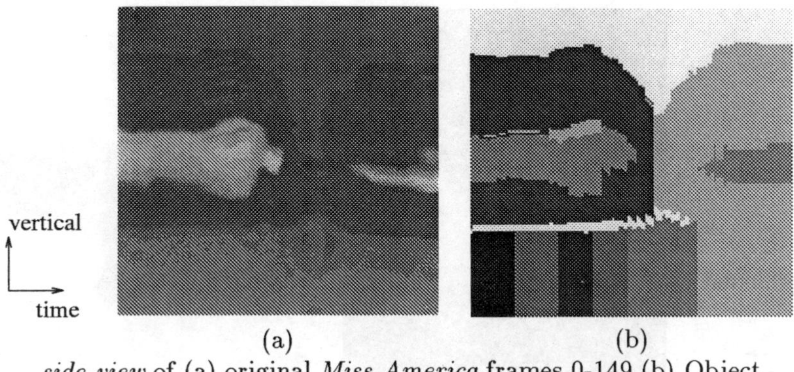

side-view of (a) original *Miss America* frames 0-149 (b) Object
segmentation mask

FIGURE 3. Objects in vertical-time space (side-view).

In Fig. 2, the motion estimation and segmentation results for *Miss America* are illustrated. A three-level pyramid was used in speeding up the algorithm, using the two-step iterations as described earlier. The motion field was compared to that obtained by hierarchical block matching. The block size used was 16x16. We can see that the MRF model produced smooth vectors within the objects with definitive discontinuities at the image intensity boundaries. Also, it can be observed that the object boundaries more or less define the "real" objects in the scene.

The temporal linkage of the object segments is illustrated in Fig. 3, which represents a "side view" of the 3-D image sequence, and Fig. 4, which represents a "top view". We can see that our segments are somewhat accurate and follow the true movement. Note that Fig. 3 is analogous to our ideal representation in Fig. 1 (b).

3 Parametric Representation of Dense Object Motion Field

The motion analysis from the previous section provides us with the boundaries of the moving objects and a dense motion field within each object. In this section, we are interested in efficiently representing and coding the found object information.

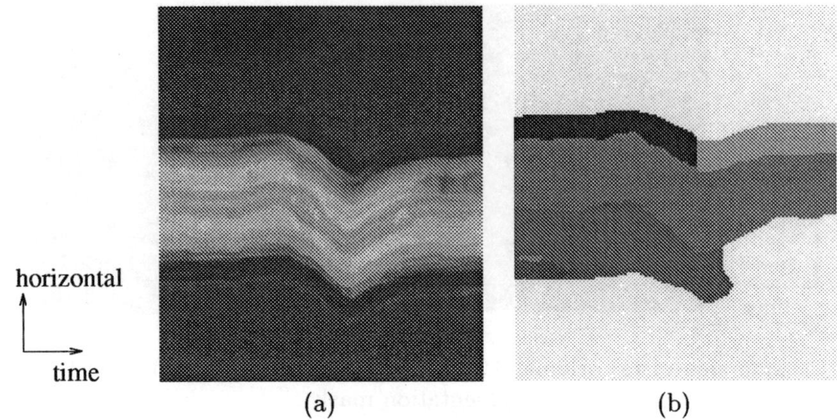

(a) (b)

top-view of (a) original *Miss America* (b) Object segmentation mask

FIGURE 4. Objects in horizontal-time space (top-view).

3.1 Parametric motion of objects

A 2-D planar surface undergoing rigid 3-D motion yields the following affine velocity field under orthographic projection [2]

$$v_x = a_1 + a_2 x + a_3 y$$
$$v_y = a_4 + a_5 x + a_6 y,$$

(1.8)

where $\mathbf{v} = (v_x(x, y), v_y(x, y))$ refers to the apparent velocity at pixel (x, y) in the x and y directions respectively. Thus, the motion of each object can be represented by the six parameters of (1.8). In [12], Wang and Adelson employ a simple least-squares fitting technique, and point out that this process is merely a plane fitting algorithm in the velocity space. In our work, we improve on this method by introducing a matrix $\mathbf{W}$ so that data with higher confidence can be given more weight in the fitting process. Specifically, we denote the six parameter set of (1.8) by

$$\mathbf{p} = \begin{bmatrix} a_1 & a_4 \\ a_2 & a_5 \\ a_3 & a_6 \end{bmatrix}.$$

(1.9)

For a particular object, we can order the M pixels that belong to the object as $(x_1, y_1), ..., (x_M, y_M)$, and define the weighting matrix $\mathbf{W}$ as

$$\mathbf{W} = diag[w_1, w_2, ..., w_M],$$

where $w_i (i = 1, 2, .., M)$ corresponds to the weight at pixel i. Then, the *weighted* least-squares solution for $\mathbf{p}$ is given by

$$\mathbf{p} = \mathbf{\Phi}_W^{-1} \mathbf{V}_W,$$

(1.10)

with

$$
\Phi_W \equiv
\begin{bmatrix}
\sum_i^M w_i^2 & \sum_i^M w_i^2 x_i & \sum_i^M w_i^2 y_i \\
\sum_i^M w_i^2 x_i & \sum_i^M w_i^2 x_i^2 & \sum_i^M w_i^2 x_i y_i \\
\sum_i^M w_i^2 y_i & \sum_i^M w_i^2 y_i x_i & \sum_i^M w_i^2 y_i^2
\end{bmatrix}
$$

and

$$
V_W \equiv
\begin{bmatrix}
\sum_i^M w_i^2 v_x(x_i, y_i) & \sum_i^M w_i^2 v_y(x_i, y_i) \\
\sum_i^M w_i^2 x_i (v_x(x_i, y_i)) & \sum_i^M w_i^2 x_i (v_y(x_i, y_i)) \\
\sum_i^M w_i^2 y_i (v_x(x_i, y_i)) & \sum_i^M w_i^2 y_i (v_y(x_i, y_i))
\end{bmatrix} .
$$

We designed the weighting matrix $\mathbf{W}$ based on experimental observations on our motion field data. For one thing, we would like to eliminate (or lessen) the contribution of inaccurate data on the least-squares fitting. This can be done using the displaced frame difference (DFD),

$$
\text{DFD}(\mathbf{x}_i) = \mathbf{I}^t(\mathbf{x}_i) - \mathbf{I}^{t-1}(\mathbf{x}_i - d(\mathbf{x}_i)). \tag{1.11}
$$

Obviously, we want pixels with higher DFD to have a lower weight, and thus define

$$
\alpha_i \equiv 1 - \text{DFD}(\mathbf{x}_i)/\text{MAX\_DFD}, \tag{1.12}
$$

where

$$
\text{MAX\_DFD} = \max_i \text{DFD}(\mathbf{x}_i).
$$

Also, we found that in image regions with almost homogeneous gray level distribution, the mean field solution favored the zero motion vector. This problem was solved by measuring the busyness in the search region of each pixel, represented by a binary weight function

$$
\beta_i = \begin{cases} 0 & \text{not busy} \\ 1 & \text{busy} \end{cases}
$$

The business is decided by comparing the gray-level variance in the search region of pixel i against a pre-determined threshold. Combining these two effects, the final weight for pixel i is determined as

$$
w_i = \lambda \alpha_i + (1 - \lambda)\beta_i \tag{1.13}
$$

where $0 < \lambda < 1$ to ensure that $w_i \in [0, 1]$. Fig. 5 images the weights for a selected object in *Miss America*.

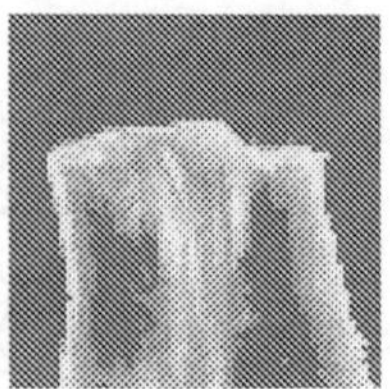

FIGURE 5. Least-squares weights for *Miss America*'s right shoulder: pixels with lighter gray-level values are given more weight.

3.2   Appearance of new regions

To extract meaningful new objects, additional processing was necessary based on least-squares fitting. The basic idea is taken from the "top-down" approach of Musmann *et al* [1], in which regions where the motion parametrization fail are assigned as new objects. However, we begin the process by splitting a given object into subregions using our spatial color segmentator. Then, a subregion is labeled as a new object only if all three of the following conditions are met:

1. The norm difference between the synthesized motion vectors and the original dense motion vectors is large.

2. The prediction error resulting from the split is significantly reduced.

3. The prediction error within the subregion is high without a split.

Because of the smoothness constraint, splitting within objects merely based on affine fit failure, did not produce meaningful objects. The second condition ensures that the splitting process decreases the overall coding rate. Finally, the third condition guards against splitting the object when there is no need to in terms of coding gain.

3.3   Coding the object boundaries

We have already seen that temporally linked objects in an object-based coding environment offer various advantages. However, the biggest advantage comes in reducing the contour information rate. Using the object boundaries from the previous frame and the affine transformation parameters, the boundaries can be predicted with a good deal of accuracy. Some error occurs near boundaries, and the difference is encoded by chain coding. These errors are usually small because the MRF formulation explicitly *makes* them small. It is interesting to note that in [13], this last step of updating is omitted, thus eliminating the need to transmit the boundary information altogether.

4 Object Interior Coding

Two methods of encoding the object interiors have been investigated. One is to code the objects, possibly motion-compensated, at each frame. The other is to explicitly encode the spatiotemporal objects in the 3-D space-time domain.

4.1 Adaptive Motion-Compensated Coding

In this scheme, objects that can be described well by the motion are encoded by motion compensated predictive (MCP) coding, and those that cannot are encoded in "Intra" mode. This adaptive coding is done independently on each object using spatial subband coding. Since the objects are arbitrarily shaped, the efficient signal extension method proposed by Barnard[14] was applied.

Although motion compensation was relatively good for most objects at most frames, the flexibility to switch to intra-mode (I-mode) in certain cases is quite necessary. For instance, when a new object appears from outside the scene, it cannot be properly predicted from the previous frame. Thus, these new objects must be coded in I-mode. This includes the initial frame of the image sequence, where all the objects are considered new. Even for "continuing" objects, the motion might be too complex at certain frames for our model to properly describe, resulting in poor prediction. Such classification of objects into I-objects and P-objects is analogous to P-blocks and I-blocks in current video standards MPEG and H.263 [15].

4.2 Spatiotemporal (3-D) Coding of Objects

Alternatively, to overcome some of the generic deficiencies of MCP coding [16], the objects can be encoded by object-based 3-D subband/wavelet coding (OB-3DSBC). This is possible because our segmentation algorithm provides objects linked in time. In OB-3DSBC, the temporal redundancies are exploited by motion-compensated 3-D subband/wavelet analysis, where the temporal filtering is performed along the motion trajectories within each object (Figure 6). The object segmentation/motion and covered/uncovered region information enables the filtering to be carried out in a systematic fashion. Up to now, rather *ad-hoc* rules had been employed to solve the temporal region consistency problem in filter implementation [3, 17]. In other words, the object-based approach allows us to make a better decision on where and how to implement the motion-compensated temporal analysis.

Following the temporal decomposition, the objects are further analyzed by spatial subband/wavelet coding. The generalized BFOS algorithm [18] is used in distributing the bits among the spatiotemporal subbands of the objects. The subband/wavelet coefficients are encoded by uniform quantization followed by adaptive arithmetic coding.

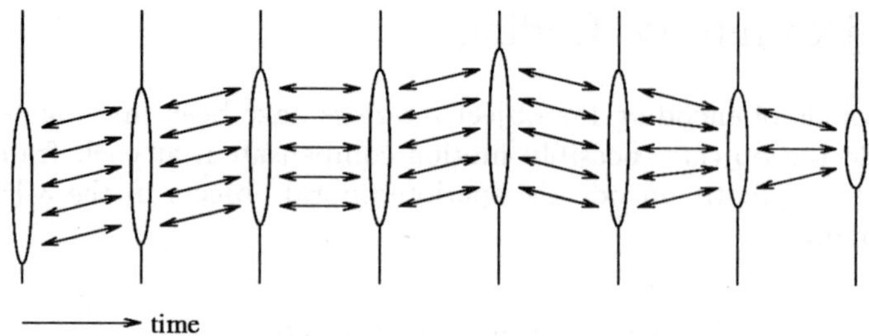

FIGURE 6. Object-based motion-compensated filtering

5   Simulation results

Our proposed object-based coding scheme was applied to three QCIF test sequences, *Miss America, Carphone*, and *Foreman*. They were compared to the Telenor research group's H.263 implementation[1]. Table 1.1 gives PSNR results comparing the object-based motion-compensated predictive (OB-MCP) coder and block-based H.263 coder. Table 1.2 shows the performance of our object-based 3-D subband/wavelet coder.

In terms of PSNR the proposed object-based coder is comparable in performance to the conventional technique at very low bit-rates. However, more importantly, the object-based coder produced visually more pleasing video. Some typical reconstructed frames are given in Fig. 7 and Fig. 8. The annoying blocking artifacts that dominate the block-based methods at low bit-rates are not present. Also, the object-based coder gave clearer reconstructed frames with less blurriness.

6   Conclusions

We have presented an object-based video compression system with improved coding performance from a visual perspective. Our motion estimation/segmentation algorithm enables the extraction of moving objects that correspond to the true scene. By following the objects in time, the object motion and contour can be encoded efficiently with temporal updating. The interior of the objects are encoded by 2-D subband analysis/synthesis. The objects are encoded adaptively based on the scene contents. No *a priori* assumptions about the image content or motion is needed. We conclude from our results that object-based coding could be a viable alternative to the block-based standards for very low bit-rate applications. Further research on reducing the computation is needed.

---

[1] `http://www.nta.no/brukere/DVC/`

sequence	bit-rate (kbps)	channel	OB-Coder (PSNR)	H.263 (PSNR)
Miss America (7.5 fps)	8	Y	36.0	35.9
		U	37.5	37.4
		V	35.5	35.3
	16	Y	38.0	38.2
		U	38.2	38.4
		V	37.2	37.6
Carphone (7.5 fps)	24	Y	30.0	30.0
		U	35.6	35.8
		V	36.4	36.4
	32	Y	30.8	31.1
		U	36.1	36.5
		V	36.9	37.2
Foreman (10 fps)	32	Y	30.8	30.7
		U	39.8	36.2
		V	40.7	36.9
	65	Y	32.5	32.5
		U	40.3	37.5
		V	41.4	38.5

TABLE 1.1. PSNR results for OB-MCP coder.

sequence	bit-rate (kbps)	channel	OB-Coder (PSNR)	H.263 (PSNR)
Miss America (15 fps)	20	Y	37.2	37.9
		U	38.9	38.5
		V	37.6	37.4
Carphone (15 fps)	40	Y	32.8	33.4
		U	38.1	38.6
		V	38.9	38.1

TABLE 1.2. PSNR results for OB-3DSBC.

7 References

[1] H. Musmann, M. Hotter, and J. Ostermann, "Object-oriented analysis-synthesis coding of moving images," *Signal Processing: Image Communications*, vol. 1, pp. 117–138, Oct. 1989.

[2] A. M. Tekalp, *Digital Video Processing*. Upper Saddle River, NJ: Prentice Hall, 1995.

(a) Object-based coder
(Frame PSNR = 34.0 dB)

(b) H.263 coder
(Frame PSNR = 34.1 dB)

FIGURE 7. Decoded frame 112 for *Miss America* at 8 kbps.

(a) Object-based coder
(Frame PSNR = 29.1 dB)

(b) H.263 coder
(Frame PSNR = 29.1 dB)

FIGURE 8. Decoded frame 196 for *Carphone* at 24 kbps.

[3] S. Choi and J. Woods, "Motion-compensated 3-D subband coding of video," *IEEE Trans. Image Process.* submitted for publication, 1996.

[4] D. W. Murray and B. F. Buxton, "Scene segmentation from visual motion using global optimization," *IEEE Trans. Pattern Analysis and Machine Intelligence*, pp. 220–228, Mar. 1987.

[5] J. Konrad and E. Dubois, "Bayesian estimation of motion vector fields," *IEEE Trans. Pattern Analysis and Machine Intelligence*, vol. 14, pp. 910–927, Sept. 1992.

[6] P. Bouthemy and E. François, "Motion segmentation and qualitative dynamic scene analysis from an image sequence," *International Journal of Computer Vision*, vol. 10, no. 2, pp. 157–182, 1993.

[7] C. Stiller, "Object-oriented video coding employing dense motion fields," in *Proc. IEEE Int. Conf. Acoust., Speech, Signal Processing*, vol. V, pp. 273–276, Adelaide, Australia, 1994.

[8] M. Chang, I. Sezan, and A. Tekalp, "An algorithm for simultaneous motion estimation and scene segmentation," in *Proc. IEEE Int. Conf. Acoust., Speech, Signal Processing*, vol. V, pp. 221–224, Adelaide, Australia, 1994.

[9] J. Zhang and G. G. Hanauer, "The application of mean field theory to image motion estimation," *IEEE Trans. Image Process.*, vol. 4, pp. 19–33, 1995.

[10] S. Geman and D. Geman, "Stochastic relaxation, Gibbs distributions, and Bayesian restoration of images," *IEEE Trans. Pattern Analysis and Machine Intelligence*, vol. PAMI-6, pp. 721–741, Nov. 1984.

[11] R. Haralick and L. Shapiro, *Computer and Robot Vision*. Reading, MA: Addison-Wesley Pub. Co., 1992.

[12] J. Wang and E. Adelson, "Representing moving images with layers," *IEEE Trans. Image Process.*, vol. 3, pp. 625–638, Sept. 1994.

[13] Y. Yokoyama, Y. Miyamoto, and M. Ohta, "Very low bit rate video coding using arbitrarily shaped region-based motion compensation," *IEEE Trans. Circuits and Systems for Video Technology*, vol. 5, pp. 500–507, Dec. 1995.

[14] H. J. Barnard, *Image and Video Coding Using a Wavelet Decomposition*. PhD thesis, Delft University of Technology, The Netherlands, 1994.

[15] ITU-T Recommendation H.263, *Video Coding for Low Bitrate Communication*, Nov. 1995.

[16] S. Han and J. Woods, "Three dimensional subband coding of video with object-based motion information," *Proceedings of IEEE International Conference on Image Processing*, Oct. 1997.

[17] J. Ohm, "Three-dimensional subband coding with motion compensation," *IEEE Trans. Image Process.*, vol. 3, pp. 559–571, Sept. 1994.

[18] E. Riskin, "Optimal bit allocation via the generalized BFOS algorithm," *IEEE Trans. Inform. Theory*, vol. IT-37, pp. 400–402, Mar. 1991.

A COMPUTATIONAL APPROACH TO
SEMANTIC EVENT DETECTION IN VIDEO

Richard J. Qian

Intel Labs
2111 NE 25th Ave
Hillsboro, OR 97124
U.S.A.
richard.j.qian@intel.com

Niels Haering

DiamondBack Vision
11600 Sunrise Valley Dr
Reston, VA 20191
U.S.A.
niels@dbvision.net

M. Ibrahim Sezan

Sharp Labs of America
5750 Pacific Rim Blvd
Camas, WA 98607
U.S.A.
sezan@sharplabs.com

1. Introduction

The amount of video information that can be accessed and consumed from people's living rooms has been ever increasing. This trend may be further accelerated due to the convergence of both technology and functionalities supported by future television receivers and personal computers. To obtain the information that is of interest and to provide better entertainment, tools are needed to help users extract relevant content and to effectively navigate through the large amount of available video information. For ordinary users, such tools may also have to satisfy the following requirements: (1) they should be easy to use in terms of operations; and (2) they should be easy to understand and predict in terms of their behaviors.

Existing content-based video indexing and retrieval methods do not provide the tools called for in the above applications. Most of those methods may be classified into the following three categories: (1) syntactic structurization of video; (2) video classification; and (3) extraction of semantics.

Work in the first category has concentrated on (a) shot boundary detection and key frame extraction [1,34]; (b) shot clustering [32]; (c) table of content creation [9]; (d) video summarization [22,35]; and (e) video skimming [28]. These methods are in general computationally simple and their performance is relatively robust. Their results, however, may not necessarily be semantically meaningful or relevant since they do not attempt to model and estimate the semantic content of the video. For consumer oriented applications, semantically irrelevant results may distract the user and lead to frustrating search or browsing experiences.

Work in the second category tries to classify video sequences into categories such as news, sports, action movies, close-ups, crowd, etc. [19,29]. These methods provide classification results which may facilitate users to browse video sequences at a coarse level. Video content analysis at a finer level is probably needed, to help users more effectively to find what they are looking for. In fact, consumers often express their search items in terms of more exact semantic labels, such as keywords describing objects, actions, and events.

Work in the third category has been mostly specific to particular domains. For example, methods have been proposed to detect events in (a) football games [18]; (b) soccer games [33]; (c) basketball games [27]; (d) baseball games [20]; and (e) sites under surveillance [4]. The advantages of these methods include that the detected events are semantically meaningful and usually significant to users. The major disadvantage, however, is that many of these methods are heavily dependent on specific artifacts such as editing patterns in the broadcast programs, which makes them difficult to extend for the detection of other events. A more general method for the detection of events [17] uses "Multijects" that are composed of sequences of low-level features of multiple modalities, such as audio, video, and text.

Query-by-sketch or query-by-example methods have also been proposed recently [7,36] to detect motion events. The advantage of these methods is that they are domain-independent and therefore may be useful for different applications. For consumer applications, however, sketching requires cumbersome input devices, specifying a query sketch may take undue amounts of time, and learning the sketch conventions may discourage users from using such tools.

Addressing these issues, we propose a computational method and several algorithmic components towards an extensible solution to semantic event detection. The automated event detection algorithm facilitates the detection of semantically significant events in their video content and helps to generate semantically meaningful highlights for fast browsing. In contrast to most existing event detection work, our goal is to develop an extensible computational approach which may be adapted to detect different events in a wide range of domains. To achieve this goal, we propose a three-level video event detection algorithm.

The first level extracts color, texture, and motion features, and detects shot boundaries and moving object blobs. The processing at this level is not affected by the event of interest.

The mid-level uses motion information from the first level to detect moving areas in each frame. A neural network determines the most likely object class for each pixel of each frame of the video. Combining the object and motion information we begin to gather evidence for *what* is moving *where* and *how*. This is the first important step towards extracting meaningful information from the vast amount of information contained in the billions of pixels that comprise videos. This level also generates shot descriptors that combine features from the first level and inferences from the mid-level.

The shot descriptors are then used by the domain-specific inference process at the third level to detect video segments that match the user defined event model. To test the effectiveness of our algorithm, we have applied it to detect animal hunt events in wildlife documentaries. In our implementation we do not attempt to detect the stalking phase that precedes many hunts, rather we aim to detect the swift or rapid chase of a fleeing or running animal. Since hunts are among the most interesting events in a wildlife program, the detected hunt segments can be composed into a program highlight sequence. The proposed approach can be applied to different domains by adapting the mid and high-level inference processes while directly utilizing the results from the low-level feature extraction processes [15].

In the following section, we describe the proposed computational method and its algorithmic components. In Section 3, we describe implementational details and present experimental results obtained as we have applied the proposed algorithm to the detection of animal hunt events in a number of commercially available wildlife video tapes. Finally, in Section 4, we summarize our work and discuss some future directions.

2. Methodology

The problem of detecting semantic events in video, e.g., hunts in wildlife video, can be solved by a three-level approach as shown in Fig. 1. At the lowest level the input video is decomposed into shots, global motion is estimated, and color and texture features are extracted. At this level we also estimate and compensate for global motion and detect motion blobs, i.e., areas containing independent object motion.

At the intermediate level the detected motion blobs are classified as moving object regions by a neural network. The network uses the color and texture features extracted at the lower level, and performs a crude classification of image regions into sky, grass, tree, rock, animal, etc.. This level also generates shot summaries which describe each individual shot in terms of intermediate-level descriptors.

At the highest level the generated shot summaries are analyzed and the presence of the events of interest are detected based on an event inference model which may incorporate domain-specific knowledge.

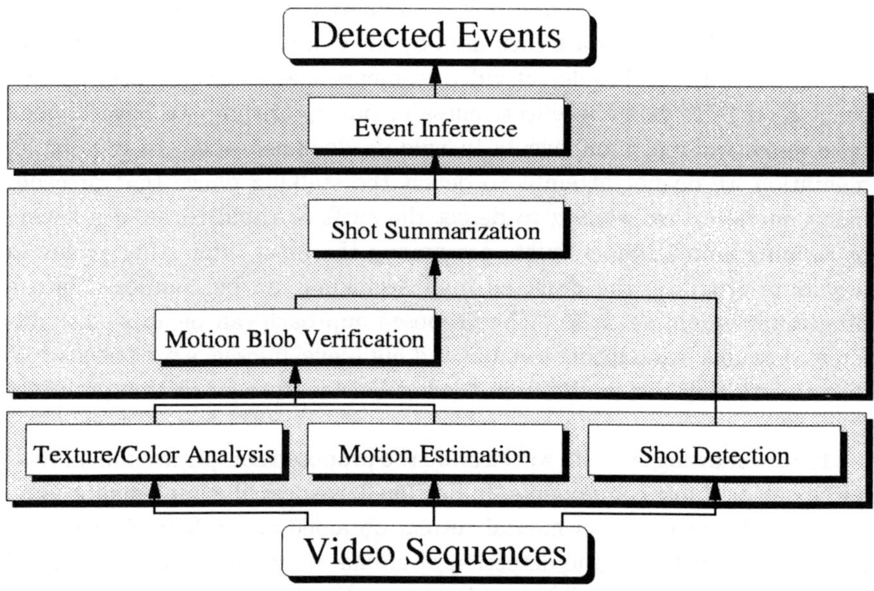

Fig. 1.   The flowchart of our method.

The feature extraction at the lowest level is entirely domain and event independent. The classifier at the intermediate level is only domain dependent. The event detection level is event specific (it describes and defines the event of interest). We will show object classification and event detection results for hunts in wildlife documentaries, and landings and rocket launches in unconstrained videos.

2.1. *Global Motion Estimation and Motion Blob Detection*

We assume that the motion in many videos can be decomposed into a global (or background) motion component and independent object motion components. We further assume that the global motion can be modeled by a three parameter system allowing only for zoom, horizontal and vertical translation.

$$u(x,y) = a_0 + a_2 x$$

$$v(x,y) = a_1 + a_2 y$$

We correlate patches from consecutive frames to estimate the global motion parameters. To improve the robustness and reduce the computation of the estimation process, we use a 5-level pyramid of reduced resolution representation of each frame. At each level of the pyramid we consider matches from a 5×5 neighborhood around the location of the patch in the source frame, enabling a maximum matching distance of 62 pixels.

At the lowest level of the pyramid, i.e. the full resolution representation of the frame, the patches used for matching are of size 64×64. Patches that overlap motion blobs are ignored since we cannot expect to find good background matches for them in adjacent frames. Patches from uniform areas also often result in erroneous motion estimates. To reduce the impact of unreliable motion estimates we discard patches with insufficient "texture". We use a 2D variance measure to determine the "amount of texture".

$$var_x = \frac{1}{m} \sum_{x=0}^{m-1} (\frac{1}{n} \sum_{y=0}^{n-1} (p(x,y) - p(x,.))^2 - q_x)^2$$

$$var_y = \frac{1}{n} \sum_{y=0}^{n-1} (\frac{1}{m} \sum_{x=0}^{m-1} (p(x,y) - p(.,y))^2 - q_y)^2$$

where p is an $m \times n$ image patch, $p(x,.)$ and $p(.,y)$ are the means of the xth column and y^{th} row of p, and q_x and q_y are the means $\frac{1}{n} \sum_{y=0}^{n-1} ((p(x,y) - p(x,.))^2$ and $\frac{1}{m} \sum_{x=0}^{m-1} (p(x,y) - p(.,y))^2$ for all x and y within p, respectively.

We compute motion estimates at each of the four corners of a frame, as shown in Fig. 5(a). Since the motion of the tracked objects often does not vary drastically between consecutive frames (i.e. their acceleration is small) we also use the previous best motion estimate to predict the location of the four patches in the next frame. A limited search in a 5×5 neighborhood around the predicted location, improves the motion estimates in many cases. Therefore, we obtain up to eight motion estimates, one pyramid based estimate for each of the four patch locations, and one for each of the four estimates based on a limited search around the predicted match locations. Since some patches may not pass the "texture" test we may have fewer than eight motion estimates. The highest normalized dot product between a source patch P_1 and matched patch P_2 determines the "correct" global motion estimate between the current and next frame. The normalized dot product is equal to the cosine of the angle (α) between the two patches (vectors) P_1, and P_2:

$$cos(\alpha)_{P_1,P_2} = \frac{\sum_{i,j} P_1(i,j)P_2(i,j)}{\sum_{i,j} P_1(i,j) \sum_{i,j} P_2(i,j)}$$

The estimated global motion parameters are used to compensate for the background motion between two consecutive frames. The difference between the current and the motion compensated previous frame is then used to detect motion blobs. Areas with low residual differences are assumed to have motion values similar to those of the background and are ignored. The independent motion of foreground objects on the other hand usually causes high residual differences between the current frame and the following motion compensated frame. We use a robust estimation technique developed in [26] to detect motion blobs. Based on the frame difference result, the algorithm constructs two 1D projections of the frame difference map along its x and y direction, respectively. These projections, therefore, represent the spatial distributions of the motion pixels along the corresponding axes. Fig. 2(a) illustrates an ideal frame difference map where there is only one textured elliptical moving object in the input sequence, and the corresponding projections on the x and y axes. The center position and size of a moving object in the video can be estimated from statistical measurements of the two 1D projections. To locate an object in the presence of multiple moving objects, a robust statistical estimation routine has been adopted and described below. Fig. 2(b) illustrates this recursive process.

The center position and size of a object in the image can be estimated based on statistical measurements derived from the two 1D projections. For example, a simple method estimates the center position and size of a dominant moving object in an input sequence using the sample means and standard deviations of the distributions. More specifically, let $h_x(i), i = 0, 1, \ldots$, and $h_y(i), i = 0, 1, \ldots$, denote the elements in the projections along

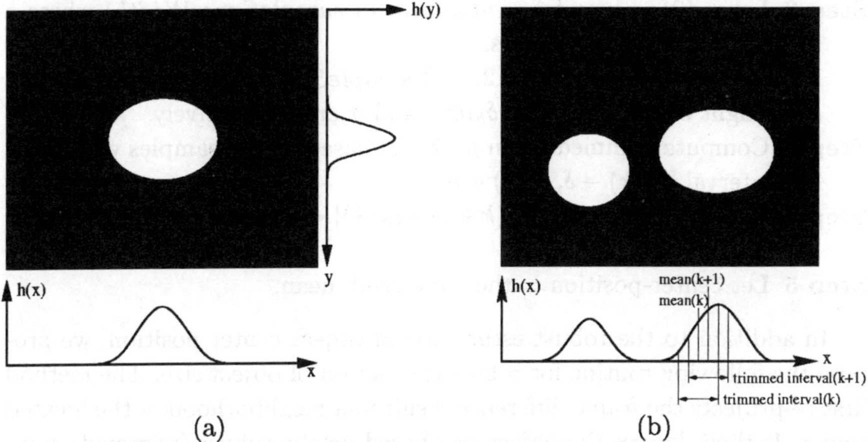

Fig. 2. (a) Two 1D projections constructed by projecting the frame difference map along the x and y direction, respectively. (b) Robust mean estimation for locating the center position of a *dominant* moving object.

the x and y direction, respectively. Then the object's position (x_c, y_c) and its width and height (w, h) may be estimated as:

$$x_c = \frac{\sum_i x_i h_x(i)}{\sum_i h_x(i)}, \quad y_c = \frac{\sum_i y_i h_y(i)}{\sum_i h_y(i)},$$

$$w = \alpha \left[\frac{\sum_i (x_i - \mu_x)^2 h_x(i)}{\sum_i h_x(i)} \right]^{\frac{1}{2}}, \quad h = \beta \left[\frac{\sum_i (y_i - \mu_y)^2 h_y(i)}{\sum_i h_y(i)} \right]^{\frac{1}{2}}$$

where α and β are constant scaling factors.

However, the object center position and size derived from the sample means and standard deviations may be biased in the cases where other moving objects appear in the scene. It is therefore necessary to develop a more robust procedure to address this problem. We propose the use of robust statistical estimation routines to achieve robust measurements for object center position and size [31]. More specifically, the center position of a dominant moving object in an input sequence is estimated based on the robust (trimmed) means of the two 1D projections in the x and y directions. Fig. 2(b) illustrates the process of the estimation of the motion center.

Step 1 Compute sample mean μ and standard deviation σ based on all the samples of the distribution.

Step 2 Let $\mu_t(0) = \mu$ and $\delta = max(a\ \sigma, b * sampleSpaceWidth)$ where a and b are scaling factors,
e.g., $a = 1.0$ and $b = 0.2$, and $sampleSpaceSize$ is the width and height of the image for δ_horiz and δ_vert, respectively.

Step 3 Compute trimmed mean $\mu_t(k+1)$ based on the samples within the interval $[\mu_t(k) - \delta, \mu_t(k) + \delta]$.

Step 4 Repeat Step 3 until $|\mu_t(k+1) - \mu_t(k)| < \epsilon$ where ϵ is the tolerance, e.g., $\epsilon = 1.0$.

Step 5 Let center-position $=$ the converged mean.

In addition to the robust estimation of object center position, we propose the following routine for robust estimation of object size. The method first re-projects the frame difference result in a neighborhood of the located center. It then derives the object size based on the robust (trimmed) standard deviation. Given the robust mean μ^* and δ obtained from the above center locating routine, the routine for estimation the size in either x or y direction is as follows.

Step 1 Construct a clipped projection H^{clip} by projecting the color filtering map within the range $[\mu^*_{opp} - \Delta, \mu^*_{opp} + \Delta]$ in the opposite direction, where μ^*_{opp} is the robust mean in the opposite direction and Δ determines the number of samples used in the calculation.

Step 2 Based on H^{clip}, compute the trimmed standard deviation δ_t based on the samples within the interval $[\mu^* - \delta, \mu^* + \delta]$.

Step 3 IF $H^{clip}(\mu^*+d\delta_t) \geq g\ H^{clip}(\mu^*)$ OR $H^{clip}(\mu^*-d\delta_t) \geq g\ H^{clip}(\mu^*)$, where e.g., $d = 1.0$ and $g = 0.4$, THEN increase δ_t until the condition is no longer true.

Step 4 Let $size = c\ \delta_t$ where c is a scaling factor, e.g., $c = 2.0$.

Multiple motion blobs can be located by repeating the above proposed method in an iterative manner. More specifically, the area of the already detected motion blob can be zeroed out in the frame difference map and the above method can be applied to the modified frame difference map to locate the subsequent motion blobs.

2.2. *Texture and Color Analysis*

To obtain rich, and hence robust and expressive descriptions of the objects in the video frames we describe each pixel in terms of 76 color and texture measures: 56 of them are based on the Gray Level Co-occurrence Matrix (GLCM), 4 on fractal dimension estimation methods, 12 on Gabor filters, and 4 on color. The feature space representations of each pixel are classified into categories, such as, sky/clouds, grass, trees, animal, rock, etc. using a back-propagation neural network. The use of these features in conjunction with the back-propagation classifier have previously been shown to enable the detection of deciduous trees in unconstrained images [13]. We decided not to use shape for our description of objects in video frames mostly because the recognition of the following important objects is far beyond the current state-of-the-art in object recognition: (1) Clouds, dust, fire, water, and smoke are amorphous "objects" for which shape models are difficult to construct. (2) Rocks, trees, grass, sky, etc. although not amorphous can occur in an almost infinite number of different shapes. Furthermore they rarely appear in isolation, trees grow near other trees, rocks lie with other rocks, etc. The overlap and occlusion makes it difficult to determine the spatial extent of these objects. (3) Articulated and non-rigid objects such as running animals are difficult to describe using their shape. (4) Occlusions by other objects and self-occlusion further complicate shape-based methods. Each of these object classes have distinct spatial or spatio-temporal color and texture characteristics. We will demonstrate the detection of many of these object classes in Section 3.

Each type of measure discussed in this section contributes significantly to the robustness of the neural network based object classifier described in Section 2.3. An analysis of the entire feature set shows that although each feature adds only a small amount of information to the pool, the classifier performs best when all the measures are used rather than a carefully selected subset [14]. The authors have also found that spatio-temporal entropy measures, the Kullback-Leibler divergence, and mutual information information measures can further aid the classification task. Gathering the features is time consuming if done at each pixel location. Fortunately, spatial redundancy between the pixels in a frame allows us to subsample and to calculate the features at a sparse grid of pixel locations. We found that pixel locations separated by 5 rows and columns from their nearest neighbors yielded sufficient resolution at computationally acceptable run times. Note, that since the texture measures are based on 64×64 image patches the overlap between adjacent pixel locations is still significant.

2.2.1. *Gabor Filter Measures*

The image (in the spatial domain) is described by its 2-D intensity function. The Fourier Transform of an image represents the same image in terms of the coefficients of sine and cosine basis functions at a range of frequencies and orientations. Similarly, the image can be expressed in terms of coefficients of other basis functions. Gabor [12] used a combined representation of space and frequency to express signals in terms of "Gabor" functions:

$$f(x,y) = \sum_i a_i \, g_i(x,y) \tag{1}$$

where a_i weights the ith complex Gabor basis function:

$$g_i(x,y) = e^{j\omega_i(x cos(\theta_i)+y sin(\theta_i))} e^{-(\alpha_i^2 \, x^2 + \beta_i^2 \, y^2)} \tag{2}$$

Gabor filters have gained popularity in multi-resolution image analysis [11,12], despite the fact that they do not form an orthogonal basis set. Gabor filter based wavelets have recently been shown [23] to be fast and useful for the retrieval of image data. We obtain 12 features, per pixel, by convolving each frame with Gabor filters tuned to 4 different orientations at 3 different scales.

2.2.2. *Graylevel Co-occurrence Matrix Measures*

Let $p(i,j,d,\theta) = \frac{P(i,j,d,\theta)}{R(d,\theta)}$, where $P(.)$ is the graylevel co-occurrence matrix of pixels separated by distance d in orientation θ and where $R(.)$ is a normalization constant that causes the entries of $P(.)$ to sum to one. In texture classification the following measures have been defined [3,16]:

The **Angular Second Moment (E)** (also called the Energy) assigns larger numbers to textures whose co-occurrence matrix is sparse.

$$E(d,\theta) = \sum_{j=1}^{N_g} \sum_{i=1}^{N_g} [p(i,j,d,\theta)]^2$$

The **Difference Angular Second Moment (DASM)** assigns larger numbers to textures containing only a few graylevel patches. This and other features use $p_{x-y}(n,d,\theta) = \sum_{\substack{j=1 \\ |i-j|=n}}^{N_g} \sum_{i=1}^{N_g} p(i,j,d,\theta)$

$$DASM(d,\theta) = \sum_{n=0}^{N_g} p_{x-y}(n,d,\theta)^2$$

The **Contrast (Con)** is the moment of inertia around the co-occurrence matrix's main diagonal. It is a measure of the spread of the matrix values and indicates whether pixels vary smoothly in their local neighborhood.

$$Con(d,\theta) = \sum_{n=0}^{N_g-1} n^2 \left[\sum_{\substack{j=1 \\ |i-j|=n}}^{N_g} \sum_{i=1}^{N_g} p(i,j,d,\theta) \right]$$

The other GLCM based measures we use for our texture analysis are the **Inverse Difference Moment, Mean, Entropy, Sum Entropy, Difference Entropy, Difference Variance, Correlation, Shade, Prominence.** These features are described in [3,16,30].

Note that the directionality of a texture can be measured by comparing the values obtained for a number of the above measures as θ is changed. The above measures were computed at $\theta = \{0^o, 45^o, 90^o, \text{and } 135^o\}$ using $d = 1$. For further discussion of these graylevel co-occurrence matrix measures, see [3,16,30].

2.2.3. *Fractal Dimension Measures*

The underlying assumption for the use of the Fractal Dimension (FD) for texture classification and segmentation is that images or parts of images are self-similar at some scale.

Various methods that estimate the FD of an image have been suggested:

- Fourier-transform based methods [25],
- box-counting methods [2,21], and
- 2D generalizations of Mandelbrot's methods [24].

The principle of self-similarity may be stated as: If a bounded set A (object) is composed of N_r non-overlapping copies of a set similar to A, but scaled down by a reduction factor r, then A is self-similar. From this definition, the Fractal Dimension D is given by

$$D = \frac{\log N_r}{\log r}$$

The FD can be approximated by estimating N_r for various values of r and then determining the slope of the least-squares linear fit of $\frac{\log N_r}{\log \frac{1}{r}}$. The differential box-counting method outlined in Chaudhuri, *et al* [2] are used to achieve this task.

Three features are calculated based on

- the actual image patch $I(i,j)$,
- the high-graylevel transform of $I(i,j)$,

$$I_1(i,j) = \begin{cases} I(i,j) - L_1 & I(i,j) > L_1 \\ 0 & otherwise \end{cases}$$

- the low-graylevel transform of $I(i,j)$,

$$I_2(i,j) = \begin{cases} 255 - L_2 & I(i,j) > 255 - L_2 \\ I(i,j) & otherwise \end{cases}$$

where $L_1 = g_{min} + \frac{g_{avg}}{2}$, $L_2 = g_{max} - \frac{g_{avg}}{2}$, and g_{min}, g_{max}, and g_{avg} are the minimum, maximum and average grayvalues in the image patch, respectively.

The fourth feature is based on multi-fractals which are used for self-similar distributions exhibiting non-isotropic and inhomogeneous scaling properties. Let k and l be the minimum and maximum graylevel in an image patch centered at position (i,j), let $n_r(i,j) = l - k + 1$, and let $\mathcal{N}_r = \frac{n_r}{N_r}$, then the multi-fractal, D_2 is defined by

$$D_2 = \lim_{r \to 0} \frac{log \sum_{i,j} \mathcal{N}_r^2}{log\, r}$$

A number of different values for r are used and the linear regression of $\frac{log \sum_{i,j} \mathcal{N}_r^2}{log\, r}$ yields an estimate of D_2.

2.2.4. *Color Measures*

The final set of features are the 3 normalized color measures r, g, b and the intensity I

$$r = \frac{R}{R+G+B}\,, \quad g = \frac{G}{R+G+B}\,, \quad b = \frac{B}{R+G+B},$$

$$I = \frac{R+G+B}{R_{max} + G_{max} + B_{max}}$$

2.3. *Region Classification and Motion Blob Verification*

We use a back-propagation neural network to arbitrate between the different features describing each pixel in each frame. Our back-propagation neural network [10] has a single hidden layer with 20 hidden units and uses the sigmoidal activation function $\Phi(act) = \frac{1}{1+e^{-act}} - 0.5$, where act is the activation of the unit before the activation function is applied. A single hidden layer in a back-propagation neural network has been shown to be sufficient to uniformly approximate any function (mapping) to arbitrary precision [5]. Although this existential proof doesn't state that the best network for some task has a single hidden layer, we found one hidden layer adequate. The architecture of the network is shown in Fig. 3. The back-propagation algorithm propagates the (input) function values layer by layer, left to right (input to output) and back-propagates the errors layer by layer, right to left (output to input). As the errors are propagated back to the input units, part of each unit's error is being corrected.

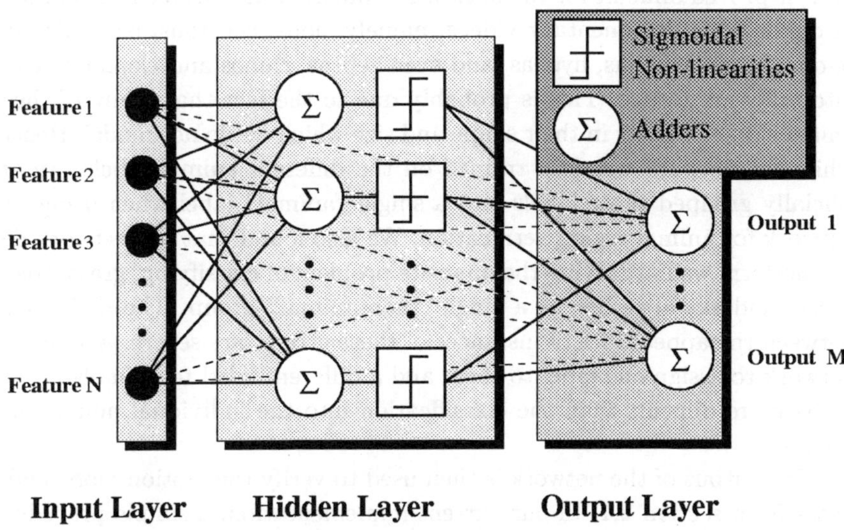

Fig. 3.   The Neural Network architecture.

A number of factors prevent zero error classification results. A few of these complicating factors are that *often there is no correct classification.* For instance, should bushes be labeled as tree or non-tree areas? What if a bush is actually a small tree? In general it is difficult to label class border pixels correctly; and misclassifications need not all be equally important. Misclassifying a distant herd of animals as trees or rocks is not as severe a mistake as, for example, classifying a nearby lion as sky.

212

For our hunt and landing events we trained the network using a total
of M = 15 labels. 9 animal labels (lion, cheetah, leopard, antelope, impala,
zebra, gnu, elephant, and an all-other-animal class) and 5 non-animal labels (rock, sky/clouds, grass, trees, and an all-other-non-animal class) as
well as a don't care label. For the detection of rocket launch events knowledge about exhaust gases, smoke, clouds, and human made structures were
useful. We retrained an new network that had the same number and con-
nectivity between the input and hidden layer, but had 4 additional output
units corresponding to the object classes smoke, hot exhaust gases, clouds,
and human made structures.

Both networks performed well at classifying animals, grass, trees, rocks,
sky, clouds/smoke, hot exhaust gases, and human made structures . However, it proved difficult for the network to differentiate between the animals
in our wildlife documentary videos, namely, lions, cheetahs, leopards, an-
telopes/impalas, gnus, hyenas, and even zebras, rhinos and elephants each
into different groups. This is probably due to the fact that many of these
animals differ mostly in their shape and size which we do not model. Hence,
while the network was still trained on the different animal labels, we artificially grouped those labels into a single "animal" label when using the
network for animal region verification. We also found that the network did
not perform well at solving the opposite problem of classifying, grass, trees,
rocks, and sky together as a single "non-animal" group. The differences
between the appearance of instances of these groups are severe. Asking the
network to assign one label to them and a different label to animals proves
to be more difficult than the classification into the individual non-animal
groups.

The output of the network is then used to verify the motion blob candidates from section 2.1. In our current implementation, a simple procedure
is employed which implements the following test. A region that has high
residual motion after motion compensation and that contains a significant
amount of animal labels, as detected by the neural network, is considered
as a possible moving animal region.

2.4. *Shot Summarization*

We use a simple color histogram based technique to decompose video sequences into shots. Since some shots last for 50 frames or less and others
last for 1000s of frames we also *force* a shot summary every 200 frames to

impose a degree of regularity onto the shot summaries and to avoid missing important events in extended shots. A third kind of shot boundary is inserted whenever the direction of the global motion changes. Shot boundaries of this last kind ensure that the motion within shots is homogeneous. Each shot is then summarized in terms of intermediate-level descriptors. The purpose of generating intermediate-level shot summaries is two-fold. First, the shot summaries provide a way to encapsulate the low-level feature and motion analysis details so that the high-level event inference module may be developed independent of those details, rendering it robust against implementational changes. Second, the shot summaries abstract the low-level analysis results so that they can be read and interpreted more easily by humans. This simplifies the algorithm development process and may also facilitate video indexing, retrieval and browsing in video database applications.

In general, the intermediate-level descriptors may consist of (1) *object*, descriptors, e.g., "animal", "tree", "sky/cloud", "grass", "rock", etc. indicate the existence of certain objects in the video frames, (2) *spatial* descriptors, e.g., "inside", "next to", "on top of", etc., that represent the location and size of objects and the spatial relations between them and (3) *temporal* descriptors, e.g., "beginning of", "while", "after", etc. [6,8], that represent motion information about objects and the temporal relations between them.

For the hunt detection application, we employ a particular set of intermediate-level descriptors which describe: (1) whether the shot summary is due to a forced or detected shot boundary; (2) the frame number of the beginning of the shot; (3) the frame number of the end of the shot; (4) the global motion; (5) the object motion; (6) the initial object location; (7) the final object location; (8) the initial object size; (9) the final object size; (10) the smoothness of the motion; (11) the precision throughout shot; and (12) the recall throughout shot. More precisely, the motion descriptors provide information about the x- and y- translation and zoom components of motion. The location and size descriptors indicate the location and size of the detected dominant motion blob at the beginning and the end of the shot. The precision is the average ratio of the number of animal labels within the detected dominant motion blob versus the size of the blob, while the recall is an average of the ratio of the animal labels within the detected dominant motion blob versus the number of animal labels in the entire frame. In addition, we also employ descriptors indicating (13) that tracking is engaged; (14) that object motion is fast; (15) that an animal is present; (16) the beginning of a hunt; (17) number of consecutive hunt shot candidates found; (16) the end of a hunt; and (19) whether a valid hunt is found. See Section 3.4 for an example and further explanation.

2.5. *Event Inference*

The event inference module determines whether segments of video contain events of interest. If a contiguous sequence of shot summaries matches the event model then the presence of that event is asserted. We decided to design the event inference module manually for two reasons:

- the design of many events is straightforward given the intermediate representation of the depicted objects and their qualitative motions,
- a rule-based event model allows a high level of transparency.

Hunt events are detected by an event inference module which utilizes domain-specific knowledge and operates at the shot level based on the generated shot summaries. From observation and experimentation with a number of wildlife documentaries, a set of rules have been deduced for detecting hunts. The rules reflect the fact that a hunt usually consists of a number of shots exhibiting smooth but fast animal motion which are followed by subsequent shots with slower or no animal motion. In other words, the event inference module looks for a prescribed number of shots in which (a) there is at least one animal of interest; (b) the animal is moving in a consistently fast manner for an extended period; and (c) the animal stops or slows down drastically after the fast motion. Fig. 4 shows and describes a state diagram of our hunt detection inference model.

Automatic detection of the properties and sequences of actions in the state digram is non-trivial and the low-level feature and motion analysis described earlier in this chapter are necessary to realize the inference. Since many events can be defined by the occurrence of objects involved and the specification of their spatio-temporal relationship, the proposed mechanism, of combining low-level visual analysis and high-level domain-specific rules, may be applicable to detect other events in different domains. In Section 3.5, we provide an example and further explanation for using this inference model for hunt detection.

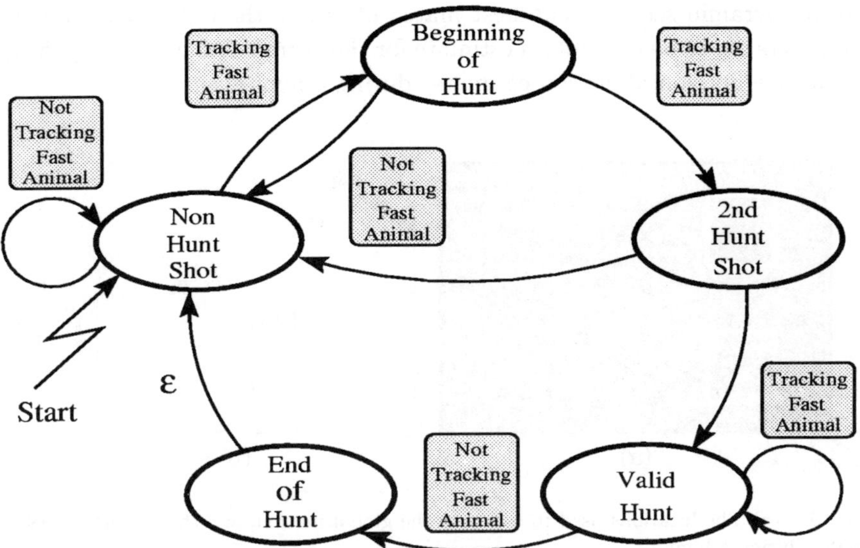

Fig. 4.   The state diagram of our hunt detection method. Initially the control is in the Non-Hunt state on the left. When a fast moving animal is detected the control moves to the Beginning of hunt state at the top of the diagram. When three consecutive shots are found to track fast moving animals then the Valid Hunt flag is set. The first shot afterwards that does not track a fast moving animal takes the control to the End of Hunt state, before again returning to the Non-Hunt state.

3. Experimental Results

The proposed algorithm has been implemented and tested on wildlife video footage from a number of commercially available VHS tapes from different content providers. In the following sections we show example results of the global motion estimation, motion blob detection, extracted texture and color features, region classification, and shot summarization. Then we present the final hunt event detection results.

3.1. *Global Motion Estimation*

Fig. 5(a) shows the size (64×64) and locations of the four regions at which we attempt to estimate the global motion between consecutive frames. Two motion estimates are computed at each of the four locations. The two motion estimates are based on (a) a local search around the best motion estimate from the previous pair of frames, and (b) a global search using a

5-level pyramid scheme. The best match of any of these 8 patch comparisons is taken to be the motion estimate for the current frame pair. Fig. 5(b) shows the horizontal motion estimates during a hunt event.

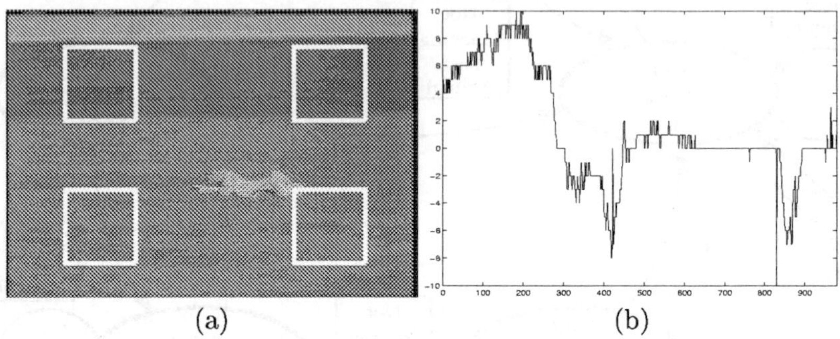

Fig. 5. (a) The locations used to estimate the global motion, and (b) the motion estimates during a hunt.

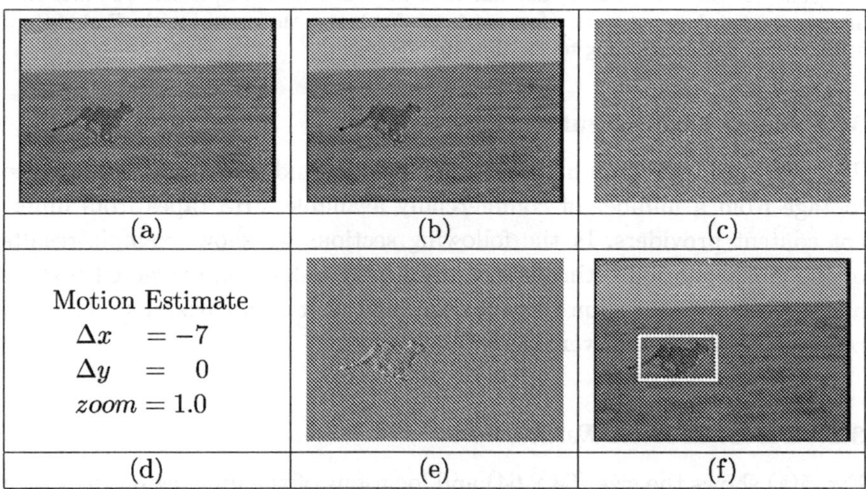

Fig. 6. Two consecutive frames from a hunt (a) and (b), the difference image (c), the estimated motion between the two frames (d), the motion compensated difference image (e) using the motion estimate in (d), and the box around the area of largest residual error in the motion compensated difference image.

3.2. *Motion Blob Detection*

Fig. 6 shows an example of the motion blob detection results. It is apparent that reliable estimation and compensation of global motion simplifies the motion blob detection task. When the accuracy of the global motion estimation results are poor, the performance of the motion blob detection relies largely on the robustness of the motion blob detection and tracking algorithm described in Section 2.1.

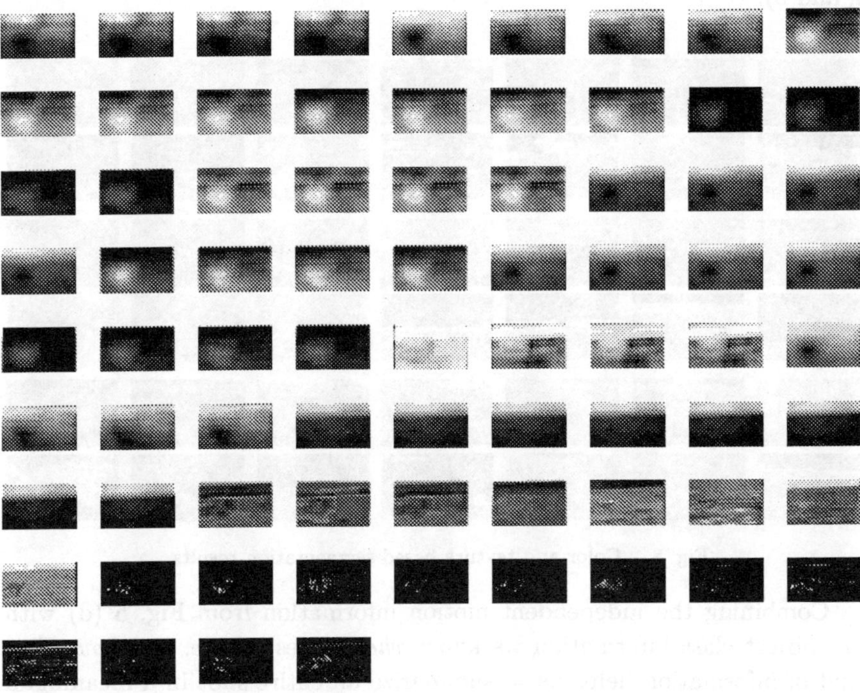

Fig. 7.   The feature space representation of the first frame in Fig. 6.

3.3. *Region Classification*

Global motion estimates such as the ones in Fig. 5 are used to detect moving objects as shown in Fig. 6. This tells us where in each frame independent object-motion occurs. Next we integrate this information with object class information to determine what moves where and how.

Fig. 7 shows the feature space representation of the first frame in Fig. 6. The features shown in order are the results of the 56 Gray-Level Co-occurrence Matrix based measures, the 4 fractal dimension based measures, the 4 color based measures, and the 12 Gabor filter bank measures.

A neural network classifier combines this color and texture information and assigns each pixel a label indicating its most likely object class. The classifier is trained on a number of training frames. Rows 1, 3, and 5 of Fig. 8 show frames from hunts together with their classification results (rows 2, 4, and 6).

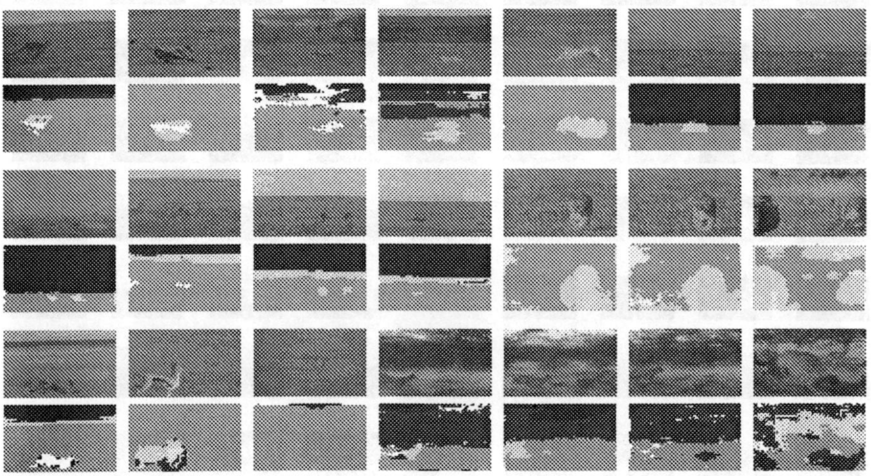

Fig. 8. Color and texture based segmentation results.

Combining the independent motion information from Fig. 5 (d) with this object class information we know *what* moves, *where*, and *how*. This kind of information helps us to summarize an entire shot in a meaningful way, as we will see in the next section.

3.4. *Shot Summarization*

The intermediate level process consists of two stages. In the first stage the global motion estimates are analyzed and directional changes in the camera motion are detected in the x and y directions. When the *signs* of a 50 frame global motion averages before and after the current frame differ and their *magnitudes* are greater than 1 pixel per frame we insert an artificial shot boundary. This ensures that the direction of motion within each shot is consistent, and it prevents us from canceling significant motions in opposite directions when computing the shot averages computed in the second stage. The first example shows the shot summary used by our hunt event detector.

```
GENERAL INFORMATION
Forced/real shot summary                          : 0
First frame of shot                               : 64
Last frame of shot                                : 263
Global motion estimate (x,y)                      : (-4.48, 0.01)
Within frame object motion estimate (x,y)         : (-0.17, 0.23)
Initial position (x,y)                            : (175,157)
Final position (x,y)                              : (147,176)
Initial size (w,h)                                : ( 92, 67)
Final size (w,h)                                  : (100, 67)
Motion smoothness throughout shot (x,y)           : ( 0.83, 0.75)
Precision throughout shot                         : ( 0.84)
Recall throughout shot                            : ( 0.16)

HUNT INFORMATION Tracking                         : 1
Fast                                              : 1
Animal                                            : 1
Beginning of hunt                                 : 1
Number of hunt shot candidates                    : 1
End of hunt                                       : 0
Valid hunt                                        : 0
```

The summary consists of two parts, the first part, General Information shows general statistics extracted for this shot, while the second, under Hunt Information consists of inferences based on those statistics for the hunt detection application.

The first row of the general Information part of the summary shows whether the shot boundary corresponding to this shot summary was real, i.e. whether it was detected by the shot boundary detector, or if it was forced because the maximum number of frames per shot was reached or the global motion has changed. The next two rows show the first and last frame numbers of this shot. The following measurements are shot statistics, i.e., the average global motion over the entire shot on row four, and the average object motion within the shot on row five. The next four rows measure the initial position and size, as well as the final position and size of the detected dominant motion blob. The third last row shows the smoothness of global motion where values near 1 indicate smooth motion and values near 0 indicate unstable motion estimation. Equation 3 shows how the smoothness measure is computed.

$$S = \frac{1}{N} \sum_{i=1}^{N} v_i, \tag{3}$$

where N is the number of frames in the shot and v_i is defined as follows:

$$v_i = \begin{cases} 1 & q_i * r_i \geq 0 \\ 0 & otherwise \end{cases},$$

where q_i and r_i are the minimum and maximum values of the horizontal components of the global motion estimates for the 5 most recent frames. The smoothness measure is large when consecutive horizontal motion estimates have the same sign. Likewise the smoothness measure is small when the motion estimates of consecutive frames frequently differs in sign. The smoothness measure, therefore, provides a *quantitative* measure of the smoothness of the estimated motion. The smoothness measure should really consider both the horizontal and the vertical motion components, but we have not noticed any related limitations for the event detectors we constructed.

The detection of a reversal of the global motion direction, described above, is based on a long term average of the motion estimates around the current frame, indicates a *qualitative* change in the global motion. Finally the last two rows show the average precision and recall for the entire shot. As defined in Section 2.4, the precision is the average ratio of the number of animal labels within the detected dominant motion blob versus the size of the blob, while the recall is an average of the ratio of the animal labels within the detected dominant motion blob versus the number of animal labels in the entire frame.

The hunt information part of the shot summary shows a number of predicates that were inferred from the statistics in part one. The shot summary shown above summarizes the first hunt shot following a **forced** shot boundary. The system is indicating that it is **Tracking a Fast** moving **Animal** and hence, that this could be the **Beginning of a hunt**. The **Tracking** predicate is true when the motion smoothness measure is greater than a prescribed value and the motion blob detection algorithm detects a dominant motion blob. The **Fast** predicate is true if the translational components of the estimated global motion are sufficiently large in magnitude, and the **Animal** predicate is true if the precision, i.e. the number of animal labels

within the tracked region, is sufficiently large. (The recall measure has not
been used in our current implementation.) The remaining predicates are
determined and used by the inference module as described below.

The next example shows the second part of a shot summary used by our
landing event detector. The first part again extracts the same information
as described in the hunt event detector example, above. This shot summary

```
LANDING INFORMATION
Tracking                    : 1
Fast horizontal motion      : 1
Descending                  : 1
Object                      : 1
Sky below object            : 1
Approach                    : 1
Touch-down                  : 0
Deceleration                : 0
First frame of shot         : 41
Last frame of shot          : 80
```

represents a shot during which we were tracking a descending object that
had a fast horizontal velocity and sky below it. The Approach, Touch-
down, and Deceleration fields keep track of the state of the landing within
the landing event model, described below.

Our last example shows a shot summary used by our rocket launch event
detector. The first part of the summary again extracts the same information as described in the hunt event detector, above. For this example it also
proved helpful to extract the following frame statistics. The second part of

```
SHOT INFORMATION
Amount of sky in frame          : (0.42)
Amount of sky above center      : (0.37)
Amount of sky below center      : (0.27)
Amount of clouds in frame       : (0.00)
Amount of clouds above center   : (0.00)
Amount of clouds below center   : (0.00)
Amount of exhaust in frame      : (0.00)
Amount of exhaust below center  : (0.00)
Amount of ground in frame       : (0.32)
```

the shot summary takes the following form. This shot summary represents

LAUNCH INFO

Shot type	: Frame time-out	Clouds appearing	: 0
Tracking	: 1	Exhaust appearing	: 0
Horizontal motion	: 0	Ground visible	: 1
Vertical motion	: 0	Ground disappearing	: 0
Ascending	: 0	Ignition	: 0
Object	: 1	Just saw ignition	: 0
Sky	: 1	Lift-off	: 0
Clouds	: 0	Flight	: 0
Exhaust	: 0	Flight candidate	: 0
Sky or clouds above center	: 1	Just saw flight	: 0
Sky or clouds below center	: 1	First frame of shot	: 1
Exhaust below center	: 0	Last frame of shot	: 40

a shot during which the program was tracking a slow moving object (fast enough to activate tracking but too slow to trigger the horizontal and vertical motion flags. We also saw evidence of sky below and above the center of the frame and ground near the bottom of the frame. We have not seen anything indicating an ignition phase of a rocket launch and thus have not entered the active states of the rocket launch model, described below.

3.5. *Event Inference and Final Detection Results*

The event inference module models the spatial and temporal characteristics of an event. In Section 2.5, above, we showed the event. model for our hunt event detector.

3.5.1. *Hunt Events*

The event inference module infers the occurrence of a hunt based on the intermediate descriptors as described in Section 3.4. It employs four predicates, **Beginning of hunt**, **Number of hunt shot candidates**, **End of hunt**, and **Valid hunt**. If the intermediate descriptors **Tracking**, **Fast** and **Animal** are all true for a given shot, **Beginning of hunt** is set to be true.

The value of **Number of hunt shot candidates** is incremented for every consecutive shot during which the three descriptors remain true. When the **Number of hunt shot candidates** is equal to or greater than 3, **Valid hunt** is set to be true. Finally the inference module sets **End of hunt** to be true if one of the intermediate descriptors **Tracking**, **Fast** and **Animal** becomes false, which implies either the animal is no longer visible or trackable, or the global motion is slow enough indicating a sudden stop after fast chasing.

In our results, hunt events are specified in terms of their starting and ending frame numbers. There are 7 hunt events in the 10 minutes (18000 frames) of wildlife video footage we have processed, Table 1 shows the actual and the detected frames of the 7 hunts. The table also shows the retrieval performance of our method in terms of the two commonly used retrieval evaluation criteria (1) precision and (2) recall.

Table 1. A comparison of the actual and detected hunts in terms of the first and last hunt frame, and the associated precision and recall.

Sequence Name	Actual Hunt Frames			Detected Hunt Frames			Precision	Recall
hunt1	305	-	1375	305	-	1375	100 %	100 %
hunt2	2472	-	2696	2472	-	2695	100 %	99.6%
hunt3	3178	-	3893	3178	-	3856	100 %	94.8%
hunt4	6363	-	7106	6363	-	7082	100 %	96.8%
hunt5	9694	-	10303	9694	-	10302	100 %	99.8%
hunt6	12763	-	14178	12463	-	13389	67.7%	44.2%
hunt7	16581	-	17293	16816	-	17298	99.0%	67.0%
Average							95.3%	86.0%

Our method detected the first five hunt events very accurately. The frame numbers of the detected and actual hunt frames match so closely because they coincide with shot boundaries which both humans as well as our method take as the boundaries of events. Hunt 6 was detected rather poorly because (1) at the beginning of the hunt the well camouflaged animals chasing each other in tall grass were not detected and (2) at the end of the hunt both animals disappear behind a hill. The camera keeps panning and the two eventually re-emerge on the other side of the hill before the predator catches the prey. Since both animals are occluded for a prolonged period of time the event inference module resets itself, signaling a premature end of this hunt. For Hunt 7 the recall measure indicates that our method missed quite a few frames at the beginning of that hunt. Human observers we had asked to determine the "actual" beginning and end of the hunt included part of the stalking phase into the hunt. Indeed, it is difficult to draw a clear line between the stalking phase and the hunt phase of that hunt. The detection of stalking animals requires a detailed animal gesture analysis which goes well beyond the scope of our coarse motion and object analysis.

3.5.2. *Landing Events*

Landing events may involve objects such as birds, aircraft, space-shuttles, etc. Appearance and shape of these objects varies greatly between the instances of these classes, for example, space shuttles have large bodies with small wings, owls on the other hand often have large wings that dwarf their bodies, and aircraft are human-made objects that occur in almost all colors and textures. Just as in the case of hunts it is often possible to trade some detailed object information for some coarse motion information to assert the presence or absence of landing events. Therefore, our landing event model depends heavily on simple motion characteristics and the detection of sky/cloud and non-sky/cloud image regions. This is reflected in the stages and the conditions on the transitions between the stages of the model of landing events. In broad terms the model aims to detect shot sequences during which a formerly flying non-sky/cloud motion blob first turns much of its potential energy into horizontal motion energy before touching the ground and slowing down significantly. These characteristics of landing events are modeled by four stages, an Approach, Touch-down, Deceleration, and Non-landing stage, as shown in Fig. 9.

The event inference module infers the occurrence of a landing when the accepting state (here the deceleration state) of Fig. 9 is reached, According to this event diagram landing events have three phases:

Approach: Initially the tracked object is seen with sky below it.

Touch-down: Following the Approach the tracked, descending object can be seen to have a large horizontal motion component.

Deceleration: A significant reduction of the horizontal speed of the tracked and now grounded object represent this final phase of the landing event.

If the descriptors Tracking, Descending, Object, and Sky-below-object are all true for the first time, we may assert that the current shot could be the Approach phase of a landing. When the control is in the Approach state, the Tracking, Descending, and Object descriptors are true, and the object has a Fast-horizontal-motion component, the control moves to the Touch-down state. From this state the control moves to the accepting Deceleration state when the Tracking and Object flags remain set but neither the Fast-horizontal-motion nor the Sky-below-object flags are set. A sequence of shots that does not contain at least an Approach,

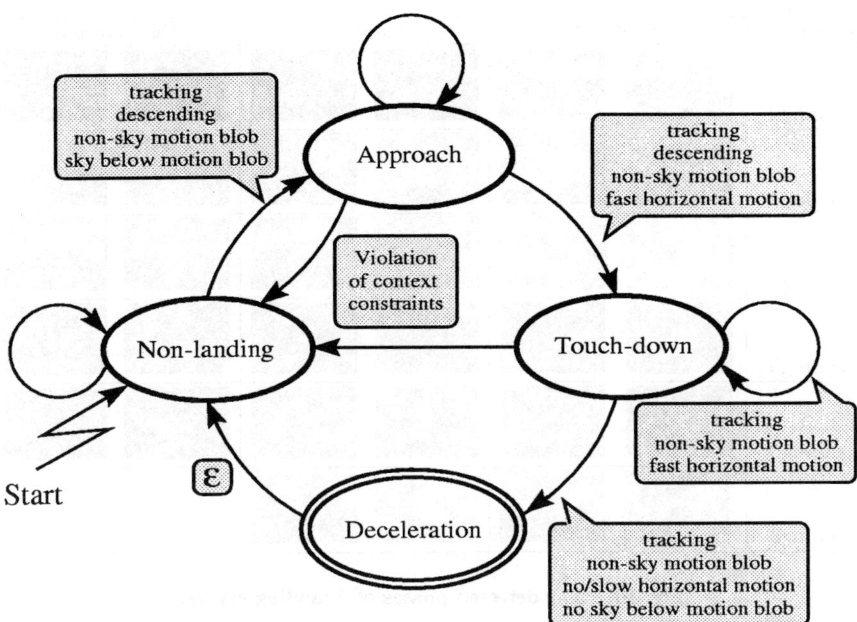

Fig. 9. The state diagram of our landing detection method. Initially the control is in the Non-Landing state on the left. When a descending object, surrounded by sky, is tracked the control moves to the Approach state at the top of the diagram. When a descending object is tracked and found to be moving with a fast horizontal motion component, the control moves to the Touch-down state on the right of the diagram. Tracking a slow moving or stationary object that is not surrounded by sky causes the control to move the Deceleration state at the bottom before returning to the Non-landing state.

Landing, and Deceleration phase is not considered a landing event. The landing event ends after the first shot in the Deceleration phase.

Fig. 10 shows these three phases for 6 landing sequences. The phases of the 6 landing events were correctly detected in all but the last landing sequence. In this last sequence only the approach and touch-down phases were found. The deceleration phase was not detected since the frames following the landing phase slowly fade to black before the aircraft slows down sufficiently, as shown in Fig. 11.

The left of Fig. 12 shows a frame from one of the two sequences for which the event detector failed. The object classifier misclassified the salt lake on which the space shuttle is landing as a sky/cloud region in the sequence.

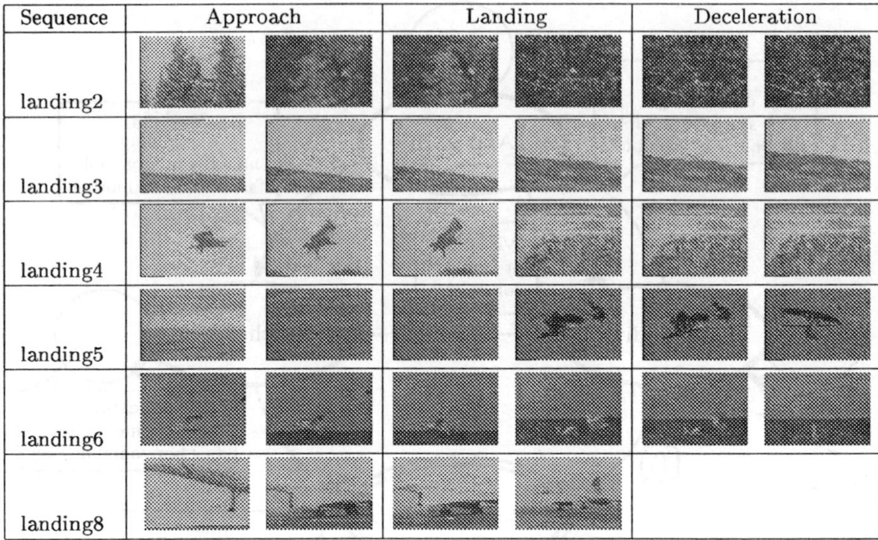

Sequence	Approach		Landing		Deceleration	
landing2						
landing3						
landing4						
landing5						
landing6						
landing8						

Fig. 10.   The detected phases of 6 landing events.

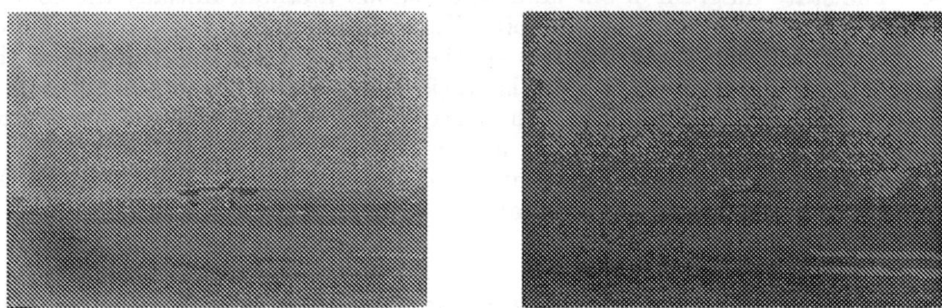

Fig. 11.   Before the aircraft slows down significantly the video fades to black.

Due to this misclassification the landing detector located sky below the motion blob and prevented the control from moving to the landing state (since for this state the moving object must touch down on a non-sky part of the image). It is unclear whether humans can visually determine that the space shuttle is rolling on a salt lake or for example on a uniform white cloud. Removing the space shuttle from the frame, as on the right in Fig. 12 makes it obvious that the classification task is difficult without context and background knowledge.

Fig. 12. Most of this frame is labeled as sky/clouds by the classifier.

3.5.3. *Rocket Launch Events*

Rocket launches are another example of events that are easily described without detailed object and motion characteristics, but rather depend on the detection of certain key objects and key motions. If we had to describe the visual characteristics of rocket launches to a child it is difficult to see how we could avoid mentioning the rocket engines' exhaust, human-made objects such as the rocket and the launch pad, and clouds or sky. Furthermore it is difficult to define the shape or appearance of launch pads or rockets. Some rockets consist of a single tube shaped object, while the space shuttle has two rocket boosters, a large Hydrogen tank and the shuttle itself. Older or future rockets may have yet other shapes and appearance. Rocket launches are another instance of events that are best described in terms of coarse, abstract, and salient characteristics, rather than more detailed models. In particular it proves difficult to extract motion information reliably. After the ignition of the rocket engines large amounts of clouds may be created, which depending on the relative camera viewpoint may occlude the rocket itself. Their non-rigid deformation and expansion severely complicates the detection of background/foreground motion. Likewise, the sky or clouds behind the rocket may be to texture less to allow reliable motion estimation.

The proposed rocket launch event model has four states, `Ignition`, `Lift-off`, `Flight`, and `Non-launch`, as shown in Fig. 13. If the descriptors `Sky-visible`, `Ground-visible`, `Clouds-forming`, are all true while there is no motion other than that of cloud regions in the video frames then control moves to the `Ignition` state. When the control is in the `Ignition` state, and the `Tracking`, `Object`, `Sky-visible` and `Upward-motion` descriptors are true while the `horizontal-motion` is not set, the control

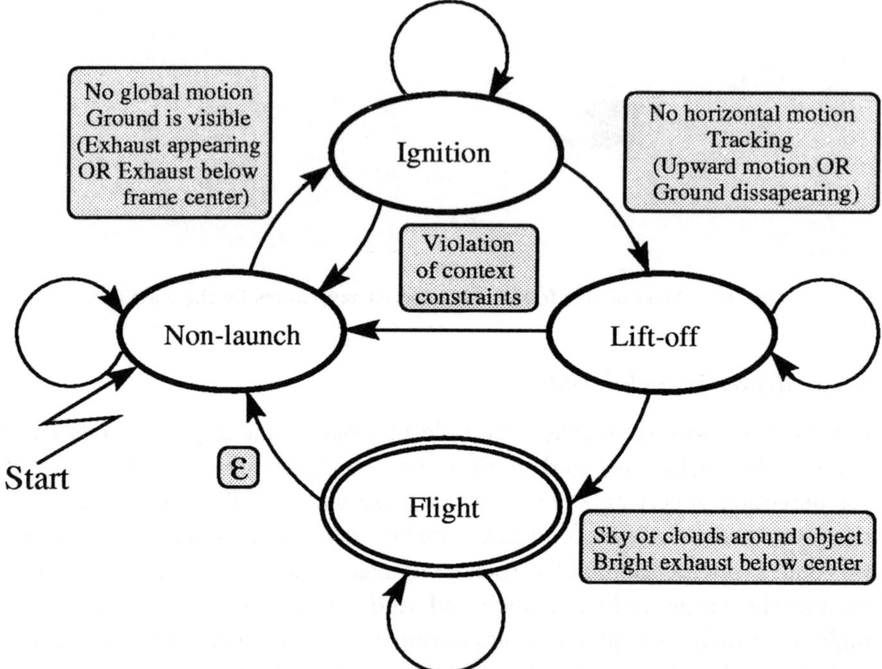

Fig. 13.   The state diagram of the proposed rocket launch detection method. Initially the control is in the **Non-launch** state on the left. If sky and ground are visible at the top and bottom of the video frames, respectively, and the only motion is due to developing cloud regions then the control moves to the **Ignition** state. When a non-sky motion-blob can be tracked in front of a sky background with an upward motion and no horizontal motion then the control moves on to the **Lift-off** state. Finally, if the tracked non-sky motion blob continues it's (mostly) upward motion, the ground disappears from the frames and a bright exhaust plume can be seen then the control moves to the accepting **Flight** state, thus concluding the rocket-launch.

moves to the **Lift-off** state. From this state the control moves to the accepting **Flight** state when the **Tracking, Object, Sky-visible,** and **Upward-motion** flags remain set but the **Exhaust-below-** object flag appears and the **Ground-visible** flag disappears. A sequence of shots that does not contain at least an **Ignition, Lift-off,** and **Flight** phase is not considered a rocket launch event. The launch event ends after the first shot in the **Flight** phase.

According to the event model in Fig. 13 rocket launches can be broken into three phases.

Ignition: Initially the engines are started, bright exhaust becomes visible, and clouds of exhaust begin to form. The only noticeable motion is due to the non-rigid deformation (growth) of these clouds.

Lift-off: After the ignition the onset of an upward motion and the presence of sky or clouds all around the moving object indicate the transition to the Lift-off.

Flight: Finally, the moving object is completely surrounded by sky and clouds and the bright exhaust plume is visible immediately below it.

Fig. 14 shows the three phases for 7 rocket launching sequences. The phases of 7 rocket launch events were correctly detected except in the third sequence, where the correct and an incorrect launch were detected.

All 7 launch events in the test set were correctly detected, with one additional, false detection during launch 3. Furthermore, the rocket launch phases detected in sequences 1 and 7 closely match the phases of the depicted launch events. The fact that not all the launch *phases* of the remaining video sequences were detected correctly has a number of reasons and implications. Sequence 4, for instance, does not have an "ignition" phase. The sequence shows shots in and outside a space shuttle in orbit, followed by an ascending shuttle after its lift-off, followed by further shots outside the orbiting shuttle. Since the rocket launch model in Fig. 13 does not state the presence of non-sky/clouds/exhaust regions below the rocket during the ignition phase, the appearance of exhaust in the first launch shot of the sequence is treated as the ignition phase of the launch. Sequences 2, 5, and 6 show that the exact detection of the boundaries between the phases of rocket launch events is not necessary in order to detect the event as a whole. In sequences 2 the beginning and end of the lift-off phases was detected incorrectly. In sequence 5 part of the ignition sequence was missed and in sequence 6 the detected lift-off phase ends prematurely. In sequence 3a a false rocket launch was detected for two reasons, 1) skin color was mistaken for exhaust (possibly because the training set for exhaust did not contain negative examples showing human skin), and 2) the motion estimation failed (largely due to the multiple motions of the people in the sequence, which violates the assumption of a uniform background motion).

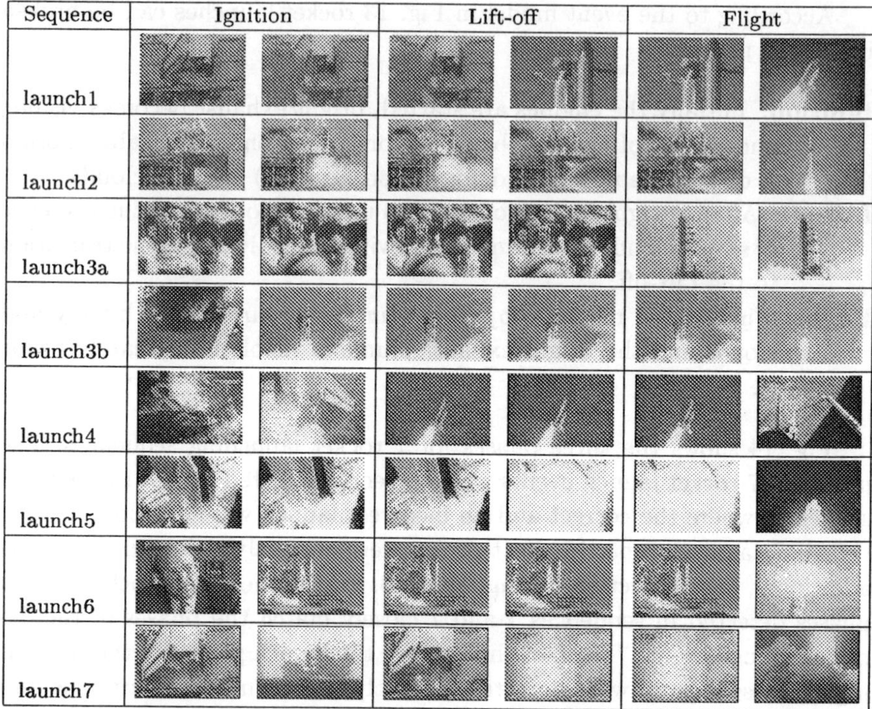

Fig. 14. The detected phases of 7 rocket launch events.

However, the correct launch event was still detected, albeit with a slightly shortened "ignition" phase, as shown in sequence 3b in Fig. 14.

This indicates that the detection of rocket launches is rather straight forward when simple motion information is combined with image regions are categorized into sky, cloud, exhaust and human-made/structured object regions. Humans quickly associate the presence of exhaust below an ascending object surrounded by sky or clouds to infer a rocket launch, even from still images. A missing launch phase or the imprecise detection of its beginning or endpoints can be compensated for by the information gathered in the other phases.

Further redundancy in rocket launch events is added when a number of sources are edited into a single launch sequence. The relatively short launch process is often artificially stretched by (a) showing a number of different views of the same visual event, (b) showing parts of the event in slow motion, or (c) repeating shots. Not only can the well developed human visual recognition system easily cope with these distortions but slight challenges to our pattern detection abilities are even considered good film-making practice and often make simple events more interesting to watch.

The three presented events show that some classes of events are sufficiently described by their approximate motion characteristics (e.g., landing events), while others are robustly described by the spatial relationships between a number of key object classes and very simple motion information (e.g., rocket launches), and yet others require a mix of both, as in the case of hunts in wildlife documentaries. The presented approach, thus, offers a simple framework for the detection of events with typical spatial and temporal characteristics, and can easily and quickly be adapted to capture the characteristics of a wide range of video events. The proposed automatic extraction of spatial and temporal primitives provides a solid basis for the description of a wide range of such events.

4. Summary and Discussion

In this chapter, we have presented a new computational method and a number of enabling algorithmic components for automatic event detection in video and applied it to detect hunts in wildlife documentaries. Our experimental results have verified the effectiveness of the proposed algorithm. The developed method decomposes the task of extracting semantic events into three stages where visual information is analyzed and abstracted. The first stage extracts low-level features and is entirely domain-independent. The second stage analyzes the extracted low-level features and generates intermediate-level descriptors some of which may be domain-specific. In this stage, shots are summarized in terms of both domain-independent and domain-specific descriptors. To generate the shot summaries, regions of interest are detected, verified and tracked. The third and final stage is domain-specific. Rules are deduced from specific domains and an inference model is built based on the established rules. In other words, each lower stage encapsulates low-level visual processing from the higher stages. Therefore, the processes in the higher stages can be stable and relatively independent of any potential detail changes in the lower level modules. In order to detect different events, (a) the object classifier may need to be adjusted in the second stage of our method and (b) a new set of rules describing and defining the event are needed in the third stage. The proposed algorithm also provides several reusable algorithmic components. In fact, the extracted low-level texture and color features are entirely domain independent since many objects have texture and color signatures. The neural network used for image region classification can be easily re-configured or extended to handle other types of objects [13]. The robust statistical estimation based object tracking method has already been used in different applications and its robustness and simplicity are verified in experiments repeatedly [26].

We would like to point out that the proposed algorithm detects hunt events by detecting spatial-temporal phenomena which are physically associated with a hunt event in nature. More precisely, the physical phenomenon which we attempt to capture is the combination of the presence of animals in space and their movement patterns in time. This is in contrast to many existing event detection methods which detect events by detecting artificial post-production editing patterns or other artifacts. The drawbacks of detecting specific editing patterns or other artifacts are that those patterns are often content provider dependent and it is difficult, if not impossible, to modify the detection methods and apply them to the detection of other events. It is also important to point out that our algorithm solves a practical problem and the solution is needed in the real world. In the wildlife video tapes which we obtained, the speech from the audio track and the text from the close-caption are loosely correlated with the visual footage. It is therefore unlikely that the hunt segments may be accurately located by analyzing the audio track and close-caption. In other words, given the existing wildlife tapes, a visual-information-based detection algorithm is needed to locate the hunt segments otherwise manual annotation is required. We believe the limitation to a specific domain, such as wildlife documentaries, does not limit our approach significantly, since such high-level information is readily available from the content provider.

The use of audio information represents one important difference to related work [17] that proposes a two level method using "Multijects" to combine low-level feature information directly. Two other differences are (1) the simplicity of the visual features they use to represent video frames, and (2) their use of adaptive components (Hidden Markov Models) to learn the entire event from examples. At present the authors only use color histograms and color histogram differences of entire frames to represent the video content. In contrast, our approach captures information on what is moving, where and how based on a richer analysis using color, texture, and motion. Although adaptive components are desirable for a general event detection scheme, they tend to reduce the transparency of the event inference process. Seeing that many events are easily described in terms of intermediate object and motion descriptors, we decided to describe and design the event inference processes manually.

An immediate focus of future work is to develop a richer set of intermediate-level descriptors for generating shot summaries. The purpose of developing the descriptors is to provide a wider coverage over different domains and events so that fewer domain-specific descriptors need to be added in new applications. Other future work is to improve the procedure which detects and tracks regions of interest. It would also be interesting to investigate the usefulness of learning techniques for the event inference engine. One goal might be the automatic tuning of the performance of the event inference module.

Finally, we would like to point out that since the submission of this article we have successfully applied the proposed method to two other events, namely landings and rocket launches in unconstrained videos [15]. As described in this article the only changes necessary to handle these new events were the classifier and the event inference module. The absence of shape based object information in our method allows us to detect landing events independent of the exact identity of the landing object (aircraft, bird, space shuttle, etc.) or the exact type of rocket, or launch pad. It is not surprising that approximate object motion information can aid object recognition and the interpretation of events in which these objects are involved.

References

1. F. Arman, R. Depommier, A. Hsu, and M.-Y. Chiu, "Content-based Browsing of Video Sequences," in proceedings of *ACM Multimedia*, pp. 97-103, 1994.
2. B.B. Chaudhuri, N. Sarkar, and P. Kundu, "Improved Fractal Geometry Based Texture Segmentation Technique," in proceedings of *IEE*, part E, vol. 140, pp. 233-241, 1993.
3. R.W. Conners, C.A. Harlow, "A Theoretical Comparison of Texture Algorithms," in *IEEE Transactions on Pattern Analysis and Machine Intelligence*, vol. 2, no 3, pp. 204-222, 1980.
4. J.D. Courtney, "Automatic Video Indexing via Object Motion Analysis," in proceedings of *Pattern Recognition*, vol. 30, no. 4, pp. 607-626, 1997.
5. G. Cybenko, "Approximation by Superposition of Sigmoidal Function," *Mathematics of Control, Signals, and Systems*, Chapter 2, pp. 303-314, 1989.
6. A. Del Bimbo, E. Vicario, D. Zingoni, "A Spatial Logic for Symbolic Descrip-

234

tion of Image Contents," in *Journal of Visual Languages and Computing*, vol. 5, pp. 267-286, 1994.

7. Y. Deng and B.S. Manjunath, "Content-base Search of Video Using Color, Texture, and Motion," in proceedings of *IEEE International Conference on Image Processing*, Vol. 2, pp. 534-537, 1998.

8. N. Dimitrova and F. Golshani, "Motion Recovery for Video Content Classification," in *ACM Transactions on Information Systems*, vol. 13, no 4, pp 408-439, 1995.

9. P. England, R.B. Allen, M. Sullivan, and A. Heybey, "I/Browse: The Bellcore Video Library Toolkit," in proceedings of *SPIE Storage and Retrieval for Image and Video Databases*, pp. 254-264, 1996.

10. S. Fahlman, "Faster-Learning Variations on Back-Propagation: An Empirical Study," in proceedings of *Connectionist Models Summer School*, Morgan Kaufmann, 1988.

11. I. Fogel and D. Sagi, "Gabor Filters as Texture Discriminator," in *Journal of Biological Cybernetics*, vol. 61, pp. 103-113, 1989.

12. D. Gabor, "Theory of communication," in *Journal of IEE*, vol. 93, pp. 429-457, 1946.

13. N. Haering, Z. Myles, and N. da Vitoria Lobo, "Locating Deciduous Trees," in proceedings of *IEEE Workshop on Content-based Access of Image and Video Libraries*, pp. 18-25, 1997.

14. N. Haering and N. da Vitoria Lobo, "Features and Classification Methods to Locate Deciduous Trees in Images," in *Journal of Computer Vision and Image Understanding*, 1999.

15. N. Haering, "A Framework for the Design of Event Detectors," Ph.D. thesis, University of Central Florida CS-TR-99-10, 1999.

16. R.M. Haralick, K. Shanmugam, and I. Dinstein, "Textural Features for Image Classification," in *IEEE Transactions Systems Man and Cybernetics*, vol. 3, no 6, pp. 610-621, 1973.

17. M.R. Naphade, T. Kristjansson, T.S. Huang, Probabilistic Multimedia Objects (MULTIJECTS): A Novel Approach to Video Indexing and Retrieval in Multimedia Systems," in proceedings of *IEEE International Conference on Image Processing*, Vol. 3, pp. 536-540, 1998.

18. S.S. Intille, "Tracking Using a Local Closed-World Assumption: Tracking in the Football Domain," *Master Thesis, M.I.T. Media Lab*, 1994.

19. G. Iyengar and A. Lippman, "Models for Automatic Classification of Video Sequences", in proceedings of *SPIE Storage and Retrieval for Image and Video Databases*, pp. 216-227, 1997.

20. T. Kawashima, K. Tateyama, T. Iijima, and Y. Aoki, "Indexing of Baseball Telecast for Content-based Video Retrieval," in proceedings of *IEEE International Conference on Image Processing*, pp. 871-875, 1998.

21. J.M. Keller and S. Chen, "Texture Description and Segmentation through Fractal Geometry," in *Journal of Computer Vision, Graphics and Image Processing*, vol. 45, pp. 150-166, 1989.

22. R.L. Lagendijk, A. Hanjalic, M. Ceccarelli, M. Soletic, and E. Persoon, "Visual Search in a SMASH System", in proceedings of *IEEE International Conference on Image Processing*, pp. 671-674, 1997.

23. B.S. Manjunath and W. Ma, "Texture Features for Browsing and Retrieval of Image Data," in *IEEE Transactions on Pattern Analysis and Machine Intelligence*, vol. 18, no. 8, pp. 837-859, 1996.

24. S. Peleg, J. Naor, R. Hartley, and D. Avnir, "Multiple Resolution Texture Analysis and Classification," in *IEEE Transactions on Pattern Analysis and Machine Intelligence*, vol. 6, no 4, pp. 518-523, 1984.

25. A.P. Pentland, "Fractal-based Description of Natural Scenes," in *IEEE Transactions on Pattern Analysis and Machine Intelligence*, vol. 6, no 6, pp. 661-674, 1984.

26. R.J. Qian, M.I. Sezan and K.E. Matthews, "A Robust Real-Time Face Tracking Algorithm", in proceedings of *IEEE International Conference on Image Processing*, pp. 131-135, 1998.

27. D. Saur, Y.-P. Tan, S.R. Kularni, and P.J. Ramadge, "Automated Analysis and Annotation of Basketball Video," in proceedings of *SPIE Storage and Retrieval for Image and Video Databases*, pp. 176-187, 1997.

28. M. Smith and T. Kanade, "Video Skimming for Quick Browsing Based on Audio and Image Characterization," *CMU Computer Science Department Technical Report CMU CS-95-186*, 1995.

29. N. Vasconcelos and A. Lippman, "A Bayesian Framework for Semantic Content Characterization," in proceedings of *IEEE Computer Vision and Pattern Recognition*, pp. 566-571, 1998.

30. J.S. Weszka, C.R. Dyer, and A. Rosenfeld, "A Comparative Study of Texture measures for Terrain Classification," in *IEEE Transactions on Systems Man and Cybernetics*, vol. 6, no 4, pp. 269-285, 1976.

31. R.R. Wilcox, *Introduction to Robust Estimation and Hypothesis Testing*, Statistical Modeling and Decision Science Series, Academic Press, 1997.

32. M. Yeung, and B.-L. Yeo, "Video Visualization for Compact Presentation and Fast Browsing of Pictorial Content," in *IEEE Transactions on Circuits and Systems for Video Technology*, vol. 7, no 5, pp. 771-785, 1996.

33. D. Yow, B.L.Yeo, M. Yeung, and G. Liu, "Analysis and Presentation of Soccer Highlights from Digital Video," in proceedings of *Asian Conference on Computer Vision*, 1995.

34. H.J. Zhang, S.W. Smoliar, and J.H. Wu, "Content-Based Video Browsing Tools," in proceedings of *SPIE Storage and Retrieval for Image and Video Databases*, pp. 389-398, 1995.

35. H.J. Zhang, J.Y.A. Wang, and Y. Altunbasak, "Content-Based Video Retrieval and Compression: A Unified Solution," in proceedings of *IEEE International Conference on Image Processing*, Vol. 1, pp. 13-16, 1997.

36. D. Zhong and S.-F. Chang, "Spatio-Temporal Video Search Using the Object Based Video Representation," in proceedings of *IEEE International Conference on Image Processing*, Vol. 1, pp. 21-24, 1998.

22 R.L. Lagendijk, A. Hanjalic, M. Ceccarelli, M. Soucic, and E. Petkovic, "Visual Search in a SMASH System", in proceedings of IEEE International Conference on Image Processing, pp. 611-671, 1997.

23 B.S. Manjunath and W. Ma, "Texture Features for Browsing and Retrieval of Image Data," in IEEE Transactions on Pattern Analysis and Machine Intelligence, vol. 18, no. 8, pp. 837-842, 1996.

24 S. Peleg, J. Naor, R. Hartley, and D. Avnir, "Multiple Resolution Texture Analysis and Classification," in IEEE Transactions on Pattern Analysis and Machine Intelligence, vol. 6, no 4, pp. 518-523, 1984.

25 A.P. Pentland, "Fractal-based Description of Natural Scenes," in IEEE Transactions on Pattern Analysis and Machine Intelligence, vol. 6, no 6, pp. 661-674, 1984.

26 J. Kim, M. Sorand, K.R. Matthews, "A Robust Real Time Face Tracking Algorithm," in proceedings of IEEE International Conference on Image Processing, pp. 151-156, 1998.

27 Sun, Y.P. Tan, N.C. Kuhn, and T. Banada, "Automated Analysis and Annotation of Basketball Video," in proceedings of SPIE Storage and Retrieval for Image and Video Database, pp. 176-187, 1997.

28 M. Smith and T. Kanade, "Video Skimming for Quick Browsing based on Audio and Image Characterization," CMU Computer Science Department Technical Report CMU-CS-95-186, 1995.

29 N. Vasconcelos and A. Lippman, "A Bayesian Framework for Semantic Content Characterization," in proceedings of IEEE Computer Vision and Pattern Recognition, pp. 566-571, 1998.

30 J.S. Weszka, C.R. Dyer, and A. Rosenfeld, "A Comparative Study of Texture measures for Terrain Classification," in IEEE Transactions on Systems Man and Cybernetics, vol. 9, no 4, pp. 269-586, 1977.

31 P. Winn, Introduction to the Phase Contrast Microscope, Unilever Research, McCrone Research and Ceruleum Research Institute, Academic Press, 1991.

32 M. Young, and R.L. Van VdMa, "Visualization for Computer Presentation and Fast Browsing of Pictorial Content," in IEEE Transactions on Graphics and Systems for Video Techniques, vol. 7, no 5, pp. 771-778, 1996.

33 M. Yow, B.L. Yeo, M. Yeung, and G. Liu, "Analysis and Presentation of Soccer Highlights from Digital Video," in proceedings of Asian Conference on Computer Vision, 1995.

34 H.J. Zhang, S.W. Smoliar, and J.H. Wu, "Content-Based Video Browsing Tools," in proceedings of SPIE Storage and Retrieval for Image and Video Databases pp. 389-398, 1994.

35 H.J. Zhang, J.Y.A. Wang, and Y. Altunbasak, "Content-Based Video Retrieval and Compression: A Unified Solution," in proceedings of IEEE International Conference on Image Processing, Vol. 1, pp. 13-16, 1997.

36 D. Zhong and S.-F. Chang, "Spatio-Temporal Video Search Using the Object Based Video Representation," in proceedings of IEEE International Conference on Image Processing, Vol. 1, pp. 21-24, 1998.

Robust Video Transmission for Feedback Channels

Steven D. Blostein and Qianfu Jiang
Department of Electrical and Computer Engineering
Queen's University
Kingston, Ontario
Canada K7L 3N6

10.1 Introduction

There has been a very large amount of activity in the development of source coding algorithms for video compression. We do not attempt to list these here, but special issues devoted to this topic such as [MOB 1999] are plentiful. A distinctive aspect of low-bit rate video compression is the requirement for low error rates, while at the same time, a tolerance for loss. Delay requirements are application-specific ranging from low-delay(for videoconferencing) to high-delay (for broadcast). Although the number of compression methods proposed has been nearly limitless, the impact of the networks within which the compression takes place has been given much less attention.

This chapter tries to fill in the gap between standardization in video compression, which has spanned over two decades, and the rise of new delivery mechanisms involving packet-based networks over wireless channels that have neither a guaranteed delivery time or packet-error-rate. The chapter will focus on extending widely-adopted motion-compensated video compression methods by taking into account delayed channel feedback information obtained from network protocols. In particular, the chapter advocates a standards-extension whereby the source coder adapts itself to an error-prone channel. This work builds upon previous research described in [STEI 1997], as well as analyzes coding performance in unrealible channels.

By way of introduction, present-day video coding techniques are very efficient in compressing data, but they are also highly sensitive to transmission errors. To exploit existing temporal redundancy, motion-compensated predictive coding is used, where the current frame is coded as a difference signal with respect to a reference frame. Usually the previously reconstructed frame serves as the reference frame, both at the transmitter and the receiver.

When there are channel errors present in the receiver's reference frame, the current frame cannot be correctly reconstructed, because the difference signal is calculated from the uncorrupted transmitter reference. Errors occurring in one frame will therefore propagate to the following frames. If motion compensation is used in prediction, errors occurring in one spatial position can propagate to other spatial positions over time in the reconstructed image sequence. This problem becomes severe for video transmission over wireless channels which have higher error rate than wireline channels. Fig. 10.1 shows an example of spatial-temporal error propagation caused by an error in a row of blocks in motion-compensated prediction decoding. The shaded areas denote corrupted pixels in three successive frames.

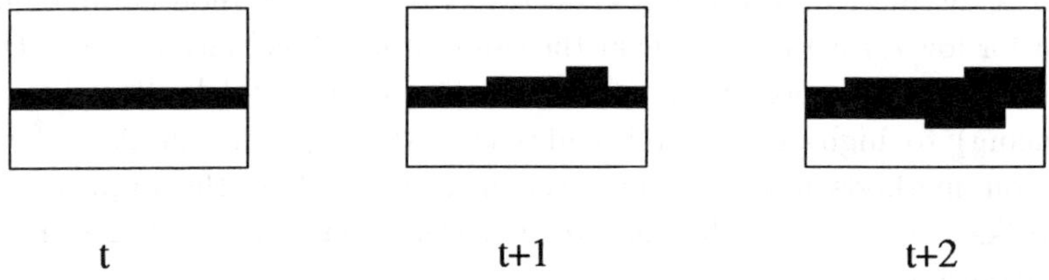

Fig. 10.1 An example of spatial-temporal error propagation in motion-compensated prediction decoding.

Another error-sensitive characteristic of video coding is that variable-length coding (VLC) is commonly used to further compact the quantizer output. In VLC, a single bit error can cause the decoder to lose synchronization and make the bit stream undecodable. If remedial measures are not taken, the whole image sequence could be corrupted.

Although channel codes can correct a certain number of errors, such coding may be too costly to guarantee error-free video bit streams at the receiver due to the high rate requirements of video transmission. Unlike data, video can tolerate some errors. The real problem is that small errors may propagate and accumulate into annoying distortions in conventional motion-compensated predictive decoding.

To stop error propagation, a common technique [MPEG 1994] is to periodically switch from motion-compensated predictive coding to intra-frame coding to refresh the coder. Unfortunately intra-frame coding typically requires many more bits than inter-frame coding because temporal correlation is not exploited. This makes frequent intra-frame refreshing very expensive.

In the presence of a feedback channel with the error detection capability (which would typically include header information, synchronization code bits, forward error correction code code, etc.), the locations of the corrupted regions can be detected and sent back to the transmitter. The corresponding lost data can then be retransmitted [LIN 1984]. However, retransmission causes additional delay which is intolerable in real-time applications such as interactive video and live broadcasting, especially for channels with large transmission delay.

Recently, partial intra-frame refreshing has been proposed to address the problem of high cost intra-coding [STEI 1997]. In [STEI 1997], fed back error locations are used by the transmitter to reconstruct the spatial-temporal error propagation in the decoding process at the receiver. The regions in the current frame affected by the transmission errors in the previous frames are determined. To avoid retransmission and to reduce bit rate, intra-coding is only performed in regions with severe visual distortion while other regions in the current frame are inter-frame coded.

In this chapter, we present and quantitatively analyze a novel coding mode for video transmission over unreliable channels which we denote as transmitter-receiver-identical-reference-frame (TRIRF) based coding. TRIRF was recently proposed in [JIAN 1999], and is elaborated upon and analyzed in the following sections. This coding uses motion estimation and compensation on a new type of reference frame, called the TRIRF-frame, which is identical both at the receiver and the transmitter and is constructed based on correctly received data, identified by a feedback channel. In Section 10.2, the construction of the TRIRF-frame is described. In Section 10.3, we propose an adaptation layer that enables the variable-length-coded video bit stream to be transmitted as fixed-length packets, such as encountered in ATM netwroks. This *packetization* scheme enables the decoder to quickly regain synchronization with the encoder. In Section 10.4, experiments show that TRIRF-frame coding effectively reduces transmission error propagation and reduces bit rates compared to intra-frame coding. Section 10.5 presents an analysis of TRIRF coding peformance in the presence of packet errors. For the sake of tractability of the analysis, variable length packets are assumed, i.e., each packet contains an integer number of encoded image blocks, such as might be encountered in IP networks.

10.2 TRIRF-frame Coding

10.2.1 *Construction of the TRIRF-frame*

As mentioned in the introduction, the receiver reference frame differs from the transmitter reference frame when channel errors occur and generates distortion propagation in conventional motion-compensated prediction. Instead of using the previous frame as a reference for motion estimation and compensation, we propose to construct a new type of reference frame, the TRIRF-frame, which is dynamically kept identical at both sides even when channel errors occur. To maximize correlation between the TRIRF-frame and the current frame, the TRIRF-frame is updated as soon as correctly received data is available. The result is an improved trade-off between error resilience and compression efficiency.

There are two basic assumptions required for TRIRF-frame construction: (1) The existence of a feedback channel and that error feedback is received at the transmitter without loss. Since only a few bits are needed to represent the feedback information, we assume that there is enough error protection for error free feedback. (2) We assume that the receiver is capable of detecting transmission errors and providing feedback of the locations of the corrupted regions in the reconstructed image. In practice, the feedback could be negative acknowledgment (NACK) or positive acknowledgment (ACK) messages which specify the locations of the regions (blocks) which are either corrupted or correctly received.

The process of TRIRF-frame construction is illustrated in Fig. 10.2, where the frames are represented by line segments. Suppose the feedback information about frame $t - t_d$ arrives before frame t is encoded, where t_d is the round trip delay, (transmission delay plus coding delay) expressed in terms of number of frames. The correctly received regions then replace the corresponding spatial regions in the TRIRF-frame. The other regions in the TRIRF-frame remain as before. Once the TRIRF-frame is updated, motion estimation and compensation will be performed on the TRIRF-frame, instead of on frame *t-1* as in conventional motion-compensated. The decoder updates its TRIRF-frame in identical fashion before decoding frame *t*.

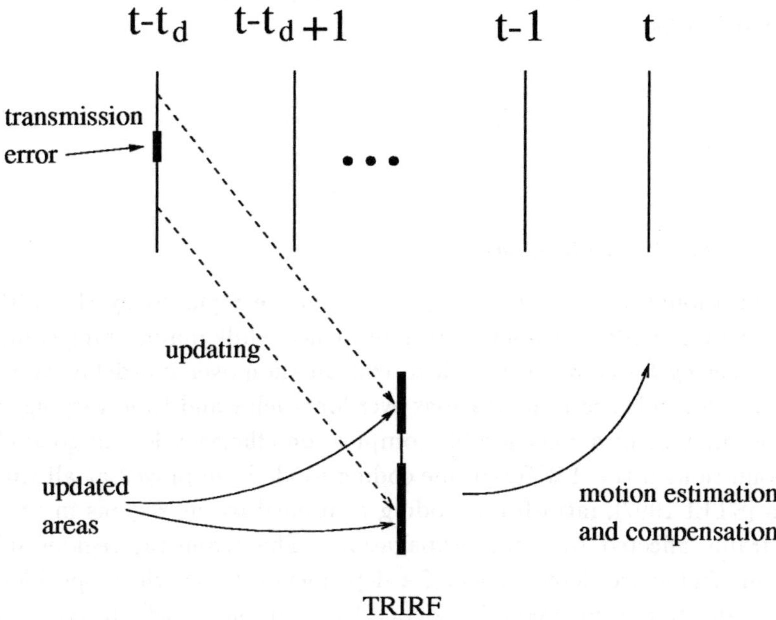

Fig. 10.2   TRIRF-frame updating and motion estimation and compensation for frame *t*.

Since motion-compensated prediction is based on TRIRF-frame at both transmitter and receiver, synchronization between both sides is maintained. Transmission errors occurring in one frame will not propagate to subsequent frames.

The efficiency of the TRIRF-frame based motion-compensated prediction is determined by the amount of correlation between the TRIRF-frame and the current frame, which depends on the transmission delay t_d, the channel conditions and the video content. Since TRIRF-frame coding exploits some degree of temporal redundancy, the compression efficiency would normally be higher than intra-frame coding. In short, the TRIRF-frame coding may achieve a better trade-off between compression efficiency and error resilience than conventional inter-frame coding and intra-frame coding. An analysis of the efficiency of the TRIRF-frame coding will be presented in Section 10.5.

As a disadvantage, TRIRF-frame coding requires storing $t_d + 1$ frames. To save memory in an implementation, some frames can be stored in compressed form and a separate decoder can be used to obtain TRIRF reconstructed blocks.

10.2.2 *Multi-Mode Coding*

The traditional inter-frame coding mode can be replaced by the TRIRF-frame coding mode to enhance error resilience while maintaining compression efficiency for slow-motion video transmission over low-delay channels. However, for video communications over long-delay and time-varying channels, we may incur a considerable compression efficiency loss in good channel conditions if the TRIRF-frame coding mode is employed at all times.

In [STEI 1997], intra-frame coding is applied to the regions in the current frame affected by error propagation. The erroneous regions in the previous frame are detected using a dependency table which specifies the spatial and temporal prediction dependency among blocks in consecutive frames. Using this table lookup, the intra-refresh can be selectively applied [STEI 1997].

We adopt a similar scheme for video transmission over long-delay and time-varying channels. However, while [STEI 1997] switches to intra-frame coding for damaged areas, we propose to update the TRIRF-frame and maintain inter-frame coding. Fig. 10.3 shows the selection process between conventional inter-frame coding and the TRIRF-frame coding. When the feedback for frame $t - t_d$ arrives at the transmitter, the affected areas in frame *t-1* are determined based on motion information. The unaffected areas in frame *t-1* are assumed error-free and serve as the reference for conventional inter-frame motion estimation and compensation. Less efficient TRIRF-frame coding is only activated when the conventional inter-frame motion estimation involves regions affected by errors.

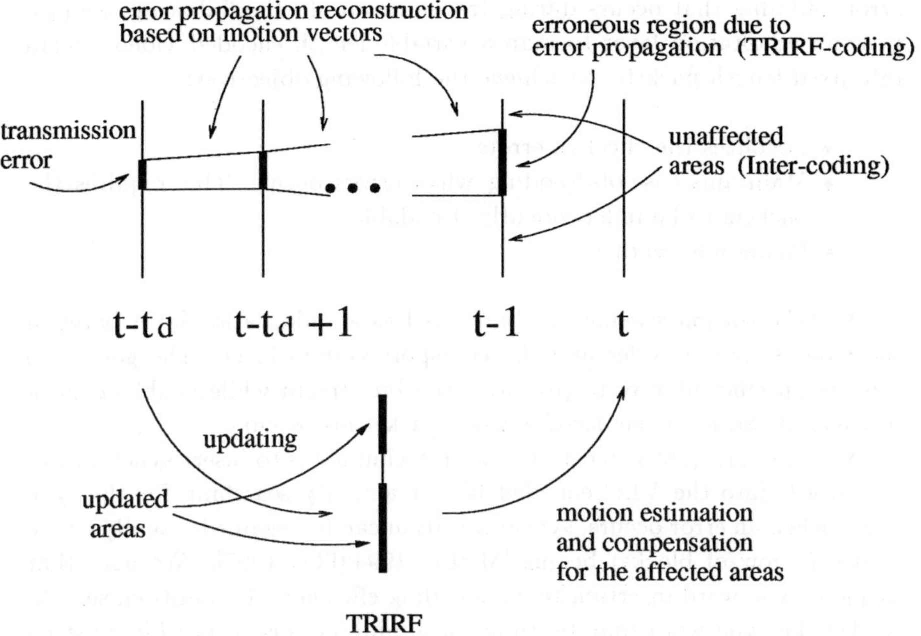

Fig. 10.3   Hybrid inter-frame/TRIRF-frame coding of frame t based on error propagation reconstruction.

10.3   Video Stream Packetization

10.3.1   *Basic Considerations*

Due to variable-length compaction of video data, transmission errors cause the decoder to lose synchronization with the encoder. Directly transmitting the bit stream over noisy channels would have very poor error resilience. By segmenting the continuous bit stream into packets, it is possible to confine the errors to lie within a damaged packet and prevent propagation into subsequent packets.

The video data may be segmented into either *variable-length* or *fixed-length* packets. Variable packet lengths as encountered in IP networks permit a straightforward image block-to-packet mapping of the video data avoiding catastrophic error propagation across blocks. On the other hand, fixed-length packets simplify the design of the transport system layer and error handling that occurs during transmission. In the following, we propose an adaptation layer to map a variable-length encoded video stream into fixed length packets, to achieve the following objectives:

- Localizes the effect of errors.
- Maintains ease-of-decoding when errors occur. This requires the packets to be independently decodable.
- Incurs low overhead.

A packetization scheme can be viewed as an adaptation layer between the video source encoder and the transport system layer. The goal is to provide an efficient way to packetize the bit stream while enabling quick resynchronization of the decoder when packet loss occurs.

A commonly used resynchronization technique is to insert synchronization words into the VLC encoded bit stream. By searching for the sync words when an error occurs, synchronization can be regained, usually where a slice (a row of blocks) begins [MPEG 1994][ITU 1995]. We note that frequent sync word insertion reduces coding efficiency. In addition, searching for the sync word may be time consuming because every bit must be checked.

We propose an alternative resynchronization method that exploits packetization and is consistent with the TRIRF feedback strategy. We record the position of the first bit of the first macroblock (MB boundary) in the packet header. This MB boundary pointer usually needs fewer bits than a sync word and allows a macroblock to span over consecutive packets. There are no unused bits in a packet. (If variable-length packets are used, packetization is performed by packing the bit stream section between macroblock boundaries.) Including the resynchronization information in the packet header provides the decoder with synchronization points spaced almost evenly in the bit stream. This allows for improved error localization in high-activity areas which are usually visually important, because the active areas usually require more bits to be encoded than low-activity areas. Fig. 10.4 shows an example of two consecutive packets, where the last macroblock of the previous packet is stored in both packets.

Encoder parameters such as frame coding mode (INTRA or INTER) and quantization step size, are also included in the header. To allow for correct reconstruction, the absolute macroblock number of the first macroblock in the packet is also included.

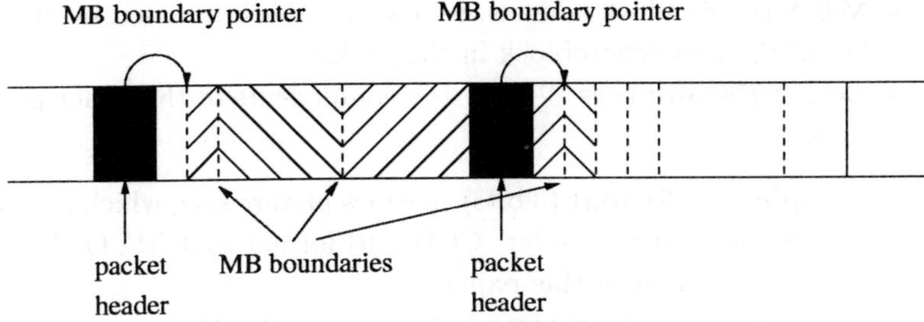

Fig. 10.4   Fixed-length packetization using boundary pointers

10.3.2 *Packet Header Specification*

The packet header structure is illustrated in Fig. 10.5. The fields in the header have the following meanings:

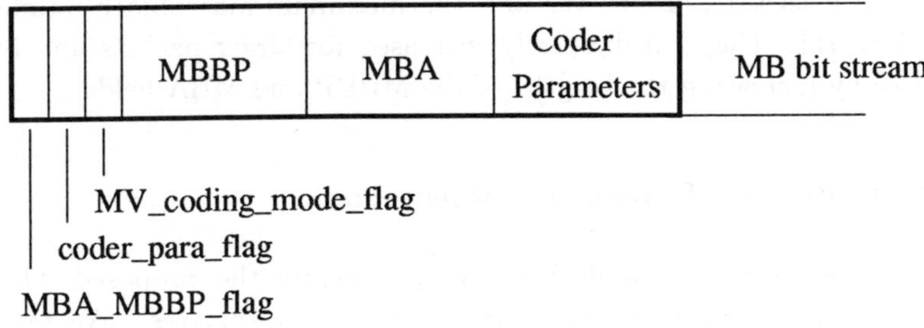

Fig. 10.5   Video adaptation header format

- **MBA_MBBP_flag** (1 bit) 1 indicates the presence of the MBA and MBBP fields.
- **coder_para_flag** (1 bit) 1 indicates the presence of the coder parameter field.
- **MV_coding_mode_flag** (1 bit) 1 indicates the motion vectors of the first macroblock are encoded differentially. 0 indicates the MVs are encoded independently.
- **MBBP** (macroblock boundary pointer, 9 bits) specifies the position of the boundary of the first macroblock in the packet. Since a macroblock is allowed to span over consecutive packets to reduce overhead of fixed-length packetization, the first few bits may contain the data of the last macroblock of the previous packet.

- **MBA** (macroblock address, 9 bits) the absolute macroblock number of the first macroblock in the packet.
- **Coder Parameters** (9 bits) the components of the coder parameters are:

  - **picture_format** (3 bits) specifies picture size, which is defined by the source encoder. CCIR 601 format (SQCIF, QCIF, CIF, etc.) is used in this paper.
  - **picture_coding_type** (1 bit) 1 indicates the current frame is INTER-coded. 0 indicates the current frame is INTRA-coded.
  - **quantization parameter** (5 bits) specifies the quantization step size.

The three 1-bit flags provide an easy way to reduce overhead when small packets (e.g. ATM cells) are adopted. Currently, the maximum length of a packet is $2^9 = 512$ and the maximum macroblock number is $2^9 - 1 = 511$. They can be easily increased for larger packets and larger pictures by increasing the lengths of the MBBP and MBA fields.

10.4   Coding Performance Comparisons

Using software codec simulations, we investigate the proposed TRIRF-frame coding performance as compared to its alternatives. We test the performance of the multi-mode coding scheme presented in Section 10.2.2 in a variety of conditions and compare to that in [STEI 1997]. The packetization scheme described in Section 10.3 is used.

Generally there are three possible scenarios regarding unsuccessful delivery of a packet: (1) The packet is lost; (2) There are uncorrectable errors in the packet; (3) The packet is received beyond the specified time limit. In all three cases, the packet is considered lost. We use a uniform packet loss model to describe packet transmission. In this model, every packet has the same probability of being lost, denoted by the packet loss rate (PLR).

Two video bit-stream codecs based on the two schemes described in Section 10.2.2 were implemented in software and compared. The basic coding elements (motion estimation and compensation, transform coding, quantization and entropy coding) are similar to the video coding standard H.263 [ITU 1995]. One codec, based on [STEI 1997], is denoted by ST97 in the simulation results. The other codec, based on the proposed TRIRF-frame coding, is denoted by TRIRF. For error concealment, **both decoders** discard the damaged blocks and replace them with the corresponding data from the previously reconstructed frame. The receiver sends back the block identification number of the corrupted regions as the feedback information.

Fig. 10.6 **Sample image frames from four test sequences, clockwise from upper left corner: Carphone frame 209, Miss America frame 48, Foreman frame 128, and Salesman frame 18.**

Standard test sequences in CCIR 601 QCIF (176×144 resolution) format were used (see Fig. 10.6). The original frame rate is 30 frames/sec. The sequences were coded at a frame rate of 10 frames/sec, which means that for every three frames in the original sequence one frame was encoded. Twenty-five Monte-Carlo simulations were run on each test sequence for different random bit error sequences. We assume a round-trip frame delay of $t_d = 3$ (*encoded frames*). Tables 10.1 and 10.2 show the averaged performance comparison of the test sequences for the PLR's of 10^{-1} and 10^{-2} respectively.

Sequence	Lum-PSNR(dB)		Bitrate (kb ps)	
	TRIRF	ST97	TRIRF	ST97
Carphone	27.3	27.6	64.7	80.5
Foreman	23.7	24.3	87.5	102.1
Miss-Amer	34.9	34.6	17.8	26.3
Mthr-Dotr	31.1	31.2	28.2	42.9
Salesman	30.5	30.7	24.7	45.1
Suzie	29.0	29.5	41.3	47.7

Table 10.1   PSNR and bitrate comparisons averaged over the entire sequence. PLR = 10^{-1}, T_d = 300ms.

Sequence	Lum-PSNR(dB)		Bitrate (kb ps)	
	TRIRF	ST'97	TRIRF	ST'97
Carphone	31.3	31.4	59.4	61.3
Foreman	29.9	30.2	74.2	75.9
Miss-Amer	36.8	36.8	16.9	18.1
Mthr-Dotr	32.6	32.6	25.8	27.7
Salesman	31.5	31.6	22.7	25.4
Suzie	33.3	33.5	36.6	37.5

Table 10.2   PSNR and bitrate comparisons averaged over the entire sequence. PLR = 10^{-2}, T_d = 300ms.

Fig. 10.7 shows bit rate comparisons for the Mother- and-Daughter sequence for the same reconstruction quality, expressed in terms of peak signal-to-noise ratio (PSNR) in dB.

Fig. 10.8 shows the results for another sequence, Salesman. From Table 10.1, 10.2, Figs. 10.7 and 10.8, TRIRF-coding outperforms Intra-coding in coding efficiency, as predicted, although at a higher computational cost.

10.5   Efficiency Analysis of TRIRF Coding

The efficiency of TRIRF-frame coding is determined by the amount of correlation between the TRIRF-frame and the current frame, which depends on three factors: *the round trip delay t_d, the channel conditions and the video content*. Each of these factors is discussed briefly below:

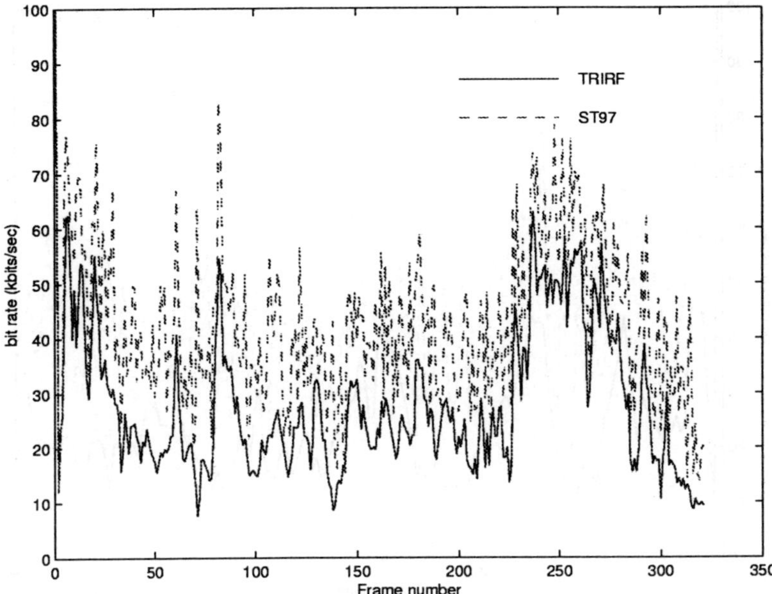

Fig. 10.7 Average frame bit rates for Mother-and-Daughter sequence. $(PLR = 10^{-1}, T_d = 300ms, PSNR = 31.1dB)$

- *Round trip delay t_d*. The TRIRF-frame contains regions from the reconstructed frames which are at least t_d frames old in time. The value t_d specifies the temporal gap between the current frame and the reference frame. Generally, as temporal redundancy decreases with increasing temporal gap, so does the coding efficiency decrease. An example is shown in Table 10.3, where the average rate of motion-compensated predictive coding of a block (luminance component plus motion vector) in frame 209 of the Carphone sequence, with respect to the temporal distance of prediction reference $t_d = 1\ to\ 5$, is given.

$t_d (frames)$	1	2	3	4	5
$Rate(bits/block)$	52.8	60.0	70.8	83.2	93.4

Table 10.3 Average rate (bits/block) of motion-compensated predictive coding (luminance component and motion vector) in frame 209 of Carphone The average rate of intra-coding of a block is 218.3 bits/block.

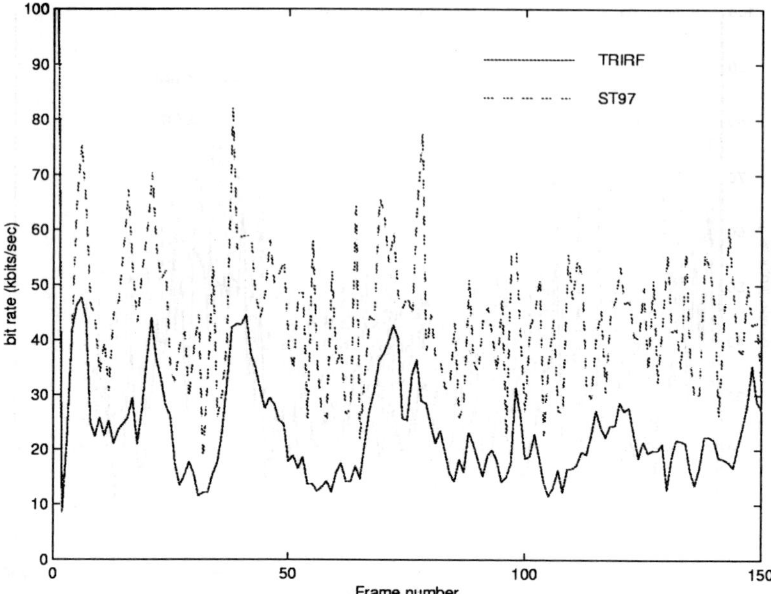

Fig. 10.8 Average frame bit rates for Salesman sequence. $(PLR = 10^{-1}, T_d = 300ms, PSNR = 30.5dB)$

- *Video content.* Scene content plays an important and complicated role in TRIRF-frame coding. Using frames older than *t-1* as a prediction reference generally results in higher bit rates. However, the rate increase is different for different sequences. For video sequences with small amounts of motion or regular (linear) motion, e.g. head and shoulder images in video phone and videoconference applications, the loss of coding efficiency may be quite small even for large delays. Table 10.4 shows another example, where the coding result of frame 48 of the Miss America sequence is given. The coding rate increase due to the round-trip delay is slower than that of Table 10.3, because the temporal correlation decrease is slower.

- *Channel conditions.* Channel conditions determine the proportion of the TRIRF-frame that requires updating. Perfect channel conditions allow a complete update by frame $t - t_d$. More channel errors can result in fewer TRIRF-frame updates. This in turn results in older content than frame $t - t_d$, reducing correlation and compression further.

$t_d(frames)$	1	2	3	4	5
$Rate(bits/block)$	10.9	12.8	13.3	13.5	13.8

Table 10.4 Average rate (bits/block) of motion-compensated predictive coding (luminance component and motion vector) in frame 48 of Miss-America. The average rate of intra-coding of a block is 78.2 bits/block.

In the following subsection, we analyze the coding efficiency of the TRIRF-frame coding using a statistical model for the video signals. In Section 10.5.1, we first investigate the problem of how the coding rate changes with respect to the round trip delay t_d and the content for error-free transmission. We then consider imperfect channel conditions in Section 10.5.2. Simulation results and analytical comparisons are given in Section 10.5.3.

10.5.1 *Error-Free Analysis*

10.5.1.1 *Problem formulation*

We assume block-based motion compensated predictive coding, in which the prediction errors of a block are DCT transformed, quantized with a step size of Q and then entropy coded. The analysis is also suitable for region-based prediction without major modification. Denote the block to be encoded in the current frame t as $I(t, \mathbf{p})$, where $\mathbf{p}$ is the position of the block. Denote the TRIRF-frame prediction of the current block, which is a block in the reconstructed frame $t - t_d$ with a displacement of $\mathbf{mv}$, as $\tilde{I}(t - t_d, \mathbf{p} - \mathbf{mv})$. Then the TRIRF-frame coding rate of block $\mathbf{p}$ can be expressed as

$$R_{trirf}(t_d, \mathbf{p}) = R\left(I(t, \mathbf{p}) - \tilde{I}(t - t_d, \mathbf{p} - \mathbf{mv}), Q\right) + R(\mathbf{mv}) \qquad (10.1)$$

where R() denotes a general rate function. The rate of a block consists of the rate of the motion compensated prediction errors $I(t, \mathbf{p}) - \tilde{I}(t - t_d, \mathbf{p} - \mathbf{mv})$ and the rate of the motion vector $\mathbf{mv}$.

The problem is then to derive an expression of the TRIRF-frame coding rate of the block $\mathbf{p}$ with respect to the round trip delay t_d and the video content.

252

10.5.1.2 *Rate computation for prediction errors*

Since variable length coding (VLC) is performed after quantizing the DCT transformed prediction errors, the entropy of the quantizer output is an appropriate measure of the coding rate of a block.

For high rate quantization, the quantizer output entropy can be approximated as [GRAY 1990]

$$H_Q = h(s) - \log_2 Q \tag{10.2}$$

where h(s) is the differential entropy of the input s. However, we are more interested in low rate coding where the above approximation is not valid. In the low rate case, the rate expression is much more complicated.

A model-based rate expression for directly quantized prediction errors is presented in [DUFA 1994]. In the following, a model-based analysis of the coding length of the DCT transformed prediction errors is performed and a block rate function is presented. The rate of the motion compensated prediction errors of a block is a function of the ratio of σ_e to Q, where σ_e is the standard deviation of the prediction errors within that block. Several other rate measures are also described in [WEBB 1997], [YANG 1997], and [RIBA 1996], all of which are functions of $\frac{\sigma_e}{Q}$. Indeed the transform coding rate of prediction errors is function of σ_e for a given Q, although the residual spatial redundancy and the distribution of the prediction errors also affects the rate. In this work, we use a function of $\frac{\sigma_e}{Q}$ as our DCT coding rate estimate, denoted by $F(\frac{\sigma_e}{Q})$, which could be one of those described in [DUFA 1994],[RIBA 1996]. This rate model is used in the experiments to be described later.

- Rate derivation of Laplacian model
  Without loss of generality, we denote the estimated transform-coded bit rate for an 8x8 motion-compensated prediction error block $\mathbf{b}$ as $\hat{R}_{res}(\mathbf{b})$. The 8x8 two-dimensional DCT coefficients of $\mathbf{b}$ is given by

$$\mathbf{C} = \mathbf{A}\mathbf{b}\mathbf{A}^{\mathbf{T}} \tag{10.3}$$

  where $\mathbf{A}$ is the DCT basis vector matrix and T denotes transposition.
  Assume the 8x8 error block can be modeled by a stationary sepa-

rable first-order Markov random field with the covariance function

$$r(m, n) = \sigma_e^2 \rho^m \rho^n \tag{10.4}$$

Then the variances of the DCT coefficients are [JAIN 1989]

$$\sigma^2(m, n) = \left[\mathbf{A}\mathbf{R}\mathbf{A}^T\right]_{m,m} \left[\mathbf{A}\mathbf{R}\mathbf{A}^T\right]_{n,n} \tag{10.5}$$

where

$$\mathbf{R} = \sigma_e^2 \begin{bmatrix} 1 & \rho & \rho^2 & \cdots & \rho^7 \\ \rho & 1 & \rho & \cdots & \rho^6 \\ \vdots & \vdots & \vdots & \ddots & \vdots \\ \rho^7 & \rho^6 & \rho^5 & \cdots & 1 \end{bmatrix} \tag{10.6}$$

It has been shown in [BELL 1992] [SMOO 1996] that the statistics of the DCT coefficients of the motion-compensated prediction errors are well approximated by a Laplacian pdf. Assume the quantizer has quantization step size Q and dead zone dz. Given the variance of the DCT coefficient c(m,n), $\sigma_{m,n}^2$, the entropy of quantized c(m,n) in (5) can be derived as

$$\begin{aligned} H_q(m, n) &= -(1 - \alpha_1) \log_2(1 - \alpha_1) - \alpha_1 \left[\log_2 \alpha_1 (1 - \alpha)\right. \\ &\quad + \left. \frac{\alpha}{1 - \alpha} \log_2 \alpha - 1\right] \end{aligned} \tag{10.7}$$

where $\alpha = e^{-\sqrt{2}Q/\sigma_{m,n}}$, $\alpha_1 = e^{-\sqrt{2}(Q+dz)/\sigma_{m,n}}$.
Finally, based on the decorrelation property of DCT, the estimate of the coding rate for error block $\mathbf{b}_i$ is given by

$$R_{est}(\mathbf{b}_i) = \sum_{m=1}^{8} \sum_{n=1}^{8} H_q(m, n) \tag{10.8}$$

For the case of motion-compensated interframe coding with frame delay t_d, we propose to use a Markov model to quantify the correlation between the projections of a moving object or the background onto the 2-D image plane. The projections form a sequence of corresponding blocks in the video frames, $\{I(t, \mathbf{p}_t)\}_{t=-\infty}^{\infty}$. We model $I(t, \mathbf{p}_t)$ as a displaced sample of a three-dimensional discrete random field, with a displacement of $\mathbf{p}_t$ at time t,

$$s(x, y, t), \qquad (x, y, t) \in \mathcal{Z}^3 = \mathcal{Z} \times \mathcal{Z} \times \mathcal{Z}$$

where (x, y) are spatial coordinates, t is temporal coordinate, and $\mathcal{Z}$ is the integer set. Conversely, we may view $s(x, y, t)$ as a motion-compensated version of $I(t, \mathbf{p}_t)$. The mean and autocovariance function of $s(x, y, t)$ are, respectively,

$$E\{s(x, y, t)\} = \mu(x, y, t) \tag{10.9}$$

$$\begin{aligned} c\left[s(x, y, t)s(x', y', t')\right] &= E\{[s(x, y, t) - \mu(x, y, t)] \\ &\quad [s(x', y', t') - \mu(x', y', t')]\} \\ &= c(x, y, t; x', y', t') \end{aligned} \tag{10.10}$$

If we assume that $s(x, y, t)$ is wide-sense stationary, then

$$\mu(x, y, t) = \mu \tag{10.11}$$

$$\begin{aligned} c(x, y, t; x', y', t') &= c(x - x', y - y', t - t') \\ &\equiv c(d_x, d_y, \tau) \end{aligned} \tag{10.12}$$

We further assume the autocovariance function is spatial-temporal separable and spatially isotropic, then (10.12) becomes

$$\begin{aligned} c(d_x, d_y, \tau) &= c_1(d)c_2(\tau) \\ &\equiv c(d, \tau) \end{aligned} \tag{10.13}$$

where d is the spatial Euclidean distance between $s(x, y, t)$ and $s(x', y', t')$, $d \stackrel{\Delta}{=} \sqrt{d_x^2 + d_y^2}$.

Finally assuming a first-order Markov statistical dependence [PAPO 1991] along each dimension, we have the model

$$c(d, \tau) = \sigma_I^2 \gamma^{|\tau|} \rho^{|d|} \tag{10.14}$$

where σ_I^2 is the variance of the original luminance pixels in the block, γ is the temporal autocovariance coefficient, $0 \leq \gamma \leq 1$, and ρ is the spatial autocovariance coefficient, $0 \leq \rho \leq 1$.

Exponential functions have long been used in modeling spatial correlation among neighboring pixels [JAIN 1989]. Here, we use an exponential function to describe the spatial-temporal correlation of the video signal, which is a simple but reasonable approximation. According to this model, the correlation between two pixels decreases with their spatial distance d and temporal distance τ, if $\gamma \neq 1$ or $\rho \neq 1$.

In TRIRF-frame coding, under error-free channel conditions, the reference for motion compensated prediction of a pixel in the current frame t, $s(x, y, t)$, is a pixel in the reconstructed frame $t - t_d$, $\tilde{s}(x', y', t - t_d)$,

$$\tilde{s}(x', y', t - t_d) = s(x', y', t - t_d) + n(x', y', t - t_d) \tag{10.15}$$

where $n(x', y', t - t_d)$ is the reconstruction error, which is quantization noise modelled as wide-sense stationary with zero mean and variance σ_0^2.

Denote the motion vector estimation error vector as (δ_x, δ_y), $\delta_x, \delta_y \geq 0$, which is the absolute value of the difference between the true motion vector and its estimate, then (10.15) can be expressed via

$$\tilde{s}(x', y', t - t_d) = s(x - \delta_x, y - \delta_y, t - t_d) + n(x - \delta_x, y - \delta_y, t - t_d) \tag{10.16}$$

The prediction error of $s(x, y, t)$ is denoted as

$$
\begin{aligned}
e_t &= s(x, y, t) - \tilde{s}(x', y', t - t_d) \\
&= s(x, y, t) - s(x - \delta_x, y - \delta_y, t - t_d) \\
&\quad - n(x - \delta_x, y - \delta_y, t - t_d)
\end{aligned} \tag{10.17}
$$

The variance of the prediction error e_t is calculated to be

$$
\begin{aligned}
\sigma_e^2 &= E\{[s(x, y, t) - s(x - \delta_x, y - \delta_y, t - t_d) - n(x - \delta_x, y - \delta_y, t - t_d)]^2\} \\
&= E\{s(x, y, t)^2\} + E\{s(x - \delta_x, y - \delta_y, t - t_d)^2\} \\
&\quad - E\{n(x - \delta_x, y - \delta_y, t - t_d)^2\} \\
&\quad - 2E\{[s(x, y, t) - s(x - \delta_x, y - \delta_y, t - t_d)]n(x - \delta_x, y - \delta_y, t - t_d)\} \\
&\quad - 2E\{s(x, y, t)s(x - \delta_x, y - \delta_y, t - t_d)\}
\end{aligned} \tag{10.18}
$$

Assuming no correlation between the displaced frame difference $(s(x, y, t) - s(x - \delta_x, y - \delta_y, t - t_d))$ and the quantization error $n(x - \delta_x, y - \delta_y, t - t_d)$, after some manipulations involving (10.18) and (10.14), we have

$$\sigma_e^2 = 2\sigma_I^2(1 - \gamma^{t_d}\rho^d) + \sigma_0^2 \tag{10.19}$$

where $d = \sqrt{\delta_x^2 + \delta_y^2}$, is the spatial Euclidean distance between $s(x, y, t)$ and its prediction, and t_d is the temporal distance between $s(x, y, t)$ and its prediction.

Eqn. (10.19) expresses σ_e^2, the prediction error variance, which is the determining factor of the coding rate of the prediction errors, based on our spatial-temporal covariance model (Eqn. (10.14)). This equation indicates the dependence of σ_e^2 on video content (luminance activity σ_I^2, temporal correlation γ, and spatial correlation ρ), round trip delay t_d, motion vector estimation error d, and quantization error of the reference frame σ_0^2.

For a given quantizer step size Q, a delayed motion compensated prediction error block is coded at rate

$$R_{mcpe}(t_d, \mathbf{p}) = R\left(I(t, \mathbf{p}) - \tilde{I}(t - t_d, \mathbf{p} - \mathbf{mv}), Q\right) \equiv F\left(\frac{\sigma_e}{Q}\right) \qquad (10.20)$$

where σ_e^2 is given by Eq. (10.19), which is then substituted into Eqs. (10.4)-(10.8).

10.5.1.3 *Rate computation for motion vectors*

Coding of motion vectors typically employs variable length coding [ITU 1995] [MPEG 1994]. If we know the probability mass function of the motion vector, $P(\mathbf{mv})$, an appropriate measure of its coding length is the Shannon code length [COVE 1991]

$$R(\mathbf{mv}) = -\log_2 P(\mathbf{mv}) \qquad (10.21)$$

Generally, the distribution of the motion vector is approximately symmetrical about zero (assuming no global motion) and it tends to have a peak at zero and falls off as the amplitude value increases. Since the block displacement as represented by $\mathbf{mv}$ increases with t_d, the temporal distance between the current frame and the reference frame, $P(\mathbf{mv})$ decreases when t_d gets larger, resulting in a longer coding length.

Note that in practice, the coding length of a particular $\mathbf{mv}$ can be simply obtained by a code-book table lookup.

10.5.1.4 *Rate derivation based on block motion*

To further investigate the space and time-varying behavior of the coding rate of a block with respect to t_d and video content, we partition the blocks into four types: *(1) background, (2) regular motion , (3) irregular motion and (4) newly appearing.* The block types are defined and discussed in the following paragraphs:

(1) Background block (B)

A background block, denoted here as a B block, is a block which does not change from $t - t_d$ to t. The prediction of a B block is the same block in frame $t - t_d$, i.e., $\mathbf{mv} = \mathbf{0}$. The temporal covariance coefficient for the corresponding B block sequence is unity, $\gamma = 1$. We assume the motion estimation algorithm can very accurately identify a B block, i.e., the motion estimation error $d = 0$. The prediction error variance (10.19) with $\gamma = 1$ and $d = 0$ becomes

$$\begin{aligned} \sigma_e^2 &= 2\sigma_I^2(1 - \gamma^{t_d}\rho^d) + \sigma_0^2 \\ &= \sigma_0^2 \end{aligned} \tag{10.22}$$

Based on Eqns. (10.1), (10.20) and (10.22), the coding rate of a B block is

$$R_{trirf\_B}(t_d, \mathbf{p}) = F\left(\frac{\sigma_0}{Q}\right) + R(\mathbf{0}) \tag{10.23}$$

where $R(\mathbf{0})$ is the coding length of the zero vector $(0,0)$, which is very small, since stationary blocks occur most frequently. For example, $R(\mathbf{0}) = 2$ bits in H.263 [ITU 1995].

(2) Regularly moving block (R)

A regularly moving block, denoted as an R block, is a block that can be accurately tracked by the motion model. Here we assume translational motion described by motion vector $\mathbf{mv}$. As in the B block case, the temporal covariance coefficient is unity, $\gamma = 1$. The prediction error variance is then

$$\begin{aligned} \sigma_e^2 &= 2\sigma_I^2(1 - \gamma^{t_d}\rho^d) + \sigma_0^2 \\ &= 2\sigma_I^2(1 - \rho^d) + \sigma_0^2 \end{aligned} \tag{10.24}$$

From Eqns.(10.1), (10.20) and (10.24), the coding rate of an R block is

$$R_{trirf\_R}(t_d, \mathbf{p}) = F\left(\left(\frac{2\sigma_I^2(1 - \rho^d) + \sigma_0^2}{Q^2}\right)^{\frac{1}{2}}\right) + R(\mathbf{mv}(t_d)) \tag{10.25}$$

where $R(\mathbf{mv}(t_d))$ can be calculated from Eqn. (10.21) or obtained from the code-book table.

(3) Irregularly moving block (IR)

258

An irregularly moving block, denoted as an *IR* block, is a block whose temporal change cannot be completely described by the motion model. We avoid the term *I block* which has already been used for intra-block in the literature. The temporal covariance coefficient falls in the range, $0 < \gamma < 1$. The correlation between the *IR* block and its prediction decays with t_d and prediction error variance increases with t_d. We have the general expression (10.19), repeated here for convenience

$$\sigma_e^2 = 2\sigma_I^2(1 - \gamma^{t_d}\rho^d) + \sigma_0^2 \tag{10.26}$$

From Eqns.(10.1) and (10.20), the coding rate of an *IR* block is

$$R_{trirf\_IR}(t_d, \mathbf{p}) = F\left(\left(\frac{2\sigma_I^2(1 - \gamma^{t_d}\rho^d) + \sigma_0^2}{Q^2}\right)^{\frac{1}{2}}\right) + R(\mathbf{mv}(t_d)) \tag{10.27}$$

where $R(\mathbf{mv}(t_d))$ can be calculated from (10.21) or obtained from the code-book table.

(4) New block (N)

A new block, denoted as an N block, is a block that is statistically independent of the reconstructed frame $t - t_d$, which means that $\gamma = 0$. For an N block, motion compensated predictive coding does not have a compression advantage over single-frame coding (intra-frame coding) and can produce a higher coding rate than intra-frame coding. The prediction error variance of an N block is

$$\begin{aligned}
\sigma_e^2 &= 2\sigma_I^2(1 - \gamma^{t_d}\rho^d) + \sigma_0^2 \\
&= 2\sigma_I^2 + \sigma_0^2
\end{aligned} \tag{10.28}$$

The coding rate of an N block is

$$R_{trirf\_N}(t_d, \mathbf{p}) = F\left(\left(\frac{2\sigma_I^2 + \sigma_0^2}{Q^2}\right)^{\frac{1}{2}}\right) + R(\mathbf{mv}(t_d)) \tag{10.29}$$

10.5.2 *TRIRF Coding: Channels with Error*

Since the analysis in the previous section is performed under perfect channel conditions, the results are lower bounds for all channel conditions. However, TRIRF-frame coding is proposed to improve the error resilience of motion compensated predictive coding for unreliable delivery of video signals. Therefore, to quantify the advantage of TRIRF-frame coding, it is necessary to analyze the coding performance with respect to error-prone channel conditions.

Fig. 10.9 gives a two-dimensional view of the TRIRF-frame update process at time t when transmission errors occur. Suppose some area containing block A of frame $t - t_d$ (denoted as $A(t - t_d)$), is damaged during transmission, then all blocks in TRIRF-frame t are updated by the corresponding blocks in frame $t - t_d$ except those in the damaged area, which are replaced by the corresponding blocks in TRIRF-frame $t - 1$. Note that

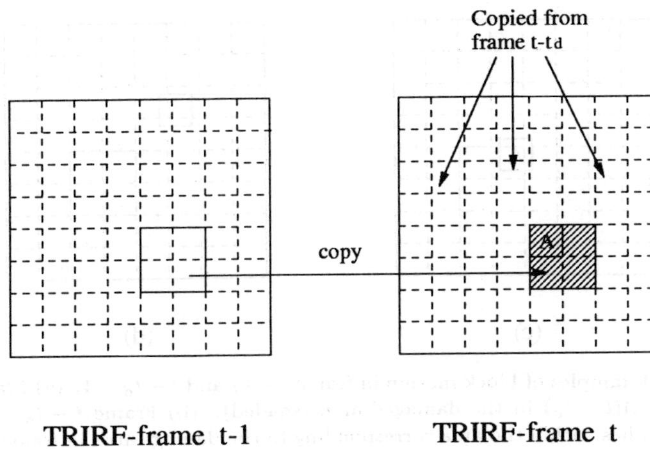

Fig. 10.9   TRIRF-frame update at time t.

for a perfect channel, TRIRF-frame t and $t - 1$ are actually frame $t - t_d$ and $t - t_d - 1$, respectively. Because of the loss of $A(t - t_d)$, which is the prediction of block A in the current frame, $A(t)$, the TRIRF-frame coding rate of $A(t)$ will be affected. If we assume that block $A(t - t_d - 1)$ is delivered successfully, then there are three cases in the TRIRF-frame update at time t, depending on the motion of the block-object A and the area of the damage.

- *Case 1:* $A(t - t_d - 1)$ is completely copied from TRIRF-frame $t - 1$. This occurs when $A(t - t_d - 1)$ is located within the area corresponding to the damaged area of frame $t - t_d$, illustrated in (b) of Fig. 10.10.

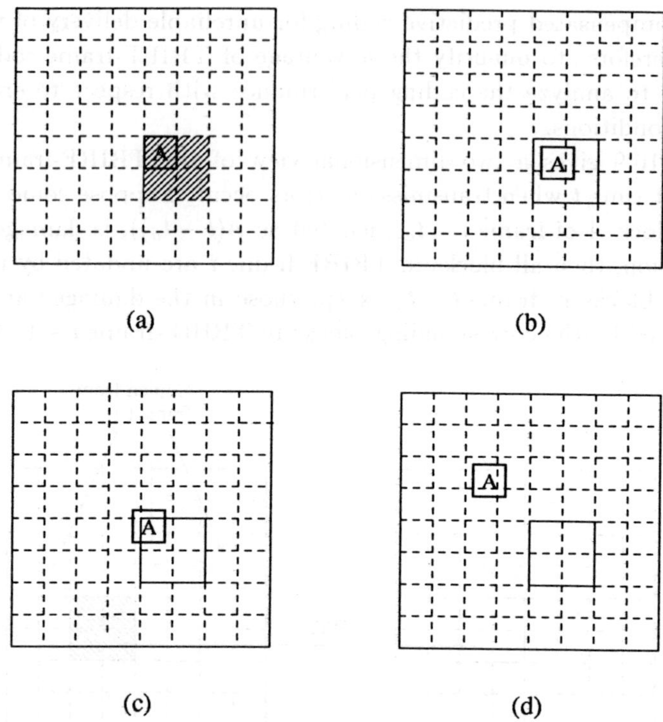

Fig. 10.10   Examples of block motion in frame $t - t_d$ and $t - t_d - 1$. (a) Frame $t - t_d$: block-object $A(t - t_d)$ in the damaged area (shaded). (b) Frame $t - t_d - 1$, case 1: $A(t - t_d - 1)$ lies within the area corresponding to the damage area in frame $t - t_d$. (c) Frame $t - t_d - 1$, case 2: $A(t - t_d - 1)$ is partially within that area. (d) Frame $t - t_d - 1$, case 3: $A(t - t_d - 1)$ is outside that area.

- *Case 2:* $A(t - t_d - 1)$ is partially copied from TRIRF-frame $t - 1$. This occurs when $A(t - t_d - 1)$ lies on the border of the area corresponding to the damaged area of frame $t - t_d$, illustrated in (c) of Fig. 10.10.
- *Case 3:* $A(t - t_d - 1)$ is not copied into TRIRF-frame t. This occurs when $A(t - t_d - 1)$ is outside the area corresponding to the damaged area of frame $t - t_d$, illustrated in (d) of Fig. 10.10.

In Section 10.5, we derived the block prediction error variance formulation (Eqn.(10.19)) for error-free transmission, which is repeated here

$$\sigma_e^2 = 2\sigma_I^2(1 - \gamma^{t_d}\rho^{d_o}) + \sigma_0^2 \tag{10.30}$$

where d_0 is the motion estimation error.

For Case 1, if the motion estimation algorithm chooses $A(t - t_d - 1)$ as the prediction of $A(t)$, then the prediction error variance (10.30) is modified to

$$\sigma_e^2 = 2\sigma_I^2(1 - \gamma^{t_d+1}\rho^{d_1}) + \sigma_0^2 \qquad (10.31)$$

where d_1 is the motion estimation error in this case. For B and R blocks ($\gamma = 1$), there is no prediction efficiency loss. However, for IR blocks ($\gamma < 1$), σ_e^2 increases, due to the correlation decrease over time.

For Cases 2 and 3, object A is either partially or totally lost in TRIRF-frame t. Here, the spatial content in the motion vector search range determines the efficiency of the block A prediction. The block which best matches $A(t)$ found by the motion estimation algorithm may or may not contain $A(t-t_d-1)$. However, the best block should normally have a similar spatial pattern to $A(t-t_d-1)$. Generally, the correlation between the best matching block and $A(t)$ is less than the correlation between $A(t - t_d - 1)$ and $A(t)$, resulting in a higher σ_e^2 than that in Case 1. We view TRIRF-frame based motion compensation in these two cases as equivalent as when using a block in frame $t-t_d-1$ which is located a certain distance away from $A(t-t_d-1)$ as the prediction of $A(t)$. This interpretation enables us to use the same formulation as Eqn.(10.31) while incorporating the transmission error effect into the parameter d_1.

We will use Eqn.(10.31) to evaluate the TRIRF-frame prediction error variance of the three cases when the block object $A(t - t_d)$ of frame $t - t_d$ is totally damaged during transmission.

Generally, due to the uncertainty of the error locations in frame $t - t_d$, the projection of object A on frame $t - t_d$, $A(t - t_d)$, can be completely outside the damaged area (intact), on the border of the damaged area (partially damaged), or completely inside the damaged area (totally damaged). We categorize these three cases into two situations depending on the percentage of the damage in the area of $A(t - t_d)$: (I) $A(t - t_d)$ is intact or just slightly impaired, if the fraction of damaged pixels in $A(t-t_d)$ is below θ, $0 < \theta < 1$; (II) $A(t - t_d)$ is severely damaged, if the erroneous part is above θ. Here, θ is a threshold which is set *a priori*.

In summary, when transmission errors occur in frame $t-t_d$, the TRIRF-frame based motion compensated prediction of a block $A(t)$ can be simplified to have two outcomes:

- I: The prediction is based on the content of frame $t - t_d$. This is when $A(t - t_d)$ is successfully delivered or slightly impaired. The prediction error variance is given by Eqn.(10.30), where the temporal distance is t_d and the motion estimation error is d_0. We assume that d_0 is uniformly distributed, $d_0 \sim U(0, a)$, where parameter a depends on the motion estimation accuracy and θ. The expected value of σ_e^2 with respecct to d_0 is

$$
\begin{aligned}
\sigma_e^2(I) &= E\{\sigma_e^2(d_0)\} \\
&= \int_0^a \sigma_e^2(d_0)p(d_0)dd_0 \\
&= \int_0^a \frac{1}{a}\left[2\sigma_I^2(1 - \gamma^{t_d}\rho^{d_0}) + \sigma_0^2\right]dd_0 \\
&= 2\sigma_I^2\left(1 - \frac{\rho^a - 1}{a\ln\rho}\gamma^{t_d}\right) + \sigma_0^2 \qquad (10.32)
\end{aligned}
$$

- II: The prediction is based on the content of frame $t - t_d - 1$. This occurs when $A(t - t_d)$ is severely damaged. The prediction error variance is given by Eqn.(10.31). where the temporal distance is $t_d + 1$ and the motion estimation error is d_1. We assume that d_1 is uniformly distributed, $d_1 \sim U(0, b)$, where parameter b depends on the motion in the scene, the distribution and size of the erroneous areas, and θ. The expected value of σ_e^2 with respect to d_1 is

$$
\begin{aligned}
\sigma_e^2(II) &= E\{\sigma_e^2(d_1)\} \\
&= \int_0^b \sigma_e^2(d_1)p(d_1)dd_1 \\
&= \int_0^b \frac{1}{b}\left[2\sigma_I^2(1 - \gamma^{t_d+1}\rho^{d_1}) + \sigma_0^2\right]dd_1 \\
&= 2\sigma_I^2\left(1 - \frac{\rho^b - 1}{b\ln\rho}\gamma^{t_d+1}\right) + \sigma_0^2 \qquad (10.33)
\end{aligned}
$$

We now calculate the probabilities of the two mutually exclusive outcomes I and II, $P(I)$ and $P(II)$, where

$$
P(I) + P(II) = 1 \qquad (10.34)
$$

These probabilities depend on the network transmission protocols. We assume transmission over a packet network and use the packet error probability (P_{PE}) to characterize the quality of the channel. We consider a simple packetization scheme where variable packet length is allowed, each packet contains fixed number of complete blocks in the raster scan order (the data of a block will not be split into two packets), and the number of the blocks in one packet is less than the number of blocks in one row. This kind of packetization can be easily supported by IP networks without the need to design an adaptation layer above the transport layer. Fig. 10.11 shows a packetization example, where half a row of blocks are placed into one packet. When a packet has an error, all blocks in that packet are considered as corrupted. How $A(t - t_d)$ intersects with the packetized blocks in frame $t - t_d$ depends on its location and the packetization scheme. For

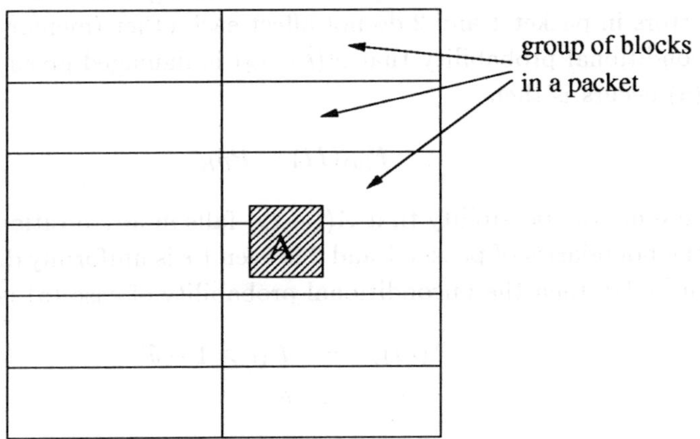

Fig. 10.11 Example of a packetization scheme. Shaded area shows the motion-compensated predicted location of block $A(t - t_d)$. in the TRIRF-frame

example, in the case of Fig. 10.11, $A(t - t_d)$ can intersect one, two, or four neighboring packets. However, most of the time $A(t - t_d)$ intersects two packets and we only consider this situation. There are three cases regarding the type of intersection: Fig. 10.12 depicts $A(t - t_d)$ intersecting with two vertically neighboring packets 1 and 2. Denoting the portion of $A(t - t_d)$ pixels in packet 2 as ϵ ($0 \leq \epsilon \leq 1$), there are two situations depending the value of θ, which is the value of the threshold by which we decide if $A(t-t_d)$ is damaged or not:

- $\theta \leq \frac{1}{2}$

    (a) $\epsilon \geq 1 - \theta$. Since the part of $A(t - t_d)$ in packet 2, ϵ, is larger than θ, $A(t - t_d)$ is damaged if packet 2 has an error. Since the

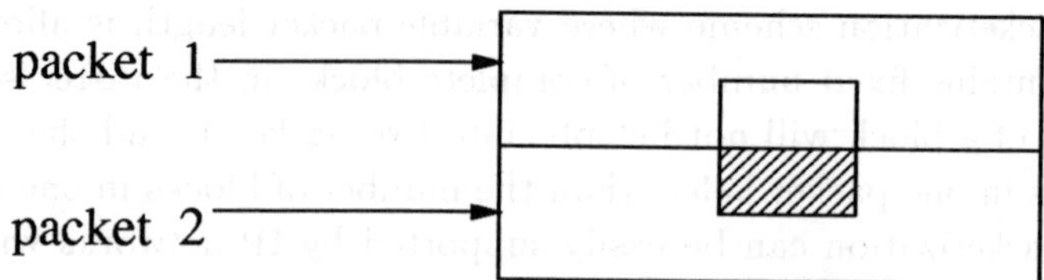

Fig. 10.12 $A(t - t_d)$ intersects two vertically neighboring packets. The shaded area is the part of $A(t - t_d)$ which contains pixels frame packet 2.

part in packet 1, $1 - \epsilon$, is less than θ, $A(t - t_d)$ is intact if packet 2 is error free, whenever packet 1 is damaged or not. Assuming errors in packet 1 and 2 do not affect each other (memoryless), the conditional probability that $A(t - t_d)$ is damaged given that case (a) occurs is then

$$P_{(a)}(II) = P_{PE} \tag{10.35}$$

Assume the possibility that $A(t - t_d)$ falls in any position between the boundaries of packet 1 and 2 is even (ϵ is uniformly distributed in $[0, 1]$), then the unconditional probability of case (a) is

$$\begin{aligned} P((a)) &= P(\epsilon \geq 1 - \theta) \\ &= \theta \end{aligned} \tag{10.36}$$

(b) $1 - \theta > \epsilon > \theta$. Since both parts of $A(t - t_d)$ in packet 1 and 2 are larger than θ, $A(t - t_d)$ is damaged if packet 1 or 2 has an error. In this case, the conditional probability is

$$\begin{aligned} P_{(b)}(II) &= (1 - P_{PE}) \cdot P_{PE} + P_{PE}^2 + (1 - P_{PE}) \cdot P_{PE} \\ &= 2P_{PE} - P_{PE}^2 \end{aligned} \tag{10.37}$$

and the unconditional probability of case (b) is

$$\begin{aligned} P((b)) &= P(1 - \theta > \epsilon > \theta) \\ &= 1 - 2\theta \end{aligned} \tag{10.38}$$

(c) $\epsilon \leq \theta$. Since the part of $A(t - t_d)$ in packet 1, $1 - \epsilon$, is larger than θ, $A(t - t_d)$ is damaged if packet 1 has an error. Since the part in packet 2, ϵ, is less than θ, $A(t - t_d)$ is intact if packet 1 is error free, whenever packet 2 is damaged or not. Then the conditional probability given case (c) is

$$P_{(c)}(II) = P_{PE} \tag{10.39}$$

and the unconditional probability of case (c) is

$$\begin{aligned} P\left((c)\right) &= P(\epsilon \leq \theta) \\ &= \theta \end{aligned} \tag{10.40}$$

Combining (10.35)-(10.40) gives the probability of a block being severely damaged when $\theta \leq \frac{1}{2}$

$$\begin{aligned} P(II) &= P_{(a)}(II) \cdot P((a)) + P_{(b)}(II) \cdot P((b)) + P_{(c)}(II) \cdot P((c)) \\ &= 2(1 - \theta)P_{PE} - (1 - 2\theta)P_{PE}^2 \end{aligned} \tag{10.41}$$

- $\theta > \frac{1}{2}$
  (a) $\epsilon \geq \theta$. Analogous to case (a) when $\theta \leq \frac{1}{2}$, we have

$$P_{(a)}(II) = P_{PE} \tag{10.42}$$

and

$$\begin{aligned} P\left((a)\right) &= P(\epsilon \geq \theta) \\ &= 1 - \theta \end{aligned} \tag{10.43}$$

(b) $\theta > \epsilon > 1 - \theta$. Since both parts of $A(t - t_d)$ in packet 1 and 2 are less than θ, $A(t - t_d)$ is considered to be damaged if packet 1 and 2 has an error. We then have

$$P_{(b)}(II) = P_{PE}^2 \tag{10.44}$$

and

$$\begin{aligned} P\left((b)\right) &= P(\theta > \epsilon > 1 - \theta) \\ &= 2\theta - 1 \end{aligned} \tag{10.45}$$

(c) $\epsilon \leq 1 - \theta$. Based on similar deduction as in case (c) when $\theta \leq \frac{1}{2}$, we have

$$P_{(c)}(II) = P_{PE} \tag{10.46}$$

and

$$P((c)) = P(\epsilon \leq 1 - \theta)$$
$$= 1 - \theta \tag{10.47}$$

Combining (10.42)-(10.47) results in $P(II)$ for case when $\theta > \frac{1}{2}$:

$$P(II) = P_{(a)}(II) \cdot P((a)) + P_{(b)}(II) \cdot P((b)) + P_{(c)}(II) \cdot P((c))$$
$$= 2(1 - \theta)P_{PE} - (1 - 2\theta)P_{PE}^2 \tag{10.48}$$

It turns out that the formula of $P(II)$ is the same for $\theta \leq \frac{1}{2}$ and $\theta > \frac{1}{2}$. This is because of symmetry in the $P(II)$ computation. Finally, the probability that $A(t - t_d)$ is considered intact is found from (10.34) as

$$P(I) = 1 - P(II)$$
$$= 1 - 2(1 - \theta)P_{PE} + (1 - 2\theta)P_{PE}^2 \tag{10.49}$$

For different packetization schemes than the above mentioned, especially for those in which there are more than one row of blocks per packet, the expressions for $P(I)$ and $P(II)$ would change.

Finally, the expected value of the TRIRF-frame based motion compensated prediction error variance is

$$\bar{\sigma}_e^2 = E\left\{\sigma_e^2\right\}$$
$$= P(I) \cdot \sigma_e^2(I) + P(II) \cdot \sigma_e^2(II)$$
$$= 2\sigma_I^2 \left[1 - \frac{\rho^a - 1}{a \ln \rho} \gamma^{t_d} P(I) - \frac{\rho^b - 1}{b \ln \rho} \gamma^{t_d+1} P(II) \right] + \sigma_0^2 \tag{10.50}$$

where $P(I)$ and $P(II)$ are given by Eqn.(10.48) and (10.49) respectively. Here we assume that the reconstruction error variance σ_0^2 does not change from frame to frame.

10.5.3 *Simulations*

To verify the expressions in Section 10.5 and 10.5.2, we developed a software video codec for TRIRF-frame coding evaluation. Block-based motion prediction with half-pixel accuracy is performed on image sequences with delayed references ranging from frame $t - 1$ to frame $t - 5$. Motion vector search distance is 15, 25, 35, 45 and 50 for $t_d = 1$ to 5, respectively. The block size is 16×16 pixels. Test sequences of CCIR 601 QCIF (176×144

resolution) format are used. Prediction errors are 8×8 DCT transformed and quantized with a step size of Q. For intra-frame coding, each 16×16 block are 8×8 DCT transformed and quantized with a step size of IQ. We use the same quantizer and VLC code books as that of H.263 [ITU 1995], except that the code book for motion vectors is modified to allow larger numbers to be encoded.

10.5.3.1 *Results for Reliable Channels*

In this subsection, we test the motion-compensated prediction error variance model formulated in Eqn. (10.19) of Section 10.5.1.2, and additionally in Eqn. (10.22), (10.24) and (10.26) for different types of blocks. For the blocks tested, temporal and spatial autocovariance coefficients γ and ρ are determined *a priori*. The motion vector estimation error d is viewed as the difference between the estimated block displacement and the best displacement which minimizes the mean squared error (MSE) or mean absolute error (MAE). The error d is not only affected by the motion estimation precision, but also by the block size and the motion model. For instance, due to the inaccuracy of the block-based translational motion model in describing the real world, increasing the motion search precision may not necessarily further decrease prediction errors significantly. We observed in the experiments that for some sequences, $\frac{1}{4}$-pixel motion search does not improve motion compensation much over half-pixel search. This shows that d is not directly related to the motion search precision. In our simulations, we observed that d is very small for the test sequences and can be ignored.

Here we present some coding examples of different block types listed in Section 10.5.1.4.

- *B* blocks

  Table 10.5 illustrates the measured prediction error variance $\hat{\sigma}_e^2$ and the model-based prediction error variance σ_e^2 of the luminance component of some *B* blocks in frame 18 of the Salesman sequence, as a function of t_d. The estimation of the *B* block prediction error variance, based on Eqn.(10.22), shows that $\hat{\sigma}_e^2$ matches σ_e^2 very closely, and that σ_e^2 has a nearly horizontal slope. This is expected since temporal prediction for static backgrounds is efficient and usually only affected by reconstruction errors of the reference block. Table 10.6 depicts the average coding rate for the luminance component

$t_d(frames)$	1	2	3	4	5
Empirical	36.5	36.5	36.5	36.5	36.5
Predicted	36.8	36.5	36.8	36.5	36.7

Table 10.5   Average σ_e^2 comparison of the luminance component of 55 B blocks in frame 18 of Salesman.

of the B blocks. *Actual rate* is the coding rate produced by the en-

$t_d(frames)$	1	2	3	4	5
Actual	4.0	4.1	4.1	4.1	4.1
Predicted 1	4.0	4.0	4.0	4.0	4.0
Predicted 2	4.0	4.0	4.0	4.0	4.0

Table 10.6   Average coding rate (bits/block) of the luminance component of 55 B blocks in frame 18 of Salesman.

coder. *Predicted 1* is the rate calculated from the rate function $F()$, based on measured values, $\hat{\sigma}_e^2$. *Predicted 2* is the rate calculated from the same rate function, but based on the analytical prediction error variance, σ_e^2. Again, we can see a close match between the actual coding rate and the predicted coding rate.

- R blocks

  Table 10.7 illustrates the measured prediction error variance $\hat{\sigma}_e^2$ and the measured prediction error variance σ_e^2 based on Eqn.(10.24) of the luminance component of a sample of R blocks in frame 128 of Foreman sequence, as a function of delay, t_d.

$t_d(frames)$	1	2	3	4	5
Measured	26.2	27.8	28.1	27.3	27.5
Predicted	27.4	27.2	26.6	27.6	28.5

Table 10.7   Average σ_e^2 comparison of the luminance component of 25 R blocks in frame 128 of Foreman.

Table 10.8 shows the average coding rate for the luminance component of the R blocks, where the rows of the table are the same as those in Table 10.6 above. It is clear that the analytical model accurately describes the behavior of these blocks.

- IR blocks

$t_d(frames)$	1	2	3	4	5
Actual	4.7	5.6	6.4	6.0	6.9
Predicted 1	6.0	6.6	6.6	6.6	6.2
Predicted 2	6.0	5.7	6.2	6.7	6.8

Table 10.8   Average coding rate (bits/block) of the luminance component of 25 R blocks in frame 128 of Foreman.

Fig. 10.13 illustrates the measured prediction error variance $\hat{\sigma}_e^2$ and the model-calculated prediction error variance σ_e^2 of the luminance component of a sample of IR blocks in frame 108 of the Carphone sequence as t_d varies from 1 to 5. The estimation of the IR block

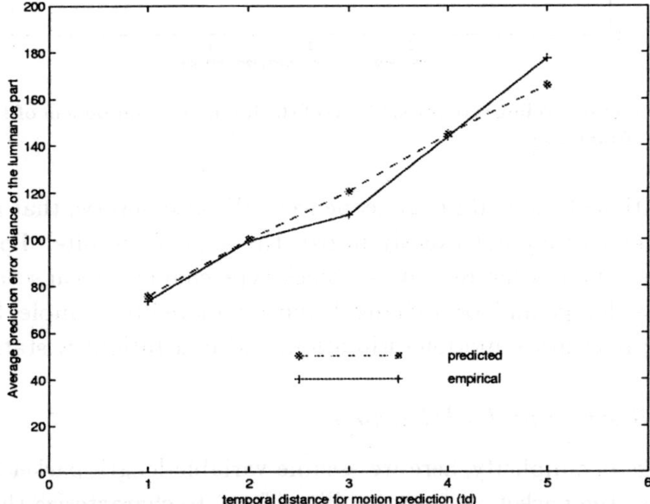

Fig. 10.13   Average σ_e^2 comparison of the luminance component of 13 IR blocks of Carphone, frame 108.

σ_e^2, based on Eqn.(10.26), increases with t_d because the temporal covariance coefficient γ is less than unity for IR blocks. Again, the estimated variance follows the measured variance closely. Fig. 10.14 shows the average rate for the luminance component of the IR blocks.

The above experimental results show that the exponential function used to quantify the spatial-temporal correlation of video signals is a reasonable

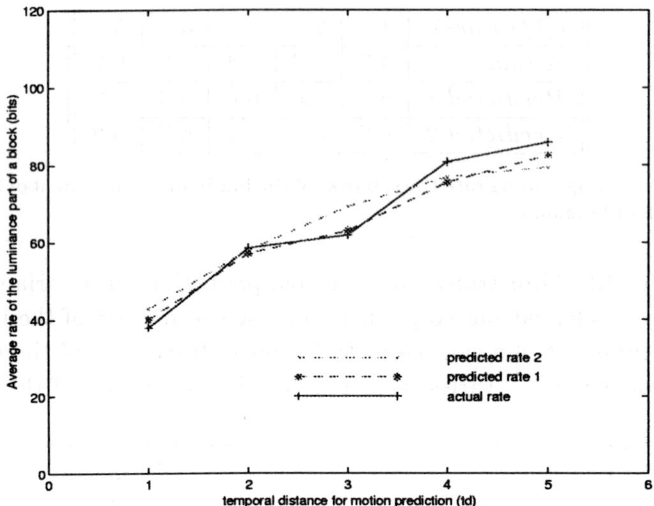

Fig. 10.14   Average coding rate (bits/block) of the luminance component of 13 *IR* blocks of Carphone, frame 108.

approximation of the real image sequences. We also observe that results on video sequences may not exactly mirror the analysis results. Possible explanations include scene repetition (block type change); local scene change (block type change and/or γ change); motion model too simple; block size and shape; inaccurate motion estimation; and nonstationary statistics.

10.5.3.2   *Results with Packet Errors*

For the sake of simplicity, here we assume variable-length packet transmission and use the packet error probability (P_{PE}) to characterize the channel conditions. Rather than the adaptation layer required for fixed-length packets as described in Section 10.3, a row of 11 blocks of QCIF data are put into one packet. If a packet has an error, the whole row of blocks is considered to be damaged. The location of the erroneous row is fed back to the encoder. Then the TRIRF-frame update is based on the replacement of the rows of blocks. We test the prediction error variance model presented in Eqn. (10.50) for this codec and packetization scheme. Twenty Monte-Carlo simulations were run on each test sequence for different packet error probabilities. Without loss of generality, the damage threshold θ is set to 0.5. The parameters a and b are set *a priori* based on the training data for each test sequence.

Fig. 10.15 depicts the measured prediction error variance $\hat{\sigma}_e^2$ and the analytically derived prediction error variance σ_e^2 of the luminance component of a block in frame 38 of the Foreman sequence for a packet error rate of 10^{-1}. Fig. 10.16 shows the corresponding coding rate and the estimated rate under the same conditions. Fig. 10.17 and Fig. 10.18 illustrate the results for $P_{PE} = 3 \times 10^{-1}$. The average intra-frame coding rate of the luminance is 226 bits/block. For this test sequence, the model parameters a and b are 0 and 0.1, respectively. The results show that the prediction error variance model in Eqn. (10.50) accurately describes the coding performance of TRIRF-frame coding for unreliable channels.

10.6   Conclusions

Under the assumption of the existence of a feedback channel, a novel coding mode for video transmission, TRIRF-frame coding, was introduced. This coding constructs a new type of motion compensation reference frame from correctly received data, and is identical at receiver and transmitter. Compression and distortion recovery performance is compared to that proposed in [STEI 1997]. Simulations show that TRIRF-based inter-frame coding can prevent error propagation as effectively as intra-coding while improving compression efficiency.

We also proposed a packetization scheme that serves as an adaptation layer between video source encoder and transport layer, which enables rapid decoder resynchronization when packet losses occur.

A Markov model quantifies the spatial-temporal correlation, and the prediction error variance is derived for error-free transmission. Based on an error variance formulation, the coding rate of prediction errors is obtained and verified using a software TRIRF codec.

The effects of channel packet errors in TRIRF coding were also analyzed and simulated. In the analysis, prediction of a block in the current frame was partitioned into two cases and the probabilities for each case was derived. Finally, the expected value of prediction error variance is derived in Eqn. (10.50). Experimental results for several error conditions showed that our analysis reasonably well describes TRIRF-frame coding efficiency when transmission errors occur.

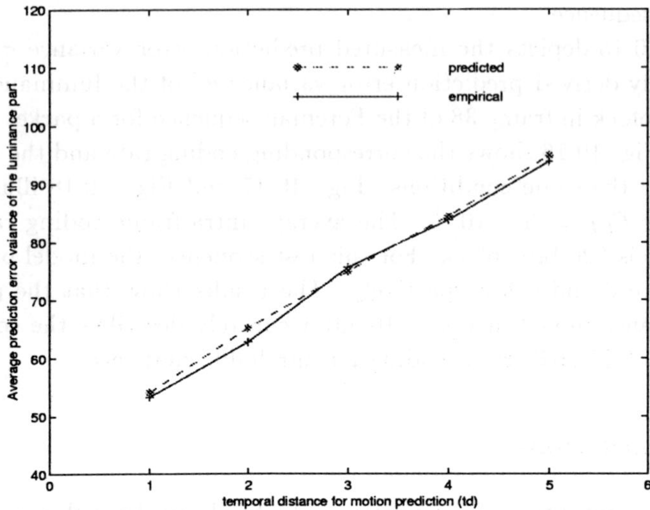

Fig. 10.15   Average σ_e^2 comparison of the luminance component of a block in frame 38 of Foreman for $P_{PE} = 10^{-1}$.

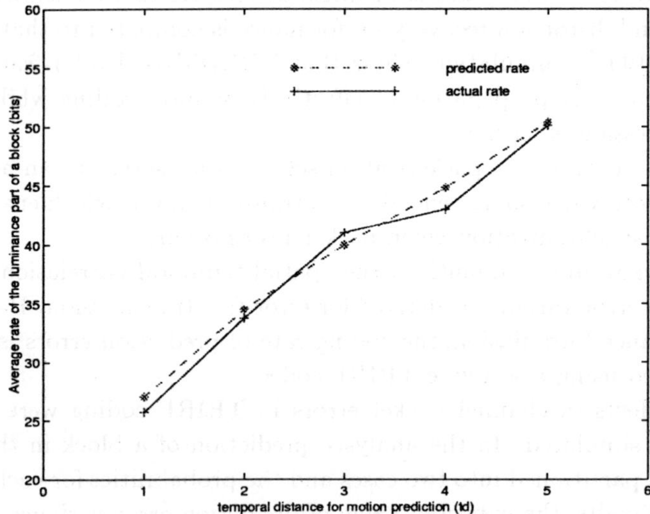

Fig. 10.16   Average coding rate (bits/block) of the luminance in frame 128 of Foreman for $P_{PE} = 10^{-1}$.

Similar results were obtained with the Salesman sequence but are not displayed here.

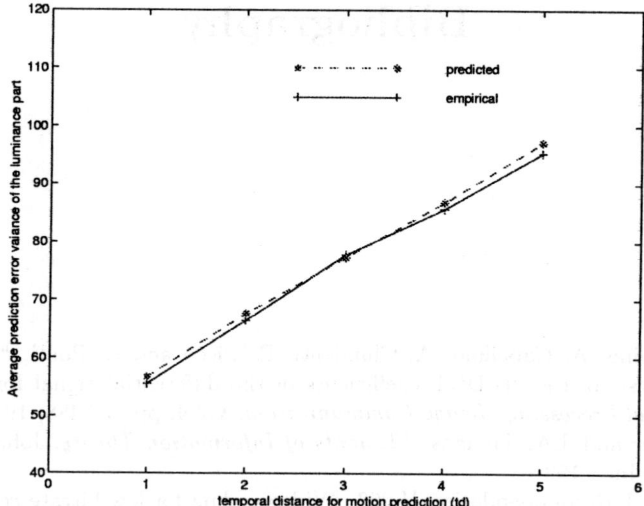

Fig. 10.17 Average σ_e^2 comparison of the luminance component of a block in frame 38 of Foreman for $P_{PE} = 3 \times 10^{-1}$.

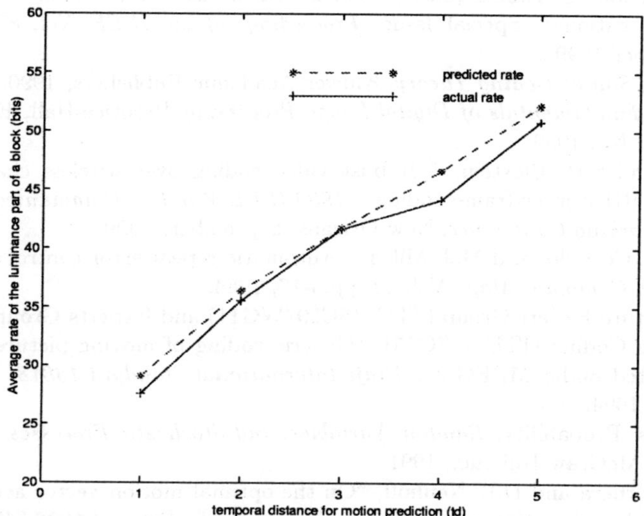

Fig. 10.18 Average coding rate (bits/block) of the luminance in frame 128 of Foreman for $P_{PE} = 3 \times 10^{-1}$.

Bibliography

F. Bellifemine, A. Capellino, A. Chimienti, R. Picco and R. Ponti, "Statistical analysis of the 2D-DCT coefficients of the differential signal for images", *Signal Processing: Image Communication*, Vol.4, pp.477-488, 1992.

T.M. Cover and J.A. Thomas, *Elements of Information Theory*, John Wiley & Sons Inc., 1991.

Draft ITU-T Recommendation H.263, "Video coding for low bitrate communication", *Draft*, Dec. 1995.

F. Dufaux, "Multigrid block matching motion estimation for generic video coding", *Ph.D. dissertation*, the Swiss Federal Institute of Technology, Lausanne, Switzerland, 1994.

H. Gharavi and L. Hanzo (eds.), "Video Transmission for Mobile Multimedia Appli cations", Special Issue, *Proceedings of the IEEE*, Vol. 87, No. 10, October 1999.

R.M. Gray, *Source Coding Theory*, Kluwer Academic Publishers, 1990.

A.K. Jain, *Fundamentals of Digital Image Processing*, Prentice-Hall, Englewood Cliffs, NJ, 1989.

Q. Jiang and S.D. Blostein, " Robust video coding over wireless channels using TRIRF inter-frame coding", *1999 IEEE Wireless Communications and Networking Conference*, New Orleans, September, 1999.

S. Lin, D.J. Costello, and M.J. Miller, "Automatic repeat error control schemes", *IEEE Commun. Mag.*, Vol. 22, pp.5-17, 1984.

Motion Picture Expert Group (JTC1/SC29/WG11) and Experts Group on ATM Video Coding (ITU-T SG15), "Generic coding of moving pictures and associated audio MPEG-2", *Draft International Standard 13818, ISO/IEC*, Nov. 1994.

A. Papoulis, Probability, *Random Variables, and Stochastic Processes*, third edition, McGraw-Hill Inc., 1991.

J. Ribas-Corbera and D.L. Neuhoff, "On the optimal motion vector accuracy for block-based motion-compensated video coders", *Proc. of 1996 SPIE Digital*

Video Compression: Algorithms and Technologies, San Jose, 1996.

S.R. Smoot, "Study of DCT coefficient distributions", *Proc. of SPIE*, Vol.2657, pp.403-411, 1996.

E. Steinbach, N. Färber, and B. Girod, "Standard Compatible Extension of H.263 for Robust Video Transmission in Mobile Environments", *IEEE Trans. Circuits and Systems for Video Technology*, Vol.7, No.6, pp.872-881, Dec. 1997.

J.L.H. Webb and K. Oehler, "A simple rate-distortion model, parameter estimation, and application to real-time rate control for DCT-based coders", *Proc. of 1997 IEEE Int. Conf. Image Processing*, Santa Barbara, CA, USA, 1997.

K.H. Yang, A. Jacquin, and N.S. Jayant, "A normalized rate-distortion model for H.263-compatible codecs and its applications to quantizer selection", *Proc. of 1997 IEEE Int. Conf. Image Processing*, Santa Barbara, CA, USA, 1997.

MULTIDIMENSIONAL AM-FM MODELS WITH IMAGE PROCESSING APPLICATIONS

MARIOS S. PATTICHIS

Dept of EECE, The University of New Mexico, Albuquerque, NM 87131-1356, USA
E-mail: pattichis@eece.unm.edu

JOSEPH P. HAVLICEK

School of ECE, The University of Oklahoma, Norman, OK 73019-1023, USA
E-mail: joebob@ou.edu

SCOTT T. ACTON

Dept of EE, The University of Virginia, Charlottesville, VA 22904-4743, USA
E-mail: acton@virginia.edu

ALAN C. BOVIK

Dept of ECE, The University of Texas at Austin, Austin, TX 78712-1084, USA
E-mail: bovik@ece.utexas.edu

Preliminary Comments

In the Signal Processing Group at the University of Illinois, Urbana-Champaign, there is an old tradition of identifying the academic family tree of an academic advisor. In this regard, one of us (ACB) is one of the many sons of Thomas Huang, while the others (MSP, JPH, and STA) are three of Tom's innumerable grandchildren - too many to count! The tree is constructed both ways in time, of course, but the conventional belief is that Tom, being one of the Immortal Titans, a Founder of the field, can only be traced to some mythological beginning at some Far East-Coast university. However, as a son, privy to the family secrets, I (ACB) can attest that Tom did have a flesh-and-blood academic father, and I think (but am not sure) that it was Bill Schreiber.

Many other of Tom's academic children are also presenting papers in this volume, work that represents some of the latest advances in image processing and analysis research. Festschrifts of this type typically are composed of papers drawn from the Honored One's area of expertise, from back when he or she was still an active researcher. The difference here is that Tom is still active and defining the field of Image Processing and Understanding, and is still publishing and creating new ideas. We're all still trying to keep up.

Before delving into the details of our chapter, I (ACB) would like to relate some of the experience of being Tom's academic son. Those readers that are acquainted with Tom know that he is a friendly man, but of very few words, except when giving talks, when he is always very warm, funny, and expansive. My experience as a graduate student in this regard was notable. Each semester, I would appear in Tom's office after several weeks or months of slavish research effort, with a wad of simulations crammed into a folder. Then, for the next hour, I would talk about them nonstop, flashing charts, graphs, and image processing print-outs as need be, all the while watching Tom's reactions. Inevitably, these were nearly imperceptible nods of his head, although his eyes communicated an intense concentration on my words. When I had completed my research deposition, I would stare expectantly at Tom and he would stare back. Uneasy about my progress, I would gabble about how nice I thought the results were, and also how promising my ideas were for moving the research forward, and didn't he think so too? Most of the time, perhaps 90 percent of my visits, I would finish my pitch, and we would commence staring again. And then Tom would say "Yes." At that time, I knew that Tom approved, and that the interview had successfully concluded, so I grabbed my things and went out as fast as possible.

The more interesting interviews occurred when I was at a research transition, or between degrees looking for new thesis topics. At these times, Tom would wax loquacious, offering as much as a single partial sentence or phrase that would engender a brilliant idea that would result in many months of research. As an example of this relative garrulousness, when I first commenced my master's degree work, I went to Tom with an expressed interest in the then-new "median filter," which was based on using the center ordered sample of a moving window as output, and which seemed to perform wonders in cleaning noisy images. Tom knew all about them, could he suggest a research topic? He scratched his head, and said simply, "weight the ordered samples" and off I went to get a MS degree, and to study those weighted samples for years beyond.

I relate these stories in hopes that the reader can glimpse the working of Tom's unusually brilliant, clear and creative mind, which combined with his dedication and work ethic, has worked to define much of what has become known about Image Processing.

So now I join my co-authors, three of Tom's bright grandchildren, on work that I hope will cause Tom to say ... "Yes."

1 Fundamentals of 2D AM-FM Modeling

In this chapter we review the fundamentals of *AM-FM image modeling* and present several practical image processing applications of the basic theory. Two-dimensional AM-FM models are useful for representing, analyzing, and processing nonstationary images. By *nonstationary*, we mean that the spectral characteristics of the image vary from region to region. For such images, classical **Fourier** representations are neither efficacious nor naturally intuitive in general. Because Fourier representations consist of pure sinusoids, they can create nonstationary structure only by constructive and destructive interference between multiple stationary Fourier components. For images encountered in real-world applications, the nature of this interference can be quite complicated. Indeed, observing the Fourier spectrum of a nonstationary image typically lends little insight into the spatially local structure of the image, and this fact is one of the main motivations for performing time-frequency analysis.

AM-FM models offer an alternative to conventional methods such as the windowed Fourier transform and quadratic time-frequency distributions that can be advantageous in terms of facilitating a well-motivated interpretation of both the spatially local and spectrally local structure that is present in an image. Given a real-valued image $s(x_1, x_2)$, the fundamental idea is to represent the image not as a sum of pure sinusoids, but rather as the real part of a sum $t(x_1, x_2)$ of *complex-valued* nonstationary AM-FM components according to

$$t(x_1, x_2) = s(x_1, x_2) + jq(x_1, x_2) = \sum_{n=1}^{K} a_n(x_1, x_2) \exp[j\phi_n(x_1, x_2)], \quad (1.1)$$

where an imaginary part $q(x_1, x_2)$ has been added to the image for agreement with the complex model. Assuming that such a model can be constructed, it then becomes possible to analyze and process the image in terms of the K AM functions $a_n(x_1, x_2)$ and the K FM functions $\nabla\phi_n(x_1, x_2)$. Taken together, this set of $2K$ modulating functions constitutes the modulation domain representation of $s(x_1, x_2)$. As a simple example, consider a 2D chirp given by $s(x_1, x_2) = \cos[u_0 x_1^2 + v_0 x_2^2]$. Setting $q(x_1, x_2) = \sin[u_0 x_1^2 + v_0 x_2^2]$ in (1.1) yields $t(x_1, x_2) = \exp[j(u_0 x_1^2 + v_0 x_2^2)]$, $K = 1$, $a_1(x_1, x_2) = 1$ and $\nabla\phi_1(x_1, x_2) = [2u_0 x_1 \quad 2v_0 x_2]^T$. Thus we obtain an interpretation that this image is a single AM-FM component with an instantaneous frequency vector that is linear in both spatial coordinates.

The simple elegance of the foregoing example notwithstanding, the problem of computing an AM-FM model for an arbitrary image $s(x_1, x_2)$ is in general an exceptionally challenging one. Consider that the model (1.1) is ill-posed on two separate levels. First, $s(x_1, x_2)$ can generally be decomposed into a sum of components in infinitely many different ways – the decomposition is not unique. Second, even if the component $s_n(x_1, x_2)$ were available, its values alone are not sufficient to determine the modulating functions $a_n(x_1, x_2)$ and $\nabla\phi_n(x_1, x_2)$ uniquely unless an imaginary part $jq_n(x_1, x_2)$ can somehow be added. We will address these issues in Sections 2 and 3. For the remainder of this section we concentrate on the interpretation of 2D AM-FM models.

We are interested in AM-FM models that can reasonably approximate an image using only a relatively small number of components. For example, consider the *mandrill* image shown in Fig. 1(a). A 43-component AM-FM model of the image was computed using the *channelized components analysis* technique (CCA) described in [1] and in Section 3 below. An approximate reconstruction of the image from all 43 components is shown in Fig. 1(b), while one of the individual AM-FM components appears in Fig. 1(c). If the modulating functions corresponding to the locally dominant AM-FM component at each pixel are extracted, they can be aggregated to construct a dominant AM function and a dominant FM function for the entire image. This approach is called *dominant component analysis*, or *DCA* [1], which will also be discussed in Section 3.

The computed dominant AM function of the *mandrill* image is shown in Fig. 1(d), while the dominant FM function is shown in Fig. 1(e). In Fig. 1(e), each arrow depicts the frequency vector $\nabla \phi_n (x_1, x_2)$ that was computed for the dominant AM-FM component at the pixel corresponding to the arrow point of origin. In the figure, only one arrow is shown for each 8×8 block of pixels. The direction of each arrow gives the orientation of the dominant frequency vector. The arrow lengths are inversely proportional to the dominant frequency magnitude $|\nabla \phi_n (x_1, x_2)|$; *i.e.*, they are proportional to the dominant instantaneous period. With this convention, long arrows indicate low frequencies that correspond to large structures in the image, whereas short arrows indicate high frequencies that correspond to more granular structures.

Dominant AM and FM functions computed for the images *Tree* and *Lena* are shown in Fig. 2. The dominant AM-FM component of each image as reconstructed from the dominant modulations is also given in Fig. 2. With reference to the dominant modulations and dominant component reconstructions shown in Figs. 1 and 2, we now discuss interpretation of the component modulating functions $a_n (x_1, x_2)$, $\nabla \phi_n (x_1, x_2)$ in (1.1). For any component $a_n (x_1, x_2) \exp[j \phi_n (x_1, x_2)]$, the FM function characterizes the local texture orientation and coarseness or granularity. The AM function, which we usually constrain to be everywhere non-negative, captures local contrast. For example, bright regions in the computed dominant AM functions of Fig. 1 and 2 generally correspond to regions of high contrast in the reconstructed dominant components.

The dominant modulations provide a powerful nonstationary description of the local texture structure in an image. Computed dominant modulations have been used for nonstationary image analysis [2-5, 31, 32, 37, 40, 41, 43], texture segmentation and classification [6, 4, 7, 14, 15, 31, 33, 35, 37], edge detection and image enhancement [8, 31], recovery of 3D shape from texture [4, 9, 10], and computational stereopsis [11, 12, 13]. By using a multicomponent model such as the

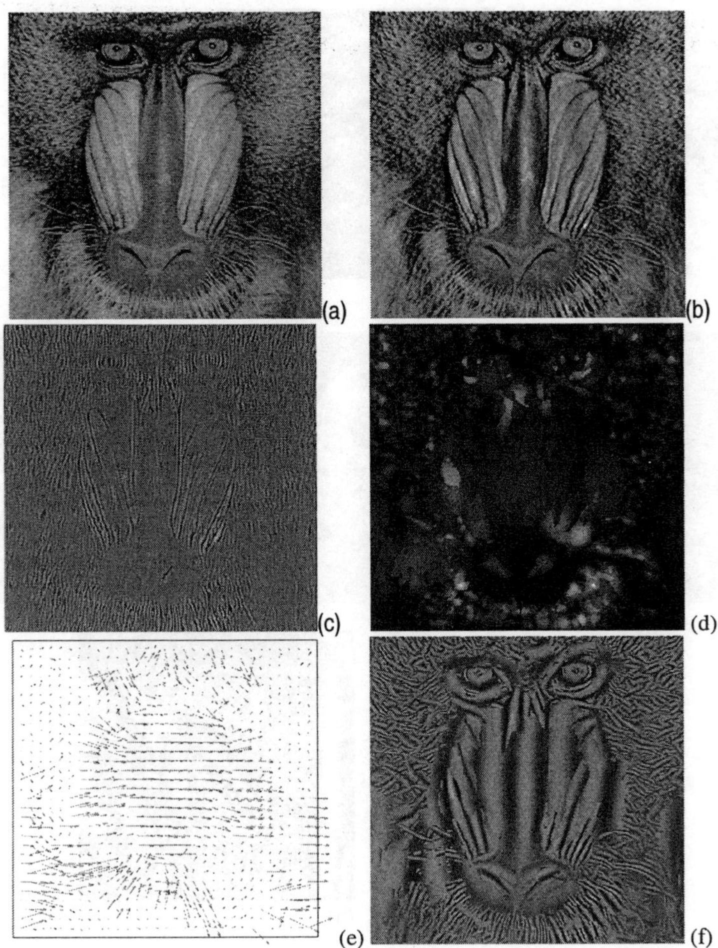

Figure 1: AM-FM modeling of *Mandrill* image. (a) Original image. (b) Reconstruction from a 43-component computed AM-FM model. (c) Reconstruction of one of the 43 components from (b). (d) Dominant AM function. (e) Dominant FM function; arrow length is proportional to the instantaneous period. (f) Reconstruction of the dominant AM-FM component from (d) and (e).

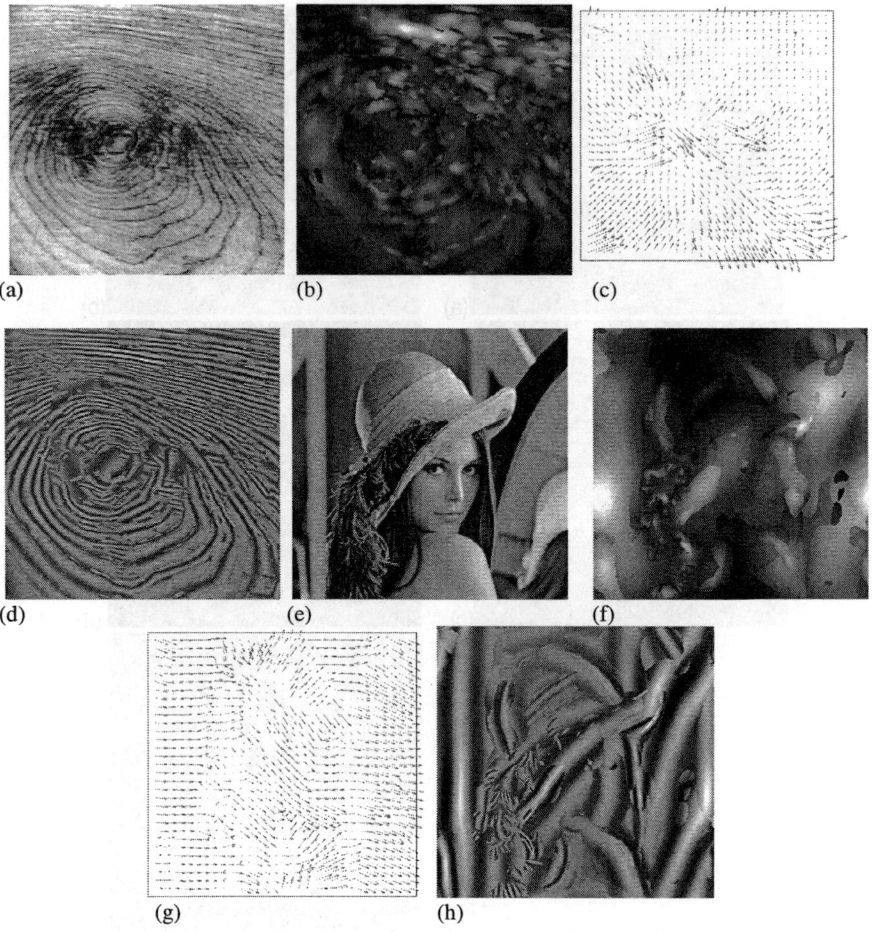

Figure 2: AM-FM modeling examples. (a) Original *Tree* image. (b) Dominant AM function. (c) Dominant FM function; arrow length is proportional to the instantaneous period. (d) Reconstruction of the dominant AM-FM component from (b) and (c). (e) Original *Lena* image. (f) Dominant AM function. (g) Dominant FM function; arrow length is proportional to the instantaneous period. (h) Reconstruction of the dominant AM-FM component from (f) and (g).

one depicted in Fig. 1(b), one obtains in addition a characterization of the various subemergent components and their interactions with each other as well as with the dominant component [1, 16, 17, 18].

A reasonable question to ask at this point is: given a real $N \times N$ digital image $s(n_1, n_2)$ with suitable complex extension $t(n_1, n_2)$, can we always compute a discrete-space AM-FM model that can represent the image exactly? The answer is yes. In particular, it is always possible to derive an orthogonal FM transform representation

$$t(n_1, n_2) = \frac{1}{K_\Phi} \sum_{k_1, k_2} T(k_1, k_2) \exp\left[j\frac{2\pi}{N} (k_1 \phi_1(n_1, n_2) + k_2 \phi_2(n_1, n_2)) \right] \quad (1.2)$$

where the discrete FM spectra are expressed by

$$T(k_1, k_2) = \frac{1}{K_\Phi} \sum_{n_1, n_2} t(n_1, n_2) \exp\left[-j\frac{2\pi}{N} (k_1 \phi_1(n_1, n_2) + k_2 \phi_2(n_1, n_2)) \right] \quad (1.3)$$

and K_Φ is a constant associated with the transform. We will investigate general M-dimensional FM transform representation of the form (1.2) and (1.3) in Section 6 on multidimensional orthogonal FM transforms.

The rest of the chapter is organized into five sections. In Section 2, we discuss the problem of isolating multiple AM-FM components, and using them to approximate any given image. In Section 3, we describe the dominant component analysis and channelized component analysis methods for AM-FM demodulation. In Section 4, we describe image segmentation applications and in Section 5 we introduce an AM-FM model for reaction-diffusion applications. In Section 6, we present results on multidimensional, orthogonal FM-transforms.

2 Isolating the Multiple Image Components

As we saw with the 2D chirp $t(x_1, x_2) = \exp\left[j(u_0 x_1^2 + v_0 x_2^2) \right]$ considered in Section I, any complex-valued continuous-domain image $t(x_1, x_2)$ admits representation as a single AM-FM function $a(x_1, x_2) \exp\left[j\phi(x_1, x_2) \right]$. Single-component models are undesirable for virtually *all* images of practical interest, however. For any but the simplest of images, the functions $a(x_1, x_2)$ and $\nabla\phi(x_1, x_2)$ required to represent the image as a single AM-FM component fail to be locally smooth, whereas it is well known that the AM and FM functions of a component are most physically meaningful when they are at least piecewise smooth [18, 19, 49].

In general, therefore, it is preferable to consider an image $t(x_1, x_2)$ to be a sum of several AM-FM components as indicated in (1.1) and to furthermore require that the modulating functions of each component be locally smooth almost everywhere. Such components are called *locally narrowband* or *locally coherent*. Although a locally coherent image component may be wideband and highly nonstationary on a global scale, it is approximately sinusoidal over *sufficiently small* neighborhoods. The notion of local coherency may be rigorously quantified in terms of the instantaneous bandwidth and certain Sobolev norms of the modulating functions [1, 4, 18, 20]. For digital images there is an even more compelling reason that representations in terms of multiple locally coherent components are desirable: all current discrete AM-FM demodulation algorithms are based on approximations of one form or another. For components that are not locally narrowband, the approximation errors can be *large*. Thus, although single-component AM-FM models exist for digital images in theory, it is generally impossible to compute them with any reasonable accuracy.

As we mentioned in Section I, one of the two respects in which computation of the model (1.1) is ill-posed involves non-unique decompositions. In this section we discuss strategies for obtaining components that are locally coherent. Linear bandpass filtering is by far the most popular approach. For example, nonlinearities in human speech were studied in [21] where short-time Fourier analysis was used to estimate the center frequencies of resonant speech components or *formants*. These center frequencies were then used to design Gabor filters for extracting individual AM-FM components from the composite speech signal. The technique was extended in [22], where an automated system for designing the Gabor filter center frequencies and bandwidths was described. Techniques for designing 2D Gabor filters to extract individual AM-FM image components were described in [6] and [23]. In each of these approaches, the main idea was to extract one or a few salient AM-FM components from each region of the signal by designing a small set of spectrally localized filters that were simultaneously spatially localized within the current region of interest.

An alternative approach is to process the signal with a multiband linear filterbank that provides reasonably complete coverage of the entire frequency domain. Gabor filterbanks of this type were utilized in [20] and [24] for the 1D case and in [1, 2, 4, 5, 7, 9-17, 31-33, 35] for the 2D case. Detailed discussions of the 2D filterbank design issues may be found in [4] and [25]. The key point is that the filters must be spatially concentrated to capture local structure in the image, but also spectrally concentrated to resolve the multiple image components from one another. Specific technical arguments supporting the idea that such jointly localized filters are powerful in their ability to extract locally coherent signal components were given in [1, 4, 6, 20, 23, 24]. It is for precisely these reasons that Gabor filters are so popular in this application – they are the unique filters that realize the uncertainty principle lower bound on joint localization [26, 27].

Let us assume that a complex image $t(x_1, x_2)$ corresponding to a given real image $s(x_1, x_2)$ has been processed with an M-channel multiband filterbank to obtain M responses $y_m(x_1, x_2)$, $0 \leq m \leq M - 1$. The most straightforward approach for computing the model (1.1) is to define the decomposition into components by assuming that the filterbank isolates components from one another on a global basis, *i.e.*, that each response $y_m(x_1, x_2)$ is globally dominated by a single AM-FM image component. This is the approach employed by the CCA technique that was used to produce the 43-component AM-FM image reconstruction of Fig. 1(b) [1]. As will be discussed in Section III, a demodulation algorithm can then be applied globally to each response image $y_m(x_1, x_2)$ to obtain estimates of the AM and FM functions for the dominating component, provided that this algorithm accounts for the action of the channel filter. When the filters are reasonably localized on a joint basis in space and frequency, the resulting components, which are known as *channelized components*, generally exhibit a reasonably high degree of local coherency. However, such computed models are only approximate unless the filterbank is orthogonal.

Therefore, if perfect reconstruction is a design goal then alternative filter types besides Gabor filters must be used. For example, one could compute AM-FM models with perfect reconstruction using wavelet filterbanks [28]. A basic issue with this is that any alternative filter type has suboptimal joint localization relative to Gabor filters. Thus, while perfect reconstruction could be achieved in theory, the image components obtained with alternative filters are generally expected to exhibit a lower degree of local coherency than those that would be obtained using Gabor filters. This in turn tends to increase the approximation errors that are expected in estimating the component modulating functions from the filterbank channel responses, once again precluding perfect reconstruction in general. Fortuitously, a complete multicomponent representation with perfect reconstruction is unnecessary for many image processing and computer vision problems of great practical interest, and Gabor filters can therefore be used to advantage. For example, most of the applications mentioned in the last paragraph of Section I utilized only the AM and FM functions corresponding to the dominant image component at each pixel.

Irrespective of what type of filterbank is used, there are alternatives to assuming that each channel response $y_m(x_1, x_2)$ is globally dominated by a single image component. When this assumption is relaxed, it becomes possible for a single component in (1.1) to exist in different filterbank channels at different points in the image. Some means must then be devised for tracking the components across the filterbank channels. A Kalman filter was used for this purpose in the *Tracked Multicomponent Analysis*, or *TMCA*, technique presented in [16].

3 AM-FM Demodulation

In this section, we review the fundamental AM-FM demodulation problem and discuss the *Dominant Component Analysis* (*DCA*) and *Channelized Components Analysis* (*CCA*) AM-FM image modeling techniques. Given a real-valued image component $s_n(x_1,x_2)$, the demodulation problem is to find a pair of modulating functions $a_n(x_1,x_2)$, $\nabla\phi_n(x_1,x_2)$ such that $s_n(x_1,x_2) = a_n(x_1,x_2)\cos[\phi_n(x_1,x_2)]$. This problem is ill-posed because the values of the component $s_n(x_1,x_2)$ are not by themselves sufficient to determine the modulating functions uniquely. The problem can be regularized by adding an imaginary part to the image component to obtain $t_n(x_1,x_2) = s_n(x_1,x_2) + jq_n(x_1,x_2) = a_n(x_1,x_2)\exp[j\phi_n(x_1,x_2)]$. The modulating functions of $t_n(x_1,x_2)$ are then unique. We therefore view addition of the imaginary part $jq_n(x_1,x_2)$ to the component s_n as being equivalent to selecting a unique pair of modulating functions; once $t_n(x_1,x_2)$ has been constructed, the AM and FM functions may be obtained using the demodulation algorithms [1]

$$\nabla\phi_n(x_1,x_2) = \mathrm{Re}\left[\frac{\nabla t_n(x_1,x_2)}{jt_n(x_1,x_2)}\right] \quad (3.1)$$

and

$$a_n(x_1,x_2) = |t_n(x_1,x_2)| . \quad (3.2)$$

The validity of these algorithms may be verified by direct calculation. An important issue that must now be addressed is how $q_n(x_1,x_2)$ should be chosen when constructing $t_n(x_1,x_2)$, for this choice determines the modulating functions and in so doing also determines the AM-FM interpretation of the real-valued component $s_n(x_1,x_2)$. Our choice is to set $q_n(x_1,x_2)$ equal to the directional multidimensional Hilbert transform of $s_n(x_1,x_2)$ [1, 16, 30]. With this choice, the complex-valued image component admits multidimensional analogues of most of the important properties of the well-known one-dimensional analytic signal, notably, stability of the solution in the presence of perturbations [19]. It should be noted that alternative techniques including the multidimensional Teager-Kaiser operator [2,8] can also be used to obtain a pair of AM and FM functions directly from the real image component $s_n(x_1,x_2)$ without constructing a complex extension $t_n(x_1,x_2)$ explicitly; these techniques typically deliver results in reasonable agreement with those obtained by applying the Hilbert transform followed by (3.1) and (3.2).

As we discussed in Section II, multiband linear filtering is often used to isolate the multiple AM-FM image components from one another prior to demodulation. Since the Hilbert transform is linear, it may be applied directly to a real image $s(x_1,x_2)$ prior to filtering. This provides in one step an imaginary part for the image $t(x_1,x_2)$ in (1.1) that is equal to the sum of the imaginary parts of the image components indicated in the right-hand side of (1.1). The complex image $t(x_1,x_2)$ is then processed with the filterbank. In [1], *quasi-eigenfunction approximations* [1,4,20] were used to establish the validity of applying (3.1) directly to the filterbank channel responses $y_m(x_1,x_2)$ to estimate the FM functions of the multiple image components $t_n(x_1,x_2)$. Having obtained these, the AM functions are then estimated by [1]

$$a_n(x_1,x_2) = \left| \frac{y_m(x_1,x_2)}{G_m\left[\nabla \phi_n(x_1,x_2)\right]} \right|, (3.3)$$

where the FM estimate $\nabla \phi_n(x_1,x_2)$ was obtained from filterbank channel m and G_m is the channel filter frequency response. Whereas (3.2) obtains the AM function directly from $t_n(x_1,x_2)$, the denominator of (3.1) accounts for the action of the channel filter when $a_n(x_1,x_2)$ is estimated instead from the channel response $y_m(x_1,x_2)$.

As we have said, any given real image $s(x_1,x_2)$, and equivalently its complex extension $t(x_1,x_2)$, can be decomposed into a sum of AM-FM components in infinitely many different ways. The goal is usually to obtain a reasonably small number of locally coherent components. The defining characteristic of CCA is that the component-wise decomposition is determined by the filterbank: it is assumed that the response of each filterbank channel $y_m(x_1,x_2)$ is dominated by one image component $t_n(x_1,x_2)$ on a global basis. The components obtained in this way are referred to as *channelized components*. For each channelized component, the modulating functions are obtained by applying (3.1) and (3.3) to the corresponding filterbank channel response. If the channel filters are reasonably well localized in space and frequency, then the channelized components are almost always highly locally coherent. However, CCA is inherently inefficient in the sense that the number of image components in the model (K in (1.1)) is by necessity equal to the number of channels in the filterbank (a 43-channel Gabor filterbank was used to compute the CCA AM-FM model depicted in Fig. 1(b)). Also, when non-orthogonal filterbanks such as Gabor filterbanks are utilized, the multicomponent CCA model is only approximate, as can be verified by close comparison of Fig. 1(b) with the original image shown in Fig. 1(a).

In DCA, the goal is to extract only a single pair of modulating functions − the so called *dominant modulations* − that correspond on a pointwise basis to that AM-FM component which dominates the image structure on a spatially local basis. At each point in the image, the dominant modulations are obtained by applying (3.1) and (3.3) to the response $y_m(x_1,x_2)$ that maximizes the selection criterion

$$\Psi_m(x_1,x_2) = \frac{\left|y_m(x_1,x_2)\right|}{\left|\max_\Omega G_m(\Omega)\right|}. (3.4)$$

As explained in [1,7], this criterion is approximately

$$\Psi_m(x_1, x_2) \approx |t_n(x_1, x_2)| \frac{|G_m[\nabla\phi_n(x_1, x_2)]|}{|\max_\Omega G_m(\Omega)|}, \quad (3.5)$$

where $t_n(x_1, x_2)$ is the AM-FM image component that dominates the channel response $y_m(x_1, x_2)$ at the point (x_1, x_2). Thus, (3.4) tends to select as dominant a large amplitude component and to estimate its modulating functions from a channel for which the dominant FM function is near the maximum transmission frequency. This approach minimizes approximation errors and numerical instabilities in the demodulation algorithms while concomitantly providing increased rejection of cross-component interference and noise. All of the dominant modulations and dominant component reconstructions given in Fig. 1 – Fig. 3 were computed using (3.1) – (3.4) with the 43-channel Gabor filterbank described in [25].

4   AM-FM Image Segmentation

In this section we describe a fully unsupervised technique for performing textured image segmentation using dominant image modulations. We will restrict our attention to the case of a discrete domain where the images are defined on a finite subspace of Z^2; discrete versions of the demodulation algorithms described in Section III were given in [1, 30]. Suppose that DCA has been applied to compute estimates $A(n_1, n_2)$ and $\nabla\phi(n_1, n_2)$ of the dominant AM and FM function at every pixel in the image. Our strategy is to map these computed functions to a modulation domain feature space and apply statistical clustering to segment the image [51–53]. An alternate, supervised segmentation method can be found in [35].

We begin by converting the dominant frequency vectors to polar coordinates according to $R(n_1, n_2) = |\nabla\phi(n_1, n_2)|$ and $\theta(n_1, n_2) = \arg[\nabla\phi(n_1, n_2)]$. To prevent any one of these features from dominating the clustering procedure, we divide each one by the respective sample standard deviation to obtain normalized features $\tilde{A}, \tilde{R}$ and $\tilde{\theta}$.

To obtain an upper bound M on the number of regions in the image, we apply a 3-D Gaussian filter to the $\tilde{A}$ - $\tilde{R}$ - $\tilde{\theta}$ feature space to estimate the local density of feature vectors about each point. Gradient ascent is then used to identify local maxima in the filtered result and group the feature vectors into clusters [54]. By thresholding on the number of feature vectors in each cluster, we remove the minor clusters and merge them with larger clusters via the nearest neighbor rule. We denote the number of remaining cluster by M, our estimated upper bound on the number of regions present in the image. The centroids of these M clusters are then used to initialize a k-means clustering algorithm [32] to segment the image.

For k-means clustering, we augment the $\tilde{A}$-$\tilde{R}$-$\tilde{\theta}$ feature vectors with two additional spatial position features to encourage the formation of clusters corresponding to spatially connected regions in the image. For each pixel, normalized position features $\tilde{X}$ and $\tilde{Y}$ are computed by dividing the row and column coordinates of the pixel by the respective sample standard deviations. The centroid of each of the M clusters obtained by density clustering are extended to this 5-D feature space by averaging the normalized position features over all pixels in the cluster.

The similarity measure used for k-means clustering is based on modulation domain entropy [51], [52]. We reason that a feature that has a flat, unimodal, or extremely narrow histogram provides little class separability information. If the histogram exhibits multiple well-defined modes, however, we expect that the feature is powerful for discriminating between the various textured regions in the image. Hence, a feature with lower modulation domain entropy is generally expected to provide greater class separability, provided that the feature histogram is not *too narrow*. Motivated by this reasoning, we define the entropy for each of the three modulation features in the usual way according to, *e.g.*,

$$E_{\tilde{A}} = -\sum_q p_{\tilde{A}}(q)\log_2 p_{\tilde{A}}(q). \quad (4.1)$$

where the $p_{\tilde{A}}(q)$ are the histogram values normalized to be probabilities. We then define a corresponding normalized entropy figure

$$\varepsilon_{\tilde{A}} = \frac{E_{\tilde{A}}}{\max_q p_{\tilde{A}}(q) - \min_q p_{\tilde{A}}(q)}, \quad (4.2)$$

that penalizes features with overly narrow histograms, where a small normalized entropy is indicative of a feature possessing high class discrimination capability.

The total normalized modulation domain entropy for the dominant image modulations is then given by $\varepsilon_T = \varepsilon_{\tilde{A}} + \varepsilon_{\tilde{R}} + \varepsilon_{\tilde{\theta}}$, which we use to calculate entropy scaling factors $\alpha = \left(\varepsilon_T - \varepsilon_{\tilde{A}}\right)/\varepsilon_{\tilde{A}}$, $\beta = \left(\varepsilon_T - \varepsilon_{\tilde{R}}\right)/\varepsilon_{\tilde{R}}$, and $\gamma = \left(\varepsilon_T - \varepsilon_{\tilde{\theta}}\right)/\varepsilon_{\tilde{\theta}}$ that will be used to weight the modulation domain features in the k-means similarity measure. The factors α, β, γ take larger large when the corresponding features contribute only smaller fractions of the total normalized entropy. The similarity measure between pixels (n_1, n_2) and (m_1, m_2) is then given by

$$S(m_1, m_2, n_1, n_2) = \left\{\alpha\left[\tilde{A}(m_1, m_2) - \tilde{A}(n_1, n_2)\right]^2\right.$$

$$+ \beta\left[\tilde{R}(m_1, m_2) - \tilde{R}(n_1, n_2)\right]^2 + \gamma\left[\tilde{\theta}(m_1, m_2) - \tilde{\theta}(n_1, n_2)\right]^2 \quad (4.3)$$

$$\left. + \left[\tilde{X}(m_1, m_2) - \tilde{X}(n_1, n_2)\right]^2 + \left[\tilde{Y}(m_1, m_2) - \tilde{Y}(n_1, n_2)\right]^2\right\}^{\frac{1}{2}}.$$

290

Using the similarity measure (4.3), the k-means algorithm is run for $1 \le k \le M$. Within each iteration, the centroids of the k largest clusters found by the density based clustering approach are used as initial cluster centers. Thus, since the cluster seeds are deterministic rather than random, only one execution of the k-means algorithm is required for each $k \in [1, M]$. The squared-error validation criterion is used to select the best one from among the M k-means results, and the selected cluster configuration is mapped back to the image domain to obtain an initial segmentation. Since this initial segmentation often contains many small regions and long "streaks" of misclassified pixels and usually exhibits irregularly shaped region boundaries, we apply two post processing steps to refine it and arrive at the final segmentation. First, connected components labeling with minor region removal is used to correct the small regions of misclassified pixels. Second, a morphological majority filter is applied to remove any remaining streaks and smooth the boundaries between regions.

Two examples of this unsupervised texture segmentation technique are shown in Fig. 3 and Fig. 4. The original image of Fig. 3(a) is a juxtaposition of four Brodatz textures [59]. The dominant AM function computed by DCA is given in Fig. 3(b), while the computed dominant FM function is given in Fig. 3(c). A reconstruction of the dominant AM-FM component reconstructed from the modulating functions shown in Fig. 3(b) and (c) appears in Fig. 3(d). When the density clustering procedure was applied to the dominant modulations, 17 local maxima were identified and used to form candidate clusters in the modulation domain feature space. Seven of these clusters were removed by thresholding and merged with the larger clusters to obtain an upper bound of $M = 10$ on the number of image regions.

The k-means clustering algorithm was executed ten times, once for each $k \in [1, 10]$. The $k = 4$ result was selected by the squared-error validation criterion and the initial raw segmentation obtained by mapping this result back to the image domain is shown in Fig. 3(e), where a number of small misclassified regions and "streaks" are apparent. The refined segmentation obtained by connected components labeling with minor region removal is given in Fig. 3(f), while the final segmentation obtained after application of a 9×9 morphological majority filter appears in Fig. 3(g). In this example, 95.74% of the pixels were correctly classified.

Our second example is the image *building0008* from the MIT Media Laboratory *VisTex* database [60]. The original image is shown in Fig. 4(a). The computed dominant AM and FM functions are given in Fig. 4(b) and (c), while a reconstruction of the dominant AM-FM component is given in Fig. 4(d). The density clustering procedure delivered an upper bound of $M = 9$ on the number of regions present and k-means clustering was run for $1 \le k \le 9$. The $k = 2$ result was selected by the validation criterion and the initial segmentation obtained by mapping this result back to the image domain is shown in Fig. 4(e). As with the raw k-means

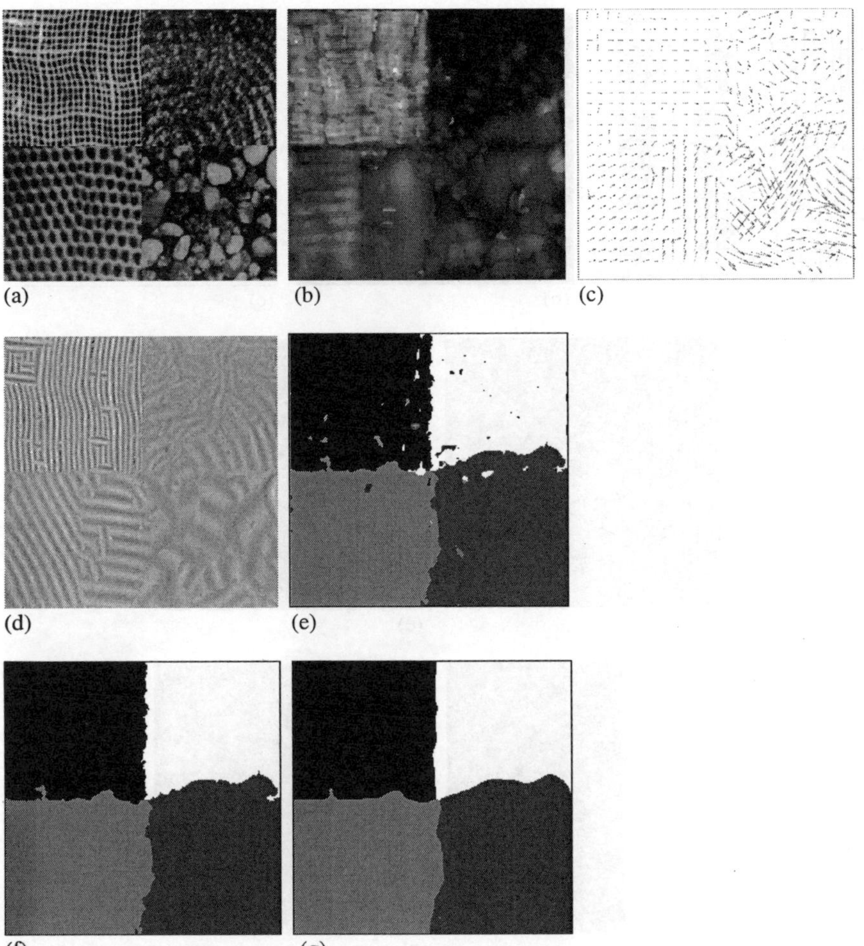

Figure 3: AM-FM texture segmentation example. (a) Original four-texture image. (b) Dominant AM function computed by DCA. (c) Dominant FM function; arrow length is proportional to the instantaneous period. (d) Reconstruction of the dominant AM-FM component from (b) and (c). (e) Initial segmentation delivered by k-means clustering and squared-error validation criterion. (f) Refined segmentation obtained by applying connected components labeling. (g) Final segmentation after application of morphological majority filter.

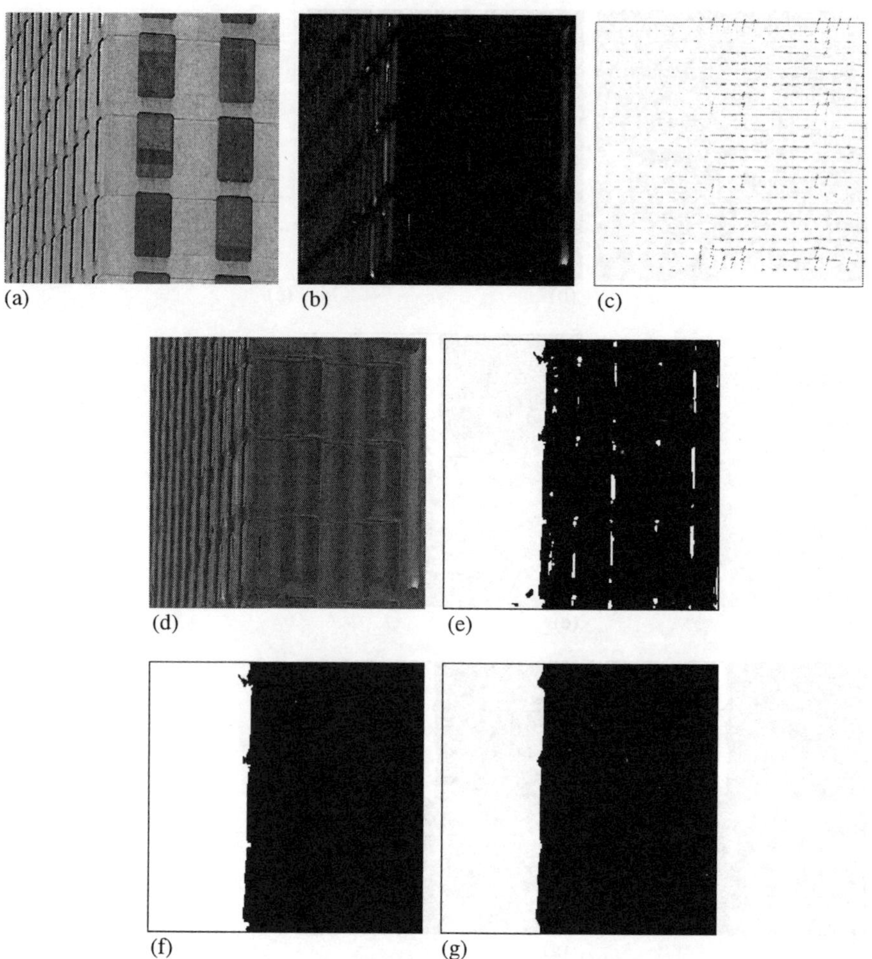

Figure 4: AM-FM texture segmentation example. (a) Original *building0008* image. (b) Dominant AM function computed by DCA. (c) Dominant FM function; arrow length is proportional to the instantaneous period. (d) Reconstruction of the dominant AM-FM component from (b) and (c). (e) Initial segmentation delivered by *k*-means clustering and squared-error validation criterion. (f) Refined segmentation obtained by applying connected components labeling. (g) Final segmentation after application of morphological majority filter.

result of Fig. 3(e), several small regions and "streaks" of misclassified pixels are clearly visible in Fig. 4(e). Connected components labeling with minor region removal was applied to obtain the refined segmentation shown in Fig. 4(f), and the final segmentation result obtained after morphological filtering is given in Fig. 4(g).

5 AM-FM Reaction-Diffusion for Texture Completion

AM-FM analysis can also be used in the process of recreating textured regions that have been obscured or occluded. Here, the input image is modeled within an AM-FM framework, and the dominant components of the oriented texture are estimated at each position. The dominant components in the region neighboring the occluded regions are used to generate the texture for the region of interest. In contrast to methods that generate a texture and attempt to insert the texture within the image in one step, our approach adapts or grows the texture via partial differential equations (PDE's). Here, texture generation and smoothing are combined using coupled PDE's that govern a *reaction-diffusion* process. The reaction mechanism utilizes the dominant component analysis to enforce a suitable pattern on the missing region. At the same time, anisotropic diffusion is used to adaptively smooth the image, producing a seamless restoration.

The reaction-diffusion mechanism used for texture completion is modeled by

$$\frac{\partial \mathbf{I}}{\partial t} = \rho_D \mathbf{D} + \rho_R \mathbf{R} \quad (5.1)$$

where $\mathbf{D}$ is the diffusion term (discussed below), $\mathbf{R}$ is the reaction term (discussed below), and ρ_D and ρ_R denote the rate of diffusion and reaction, respectively. The rate of diffusion ρ_D is constant within the occluded region. Typically, $\rho_D < 1/4$ to ensure stability. The rate of reaction ρ_R is also constant within the occluded region. In the area surrounding the occluded region, the rate of reaction is decreased linearly until a rate of zero is obtained. By enacting reaction at a reduced rate, the texture in the surrounding region is fused with that of the occluded region. Thus, the reaction-diffusion approach has the benefit of reduced boundary artifacts. For a specific image location $\mathbf{x} = (x_1, x_2)$, we have

$$\frac{\partial I(\mathbf{x})}{\partial t} = \rho_D(\mathbf{x})D(\mathbf{x}) + \rho_R(\mathbf{x})R(\mathbf{x}) . \quad (5.2)$$

A discrete Jacobi update for (5.2) is given by:

$$I_{t+1}(\mathbf{x}) \leftarrow I_t(\mathbf{x}) + \rho_D(\mathbf{x})D(\mathbf{x}) + \rho_R(\mathbf{x})R(\mathbf{x}) . \quad (5.3)$$

where $I_t(\mathbf{x})$ is the intensity of position $\mathbf{x}$ at iteration t and $\mathbf{x} \in \mathbf{Z}^2$. The initial image intensities in $\mathbf{I}_0$ are equal to those in the input image $\mathbf{I}$, except in the case of the occluded region.

For the occluded region, we "seed" the reaction-diffusion process with noise that is distributed identically to that of the surrounding region. Let Ω denote the

294

domain of the image and $\mathbf{U} \subset \Omega$ denote the unoccluded region. Let $\mathbf{B} \subset \mathbf{U}$ denote the region surrounding the occlusion/latency and $\mathbf{O} = \mathbf{U}^c$ the occluded region. If $\mathbf{x} \in \mathbf{U}$, then $I_0(\mathbf{x}) = I(\mathbf{x})$. But, if $\mathbf{x} \in \mathbf{O}$, then $I_0(\mathbf{x}) = R$, where R is a random variable with density $f_R(i) = H_\mathbf{B}(i)/|\mathbf{B}|$ where $H_\mathbf{B}(i)$ is the histogram value (number of occurrences) for intensity i within region $\mathbf{B}$, and $|\mathbf{B}|$ is the cardinality of $\mathbf{B}$. The width of $\mathbf{B}$, the region surrounding the occlusion, depends on the maximum instantaneous period of the dominant local texture pattern. Let $T_{\max}$ denote this maximum width (estimated by the AM-FM dominate component analysis presented in Section IV). Then, we define the width of $\mathbf{B}$ to be $2T_{\max}$ pixels. Using this method of defining the boundary region $\mathbf{B}$, we ensure that the boundary is more than one full pattern period in width.

Seeding the region with noise identically distributed as the intensities of the surrounding region has the effect of providing a disocclusion solution that has a similar appearance as the surrounding region in the image. If uniformly distributed noise is used, as in [50], the repaired region does not match the surrounding region in graylevel distribution and results in an unnatural appearance.

Given the basic reaction-diffusion model, we now define the diffusion and reaction terms for texture disocclusion. Diffusion and reaction have conflicting objectives. The goal of diffusion is smoothing, while the goal of reaction is pattern formation. Without diffusion, a smooth texture pattern could not be generated from the seed noise. Since anisotropic diffusion encourages intra-region, not inter-region, smoothing, the texture can be smoothed without eliminating the important intensity transitions (edges). The discrete diffusion update used in (5.3) is

$$D(\mathbf{x}) = \sum_{d=1}^{\Gamma} c_d(\mathbf{x}) \nabla I_d(\mathbf{x}) \, , \quad (5.5)$$

where Γ is the number of directions in which diffusion is computed, and $\nabla I_d(\mathbf{x})$ is the directional derivative (simple difference) in direction d at location $\mathbf{x}$. For $\Gamma = 4$, we use the simple differences $\nabla I_d(\mathbf{x})$ with respect to the "western", "eastern", "northern" and "southern" neighbors. For example, if $\mathbf{x} = (x_1, x_2)$, $\nabla I_1(x_1, x_2) = I(x_1 - 1, x_2) - I(x_1, x_2)$.

A Gaussian-convolved version of the image is then utilized in computing the gradient magnitudes used in the diffusion coefficients:

$$c(\mathbf{x}) = \exp\left\{ -\left[\frac{\nabla S(\mathbf{x})}{k} \right]^2 \right\} , (5.6)$$

where $\mathbf{S} = \mathbf{I} * \mathbf{g}_\sigma$ is the convolution of $\mathbf{I}$ with a Gaussian of standard deviation σ.

In the reaction process, we encourage formation of patterns of a given granularity and directionality, corresponding to a localized area in the frequency domain covered by a specific Gabor filter $\mathbf{G}$ given by

$$\mathbf{G} = \cos[(2\pi/N)(ux_1 + vx_2)]g_\sigma(x_1, x_2) \quad (5.7)$$

for an NxN image indexed by (x_1, x_2) and a Gaussian $g_\sigma(x_1, x_2)$, where σ is the scale parameter (standard deviation of the Gaussian). In this case, the Gabor function has standard deviation (width) of σ and center frequency u, v. The Gabor parameters are automatically determined by the AM-FM DCA method.

To produce patterns that correspond to oriented texture features, the reaction term is given by

$$R(\mathbf{x}) = \mathbf{G_x} \otimes \left[\varphi(\mathbf{G_x} * \mathbf{I})\right]. \quad (5.8)$$

Here, $\mathbf{G_x}$ is the Gabor filter matched to the dominant component at position $\mathbf{x}$. The operator $\otimes$ denotes correlation and $*$ denotes convolution. The function $\varphi(\cdot)$ weighs the contribution of the Gabor filter. For $\varphi(\cdot)$, we use the formulation proposed in [50]:

$$\varphi(\xi) = -1 - \left(\frac{1}{1 + (|\xi|/k)^2}\right) \quad (5.9)$$

where k is a scaling constant. For example, in the case of fingerprint pattern generation, a typical and useful application of this technique, we can set k according the desired contrast within the fingerprint ridges, as with (5.6).

The net effect of (5.8) is to produce a reaction where the pattern of specified granularity and directionality has not emerged. Therefore, (5.8) will stabilize when the local spectrum of $\mathbf{I}$ contains components within the localized spectral region covered by the Gabor filter frequency response. Since the patterns that emerge are not necessarily smooth, the simultaneous diffusion process allows the creation of smooth patterns localized in both space and frequency.

For example, consider the partially occluded fingerprint images shown in Figs. 5(a) and 6(a). The combination of AM-FM DCA and reaction-diffusion leads to the repaired images shown in Figs 5(b) and 6(b). Fig. 7 shows the dominant component frequencies estimated around the perimeters of the two occlusions.

6 Multidimensional Orthogonal FM Transforms

In this section, we develop and compute discrete, orthogonal FM Transforms. The fundamental application of this research is in image coding of wideband images [34, 36, 37]. Classical frequency-based approaches to image compression, e.g, based on the DCT, are less effective for wideband images since the achievable energy compaction is limited. The FM transform approach described here achieves efficiency by a process of rearranging the samples to resemble a narrowband signal, following which a DCT-like transformation becomes more effective. We will summarize the theory, and then demonstrate two orthogonal FM transform decompositions on randomly generated images.

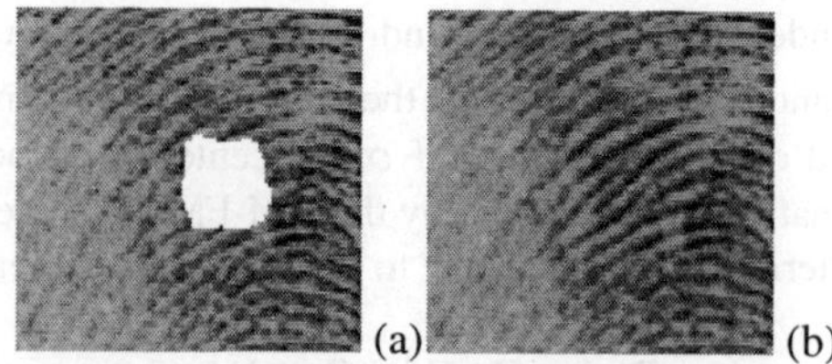

Figure 5: (a) Occluded 'oriented' fingerprint image. (b) After disocclusion using proposed AM-FM reaction-diffusion method [58].

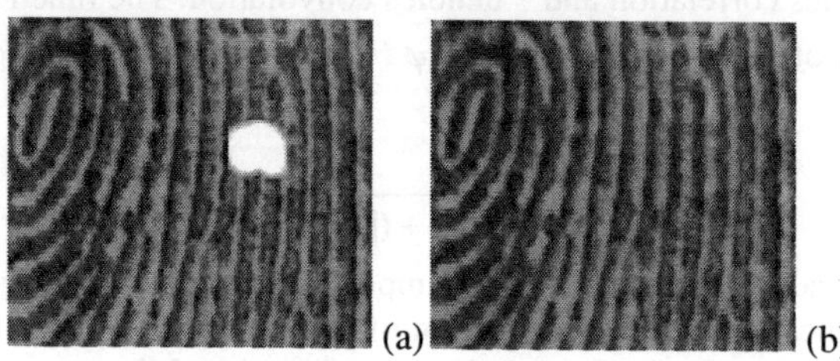

Figure 6: (a) Occluded "stripe" fingerprint image. (b) After disocclusion using AM-FM reaction-diffusion method [58].

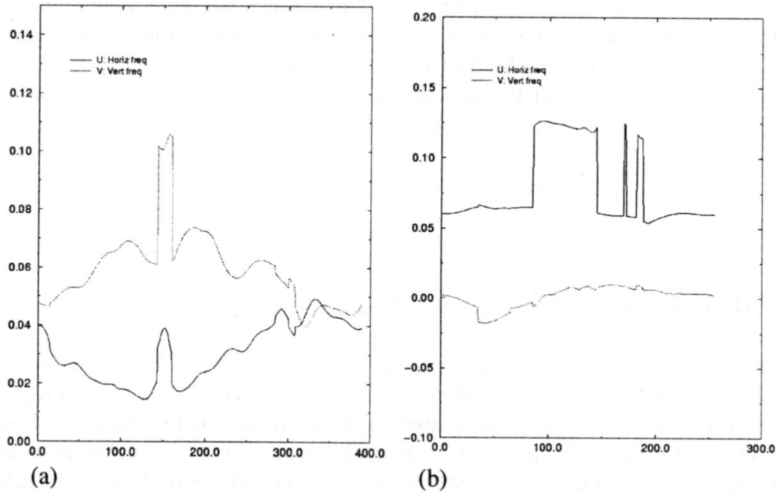

Figure 7: Graphs of dominant component frequencies (u, v) around the perimeter of the occluded area: (a) for "oriented" fingerprint image; (b) for "stripe" fingerprint image. (In each figure, the x-axis represents distance around the perimeter, and the y-axis represents frequency in cycles per sample [58].

We are interested in expressing discrete signals as a sum of FM harmonics

$$x(\mathbf{n}) = \frac{1}{K_\Phi} \sum_{\mathbf{k} \in Q} X(\mathbf{k}) \exp\left[j \frac{2\pi}{N} \mathbf{k} \cdot \Phi(\mathbf{n}) \right] \quad (6.1)$$

where the FM spectra are expressed by

$$X(\mathbf{k}) = \frac{1}{K_\Phi} \sum_{\mathbf{k} \in Q} x(\mathbf{n}) \exp\left[-j \frac{2\pi}{N} \mathbf{k} \cdot \Phi(\mathbf{n}) \right] \quad (6.2)$$

and where $\mathbf{n} = (n_1, n_2, \ldots, n_M)$ and $\mathbf{k} = (k_1, k_2, \ldots, k_M)$ are elements of $Q = (Z/N)^M$. We assume that the phase function $\Phi(\cdot) = (\phi_1(\cdot), \phi_2(\cdot), \ldots, \phi_M(\cdot))$ takes values in $(\mathbf{R}/N)^M$ where $\mathbf{R}$ denotes the real line, and define the inner product reduced mod N :

$$\mathbf{k} \cdot \Phi(\mathbf{n}) = k_1 \phi_1(\mathbf{n}) + k_2 \phi_2(\mathbf{n}) + \cdots + k_M \phi_M(\mathbf{n}) \mod N.$$

We can compute a solution of (6.1) and (6.2) in terms of the multidimensional phase function as given in the following proposition [34, 37]:

Proposition [Orthonormality condition]
Assume that Φ satisfies

$$\frac{1}{K_\Phi^2} \sum_{\mathbf{k} \in Q} \exp\left[j \frac{2\pi}{N} \mathbf{k} \cdot (\Phi(\mathbf{n}) - \Phi(\mathbf{p})) \right] = \delta(\mathbf{n} - \mathbf{p})$$

for all $\mathbf{n}, \mathbf{p} \in Q$, where $\delta(\cdot)$ denotes the Kronecker delta function. Then any bounded signal $x(\cdot)$ on Q is given by

$$x(\mathbf{n}) = \frac{1}{K_\Phi} \sum_{\mathbf{k} \in Q} X(\mathbf{k}) \exp\left[j \frac{2\pi}{N} \mathbf{k} \cdot \Phi(\mathbf{n}) \right],$$

where the FM spectrum is given by

$$X(\mathbf{k}) = \frac{1}{K_\Phi} \sum_{\mathbf{k} \in Q} x(\mathbf{n}) \exp\left[-j \frac{2\pi}{N} \mathbf{k} \cdot \Phi(\mathbf{n}) \right].$$

The converse of the orthonormality condition is that an orthogonal FM transform exists only if the orthonormality condition is satisfied. This condition is also true. The basic result is that the orthogonal FM transform exists if and only if the orthonormality condition is satisfied.

A necessary and sufficient condition for satisfying the orthonormality condition is given in the following theorem (see [34, 37]):

Theorem [M-D orthonormal FM transforms]

Let $K_\Phi = N^{M/2}$ where M is the number of spatial dimensions. Let $\Phi = (\phi_1, \phi_2, ..., \phi_M)$. Then Φ satisfies the orthonormal condition if and only if there is a symmetric function $\alpha : Q \times Q \to \{1, ..., M\}$ such that

$$\phi_{\alpha(\mathbf{n}, \mathbf{p})}(\mathbf{n}) - \phi_{\alpha(\mathbf{n}, \mathbf{p})}(\mathbf{p}) \quad (6.3)$$

is a nonzero integer mod N whenever $\mathbf{n} \neq \mathbf{p}$. By *symmetric*, we mean that $\alpha(\mathbf{n}, \mathbf{p}) = \alpha(\mathbf{p}, \mathbf{n})$ for all $\mathbf{n}, \mathbf{p} \in Q$.

The theorem states that an orthogonal FM transform can be constructed if and only if for any two distinct points $\mathbf{n}$, $\mathbf{p}$ we can find at least one of the multidimensional phase function components of Φ, say ϕ_i, such that $\phi_i(\mathbf{n}) - \phi_i(\mathbf{p})$ is a non-zero integer. The condition specified by (6.3) is fairly general. It is the most general condition possible, but it is only of interest if we can use it to build FM transforms for general wideband images. In order to find phase functions that satisfy (6.3), we must view Φ as a suitable permutation that re-arranges two-dimensional lattice points [34, 37]. The orthogonal FM transforms under this restriction are equivalent to a re-arrangement of the image samples, followed by an FFT. The inverse FM transform is simply an inverse FFT, followed by the inverse re-arrangement.

To compute optimal re-arrangements, we view the multidimensional signals as single-dimensional. For example, a 2D image is replaced by a 1D signal of the concatenated columns of the image. The optimal re-arrangement is then computed using the rearrangement algorithm given in [36].

Proposition (see proof and associated algorithms in [36])

If Φ sorts x and Ψ sorts t, then $\Phi \circ \Psi^{-1}$, where $\circ$ denotes function composition, matches x to t.

The proposition leads to an algorithm for re-arranging an arbitrary input signal into a new signal so that the mean-square error of the difference between the new and the target FM signals is minimized. When the mean-square error is minimized, we say that the two signals are matched. The target FM signal involves a small number of FM harmonics, as shown in Table 1. In Table 1, the required bits per sample denote the number of bits that are required for encoding the permutation for the FM transform. Using an optimal permutation, the FM spectrum is concentrated on a small number of FM harmonics. The number of FM harmonics is given in column 3. In column 1, we describe the optimal input signal that will have its FM spectrum concentrated in the small number of FM harmonics given in column 3. An optimal input signal is one that only allows 2, 4, 8, ..., N equally-distributed, distinct values.

Two examples of FM transforms are shown in Figures 8 and 9. In Figure 8, we show a bimodal distribution, and a four-modal distribution is shown in Figure 9. In

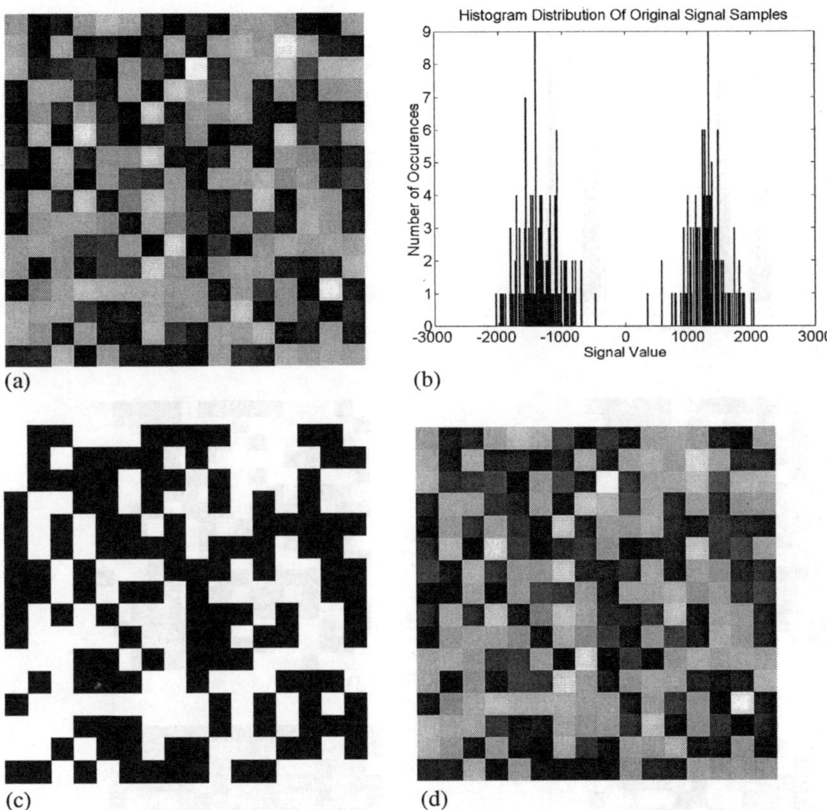

Figure 8: Multidimensional FM transform example for single bit permutations. (a) The original random image. (b) The histogram of the intensity values of the image in (a). (c) FM transform reconstruction using the DC coefficient and the dominant harmonic coefficient. (d) FM transform reconstruction using all coefficients. The FM transform DC and dominant harmonic coefficients were divided by 2, and rounded off to the nearest integer. For (d), the rest of the FM harmonic coefficients were divided by 256 (the total number of samples), and then rounded off to the nearest integer. Under these conditions, at 11.8 bits per pixel, the FM transform has a PSNR of 56 dB, while the original FFT (after quantizing the result of dividing the DC by 2, and quantizing the result of dividing the non-DC coefficients by 256), requires 13.1 bits per pixel for the same PSNR.

300

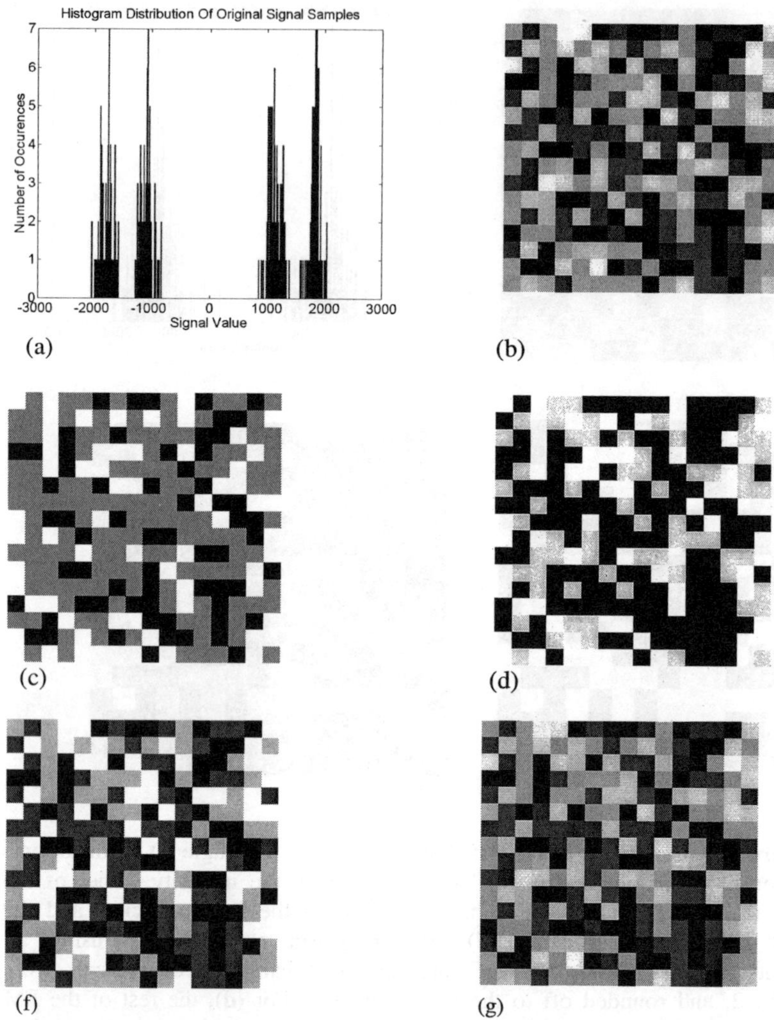

Figure 9: Multidimensional FM transform example for two bit permutations. (a) The histogram of the intensity values of the original image shown in (b). The. FM reconstruction using: (c) the DC plus one dominant FM coefficient, (d) DC plus two dominant FM coefficients, (e) DC plus three coefficients, and (f) all the FM coefficients. Quantization was done as in Figure 8. Under the same quantization scheme as in Figure 8, at 56 dB, FM requires 10.5 bpp, while FFT requires 13.1 bpp.

both cases, for the examples shown, the FM transforms provides better rate-distortion performance than the FFT. Many more examples can be found in [34, 36, 37], where the FM transform is compared against the DCT, the FFT, and JPEG. The examples demonstrate the advance in developing AM-FM representations for wide-band signals.

7 Concluding Remarks

Rather than following the usual paths of summarizing our work, or of pointing out the plethora of world-changing future research directions that it implies, we'd like to conclude with a simple note of thanks to Tom Huang for helping to make this such an interesting field of endeavor, and for serving as the inspiration for generations of students, past, present, and future of image processing.

8 Acknowledgement

The authors wish to express their gratitude to "Francis" Teck Beng Yap of the University of Oklahoma School of Electrical and Computer Engineering, who contributed substantially to the development of the texture segmentation algorithm presented in Section 4 and to production of the examples shown in Figs. 3 and 4.

References

1. J.P. Havlicek, D.S. Harding, and A.C. Bovik, "Multidimensional quasi-eigenfunction approximations and multicomponent AM-FM models," *IEEE Trans. Image Proc.*, vol 9, no. 2, pp. 227-242, Feb. 2000.
2. P. Maragos and A.C. Bovik, "Image Demodulation Using Multidimensional Energy Separation," J. Opt. Soc. Amer. A, vol. 12, no. 9, pp. 1867-1876, Sept. 1995.
3. B. Friedlander and J.M. Francos, "An Estimation Algorithm for 2-D Polynomial Phase Signals," *IEEE Trans. Image Proc.*, vol. 5, no. 6, pp. 1084-1087, Jun. 1996.
4. A.C. Bovik, N. Gopal, T. Emmoth, and A. Restrepo, "Localized measurement of emergent image frequencies by Gabor wavelets," *IEEE Trans. Info. Theory*, vol. 38, no. 2, pp. 691-712, Mar. 1992.
5. J.P. Havlicek, A.C. Bovik, and P. Maragos, "Modulation models for image processing and wavelet-based image demodulation," in *Proc. 26th IEEE*

Asilomar Conf. Signals, Syst., Comput., Pacific Grove, CA, pp. 805-810, Oct. 26-28, 1992.

6. A.C. Bovik, M. Clark, and W.S. Geisler, "Multichannel texture analysis using localized spatial filters," *IEEE Trans. Pattern Anal. Machine Intell.*, vol. 12, no. 1, pp. 55-73, Jan. 1990.

7. J.P. Havlicek, "The evolution of modern texture processing," *Elektrik, Turkish J. Elect. Eng., Computer Sci.,*" vol. 5, no. 1, pp. 1-28, 1997.

8. S.K. Mitra, S. Thurnhofer, M. Lightstone, and N. Strobel, "Two-dimensional Teager operators and their image processing applications," in *Proc. 1995 IEEE Workshop Nonlin. Signal and Image Proc.*, Neos Marmaras, Halkidiki, Greece, pp. 959-962, Jun. 20-22, 1995.

9. B.J. Super and A.C. Bovik, "Planar surface orientation from texture spatial frequencies," *Pattern Recog.*, vol. 28, no. 5, pp. 728-743, 1995.

10. B.J. Super and A.C. Bovik, "Shape from texture using local spectral moments," *IEEE Trans. Pattern Anal. Machine Intell.*, vol. 17, no. 4, pp. 333-343, 1995.

11. T.-Y. Chen and A.C. Bovik, "Stereo disparity from multiscale processing of local image phase," in *Proc. IEEE Int'l. Symp. Comput. Vision*, Coral Gables, FL, Nov. 20-22, 1995.

12. T.-Y. Chen, A.C. Bovik, and B.J. Super, "Multiscale stereopsis via Gabor filter phase response," in *Proc. IEEE Int'l. Conf. Syst., Man, and Cyber.*, San Antonio, TX, pp. 55-60, Oct. 2-5, 1994.

13. T.-Y. Chen, A.C. Bovik, and L.K. Cormack, "Stereoscopic ranging by matching image modulations," *IEEE Trans.Image Proc.*, vol. 8, no. 6, pp. 785-797, Jun. 1999.

14. T. Tangsukson and J.P. Havlicek, "AM-FM image segmentation," in *Proc. IEEE Int'l Conf. Image Proc.*, Vancouver, Canada, Sep. 10-13, 2000.

15. T. Tangsukson and J.P. Havlicek, "Modulation domain image segmentation," in *Proc. IEEE Southwest Symp. Image Anal., Interp.*, Austin, TX, pp. 46-50, Apr. 2-4, 2000.

16. J. P. Havlicek, D. S. Harding, and A. C. Bovik, "The multi-component AM-FM image representation," *IEEE Trans. Image Proc.*, vol. 5, no. 6, pp. 1094-1100, Jun. 1996.

17. J.P. Havlicek, D.S. Harding, and A.C. Bovik, "Extracting essential modulated image structure," in *Proc. 30th IEEE Asilomar Conf. Signals, Syst., Comput.*, Pacific Grove, CA, pp. 1014-1018, Nov. 3-6, 1996.

18. J.P. Havlicek, D.S. Harding, and A.C. Bovik, "Multicomponent multidimensional signals," *Multidimensional Syst. and Signal Proc.*, vol. 9, no. 4, pp. 391-398, Oct. 1998.

19. L. Cohen, *Time-frequency analysis*, Prentice Hall, Englewood Cliffs, NJ, 1995.

20. A.C. Bovik, J.P. Havlicek, D.S. Harding, and M.D. Desai, "Limits on discrete modulated signals," *IEEE Trans. Signal Proc.*, vol. 45, no. 4, pp. 867-879, Apr. 1997.

21. P. Maragos, J.F. Kaiser, and T.F. Quatieri, "Energy separation in signal modulations with applications to speech analysis," *IEEE Trans. Signal Proc.*, vol. 42, no. 10, pp. 3024-3051, Oct. 1993.

22. H.M. Hanson, P. Maragos, and A. Potamianos, "A system for finding speech formants and modulations via energy separation," *IEEE Trans. Speech and Audio Proc.*, vol. 2, no. 3, pp. 436-443, Jul. 1994.

23. A.C. Bovik, "Analysis of multichannel narrow-band filters for image texture segmentation," *IEEE Trans. Signal Proc.*, vol. 39, no. 9, pp. 2025-2043, Sep. 1991.

24. A.C. Bovik, P. Maragos, and T.F. Quatieri, "AM-FM energy detection and separation in noise using multiband energy operators," *IEEE Trans. Signal Proc.*, vol. 41, no. 12, pp. 3245-3265, Dec. 1993.

25. J.P. Havlicek, A.C. Bovik, and D. Chen, "AM-FM image modeling and Gabor analysis," in *Visual Information Representation, Communication, and Image Processing*, C.W. Chen and Y. Zhang, eds., Marcel Dekker, New York, 1999.

26. D. Gabor, "Theory of Communication," *J. Inst. Elect. Eng. London*, vol. 93, no. III, pp. 429-457, 1946.

27. J.G. Daugman, "Uncertainty relation for resolution in space, spatial frequency, and orientation optimized by two-dimensional visual cortical filters," *J. Opt. Soc. Am. A*, vol. 2, no. 7, pp. 1160-1169, Jul. 1985.

28. G. Strang and T. Nguyen, *Wavelets and filter banks*, Wellesley-Cambridge Press, Wellesley, MA, 1996.

29. L. Hong, Y. Wan, and A. Jain, "Fingerprint Image Enhancement: Algorithm Performance and Evaluation," *IEEE. Trans. Pattern Anal. Machine Intell.*, vol. 20, no. 8, pp. 777-789, August 1998.

30. J. P. Havlicek and A. C. Bovik, "Image Modulation Models," *The Image and Video Processing Handbook*, Ed. A.C. Bovik, Academic Press (San Diego), 1999.

31. M. S. Pattichis, A. C. Bovik, and M. Desai, "Latent Fingerprint Analysis Using An AM-FM Model", in revision, *Pattern Recognition*.

32. M.S. Pattichis and A.C. Bovik, "Non-stationary Texture Analysis Using Multidimensional Frequency Modulation," *in preparation*, to be submitted to *IEEE Trans. on Pattern Analysis and Machine Intelligence*.

33. M. S. Pattichis, G. Panayi, A. C. Bovik, and H. Shun-Pin, "Fingerprint Classification Using an AM-FM Model," *IEEE Transactions on Image Processing,* vol. 10, no. 6, pp. 951-954. June 2001.

34. M. S. Pattichis, A. C. Bovik, J. W. Havlicek, and N. D. Sidiropoulos, "Multidimensional Orthogonal FM Transforms," *IEEE Transactions on Image Processing,* vol. 10, no. 3, pp. 448-464. March 2001.

35. M. S. Pattichis, C. S. Pattichis, M. Avraam, A. C. Bovik, and K. Kyriakou, "AM-FM Texture Segmentation in Electron Microscopic Muscle Imaging,"

304

IEEE Transactions on Medical Imaging, vol. 19, no. 12, pp. 1253-1258. December 2000.

36. N.D. Sidiropoulos, M.S. Pattichis, A.C. Bovik, and J.W. Havlicek, "COPERM: Transform-Domain Energy Compaction by Optimal Permutation," *IEEE Trans. on Signal Processing*, vol. 47, no. 6, pp. 1679-1688, June 1999.

37. Marios S. Pattichis, "AM-FM Transforms with Applications", *Ph.D. Dissertation*, The University of Texas at Austin, 1998.

38. S. Lee, M.S. Pattichis, and A.C. Bovik, "Foveated Video Quality Assessment and Compression Gain," to appear, *IEEE Trans. on Multimedia.*

39. S. Lee, M. S. Pattichis, and A. C. Bovik, "Foveated Video Compression with Optimal Rate Control," *IEEE Transactions on Image Processing*, vol. 10, no. 7, pp. 977-992. July 2001.

40. M.S. Pattichis and A.C. Bovik, "Multi-Dimensional Frequency Modulation in Texture Images," in *Proc. International Conference on Digital Signal Processing*, Limassol, Cyprus, June 26-28 1995, pp. 753-758.

41. M.S. Pattichis and A.C. Bovik, "A Nonlinear Fluid Model for Describing Frequency Modulation of Image Orientations," in *Proc. IEEE Workshop on Non-Linear Signal and Image Proc.*, Neos Marmaras, Halkidiki, Greece, June 20-22 1995, pp. 198-201.

42. M.S. Pattichis and A.C. Bovik, "AM-FM Expansions for Images," in *Proc. European Signal Processing Conf.*, Trieste, Italy, Sep. 10-13 1996.

43. J.P. Havlicek, M.S. Pattichis, D.S. Harding, A.C. Christofides, and A.C. Bovik, "AM-FM Image Analysis Techniques," in *Proc. IEEE Southwest Symp. Image Anal., Interp.*, San Antonio, TX, April 1996, pp. 195-199.

44. M.S. Pattichis and A.C. Bovik, "A Fluid Model for Texture Images," in *Proc. Workshop on Image and Multidimensional Signal Processing*, Belize City, Belize, March 3-6 1996, pp. 18-19.

45. M.S. Pattichis, A.C. Bovik, J.W. Havlicek, and N.D. Sidiropoulos, "On the Representation of Wideband Images Using Permutations for Lossless Coding," *IEEE Southwest Symp. Image Anal., Interp.*, Austin, Texas, April 2000, pp. 237-241.

46. S. Lee, M.S. Pattichis, and A.C. Bovik, "Foveated Image/Video Quality Assessment in Curvilinear Coordinates", *Int. Workshop on Very Low Bitrate Video Coding 98*, Oct. 1998, pp. 189-192.

47. S. Lee, M.S. Pattichis, and A.C. Bovik, "Rate Control for Foveated MPEG/H.263 Video," in *Proc. IEEE Int. Conf. on Image Processing 98*, vol. 2, pp. 365-369, Oct., 1998.

48. P. Perona and J. Malik, "Scale-space and edge detection using anisotropic diffusion," *IEEE Trans. on Pattern Anal. and Mach. Intell.*, vol. PAMI-12, pp. 629-639, 1990.

49. D. Wei and A. C. Bovik, "On the Instantaneous Frequencies of Multicomponent AM-FM Signals," *IEEE Signal Proc. Let.*, vol. 5, no. 4, pp. 84-86, April 1998.

50. S. Zhu and D. Mumford, "Prior Learning and Gibbs reaction-diffusion," *IEEE Trans. Pattern. Anal., Machine Intell.*, vol. 19, no. 11, November 1997.

51. T. Tangsukson and J.P. Havlicek, "Modulation domain image segmentation," *Proc. IEEE Southwest Symp. Image Anal., Interp.*, Austin, TX, pp. 46-50, April 2-4, 2000.

52. T. Tangsukson and J.P. Havlicek, "AM-FM image segmentation", *Proc. IEEE Int'l. Conf. Image Proc.*, Vancouver, Canada, September 10-13, 2000.

53. T.B. Yap, T. Tangsukson, P.C. Tay, N.D. Mamuya, and J.P. Havlicek, "Unsupervised texture segmentation using dominant image modulations," *Proc. 34th IEEE Asilomar Conf. Singals, Syst., Comput.*, Pacific Grove, CA, October 29, November 1, 2000.

54. E.J. Pauwels and G. Frederix, "Finding salient regions in images", *Comput. Vision, Image Understand.*, vol. 75, no. 1/2, July/August 1999, pp. 73-85.

55. A.K. Jain and R.C. Dubes, *Algorithms for Clustering Data*, Prentice Hall, Englewood Cliffs, NJ, 1988.

56. B. Santhanam, and P. Maragos, "Harmonic Analysis and Restoration of Separation Methods for Periodic Signal Mixtures: Algebraic Separation Vs. Comb Filtering," *Signal Proc.*, Vol. 69, No. 1, pp. 81-91, 1998.

57. B. Santhanam, and P. Maragos, "Multicomponent AM-FM Demodulation via Periodicity-Based Algebraic Separation and Energy-based Demodulation," *IEEE Trans. on Comm.*, Vol. 48, No. 3, pp. 473-490, 2000.

58. S.T. Acton, D.P. Mukherjee, J.P. Havlicek, and A.C. Bovik, "Oriented texture completion by AM-FM reaction-diffusion," submitted to *IEEE Transactions on Image Processing*.

59. P. Brodatz, *Textures.* New York: Dover Publications, Inc., 1966.

60. http://www-white.media.mit.edu/vismod/imagery/VisionTexture/vistex.html

Table 1. Permutation bits overhead for optimal FM transforms.

Number of equally-distributed signal values	Permutation bits per sample	FM spectrum coefficients plus DC coefficient
$T = 2$	1 bps	1+1
$T = 4$	2 bps	3+1
$\vdots$	$\vdots$	$\vdots$
$T = N/2$	$\log_2(N) - 1$ bps	$\log_2(N) - 1 + 1$
$T = N$	$\log_2 N$ bps	N

IMAGE TRANSMISSION OVER NOISY CHANNELS: TCQ-BASED CODING SCHEMES

Chang Wen Chen†, Zhaohui Sun‡, Hongzhi Li§, Jianfei Cai† and Lei Cao†

†*Dept of EE, University of Missouri-Columbia, Columbia, MO 65211*
‡*Kodak Research Laboratories, 1700 Dewey Avenue, Rochester, NY 14650*
§*Symbol Technologies, One Symbol Plaza, Holtsville, NY 11742*

In this chapter, we describe several fixed length coding schemes based on trellis coded quantization (TCQ) that have been developed for image transmission over noisy channels such as wireless links. In general, wireless channels are time-varying, bandwidth constrained, and error pruned. Therefore, it is desired that the images are not only appropriately coded to achieve bandwidth compression, but also coded in such a way that the coded bitstream is resilient to channel errors and robust to time-varying channel distortion and fading. The proposed schemes consist of the basic algorithm of uniform threshold TCQ (UTTCQ) and two enhanced schemes with increased computational complexity. The enhanced schemes include nonuniform threshold TCQ and UTTCQ with block classification. We demonstrate that, in the absence of channel coding, the proposed fixed length coding schemes can be designed to achieve efficient compression, error resilience, and robustness. In particular, the fixed length coding schemes will not suffer from the loss of synchronization that often causes catastrophic error effects when more efficient variable length source coding is adopted. We also present a scheme of layered transmission with unequal error protection channel coding to further improve the performance of image transmission over noisy channels.

Keywords: Trellis coded quantization, fixed length coding, DCT, noisy channels, image transmission, unequal error protection

1. Introduction

Image transmission over mobile wireless channels is a challenging task. Since mobile wireless channels are usually bandwidth constrained, error pruned, and time-varying, it is desired that the images are not only appropriately coded to achieve bandwidth compression, but also coded in such a way that the coded bitstream is resilient to channel errors and robust to time-varying channel distortion and fading. There have been significant developments in the area of image and video compression that have resulted in several standards, including JPEG, JPEG2000, MPEG-1, MPEG2, and MPEG4. Many standard image compression algorithms have been shown to perform well for transmission over noise-free channels. However, these standard image compression algorithms usually cannot be directly adopted for wireless image transmission since the compressed images are very sensitive to channel noise due to variable length coding schemes they have employed [1,2]. In the case of variable length coding, a single error may cause the loss of decoding synchronization and result in an error propagation of many data blocks. Insertion of error-resilient synchronization codes are therefore necessary to avoid the channel error from propagating beyond an acceptable range.

We describe in this chapter an alternative way to mitigate the catastrophic error propagation. This is to design fixed length coding schemes for image transmission without the insertion of synchronization codes and the explicit channel coding protection. The basic algorithm of the fixed length coding employs block DCT, subsource construction, uniform threshold TCQ (UTTCQ), and optimal bit allocation [3]. TCQ is a finite-state quantizer which has been shown relatively insensitive to channel errors [4]. Moreover, it has a moderate complexity with excellent mean square error performance. This basic algorithm is able to achieve a reasonable balance between compression and error resilience and is able to avoid the catastrophic error propagation that is frequently encountered in variable length coding.

The basic algorithm of fixed length coding can be enhanced to provide improved performance in terms of both compression and error resilience. Although the uniform threshold TCQ adopted in the basic algorithm can be easily implemented, it does not match well with the distribution of subsources that are obtained by grouping the same coefficients from all blocks. In general, the histogram of these subsources can be approximated as a generalized Gaussian distribution (GGD). A natural enhancement scheme to improve the performance of image transmission would be to adopt nonuniform threshold TCQ for the quantization of the subsources. With GGD approximation, we can design optimal (non-uniform) threshold and quantization levels to minimize the mean square quantization error. Such a non-uniform quantization clearly matches with the distribution of the subsources and would result in improved performance in terms of compression efficiency. The additional overhead that we need to transmit to the receiving end consists of only two parameters of GGD for each subsource. The experimental results confirm that noticeable performance improvement can be achieved using this non-uniform threshold TCQ scheme.

We have also investigated an enhancement scheme that attempts to examine and classify the image blocks so that more than one bit allocation map can be designed for different types of image blocks. Intuitively, high frequency coefficients from smooth blocks are of low amplitudes while those from blocks containing texture and edges are of high amplitudes. Therefore, smooth blocks can be coded with many fewer bits than those blocks containing texture and edges. The proposed enhancement scheme first classifies the blocks according to the criterion of smoothness and then constructs the subsources from blocks of same type. We show that, with block classification, the performance of the fixed length coding can be substantially improved over the basic scheme. We also show that two-class scheme is a good trade-off between the improvement and the additional overhead of bit allocation maps and necessary labeling of the type of blocks for each block.

Finally, we present an application of the channel coding to the compressed images coded with the proposed basic fixed length coding scheme. To take advantage of the fixed bit allocation map, a layered transmission strategy integrated with rate compatible punctured convolutional codes (RCPC) has been developed to facilitate unequal error protection. With additional bit budget for channel coding, the layered transmission with RCPC is able to perform very well under severe channel conditions. Comparing with non-layered transmission, the proposed scheme with layered transmission and some additional bit budget for RCPC channel coding, achieves consistent improvement, especially when the channel becomes very noisy.

2. The Basic Algorithm With UTTCQ

The basic algorithm we developed is a fixed length coding without explicit error protection. Shannon's information theory [5] states that information transmission can be implemented by source coding followed by channel coding without sacrifice of performance in terms of transmission rate and reproduction quality. However, to achieve an optimum design, the separation of source coding and channel coding may lead to long delay and high complexity. Therefore, in practical applications, combined source and channel coding is often employed to achieve optimum coding performance while keeping the complexity low and the delay tolerable. Optimum bit allocation algorithm is used to carefully arrange the encoded bits in such a way that both compression and error resilience can be simultaneously accomplished.

Transform coding based on the 2-D DCT, rather than subband coding, is employed in the proposed coding scheme. The DCT is an established transform coding scheme with very good performance and fast implementation algorithms. In the transform domain, most DCT coefficients with large amplitude are located at DC or low frequency positions. A carefully designed bit allocation map can be applied to all blocks in frequency domain. Such a fixed bit allocation map is very beneficial for decoding the position of the coefficients at the decoder when the compressed images are transmitted over noisy channels. This is because the position shifts of the coefficients due to channel noise may result in the most visible distortions to the reconstructed image. It is true that subband coding has been widely used for transmission over error-free channels, because it usually yields better coding results than DCT. However, subband coefficients with large amplitude may appear at any places in the subbands, making it non-trivial to formulate a single bit allocation map for all subbands.

The next step in error-resilient image coding is to choose the quantization scheme. There has been extensive research on quantization, and various schemes have been proposed, including a variety of scalar quantization and vector quantization schemes. One recently proposed scheme, trellis coded quantization (TCQ) [4], has been shown to be relatively insensitive to channel errors with moderate complexity. One bit error affects no more than $1 + \log_2 N$ outputs, where N is the number of trellis states. Therefore we use TCQ as the quantization scheme. It will be discussed in detail later. Furthermore, fixed-rate TCQ is used to avoid the possibility of incorrect decoding position on bitstream due to channel noise. This will facilitate robust decoding and is capable of preventing the errors from propagating.

2.1. *System Description*

Based on these considerations, we proposed an error-resilient image cod-

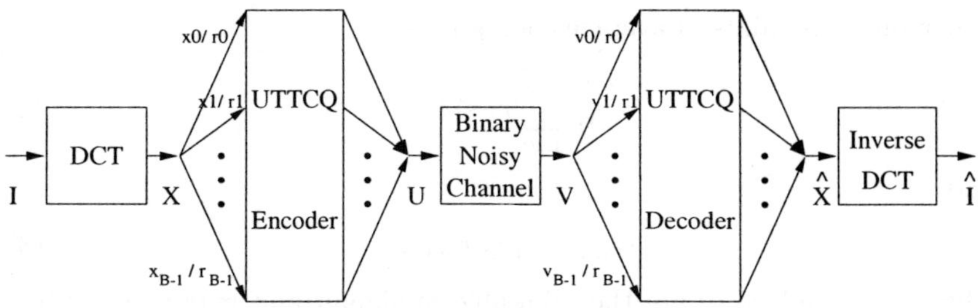

Fig. 1. Block diagram of the basic algorithm

ing system without error protection as shown in Figure 1. The input image I is divided into nonoverlapping blocks of size $B = L \times L$ and each block is transformed using the 2-D DCT. The transformed image X is decomposed into B subsources $\{x_i\}_{i=0}^{B-1}$. Each subsource is composed of coefficients with the same frequency (at the same block position) from all the blocks. For example, all the DC coefficients make up subsource x_0. After shifting with respect to the mean values, the $B-$dimensional vector source is a good representation of the original image and is fed into uniform threshold trellis coded quantizers. Subsource x_i is quantized and encoded by r_i bits/sample, where r_i is the $i-th$ component at the bit allocation map $\{r_i\}_{i=0}^{B-1}$. The bit allocation map decides how many bits (r_i) are to be allocated to the subsource x_i. The encoded bit stream U passes through the noisy channel and is corrupted. The decoder simply chops fixed-length bits from the received bitstream V based on the bit allocation map and decodes the DCT coefficients $\hat{X}$ according to the codebook. At the end, the image is reconstructed as $\hat{I}$ using the 2-D inverse DCT.

The robust image transmission problem can therefore be stated as follows : Given the coding rate of $\bar{r}$ bits/pixel, the bit error rate (BER) of the noisy channel and the input image, we attempt to minimize the average mean square error

$$D = \frac{1}{B} \sum_{i=0}^{B-1} E\left\{(\hat{x}_i - x_i)^2\right\} \tag{1}$$

under the constraints of average coding rate

$$\frac{1}{B} \sum_{i=0}^{B-1} r_i \leq \bar{r} \tag{2}$$

and

$$r_{min} \leq r_i \leq r_{max}, \tag{3}$$

where r_{min} and r_{max} are the allowable minimum and maximum coding rate. Subsources $\{x_i\}_{i=0}^{B-1}$ are quantized to $\{r_i\}_{i=0}^{B-1}$ bits/sample, and reconstructed as $\{\hat{x}_i\}_{i=0}^{B-1}$.

2.2. *Fixed-rate UTTCQ*

Trellis coded quantization [4] is a finite-state quantizer that employs a scalar codebook and a Viterbi encoding algorithm and labels the trellis branches with subsets of the codebook. This quantization scheme has low complexity with excellent mean square error (MSE) performance and is also insensitive to channel noise. TCQ borrows the ideas of signal set expansion, set partitioning and branch labeling from trellis coded modulation (TCM) [6] and finds its own theoretical foundation in alphabet constrained rate distortion theory.

To encode a memoryless source at a rate of R bits per sample, the signal set is first doubled from 2^R to 2^{R+1} and then partitioned into $2^{\widetilde{R}+1}$ subsets ($\widetilde{R} < R$). $\widetilde{R}$ bits out of the R input bits are fed into an $\widetilde{R}/\left(\widetilde{R}+1\right)$ convolutional coder, and the $\widetilde{R}+1$ output bits are used to select the subset. The remaining $R - \widetilde{R}$ bits are used to decide the codeword in the selected subset. In detail, a $R + 1$ bits scalar quantizer is constructed subject to source statistics. The scalar codebook is grouped into $2^{(\widetilde{R}+1)}$ subsets with $2^{R-\widetilde{R}}$ codewords in each subset. TCQ maps every input symbol to an integer pair (i,j) according to the current symbol magnitude and the previous trellis state, where $\widetilde{R} + 1$ bits integer i decides subset and trellis state and $R - \widetilde{R}$ bits integer j selects a codeword within the specified subset. Next, the Viterbi algorithm [7], an asymptotically optimum decoding technique for convolutional codes, is employed to find the codeword sequence that minimizes the mean square error between the input data and the codeword sequence. TCQ uses an expanded signal set and thus has better granular quantization performance than the corresponding scalar quantization at

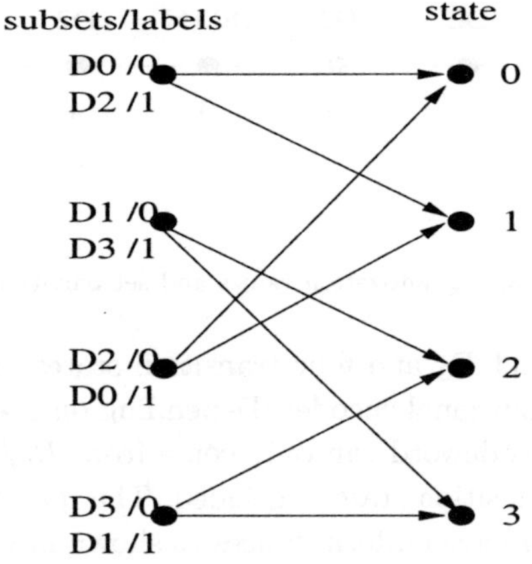

Fig. 2.   Four-state trellis with four subsets

the same coding rate. With the Viterbi algorithm, TCQ is also capable of achieving excellent MSE performance.

Most importantly, TCQ is relatively insensitive to channel noise. If the $R - \widetilde{R}$ bits integer j is corrupted, only the wrong codeword (close to the real one) in the same subset may be picked and there is no effect on the trellis state. As long as the trellis state is correct, the channel error will not propagate to subsequent quantizer outputs. If the $\widetilde{R} + 1$ bits integer i is corrupted, then the wrong subset is picked and the trellis state may also become incorrect. However, due to the trellis structure, such bit error affects no more than $1 + \log_2 N$ outputs, where N is the number of trellis states. As a result, the effects of channel errors will not propagate beyond the upper limit. Therefore, TCQ is preferred for noisy channel image transmission over other entropy coding and large dimensional vector quantization schemes because in these cases a single bit channel error may destroy an entire block of data.

The quantization scheme employed in this research is based on the uniform threshold trellis coded quantization proposed in the scheme of ACTCQ [8]. The suboptimal UTTCQ has certain practical advantages because of its uniform codebooks. A simple example is given in Figure 2 with four

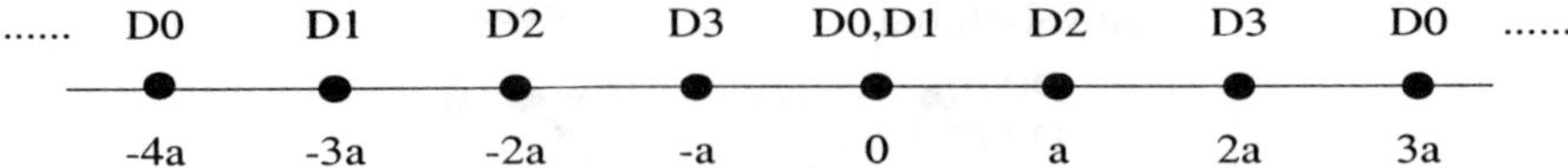

Fig. 3.   Quantization values and set partition

subsets D_0, D_1, D_2 and D_3 and four transition states. This is a TCQ defined by an 1/2 convolutional encoder. Depending on the present state and the input symbol, a codeword can only come from D_0/D_2 or D_1/D_3 and therefore the next transition state is decided. The quantization thresholds $T = (T_0, T_1, ..., T_{N-1})$ have uniform spaces as shown in Figure 3. The space is decided by the variance of the source. Zero is in D_0 as well as D_1 so that the zero codeword is always available no matter what the present trellis state is.

Given a subsource x_i and the coding rate of $r_i > 1$, the variance of the zero-mean subsource x_i is estimated. The number of quantization levels is set as 2^{r_i+1}, and the uniform quantization step is determined according to the variance of the subsource. The source symbol is quantized by the UTTCQ and the integer pair (i, j) is encoded at $r_i + 1$ bits/sample.

Fixed-rate TCQ needs at least one bit to select the subset and one bit to select the codeword in the subset. Therefore the coding rate r_i cannot be less than 1 bit/sample. When coding rate $r_i = 1$, a 2-level scalar quantizer is employed instead. When $r_i = 0$, then the source x_i is not coded and transmitted at all and all the corresponding frequency components are neglected.

2.3. *Bit Allocation Scheme*

Given a coding rate of $\bar{r}$ bits/sample for a source X, the bit allocation problem in this research is to decide the bit allocation map $\{r_i\}_{i=0}^{B-1}$ for the subsources $\{x_i\}_{i=0}^{B-1}$ so that the MSE (1) is minimized subject to the constraints of (2) and (3).

As shown in Figure 1, errors are only incurred by quantization and transmission. The transformed source image X is quantized to U and then corrupted by channel noise to become V. The mean-square reconstruction error can be written as [9]:

$$E\left\{(V-X)^2\right\} = E\left\{[(V-U)+(U-X)]^2\right\}$$
$$= \sigma_q^2 + \sigma_c^2 + 2\sigma_m^2, \tag{4}$$

where $\sigma_q^2, \sigma_c^2, \sigma_m^2$ are the quantization error, channel error, and mutual error, respectively.

The quantization error depends only on the selected quantization scheme, the channel error depends only on the channel characteristics, and the mutual error term depends on both of them and can generally be neglected when the channel bit error rate is low. When the mutual error term is considered, it is usually very difficult to obtain a close-form solution for the mean square reconstruction error except for the one-bit quantizer or the specific input (such as the uniform probability density function) with known channel transition matrix. Due to the lack of a general close-form solution for the above distortion, we resort to the integer programming algorithm proposed in [1] with a small modification. Bits are allocated to the subsources that would minimize the total distortion.

To explicitly express the block positions, the bit allocation map is written from vector $\{r_i\}_{i=0}^{B-1}$ to matrix form as $\{r_{ij}, i, j = 0, 1, ..., L-1\}$ where $B = L \times L$. A set $P = \{(i,j)|r_{ij} \neq 0\}$ is defined as all the positions in which we have allocated bits. Source symbols at P are then quantized. An operator Θ on set P, $\Theta(P) = \{(i,j), (i+1,j), (i,j+1)|r_{ij} \neq 0\}$, is defined as the expansion of P where the right neighbors and lower neighbors are also included. Here sets P and $\Theta(P)$ are introduced to limit the searching space. Instead of searching all $L \times L$ possible positions in every iteration to allocate one bit, only the positions in $\Theta(P)$, i.e. the positions already have bits allocated and their nearest neighbors, are searched. In this way, fewer trials are tested to obtain the final bit allocation. When $r_{ij} = 0$, no bit is allocated to the position (i,j) and the corresponding coefficients are not quantized and transmitted. The basic idea behind the optimum bit allocation algorithm is to allocate one bit a time at the place (i,j) on bit allocation map which improves the distortion function most. The optimum bit allocation algorithm can be stated as:

(1) Set $k = 0$, $r_{00} = 1$ and all other $r_{ij} = 0$, $P = \{(0,0)\}$.

(2) Set $k = k+1$; Compute the indices i_k and j_k which satisfy

$$D(r_{i_k j_k}) - D(r_{i_k j_k} + 1)$$

$$= \max_{(i,j)\in\Theta(P)} \{D(r_{ij}) - D(r_{ij}+1)\}. \tag{5}$$

This means allocating one more bit to (i_k, j_k) on the current bit allocation map that makes the largest improvement on distortion function (1).

(3) Set $r_{i_k j_k} = r_{i_k j_k} + 1$ and update $P = P \cup \{(i_k, j_k)\}$. If $k < B \times \bar{r}$, go back to 2; else stop.

Successful implementation of this basic algorithm of UTTCQ has been reported in a recent paper [3]. The experimental results presented in Section 6 also confirm that, without error protection channel coding, this fixed length coding scheme is still able to achieve gracious degradation as the channel becomes more noise corrupted.

3. Nonuniform Threshold TCQ

One limitation of the UTTCQ scheme presented in Section 2 is that the uniform threshold does not match well with the distribution of the subsources obtained from all image blocks. The idea of a non-uniform threshold TCQ (NUTTCQ) can be derived directly from the UTTCQ proposed in Section 2 with minor modifications. Instead of using uniform thresholds, which have certain practical advantages because of the uniform codebooks, the proposed nonuniform threshold quantizers are based on the GGD parameters and yield better performance because GGD employs higher order statistics and matches better with the subsource distributions. In fact, the performance is near optimal. In this case, only the GGD parameters need to be transmitted to reconstruct the codebooks at the decoder, therefore there is little extra transmission burden. Certainly, extra computation effort is needed at the decoder to reconstruct the codebooks from the GGD statistics. Furthermore, the quantization thresholds in the case of NUTTCQ have nonuniform spaces, which would be different from the uniform spaces shown in Figure 3.

The probability density function of the generalized Gaussian distribution is given by

$$p(x) = \left[\frac{\nu\eta(\nu,\sigma)}{2\Gamma(1/\nu)}\right] \exp\left(-\left[\eta(\nu,\sigma)|x|\right]^\nu\right) \tag{6}$$

where

$$\eta\left(\nu,\sigma\right) = \frac{1}{\sigma}\left[\frac{\Gamma\left(3/\nu\right)}{\Gamma\left(1/\nu\right)}\right]^{1/2} \tag{7}$$

with ν describing the exponential rate of decay and σ^2 representing the variance of the random variable. Equation (6) becomes the Gaussian distribution when $\nu = 2$, the Laplacian distribution when $\nu = 1$, and the uniform distribution as $\nu \to \infty$.

A generalized Gaussian model can be found for subsource $\{x_i\}$ by solving

$$\nu = F^{-1}\left(\frac{E\left[|X|\right]}{\sigma}\right) \tag{8}$$

where

$$F\left(\alpha\right) = \frac{\Gamma\left(2/\alpha\right)}{\sqrt{\Gamma\left(1/\alpha\right)\Gamma\left(3/\alpha\right)}}. \tag{9}$$

$E[|X|]$ is the estimated mean absolute value and σ^2 is the estimated variance of the subsource $\{x_i\}$.

The implementation of NUTTCQ is similar to that of UTTCQ with slightly more complicated nonuniform quantization and the additional parameters of GGD. Such a nonuniform quantization clearly matches with the distribution of the subsources and would result in an improved performance in terms of compression efficiency. The additional overhead that we need to transmit to the receiving end consists of only two parameters of GGD. The experimental results presented in Section 6 confirm that noticeable performance improvement can be achieved using this nonuniform threshold TCQ scheme.

4. UTTCQ With Block Classification

Another limitation of the scheme proposed in Section 2 is the use of a single bit allocation map. For a block-based DCT coding, since each image block has a different degree of spatial activity, contrast, and detail, the transform blocks can be quite different from each other in terms of the distribution of the coefficients. A single allocation map for all the transform blocks may cause significant distortions, especially using a uniform threshold. In order to improve the coding performance, we propose to apply a classification method – equal mean-normalized standard deviation (EMNSD) method [10] – before the quantization process with UTTCQ. Transform blocks are classified into several classes according to the level of image activity. Bit allocation among classes and individual transform coefficients is determined by an optimal joint source-channel algorithm similar to the optimization described in Section 2. We also apply noise reduction filters at the decoder end to further improve the rate-distortion performance.

4.1. *Description of the Enhanced Scheme*

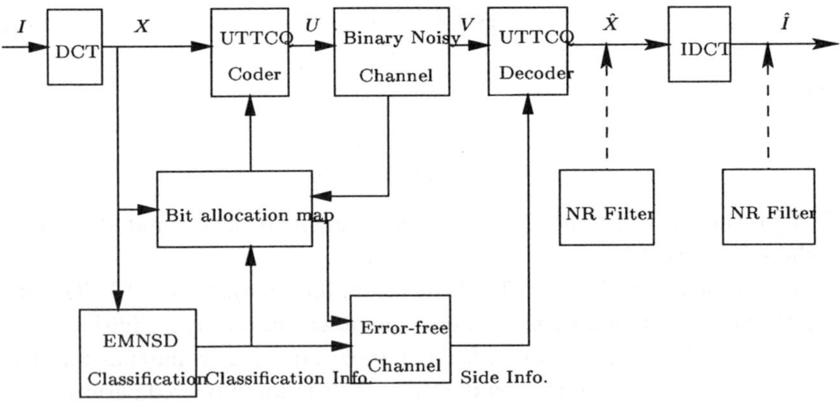

Fig. 4.   UTTCQ with block classification.

The system of the proposed enhanced scheme is shown in Figure 4. Input image I $(M \times N)$ is divided into non-overlapping blocks of size $B = L \times L$ and each block is transformed using 2-D DCT. Transform blocks are grouped into K classes using the EMNSD classification method. Blocks in the kth class are decomposed into B subsources $\{x_{k,i}\}_{i=0}^{B-1}$; each subsource is composed of the coefficients with the same frequency (at the same block position) from all the blocks in a class. Subsource $x_{k,i}$ is quantized and encoded by $r_{k,i}$ bits/sample, where $r_{k,i}$ is the ith component at the bit allocation map $\{r_{k,i}\}_{i=0}^{B-1}$ for the kth class. In this work, we use two types of maps: a classification map and bit allocation maps. The classification map serves as an index or a reference to a proper bit allocation map. After shifting with respect to the mean values, each subsource is fed into uniform threshold trellis coded quantizers [3,8]. The encoded bit stream U passes through the noisy channel and becomes error corrupted. The decoder chops known bits from the received bitstream V and decodes the DCT coefficients $\hat{X}$ according to the codebook. To make use of the high correlation among neighbor DC coefficients, a noise reduction filter is applied to correct some obvious errors in the DC coefficients. The image is then reconstructed as $\hat{I}$ using 2-D IDCT. In the case of very noisy channel, we also exploit spatial correlation among neighboring pixels by using a spatial low-pass filter to alleviate the error effect.

An optimization problem similar to the one presented in Section 2 can be formulated for the proposed UTTCQ fixed length coding with block classification. The bit allocation maps are determined by an optimum algorithm similar to the one described in Section 2. The overhead information consists of one classification map, K bit allocation maps, and the mean and variance values of the subsources. We assume that the side information can be transmitted error free by appropriate error correction coding.

4.2. *Classification Methods*

Classification has frequently been used in the compression of real-word signals. Chen and Smith [11] proposed the use of spatially adaptive quantization in DCT coding. They classified the DCT blocks according to their AC energy and made the quantizer adaptive to the class to be encoded. However, this classification scheme suffers from the unnecessary constraint that all classes contain an equal number of blocks. Joshi et al. [10] recently proposed two new algorithms, maximum classification gain and EMNSD classification methods, both of which allow an unequal number of blocks in each class. All three schemes are gain-based classification. Block features other than the gain have also been studied for classification. For instance, Ramamurthi and Gersho [12] investigated the classification in vector quantization, in which blocks are classified according to distinct perceptual features, such as edges. Pearlman [13] proposed an adaptive DCT image coding system in which the rates vary to match the changing spectral characteristics of the blocks.

In this research, a modified EMNSD classification is adopted because it is simple yet offers good performance. Instead of average energy, we choose to use AC energy as the criterion for classification. The block gain is now defined as the square root of the AC energy. All the blocks are arranged in increasing order of gain. The first N_1 blocks are assigned to class 1, the next N_2 blocks to class 2, and so on. The proposed classification finds N_1, N_2, ..., N_{K-1} such that the mean-normalized standard deviation of the gains in the resulting classes is equal. The idea behind this approach is to allow the possibility of having a different number of blocks in each class and to have similar statistical properties within each class [10].

For example, suppose the transformed blocks are divided into 2 classes. The total N blocks are organized in an increasing order of their gain values $g_j, j = 1, 2, ..., N$. The AC energy E_j and g_j of the jth block can be computed as following:

$$E_j = \sum_{u=0}^{L-1} \sum_{v=0}^{L-1} [F_j(u,v)]^2 - [F_j(0,0)]^2 , \quad g_j = \sqrt{E_j} , \tag{10}$$

where $F_j(u,v)$ is the DCT coefficient in position (u,v) of the jth block. We seek an integer N_1 such that blocks indexed 1 to N_1 belong to the first class and the remaining blocks belong to the second class. The mean m_k and standard deviation σ_k of class $k, k = 1, 2$, are defined by

$$m_1 = \frac{1}{N_1} \sum_{j=1}^{N_1} g_j , \quad m_2 = \frac{1}{N - N_1} \sum_{j=N_1+1}^{N} g_j ,$$

$$\sigma_1^2 = \frac{1}{N_1} \sum_{j=1}^{N_1} (g_j - m_1)^2 , \quad \sigma_2^2 = \frac{1}{N - N_1} \sum_{j=N_1+1}^{N} (g_j - m_2)^2 , \tag{11}$$

where N_1 is chosen such that

$$q_1 = q_2 , \tag{12}$$

where

$$q_k = \frac{\sigma_k}{m_k}, \quad k = 1, 2. \tag{13}$$

An iterative algorithm to find N_1 satisfying Equation (12) is provided in [10]. If there is no integer N_1 such that $q_1 = q_2$, the algorithm finds an N_1 which minimizes $|q_1 - q_2|$.

4.3. *Noise Reduction Filters*

It is well-known that, in the spatial domain, neighboring pixels tend to be highly correlated; likewise, in frequency domain, the DC coefficients of neighboring blocks also exhibit significant mutual correlation. In order to exploit this redundancy, noise reduction filters are used at the decoder side.

In the case of low bit error rate (say less than 1%), we use a threshold filter, similar to that in [14]. It begins by examining eight neighbor DC coefficients of the central block, and sorting them in ascending order of the coefficients. It then discards the highest and lowest values on the basis that they might be erroneous, and determines if the central coefficient falls within the range determined by the remaining values [14]. If the central coefficient falls outside of that range and it is also above an upper bound threshold or below a lower bound threshold, it is deemed a probable error.

For high BER (0.1), the well-known median filter is used for DC coefficients. In addition, an average filter is also applied to the reconstructed image. The effect of noise-reduction filters should be considered in the joint source-channel bit allocation algorithm. For example, the optimum quantizer design in [15] shows that in general, the noisier the channel is, the coarser the quantization should be. This translates into allocating less bits. However, in our research, we use the noise reduction filter for DC coefficients so that some errors can be easily corrected. In general, DC coefficients are allocated more bits. With an integrated optimal bit allocation, a better tradeoff can be obtained.

5. Layered Transmission with RCPC Channel Coding

To further improve the performance of the TCQ-based fixed length coding, RCPC channel coding can be applied to the compressed images. Traditional approaches to unequal error protection are usually based on the position of the spatial frequency components. Typically, low frequency components receive more protection while high frequency components receive less protection. However, this frequency-based unequal error protection is not optimal in terms of rate-distortion performance. This is because the distortion caused by the error from the most significant bit of a coefficient may be significantly more than the distortion caused by the least significant bit of the same coefficient. We can therefore conclude that unequal error protection should be designed according to bit location rather than the frequency location.

Notice that the bit allocation map exhibits a pyramid shape if the number of bits allocated to a particular coefficient is considered as the height at its location. Such a pyramid shape facilitates efficient layered grouping of the quantized coefficients according to the bit planes. In the case of a fixed bit allocation map in UTTCQ, the number of bits that need to be grouped is fixed. There are usually only few bits in the higher bit planes. Once we apply the layered grouping according to the bit plane location, an RCPC channel coding can be developed to facilitate unequal error protection. With additional bit budget for channel coding, the layered grouping with RCPC is able to perform very well under severe channel conditions. Compared with non-layered protection based on the frequency components, the proposed bit plane-based scheme achieves consistent improvement under the same RCPC channel coding budget, especially when the channel becomes extremely noisy. A block diagram of the proposed scheme is shown in Figure 5.

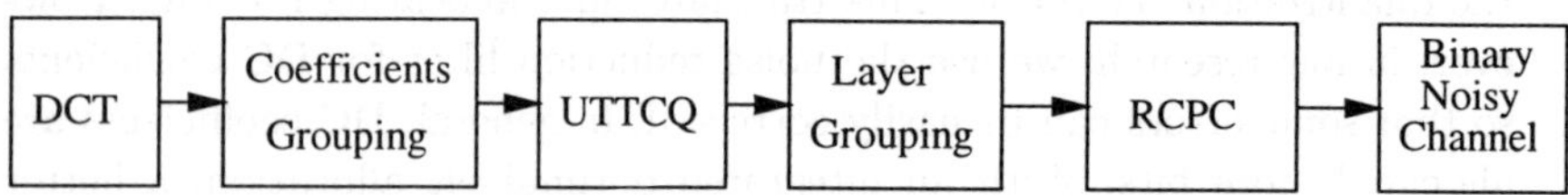

Fig. 5.   Block diagram for layered transmission with RCPC.

5.1. *Layered Grouping and RCPC coding*

In general, the more significant a bit is in a symbol, the more important it is in the decoding process. For example, using a uniform N-bit scalar quantizer with quantization step Δ, x is quantized to:

$$\hat{x} = Q(x) = \sum_{i=1}^{N} a_i 2^{i-1} \Delta \tag{14}$$

where a_i is the bit in layer i. If a single a_i is changed to opposite $\overline{a_i}$, the distortion energy will be:

$$D = [2^{i-1}]^2 \Delta^2 = 2^{2(i-1)} \Delta^2. \tag{15}$$

We can see that the distortion energy caused by a single error bit in layer i is 4 times as large as a single error bit in layer $i - 1$.

In the scheme shown in Figure 1, because the high layer indices of UTTCQ are obtained in the same fashion as uniform scalar quantization, the higher layer the bits are located, the more important they are. For simplicity, we regard all the bits in the same layer as of the same importance and organize these bits into one data block.

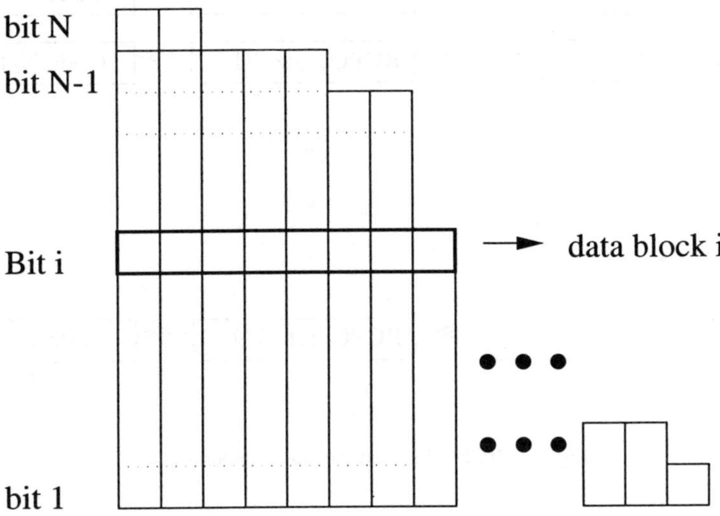

Fig. 6.   Bits in same layer are grouped as one data block.

Assuming N is the largest number in an optimal bit allocation map, we have N data block layers ranging from 1 to N. In this case layer N is the most significant layer and layer 1 is the least significant layer. For each layer, find the quantized subsources that have such layer, and then group all the bits in that layer into a block. Eventually we obtain N data blocks of different importances in the process to reconstruct the transmitted image. Figure 6 illustrates the concept of the layered grouping.

The RCPC codes are adopted since we can take advantage of a hierarchical structure of the layered grouping of the bitstream to achieve the desired unequal error protection. Another desired feature of the RCPC channel coding is that only single decoder is needed for different code rates as these codes can be made compatible within a data block. The RCPC codes are also able to provide a balanced overhead redundancy so that we can meet the constraints of channel bandwidth during the image transmission.

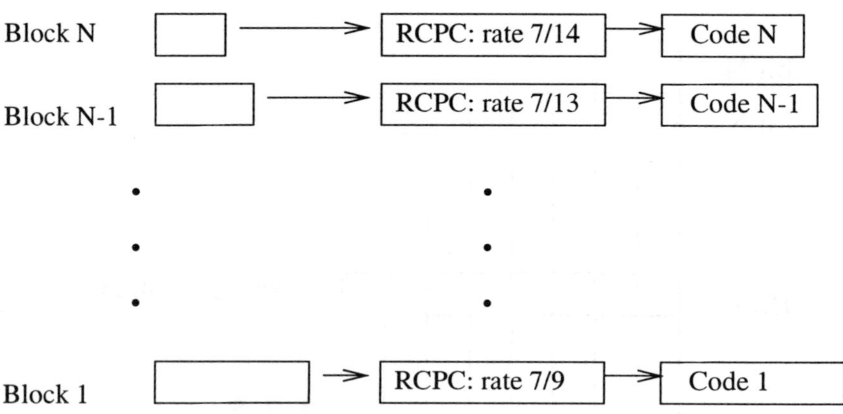

Fig. 7.   RCPC Layered channel protection.

6. Experimental Results and Comparisons

We conducted experiments on the 256×256 grey scale Lena image. The image was divided into nonoverlapping blocks of size 8×8. The 2-D DCT was applied to each block. In the case of UTTCQ and NUTTCQ, all DCT coefficients at the same position were grouped into one subsource and then quantized by either UTTCQ or NUTTCQ according to the optimal bit allocation map. The bitstream of the quantized coefficients was then transmitted through noisy channels and reconstructed at the receiving end. Figure 8 shows that, without RCPC channel coding, both UTTCQ and

NUTTCQ performed well with gracious degradation as the channel BER increased.

As expected, the enhanced NUTTCQ performed better than UTTCQ because the optimal nonuniform quantization matches the subsource distribution better than UTTCQ does. The improvements were more than one dB for high BER channels.

In the case of UTTCQ with block classification, we used the EMNSD classification method to divide blocks into two classes or four classes. The two-class and four-class classification maps are shown in Fig. 9. We can see that the texture and edge regions of Lena were classified as high activity blocks, while the smooth regions were classified as low activity blocks. The more active the blocks are, the more bits should be assigned. After classification, the coefficients were partitioned to subsources according to their positions in the blocks. These subsources were quantized by UTTCQ and transmitted through a noisy channel. Compared with the UTTCQ scheme without classification, the additional overhead for the two-class classification scheme was 0.041 bpp, and the four-class classification scheme yielded 0.088 bpp. Our experiments show that the four-class classification achieveed negligible additional gains over two-class classification because the the overhead is more than doubled.

In the case of UTTCQ with RCPC channel coding, the quantized coefficients were grouped into layers for unequal error protection. Since $N = \max r_i = 7$, all TCQ indices were grouped into 7 data blocks. We employed an 1/2 RCPC mother code with memory 6 and puncture period 7 [16]. Six different coding rates were applied to these 7-layer data blocks. The code rates for these 7-layer data are $7/14, 7/13, 7/12, 7/11, 7/10, 7/9, 7/9$, respectively.

The image was coded at 0.5 bpp in all the experiments. PSNR results under various noisy channels were obtained based on an average over 30 simulations. Figure 8 shows the comparison of UTTCQ, NUTTCQ and UTTCQ with block classification. It is shown that the TCQ with block classification consistently outperformed both UTTCQ and NUTTCQ. This is essentially due to the bipolar distribution of the DCT coefficients, in which the distribution of the coefficients from smooth blocks is centralized and the distribution of the coefficients from edge blocks is heavy tailed. As a result, two bit allocation maps based on classified blocks facilitate better coding performance than the single bit allocation map. Figure 10 shows the comparison between UTTCQ with and without RCPC channel coding, as well as layered and non-layered RCPC channel coding. With additional bit budget, the layered RCPC scheme was able to offer significant improvement of 4-8 dB over the original UTTCQ scheme. The layered RCPC channel coding was able to provide consistent improvement over non-layered channel coding, especially when the channel was noisy.

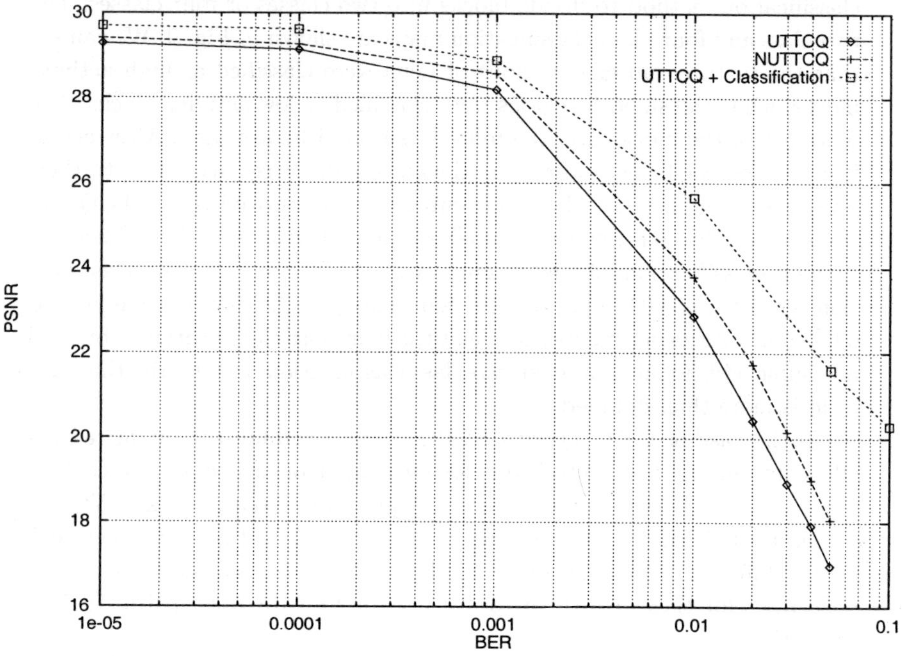

Fig. 8. The performance comparison of UTTCQ, NUTTCQ and UTTCQ with block classification.

7. Conclusion and Discussion

We have presented several fixed length coding schemes based on TCQ and optimal block bit allocation map for image transmission over noisy

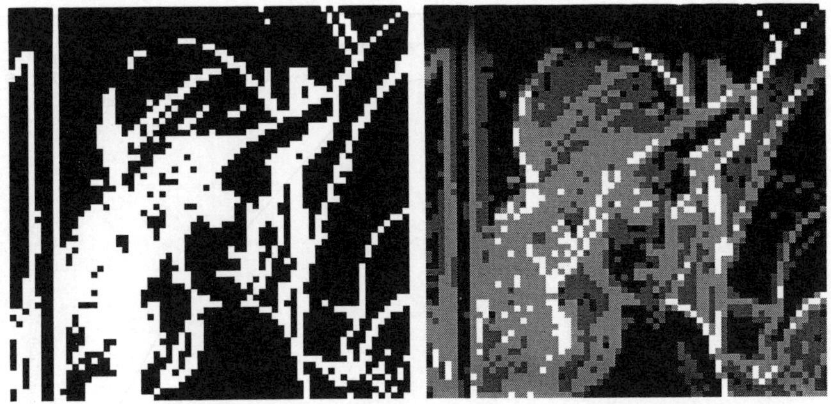

Fig. 9.   Images of classification maps. Left: 2 classes; Right: 4 classes.

channels. The performance of each scheme was analyzed and confirmed by experimental simulations. It is evident that all these schemes are able to perform graciously under various noisy channel conditions. These schemes are of different computational complexity. Among all schemes, the basic UTTCQ scheme is the simplest one in terms of its implementation. However, its PSNR performance is also the most inferior one. This investigation and comparison offers us flexibility in adopting an appropriate scheme for a particular application. When the encoding end can afford high computational complexity, UTTCQ with block classification should be adopted. Otherwise, computationally less complicated UTTCQ or NUTTCQ should be adopted. When the channel is very noisy and the bit budget allows additional channel coding, layered RCPC coding should be adopted. The choice of channel coding rate presented in this research is not optimized. Future research includes investigating an optimal allocation of fixed bit budget between source coding and channel coding when an image transmission scheme employs both source coding and channel coding.

Acknowledgements

The research was supported by NSF Grant EEC-92–09615, a New York State Science and Technology Foundation Grant to the Center for Elec-

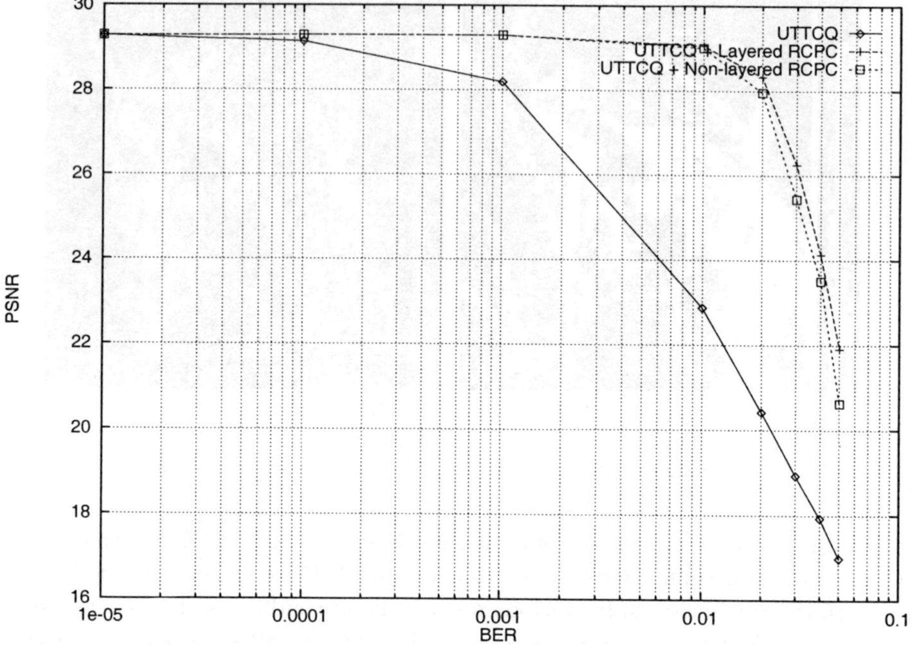

Fig. 10. The performance comparison of UTTCQ, non-layered RCPC, and Layered RCPC.

tronic Imaging Systems at the University of Rochester, and the University of Missouri Research Board Grant URB-98-142.

References

1. V. A. Vaishampayan and N. Farvardin, "Optimal block cosine transform image coding for noisy channels," *IEEE Trans. Communication*, vol. 38, pp. 327–336, 1990.
2. M. Y. Cheung and J. Vaisey, "A comparison of scalar quantization strategies for noisy channel data transmission," *IEEE Trans. Communications*, vol. 43, pp. 738–742, 1995.
3. C. W. Chen and Z. Sun, "Uniform trellis coded quantization for image transmission over noisy channels," *Signal Processing: Image Communication*, vol. 14, pp. 575–584, May 1999.

329

4. M. W. Marcellin and T. R. fischer, "Trellis coded quantization of memoryless and gauss-markov sources," *IEEE Trans. Communication*, vol. 38, pp. 82–93, 1990.

5. C. E. Shannon, "A mathematical theory of communication," *The Bell System Technical Journal*, vol. XXVII, 1948.

6. G. Ungerboeck, "Channel coding with multilevel/phase signals," *IEEE Trans. Information Theory*, vol. IT28, pp. 55–67, 1982.

7. G. D. Forney Jr., "The viterbi algorithm," *Proc IEEE*, vol. PROC-61, pp. 268–278, 1973.

8. R. L. Joshi, V. J. Crump, and T. R. Fischer, "Image subband coding using arithmetic coded trellis coded quantization," *IEEE Trans. Circuits and Systems for Video Technology*, vol. 5, pp. 515–523, 1995.

9. N. S. Jayant and P. Noll, *Digital Coding of Waveforms*. Prentice-Hall Inc., 1984.

10. R. L. Joshi, H. Jafarkhani, J. H. Kasner, T. R. Fishcer, N. Farvardin, M. W. Marcellin, and R. H. Bamberger, "Comparison of different methods of classification in subband coding of image," *IEEE Trans. on Image Proc.*, vol. 6, No.11, pp. 1473–1485, Nov. 1997.

11. W. H. Chen and C. H. Smith, "Adaptive coding of monochrome and color images," *IEEE Trans. Commun.*, vol. COM-25, pp. 1285–1292, Nov. 1977.

12. B. Ramamurthi and A. Gersho, "Classified vector quantization of images," *IEEE Trans. Commun.*, vol. COM-34, pp. 1105–1115, Nov. 1986.

13. W. A. Pearlman, "Adaptive cosine transform image coding with constant block distortion," *IEEE Trans. Commun.*, vol. 38, No.5, pp. 698–703, May 1990.

14. A. E. Mohr, E. A. Riskin, and R. E. Ladner, "Recovering from bit errors in scalar-quantized discrete wavelet transformed images," in *ICIP98*, pp. 502–506, Oct. 1998.

15. A. J. Kurtenbach and P. A. Wintz, "Quantizing for noisy channels," *IEEE Trans. Communication*, vol. COM-17, pp. 291–302, 1969.

16. L. H. C. Lee, "New rate-compatible punctured convolutional codes for Viterbi decoding," *IEEE Trans. Communications*, vol. 42, pp. 3073–3079, 1994.

Motion and Structure from Feature Correspondences: A Review

THOMAS S. HUANG, FELLOW, IEEE, AND ARUN N. NETRAVALI, FELLOW, IEEE

We present a review of algorithms and their performance for determining three-dimensional (3D) motion and structure of rigid objects when their corresponding features are known at different times or are viewed by different cameras. Three categories of problems are considered, depending upon whether the features are two- (2D) or three-dimensional (3D) and the type of correspondence: a) 3D to 3D (i.e., locations of corresponding features in 3D space are known at two different times), b) 2D to 3D (i.e., locations of features in 3D space and their projection on the camera plane are known), and c) 2D to 2D (i.e., projections of features on the camera plane are known at two different times). Features considered include points, straight lines, curved lines, and corners. Emphasis is on problem formulation, efficient algorithms for solution, existence and uniqueness of solutions, and sensitivity of solutions to noise in the observed data. Algorithms described have been used in a variety of applications. Some of these are: a) positioning and navigating 3D objects in a 3D world, b) camera calibration, i.e., determining location and orientation of a camera by observing 3D features whose location is known, c) estimating motion and structure of moving objects relative to a camera. We mention some of the mathematical techniques borrowed from algebraic geometry, projective geometry, and homotopy theory that are required to solve these problems, list unsolved problems, and give some directions for future research.

I. INTRODUCTION

Human beings are endowed with the ability to see, discern objects, estimate and understand motion, and navigate in the three-dimensional (3D) space. Incorporating such ability in machines has been a challenging task and has occupied scientists and engineers working in computer vision for a long time [1], [2]. In this paper we review a subset of this activity which deals with observing some features on the surface of an object in the environment at different points in time and using this information to derive 3D motion and structure of these objects. Depending on the nature of the features observed (two- or three-dimensional, points or lines on the surface of the object, etc.), different formulations and algorithms come into play. However, the underlying mathematics has much in common: all the different cases can be formulated in

such a way that they require solution of simultaneous transcendental, polynomial, or linear equations in multiple variables which represent the structure of the object and its 3D motion as characterized by rotation and translation. It is this commonality that we wish to exploit by formulating the problems in seemingly disparate applications in a common format and then discussing mathematical tools for solving them.

The list of applications in sensing, modeling, and interpretation of motion and structure from corresponding features observed at different times is rather long. It depends upon the type of features observed. We categorize the problems discussed in this paper and their applications as follows:

i) 3D-to-3D feature correspondences.
   applications:

   a) Motion estimation using stereo or other range finding devices
   b) positioning a known 3D object using stereo or other range-finding devices.

ii) 2D-to-3D feature correspondences.
   applications:

   a) single camera calibration, i.e., determination of position and orientation of a camera knowing some features of 3D objects as imaged on the camera.
   b) passive navigation of a vehicle using a single camera and based on the knowledge of 3D landmarks.

iii) 2D-to-2D feature correspondences.
   applications:

   a) finding relative attitudes of two cameras which are both observing the same 3D features.
   b) Estimating motion and structure of objects moving relative to a camera.
   c) passive navigation, i.e., finding the relative attitude of a vehicle at two different time instants.

Manuscript received May 23, 1993; revised October 16, 1993.
T. S. Huang is with Beckman Institute and Coordinated Science Laboratory, University of Illinois, Urbana, IL 61801.
A. N. Netravali is with AT&T Bell Laboratories, Murray Hill, NJ 07974.
IEEE Log Number 9214859.

    d)   efficient coding and noise reduction of image sequences by estimating motion of objects.

We consider a variety of different features, such as points, straight lines, corners, etc., on the surface of 3D objects. By correspondence is meant observing the same feature at two or many different instants of time or viewing the same feature by two different cameras. In cases where features are 2D, they are obtained usually by perspective transformations of the 3D features on the camera plane. Although most of the paper deals with the perspective transformation, to a lesser extent, orthographic transformation is also considered. For the many cases that result, we formulate the problems, give algorithms for solution, and discuss conditions for existence and uniqueness of solutions and sensitivity of algorithms and solutions to noise. The approach we shall consider for motion/structure determination consists of two steps: i) Extract, match and determine locations (2D or 3D) of corresponding features. ii) Determine motion and structure parameters from the feature correspondences. It is to be emphasized that in this paper we discuss only the second step.

We start with the general statement of the problem and the relevant notation in the next section. We then go through the above three categories of problems, in each case reviewing the formulations and their solutions. The relevant mathematics that deals with solutions of simultaneous linear and nonlinear (especially polynomial) equations in multiple variables is described along the way. Some of these mathematical tools are new to workers in computer vision, but we believe that many of the unsolved questions that we raise in the end require such tools and hope that answers to these questions will be forthcoming using these tools.

II. General Problem and Notation

Consider an isolated rigid body viewed by an imaging system. Figure 1 shows a typical geometry for imaging. In this figure, object space coordinates are denoted by lower case letters and the image space coordinates are denoted by the upper case letters. Optical center of a pin-hole camera coincides with the origin of a cartesian coordinate system $(oxyz)$ and the positive z-axis is the direction of view. The image plane is located at a distance equal to the focal length F (which is assumed to be unity) from o along the direction of view. Using a perspective projection model, a point $p(=(x,y,z))$ on the surface of an object is projected at a point $P(=(X,Y))$ on the image plane, where

$$X = \frac{x}{z}$$
$$Y = \frac{y}{z}. \tag{1}$$

In some cases, we also use the orthographic projection instead of the perspective projection. In such cases, the image coordinates of point $P(=(X,Y))$ are related to the

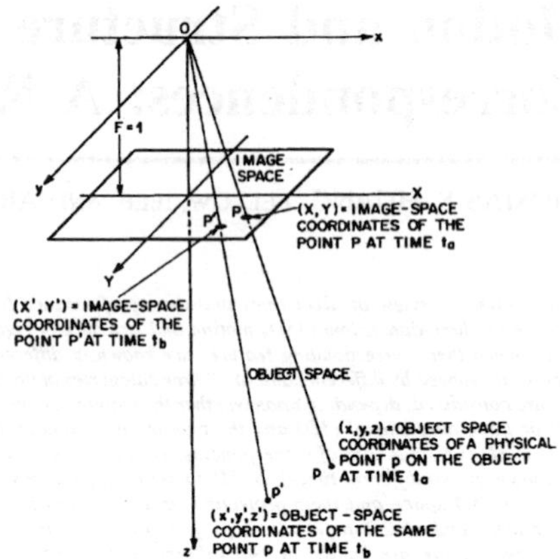

Fig. 1. Basic perspective geometry for imaging. Lower case letters refer to coordinates in the object space and upper case letters refer to coordinates on the image plane. Focal length F is assumed to be equal to one.

object space coordinates of point $p(=(x,y,z))$ by

$$X = x$$
$$Y = y. \tag{2}$$

The problem that we wish to tackle can be stated generally as follows. Consider two features f_1 and f_1'. These may be points, lines, conics, corners, etc. f_1 and f_1' refer to description of these features, e.g., their location in either 3 or 2 dimensions. f_1 may be at time t_a and f_1' is the same corresponding feature at time t_b; or, f_1 may be specified in 3D space and f_1' may be its corresponding projection on the image plane. In any case, we are given N such corresponding features on the same rigid object and our problem is to infer motion (where appropriate) and structure of this rigid body with respect to the imaging system. Broadly speaking, there are three different cases:

1) 3D-to-3D Correspondences: In this case, we are given 3D locations (e.g., object space coordinates in the case of point features) of N corresponding features (points or lines) at two different times and we need to estimate 3D motion of the rigid object. Thus the problem has application in either motion estimation using 3D information which can be obtained by stereo or other range-finding techniques, or positioning a 3D object with known feature locations using stereo techniques.

2) 2D-to-3D Correspondences: In this case, we are given correspondence of N features (f_i, f_i') such that f_i are specified in three dimensions and f_i' are their projection on the 2D image plane. The problem is to find location and orientation of the imaging camera. This has applications in either calibration (= determining location and orientation of the camera plane) of a single camera or passive navigation through known 3D landmarks (i.e., f_i) using projection of f_i on a single camera (i.e., f_i').

3) 2D-to-2D Correspondences: Here, N corresponding features are specified on the 2D image plane either at two different times for a single camera or at the same instant of time but for two different cameras. In the former case, the problem is to determine 3D motion and structure of the rigid object and in the latter case, the problem is to determine the relative orientation and location of the two imaging cameras.

As mentioned before, in each of the above cases, different formulations are necessary for different kinds of features. In fact, since the problems almost always result in solution of simultaneous linear and nonlinear (mostly polynominal) equations, ability to solve and gain insight depends to a large extent on the proper formulation. Our interest is in pointing out various formulations, algorithms for solution and determining the number of possible solutions as a function of the number of features considered.

A. Motion Model

Since a large part of the paper is concerned with estimating motion of rigid bodies, we state some well known results from kinematics of rigid bodies [3]. Consider a point $p(=(x,y,z))$ at time t_a which moves to location $p'(=(x',y',z'))$ at time t_b as a result of the motion of the rigid body. Then

$$
\begin{bmatrix} x' \\ y' \\ z' \end{bmatrix} = R \begin{bmatrix} x \\ y \\ z \end{bmatrix} + t
$$

$$
= \begin{bmatrix} r_{11} & r_{12} & r_{13} \\ r_{21} & r_{22} & r_{23} \\ r_{31} & r_{32} & r_{33} \end{bmatrix} \begin{bmatrix} x \\ y \\ z \end{bmatrix} + \begin{bmatrix} t_1 \\ t_2 \\ t_3 \end{bmatrix} \tag{3}
$$

where R represents rotation and t represents translation. Rotation can be specified in a number of equivalent ways. For example, rotation can be around an axis passing through the origin of our coordinate system. Let $\hat{n} = (n_1, n_2, n_3)^T$ be a unit vector along the axis of rotation and let χ be the angle of rotation from time t_a to time t_b. Then the rotation matrix R can be expressed as

$$R = S + K$$
$$S = \cos\chi I + (1 - \cos\chi)\hat{n}\hat{n}^T \text{(symmetric part)}$$
$$K = \sin\chi N \text{ (skew-symmetric part)}$$
$$\tag{4}$$

where I is the 3×3 identity matrix and

$$
N = \begin{bmatrix} 0 & -n_3 & n_2 \\ n_3 & 0 & -n_1 \\ -n_2 & n_1 & 0 \end{bmatrix} \tag{5}
$$

and $\hat{n}^T$ is the transpose of $\hat{n}$.

Alternatively, R can be specified as three successive rotations around the x-, y-, and z-axis, by angles θ, ψ, and ϕ, respectively, and can be written as a product of these three rotations

$$
R = \begin{bmatrix} \cos\phi & \sin\phi & 0 \\ -\sin\phi & \cos\phi & 0 \\ 0 & 0 & 1 \end{bmatrix} \begin{bmatrix} \cos\psi & 0 & -\sin\psi \\ 0 & 1 & 0 \\ \sin\psi & 0 & \cos\psi \end{bmatrix}
$$
$$
\cdot \begin{bmatrix} 1 & 0 & 0 \\ 0 & \cos\theta & \sin\theta \\ 0 & -\sin\theta & \cos\theta \end{bmatrix}. \tag{6}
$$

In the first case, motion is represented by seven parameters $n_1, n_2, n_3, \chi, t_1, t_2$, and t_3, with a relationship $n_1^2 + n_2^2 + n_3^2 = 1$ since $\hat{n}$ is a unit vector. In the second case, motion is represented by $\theta, \phi, \psi, t_1, t_2$, and t_3. Thus in either case, there are six free parameters that express 3D motion. In some cases, we want to specify rotation matrix R using all its nine components $\{r_{ij}\}_{i,j=1,\cdots,3}$. In such a case, it is important to realize that all these nine components are not independent, but the following relationships always hold:

$$
\begin{aligned}
r_{11}^2 + r_{12}^2 + r_{13}^2 &= 1 \\
r_{21}^2 + r_{22}^2 + r_{23}^2 &= 1 \\
r_{31}^2 + r_{32}^2 + r_{33}^2 &= 1 \\
r_{22}r_{33} - r_{23}r_{32} &= r_{11} \\
r_{23}r_{31} - r_{21}r_{33} &= r_{12} \\
r_{21}r_{32} - r_{22}r_{31} &= r_{13}.
\end{aligned} \tag{7}
$$

Thus in this representation of motion, we have twelve unknowns (nine rotation and three translation), but these six independent relationships among the components of R result again in six free parameters that express motion.

Finally, we briefly review the quaternion representation of 3D rotation. A rotation around an axis with direction cosines (n_1, n_2, n_3) and rotation angle χ can be represented by the unit quaternion

$$
q = (s; l, m, n) = \left[\cos\frac{\chi}{2}; n_1 \sin\frac{\chi}{2}, n_2 \sin\frac{\chi}{2}, n_3 \sin\frac{\chi}{2}\right] \tag{8}
$$

specifically

$$(0; p_i') = q(0; p_i)q^* \tag{9}$$

where * denotes complex conjugation. In terms of q, the rotation matrix becomes (10); see below. We start now with the different cases.

III. 3D-TO-3D CORRESPONDENCES

1) Point Features: Our first case is when the features (f_i, f_i') are 3D coordinates of points on the surface of the rigid body in motion. These are observed at times t_a and

---

$$
R = \begin{bmatrix} s^2 + l^2 - m^2 - n^2 & 2(lm + sn) & 2(ln + sm) \\ 2(lm + sn) & s^2 - l^2 + m^2 - n^2 & 2(mn - sl) \\ 2(ln - sm) & 2(mn + sl) & s^2 - l^2 - m^2 + n^2 \end{bmatrix} \tag{10}
$$

t_b. Suppose we **are given** N corresponding points $(p_i, p_{i'})$ which obey the relationship of (3), i.e.

$$p_i' = Rp_i + t, \quad i = 1, \cdots, N. \tag{11}$$

The problem is: given(11), find R and t. Since for $N = 1$, the number of independent linear equations is fewer than the number of variables (six), there are always infinitely many solutions. For $N = 2$, there are also infinitely many solutions. It is well known [3] that three noncollinear-point correspondences are necessary and sufficient to determine R and t uniquely.

Equation (11), when expanded represents three scalar equations in six unknown motion parameters. With three point correspondences, we will get nine nonlinear equations. Iterative methods can be used to obtain the "best" fits of the six unknowns. However, it is possible to get stuck in the local minima.

It is therefore advisable to use linear algorithms [4] by observing that (11) is linear in components of R (i.e., r_{ij}) and t. For example, one of the scalar equations from (11) can be written as

$$x_i' = r_{11}x_i + r_{12}y_i + r_{13}z_i + t_1. \tag{12}$$

Therefore, if we have four point correspondences, then we have enough linear equations to solve for the twelve unknowns. In fact, it can be readily seen that if three point correspondences are known, the fourth point correspondence can be found on the basis of rigidity of the body and that if the three points are not collinear then the system of equations (11) is invertible for the unknown parameters.

In practice, since the point correspondences are obtained from measurements, they are subject to error and therefore one prefers to work with more than three point correspondences. In this case, R and t can be obtained as a solution to the following least squares problem:

$$\underset{\text{w.r.t. } R, t}{\text{minimize}} \left\{ \sum_{i=1}^{N} \|p_i' - (Rp_i + t)\|^2 \right\} \tag{13}$$

subject to the constraint that R is a rotation matrix (e.g., subject to (7)). Here $\|\cdot\|$ represents the Euclidean norm. (As in any such procedure, if there are some measurements with a large amount of error, it is advisable to throw them away, rather than average over them.) Such a constrained least square problem can be solved by linear procedures using quaternions [5], [6] or by singular value decomposition [7], [8]

2) Motion from Stereo Images Sequences: Of particular interest is the case of motion estimation from stereo image sequences [10] Here it is assumed that p_i and $p_{i'}$ are measured by stereo triangulation. When the ratio of object range (i.e., z) to the camera baseline is large (say $>$ 10), the measurement error due to image sampling is much bigger in z than in x and y [10]. In such a case, weighted least squares can be used to give less importance to z in (13). However, it is difficult to estimate proper weights [11]. Alternatively, maximum likelihood [12] or its approximations [13] can be tried. All these approaches

are computationally time-consuming. It appears that when errors in z are really large, it is better to throw the z's away and use orthographic approximations [14].

B. 3D-to-3D Straight-Line Correspondences

Suppose, instead of point correspondences, we are given correspondences of straight lines. Thus let l_i and l_i' be two corresponding straight lines at times t_a and t_b, respectively. We note that these lines are considered infinitely long and that no point correspondences on these lines are assumed to be known. Thus our problem is: given corresponding $(l_i, l_i')_{,i=1}, \cdots, N$, find R and t.

If $N = 1$, the number of equations is fewer than the number of unknowns and therefore the number of solutions is infinite. Moreover, *it can be proved* that two nonparallel "sensed" lines are necessary and sufficient to determine R and t uniquely.

The following two types of algorithms may be used.

i) From the nonparallel sensed lines, we can generate three noncollinear point correspondences and then use the algorithms of Section III-A1.

ii) Alternatively, if v_i and v_i' are unit vectors along the direction of lines l_i and $l_i'(i = 1, 2)$, respectively, and if[1]

$$v_3 = v_1 \times v_2 \tag{14}$$

and

$$v_3' = v_1' \times v_2'$$

then

$$v_i' = Rv_i, i = 1, \cdots, 3. \tag{15}$$

This gives us enough equations to determine the rotation matrix R. The translation can be obtained by creating a point correspondence on the lines Rl_1 and l_1'. For example, the point on Rl_1 which is closest to Rl_2 corresponds to the point on l_1' which is closest to l_2'.

To combat noise, rotation can be determined by constrained least squares, i.e.

$$\underset{\text{w.r.t. } R}{\text{minimize}} \left\{ \sum_{i=1}^{N} \|v_i' - Rv_i\|^2 \right\} \tag{16}$$

subject to R being a rotation matrix. Typically, translation is more sensitive to noise and additional information is necessary to obtain reasonable estimate of the translation [15].

IV. 2D-TO-3D CORRESPONDENCES

As we mentioned in the Introduction, this situation arises when each of the features is 3D and their corresponding features are 2D. If 3D locations of features are known along with their projection on the camera plane which is at unknown location, then the algorithms described in this

---

[1] $\times$ denotes the usual cross product.

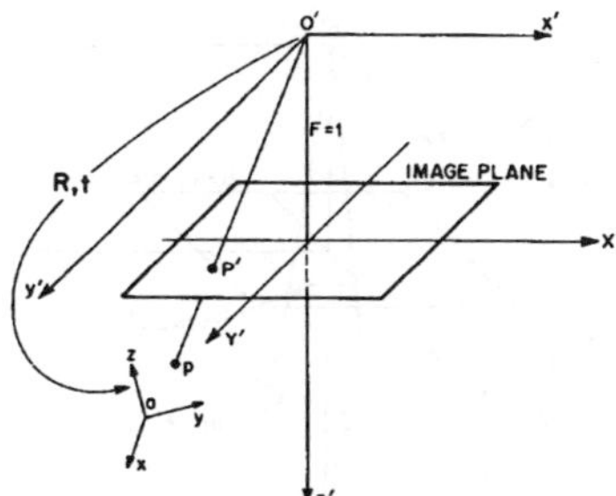

Fig. 2. Imaging geometry for 2D-to-3D correspondence problem. A point p in coordinate system $oxyz$ is imaged at location P' on the image plane which is specified in coordinate system $ox'y'z'$.

section allow us to determine the attitude, i.e., the location and the orientation of the camera (known as the camera calibration problem in classical photogrammetry [16]). A related problem is when the camera is attached to a vehicle which is moving in a 3D environment with landmarks at known locations and the goal is to guide this vehicle by observing images of these landmarks. Since the camera is attached to the vehicle, determining the camera attitude, obtains the attitude of the vehicle, which helps navigate it. We consider two types of features: points and straight lines.

A. 2D-to-3D Point Correspondences

As shown in Fig. 2, consider two coordinate systems. $oxyz$ is a coordinate system in which the 3D point features are located. Thus p_i are points in this coordinate system with coordinates (x_i, y_i, z_i). The camera is referenced to the other coordinate system $(o'x'y'z')$. In particular, we assume as before, that the camera plane is perpendicular to the $o'z'$-axis and at location $z' = 1$. Image coordinates on the camera plane are obtained by perspective projection and denoted by (X', Y'). Thus the image of point p_i is at P'_i whose coordinates are given by

$$X'_i = \frac{x'_i}{z'_i}$$

and

$$Y'_i = \frac{y'_i}{z'_i}. \tag{17}$$

Coordinate system $oxyz$ is obtained by a rotation R and translation t of the coordinate system $o'x'y'z'$ and our goal in camera calibration is to determine R and t, knowing the N point correspondences $(p_i, P'_i)_{i=1,\cdots,N}$.

The 3D coordinates of p'_i are related to those of p_i by

$$p'_i = R\, p_i + t \tag{18}$$

or

$$\begin{pmatrix} x' \\ y' \\ z' \end{pmatrix} = R \begin{pmatrix} x \\ y \\ z \end{pmatrix} + t.$$

1) Church's Method [16]: **Combining (17) and (18), we get**

$$X'_i = \frac{r_{11}x_i + r_{12}y_i + r_{13}z_i + t_1}{r_{31}x_i + r_{32}y_i + r_{33}z_i + t_3}, \quad i = 1, \cdots, N$$

$$Y_i = \frac{r_{21}x_i + r_{12}y_i + r_{13}z_i + t_2}{r_{31}x_i + r_{32}y_i + r_{33}z_i + t_3}, \quad i = 1, \ldots, N. \tag{19}$$

As in the previous section, there are six unknowns (three for rotation and three for translation) and therefore with three point correspondences, we have enough (i.e., six) equations. Unfortunately, these are nonlinear transcendental equations, since r_{ij} are related to the three unknowns of the rotation matrix (e.g., Euler angles of (6)) in a transcendental manner. Iterative methods are required to solve these nonlinear algebraic equations. In practice, the data (i.e., p_i and P'_i) are known only approximately and therefore one may use more than three point correspondences. In such a case, the following nonlinear least squares problem may be solved iteratively:

$$\begin{aligned} \underset{\text{w.r.t. } R, t}{\text{minimize}} \Bigg\{ \sum_{i=1}^{N} \bigg(X'_i - \frac{r_{11}x_i + r_{12}y_i + r_{13}z_i + t_1}{r_{31}x_i + r_{32}y_i + r_{33}z_i + t_3} \bigg)^2 \\ + \bigg(Y_{i'} - \frac{r_{21}x_i + r_{22}y_i + r_{23}z_i + t_2}{r_{31}x_i + r_{32}y_i + r_{33}z_i + t_3} \bigg)^2 \Bigg\} \end{aligned} \tag{20}$$

subject to R being a rotation matrix (i.e., subject to (7)). The disadvantages of these approaches is that unless one starts with a good initial guess, the iterative procedure may not converge to the right solution. Moreover, no insight is obtained about the nature, uniqueness or the number of solutions.

2) Ganapathy's Method [17], [18]: If three noncollinear point correspondences are given, then without loss of generality we can assume that the three points lie in the plane $z = 0$. Then (19) becomes

$$X'_i = \frac{r_{11}x_i + r_{12}y_i + t_1}{r_{31}x_i + r_{32}y_i + t_3}$$

$$Y'_i = \frac{r_{21}x_i + r_{22}y_i + t_2}{r_{31}x_i + r_{32}y_i + t_3}. \tag{21}$$

Thus the three point correspondences give six linear and homogeneous equations in nine unknowns $r_{11}, r_{12}, r_{21}, r_{22}, r_{31}, r_{32}, t_1, t_2, t_3$. Assuming $t_3 \neq 0$, we can divide by t_3, to get six linear equations in eight unknowns

$$\frac{r_{11}}{t_3}, \frac{r_{12}}{t_3}, \frac{r_{21}}{t_3}, \frac{r_{22}}{t_3}, \frac{r_{31}}{t_3}, \frac{r_{32}}{t_3}, \frac{t_1}{t_3}, \frac{t_2}{t_3}.$$

Additional constraints on $\{r_{ij}\}$ can be obtained from (7) as

$$\left(\frac{r_{11}}{t_3}\right)^2 + \left(\frac{r_{21}}{t_3}\right)^2 + \left(\frac{r_{31}}{t_3}\right)^2$$
$$= \left(\frac{r_{12}}{t_3}\right)^2 + \left(\frac{r_{22}}{t_3}\right)^2 + \left(\frac{r_{32}}{t_3}\right)^2 \tag{22}$$

and

$$\left(\frac{r_{11}}{t_3}\right)\left(\frac{r_{12}}{t_3}\right) + \left(\frac{r_{21}}{t_3}\right)\left(\frac{r_{22}}{t_3}\right) + \left(\frac{r_{31}}{t_3}\right)\left(\frac{r_{32}}{t_3}\right) = 0.$$

Thus we have six linear and two quadratic equations in eight unknowns. According to Bézout's theorem [19], the maximum number of solutions (real or complex) is four, assuming that the number of solutions is finite. Solutions can be obtained by computing the resultant which in this case will be a fourth-degree polynominal in one of the unknowns. Note that the unknown "scale factor" t_3 can be determined by using, e.g., the constraint $r_{11}^2 + r_{12}^2 + r_{13}^2 = 1$.

With four coplanar point correspondences, (21) yields eight linear homogeneous equations in nine unknowns. If this system of equations is nonsingular R, t can be obtained uniquely.

If four or five point correspondences are known, then one can either solve a linear least squares problem or use the above method by taking three point correspondences at a time. In the latter case, one expects that the different solution sets have only one common solution. However, precise conditions under which a unique solution is guaranteed are not yet known and in fact, it is easy to construct examples where more than one solution exists with four or five point correspondences.

If six point correspondences are known, then (21) gives twelve linear homogeneous equations in twelve unknowns $\{r_{ij}\}_{i,j=1,\cdots,3}$, $\{t_i\}_i = 1, \cdots 3$. R, t can be determined uniquely, if the system is nonsingular. Thus with six or more point correspondences, one expects a unique solution generally.

3) Fischler and Bolles' Method [20]: Fischler and Bolles presented a geometric formulation of the problem for three general point correspondences and four coplanar point correspondences. For the three-point case, assume that we are given the three angles $\angle p_2 o' p_3$, and $\angle p_3 o' p_1$ and our problem is to find the lengths $\overline{o'p_1}$, $\overline{o'p_2}$, and $\overline{o'p_3}$. By the law of cosines,

$$(\overline{p_1 p_2})^2 = (\overline{o'p_1})^2 + (\overline{o'p_2})^2 - 2(\overline{o'p_1})(\overline{o'p_2})\cos(\angle p_1 o' p_2)$$
$$(\overline{p_2 p_3})^2 = (\overline{o'p_2})^2 + (\overline{o'p_3})^2 - 2(\overline{o'p_2})(\overline{o'p_3})\cos(\angle p_2 o' p_3)$$
$$(\overline{p_3 p_1})^2 = (\overline{o'p_3})^2 + (\overline{o'p_1})^2 - 2(\overline{o'p_3})(\overline{o'p_1})\cos(\angle p_3 o' p_1).$$
$$(23)$$

Thus we have three quadratic equations in three unknowns, $\overline{o'p_1}, \overline{o'p_2}$ and $\overline{o'p_3}$. From Bézout's theorem, the maximum number of solution can be eight. However, because of symmetry, if $(\overline{o'p_1}, \overline{o'p_2}, \overline{o'p_3}) = (a, b, c)$ is a solution, so is $(\overline{o'p_1}, \overline{o'p_2}, \overline{o'p_3}) = (-a, -b, -c)$. Thus there are at most four positive solutions. One can show this, alternatively, by computing the resultant of the system of equations (23) and showing that it is only a fourth-degree polynominal.

In practice, if the measurements are noisy, Fischler and Bolles proposed a robust approach which they called RANSAC.

4) Horaud, et al.'s Method [21]: For the four-point case, Horaud, Conio, Leboulleux, and Lacolle have presented a formulation which results in the solution of a fourth-order polynomial equation in one unknown.

5) Multiplicity of Solutions and Degeneracy: Fischler and Bolles [20] showed that with three point correspondences one can have as many as four solutions. Wolfe, Weber-

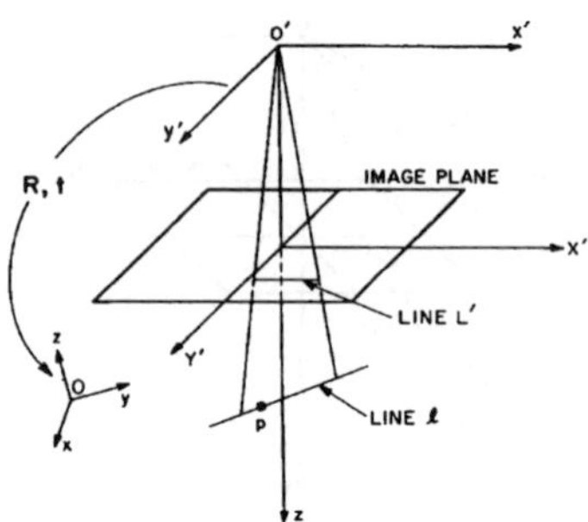

Fig. 3. Imaging geometry for line correspondences. A line l in 3D object space is mapped perspectively into a line L on the 2D image plane.

Sklair, Mathis, and Magee [22] have used a geometrical approach to study this problem of the number of solutions for the three-point case. They exhibited examples of point configurations which give rise to one, two, three, or four solutions. However, to date there is no complete answer to the question: For the N-point case, what geometrical configurations give rise to how many solutions?

Holt and Netravali [23] have given a complete answer to the question: Under what conditions is the number of solutions infinite? The necessary and sufficient condition for infinitely many solutions is essentially that the image points are collinear on the image plane.

B. 2D-to-3D Line Correspondences

Consider the geometry of Fig. 3. Let a straight line l_i in 3D space be perspectively projected on the image plane to give a line L_i'. Also, let the 3D line l_i be characterized by its direction $\boldsymbol{n}_i = (a_i, b_i, c_i)$ and a point $\boldsymbol{p}_i$ on it. $(\boldsymbol{n}_i, p_i)$ are with respect to the coordinate system $oxyz$. The projected line L_i' is characterized by the following equation in the image plane:

$$A_i X' + B_i Y' + C_i = 0 \qquad (24)$$

i.e., by the parameter vector

$$\boldsymbol{N}_i' \triangleq (A_i, B_i, C_i)^T. \qquad (25)$$

As before the two coordinate systems are related by a rotation R and translation t and our goal is to determine them. Thus the problem is as follows: given N correspondences $(l_i, L_{i'})_{i=1,\cdots,N}$, determine R and t.

1) Liu, Huang and Faugeras Algorithms [24]: We first note that the plane containing o' and L' has an equation

$$A_i x' + B_i y' + C_i z' = 0 \qquad (26)$$

and therefore the normal of the plane is $\boldsymbol{N}_i$. Since l_i lies in this plane, we know that $R\boldsymbol{n}_i$ is orthogonal to $\boldsymbol{N}_i'$ and this gives us

$$\boldsymbol{N}_i'^T R\boldsymbol{n}_i = 0. \qquad (27)$$

Thus we have succeeded in decoupling rotation from translation. Since R contains only three independent variables, with three line correspondences we can solve the nonlinear transcendental equations of (27) iteratively to get R. Additionally, with eight line correspondences, (27) gives eight linear homogeneous equations in elements of R (i.e., $\{r_{ij}\}$). If this system of equations is nonsingular, then a unique solution to within a scale factor can be obtained for R. The scale factor can be determined from the nonlinear constraints on R of (7). Conditions for nonsingularily are not yet known.

From geometrical considerations, it can be shown that

$$(N_i')^T t = (N_i')^T (R p_i). \tag{28}$$

Therefore, once R has been found, (28) can be used to solve for t from three or more line correspondences.

By decomposing R in an appropriate way, Chen [25] showed that with three line correspondences, there are at most eight solutions to R from (27); for each solution of R, t can be found from (28). He also demonstrated that eight solutions are attainable for some line configurations. With four, five, six, or seven line correspondences, the exact number of solutions is not yet known. It is expected to be less than eight, since in each of these cases one can take sets of three line correspondences and get eight solutions. The intersection of all these solutions will then be the solution. However, the precise number of these intersections and conditions under which they hold is not yet known. With eight line correspondences, (27) gives a linear system of equations for R. However, conditions for nonsingularity are not yet known. Chen did succeed in obtaining a necessary and sufficient condition for the number of solutions to be infinite.

More recently, Navab and Faugeras [74] showed that if the feature points lie on a one-sheet hyperboloid passing through the camera center, then the number of solutions to the translation is infinite.

In practice, if the measurements are noisy, by using a larger number of line correspondences, one can pose a variety of least square problems. In most cases, $(3 < N < 8)$, the result is a linear least square problem with quadric constraints.

2) Using Line Correspondence Methods for Point Correspondences: Given N-point correspondences, we can connect every point pair by a straight line to get $N - (N-1)/2$ line correspondences, out of which only $3N - 6$ are independent (assuming $N \geq 3$). Then the line correspondence methods of this section can be used to find R, t. The advantage of this approach is that R and t are decoupled and therefore in a sense the dimensionality of the problem is reduced.

It is interesting to examine the number of solutions obtained by the line and point correspondence method. Three point correspondences generate three line correspondences. However these three lines are coplanar and this appears to ensure that out of the eight possible solutions only four are real. With five point correspondences, we get nine line correspondences and therefore can use the linear method of line correspondences. Similarly, with six point correspondences, we get twelve line correspondences. Although conditions on uniqueness of solution are not known, empirically a unique solution is obtained for six or more point correspondences.

V. 2D-TO-2D CORRESPONDENCES

Consider a situation where the features of a rigid body are projected on the image plane and only these projections are known. If the camera geometry is fixed, and the object is in motion, then our problem is to obtain 3D motion and structure of this rigid body by observing corresponding projected features at two different instants of time. In this context, by structure is meant the z coordinate (depth or distance along the camera axis) of these features in the 3D space. If, on the other hand, the same rigid body features are observed by projecting them on two different cameras, then the problem is to determine the location and orientation of one camera relative to the other. Both these problems are mathematically equivalent. Different formulations and solutions occur depending on the nature of features. We start with point features.

A. 2D-to-2D Point Correspondences

Consider the problem in which a point $p_i(= (x_i, y_i, z_i))$ on a rigid body moves to a point $p_i'(= (x_i', y_i', z_i'))$ with respect to a camera fixed coordinate system shown in Fig. 4. Let the perspective projection of p_i be $P_i(= (X_i, Y_i, 1))$ and that of p_i' be $P_i(= (X_i', Y_i', 1))$. Due to the rigid body motion, p_i and p_i' are related by

$$p_i' = R p_i + t \tag{29}$$

where R and t are rotation and translation, respectively. Our problem is: given N correspondences $(P_i, P_i')_{i=1,\cdots,N}$, determine R and t. It is obvious that from two perspective views, it is impossible to determine the magnitude of translation. If the rigid body were two times farther away from the image plane, but twice as big, and translated at twice the speed, we would get exactly the same two images. Therefore, the translation t and object-point ranges (z_i) can only be determined to within a global positive scale factor. The value of this scale factor can be found if we know the magnitude of t or the absolute range of any observed object point. Therefore, our problem is to determine rotation R, $t/\|t\|$ and $z_i/\|t\|$ (= structure). Since the motion and structure are coupled together, different algorithms result depending on whether structure or motion is determined first. We start with the "structure first" algorithm.

1) "Structure-First" Algorithms [26]: In this approach, from the rigidity constraints, object-point ranges z_i and z_i' are determined first. Then the motion parameters R and t can be determined by solving (29) using the methods of Section III. The points p_i and $p_{i'}'$ are on a rigid body only if the distance between any pair of them does not change in two different views taken at two different times. Thus we must have

$$\|p_i - p_j\|^2 = \|p_i' - p_j'\|^2, \quad 1 \leq i, j \leq N. \tag{30}$$

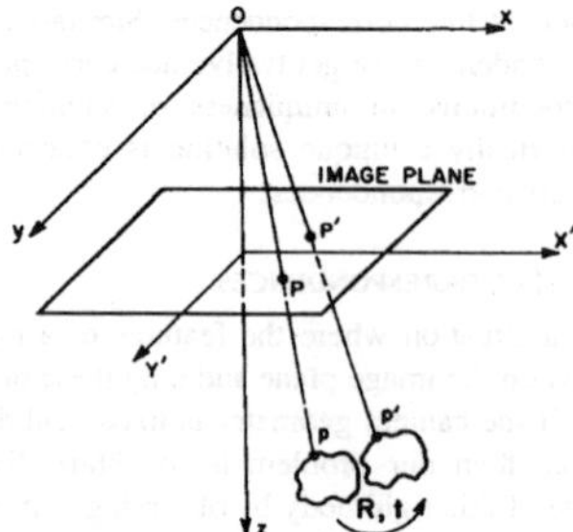

Fig. 4. Imaging geometry for 2D point correspondences. On the image plane, a point P moves to point P' as a result of motion of a rigid body.

For $N(N \geq 3)$ point correspondences, there are $3N - 6$ independent equations. Equation (30) can be expanded as

$$(x_i - x_j)^2 + (y_i - y_j)^2 + (z_i - z_j)^2$$
$$= (x_i' - x_j')^2 + (y_i' - y_j')^2 + (z_i' - z_j')^2. \quad (31)$$

By using the relationships of perspective projection as in (1)

$$(X_i z_i - X_j z_j)^2 + (Y_i z_i - Y_j z_j)^2 + (z_i - z_j)^2$$
$$= (X_i' z_i' - X_j' z_j')^2 + (Y_i' z_i' - Y_j' z_j')^2 + (z_i' - z_j')^2. \quad (32)$$

In this equation, unknowns are $\{z_i, z_i', z_j, z_j'\}$. The equation is a homogeneous quadratic in these unknowns.

With five point correspondences, we have ten unknowns and nine homogeneous equations and iterative algorithms can be used to obtain solutions to within a scale factor. From Bézout's theorem, the number of possible solutions is no more than $2^9 = 512$. Various attempts to obtain bounds on the number of solutions by computing resultants have not been successful. Also, obtaining all the real solutions by using homotopy methods have not been successful due to the large dimensionality of this formulation. For a discussion on resultants, the reader is referred to [27]. For homotopy methods for polynomials, to [28].

2) "Motion-First" Algorithms: In this approach, equations are first formulated that only involve motion parameters. The structure values z_i, z_i' are then obtained from (33) below.

a) Transcendental equations [29], [30]: From (1) and (29), we get (omitting the subscripts)

$$X' = \frac{r_{11}X + r_{12}Y + r_{13} + \frac{t_1}{z}}{r_{31}X + r_{32}Y + r_{33} + \frac{t_3}{z}}$$

and

$$Y' = \frac{r_{21}X + r_{22}Y + r_{23} + \frac{t_2}{z}}{r_{31}X + r_{32}Y + r_{33} + \frac{t_3}{z}}. \quad (33)$$

Eliminating z between these two equations

$$(t_1 - t_3 X')\{(r_{31}X + r_{32}Y + r_{33})Y' - (r_{21}X + r_{22}Y + r_{23})\}$$
$$= (t_2 - t_3 Y')\{(r_{31}X + r_{32}Y + r_{33})X'$$
$$- (r_{11}X + r_{12}Y + r_{13})\}. \quad (34)$$

If we use the Euler angle representation of the rotation (6), then (34) is a transcendental equation in terms of these angles and linear and homogeneous in terms of t_i. With five point correspondences, we have five equations in five unknowns (setting the scale factor $= 1$, e.g., by setting $t_3 = 1$). Iterative methods can be used to solve these nonlinear equations. However, no insight is gained in nature, uniqueness or number of solutions.

b) Polynomial equations: Equation (34) is a second-degree polynominal in eleven unknowns, $\{r_{ij}\}_{i,j=1,\cdots 3}$, t_1, t_2 (setting $t_3 = 1$). Then, with five point correspondences, we have five equations from (34) and the six quadratic constraints on the components of the rotation matrix $\{r_j\}$ (7). Thus the number of equations is equal to the number of unknowns and iterative methods can be used for solution. The number of solutions is no more than 2^{11}, but no insight is gained about the number of real solutions. Neither are these particularly suited for numerical computation due to the high dimensionality of search space.

A better approach is due to Jerian and Jain [31] who show that with three point correspondences, a quartic equation can be derived which contains three unknowns; namely, the three components of the "tangent quaternions," representing R. These tangent quaternion components can be expressed as: $n_1 \tan \theta/2$, $n_2 \tan \theta/2$, and $n_3 \tan \theta/2$, where the axis of rotation has direction cosines (n_1, n_2, n_3) and the rotation angle is θ.

Any additional point correspondence gives one more such quartic equation. Therefore, five point correspondences gives three quartic equations in three unknowns. The maximum number of solutions is $4^3 = 64$. In principle, one can reduce the three equations (using resultants) to a single 64th-order equation in one unknown. Then Sturm's method can be used to find all the real solutions. In practice, Jerian and Jain were not able to get the 64th-order equation. They did succeed in reducing two quartics to a single 16th-order equation (using MACSYMA). Thus their method is as follows. Do a global search on one of the three variables. For each fixed value of this variable, the other two variables are solved by reducing two of the three quartics to a single 16th-order equation in one variable whose real roots are determined by Sturm's method. Then each real candidate solution for the three variables is substituted into the remaining quartic equation to check whether it is satisfied. Empirically, Jerian and Jain found that with five point correspondences, the number of real solutions could be two, four, or eight.

c) Linear algorithms [32], [33]: Given eight or more point correspondences, a linear algorithm can be devised. It is obvious from the geometry of Fig. 4, that the three vectors Rp (not shown), p', and t are coplanar and therefore

$$(p') \cdot (t \times Rp) = 0 \quad (35)$$

which can be written in matrix form as

$$(p')^T E p = 0 \quad (36)$$

where E is a 3×3 matrix defined as

$$E = \begin{bmatrix} e_1 & e_2 & e_3 \\ e_4 & e_5 & e_6 \\ e_7 & e_8 & e_9 \end{bmatrix} \triangleq GR \qquad (37)$$

and G is defined as

$$G \triangleq \begin{bmatrix} 0 & -t_3 & t_2 \\ t_3 & 0 & -t_1 \\ -t_2 & t_1 & 0 \end{bmatrix}. \qquad (38)$$

Dividing both sides of (36) by the positive quantity zz' (i.e., dividing p by z and p' by z'),

$$(P')^T E P = 0 \qquad (39)$$

or

$$[X'Y'1]E \begin{bmatrix} X \\ Y \\ 1 \end{bmatrix} = 0. \qquad (40)$$

Equation (40) is linear and homogeneous in the nine unknowns $\{e_i\}_{i=1,\cdots,9}$. Given N point correspondences, we can write (40) in the form

$$B[e_1, e_2, e_3, e_4, e_5, e_6, e_7, e_8, e_9]^T = 0 \qquad (41)$$

where the coefficient matrix B is $N \times 9$. With eight point correspondences, if the rank $(B) = 8$, (41) can be used to uniquely determine E to within a scale factor. Once E is determined, R and t can be determined uniquely, as described, e.g., in [34]. In practice, the data are noisy. Various least squares techniques can be used. See, e.g., [35].

d) Polynomial methods again: Given N point correspondences, if the rank $(B) < 8$, then the linear algorithm cannot be used. However, if rank $(B) = 5$, 6, or 7, then the linear equations (41) can be solved along with the polynominal constraints on the components of matrix E [36], [37]. Specifically, E is equal to a skew-symmetric matrix post multiplied by a rotation matrix only if $\{e_i\}_{i=1,\cdots,9}$, satisfy the following three constraint equations. Let $\{\varepsilon_i\}_{i=1,\cdots,3}$ be the ith row of E, then

$$\varepsilon_3 \cdot (\varepsilon_1 \times \varepsilon_2) = 0$$
$$(\|\varepsilon_2\|^2 + \|\varepsilon_3\|^2 - \|\varepsilon_1\|^2)(\varepsilon_2 \cdot \varepsilon_3) + 2(\varepsilon_1 \cdot \varepsilon_2)(\varepsilon_1 \cdot \varepsilon_3) = 0$$
$$\|\varepsilon_3\|^4 = (\|\varepsilon_2\|^2 - \|\varepsilon_1^2\|^2)^2 + 4(\varepsilon_1 \cdot \varepsilon_2)^2. \qquad (42)$$

Thus we get three polynomial equations in $\{e_i\}_{i=1,\cdots,9}$ of degree 3, 4, 4, respectively.

If Rank $(B) = 5$, we have a set of five independent linear honomogeneous equations (41) and three homogeneous polynomial equations (42) in the nine unknowns $\{e_i\}$. We can solve these equations to determine $\{e_i\}$ to within a scale factor. From Bézout's theorem, the maximum number of solutions (real or complex) is $3 \times 4 \times 4 = 48$.

One method of solution is to first solve the five linear equations to get $(e_1, \cdots, e_9)$ as a linear combination of four known 9-vectors (a basis of the nullspace of B) with unknown weights. Substituting these into (42), we get three homogeneous equations in the four unknown weights. Then,

we solve these three polynomial equations to determine these four weights (to within a scale factor).

If Rank $(B) = 6$, we have a set of six independent linear homogeneous equations in the nine unknowns $\{e_i\}$. We solve these together with the first two equations in (42) to determine $\{e_i\}$ to within a scale factor. The maximum number of solutions (real or complex) is $3 \times 4 = 12$. For each real solution, we substitute it into the third equation of (42) to see whether it is satisfied.

If Rank $(B) = 7$, we have a set of seven independent linear homogeneous equations in the nine unknowns $\{e_i\}$. We solve these together with the first equation in (42). The maximum number of solution is 3. For each real solution we substitute it into the second and third equations in (42) to check if they are satisfied.

For a detailed discussion on such polynomial methods for the cases of Rank $(B) = 5$, 6, 7, see [37].

If Rank $(B) = 8$, then a unique solution to E (to within a scale factor) is ensured. Longuet-Higgins [38] established a necessary and sufficient condition for Rank $(B) = 8$. For convenience, assume the object is stationary and the camera is moving (in particular, the focal point 0 at time t_a moves to $0'$ at time t_b). Then, Rank $(B) = 8$ if and only if the N points lie on a quadratic surface passing through 0 and $0'$. (Note that any nine points lie on a quadratic surface.) Rank $(B) = 8$ is a sufficient but *not* necessary condition for uniqueness of the solution to E.

For Rank $(B) = 5$, which is equivalent to having five point correspondences in general positions, some very loose upper bounds on the number of solutions have been established in earlier sections. Way back in 1913, using projective geometry, Kruppa [39] showed that the number of solutions to E is no more than 11. Recently, Faugeras and Maybank [40], Demazure [41], and Netravali *et al.* [42] sharpened this result to 10.

For Rank $(B) = 6$ or 7, the number of independent equations in (41) and (42) is larger than the number of unknowns (remembering that the equations are homogeneous so we can set one of the e_i's equal to 1, thus *heuristically* one would expect that the solution to E is almost always unique. However, it can be shown that for Rank $(B) = 6$ or 7, it is possible to have up to three solutions in special cases [43], [44].

One point should be clarified here. For a given E matrix (determined to within a scale factor), four pairs of R, t can be derived. However, at most one of the four is physically realizable (i.e., corresponding to 3D points which are in front of the camera both at t_a and t_b) and compatible with the given point correspondences [45].

In practice, since the measurements may be inaccurate and noisy, a larger number of point correspondences should be used. In such cases, a variety of least squares problems can be formulated. Using nonlinear transcendental equations, least squares can be set up as in [46]. If the linear equations (41) are used along with the polynominal constraints (42), then a constrained linear least squares problem has to be solved [47]. Finally, for a large number of points, linear least squares can be formulated [48]. In this case, error estimates have been derived. One can compute the error estimates alongside the calculation of motion and structure parameters and trust the latter only if the former are sufficiently small.

3) 2D-to-2D Point Correspondences—Planar Case: Previous sections dealt with situations in which the correspondences of points at any general location were known. If these points have some structure, then this structure can be exploited to generate additional equations and this results in requiring fewer points for solution of the problem. As an example, with four point correspondences, methods of previous sections would yield an infinite number of solutions since the number of equations is smaller than the number of unknowns required to specify motion and structure. However, if the four points are coplanar, then in addition to the six equations from (30), we have the following condition for coplanarity:

$$(\boldsymbol{p}_1 - \boldsymbol{p}_2) \cdot (\boldsymbol{p}_1 - \boldsymbol{p}_3) \times (\boldsymbol{p}_1 - \boldsymbol{p}_4) = 0. \tag{43}$$

This gives us seven homogeneous equations in eight unknowns (z_i, z_i'). From Bézout's theorem, this system can have at most 192 ($= 3 \times 2^6$) solutions. In fact, as we shall shortly see, the number of solutions is almost always two. In many ways, this conclusion is similar to the 2D-to-3D point correspondence case that we discussed in Section IV-A.

With the motion-first approach, the condition of coplanarity is more difficult to include since perspective projection of coplanar points is not constrained in general on the image plane. Thus with four coplanar points, we still have four linear homogeneous equations from (36). Together with (42), we have seven equations in nine unknowns and therefore if coplanarity is used to generate an additional equation, the number of solutions will be infinite. We do not yet know how to include coplanarity in this formulation. The following linear formulation [49] is more appropriate.

Let the equation of the plane containing the four points at time t_a be given by

$$\boldsymbol{g}^T \boldsymbol{p} = 1 \tag{44}$$

where

$$\boldsymbol{g}^T = (a, b, c). \tag{45}$$

Then at time t_b,

$$\begin{aligned} \boldsymbol{p}' &= R\boldsymbol{p} + \boldsymbol{t} \\ &= R\boldsymbol{p} + \boldsymbol{t}\boldsymbol{g}^T \boldsymbol{p} \\ &= (R + \boldsymbol{t}\boldsymbol{g}^T)\boldsymbol{p} \\ &= A\boldsymbol{p} \end{aligned} \tag{46} \tag{47}$$

where

$$A = R + \boldsymbol{t}\boldsymbol{g}^T \tag{48}$$

$$\triangleq \begin{bmatrix} a_1 & a_2 & a_3 \\ a_4 & a_5 & a_6 \\ a_7 & a_8 & a_9 \end{bmatrix} \tag{49}$$

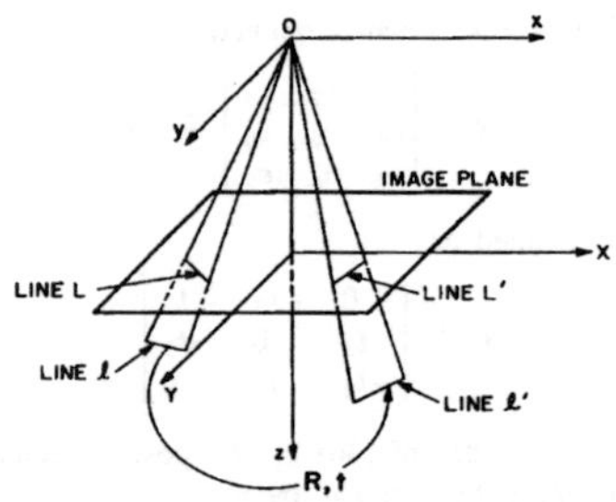

Fig. 5. Imaging geometry for 2D line correspondences. Line l which projects to line L at time t_a moves to line l' at time t_b and projects to line L'.

From (1) and (47)

$$\begin{aligned} X' &= \frac{a_1 X + a_2 Y + a_3}{a_7 X + a_8 Y + a_9} \\ Y' &= \frac{a_4 X + a_5 Y + a_6}{a_7 X + a_8 Y + a_9}. \end{aligned} \tag{50}$$

Thus with four point correspondences, we have eight homogeneous linear equations in nine unknowns $\{a_i\}_{i=1,\cdots,9}$ from (50). It can be easily shown that if no three points out of the four are collinear, then this system of linear equations has rank 4. Therefore, we have a unique solution to $\{a_i\}$ to within a scale factor. Once matrix A is determined to within a scale factor, $\{R, \boldsymbol{w}\boldsymbol{t}, \boldsymbol{g}/w\}$ can be determined, where w is an unknown positive scale factor [49]. It is shown in [49], [50] that there are in general only two solutions. It is also easy to see that additional coplanar points will not yield any more linearly independent equations in $\{a_i\}$. Also, it is known that if we track four coplanar points over three views, then the solution is unique [51]. In practical situations, where the point correspondences may be known only approximately, a least squares algorithm as described in [52] may be used, where a procedure for computing the error estimates is also given.

B. 2D-to-2D Line Correspondences

Consider the geometry of Fig. 5, where l_i is the 3D line on a rigid object at time t_a and L_i is its perspective projection on the image plane. As a result of object motion, this 3D line l_i becomes line l_i' in three dimensions at time t_b and its corresponding projection on the image plane becomes L_i'. Our problem then is as follows: given $\{L_i, L_i'\}_{i=1,\cdots,N}$, the corresponding lines on the image plane, determine the rotation R, translation $\boldsymbol{t}/\|\boldsymbol{t}\|$, and the 3D line positions to within a scale factor, e.g., $\|\boldsymbol{t}\|$.

We shall see presently that the number of solutions is infinite no matter how large N is. One way to make solutions unique (or finite in number) is to take three views, i.e., take the projection at another time t_c. Thus let l_i'' and L_i'' be the corresponding lines at t_c. Assume that the motion from t_a to t_b and t_b to t_c is represented by $\{R_{ab}, \boldsymbol{t}_{ab}\}$ and $\{R_{bc}, \boldsymbol{t}_{bc}\}$, respectively. Our problem is then modified to: given three corresponding 2D views $\{L_i, L_i', L_i''\}_{i=1,\cdots,N}$ of lines, determine motion parameters $\{R_{ab}, R_{bc}, \kappa t_{ab}, \kappa t_{bc}\}$ and the 3D positions at t_a of the lines l_i, where the κ is a scale factor. As before, we assume that no point correspondences on the lines are known.

1) Structure-First Algorithm [53]: Let us consider the two-view case first. At each time instant t_a and t_b, given the projected line L, the 3D line l is restricted to lie in the plane containing the origin O and line L. Two additional parameters are needed to fix l. Thus there are four "structure" parameter unknowns (two at t_a and t_b, each) associated with each line. Given two lines, we can write two equations representing the rigidity constraints which imply that the angle and the distance between the two lines remains constant from time t_a to t_b. Any additional line adds four more unknowns and four more rigidity equations (representing the angle and distance constraints between the new line and two of the old lines). Thus no matter how many line correspondences we have, the number of equations is always smaller (by 2) than the number of unknowns. One would expect then that the number of solutions is infinite.

Now consider the three-view case (t_a, t_b, and t_c). Given N line correspondences over three views, the number of "structure" unknowns is $6N$. The number of equations is $2 \times 2 + (N - 2) \times 8 = 8N - 12$. The number of equations is larger than or equal to the number of unknowns when $N \geq 6$. Thus at least six line correspondences over three views are needed to get a finite number of solutions to the motion/structure parameters. Heuristically, seven or more line correspondences over three views probably make the solution unique (to within a scale factor for the translation and structure parameters), although no proof is yet available.

2) A Motion-First Algorithm [54], [55]: Consider the geometry of Fig. 6, where 3D lines l, l', and l'' (at times t_a, t_b, and t_c, respectively) are projected on the image plane to get 2D lines L, L' and L''. Let M, M', and M'' be the planes containing origin O and lines L, L', and L'', respectively. If the lines L, L', and L'' are represented by

$$
\begin{aligned}
L &: AX + BY + C &&= 0 \\
L' &: A'X + B'Y + C' &&= 0 \\
L'' &: A''X + B''Y + C'' &&= 0
\end{aligned}
\tag{51}
$$

then the normals to planes M, M', and M'' are given by $N^T (= (A, B, C))$, $N'^T (= (A', B', C'))$, and $N''^T (= (A'', B'', C''))$, respectively. Obviously, N, N', and N'' are perpendicular to l, l', l'', respectively. If we rotate M (together with l) by R_{ab} and rotate M'' (together with l'') by R_{bc}^{-1}, then $R_{ab}l, l'$ and $R_{bc}^{-1}l''$ will be parallel to each other, which implies that $R_{ab}N, N'$ and $R_{bc}^{-1}N''$ are coplanar, i.e.,

$$
(R_{ab}N) \cdot N' \times (R_{bc}^{-1}N'') = 0. \tag{52}
$$

This is a nonlinear (transcendental) equation in the six rotation unknowns (e.g., the Euler angles). With six line correspondences over three views, we can solve the resulting six equations (52) iteratively to find the rotations.

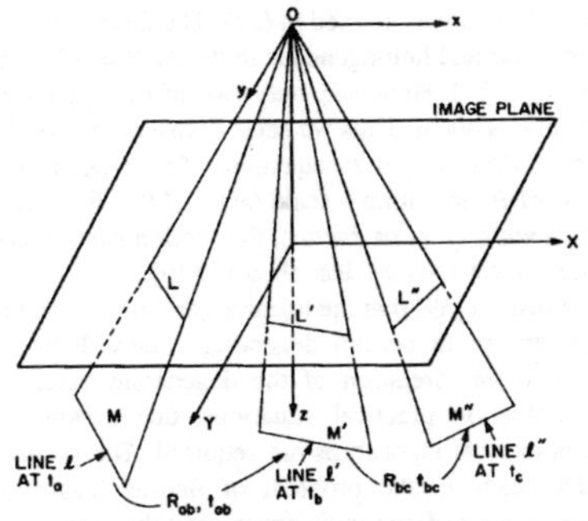

Fig. 6. Line correspondences for the three-view system.

It can be shown [55] that the translations satisfy

$$
t_{ab} \cdot (R_{ab}N) = \frac{\|N' \times R_{ab}N\|}{\|N' \times R_{bc}^{-1}N''\|} R_{bc}^{-1} t_{bc} \cdot (R_{bc}^{-1}N'')
\tag{53}
$$

which is a linear homogeneous equation in the six translation components (after the rotations have been found). Thus the translations can be determined to within a scale factor from five line correspondences over three views.

We note that the problem of finding the rotations can be formulated as a solution of polynomials in several variables. Equation (52) is quadratic (and homogeneous) in the 18 unknowns which are the elements of R_{ab} and R_{bc}^{-1}. With six line correspondences over three views, we have six equations similar to (52) plus the 12 constraint equations on the elements of the rotation matrices. Thus we have a total of 18 quadratic equations in 18 unknowns. This admits a maximum of 2^{18} solutions, by Bezout's Theorem. However, only a few of these will be real, but this number is not yet known. An upper bound of 600 was established recently by Holt and Netravali [75].

Buchanan [56], [76] has established some results on the conditions under which the line case fails to get a unique solution. Specifically, he showed that the algorithm based on (52) will fail to get a unique solution if the lines lie on a line complex, and that any algorithm will fail if the lines lie on a line congruence. The rather abstract results of Buchanan have been given some nice geometrical interpretation by Navab *et al.* [77].

3) A Linear Algorithm [57], [58]: For convenience, we shall try to determine (R_{ab}, t_{ab}) and (R_{ac}, t_{ac}), the latter being the motion from t_a to t_c. We use $R^{(i)}$ to denote the ith column of R. Let

$$
F_i \triangleq t_{ac}(R_{ab}^{(i)})^T - (R_{ac}^{(i)})t_{ab}^T, \quad i = 1, 2, 3. \tag{54}
$$

Then it can be shown that

$$
\begin{aligned}
AN'' \cdot F_2N' - BN'' \cdot F_1N' &= 0 \\
BN'' \cdot F_3N' - CN'' \cdot F_2N' &= 0 \\
CN'' \cdot F_1N' - AN'' \cdot F_3N' &= 0
\end{aligned}
\tag{55}
$$

where A, B, C are as defined in (51). The three equations in (55) are linear and homogeneous in the $3 \times 9 = 27$ elements of $F_i; i = 1, 2, 3$. However, only two of the equations are linearly independent. Thus we need 13 line correspondences over three views to get 26 equations (55) to determine the elements of F_i to within a scale factor. After F_i have been found (to within a scale factor), the motion parameters can be obtained via (54) as described in [59].

It is shown in [59] that the linear algorithm gives a unique solution except in certain degenerate cases. However, a geometrical interpretation of the degenerate cases is not yet available. In practical situations, due to noisy data, robust numerical algorithms are required. The polynomial approach leads to the problem of finding least squares solutions to a set of quadratic equations subject to quadratic equality constraints. Sufficient numerical experience with such problems is not yet available. Linear algorithms can be made robust more easily as shown in [59].

C. 2D-to-2D Point Correspondences: Orthographic Projections

If a point $p(= (x, y, z))$ in 3D space is projected orthographically to a point $P(= (x, y))$ on the image plane, then

$$X = x$$

and

$$Y = y. \tag{56}$$

The problem then is as follows: given corresponding points $\{P_i, P'_i\}_{i=1,\cdots,N}$, determine rotation R, translation t, and depth z_i. A little reflection indicates that t_3 is irrecoverable and the z_i's can be recovered at best to within an additive constant.

We can decompose the motion into a rotation R around one of the points (say p_1) and translation $t = p'_1 - p_1$. Then the x- and y- components of t can be found simply from $p'_1 - p_1$. Thus without loss of generality, we can fix p_1 and p'_1 at the origin and the problem is then reduced to finding R and $\{z_i\}_{i=2,\cdots,N}$. Therefore, our modified problem is as follows: given correspondences $\{P_i, P'_i\}_{i=2,\cdots,N}$ and assuming $P_1^T = P_0^T = (0, 0, 0)$, determine R and $\{z_i\}_{i=2,\cdots,N}$.

1) Two-View Case [60]: Since $p'_i = Rp_i, i = 2, \cdots, N$ and from (56), we have

$$X'_i = r_{11}X_i + r_{12}Y_i + r_{13}z_i$$
$$Y'_i = r_{21}X_i + r_{22}Y_i + r_{23}z_i. \tag{57}$$

Eliminating z_i and using properties of R, we get

$$r_{23}X'_i - r_{13}Y'_i + r_{32}X_i - r_{31}Y_i = 0 \tag{58}$$

which is linear and homogeneous in the four unknowns: $r_{23}, r_{13}, r_{32}, r_{31}$. With four point correspondences, we have three eqations (58). Assuming the four points are noncoplanar, it can be shown that the coefficient matrix has rank 3. Thus we can determine $(r_{13}, r_{23}, r_{31}, r_{32})$ uniquely

to within a scale factor. Note that any additional point correspondences will only give redundant (58).

By changing the scale factor, we can get an uncountably infinite number of solutions to $(r_{13}, r_{23}, r_{31}, r_{32})$ which satisfy

$$r_{13}^2 + r_{23}^2 = r_{31}^2 + r_{32}^2 < 1 \tag{59}$$

and for each of these solutions we can construct a rotation matrix R. Thus our conclusion is that with two orthographic views, there are an uncountably infinite number of solutions to motion/structure, no matter how many point correspondences are given.

2) Three-View Case: Ullman [61] showed that four point correspondences over three orthographic views yield a unique solution to motion/structure (up to a reflection). He also provided a nonlinear algorithm for finding the solution. More recently, Lee [62] and Huang and Lee [60] have found a number of linear algorithms. The basic idea of the linear algorithm in [60] is the following: Let

$$P' = Rp \tag{60}$$
$$P'' = Sp'$$

and

$$P'' = Wp$$

where

$$W = SR. \tag{61}$$

Then, taking two views at a time and using the method of Section V-C1, we can find $(r_{13}, r_{23}, r_{31}, r_{32})$, $(s_{13}, s_{23}, s_{31}, s_{32})$, and $(w_{13}, w_{23}, w_{31}, w_{32})$ to within scale factors. Then these three scale factors are determined from the constraint equation (61). In [60], [63], it is also shown that three point correspondences over three orthographic views yield four solutions to the structure and 16 solutions to the motion parameters (including reflections).

3) Relationship to Perspective Projections:

i) As mentioned in Section III, in determining motion/structure from stereo image sequences (perspective projection model), the ranges of the points (obtained from triangulation) can be very inaccurate. Thus it may be a good idea to disregard z's (at least initially), and use orthographic-view techniques [14].

ii) In Section V-A we have seen that with five or more point correspondences over two *perspective* views, motion/structure can be determined. On the other hand, we have shown in the previous section that motion/structure cannot be determined no matter how many point correspondences we have over two orthographic views. Since orthographic projection is a reasonable approximation to perspective projection when the object is relatively far away from the camera, we conclude that when the object is relatively far away from the camera, the motion/structure from point correspondences over two perspective views must be ill-conditioned.

iii) A thorough analysis is needed to find out when and how the perspective projections can be approximated by orthographic projections (perhaps with a scale change). In this regard, [64] is relevant.

D. 2D-to-2D Correspondences: Other Features

1) Combined use of Points and Lines [65]: When both point and line correspondences are given over two views, the method of using rigidity constraints described in Sections V-A and V-B can be readily extended. The additional rigidity constraints between points and lines can, for example, be written in terms of the invariance of the distance from a point to a line.

It appears that adding line correspondences to point correspondences will not help (in the absence of noise), since each line brings in four additional unknowns and four additional equations. That each line yields four additional equations can be seen as follows. On the rigid configuration of N points ($N \geq 3$), we can establish a 3D coordinate system. To specify a 3D line in this coordinate system, we need four parameters.

In the presence of noise, least squares techniques are typically used. Then, the addition of line correspondences may help in getting more accurate estimates of motion/structure.

2) Using Corners and Curves: In [66], orthogonal corners are used as features. Generally, one orthogonal corner and two point or line correspondences determine motion/structure uniquely. Another feature used in [67], [68], [78] is conic arcs. The value of these variety of features is yet unknown both in terms of our ability to recognize them and then track them.

VI. FUTURE RESEARCH AND OPEN QUESTIONS

A. Noise Sensitivity

In all practical situations, the coordinates of features cannot be measured exactly. The errors in feature coordinates cause errors in motion/structure estimation. It is well known that the noise sensitivity problem can be especially severe in the 2D-to-2D feature correspondence case. However, good results can be obtained in many situations [35].

Ideally, one would like to have analytical results (both algorithm-dependent and algorithm-independent) on how noise sensitivity depends on feature configurations and motion characteristics. Unfortunately, no such results are available. Some heuristic and empirical results do exist [34], [35]. For example, it is reported that the estimates are very sensitive to data noise, if the object occupies a small part of the field of view, or if the z-component of the translation is small.

For linear algorithms, one can perform a numerical first-order error analysis along with the motion determination [35], [52]. Thus one obtains not only the motion/structure parameters but also estimates of the errors contained in them. Only if the error estimates are small, will one accept the motion/structure results. This approach becomes difficult, when the motion/structure determination algorithm is nonlinear.

B. Robust Algorithms

There are two general approaches to robustness: Least squares and RANSAC. In least squares, one tries to smooth out noise by using as much data as possible. However, in motion/structure determination, some of the feature correspondences may be incorrect. These "outliers" should be weeded out by, for example, using least squares with adaptive weights. RANSAC [20] takes the approach of using as few data as possible to obtain a good solution. To illustrate it, take the case of motion/structure estimation using 2D-to-2D point correspondences. Assume 20 point correspondences are given. In RANSAC, one would pick six point correspondences and determine the motion parameters. Then, these computed motion parameters will be checked against the remaining 14 point correspondences for consistency. If they are consistent with the majority, one would accept them. If not, one picks a different set of six point correspondences, and so on, until one gets a solution which is consistent with a majority of the 20 given point correspondences.

We have seen from the previous sections that problems of motion/structure determination lead to the solution of simultaneous equations. These equations can be transcendental (e.g., if rotation is represented by Euler angles) or polynomial (e.g., if rotation is represented by a quaternion). Even in the absence of noise, transcendental equations can be solved only by iterative methods. For polynomial equations (when the number of equations is equal to the number of unknowns), one has the option of using homotopy methods [28]. When the data are noisy (which is always the case in practice), we face the problem of nonlinear least squares. In principle, a polynomial nonlinear least squares problem can be reduced to the solution of a larger set (than the original set of polynomial equations) of polynomial equations which can be solved by homotopy methods. However, in reality, even in the simplest motion/structure estimation problems, the total degree of this new polynomial equation set will be too large to handle numerically. Thus the only option appears to be to solve the nonlinear least squares problem by iterative methods. A major difficulty is of course that unless one has a good initial guess at the solution, the iteration may lead to a local but not global minimum, or may not converge at all.

An alternative formulation of motion/structure determination problems leads to linear least squares with polynomial (usually quadratic) equality constraints (e.g., see the end of section V-A2d [47].) Another example is presented in (21) and (22) in Section IV-A2. Unfortunately, no particularly efficient algorithm for solving such problems is known.

As we have seen in the previous sections, in a number of cases, it is possible to formulate linear algorithms at the expense of a small number of additional feature correspondences. Then the least squares problems become linear. The computation is simpler, and above all one does not have to worry about being trapped in local minima. However, it has been found empirically that linear algorithms are usually more sensitive to data noise than nonlinear algorithms.

On balance, perhaps the best approach is to first use a linear algorithm (assuming that a sufficient number of feature correspondences are given) to find a rough solution; and then to use a nonlinear formulation to refine the solution iteratively [46].

C. Multiplicity of Solutions and Degeneracy

In problems of motion/structure determination, it is of both theoretical and practical interest to know how the number of solutions depends on the number of feature correspondences. Let N be the number of feature correspondences, and $m(N)$ be the number of solutions at a "generic" data set. Then, typically, for a particular problem, there is a number N_o such that: For $N < N_o$, $m(N) = \infty$ (uncountable). For $N = N_o$, $m(N) \leq m_o =$ finite positive integer. For $N > N_o$, $m(N) = 1$. We have assumed that the problem arises from a real physical situation so that there is at least one real solution; we have also assumed that there is no noise in the data. The critical case $N = N_o$ is of particular interest, because: 1) In practice, it is not easy to obtain feature correspondences. Thus it is important to know the minimum number needed. 2) To use RANSAC-like techniques, one needs to know N_o.

Two important related questions are: a) Nonuniqueness-degeneracy: For $N > N_o$, what are the necessary and sufficient conditions (on the feature configurations and the motion characteristics) such that $1 < m(N) < \infty$? b) ∞-degeneracy: For $N \geq N_o$, what are the necessary and sufficient conditions such that $m(N) = \infty$? These questions are closely related to noise sensitivity (Section VI-A). Specifically, for $N > N_o$, if the feature configuration and motion characteristics are close to be degenerate, then the estimation problem will most likely be ill-conditioned.

Unfortunately, answers to these important questions are far from complete. Our present knowledge is summarized in Table 1. In addition to the question marks in the table, it is also not known, for the 2D-to-3D and 2D-to-2D cases, under what conditions, $m(N_o) = 1, 2, \cdots, m_o$, respectively.

The mathematical tools appropriate for attacking these questions appear to be algebraic geometry [27], [42] and projective geometry [40], [69]. Numerically, homotopy methods seem to be the best for finding all solutions of a set of simultaneous polynomial equations [28], and "upper semicontinuity" arguments [63], [79] have the potential of proving general theorems by exhibiting numerical examples.

D. Long Sequences

In this paper, we have concentrated on motion/structure determination using only two (or sometimes three) time instants or frames. This is sufficient for some applications

Table 1 Solution Multiplicity and Degeneracy Conditions

	N_o	$m(N_o)$	Conditions for nonuniqueness-degeneracy	Conditions for ∞-degeneracy
3D to 3D PC	3	1	collinear	collinear
3D to 3D LC	2	1	parallel	parallel
2D to 3D PC	3	≤4 [20]	?	Essentially collinear in 2D [23]
2D to 3D LC	3	≤8 [24]	?	Some parallelism conditions [25]
2D to 2D PC	5	≤10 [40],[42]	3D points lying on certain quadratic surface [43],[44]	?
2D to 2D LC (over 3 frames)	6	?	? (some partial results in [56])	?

Note: References are in square brackets.

(e.g., passive navigation, pose determination, camera calibration), but not for others (e.g., motion prediction). For motion prediction and general understanding, it is necessary to work with longer image sequences. Furthermore, using longer image sequences is potentially a way of combatting noise in the data.

The key issue in the analysis of long image sequences is motion modeling. For a given scenario, one needs a motion model containing a small number of parameters which can be assumed to remain constant during a short period of time. Significant work in this area has been reported in [70]–[73]. Here, we shall discuss only the work of Shariat [73].

Shariat used a "constant object motion" model, where the object is assumed to be translating with a constant velocity T and rotating with a constant R around an unknown object center $C = (x_c, y_c, z_c)$. The parameters to determine are R, T, and C. He derived the following main results: 1) One point over five frames: seven second-order homogeneous polynomial equations in eight unknowns. 2) Two points over four frames: seven second-order homogeneous polynomial equations in eight unknowns. 3) Three points over three frames: eight second-order homogeneous polynomial equations in nine unknowns. Two important open questions are: i) Multiplicity of solutions and degeneracy conditions? ii) Effective linear algorithms?

VII. SUMMARY AND CONCLUSION

We have presented a review of techniques for determining motion and structure of rigid bodies, by knowing the locations of their corresponding features at different times or when they are projected on two different cameras. Three major categories of problems were considered: a) 3D features are known at two different times; b) features in 3D space and their projections on the camera plane are known; c) projections of 3D features on the camera plane are known at two different times. Features may consist of points, straight lines, curved lines, corners, etc. In each case, we reviewed a variety of formulations, efficient algorithms for solution, existence and uniqueness of solutions, and sensitivity of solutions to noise in the data. We showed that, even though problems and their formulation may be very different, for each of the above cases, the underlying mathematics has much in common. It requires solution of simultaneous, transendental, polynomial, or linear equations in multiple variables which represent the structure, and motion of the object. Thus the problems are inherently non-linear and therefore appropriate formulation is extremely important to avoid difficulties in either numerical computation of the solution or determination of nonuniqueness and multiplicity of solutions. A variety of theoretical (e.g., algebraic and projective geometry) and numerical (e.g., homotopy) techniques are being applied to these problems with varying degrees of success. Despite over two decades of work in modern time and half century of work around 1900 (by photogrammetrists) problems are far from being completely solved. Section VI contains a partial list of some of the open questions. Techniques reviewed in this paper have found a number of applications. Some of these are: a) positioning and navigating objects in a 3D world; b) Determining location and orientation of a camera by observing 3D features in its view; c) Estimating motion and structure of moving objects relative to a camera; and there are many more. We believe that the new mathematical tools will allow us to make steady progress in the future towards the resolution of many of the outstanding questions and this technology will get applied in a wide variety of situations.

REFERENCES

[1] T. S. Huang, "Motion analysis," in *Encyclopedia of Artificial Intelligence*, S. Shapiro, Ed. New York: Wiley, 1987.
[2] J. K. Aggarwal and N. Nandhakumar, "On the computation of motion from sequences of images—A review," *Proc. IEEE*, vol. 76, no. 8, pp. 917–935, Aug. 1988.
[3] H. Goldstein, *Classical Mechanics*. Reading. MA: Addison Wesley, 1981.
[4] S. D. Blostein and T. S. Huang, "Algorithms for motion estimation based on 3-D correspondences," in *Motion Understanding*, W. Martin and J. K. Aggrawal, Eds. Norewell, MA: Kluwer, 1988.
[5] O. D. Faugeras and M. Hebert, "A 3-D recognition and positioning algorithm using geometrical matching between primitive surfaces," in *Proc. Int. Joint Conf. on Artificial Intelligence* (Karlsruhe, W. Germany), Aug. 1983, pp. 996–1002.
[6] B. K. P. Horn, "Closed-form solution of absolute orientation using unit quaternions," *J. Opt. Soc. Amer.*, vol. 4, pp. 629–642, Apr. 1987.
[7] K. S. Arun, T. S. Huang, and S. D. Blostein, "Least-squares fitting of two 3-D point set," *IEEE Trans. Pattern Anal. Machine Intell.*, vol. 9, no. 5, pp. 698–700, Sept. 1987.
[8] S. Umeyama, "Least-squares estimation of transformation parameters between two point patterns," to appear in *IEEE Trans. Pattern Anal. Machine Intell.*.
[9] T. S. Huang *et al.*, "Motion/structure estimation from stereo image sequences," in *Proc. IEEE Workshop on Motion* (Kiawah Island, SC, May 7–9), 1986.
[10] S. D. Blostein and T. S. Huang, "Quantization errors in stereo triangulation," in *Proc. 1st ICCV* (London, England, June 8–11, 1987), pp. 325–344. Also, in *IEEE Trans. Pattern Alai. Machine Intell.*, vol. 9, pp. 752–765, 1987.
[11] L. Matthies and S. Shafer, "Error modeling in stereo navigation," *IEEE Trans. Robotics Automat.*, vol. 3, pp. 239–248, 1987.
[12] C. W. Chen and T. S. Huang, "Error probability based estimation of motion from stereo sequences," in *Proc. 3rd Int. workshop on Time-varying Image Processing* (Florence, Italy), May 1989.
[13] S. M. Kiang, R. J. Chou, and J. K. Aggarwal, "Triangulation errors in stereo algorithms," in *Proc. IEEE Workshop on Computer Vision* (Miami Beach, FL, Dec. 1987), pp. 72–78.
[14] T. S. Huang, "Use of orthographic-projection techniques in motion estimation from stereo image sequences," *Machine Vision for Inspection and Measurement*, H. Freeman, Ed. New York: Academic Press, 1989, pp. 127–135.
[15] H. H. Chen and T. S. Huang, "An algorithm for matching 3-D line segments with applications to multiple object motion estimation," in *Proc. IEEE Workshop on Computer Vision* (Miami Beach, FL, Nov. 30–Dec. 2, 1987),pp. 151–156.
[16] P. R. Wolf, *Elements of Photographmetry*. New York: McGraw-Hill, 1974.
[17] S. Ganapathy, "Camera location determination problem," Tech. Memo., AT&T Bell Laboratories, Holmdel, NJ, Nov. 2, 1984.
[18] S. Ganapathy, "Decomposition of transformation matrices for robot vision," *Pattern Recogn. Lett.*, vol. 2, pp. 401–412, Dec. 1989.
[19] B. L. van der Waerdern, *Modern Algebra*, vol. 2. Berlin, Germany: , Springer, 1940.
[20] M. Fischler and "R. C. Bolles, "Random sample consensus: a paradigm for model fitting with applications to image analysis and automated cartography," *Commun. ACM*, vol. 24, no. 6, pp. 381–395, June 1981.
[21] R. Horaud, B. Conio, O. Leboullenx, and B. LaColle, "An analytic solution for the perspective 4-point problem," *Comput. Vis., Graphics. Image Process.*, vol. 47, no. 1, pp. 33–44, July 1989.
[22] W. J. Wolfe, C. Weber-Sklair, D. Mathis, and M. Magee, "The perspective view of three points," to appear in *IEEE Trans. Pattern Anal. Machine Intell.*.
[23] R. J. Holt and A. N. Netravali, "Camera calibration problem: Some new results," Tech. Memo., AT&T Bell Laboratories, Murray Hill, NJ, July 1989.
[24] Y. Liu, T. S. Huang, and O. D. Faugeras, "Determination of camera location from 2D to 3D line and point correspondences," in *Proc. CVPR*, (Ann Arbor, MI, June 1988).
[25] H. H. Chen, "Locating polyhedral objects with dextrous hand by straight finger motion," Tech. Memo., AT&T Bell Laboratories, Holmdel, NJ, May 1989.
[26] A. Mitiche and J. K. Aggarwal, "A computational analysis of time-varying images," in *Handbook of Pattern Recognition and Image Processing*, T. Y. Young and K. S. Fu, Eds. New York: Academic Press, 1986.
[27] W. V. D. Hodge and D. Pedoe, *Methods of Algebraic Geometry*, 3 vols. London, UK: Cambridge Univ. Press, 1953.
[28] A. Morgan, *Solving Polynomial Systems using Continuation for Engineering and Science Problems*, Englewood Cliffs, NJ: Prentice-Hall, 1987.
[29] J. W. Roach and J. K. Aggarwal, "Determining the movement of objects from a sequence of images," *IEEE Trans. Pattern Anal. Machine Intell.*, vol. 2, no. 6, pp. 554–562, 1980.
[30] T. S. Huang and R. Y. Tsai, "Image sequence analysis: Motion estimation," in *Image Sequence Analysis*, T. S. Huang, Ed. New York: Springer-Verlag, 1981.
[31] C. Jerian and R. Jain, "Polynomial methods for structure from motion," in *Proc. 2nd ICCV* (Tampa, FL), Dec. 1988.
[32] H. C. Longuet-Higgins, "A computer program for reconstructing a scene from two projections," *Nature*, vol. 293, pp. 133–135, Sept. 1981.
[33] R. Y. Tsai and T. S. Huang, "Uniqueness and estimation of 3-D motion parameters of rigid bodies with curved surfaces," *IEEE Trans. Pattern Anal. Machine Intell.*, vol. 6, no. 1, pp. 13–27, Jan. 1984.

[34] T. S. Huang, "Determining 3 dimensional motion and structure from two perspective views," in *Handbook of Pattern Recognition and Image Processing*, T. Y. Young and K. S. Fu, Eds. New York: Academic Press, 1986.

[35] J. Weng, T. S. Huang, and N. Ahuja, "Motion and structure from two perspective views: algorithms, error analysis, and error estimation," *IEEE Trans. Pattern Anal. Machine Intell.*, vol. 11, no. 5, pp. 451–476, May 1989.

[36] T. S. Huang and Y. S. Shim, "Linear algorithm for motion estimation: How to handle degenerate cases," in *Proc. British Pattern Recognition Association Conf.* (Cambridge, England), Apr. 1987. Also published by Springer-Verlag, J. Kittler, Ed.

[37] T. S. Huang and O. D. Faugeras, "Some properties of the e-matrix in two-view motion estimation," *IEEE Trans. Pattern Anal. Machine Intell.*, vol. 11, no. 12, pp. 1310–1312, Dec. 1989.

[38] H. C. Longuet-Higgins, "The reconstruction of a scene from two projections-configurations that defeat the 8-point algorithm," in *Proc. 1st Conf. on AI Applications* (Denver, CO, Dec. 5–7), 1984, pp. 395–397.

[39] E. Kruppa, "Zur Ermittlung Eines Objektes Aulzwei Zwei Perspektieren Mit Innerer Orientierung," *Sitz-Ber. Akad. Wiss., Wien, math. naturw. kl., Abt-IIa*, vol. 122, pp. 1939–1948, 1913.

[40] O. D. Faugeras and S. J. Maybank, "Multiplicity of solutions for motion problems," Tech. Rep., INRIA, France, 1988. Appeared later in *Proc. 1st ICCV* (Irvine, CA, Mar. 20–22), 1989, pp. 248–255.

[41] M. Demazure, "Sur Deux Problémes de Reconstruction," Tech. Rep, INRIA, France, 1988.

[42] A. N. Netravali, T. S. Huang, A. S. Krishnakumar, and R. J. Holt, "Algebraic methods in 3D motion estimation from two-view point correspondences," *Int. J. Imaging Syst. Technol.*, vol. 1, pp. 78–99, 1989.

[43] B. K. P. Horn, "Motion fields are hardly ever ambiguous," *Int. J. of Comput. Vision*, vol. 1, pp. 263–278, 1987.

[44] H. C. Longuet-Higgins, "Multiple interpretation of a pair of images of a surface," *Proc. Royal Soc. London*, Series A, vol. 418, pp. 1–15, 1988.

[45] M. A. Snyder, "On the calculation of rigid motion parameters from the essential matrix," COINS Tech. Rep. TR 89–102, Univ. of Massachusetts at Amherst, Jan. 1990.

[46] J. Weng, N. Ahuja, and T. S. Huang, "Closed-form solution and maximum likelihood: A robust approach to motion and structure estimation," in *Proc. IEEE Conf. on CVPR* (Ann Arbor, MI, June 5–9), 1988

[47] C. Braccini, G. Gambardella, A. Grattarola, and S. Zappature, "Motion estimation of rigid bodies: effects of the rigidity constraints," in *Proc. EUSIPCO-86* (The Hague, The Netherlands, Sept. 2–5), 1986.

[48] J. Weng, N. Ahuja, and T. S. Huang, "Error analysis of motion parameter estimation from image sequences," in *Proc. 1st Int. Conf. on Computer Vision* (London, England), June 1987.

[49] R. Y. Tsai, T. S. Huang, and W. L. Zhu, "Estimating 3-D motion parameters of a rigid planar patch 2, II: Singular value decomposition," *IEEE Trans. Acoust. Speech Signal Process.*, vol. 30, no. 4, pp. 523–525, Aug. 1982.

[50] H. C. Longuet-Higgins, "The visual ambiguity of a moving plane," *Proc. Roy. Soc.*, Ser. B, vol. 223, no. 1, pp. 165–170, 1984.

[51] R. Y. Tsai and T. S. Huang, "Estimating 3-D motion parameters of a rigid planar patch, III: Finite point correspondences and the three-view problem," *IEEE Trans. Accoust. Speech Signal Process.*, vol. 32, no. 2, pp. 213–220, Apr. 1984.

[52] J. Weng, N. Ahuja, and T. S. Huang, "Motion and structure from point correspondences: a robust algorithm for planar case with error estimation," in *Proc. 9th ICPR* (Rome, Italy, Nov. 14–17), 1988.

[53] A. Mitiche and J. K. Aggarwal, "Line-based computation of structure and motion using angular invariance," in *Proc. IEEE Workshop on Motion* (Kiawah Island, SC, May 7–9), 1986, pp. 175–180.

[54] B. L. Yen and T. S. Huang, "Determining 3-D motion and structure of a rigid object using straight line correspondences," in *Image Sequence Processing and Dynamic Scene Analysis*, T. S. Huang, Ed. New York: Springer-Verlag, 1983.

[55] Y. C. Liu and T. S. Huang, "Estimation of rigid body motion using straight line correspondences," in *Proc. IEEE Workshop on Motion* (Kiawah Island, SC, May 7–9), 1986, pp. 47–52.

[56] T. Buchanan, "Notes on two recent reconstruction algorithms," unpublished report, 1987.

[57] M. E. Spetsakis and J. Aloimonos, "Closed form solutions to the structure from motion problem from line correspondences," in *Proc. AAAI* (Seattle, WA, July 1987), pp. 738–743.

[58] Y. Liu and T. S. Huang, "A linear algorithm for motion estimation using straight line correspondences," in *Proc. 9th ICPR* (Rome, Italy., Nov. 14–17), 1988.

[59] J. Weng, Y. Liu, T. S. Huang, and N. Ahuja, "Estimating motion/structure from line correspondences: A robust algorithm and uniqueness theorem," in *Proc. IEEE Conf. on CVPR* (Ann Arbor, MI, June 5–9, 1988).

[60] T. S. Huang and C. H. Lee, "Motion and structure from orthographic projections,"in *Proc. 9th ICPR* (Rome, Italy., Nov. 14–17), 1988. A longer version appeared in *IEEE Trans. Pattern Anal. Machine Intell.*, vol. 11, no. 5, pp. 536–540, May 1989.

[61] S. Ullman, *The Interpretation of Visual Motion.* Cambridge, MAAA: MIT Press, 1979.

[62] C. H. Lee, "Structure from motion: An augumented problem and a new algorithm," Tech. Rep., Dept. of CS, Purdue Univ., Sept. 1, 1986.

[63] D. D. Hoffman and B. M. Bennett, "The construction of structure from fixed-axis motion: rigid structures," *Biol. Cybern.*, vol. 54, pp. 71–83, 1986.

[64] J. Aloimonos and M. Swain, "Paraperspective projection: Between orthograph and perspective," Tech. Rep. CAR-TR-320, Center for Automation Research, Univ. of Maryland, College Park, MD, May 1987.

[65] J. K. Aggarwal and Y. F. Wang, "Analysis of a sequence of images using point and line correspondences," in *Proc. Int. Conf. on Robotics and Automation* (Raleigh, NC, Mar.1987).

[66] Y. Liu and T. S. Huang, "Motion estimation from corner correspondences," in *Proc. Int. Conf. on Image Processing* (Singapore, Sept. 5–8, 1989), pp. 785–790.

[67] R. Y. Tsai, "Estimating 3-D motion parameters and object surface structure from the image motion of curved edges," in *Proc. IEEE Conf. on CVPR* (Washington, DC), 1983, pp. 259–266.

[68] R. Y. Tsai, "3-D inference from the motion parallax of a conic arc and a point in two perspective views," in *Proc. 8th IJCAI* (Karlsruhe, W. Germany), pp. 1039–1042.

[69] J. G. Semple and G. T. Kneebone, *Algebraic Projective Geometry.* Oxford, England: Clarendon Press, 1952.

[70] A. N. Netravali and J. Salz, "Algorithms for estimation of three-dimensional motion," *AT&T Tech. J.*, pp. 335–346, Feb. 1985.

[71] T. S. Huang, J. Weng, and N. Ahuja, "3D motion from image sequences: Modeling, understanding, and prediction," in *Proc. IEEE Workshop on Motion* (Kiawah Island, SC, May 7–9), 1986, pp. 125–130.

[72] T. J. Broida and R. Chellappa, "Kinematics and structure of a rigid object from a sequence of noisy images," in *Proc. IEEE Workshop on Motion* (Kiawah Island, SC, May 7–9), 1986, pp. 95–100.

[73] H. Shariat, "The motion problem: How to use more than two-frames," Rep. IRIS-202, Univ. of Southern California, Oct. 6, 1986.

[74] N. Navab and O. D. Faugeras, "Monocular pose determination from lines: critical sets and maximum number of solutions," in *Proc. IEEE Computer Society Conf. on Computer Vision and Pattern Recognition* (New York, June 15–17, 1993), pp. 254–260.

[75] R. J. Holt and A. N. Netravali, "Motion and structure from line correspondences: some further results," AT&T Bell Labs. Tech. Memo., Sept. 29, 1992.

[76] T. Buchanan, "Critical sets for 3D reconstruction using lines," in *Proc. 2nd European Conf. on Computer Vision* (Santa Margherita, Italy, May 1992), pp. 730–738.

[77] N. Navab, "Visual motion of lines, and cooperation between motion and stereo," Dissertation, Univ. of Paris XI, Orsay, France, Jan. 1993.

[78] Song De Ma, "Conic based stereo, motion estimation, and pose determination," preprint, May 1992.

[79] R. J. Holt and A. N. Netravali, "Motion from optic flow: Multiplicity of solutions," *J. Visual Commun. Image Represent.*, vol. 4, no. 1, pp. 14–24, Mar. 1993.

Thomas S. Huang (Fellow, IEEE) received the B.S. degree in electrical engineering from NationalTaiwan University, Taipei, Taiwan, China, and the M.S. and Sc.D. degrees in electrical engineering from the Massachusetts Institute of Technology, Cambridge.

He was on the Faculty of the Department of Electrical Engineering at MIT from 1963 to 1973; and on the Faculty of the School of Electrical Engineering and Director of its Laboratory for Information and Signal Processing at Purdue University, West Lafayette, IN, from 1973 to 1980. In 1980, he joined the University of Illinois at Urbana-Champaign, where he is now Professor of Electrical and Computer Engineering and Research Professor at the Coordinated Science Laboratory, and at the Beckman Institute. During his sabbatical leaves he has worked at the MIT Lincoln Laboratory, Lexington, MA, the IBM T.J. Watson Research Center, Yorktown Heights, NY, and the Rheinishes Landes Museum in Bonn, West Germany, and held visiting Professor positions at the Swiss Institutes of Technology in Zurich and Lausanne, University of Hannover, in West Germany, INRS-Telecommunications of the University of Quebec in Montreal, Canada, and the University of Tokyo, Japan. He has served as a consultant to numerous industrial firms and government agencies both in the U.S. and abroad. His professional interests lie in the broad area of information technology, especially the trnsmission and processing of multidimensional signals. He has published 11 books and over 300 papers in Network Theory, Digital Filtering, Image Processing, and Computer Vision. He has received a Guggenheim Fellowship (1971–1972), an A. V. Humboldt Foundation Senior U.S. Scientist Award (1976–1977), and a Fellowship from the Japan Association for the Promotion of Science (1986). He received the IEEE Signal Processing Society's Technical Achievement Award in 1987 and the Society Award in 1991. He was a founding Editor, and is currently an Area Editor of the *International Journal of Computer Vision, Graphics, and Image Processing*, and Editor of the Springer Series in Information Sciences published by Springer-Verlag.

Dr. Huang is a Fellow of the Optical Society of America .

Arun Netravali (Fellow, IEEE) received the B.Tech. (Honors) degree from the Indian Institute of Technology, Bombay, India, in 1967, and the M.S. and Ph.D. degrees from Rice University, Houston, TX, in 1969 and 1970, respectively, all in electrical engineering.

He was at NASA from 1970 to 1972, where he worked on problems related to filtering, guidance, and control for the Space Shuttle. He joined Bell Laboratories in 1972 as a Member of Technical Staff, became Head of the Visual Communications Research Department in 1978, Director of Computing Systems Research in 1983, and assumed his current position as Executive Director of Research Communications Sciences Division and Technology Conversion Laboratories at AT&T Bell Laboratories, Murray Hill, NJ, in 1992 with added responsibility as a project manager for HDTV since 1990. His responsibility is research in all aspects of communication and networking. He has been an adjunct professor at the Massachusetts Institute of Technology since 1984, and has taught graduate courses at City College, New York, Columbia University, New York, MIT, Cambridge, MA, and Rutgers University, Piscataway, NJ. He served on the Editorial Board of the PROCEEDINGS OF THE IEEE from 1980 to 1984, and is currently an editor of several journals. He is an advisor to the Center for Telecommunications Research of Columbia University, the Swiss Federal Institute of Technology in Lausanne, Switzerland, and the Beckman Institute of the University of Illinois at Urbana-Champaign. He has organized and chaired sessions at several technical conferences and was the Program Chairman of the 1981 Picture Coding Symposium and the 1990 International Conference on Pattern Recognition. He has edited several special issues for IEEE publications, including two for PROCEEDINGS OF THE IEEE (Digital Encoding of Graphics, Visual Communication Systems) and one for IEEE TRANSACTIONS ON (Picture Communication Systems). He is the author of more than 100 papers and holds over 50 patents in the areas of Computer Networks, Human Interfaces to Machines, Picture Processing, and Digital Television. He is the co-author of two books: *Digital Picture Representation and Compression* (New York, Plenum, 1987) and *Visual Communication Systems* (New York, IEEE PRESS, 1989). He received the Donald G. Fink Award for the best review paper published in PROCEEDINGS OF THE IEEE in 1980, the journal award for the best paper from the Society of Motion Pictures and Television Engineers in 1982, the L. G. Abraham Award for the best paper from the IEEE Communications Society in 1985 and 1991, the Alexnder Graham Bell Medal in 1991, the OCA National Corporate Employee Achievement Award in 1991, and Engineer of the Year Award from the Association of Engineers from India in 1992. He serves on the New Jersey Governor's Committee on "Schools" programs.

Dr. Netravali is a member of Tau Beta Pi and Sigma Xi. He is also a Fellow of the AAAS, and a member of the United States National Academy of Engineering. He has served on the Digital Television Committees of the IEEE and the Society of Motion Picture and Television Engineers.

Toward Multimodal Human–Computer Interface

RAJEEV SHARMA, MEMBER, IEEE, VLADIMIR I. PAVLOVIĆ, STUDENT MEMBER, IEEE, AND THOMAS S. HUANG, FELLOW, IEEE

Invited Paper

Recent advances in various signal-processing technologies, coupled with an explosion in the available computing power, have given rise to a number of novel human–computer interaction (HCI) modalities—speech, vision-based gesture recognition, eye tracking, electroencephalograph, etc. Successful embodiment of these modalities into an interface has the potential of easing the HCI bottleneck that has become noticeable with the advances in computing and communication. It has also become increasingly evident that the difficulties encountered in the analysis and interpretation of individual sensing modalities may be overcome by integrating them into a multimodal human–computer interface.

In this paper, we examine several promising directions toward achieving multimodal HCI. We consider some of the emerging novel input modalities for HCI and the fundamental issues in integrating them at various levels—from early "signal" level to intermediate "feature" level to late "decision" level. We discuss the different computational approaches that may be applied at the different levels of modality integration. We also briefly review several demonstrated multimodal HCI systems and applications. Despite all the recent developments, it is clear that further research is needed for interpreting and fusing multiple sensing modalities in the context of HCI. This research can benefit from many disparate fields of study that increase our understanding of the different human communication modalities and their potential role in HCI.

Keywords—*Human–computer interface, multimodality, sensor fusion.*

NOMENCLATURE

AGR	Automatic gesture recognition.
ANN	Artificial neural network.
ASR	Automatic speech recognition.
BAC	Brain-activated control.
DP	Dynamic programming.
DTW	Dynamic time warping.
EBP	Error back propagation.
EEG	Electroencephalograph.
EM	Expectation maximization.
EMG	Electromyograph.
FIDO	Feature in, decision out.
FIFO	Feature in, feature out.
HCI	Human–computer interaction.
HMM	Hidden Markov model.
LRT	Likelihood ratio test.
MAP	Maximum *a posteriori* (estimator).
ML	Maximum likelihood (estimator).
MLP	Multilayer perceptron.
MOG	Mixture of Gaussians.
MS-TDNN	Multistate time-delay ANN.
OAA	Open agent architecture.
PDA	Personal digital assistant.
VR	Virtual reality.

Manuscript received July 15, 1997; revised November 30, 1997. The Guest Editor coordinating the review of this paper and approving it for publication was A. M. Tekalp. This work was supported in part by the National Science Foundation under Grant IRI-96-34618 and in part by the U.S. Army Research Laboratory under Cooperative Agreement DAAL01-96-2-0003.

R. Sharma is with the Department of Computer Science and Engineering, Pennsylvania State University, University Park, PA 16802 USA (e-mail: rsharma@cse.psu.edu).

V. I. Pavlović and T. S. Huang are with The Beckman Institute and Department of Electrical and Computer Engineering, University of Illinois, Urbana, IL 61801 USA (e-mail: vladimir@ifp.uiuc.edu; huang@ifp.uiuc.edu).

Publisher Item Identifier S 0018-9219(98)03281-2.

I. INTRODUCTION

With the ever increasing role of computers in society, HCI has become an increasingly important part of our daily lives. It is widely believed that as the computing, communication, and display technologies progress even further, the existing HCI techniques may become a bottleneck in the effective utilization of the available information flow. For example, the most popular mode of HCI still relies on the keyboard and mouse. These devices have grown to be familiar but tend to restrict the information and command flow between the user and the computer system. This limitation has become even more apparent with the emergence of novel display technology such as virtual reality [1]–[3] and wearable computers [4], [5]. Thus, in recent years, there has been a tremendous interest in introducing new modalities into HCI that will potentially resolve this interaction bottleneck.

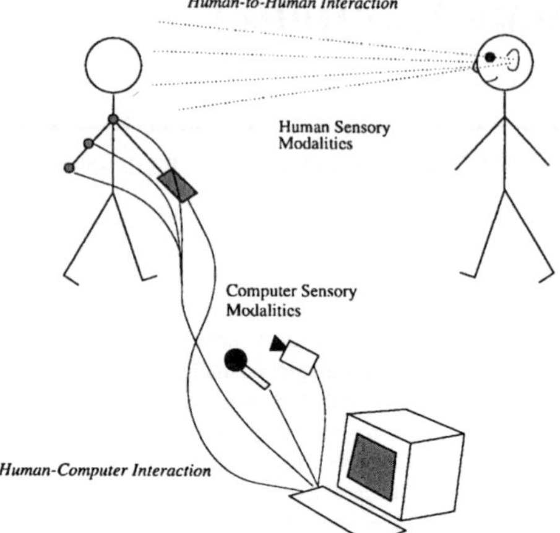

Fig. 1. Human-to-human interaction and human-to-computer interaction. Humans perceive their environment through five basic senses. HCI, on the other hand, need not be bounded to typical human senses.

One long-term goal in HCI has been to migrate the "natural" means that humans employ to communicate with each other into HCI (Fig. 1). With this motivation, ASR has been a topic of research for decades [6]. Some other techniques like automatic gesture recognition, analysis of facial expressions, eye tracking, force sensing, or EEG have only recently gained more interest as potential modalities for HCI. Though studies have been conducted to establish the feasibility of these novel modalities using appropriate sensing and interpretation techniques, their role in HCI is still being explored. A limiting feature of modern interfaces that has also become increasingly evident is their reliance on a single mode of interaction—a mouse movement, key press, speech input, or hand motion. Even though it may be adequate in many cases, the use of a single interaction mode proves to be inept in HCI. For example, in manipulating a [three-dimensional (3-D)] virtual object, a user may employ [two-dimensional (2-D)] mouse motion to select the object, then point with the mouse at a control panel to change the object's color. On the other hand, in a more natural setup, the same user would point at the object with his hand and say: "Make it green." Almost any natural communication among humans involves *multiple, concurrent modes of communication*. Surely, any HCI system that aspires to have the same naturalness should be multimodal. Indeed, studies have shown that people prefer to interact multimodally with computers, since among other things, such interaction eases the need for specialized training [3], [7]. The integration of multimodal input for HCI can also be seen from the perspective of *multisensor data fusion* [8]. Different sensors can, in that case, be related to different communication modalities. It is well known that multiple types of sensors may increase the accuracy with which a quantity can be

measured by reducing the uncertainty in decision making [8], [9]. From a biological point of view, there is a clear evidence that the integration of multiple sensory modalities occurs in the human superior colliculus [9]. Yet, the use of multiple integrated interaction modalities in the HCI systems has not been adequately explored.

In this paper, we consider four basic questions relevant for multimodal HCI:

- *Why* integrate multiple modalities?
- *Which* modalities to integrate?
- *When* to integrate multiple modalities?
- *How* to integrate multiple modalities?

There are numerous potential benefits in integrating multiple modalities into HCI. The reasons range from the fact that natural human interaction itself has a multimodal character to the statistical advantages of combining multiple observations. *Why* integrate multiple modalities is discussed in Section II.

Natural human-to-human interaction is perceived through five basic senses and expressed through various actions such as voice, hand and body movements, facial expression, etc. However, an HCI system does not have to confine itself to these sensors and actions but may also take advantage of other computer-sensing modalities, like the EEG. We discuss some of the promising new HCI modalities in Section III.

Once the desired HCI modalities are selected, an important question to be addressed is *how* to combine them. To address this problem, it is helpful to know how the integrating modalities relate in a natural environment. Some modalities, like speech and lip movements, are more closely tied than others, such as speech and hand gestures. It is also plausible to assume that integration of such different combinations of modalities should be explored at *different* levels of integration. Depending on the chosen level of integration, the actual fusion can then be performed using numerous methods, ranging from simple feature concatenation to complex interaction of interface agents. The issues and techniques of *when* and *how* to combine multiple modalities are considered in Sections IV and V, respectively.

In Section VI, we briefly review some implemented multimodal HCI systems. These systems have incorporated multiple modalities at various integration levels into their interfaces. A particular speech/gesture system for controlling virtual-reality display is considered in greater detail as a case study of multimodal integration. This is followed by our discussion in Section VII and concluding remarks in Section VIII.

II. WHY MULTIPLE MODALITIES IN HCI?

The interaction of humans with their environment (including other humans) is naturally multimodal. We speak about, point at, and look at objects all at the same time. We also listen to the tone of a person's voice and look at a person's face and arm movements to find clues about his feelings. To get a better idea about what is going on around us, we look, listen, touch, and smell. When it comes to HCI, however, we usually use only one interface device at a time—typing, clicking the mouse button, speaking, or pointing with a magnetic wand. The "ease" with which this unimodal interaction allows us to convey our intent to the computer is far from satisfactory. An example of a situation when these limitations become evident is when we press the wrong key or when we have to navigate through a series of menus just to change an object's color. We next discuss the practical, biological, and mathematical rationales that may lead one to consider the use of *multimodal interaction* in HCI.

A. Practical Reasons

Practical reasons for multimodal HCI stem from some inherent drawbacks of modern HCI systems that undermine their éffectiveness. HCI systems today are unnatural and cumbersome. They are based on "Stone Age" devices like the mouse, joystick, or keyboard, which limit the ease with which a user can interact in today's computing environments, including, for example, immersive virtual environments. Several studies have confirmed that people prefer to use multiple-action modalities for virtual object manipulation tasks [3], [7]. Such studies were based on the "Wizard of Oz" experiments, where the role of a multimodal computer is played by a human "behind the scenes" [10]. In [3], Hauptmann and McAvinney concluded that 71% of their subjects preferred to use both speech and hands to manipulate virtual objects rather than just one of the modalities alone. Oviatt has shown in [7] that 95% of the subjects in a map manipulation task tend to use gestures together with speech. Multiple modalities also *complement* each other. Cohen has shown [11], for example, that gestures are ideal for direct object manipulation, while natural language is more suited for descriptive tasks.

Another drawback of current advanced single-modality HCI is that it lacks robustness and accuracy. For example, modern ASR systems have advanced tremendously in recent years. However, they are still error-prone in the presence of noise and require directed microphones or microphone arrays. Automatic gesture-recognition systems have just recently gained popularity. Whether they use a stylus or a glove or are vision based, they are still constrained to the recognition of few predefined hand movements and are burdened by cables or strict requirements on background and camera placement [12]. However, concurrent use of two or more interaction modalities may loosen the strict restrictions needed for accurate and robust interaction with the individual modes. For instance, spoken words can *affirm* gestural commands, and gestures can *disambiguate* noisy speech. Gestures that complement speech, on the other hand, carry a complete communicational message only if they are interpreted together with speech and, possibly, gaze. The use of such multimodal messages can help reduce the complexity and increase the naturalness of the interface for HCI. For example, in computer-vision-based gesture recognition, in addition to the input from the images, the gesture recognition could be influenced by the speech, gaze direction, and content of the virtual display. To exploit this multimodality, for example, instead of designing a complicated gestural command for the object selection, which may consist of a deictic gesture followed by a symbolic one (to symbolize that the object that was pointed at by the hand is supposed to be selected), a simple concurrent deictic gesture and verbal command "this" can be used (as will be discussed in Section VI).

Another pragmatic reason for using multiple modalities in HCI, particularly with redundant input, is to enable physically or cognitively handicapped people access to computers (or computer-controlled devices). For example, the use of hand gestures and American Sign Language with the help of computer vision, the use of eye tracking combined with speech recognition, and the use of EEG-based control would help the physically challenged. With multimodality built into the HCI, the need for building special-purpose interfaces for individual disability will be greatly eased.

B. Biological Reasons

A rationale for integration of multiple sensory modalities can be found in nature. Human beings as well as other animals integrate multiple senses.

Studies of superior colliculus have shown that different senses are initially segregated at the neural level. When they reach the brain, sensory signals converge to the same target area in the superior colliculus, which also receives signals from the cerebral cortex, which, in turn, modulates resultant behavior. A majority (about 75%) of neurons leaving the superior colliculus are *multisensory*. This strongly suggests that the use of multimodality in HCI would be desirable, especially if the goal is to incorporate the naturalness of human communication into HCI. We further expose these issues in a related section on biological foundations for multimodal integration (see Section V-A). Another thorough discussion pertaining to this topic, including additional references, can be found in [9].

C. Mathematical Reasons

More insight on *why* but also *how* and *when* to integrate multiple modalities comes from the field of *sensory data fusion*. Data fusion as a field of study has existed for many decades. However, its main thrust has been in the area of target detection. The goal of data fusion for target detection is to find optimal ways of integrating different sensory data (radar, infrared, etc.), which produce "best" detection rates. The reason for combining different sensors has its origins in statistical data analysis. The disadvantage of using a single sensor system is that it may not be able adequately to reduce the uncertainty for decision making. Uncertainty arises when features are missing, when the sensor cannot measure all relevant attributes, or when observations are ambiguous [9]. On the other hand, it is well known that it is statistically advantageous to combine multiple observations from the same source because improved estimates are obtained using redundant observations [8]. It is also known

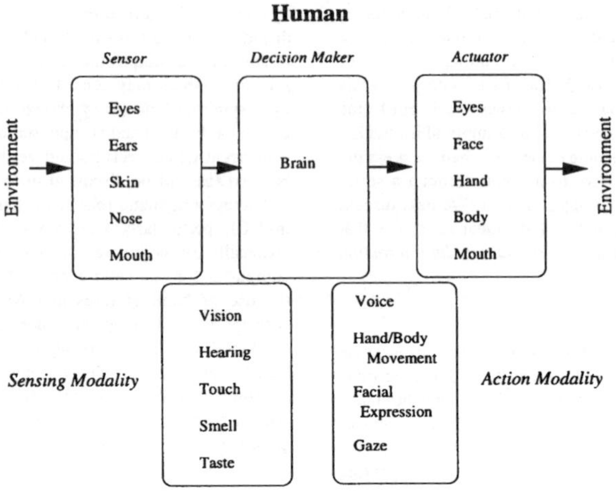

Human

Sensor   *Decision Maker*   *Actuator*

Environment

Eyes		Eyes
Ears	Brain	Face
Skin		Hand
Nose		Body
Mouth		Mouth

Environment

Sensing Modality

Vision
Hearing
Touch
Smell
Taste

Action Modality

Voice
Hand/Body Movement
Facial Expression
Gaze

Fig. 2. Modalities for human sensing and action. Human beings sense the environment in which they live through their senses. They act on the environment using numerous actuators.

that multiple types of sensors may increase the accuracy with which a quantity can be observed. Formally, if x_i and x_j are two (statistically independent) estimates of an observed quantity, the minimum mean square error (MSE) combination of the two estimates results in

$$x_{ij} = \left(\Sigma_i^{-1} + \Sigma_j^{-1}\right)^{-1} \Sigma_i^{-1} x_i + \left(\Sigma_i^{-1} + \Sigma_j^{-1}\right)^{-1} \Sigma_j^{-1} x_j \tag{1}$$

where Σ_i and Σ_j are the variances of x_i and x_j, respectively. Moreover, the variance of the fused estimate Σ_{ij} is given by

$$\Sigma_{ij}^{-1} = \Sigma_i^{-1} + \Sigma_j^{-1}. \tag{2}$$

Thus, the variance of the fused estimate Σ_{ij} is "smaller" than the variances of either of the two original estimates. This can be easily generalized to more than two redundant observations. Clearly, the advantage of having multimodal HCI is substantiated by the purely statistical point of view.

III. Modalities for HCI

Humans perceive the environment in which they live through their *senses*—vision, hearing, touch, smell, and taste. They act on and in it using their *actuators* such as body, hands, face, and voice. Human-to-human interaction is based on sensory perception of actuator actions of one human by another, often in the context of an environment (Fig. 2). In the case of HCI, computers perceive actions of humans. To have the human–computer interaction be as natural as possible, it is desirable that computers be able to interpret all natural human actions. Hence, computers should interpret human hand, body, and facial gestures, human speech, eye gaze, etc. Some computer-sensory modalities are analogous to human ones. Computer vision and ASR mimic the equivalent human sensing modalities.

However, computers also possess sensory modalities that humans lack. They can accurately estimate the position of the human hand through magnetic sensors and measure subtle changes of the electric activity in the human brain, for instance. Thus, there is a vast repertoire of human-action modalities that can potentially be perceived by a computer.

In the rest of this section, we review the individual modalities for HCI. The modalities are discussed under the two categories of *human-action modalities* and *computer-sensing modalities*. Fig. 3 shows how the two categories relate to each other. A particular human-action modality (e.g., speaking) may be interpreted using more than one computer-sensing modality (e.g., audio and video). We discuss a sampling of issues related to each of the individual modalities, some of which may be resolved by using multimodal integration in HCI.

A. Human-Action Modalities for HCI

A large repertoire of human actions could possibly be incorporated into HCI by designing suitable sensing mechanisms. Historically, the action modalities most exploited for HCI are based on hand movements. This is largely due to the dexterity of the human hand which allows accurate selection and positioning of mechanical devices with the help of visual feedback. Appropriate force and acceleration can also be applied easily using the human hand. Thus, the hand movement is exploited in the design of numerous interface devices—keyboard, mouse, stylus, pen, wand, joystick, trackball, etc. The keyboard provides a direct way of providing text input to the computer, but the speed is obviously limited and can only be improved to a certain rate. Similarly, hand movements cause a cursor to move on the computer screen (or a 3-D display). The next level of action modalities involves the use of *hand gestures*,

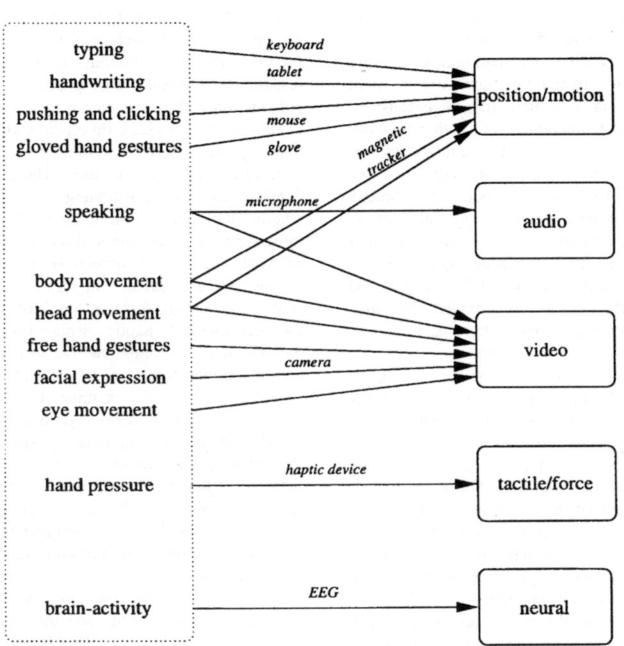

Fig. 3. Mapping of different human-action modalities to computer-sensing modalities for HCI. Multiple human actions, such as facial expressions and hand or eye movement, can be sensed through the same "devices" and used to infer different information.

ranging from simple pointing through manipulative gestures to more complex symbolic gestures such as those based on American Sign Language. With a glove-based device, the ease of hand gestures may be limited, but with noncontact video cameras, free-hand gestures would be easier to use for HCI. The role of free-hand gestures in HCI could be further improved (requiring lesser training, etc.) by studying the role of gestures in human communication. A multimodal framework is particularly well suited for embodiment of hand gestures into HCI.

In addition to hand movements, a dominant action modality in human communication is the production of sound, particularly spoken words. The production of speech is usually accompanied by other visible actions, such as lip movement, which can be exploited in HCI as well. Where the human is looking can provide a clue to the intended meaning of a particular action or even serve as a way of controlling a display. Thus, eye movements can be considered a potential action modality for HCI. The facial expression and body motion, if interpreted appropriately, can help in HCI. Even a subtle "action" like a controlled thought has been investigated as a potential candidate for HCI.

B. Computer-Sensing Modalities for HCI

What action modality to use for HCI is largely dependent on the available computer-sensing technology. We next discuss the broad categories of the computer-sensing modalities and consider how the above human-action modalities might by measured and interpreted.

1) Position and Motion Sensing: A large number of interface devices have been built to sense the position and motion of the human hand and other body parts for use in HCI. The simplest such interface is the keyboard, where the touch of a particular key indicates that one of a set of possible inputs was selected. More accurate position and motion sensing in a 2-D plane is used in interface devices such as a mouse, light pen, stylus, and tablet [7], [13]. Three-dimensional position/motion sensing is commonly done through a joystick or a trackball. For a brief history of HCI technology covering these familiar computer-sensing modalities, we refer the reader to [14]. In position/motion sensing, both relative and absolute measurements are made, dictated by the type of position/motion transducer used. With the advent of 3-D displays and virtual reality, there was a need to track the position of head, fingers, and other main body parts for controlling the display. For tracking the head (to display the graphics with the correct perspective), various forms of sensors have been employed. Electromagnetic fields [15] are the most popular method but are expensive and restricted to a small radius, typically about 5–20 ft. Ultrasonic tracking requires line of sight and is inaccurate, especially at long ranges, because of variation in the ambient temperature [16]. Other methods might include tracking of infrared light-emitting diodes or inertial trackers using accelerometers. Attempts to solve hand tracking resulted in mechanical devices that directly measure hand and/or arm joint angles and spatial position. This group is best represented by *glove-based devices* [17]–[21]. Glove-based gestural interfaces require the user to wear a cumbersome device and generally carry a load of cables that connect the device to a computer. This may hinder the ease and naturalness with which the user interacts with the computer-controlled environment.

2) Audio Sensing: The direct motivation for sensing the sound waves using a (set of) microphone(s) and processing the information using techniques known as ASR is to be able to interpret speech, the most natural human-action modality for HCI. Significant advances have been made toward the use of ASR for HCI [6]. The current ASR technology is still not robust, however, especially outside controlled environments, under noisy conditions and with multiple speakers [22]. Methods have been devised, for example, by using microphone arrays and noise cancellation techniques to improve the speech recognition. However, these tend to work only for the environments for which they are designed. An active research area is concerned with making ASR sufficiently robust for use in HCI. For instance, it has been demonstrated conclusively that the recognition rate for speech can be improved by using visual sensing to analyze the lip motion simultaneously [23]. Other visual sensing modalities such as gesture analysis may also help in improving speech interpretation [24].

3) Visual Sensing: A video camera, together with a set of techniques for processing and interpreting the image sequence, can make it possible to incorporate a variety of human-action modalities into HCI. These actions include hand gestures [12], lip movement [23], gaze [25]–[27], facial expressions [28], and head and other body movements [29], [30]. For example, with the help of specially designed cameras and lighting, eye movements can be tracked at greater than 250 Hz and can be potentially used for controlling a display, either directly or indirectly, by designing multiresolution displays [31], [32]. Similarly, visually interpreted gestures can allow a tetherless manipulation of virtual-reality [33] or augmented-reality displays [34]. Use of visual sensing for HCI suffers difficulties from both a theoretical and practical standpoint. The problem, such as visual interpretation of hand gestures, is still not well understood, particularly when it is desirable not to put restrictions on the hand movements for more natural HCI [12]. From a practical standpoint, visual sensing involves the processing of huge amounts of information in real time, which could put undue demands on the processing

power of the system being controlled. Furthermore, visual sensing requires an unoccluded view of the human, putting restrictions on the motion of the user and the physical setting for HCI. Nonetheless, the use of computer vision for improving HCI continues to be a topic of very active research [35]. Visual sensing can be especially useful in conjunction with other sensing modalities [36], such as lip reading with audio [23], lip reading with eye tracking [32], visual gesture recognition with speech [24], etc.

4) Tactile and Force Sensing: The dexterity of the human hand for accurately positioning a mechanical device can be coupled with application of "force," which can be sensed by using appropriate *haptic* devices. The computer sensing of touch and force is especially important for building a proper feel of "realism" in virtual reality. The key idea is that by exerting force or touch on virtual objects (with the corresponding haptic display for feedback), the user will be able to manipulate the virtual environment in a natural manner. Situations where such realism is especially important include, for example, simulation of surgery for training [37], [38]. Force sensing is a topic of very active research since is it difficult to design suitable devices with the desired accuracy without constraining the user [39], [40]. A better force sensing for HCI may also be obtained by simultaneously considering the sensing of position and motion.

5) Neural Sensing: One computer-sensing modality that has been explored with increasing interest is based on the monitoring of brain electrical (EEG) activity [41]–[44]. The brain activity can be monitored noninvasively from the surface of the scalp and used for directly controlling the computer display (Fig. 4). This form of interaction is also termed BAC. The "hands-free" nature of the resulting HCI makes it attractive for head-mounted displays and situations (such as aircraft piloting) where hands are being used in other tasks. Another very big impetus for pursuing this sensing modality is as a means of HCI for the physically disabled [45]. However, it requires training (using biofeedback and self-regulation) so that specific brain responses may be modulated [46]. There are many theoretical and applied open problems that need to be addressed for BAC, for example, how user distractions and/or increased workload affect such an interface, etc. An alternative approach includes sensing surface EMG signals [47]. Approaches have also been suggested for using multimodal sources that include eye tracking and monitoring of muscle tension in conjunction with EEG [48], [49].

IV. WHEN TO INTEGRATE THE HCI MODALITIES

The previous section introduced different types of modalities that may be "integrated" for multimodal HCI. Different sensing modalities yield disparate signal forms and rates. That makes successful integration of such signals a difficult and challenging task. In this section, we consider the problem of *when* to integrate the multiple modalities, which, in turn, determines the abstraction level at which the modalities are fused. Should they be fused at the "raw" sensory data level or at the higher "decision" level? How are

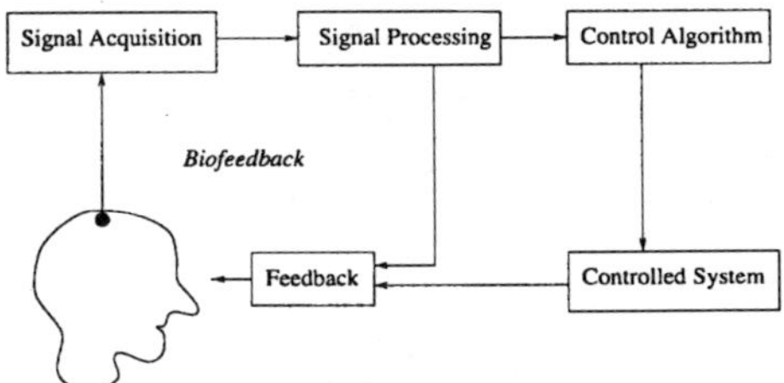

Fig. 4. The main components of an EEG-based system for controlling a display using brain activity.

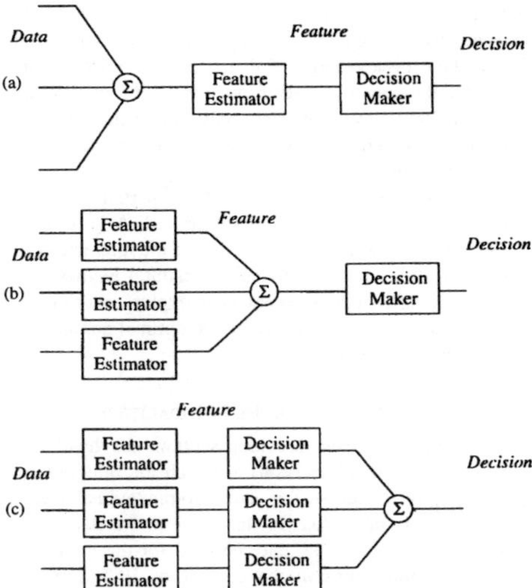

Fig. 5. The three different levels for fusing the multiple sensing modalities. (a) Data fusion fuses individual modes' data.
(b) Feature fusion combines features of individual modalities.
(c) Decision fusion integrates individual modes' decisions.

multiple modalities synchronized? In solving this problem, one should perhaps consider the following questions.

- How closely coupled are the modalities in natural human interaction?
- Does this coupling remain in HCI?
- What are the possible levels of multimodal integration in HCI?

The first question is not easy to answer. The answers mostly originate in psychobehavioral studies concerned with the interaction of modalities. For instance, it is known that gestures and speech are intimately connected and are claimed to arise from a single mental concept [50]. Gestures occur synchronously with their semantically parallel speech units or just before them [50]. It is also claimed that the gaze follows the hand during gestural actions [51]. Speech and lip movements are also closely coupled [23], even more so than gestures and speech.

A question remains, however, as to whether such coupling persists when the modalities are used for HCI. Several "Wizard of Oz"-type studies have confirmed that it does. Oviatt [7], for example, has extensively studied the interaction of drawing gestures and speech. She has concluded that the integration occurs on a semantic level where gestures are used to convey information on location, while speech conveys the information on subject and action (verb) in a sentence.

To study the levels of multimodal integration in HCI, one can use the theoretical and computational apparatus developed in the field of *sensory data fusion*. For the most part, three distinct levels of integration can be distinguished [8]:

1) data fusion;
2) feature fusion;
3) decision fusion.

Integration of sensory data according to the above levels of fusion is depicted in Fig. 5. Another, more refined version of this classification can be found in [52].

Data fusion is the lowest level of fusion [Fig. 5(a)]. It involves integration of raw observations and can occur only in the case when the observations are of the same type. This type of fusion does not typically occur in multimodal integration for HCI since the modes of interaction are of a different nature (gestures and speech, for instance) and are observed using different types of sensors (video camera and microphone, for instance). It can occur, for example, when one or more cameras are used to capture visual information on one object. Data-level fusion is characterized by the highest level of information detail out of the three fusion types. It also assumes a high level of synchronization of the multimodal observations. Unfortunately, data fusion is also highly susceptible to noise, specific nature of individual sensors, sensor failures, and sensor alignment [52].

Feature fusion is more commonly found in integration of modalities for HCI. It assumes that each stream of sensory data is first analyzed for features, after which the features themselves are fused [Fig. 5(b)]. This type of fusion is appropriate for closely coupled and synchronized modalities, possibly speech and lip movement. Feature-level fusion retains less detailed information than data fusion but is also less sensitive to noise. However, feature sets can be quite large. This high cardinality can result in soaring computational cost for this fusion approach [52].

The type of fusion most commonly found in HCI is the so-called decision-level fusion. Decision-level fusion is based on the fusion of individual mode decisions or interpretations [Fig. 5(c)]. For example, once an arm movement is interpreted as a deictic (pointing) gesture and a spoken sentence is recognized as "Make *this* box white," the two can be fused to interpret that a particular object (box) needs to be painted white. Synchronization of modalities in this case pertains to synchronization of decisions on a semantic level. Decision fusion is the most robust and resistant to individual sensor failure. It has a low data bandwidth and is generally less computationally expensive than feature fusion. One disadvantage of decision-level fusion is that it potentially cannot recover from loss of information that occurs at lower levels of data analysis and thus does not exploit the correlation between the modality streams at the lower integration levels.

Finding an optimal fusion level for a particular combination of modalities is not straightforward. A good initial guess can be based on the knowledge of the interaction and synchronization of those modes in a natural environment. However, it still remains necessary to explore multiple levels of fusion in order to determine the optimal combination of the desired modalities.

V. How to Integrate the HCI Modalities

As mentioned in the previous section, the level (data *versus* feature *versus* decision) at which the integration is done strongly influences the actual computational mechanism used for the fusion. In this section, we discuss the different mechanisms that may be used for the integration of multiple modalities in the context of HCI. First, we discuss the plausible biological basis for integration. This is followed by a general model of fusion that is used to discuss "how" to carry out the integration at the feature and decision levels.

A. Biological Foundations

An insight into *how* to combine multiple modalities can be gained from neurological models of sensor fusion. One such model was proposed by Stein and Meredith in [53]. The model suggests that the fusion of sensory neurons coming from individual sensors occurs in the brain structure know as *superior colliculus*. Superior colliculus is thought of as being responsible for orienting and attentive behavior. Two facts relevant to multimodal fusion can be gathered from their model.

1) *Evidence accruement:* Sensory evidence in superior colliculus seems to be *accrued* rather than averaged over different sensors inputs. In other words, the response of multisensory neurons leaving the colliculus is stronger when multiple weak-input sensory signals are present than when a single strong signal exists.

2) *Contextual dependency:* Besides receiving input from sensory neurons, superior colliculus also receives signals from the cerebral cortex. These signals modulate the fusion of sensory neurons, thus inducing *contextual feedback*. They are also responsible for different combinations of sensory signals based on the context.

Another important issue for multimodal fusion is addressed in the studies of perceptual sensory fusion. This issue tackles the problem of how *discordances* between individual sensors are dealt with. Discordances usually arise as a consequence of sensor malfunctioning. Dealing with them is clearly of utmost importance for the proper

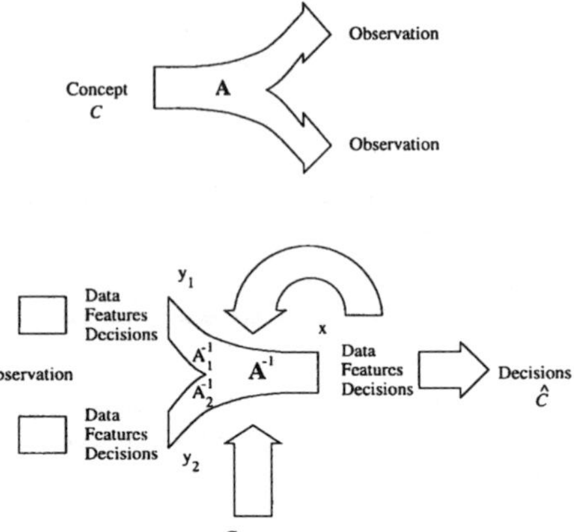

Fig. 6. A general model for multimodal production and fusion in HCI. Multiple observations are produced through different action modalities from the same concept "C." To infer the driving concept, multiple observations need to be reintegrated in the multimodal fusion process.

functioning of a system. According to Bower [54], there are four possible ways of dealing with sensory discordances:

1) *blind fusion:* sensor observations are fused without any regard for individual discordances;

2) *fusion with sensor recalibration:* an attempt is made to recalibrate discordant sensors;

3) *fusion with sensor suppression:* discordant sensors are suppressed;

4) *no fusion:* discordant sensors are not fused.

The last three fusion categories indicate the existence of feedback in the signal fusion processes in biological entities. Obviously, this provides one with a good rationale to consider those issues when tackling the problem of multimodal fusion for HCI.

B. A General Fusion Model

We consider a general model of multimodal fusion for HCI built on the foundations of sensory data fusion theory while also taking into account the biological evidence about integration of multiple senses. The model is depicted in Fig. 6. The fusion model is built under the assumption that each concept behind any human action is expressed through multiple action modalities and is perceived through multiple sensory modalities. The goal of multimodal fusion is then to integrate different abstractions of the observed actions (data, features, or decisions) such that it can best infer a decision about the driving concept. As part of such a process, contextual knowledge can be used to constrain the search space of the problem.

Let us denote by y_i, $i = 1, 2, \cdots, N$ observation abstractions of the concept C perceived through one of N sensory modalities. As mentioned before, such abstractions can be raw observations (data), features estimated from raw observations, or even individual mode decisions based on unimodal observations. Let Y_i be the set of all observations of modality i, $Y_i = \{y_{i1}, y_{i2}, \cdots\}$. Let x be an abstraction of concept C. Again, this could be the concept C itself or a feature in the concept space $\mathcal{X}$. The *production model* in additive noise environment can then be defined as

$$y_i = A_i(x) + \omega_i, \quad i = 1, 2, \cdots, N \quad (3)$$

where $A_i(\cdot)$ is the mapping that transduces a mental concept to an observable action and ω_i is an additive noise. The task of inferring the best concept $\hat{x}$ given some cost function J, sets of observations $Y_1, \cdots, Y_N$, and context $\kappa(x) = 0$ can then be formulated as the following constrained optimization problem:

$$\hat{x} = \arg, \min_{x \in \mathcal{X}} J(x|Y_1, \cdots, Y_N), \text{ such that } \kappa(x) = 0. \quad (4)$$

A common way of defining the inference problem employs the *Bayesian framework* (see, for instance, [55] for an overview of Bayesian inference). In this framework, the cost function is given as the probability of making a wrong decision $J(x|Y_1, \cdots, Y_N) = 1 - P(x|Y_1, \cdots, Y_N)$. Assuming, for the sake of simplicity, that context plays no role, this leads to

$$\hat{x}_{\text{MAP}} = \arg, \max_x P(x|Y_1, \cdots, Y_N). \quad (5)$$

Hence, (4) now assumes the form of the MAP estimator. Another equivalent form of this criterion is often found in data fusion and detection literature and follows from the *Bayes* inference rule:

$$\hat{x}_{\text{MAP}}: \frac{P(Y_1, \cdots, Y_N|\hat{x})}{P(Y_1, \cdots, Y_N|x)} > \frac{P(x)}{P(\hat{x})}, \qquad \forall x \in \mathcal{X}. \quad (6)$$

Test (6) is commonly referred to as the *Bayes LRT* [56]. The quantity on the left side of (6) is known as the likelihood ratio $\Lambda(Y)$, and the quantity on the right side is the threshold η.

A frequently used assumption in the integration of multiple modalities is that of *conditionally independent observations*. In other words

$$P(y_1, \cdots, y_N|x) = P(y_1|x) \cdots P(y_N|x). \quad (7)$$

Under this assumption, the MAP LRT reduces to

$$\hat{x}_{MAP}: \quad \frac{P(Y_1|\hat{x})}{P(Y_1|x)} \cdots \frac{P(Y_N|\hat{x})}{P(Y_N|x)} > \frac{P(x)}{P(\hat{x})} \quad (8)$$

$$: \quad \Lambda(Y_1) \cdots \Lambda(Y_N) > \eta, \forall x \in \mathcal{X}. \quad (9)$$

This equation can be viewed as the distributed version of the Bayes (fusion) rule.

Sometimes, however, the prior probabilities of individual multimodal concepts $P(x)$ are not known. In the absence of this knowledge, it is best to assume that all concepts are equally likely. This leads us to another criterion for multimodal fusion, known as the ML criterion

$$\hat{x}_{\text{ML}} = \arg, \max_x P(Y_1, \cdots, Y_N|x). \quad (10)$$

Again, using the independence-of-observations assumption from (7), the ML criterion becomes

$$\hat{x}_{\text{ML}} = \arg, \max_x \prod_{i=1}^{N} P(Y_i|x)$$

$$= \arg, \max_x \sum_{i=1}^{N} \log P(Y_i|x). \quad (11)$$

Often, a weighted form of the ML is used to emphasize the importance of individual modes

$$\hat{x}_{\text{ML}_{\text{w}}} = \arg, \max_x \sum_{i=1}^{N} w_i, \log P(Y_i|x) \quad (12)$$

where w_i are the modal weights such that $\sum_{i=1}^{N} w_i = 1$. For example, in many bimodal speech-recognition applications, weights w_i are employed to indicate the dominant communication mode in different noise environments.

Equipped with these tools, one can now approach the task of multimodal fusion from the perspective of fusion on different integration levels, as discussed in Section IV. In the following discussion, we address two categories of multimodal fusion techniques often found in HCI—feature-level and decision-level fusion techniques.

C. Feature-Level Fusion

Feature-level fusion techniques are concerned with integration of features from individual modalities into more complex multimodal features and decisions. Using the terminology from data-fusion literature [52], feature-fusion techniques can be classified as twofold:

- FIFO techniques;
- FIDO techniques.

FIFO techniques yield fused multimodal features. This implies the need for an additional feature classifier to infer the multimodal decision. Kalman filters are an often accounted type of FIFO fusers. Unlike FIFO integrators, FIDO integrators do not require a separate classification unit. Feature fusion and classification are inherently connected in this architecture. FIDO fusion frequently employs structures known as *probabilistic networks*, such as artificial neural networks and HMM's.

1) Kalman Fusion: Multimodal fusion on a feature level can easily be formulated using the *Kalman filter* approach [57], [58]. Instead of performing fusion of a time series of feature vectors, however, the fusion is in this case performed over a sequence of features belonging to different modalities. The Kalman fusion approach is based on the assumption that the production model (3) is known. For ease of discussion, we assume that this model is linear and that there are only two modalities to be fused. Assume also that the additive noise in (3) is independent across different modalities, $\omega_1 \perp \omega_2$. We can then combine observations from the two modalities into a single vector $y^T = [y_1^T y_2^T]$ and write

$$y = Ax + \omega \quad (13)$$

where

$$A^T = \begin{bmatrix} A_1^T A_2^T \end{bmatrix}$$
$$\omega^T = \begin{bmatrix} \omega_1^T \omega_2^T \end{bmatrix} \tag{14}$$
$$\Omega = E\begin{bmatrix} \omega\omega^T \end{bmatrix}.$$

Let $\hat{x}_-$ and $\hat{x}_+$ be the estimates of x before and after new observations from two modalities are fused, respectively, and let Σ_- and Σ_+ be their corresponding variances. Then

$$\hat{x}_j = \Sigma_j \begin{bmatrix} A_j^T \Omega_j^{-1} y_j + \Sigma_-^{-1} \hat{x}_- \end{bmatrix} \tag{15}$$
$$\Sigma_j^{-1} = \Sigma_-^{-1} + A_j^T \Omega_j^{-1} A_j, \quad j = 1, 2. \tag{16}$$

Similarly, from (13), we can obtain the following Kalman filter equation:

$$\hat{x}_+ = \Sigma_+ \begin{bmatrix} A^T \Omega^{-1} y + \Sigma_-^{-1} \hat{x}_- \end{bmatrix} \tag{17}$$
$$\Sigma_+^{-1} = \Sigma_-^{-1} + A^T \Omega^{-1} A. \tag{18}$$

Last, substituting (14) into (17) and using (15), we have

$$\hat{x}_+ = \Sigma_+ \begin{bmatrix} \Sigma_1^{-1} \hat{x}_1 + \Sigma_2^{-1} \hat{x}_2 - \Sigma_-^{-1} \hat{x}_- \end{bmatrix} \tag{19}$$
$$\Sigma_+^{-1} = \Sigma_1^{-1} + \Sigma_2^{-1} - \Sigma_-^{-1}. \tag{20}$$

Equation (19) clearly has the same form as (8).

From (19), it is obvious that in the Bayesian case with independent observations, the fused evidence is formed by averaging the evidence from individual modalities. However, a general Bayesian inference framework can result in a highly nonlinear evidence fusion.

The above feature fusion equations can easily be generalized for the fusion case of N conditionally independent modalities. Similarly, an *extended Kalman filter* [57], [58] approach can be used if (3) is nonlinear. Extensions to multiscale Kalman fusion have also been explored [59]. In general, the Kalman filter approach is the most commonly found approach in feature-to-feature fusion.

2) ANN's: An ANN is a type of statistical classifier often used in pattern recognition. More precisely, it is a graph where variables are associated with nodes of the graph and variable transformations are based on propagation of numerical messages along the links of the graph [60]. The network is used for classification of inputs y into N classes $X \in \mathcal{X} = \{X_1, X_1, \cdots, X_N\}$. In other words, given an observation y, the network estimates the density $P(x|y)$. To show that a structure like an ANN can indeed be used as a density estimator, consider that according to the Bayes rule

$$
\begin{aligned}
&P(x = X_1|y) \\
&= \frac{P(y|x = X_1)P(x = X_1)}{P(y)} \\
&= \frac{P(y|x = X_1)P(x = X_1)}{\sum_i P(y|x = X_i)P(x = X_i)} \\
&= \frac{1}{1 + \exp\left\{ \sum_i - \ln\left[\frac{P(y|x=X_1)}{P(y|x=X_i)} \right] - \ln\left[\frac{P(x=X_1)}{P(x=X_i)} \right] \right\}} \\
&= \frac{1}{1 + \exp(z_1)} \\
&= g(z_1).
\end{aligned}
\tag{21}
$$

$g(\cdot)$ is called the logistic sigmoid function. Assuming that conditional probabilities are Gaussian (or of general exponential family) with identical covariance matrices, it readily follows that

$$z_1 = w_1^T y + w_{11}. \tag{22}$$

Thus, the conditional density computation can be achieved using a simple one-layer linear network with the sigmoid node transfer functions. In fact, it can be shown (see [61], for example) that a network of the form

$$u_k(y) = v_k^T g[z(y)] + v_{k1} \tag{23}$$

with "properly" selected weights v and w yields $P(x = X_k|y) = u_k(y)$. The network of the above type is also known as the MLP and is frequently used in pattern-recognition tasks. Many other ANN architectures have been proposed in a variety of different contexts [62].

Selection of network weights is done through network training. Based on a corpus of training data with known classification, the network weights are modified until the network "learns" the classification. Training procedures differ widely depending on the network architecture. For MLP, for instance, a gradient-based optimization technique, also know as EBP, is often used [63]. If optimized to a global minimum of the MSE cost function, such networks indeed behave as MAP density estimators. In practice, however, the weights usually correspond to a local minimum of the cost function, and the networks only approximate MAP estimators.

One drawback of "classical" ANN architectures is their inability efficiently to handle temporal sequences of features. Mainly, they are unable to compensate for changes in temporal shifts and scales. Several modified architectures have emerged that can handle such tasks. One of the most often used architectures is the so-called MS-TDNN [64]. This architecture handles changes in pattern temporal scale using the dynamic programming approach.

The adaptation of ANN's to multimodal fusion has often been inspired by biological origins. However, fusion architectures have mostly followed the line of regular ANN architectures with straightforward concatenation of features from multiple modalities into a joint feature vector. Some attempts have been made to design specific fusion architectures and fusion nodes. For example, Meier *et al.* in [65] designed an architecture that combines two TDNN's using a layer of "combination" nodes. The combination nodes' activation is determined as the weighted sum of the individual mode networks' output scores.

3) HMM's: HMM's are, like the ANN's, a special case of probabilistic Bayes networks [60]. They have been used successfully for more than a decade in the field of ASR [6]. Unlike ANN's, HMM's are designed to model the posterior densities of observations $P(y|x = X)$ over time and can, therefore, be used as ML estimators (10). An HMM is a doubly stochastic process, a network with *hidden* and *observable* states. The hidden states "drive" the model dynamics—at each time instance, the model is in one of its hidden states. Transitions between the hidden states are governed by probabilistic rules. The observable states produce outcomes during hidden-state transitions or while the model is in one of its hidden states. Such outcomes are measurable by an outside observer. The outcomes are governed by a set of probabilistic rules. Thus, an HMM can be represented as a triplet (A, b, pi), where A is called the (hidden) state transition matrix, b describes the probabilities of the observation states, and π is the initial hidden-state distribution. It is common to assume that the hidden-state space is discrete and that the observables are allowed to assume a continuum of values. In such cases, b is usually represented as a MOG probability density functions (pdf's). The process of association of different HMM's with different concepts is denoted as training. In this process, the parameters of the HMM (A, b, pi) are modified so that the chosen model "best" describes the spatio/temporal dynamics of the desired concept. The training is, again, achieved by optimizing the likelihood measure $\log [P(y|x = X)]$ over the model parameters. Such optimization involves the use of computationally expensive EM procedures, like the Baum–Welch algorithm [66]. However, any such training procedure involves a step based on DP, which in turn has a DTW property. This means that the variability in duration of training samples is accounted for in the model. The same is true for the recognition or model-evaluation process. A probability of the observation's being produced by each HMM is evaluated using a DP *forward/backward* or *Viterbi* algorithm. Obviously, the larger the number of trained HMM's, the more computationally demanding the recognition procedure. To help address this problem successfully, an external set of rules or *grammar* is imposed, which describes the language sentence structure or how the trained units can be "connected" in time [33], [67]. Several problems are related to the typical use of the HMM as a recognition tool. For example, in its original formulation, an HMM is a first-order stochastic process. This implies that the (hidden) state of the model at time instance i depends only on the state at time $i - 1$. While this model may be adequate for some processes, it often results in lower recognition rates for the processes that do not follow the first-order Markov property. As in speech, such problems can be somewhat reduced by extending the parameter vectors with the time derivatives of the original parameters [68]. It is also possible to derive higher order HMM's; however, such models do not share the computational efficiency of the first-order models [6]. Another possible drawback of classical HMM's is the assumption that pdf's of the observables can be modeled as MOG's. The main reason for modeling the observables as MOG's is to ease the training. In such cases, the HMM parameters can be efficiently computed using the Baum–Welch algorithm. Extensions in this direction have been achieved in speech recognition by using neural networks to model the observation pdf's [61]. Unfortunately, the training procedure in that case is computationally overwhelming. Also, in the original formulation, an HMM

is assumed to be *stationary*. Nonstationary versions of HMM's have been recently formulated for speech recognition [69].

Feature fusion context can be introduced into HMM's by modeling the observations as concatenated multimodal feature vectors. Such integration architectures have been considered for the fusion of speech and lip movements [70] and speech and hand gestures [71]. However, possibly due to the differences in the time scale of the features from the two modalities, such architectures do not perform well. One attempt to alleviate this problem was introduced in [72] through an HMM-like architecture called the Boltzmann zipper. In the Boltzmann zipper, each hidden state can "belong" to only one of the multiple modalities (audio or video, for example) but not to both, as is the case in classical multimodal HMM's. This architecture has been applied to bimodal speech recognition and has shown improvement in fusion characteristics [23] over the concatenation approach. HMM's have been utilized with much more success as individual feature classifiers at the decision-level multimodal fusion (see Section V-D).

D. Decision-Level Fusion

Fusion on the decision level is the most frequently followed approach to multimodal integration. As depicted in Fig. 5, it involves fusion of concepts (decisions) from the individual modes to form a unique multimodal concept. An underlying assumption of this type of fusion is that the basic features of the individual modes are not sufficiently correlated to be fused at the feature level. Therefore, feature fusers/classifiers mentioned in Section V-C cannot be directly used for fusion. However, they are often used here too, but in a slightly different role, as decision makers for the individual modes. Several types of decision-level fusion mechanisms are commonly found in HCI systems. In the following discussion, we consider two such mechanisms: *frames* and *software agents*.

1) Frames: The concept of frames is commonly found in artificial intelligence literature. A frame is a unit of a knowledge source describing an object [73]. Each frame has a number of *slots* associated with it. The slots represent possible properties of the object, actions, or an object's relationship with other frames. This last property facilitates a mechanism for designing networks of frames for a particular context with links describing contextual semantics. Such networks are also known as semantic networks [74]. In the multimodal HCI context, different modalities can be associated with individual frame slots. Different modalities can describe particular properties of a virtual object. Speech can, for instance, designate the object's color, while gestures can imply the object's location. This is a case of the complementary role of modalities. It is also possible that multiple modalities indicate the same property of an object. In such cases, fusion can be achieved by selecting the property with the lowest joint cost. In the Bayesian framework, this is equivalent to choosing the highest prior or posterior joint probability. An alternative may be to consider the Dempster–Shafer combination of evidence

360

[75]. In that case, the evidence is actually accrued, which is consistent with the observed properties of biological data-fusion systems.

Frame-based multimodal HCI systems have been utilized ever since Bolt's early "Put-That-There" system [76]. This system used speech, gaze, and hand gestures to manipulate virtual objects. Many recent systems still use the same mechanism. For example, [77] used speech and pen-gesture frame fusion to design an interface for a calendar program. Many simple frame-based approaches have also been implemented for bimodal (audio and video) speech recognition [65], [70], [78]. Such approaches basically assume one-frame/one-slot networks for each of the two modalities. The slots describe phonemes observed through speech and lip movements. Two frames are fused by selecting the phoneme with the highest joint probability, $P(\text{video}|\text{phoneme})P(\text{audio}|\text{phoneme})$. The classifiers for the individual modes are commonly of the HMM type.

2) Software Agents: Software agents have recently emerged as a valuable tool for HCI [79]. A software agent is a software entity that functions continuously and autonomously in a particular environment, often inhabited by other agents and processes [79], [80]. Agents should be able to perform their activities without human intervention over long periods of time. They should learn from their experience and communicate and cooperate with other agents. Groups of agents can play roles of "digital butlers," "personal filters," or "digital sisters-in-law" [81]. In that respect, software agents are particularly useful in overcoming some problems of present-generation user interfaces. For example, current direct manipulation interfaces are inappropriate for large search spaces, are not adaptive and easy to learn, cannot learn from examples themselves, and, most important, cannot easily integrate multiple interaction modalities. On the other hand, software agents can be task oriented, flexible, adaptive, and can integrate modalities by delegating modal interaction to different communicating subagents.

OAA [82] is especially suitable for multimodal fusion tasks. In this architecture, one agent can autonomously handle speech recognition while another handles gestures and a third processes eye movements, for instance. The modal agents, in turn, communicate with a central agent known as a *facilitator,* which handles their interactions with other agents in the system who wish to receive multimodal information, such as a multimodal interpretation agent. This multimodal integration architecture provides an opportunity for implementation of sensor discordances detection, evidence accruement, and contextual feedback. However, the complexity of the architecture is greater compared to some of the other integration techniques. To handle this burden, the OAA facilitates distributed computing, in which different agents can exist on different computer platforms, ranging from workstations to hand-held personal assistants. One implementation of this architecture has been used in QuickSet, a multimodal interface for military simulation [83], which uses speech, handwriting, and pen gestures.

Fig. 7. A visual computing environment for structural biology (MDScope) used as a testbed for building a speech/gesture interface with decision-level fusion.

VI. Multimodal HCI Systems and Applications

Although there has been substantial research interest toward developing multimodal HCI systems, relatively few implemented HCI systems exhibit such multimodality. We first present in Section VI-A a description of an implemented speech/gesture system that can be considered as a case study of multimodal integration with fusion at the decision level. This is followed by a brief review of other reported multimodal systems and applications in Section VI-B.

A. A Gesture/Speech Interface for Controlling a 3-D Display

We summarize a case study in building a speech/gesture interface for a virtual-reality application (further details are given in [24]). The particular virtual environment that we considered is used by structural biologists in the Theoretical Biophysics Group at the University of Illinois at Urbana-Champaign. The system, called MDScope [84], is a set of integrated software components that provides an environment for simulation and visualization of biomolecular systems in structural biology (Fig. 7). To keep the interaction natural in a complex environment like MDScope, it is desirable to have as few devices attached to the user as possible. Motivated by this, we developed techniques that enable spoken words and simple free-hand gestures to be used while interacting with 3-D graphical objects in this virtual environment. The hand gestures are detected through a pair of strategically positioned cameras and interpreted using a set of computer-vision techniques that we term AGR. These computer-vision algorithms are able to extract the user hand from the background, extract positions of the fingers, and distinguish a meaningful gesture from unintentional hand movements using the context. The context of a particular virtual environment is used to place the necessary constraints to make the analysis robust and to develop a command language that attempts optimally to combine speech and gesture inputs.

The key goal of our work was to simplify model manipulation and rendering to such a degree that biomolecular modeling assumes a playful character; this will allow the researcher to explore variations of the model and concentrate on biomolecular aspects of the task without undue distraction by computational aspects. This helps in the process of developing an understanding of important properties of the molecules, in viewing simulations of molecular dynamics, and in "playing" with different combinations of molecular structures. One potential benefit of the system would be in reducing the time to discover new compounds—in research toward new drugs, for example.

The general AGR problem is difficult because it involves analyzing the human hand, which has a very high degree of freedom, and because the use of the hand gesture is not so well understood. (See [12] for a recent survey of vision-based AGR.) However, we use the context of the particular virtual environment to develop an appropriate set of gestural "commands." The gesture recognition is done by analyzing the sequence of images from a pair of cameras positioned such that they facilitate robust analysis of the hand images. The background is set to be uniformly black to further help with the real-time analysis without using any specialized image-processing hardware. In addition to recognizing a pointing finger, we have developed an HMM-based AGR system for recognizing a basic set of manipulative hand gestures. The gesture commands are categorized as being either dynamic (e.g., move back, move forward) or static (e.g., grab, release, stop, up, down). We have also developed a gesture command language for MDScope that is mainly concerned with manipulating and controlling the display of the molecular structures.

For integration of speech and gesture within the MDScope environment, a real-time decoding of the user's commands was required in order to keep pace with the hand gestures. Thus we used "word spotting," the task of detecting a given vocabulary of words embedded in unconstrained continuous speech. The recognition output stream consisted of a sequence of keywords and fillers constrained by a simple syntactical network. The recognizer that followed was developed by modifying the HMM implementation of HTK Toolkit by Entropic Research.

To utilize the information input from the user in the form of spoken words and simple hand gestures effectively, we designed a command language for MDScope that combines speech with gesture using a frame-based architecture. This command language employs the basic syntax of < action < object < modifier > and emphasizes both *complementary* and *reenforcing* roles of spoken and gestural modes. The < action > component is spoken (e.g., "rotate"), while the < object > and < modifier > are specified by a combination of speech and gesture. An example is speaking "this" while pointing, followed by a modifier to clarify what is being pointed to, such as "molecule," "helix," "atom," etc., followed by speaking "done" after moving the hand according to the desired motion. Another example of the desired speech/gesture capability is the voice command "engage" to query MDScope for the molecule that is nearest to the tip of the pointer and to make the molecule blink to indicate that it was selected and to save a reference to that molecule for future use. Once engaged, the voice command "rotate" converts the gesture commands into rotations of the chosen molecule and the command "translate" converts them into translations. When finished, the command "release" deselects the molecule and allows the user to manipulate another molecule.

This application shows a case where computer-vision and speech-recognition techniques are used for building a natural human–computer interface for a virtual-reality environment using spoken words and free hand gestures. The previous interface of MDScope was a keyboard and a magnetically tracked pointer. This is particularly inconvenient since the system is typically used by multiple (six to eight) users, and the interface hinders the interactive nature of the visualization system. Hence, incorporating voice command control in MDScope enabled the users to be free of keyboards and to interact with the environment in a natural manner. The hand gestures permitted the users easily to manipulate the displayed model and "play" with different spatial combinations of the molecular structures. The integration of speech and hand gestures as a multimodal interaction mechanism was more powerful than using either mode alone.

B. Other Multimodal HCI Systems

One of the first multimodal HCI systems can be accredited to Bolt [76]. His "Put-That-There" system fused spoken input and magnetically tracked 3-D hand gestures using a frame-based integration architecture. The system was used for simple management of a limited set of virtual objects such as selection of objects, modification of object properties, and object relocation. Even though the naturalness of the interaction was hindered by the limitations of the technology at that time, "Put-That-There" has remained the inspiration of all modern multimodal interfaces. The rest of this section focuses on some of its descendants.

QuickSet [83], [85] is a multimodal interface for control of military simulations using hand-held PDA's. It incorporates voice and pen gestures as the modes of interaction. This interface belongs to the class of decision-level fusers. It follows the OAA [82] with ten primary agents connected through a central facilitator. Recognition of pen gestures sensed through the PDA is conducted by the gesture agent. The agent utilizes ANN and HMM classifiers for concurrent gesture recognition. Multiple modalities in QuickSet play reenforcing roles. The modalities can automatically disambiguate each other using joint ML estimation. Alternatively, unimodal interaction can be enabled when one of the modes becomes unreliable. Situations like that may occur in high noise environments such as field posts during military exercises.

Another multimodal interface system was built for interacting with a calendar program called Jeanie [77]. The interface consists of autonomous speech, pen gesture, and handwriting-recognition modules. The speech-recognition module is built upon the JANUS speech translation system [86]. It includes a semantic parser that can efficiently deal with unknown words and unrecognized fragments. The pen-gesture recognition module uses TDNN's to classify a small number of pen strokes sensed through a PDA, while the handwriting recognizer employs MS-TDNN's as classifiers. The fusion of the three modalities is performed in a frame-based fashion (see Section V-D1) followed by the dialogue manager interpretation of the fused information according to the current context. In the absence of recognition errors, the multimodal interpreter performs with 80% accuracy, while in its worst case, the accuracy drops to a low 35%.

VisualMan [87] is an application-independent multimodal user interface that combines eye gaze, voice, and 3-D motion. The interface is used for a 3-D virtual object manipulation in a Windows-based environment. Three-dimensional motion and eye gaze are integrated to provide positional information about the manipulated object, whereas spoken commands independently determine manipulative actions.

Finger-Pointer [88] integrates deictic free-hand gestures and simple static hand postures with voice commands for video presentation system control. Multimodal integration of the two modalities assumes that their roles are complementary—gestures specify positional information and identify simple object attributes (number of slides, for example), while spoken commands identify actions.

Virtual-World [89] is a combination of a flexible-object simulator and a multisensory user interface. It integrates hand gestures and hand motion detected with a glove-based device with spoken input. A dialogue manager is employed to map sensing device outputs to application parameters and results using a set of rules.

The integration of speech and lip reading has been extensively explored in recent years. The main goal of this fusion task has been to improve the recognition of speech in high noise environments. Approaches ranging from feature- to decision-level fusion have been tested for that purpose. For instance, [70] experimented with HMM-based feature fusion on feature and joint ML fusion on decision level (see Section V-C3). Results from their 40 word-recognition tasks indicate that decision-level bimodal fusion yields better accuracy compared to the feature-level approach. Similar results have been observed in [65], [72], and [78]. In [78], HMM fusion on feature level was tested against the decision level using the machine-learning C4.5 algorithm and showed again the superiority of the decision-level fusion. Fusion on the two levels tested in an ANN/TDNN setup by [65] confirmed the above observations.

An interesting application of multimodal interfaces lies in the domain of virtual autonomous agents. Autonomous agents are autonomous behaving entities in a dual vir-tual/real world who perform some actions in response to their perceived environment. Natural interaction and communication between the agents on one side and a human user on the other is crucial for effective system performance. We briefly survey a few such systems from the multimodal HCI standpoint.

The Artificial Life Interactive Video Environment (ALIVE) [90] is a system that allows wireless, full-body interaction between a human and a world of autonomous agents. The system uses a real-time, vision-based interface to detect and interpret the user's body motion in the context of a current virtual world and its artificial inhabitants. ALIVE has been used in numerous applications ranging from entertainment agents and personal teachers and trainers to interface agents and PDA's.

A similar approach is used in Smart Rooms [91]. Smart Rooms play the role of an invisible butler in trying to interpret what the user is doing and help him accomplish his tasks easily. Based on agent architecture, Smart Rooms use visual and auditory sensors to interpret hand gestures and speech and identify the user, for example. Extensions of this approach have been implemented as Smart Desks, Smart Clothes, and smart car interiors [92].

Another multimodal autonomous agent system called Neuro Baby (NB) [93], [94] was designed as a form of human companion. NB employs recognition of the user's voice intonation and mood as well as eye tracking and hand shaking via robotic hand. A feedback to the user is provided through the autonomous character's facial expressions and speech. The system has also evolved into a network NB, the intent of which is to provide two users, separated by a cultural gap, a way to communicate feelings in a nonverbal fashion.

VII. DISCUSSION

With the massive influx of computers in society, the limitations of current human–computer interfaces have become increasingly evident. HCI systems today restrict the information and command flow between the user and the computer system. They are, for the most part, designed to be used by a small group of experts who have *adapted themselves* to the available HCI. For a casual user, however, the HCI systems are cumbersome and obtrusive and lack the "intelligence" expected by the user. Further, the HCI systems tend to confine the user to a less natural, *unimodal* means of communication. The ease with which such uni-modal interfaces allow one to communicate with computers is far from satisfactory.

Integration of more than one modality into an interface would potentially overcome the current limitations and ease the information-flow bottleneck between the user and the computer. Ideally, in a multimodal HCI setup, the computers would adapt to the needs of the user. Cumbersome and obtrusive devices in one interaction modality would be replaced by more natural interface devices in other modalities. Such modalities do not necessarily have to be the ones employed in an analogous human-to-human communication. Computers possess sensory modalities that could prove to be superior to those that humans possess. Inaccurate interaction in one modality can be complemented by a more accurate interpretation in another modality or can be improved by combined interpretation through multiple modalities.

Some of the reported experimental HCI systems support the evidence of the potential benefits of multimodality in HCI. However, the limitations of these current systems are quite evident. A major hindrance is perhaps still in the inadequacies of the individual modalities that are used in the multimodal interface. For example, the performance of ASR is still highly context dependent, often below the desired robustness. Visual sensing involves real-time processing of huge amounts of data and thus suffers difficulties from both a theoretical and practical standpoint. Force sensing lacks suitable devices with desired accuracy without constraining the user. Sensing of neural information requires extensive training. These problems have restricted today's multimodal interfaces to a very narrow class of domains where the problems can be minimized. Further progress is needed in developing an understanding of the limitations of the individual modalities—to help both in making them better for HCI and for making them more suitable for integration with other modalities.

Strategies and techniques for multimodal integration are only beginning to emerge. The questions of *when* and *how* to merge multiple modalities have not yet been addressed in a satisfactory manner. More tightly coupled modalities such as speech and lip reading may call for integration at lower, feature levels, whereas modalities such as hand gestures and spoken language possibly require a semantic-level integration. Current multimodal HCI systems are often built using ad hoc approaches based more on intuition rather than systematic techniques and studies on human subjects. This can result in awkward solutions where the interaction requires unnatural mode couplings or where mode transitions need to be induced by the press of a button.

To alleviate the current problems, a massive effort focusing on several fundamental questions is necessary. How to increase robustness and accuracy of individual interface devices while minimizing their obtrusiveness? How to effectively couple multiple modalities in a natural manner? How to provide flexibility and adaptivity of the interaction? Better methodologies, perhaps based on systematic human studies, may need to be developed for evaluation of the multimodal interfaces. These evaluation techniques would ultimately determine the effectiveness of proposed techniques and architectures for multimodal HCI.

VIII. Concluding Remarks

Motivated by the tremendous need to explore better HCI paradigms, there has been a growing interest in developing novel sensing modalities for HCI. To achieve the desired naturalness and robustness of the HCI, multimodality would perhaps be an essential element of such interaction. Clearly, human studies in the context of HCI should play a larger role in addressing issues of multimodal integration. Even though a number of developed multimodal interfaces seem to be domain specific, there should be more systematic means of evaluating them. Modeling and computational techniques from more established areas such as sensor

fusion may shed some light on how systematically to integrate the multiple modalities. However, the integration of modalities in the context of HCI is quite specific and needs to be more closely tied with subjective elements of "context." There have been many successful demonstrations of HCI systems exhibiting multimodality. Despite the current progress, with many problems still open, multimodal HCI remains in its infancy. A massive effort is perhaps needed before one can build practical multimodal HCI systems approaching the naturalness of human–human communication.

References

[1] J. A. Adam, "Virtual reality," *IEEE Spectrum,* vol. 30, no. 10, pp. 22–29, 1993.

[2] H. Rheingold, *Virtual Reality.* New York: Summit Books, 1991.

[3] A. G. Hauptmann and P. McAvinney, "Gesture with speech for graphics manipulation," *Int. J. Man-Machine Studies,* vol. 38, pp. 231–249, Feb. 1993.

[4] S. Mann, "Wearable computing: A first step toward personal imaging," *IEEE Computer Mag.,* vol. 30, pp. 25–32, Feb. 1997.

[5] R. W. Pickard and J. Healey, "Affective wearables," in *Proc. Int. Symp. Wearable Computing,* Cambridge, MA, Oct. 1997.

[6] L. R. Rabiner and B. Juang, *Fundamentals of Speech Recognition.* Englewood Cliffs, NJ: Prentice-Hall, 1993.

[7] S. Oviatt, A. DeAngeli, and K. Kuhn, "Integration and synchronization of input modes during multimodal human–computer interaction," in *Proc. Conf. Human Factors in Computing Systems (CHI'97),* Atlanta, GA, pp. 415–422.

[8] D. L. Hall and J. Llinas, "An introduction to multisensor data fusion," *Proc. IEEE,* vol. 85, pp. 6–23, Jan. 1997.

[9] R. R. Murphy, "Biological and cognitive foundations of intelligent data fusion," *IEEE Trans. Syst., Man, Cybern.,* vol. 26, pp. 42–51, Jan. 1996.

[10] D. Salber and J. Coutaz, "Applying the Wizard of Oz technique to the study of multimodal systems," in *Proc. EWHCI'93,* Moscow, Russia, 1993.

[11] P. R. Cohen, M. Darlymple, F. C. N. Pereira, J. W. Sullivan, R. A. Gargan, Jr., J. L. Schlossberg, and S. W. Tyler, "Synergic use of direct manipulation and natural language," in *Proc. Conf. Human Factors in Computing Systems (CHI'89),* Austin, TX, pp. 227–233.

[12] V. I. Pavlović, R. Sharma, and T. S. Huang, "Visual interpretation of hand gestures for human–computer interaction: A review," *IEEE Trans. Pattern Anal. Machine Intell.,* vol. 19, no. 7, pp. 677–695, 1997.

[13] A. Waibel, M. T. Vo, P. Duchnowski, and S. Manke, "Multimodal interfaces," *Artificial Intell. Rev.,* vol. 10, pp. 299–319, Aug. 1995.

[14] B. A. Myers, "A brief history of human computer interaction technology," Human Computer Interaction Institute, School of Computer Science, Carnegie-Mellon University, Pittsburgh, PA, Tech. Rep. CMU-CS-TR-96-163, 1996.

[15] F. H. Raab, E. B. Blood, T. O. Steiner, and H. R. Jones, "Magnetic position and orientation tracking system," *IEEE Trans. Aerosp. Electron. Syst.,* vol. 15, pp. 709–718, 1979.

[16] R. Azuma, "Tracking requirements for augmented reality," *Commun. ACM,* vol. 36, no. 7, pp. 50–52, 1993.

[17] T. Baudel and M. Baudouin-Lafon, "Charade: Remote control of objects using free-hand gestures," *Commun. ACM,* vol. 36, no. 7, pp. 28–35, 1993.

[18] S. S. Fels and G. E. Hinton, "Glove-Talk: A neural network interface between a Data-Glove and a speech synthesizer," *IEEE Trans. Neural Networks,* vol. 4, pp. 2–8, Jan. 1993.

[19] D. J. Sturman and D. Zeltzer, "A survey of glove-based input," *IEEE Comput. Graph. Applicat. Mag.,* vol. 14, pp. 30–39, Jan. 1994.

[20] D. L. Quam, "Gesture recognition with a DataGlove," in *Proc. 1990 IEEE National Aerospace and Electronics Conf.,* 1990, vol. 2.

[21] C. Wang and D. J. Cannon, "A virtual end-effector pointing system in point-and-direct robotics for inspection of surface flaws using a neural network based skeleton transform," in *Proc. IEEE Int. Conf. Robotics and Automation,* May 1993, vol. 3, pp. 784–789.

[22] B. H. Juang, "Speech recognition in adverse environments," *Comput. Speech Language,* vol. 5, pp. 275–294, 1991.

[23] D. Stork and H.-L. Lu, "Speechreading by Boltzmann zippers," in *Machines that Learn.* Snowbird, UT: 1996.

[24] R. Sharma, T. S. Huang, V. I. Pavlović, Y. Zhao, Z. Lo, S. Chu, K. Schulten, A. Dalke, J. Phillips, M. Zeller, and W. Humphrey, "Speech/gesture interface to a visual computing environment for molecular biologists," in *Proc. Int. Conf. Pattern Recognition,* Aug. 1996, pp. 964–968.

[25] F. Hatfield, E. A. Jenkins, M. W. Jennings, and G. Calhoun, "Principles and guidelines for the design of eye/voice interaction dialogs," in *Proc. 3rd Ann. Symp. Human Interaction with Complex Systems,* Dayton, OH, 1996, pp. 10–19.

[26] T. E. Hutchinson, "Computers that sense eye position on the display," *Computer,* vol. 26, pp. 65–67, July 1993.

[27] R. J. K. Jacob, "What you look at is what you get," *Computer,* vol. 26, pp. 65–67, July 1993.

[28] I. A. Essa and A. P. Pentland, "Coding analysis, interpretation, and recognition of facial expressions," *IEEE Trans. Pattern Anal. Machine Intell.,* vol. 19, no. 7, pp. 757–763, 1997.

[29] D. M. Gavrila and L. S. Davis, "Toward 3-D model-based tracking and recognition of human movement: A multi-view approach," in *Proc. IWAFGR'95,* Zurich, Switzerland, June 1995, pp. 272–277.

[30] C. R. Wren, A. Azarbayejani, T. Darrell, and A. P. Pentland, "Pfinder: Real-time tracking of the human body," *IEEE Trans. Pattern Anal. Machine Intell.,* vol. 19, no. 7, pp. 780–785, 1997.

[31] C. Nodine, H. Kundel, L. Toto, and E. Krupinski, "Recording and analyzing eye-position data using a microcomputer workstation," *Behavior Res. Methods, Instruments Comput.,* vol. 24, no. 3, pp. 475–584, 1992.

[32] C. Lansing and G. W. McConkie, "A new method for speechreading research: Tracking observers' eye movements," *J. Acad. Rehabilitative Audiology,* vol. 28, pp. 25–43, 1994.

[33] V. I. Pavlović, R. Sharma, and T. S. Huang, "Gestural interface to a visual computing environment for molecular biologists," in *Proc. Int. Conf. Automatic Face and Gesture Recognition,* Killington, VT, Oct. 1996, pp. 30–35.

[34] R. Sharma and J. Molineros, "Computer vision-based augmented reality for guiding manual assembly," *Presence: Teleoperators Virtual Environ.,* vol. 6, pp. 292–317, June 1997.

[35] F. K. H. Quek, "Eyes in the interface," *Image Vision Comput.,* vol. 13, Aug. 1995.

[36] R. Sharma, T. S. Huang, and V. I. Pavlović, "A multimodal framework for interacting with virtual environments," in *Human Interaction with Complex Systems,* C. A. Ntuen, E. H. Park, and J. H. Kim, Eds. Norwell, MA: Kluwer, 1996, pp. 53–71.

[37] R. M. Satava and S. B. Jones, "Virtual environments for medical training and education," *Presence: Teleoperators Virtual Environ.,* vol. 6, no. 2, pp. 139–146, 1997.

[38] S. L. Delp, P. Loan, C. Basdogan, and J. M. Rosen, "Surgical simulation: An emerging technology for training in emergency medicine," *Presence: Teleoperators Virtual Environ.,* vol. 6, no. 2, pp. 147–159, 1997.

[39] M. Bergamasco, "Haptic interfaces: The study of force and tactile feedback systems," in *Proc. IEEE Int. Workshop Robot on Robot and Human Communication,* 1995, pp. 15–20.

[40] T. R. Sheridan, *Telerobotics, Automation, and Human Supervisory Control.* Cambridge, MA: MIT Press, 1992.

[41] Z. A. Keirn and J. I. Aunon, "Man-machine communications through brain-wave processing," *IEEE Eng. Med. Biology Mag.,* vol. 9, pp. 55–57, 1990.

[42] D. J. McFarland, G. W. Neat, R. F. Read, and J. R. Wolpaw, "An EEG-based method for graded cursor control," *Psychobiology,* vol. 21, pp. 77–81, 1993.

[43] V. T. Nasman, G. L. Calhoun, and G. R. McMillan, "Brain-actuated control and HMDS," in *Head Mounted Displays,* New York: McGraw-Hill, 1997, pp. 285–312.

[44] W. Putnam and R. B. Knapp, "Real-time computer control using pattern recognition of the electromyogram," in *Proceedings of the Fifteenth Annual International Conference on Engineering in Medicine and Biology Society.* New York: IEEE Press, 1993, vol. 15, pp. 1236–1237.

[45] H. S. Lusted and R. B. Knapp, "Controlling computers with neural signals," *Sci. Amer.,* pp. 82–87, Oct. 1996.

[46] T. Elbert, B. Rockstroh, W. Lutzenberger, and W. Birbaumer, *Self-Regulation of the Brain and Behavior.* New York: Springer-Verlag, 1984.

[47] S. Suryanarayanan and N. R. Reddy, "EMG-based interface for position tracking and control in VR environments and teleoperation," *Presence: Teleoperators Virtual Environ.,* vol. 6, no. 3, pp. 282–291, 1997.

[48] A. M. Junker, J. H. Schnurer, D. F. Ingle, and C. W. Downey, "Loop-closure of the visual cortex response," Armstrong Aerospace Medical Research Laboratory, Wright–Patterson Air Force Base, Dayton, OH, Tech. Rep. AAMRL-TR-88-014, 1988.

[49] D. W. Patmore and R. B. Knapp, "A cursor controller using evoked potentials and EOG," in *Proc. RESNA 18th Ann. Conf.,* 1995, pp. 702–704.

[50] D. McNeill, *Hand and Mind: What Gestures Reveal About Thought.* Chicago, IL: Univ. of Chicago Press, 1992.

[51] J. Streeck, "Gesture as communication I: Its coordination with gaze and speech," *Commun. Monographs,* vol. 60, pp. 275–299, Dec. 1993.

[52] B. V. Dasarathy, "Sensor fusion potential exploitation—Innovative architectures and illustrative approaches," *Proc. IEEE,* vol. 85, pp. 24–38, Jan. 1997.

[53] B. Stein and M. A. Meredith, *The Merging of Senses.* Cambridge, MA: MIT Press, 1993.

[54] T. G. R. Bower, "The evolution of sensory system," in *Perception: Essays in Honor of James J. Gibson,* R. B. MacLeod and H. L. Pick, Jr., Eds. Ithaca, NY: Cornell Univ. Press, 1974, pp. 141–153.

[55] D. Heckerman, "A tutorial on learning with Bayesian networks," Microsoft Corp., Seattle, WA, Tech. Rep. MSR-TR-95-06, Mar. 1995.

[56] P. K. Varshney, *Distributed Detection and Data Fusion.* New York: Springer-Verlag, 1996.

[57] R. G. Brown and P. Y. C. Hwang, *Introduction to Random Signals and Kalman Filtering.* New York: Wiley, 1992.

[58] C. K. Chui and G. Chen, *Kalman Filtering with Real-Time Applications.* Berlin/Heidelberg, Germany: Springer-Verlag, 1991.

[59] K. C. Chou, A. S. Willsky, and A. Benveniste, "Multiscale recursive estimation, data fusion, and regularization," *IEEE Trans. Automat. Contr.,* vol. 39, pp. 464–478, Mar. 1994.

[60] M. I. Jordan and C. M. Bishop, "Neural networks," in *CRC Handbook of Computer Science* A. Tucker, Ed. Boca Raton, FL: CRC Press, 1996.

[61] H. A. Boulard and N. Morgan, *Connectionist Speech Recognition. A Hybrid Approach.* Norwell, MA: Kluwer, 1994.

[62] A. K. Jain, J. Mao, and K. M. Mohiuddin, "Artificial neural networks: A tutorial," *IEEE Computer Mag.,* pp. 31–44, Mar. 1996.

[63] P. J. Werbos, "Generalization of back propagation with applications to a recurrent gas market model," *Neural Networks,* vol. 1, pp. 339–356, 1988.

[64] P. Haffner, M. Franzini, and A. Weibel, "Integrating time alignment and neural networks for high performance continuous speech recognition," in *Proc. IEEE Int. Conf. Acoustics, Speech, and Signal Processing,* Toronto, Ont., Canada, Apr. 1991, pp. 105–108.

[65] U. Meier, W. Hürst, and P. Duchnowski, "Adaptive bimodal sensor fusion for automatic speechreading," in *Proc. IEEE Int. Conf. Acoustics, Speech, and Signal Processing,* 1996.

[66] L. R. Rabiner, "A tutorial on hidden Markov models and selected applications in speech recognition," *Proc. IEEE,* vol. 77, pp. 257–286, Feb. 1989.

[67] T. E. Starner and A. Pentland, "Visual recognition of American sign language using hidden Markov models," in *Proc. Int. Workshop Automatic Face and Gesture Recognition,* Zurich, Switzerland, June 1995, pp. 189–194.

[68] L. W. Campbell, D. A. Becker, A. Azarbayejani, A. F. Bobick, and A. Pentland, "Invariant features for 3-D gesture recognition," in *Proc. Int. Conf. Automatic Face and Gesture Recognition,* Killington, VT, Oct. 1996, pp. 157–162.

[69] D. X. Sun and L. Deng, "Non-stationary hidden Markov models for speech recognition," in *Image Models (and Their Speech Model Cousins),* S. E. Levinson and L. Shepp, Eds. New York: Springer-Verlag, 1996, pp. 161–182.

[70] A. Adjoudani and C. Benoit, "Audio-visual speech recognition compared across two architectures," in *Proc. Eurospeech'95 Conf.*, Madrid, Spain, 1995, vol. 2, pp. 1563–1566.

[71] V. Pavlović, G. Berry, and T. S. Huang, "Integration of audio/visual information for use in human–computer intelligent interaction," in *Proc. IEEE Int. Conf. Image Processing*, Santa Barbara, CA, 1997.

[72] M. E. Hennecke, D. G. Stork, and K. V. Prasad, "Visionary speech: Looking ahead to practical speechreading systems," in *Proc. Speechreading by Man and Machine: Models, Systems and Applications Workshop*, Aug./Sept. 1995.

[73] M. Minsky, "A framework for representing knowledge," in *The Psychology of Computer Vision*, P. H. Winston, Ed. New York: McGraw-Hill, 1975.

[74] F. Lehman, Ed., *Semantic Networks in Artificial Intelligence.* Oxford, England: Pergamon, 1992.

[75] J. Guan and D. A. Bell, *Evidence Theory and its Applications*, vol. 1. Amsterdam, The Netherlands: North-Holland, 1991.

[76] R. A. Bolt, "Put that there: Voice and gesture at the graphics interface," *ACM Comput. Graph.*, vol. 14, no. 3, pp. 262–270, 1980.

[77] M. T. Vo and C. Wood, "Building an application framework for speech and pen input integration in multimodal learning interfaces," in *Proc. IEEE Int. Conf. Acoustics, Speech, and Signal Processing*, 1996, pp. 3545–3548.

[78] R. Kober, U. Harz, and J. Schiffers, "Fusion of visual and acoustic signals for command-word recognition," in *Proc. IEEE Int. Conf. Acoustics, Speech, and Signal Processing*, 1997.

[79] J. M. Bradshaw, "An introduction to software agents," in *Software Agents*, J. M. Bradshaw, Ed. Cambridge, MA: AAAI Press/MIT Press, 1997.

[80] Y. Shoham, "An overview of agent-oriented programming," in *Software Agents*, J. M. Bradshaw, Ed. AAAI Press/MIT Press, 1997.

[81] N. Negroponte, "Agents: From direct manipulation to delegation," in *Software Agents*, J. M. Bradshaw, Ed. AAAI Press/MIT Press, 1997.

[82] D. B. Moran, A. J. Cheyer, L. E. Julia, D. L. Martin, and S. Park, "Multimodal user interface in the open agent architecture," in *Proc. ACM Int. Conf. Intelligent User Interfaces*, Orlando, FL, 1997, pp. 61–68.

[83] J. A. Pittman, I. Smith, P. Cohen, S. Oviatt, and T.-C. Yang, "QuickSet: A multimodal interface for military simulation," in *Proc. 6th Conf. Computer-Generated Forces and Behavioral Representation*, Orlando, FL, 1996, pp. 217–224.

[84] M. Nelson, W. Humphrey, A. Gursoy, A. Dalke, L. Kalé, R. Skeel, K. Schulten, and R. Kufrin, "MDScope—A visual computing environment for structural biology," *Comput. Phys. Commun.*, vol. 91, no. 1/2/3, pp. 111–134, 1995.

[85] P. R. Cohen, M. Johnston, D. McGee, S. Oviatt, and J. Pittman, "QuickSet: Multimodal interaction for simulation set-up and control," in *Proc. 5th Applied Natural Language Processing Meeting*, Washington, DC, 1997.

[86] B. Suhm, P. Geunter, T. Kemp, A. Lavie, L. Mayfield, A. McNair, I. Rogina, T. Schultz, T. Sloboda, W. Ward, M. Woszczyna, and A. Waibel, "Janus: Toward multilingual spoken language translation," in *Proc. ARPA SLT Workshop*, Austin, TX, 1995.

[87] J. Wang, "Integration of eye-gaze, voice and manual response in multimodal user interface," in *Proc. IEEE Int. Conf. Systems, Man, and Cybernetics*, 1995, pp. 3938–3942.

[88] M. Fukumoto, Y. Suenaga, and K. Mase, "'Finger-pointer': Pointing interface by image processing," *Comput. Graph.*, vol. 18, no. 5, pp. 633–642, 1994.

[89] C. Codella, R. Jalili, L. Koved, *et al.*, "Interactive simulation in a multi-person virtual world," in *ACM Conf. Human Factors in Computing Systems (CHI'92)*, pp. 329–334.

[90] P. Maes, T. Darrell, B. Blumberg, and A. Pentland, "The ALIVE system: Wireless, full-body interaction with autonomous agents," *ACM Multimedia Syst.*, 1996.

[91] A. Pentland, "Smart rooms," *Sci. Amer.*, pp. 54–62, Apr. 1996.

[92] MIT Media Laboratory, Perceptual Intelligence Group. [Online]. Available: http://casr.www.media.mit.edu/groups/casr/pentland.html.

[93] N. Tosa. (1996). Neuro-Baby. [Online]. Available: http://www.mic.atr.co.jp/tosa.

[94] M. Kakimoto, N. Tosa, J. Mori, and A. Sanada, "Tool of Neuro-Baby," *Inst. Television Eng. Jpn. Tech. Rep.*, vol. 16, pp. 7–12, June 1992.

Rajeev Sharma (Member, IEEE) received the Ph.D. degree in computer science from the University of Maryland, College Park, in 1993.

For three years, he was with the University of Illinois at Urbana-Champaign as a Beckman Fellow and Adjunct Assistant Professor in the Department of Electrical and Computer Engineering. He currently is an Assistant Professor in the Department of Computer Science and Engineering, Pennsylvania State University, University Park. His research interests lie in studying the role of computer vision in robotics and advanced human–computer interfaces.

Dr. Sharma received the ACM Samuel Alexander Doctoral Dissertation Award, an IBM Pre-Doctoral Fellowship, and an NSF CAREER award.

Vladimir I. Pavlović (Student Member, IEEE) was born in Paris, France, in 1966. He received the Dipl.Eng. degree in electrical engineering from the University of Novi Sad, Yugoslavia, in 1991 and the M.S. degree in electrical engineering and computer science from the University of Illinois at Chicago in 1993. He currently is pursuing the Ph.D. degree in electrical engineering at the Beckman Institute and the Department of Electrical and Computer Engineering, University of Illinois at Urbana-Champaign.

His research interests include vision-based human–computer interaction, multimodal signal fusion, and image coding.

Thomas S. Huang (Fellow, IEEE) received the B.S. degree in electrical engineering from National Taiwan University, Taipei, Taiwan, R.O.C., and the M.S. and Sc.D. degrees in electrical engineering from the Massachusetts Institute of Technology (MIT), Cambridge.

From 1963 to 1973, he was a Member of the Faculty of the Department of Electrical Engineering at MIT. From 1973 to 1980, he was a Member of the Faculty of the School of Electrical Engineering and Director of the Laboratory for Information and Signal Processing at Purdue University, West Lafayette, IN. In 1980, he joined the University of Illinois at Urbana-Champaign, where he is now a William L. Everitt Distinguished Professor of Electrical and Computer Engineering, a Research Professor at the Coordinated Science Laboratory, and Head of the Image Formation and Processing Group at the Beckman Institute for Advanced Science and Technology. During sabbatical leaves, he has worked at the MIT Lincoln Laboratory, the IBM T. J. Watson Research Center, and the Rheinishes Landes Museum in Bonn, West Germany. He was a Visiting Professor with the Swiss Institutes of Technology in Zurich and Lausanne, the University of Hannover in West Germany, INRS-Telecommunications of the University of Quebec, Montreal, Canada, and the University of Tokyo, Japan. He has been a Consultant to numerous industrial firms and government agencies both in the United States and abroad. His professional interests lie in the broad area of information technology, especially the transmission of processing of multidimensional signals. He has published 12 books and more than 300 papers on network theory, digital filtering, image processing, and computer vision. He is a Founding Editor of the *International Journal Computer Vision, Graphics, and Image Processing* and Editor of the Springer Series in Information Sciences published by Springer-Verlag.

Dr. Huang is a Fellow of the International Association of Pattern Recognition and the Optical Society of America. He has received a Guggenheim Fellowship, an A. V. Humboldt Foundation Senior U.S. Scientist Award, and a Fellowship from the Japan Association for the Promotion of Science. He received the IEEE Acoustics, Speech, and Signal Processing Society's Technical Achievement Award in 1987 and the Society Award in 1991.

PROCEEDINGS OF THE IEEE, VOL. 59, NO. 11, NOVEMBER 1971

Image Processing

THOMAS S. HUANG, MEMBER, IEEE, WILLIAM F. SCHREIBER, MEMBER, IEEE, AND
OLEH J. TRETIAK, MEMBER, IEEE

Invited Paper

Abstract—Image processing techniques find applications in many areas, chief among which are image enhancement, pattern recognition, and efficient picture coding. Some aspects of image processing are discussed—specifically: the mathematical operations one is likely to encounter, and ways of implementing them by optics and on digital computers; image description; and image quality evaluation. Many old results are reviewed, some new ones presented, and several open questions are posed.

I. INTRODUCTION

IN A BROAD SENSE, the field of image processing deals with the manipulation of data which are inherently two-dimensional in nature. The techniques of image processing find applications in many areas, notably: image enhancement, pictorial pattern recognition, and the efficient coding of pictures for transmission or storage. The common questions underlying these areas are: 1) How do we describe or characterize images? 2) What mathematical operations do we want to use on the images? 3) How do we implement (in hardware) these mathematical operations? 4) How do we evaluate image quality? In the present paper, we shall attempt to discuss some aspects of these questions.

In Sections II and III, we describe some of the more important mathematical operations one encounters in image processing, and in Sections IV, V, and VI the optical and digital computer implementation of these mathematical operations. Then, in Sections VII and VIII, we discuss briefly the problems of image description and image quality evaluation, respectively. Since many excellent review articles on pattern recognition are available [4], [17], [217], [134], [146], [223], and [100], we shall concentrate on image enhancement and efficient picture coding in our paper.

Although most of the techniques we shall describe have been developed and studied by many researchers both at MIT and elsewhere, the way we shall describe them reflects our own personal biases and the experimental results we shall present are mostly our own. Therefore, the reader should be warned at the outset that this is a highly personal paper.

It is impossible, even in this relatively long paper, to cover all the important aspects of image processing. The reader is referred to the Bibliography at the end of the paper for further study. He may also look forward to reading two related special issues of the PROCEEDINGS in 1972, one on digital picture processing and the other on digital pattern recognition.

II. IMAGE ENHANCEMENT

A. *The Problem*

No imaging system will give images of perfect quality. In image enhancement, we aim to manipulate the image to improve its quality. For example, in aerial reconnaissance (for classifying crops, say)

Manuscript received April 7, 1971; revised August 13, 1971. This work was supported by NIH GMS under Grant 5 P01 GM14940-05. *This invited paper is one of a series planned on topics of general interest—The Editor.*
The authors are with the Department of Electrical Engineering and Research Laboratory of Electronics, Massachusetts Institute of Technology, Cambridge, Mass. 02139.

and in photographing the planets through the atmosphere, the pictures one gets are degraded by atmospheric turbulence, aberration of the optical system, and relative motion between the camera and the object. In the medical area, a prominent example is radiographs which are usually of low resolution and low contrast. Many electron micrographs are distorted by the spherical aberration of the electron lens. In these and many other similar cases, one would like very much to work on the degraded images to improve their quality.

There are two ways of going about image enhancement. The first way might be called *a priori*. Here, we cleverly design our imaging systems to minimize degradations. Examples of *a priori* methods include the use of sensor and feedback servosystems to compensate for camera motion [25], [46], and [128], and the several unconventional methods of combating atmospherical turbulence—the use of holographic techniques [75], [47], the use of a large optical aperture as a multiple-element interferometer [73], [76], and the ingenious method of Gregory where conventional imaging is used but the camera shutter opens intermittently, exposing the film only when "the seeing is good" [81].

The second way of going about image enhancement might be called *a posteriori*. Here we are given images whose quality needs to be improved. We do not have control over how the image is formed.

Since the variety of *a priori* methods is limited only by the imagination of the inventors, one can hardly make general comments about it—except perhaps saying: "be clever." Therefore, our discussion in this section will be concentrated on *a posteriori* methods.

We shall approach the problem of *a posteriori* image enhancement from the point of view of image restoration. A general block diagram of the situation is shown in Fig. 1. We shall concern ourselves mainly with two-dimensional monochromatic images. Such an image can be characterized by a real function of two spatial variables, representing the intensity of the image at a spatial point. We assume that an ideal image $f(x, y)$ would be obtained if our imaging system were perfect. But since our imaging system is not perfect, we get a degraded image $g(x, y)$. The purpose of image restoration is to work on the degraded image to get an improved image $\hat{f}(x, y)$ which is as close to the ideal image $f(x, y)$ as possible according to, e.g., the mean-square error criterion.

B. *A Special Class of Degrading Systems*

In general, the degrading system could be very complex. However, in many cases of practical importance, such as camera motion, atmospheric turbulence, and blurring due to the optical transfer functions of lenses, the degrading systems can be modeled by the block diagram shown in Fig. 2. The ideal image $f(x, y)$ is first acted on by a linear system with impulse response $k(x, y; \alpha, \beta)$:

$$g_1(x, y) = \int\int_{-\infty}^{\infty} k(x, y; \alpha, \beta) f(\alpha, \beta)\, d\alpha d\beta. \tag{1}$$

Then g_1 goes through a nonlinear amnesic (memoryless) system with a transfer characteristic $T(\cdot)$. The output of an amnesic system at any particular spatial point depends only on the corresponding

368

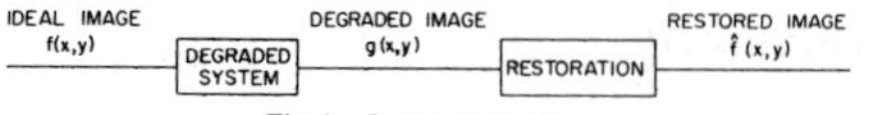

Fig. 1.   Image restoration.

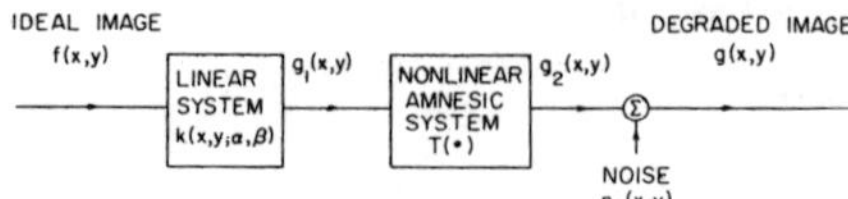

Fig. 2.   A special class of degrading systems.

point of the input but no other points. Therefore,

$$g_2(x_0, y_0) = T(g_1(x_0, y_0)) \tag{2}$$

where (x_0, y_0) is any given spatial point. Finally, a noise $n_2(x, y)$ is added to g_2 to yield the degraded image:

$$g(x, y) = g_2(x, y) + n_2(x, y). \tag{3}$$

The nonlinearity and the noise are usually due to the detector (such as film) in the imaging system.

In some cases, the linear system in Fig. 2 is shift-invariant

$$k(x, y; \alpha, \beta) = h(x - \alpha, y - \beta). \tag{4}$$

Then the superposition integral (1) can be written as a convolution

$$g_1(x, y) = \int\int_{-\infty}^{\infty} h(x - \alpha, y - \beta) f(\alpha, \beta) \, d\alpha d\beta = h \otimes f. \tag{5}$$

A linear system that is not shift-invariant will be called shift-varying.

C. Restoring Images Degraded by Linear Shift-Invariant (LSI) Systems

1) *The Fourier Transform Approach:* Let us assume that we know the transfer characteristic T of our detector and let us assume for the time being that the noise n_2 is negligible. Then by applying T^{-1}, the inverse of T, to the degraded image, we will obtain g_1 (cf., Fig. 2). The remaining task is to recover the ideal image f from g_1. This can be done easily, if the linear system is shift-invariant (LSI), because from (5) we have

$$F(u, v) = \frac{G_1(u, v)}{H(u, v)} \tag{6}$$

where F, G_1, and H are the two-dimensional Fourier transforms of f, g_1, and h, respectively, and u and v are spatial frequencies.

2) *Noise:* In reality, of course, noise is always present. Therefore, after applying T^{-1} to the degraded image g (cf., Fig. 2) we will get

$$p(x, y) = g_1(x, y) + n_1(x, y) = f \otimes h + n_1 \tag{7}$$

where $n_1(x, y)$ is noise. We can still try to estimate $F(u, v)$ by

$$\hat{F}(u, v) = \frac{P(u, v)}{H(u, v)} \tag{8}$$

where P is the Fourier transform of p. However, we will get into trouble where $H(u, v)=0$. One way to remedy this is to modify the right-hand side of (8), replacing $1/H$ by zero in the range of (u, v) over which the noise is larger than the signal [91].

Alternatively, we can find an optimum linear shift-invariant filter which, when acting upon the noisy degraded image $p(x, y)$, will give an estimation of the ideal image f with the least mean-square error. It can be shown [97] that, when f and n_1 are statistically uncorrelated, such an optimum filter has the frequency response

$$Q(u, v) = \frac{H^*(u, v)\Phi_f(u, v)}{|H(u, v)|^2\Phi_f(u, v) + \Phi_n(u, v)} \tag{9}$$

where Φ_f and Φ_n are the power density spectra of the ideal image f and the noise n_1, respectively, and $*$ denotes complex conjugation. And the minimum mean-square error is

$$E_{\min} = \int\int_{-\infty}^{\infty} \frac{\Phi_f(u, v)\Phi_n(u, v)}{|H(u, v)|^2\Phi_f(u, v) + \Phi_n(u, v)} \, du dv. \tag{10}$$

Note that when $n_1 = 0$, $Q = 1/H$, which is the simple inverse filter used in (8). Slepian [202] also solved the least mean-square estimation problem for the case where the degrading impulse response h is stochastic. The optimum filter was found to be again given by (9), except that H^* and $|H|^2$ are replaced by $\overline{H^*}$ and $\overline{|H|^2}$, where the overbars denote ensemble averages.

Experiments with laboratory-simulated degraded imagery indicated that [103], [104] the optimum filter (9) gave much better recovered images than the simple inverse filter used in (8). However, the case of finding good restoration filters is by no means closed. First of all, detector noise is not uncorrelated with the ideal image [164], [106], [61]. Secondly, the filter (9) is optimum only among all linear shift-invariant filters. There certainly may be linear shift-varying and nonlinear filters which perform much better. In searching for good filters for signal-dependent noise, one promising approach seems to be the use of adaptive filters [52a], [170].

3) *Restoration Beyond the Diffraction Limit:* Even in the absence of noise, the estimation (8) gets into trouble when $H(u, v)$ is zero outside a certain range of (u, v).

In the presence of noise, our optimum LSI filter $Q(u, v)$ is given by (9). Note that $Q(u, v)=0$ wherever $H(u, v)=0$. Therefore, by using Q, we cannot hope to recover $F(u, v)$ outside the range of (u, v) where $H(u, v)$ is nonzero.

In reality, all optical imaging systems are limited by diffraction. Therefore, the degrading frequency response $H(u, v)$ will be zero for $(u^2 + v^2) \geq A$ where A is a constant. Is there any hope of restoring image detail beyond the diffraction limit? The answer is a qualified yes. There is a way out if the ideal image $f(x, y)$ is of finite extent; because then $F(u, v)$ is analytic, and once we have determined $F(u, v)$ within a certain range of (u, v), we can use analytic continuation to extend our solution to all (u, v). Harris [90] discussed several practical methods of carrying out the analytic continuation. On a theoretical basis, the method of analytic continuation proposed by Slepian [204] is perhaps most satisfying. It makes use of prolate spheroidal wave functions. We note that the operation of analytic continuation is linear but shift-varying.

The presence of noise introduces severe errors in analytic continuation [228], [48], [66]. In one example [93] it was found that in order to succeed in analytic continuation a noise to signal amplitude ratio of around 1:1000 was required.

4) *Analytic Continuation Using Prolate Spheroidal Wave Functions (PSWF):* We now describe briefly the procedure of doing analytic continuation using PSWF. We first review the properties of PSWF [212], [63], [204], [138], [139], [200], [201], [205] following Slepian and Pollak.

Given $T > 0$ and any $\Omega > 0$, we can find a countably infinite set of real functions $\{\psi_i(t); i = 0, 1, 2, \cdots\}$ and a set of real positive numbers $\lambda_0 > \lambda_1 > \lambda_2 > \cdots$ such that:

1) $\Psi_i(\omega)$, the Fourier transform of $\psi_i(t)$, vanishes for $|\omega| > \Omega$, and $\psi_i(t)$ are orthonormal on the real line, and complete in the class of

1588

PROCEEDINGS OF THE IEEE, NOVEMBER 1971

functions whose Fourier transform vanishes for $|\omega| > \Omega$

$$\int_{-\infty}^{\infty} \psi_i(t)\psi_j(t)dt = \begin{cases} 0, & i \neq j \\ 1, & i = j \end{cases} \qquad i, j = 0, 1, 2, \cdots . \quad (11)$$

2) In the interval $-T/2 \leq t \leq T/2$, $\psi_i(t)$ are orthogonal and complete in the class of all square integrable functions:

$$\int_{-T/2}^{T/2} \psi_i(t)\psi_j(t)dt = \begin{cases} 0, & i \neq j \\ \lambda_i, & i = j \end{cases} \qquad i, j = 0, 1, 2, \cdots . \quad (12)$$

a)
$$\sum_{n=0}^{\infty} \frac{1}{\lambda_n} \psi_n(t)\psi_n(t') = \delta(t - t') \quad (13)$$

where $\delta(t)$ is the unit impulse function.

3) For all values of t, real or complex

$$\lambda_i\psi_i(t) = \int_{-T/2}^{T/2} \frac{\sin \Omega(t - S)}{\pi(t - S)} \psi_i(S)\, dS, \qquad i = 0, 1, 2, \cdots . \quad (14)$$

a)
$$K_n\psi_n(t) = \frac{1}{2\pi} \int_{-\Omega}^{\Omega} e^{j\omega t}\psi_n\left(\frac{\omega T}{2\Omega}\right) d\omega \quad (15)$$

where K_n is a constant depending on n.

4) Both $\psi_i(t)$ and λ_i are functions of $C \equiv \Omega T/2$. Note that the number of independent samples in the interval $-T/2 \leq t \leq T/2$ for a function bandlimited to $(-\Omega, \Omega)$ is $(2/\pi)C$. For a fixed value of C, the λ_i fall off to zero rapidly with increasing i once i has exceeded $(2/\pi)C$.

5)
$$\psi_n(-t) = (-1)^n\psi_n(t). \quad (16)$$

We now come back to our problem of analytic continuation. We assume that a real function $f(x, y)$ satisfies

$$f(x, y) = 0, \qquad \text{for } |x| > A \quad \text{or} \quad |y| > B \quad (17)$$

where A and B are constants. We know the value of $F(u, v)$, the Fourier transform of $f(x, y)$, in $|u| \leq \alpha/2$ and $|v| \leq \beta/2$ where α and β are constants. We want to determine the value of $F(u, v)$ for all u and v. We proceed as follows. Let $\{\psi_i(u); \lambda_i\}$ be the set of PSWF and their corresponding eigenvalues with $T = \alpha$ and $\Omega = A$, and let $\{\phi_j(v); \mu_j\}$ be those with $T = \beta$ and $\Omega = B$. Then from property 1) we can expand $F(u, v)$ in terms of ψ_i and ϕ_j

$$F(u, v) = \sum_{i=0}^{\infty} \sum_{j=0}^{\infty} a_{ij}\psi_i(u)\phi_j(v), \qquad \text{for all } u \text{ and } v. \quad (18)$$

Multiplying both sides of (18) by $\psi_m(u)\phi_n(v)$ and integrating from $u = -\alpha/2$ to $\alpha/2$ and $v = -\beta/2$ to $\beta/2$, and using (12), we get

$$a_{mn} = \frac{1}{\lambda_m\mu_n} \int_{u=-\alpha/2}^{\alpha/2} \int_{v=-\beta/2}^{\beta/2} F(u, v)\psi_m(u)\phi_n(v)\, dudv. \quad (19)$$

Since we know $F(u, v)$ in $|u| \leq \alpha/2$ and $|v| \leq \beta/2$, we can calculate a_{ij} $(i, j = 0, 1, 2, \cdots)$ from (19). Then, substituting the values of a_{ij} into (18), we get $F(u, v)$ for all u and v.

We note that the function $F(u, v)$ is in general complex. However, it is easily shown that both its real and imaginary parts have inverse Fourier transforms that vanish for $|x| > A$ or $|y| > B$. Therefore, (18) is valid with complex coefficients a_{ij}. In fact, since $f(x, y)$ is limited in extent, the real and imaginary parts of $F(u, v)$ are related by the Hilbert transform [84]; so it is necessary to work only with the real or imaginary part.

In practical calculations, (18) has to be truncated:

$$F_{MN}(u, v) = \sum_{i=0}^{M-1} \sum_{j=0}^{N-1} a_{ij}\psi_i(u)\phi_j(v), \qquad \text{for all } u \text{ and } v. \quad (20)$$

The mean-square error due to this truncation is

$$\int\int_{-\infty}^{\infty} |F(u, v) - F_{MN}(u, v)|^2 dudv = \sum_{i=M}^{\infty} \sum_{j=N}^{\infty} |a_{ij}|^2. \quad (21)$$

Also, in practice, we always have noise. Instead of knowing $F(u, v)$ we know only

$$F_C(u, v) = F(u, v) + N(u, v) \quad (22)$$

where $N(u, v)$ is noise. Using F_C instead of F in the integral of (19), we get instead of (18):

$$F_C(u, v) = \sum_{i=0}^{\infty} \sum_{j=0}^{\infty} a'_{ij}\psi_i(u)\phi_j(v), \qquad \text{for all } u \text{ and } v \quad (23a)$$

where

$$a'_{ij} = a_{ij} + n_{ij} \quad (23b)$$

and

$$n_{ij} = \frac{1}{\lambda_i\mu_j} \int_{u=-\alpha/2}^{\alpha/2} \int_{v=-\beta/2}^{\beta/2} N(u, v)\psi_i(u)\phi_j(v)\, dudv. \quad (24)$$

After truncation, we have

$$F_{C,MN}(u, v) = \sum_{i=0}^{M-1} \sum_{j=0}^{N-1} (a'_{ij})\psi_i(u)\phi_j(v), \qquad \text{for all } u \text{ and } v. \quad (25)$$

Therefore, in practice, what we get is $F_{C,MN}(u, v)$. The question is how close is $F_{C,MN}$ to the desired F over all u and v?

The error between $F_{C,MN}$ and F is

$$\varepsilon(u, v) \equiv F - F_{C,MN} = \sum_{i=M}^{\infty} \sum_{j=N}^{\infty} a_{ij}\psi_i(u)\phi_j(v)$$
$$- \sum_{i=0}^{M-1} \sum_{j=0}^{N-1} n_{ij}\psi_i(u)\phi_j(v). \quad (26)$$

The first term at the right-hand side of (26) is the error due to truncation, while the second term is the error due to noise. We denote the second term by

$$N_{MN}(u, v) \equiv \sum_{i=0}^{M-1} \sum_{j=0}^{N-1} n_{ij}\psi_i(u)\phi_j(v), \qquad \text{for all } u \text{ and } v. \quad (27)$$

Then assuming the noise $N(u, v)$ has zero mean and is white, i.e.,

$$\overline{N(u, v)} = 0 \quad (28)$$

$$\overline{N(u_1, v_1)N(u_2, v_2)} = K\delta(u_1 - u_2, v_1 - v_2) \quad (29)$$

where K is a constant and the superbars denote ensemble averages, we get

$$\overline{N_{MN}(u, v)} = 0 \quad (30)$$

$$\overline{N_{MN}^2(u, v)} = K \sum_{i=0}^{M-1} \sum_{j=0}^{N-1} \frac{1}{\lambda_i\mu_j} \psi_i^2(u)\phi_j^2(v), \qquad \text{for all } u \text{ and } v \quad (31)$$

and

$$\int\int_{-\infty}^{\infty} \overline{\varepsilon^2(u, v)}\, dudv = \sum_{i=M}^{\infty} \sum_{j=N}^{\infty} |a_{ij}|^2 + K \sum_{i=0}^{M-1} \sum_{j=0}^{N-1} \frac{1}{\lambda_i\mu_j}. \quad (32)$$

Remembering that λ_i and μ_j decrease with increasing i and j, we see from (32) that while the truncation error decreases with increasing M and N, the error due to noise increases with increasing M and N. Although we have not done any detailed noise analysis, the situation does not seem promising. On the one hand, since the number of independent samples of $F(u, v)$ in $|u| \leq \alpha/2$ and $|v| \leq \beta/2$ is $(A\alpha/\pi)(B\beta/\pi)$, we do not expect to be able to make the truncation error small unless $M \gg A\alpha/\pi$ and $N \gg B\beta/\pi$. On the other hand, when $i > A\alpha/\pi$ and $j > B\beta/\pi$, λ_i and μ_j will decrease rapidly with increasing i and j (property 4), so that the error due to noise will be large.

A more satisfying way to resolve this truncation versus noise problem is as follows. Instead of using a'_{ij} as an estimation for a_{ij} as we did in (23a), we use the least mean-square linear estimation

$$\hat{a}_{ij} = a'_{ij}\left(1 + \frac{\overline{n_{ij}^2}}{\overline{a_{ij}^2}}\right)^{-1}. \tag{33}$$

Then, when i and j are such that the noise power is much greater than the signal power, $\hat{a}_{ij}$ becomes very small, which essentially truncates the infinite series in (23a).

5) *Integral Equation Approach:* Alternatively, we can solve the problem discussed in the preceding section in the spatial domain via the solution of an integral equation [34], [181], [216]. Let

$$F_T(u, v) = F(u, v)W(u, v) \tag{34}$$

where

$$W(u, v) = \begin{cases} 1, & \text{for } |u| \leq \frac{\alpha}{2}, \text{ and } |v| \leq \frac{\beta}{2} \\ 0, & \text{elsewhere.} \end{cases} \tag{35}$$

The problem is: Given $F_T(u, v)$, find $F(u, v)$ for all u and v. Taking the inverse Fourier transform of both sides of (34), we get

$$\begin{aligned} f_T(x, y) &= f(x, y) \otimes w(x, y) \\ &= \int_{\zeta=-A}^{A} \int_{\eta=-B}^{B} f(\zeta, \eta)w(x - \zeta, y - \eta)\, d\zeta d\eta \end{aligned} \tag{36}$$

where f_T, f, and w are the inverse Fourier transforms of F_T, F, and W, respectively, and as before, we assume $f(x, y) = 0$ for $|x| > A$ or $|y| > B$. The inverse Fourier transform of $W(u, v)$ is

$$w(x, y) = \frac{\sin(x\alpha/2)}{\pi x} \cdot \frac{\sin(y\beta/2)}{\pi y}. \tag{37}$$

In the spatial domain, our problem becomes: Given $f_T(x, y)$, find $f(x, y)$. That is, we want to solve the integral equation (36).

From property 3) of the preceding section, we know that the eigenfunctions and eigenvalues for the kernel $w(x, y)$ are $\{\Psi_i(x)\Phi_j(y); i, j = 0, 1, 2, \cdots\}$, where $\{\Psi_i(x); \lambda'_i\}$ are PSWF with $\Omega = \alpha/2$ and $T = 2A$, and $\{\Phi_j(y); \mu'_j\}$ those with $\Omega = \beta/2$ and $T = 2B$. Expanding $f(x, y)$ in terms of the eigenfunctions

$$f(x, y) = \sum_{i=0}^{\infty} \sum_{j=0}^{\infty} b_{ij}\Psi_i(x)\Phi_j(y), \quad \text{for } |x| \leq A \text{ and } |y| \leq B. \tag{38}$$

Substituting in (36) and using (14),

$$f_T(x, y) = \sum_{i=0}^{\infty} \sum_{j=0}^{\infty} b_{ij}\lambda'_i\mu'_j\Psi_i(x)\Phi_j(y), \quad \text{for } |x| \leq A \text{ and } |y| \leq B. \tag{39}$$

Multiplying both sides by $\Psi_m(x)\Phi_n(y)$ and integrating from $x = -A$ to A and from $y = -B$ to B, we get

$$b_{mn} = \frac{1}{\lambda'_m\mu'_n}\int_{x=-A}^{A} \int_{y=-B}^{B} f_T(x, y)\Psi_m(x)\Phi_n(y)\, dxdy. \tag{40}$$

To summarize, the procedure is to first calculate b_{mn} from (40) and then substitute them into (38) to get $f(x, y)$. Of course, in practice, we again have errors due to truncation and noise.

6) *Boundary Conditions:* In deriving the optimum filter $Q(u, v)$ given in (9), it was assumed tacitly that we had the degraded image $p(x, y)$ of (7) available for all (x, y). In reality, we will have only a finite piece of it. For example, we may know $p(x, y)$ only in the region $R = \{|x| \leq A/2 \text{ and } |y| \leq B/2\}$, where A and B are constants. Let

$$p_r(x, y) = \begin{cases} p(x, y), & \text{in } R = \left\{|x| \leq \dfrac{A}{2} \text{ and } |y| \leq \dfrac{B}{2}\right\} \\ 0, & \text{elsewhere.} \end{cases} \tag{41}$$

Then what we can do is to apply our optimum inverse filter to p_r to get $p_r(x, y) \otimes q(x, y)$, where $q(x, y)$ is the inverse Fourier transform of $Q(u, v)$. Under what conditions will $p_r \otimes q$ equal $p \otimes q$ which is our desired result? They will be equal if the original image $f(x, y)$ consists of a small object lying in a uniform background (assuming that the object lies in R). If the original image $f(x, y)$ is not uniform outside R, things will still be all right if the extent of $q(x, y)$ is small compared with the size of R, i.e., if

$$q(x, y) \simeq 0, \quad \text{for } (x^2 + y^2) \geq D$$

where D is a constant, and $D \ll A, B$.

Then

$$p_r \otimes q \simeq p \otimes q, \quad \text{for } |x| \leq \frac{A - D}{2} \text{ and } |y| \leq \frac{B - D}{2}.$$

What can we do if the original image $f(x, y)$ is not uniform outside the region R and if the extent of $q(x, y)$, the impulse response of the inverse filter, is not small compared to the size of R? The answer is that under certain conditions, we do have a way out via analytic continuation. If either the original image $f(x, y)$ or the impulse response $h(x, y)$ of the degrading system is bandlimited, i.e., if either $F(u, v)$ or $H(u, v)$ is zero for $(u^2 + v^2) \geq K$ where K is a constant, then $f \otimes h$ will be an analytic function. Neglecting the noise n_1 in (7), we can say that $p(x, y)$ is analytic. Therefore, we can use analytic continuation to extend $p_r(x, y)$ to outside of R and thereby obtain $p(x, y)$ for all (x, y). Then we can apply the optimum inverse filter q to $p(x, y)$. In this way, we can recover $f(x, y)$ not only in R but in fact for all (x, y) [175], [176]. Again, the inevitable noise will be the limiting factor of this procedure.

7) *Linear Motion Degradation:* In the preceding sections, we discussed in general terms the restoration of images degraded by LSI systems. For any particular type of degradation, special methods may be available. A case in point is linear motion-degraded images, which were studied by various researchers [203], [92], [214].

8) *Other Approaches:* In the preceding sections we have discussed the Fourier transform approach of solving the integral equation (7). Several other approaches are worth noting.

Jansson [121], [120], [122], proposed an iterative method of solving (7), which can best be implemented digitally. A similar approach was used by Shaw [197]. In a method due to MacAdam [151], the digitized version of (7) was first transformed into a one-dimensional form, and then the inverse filtering or deconvolution was done by essentially dividing the Z transform (in polynomial form) corresponding to p by that corresponding to h. MacAdam developed an algorithm which could do the deconvolution with the constraint that the values of the samples of p, f, and h lie in prescribed ranges. The major disadvantage of these methods is that when the image to be restored contains a large number of resolvable points, the computation time may become unreasonably long.

It is interesting to mention the alternative formulation of the restoration problem by Smith [207]. He studied the problem of determining LSI filter $r(x, y)$ which would minimize the "width" of $r \otimes h$ (where h is the degrading filter) under the condition that the signal-to-noise ratio in $p \otimes h \otimes r$ is kept constant. In general, no closed-form solution can be found. However, Smith's numerical example indicates that the filter $r(x, y)$ has the same characteristics as the optimum inverse filter $q(x, y)$ of (9).

9) Multiframe Processing: In some applications, we have available to us several pictures of the same object degraded by different LSI systems. This is the case, e.g., when we take a sequence of short-exposure pictures of a relatively stationary object through a turbulent medium such as the atmosphere. Let us assume that the exposure time of each picture is short so that the turbulent medium is "frozen" for each frame, and let us assume that the object remains unchanged during our picture taking. Then the degraded images will be (if we neglect detector noise)

$$p_i(x, y) = f(x, y) \otimes h_i(x, y), \qquad i = 1, 2, \cdots, M \qquad (42)$$

where $f(x, y)$ is the ideal image, and $h_i(x, y)$ the impulse response of the turbulent medium at the instant of time when the ith picture was taken. It should be mentioned here that generally a turbulent medium can be modeled better by a linear shift-varying (LSV) system. However, under certain conditions (e.g., when the turbulent medium is very close to the entrance pupil of the camera and very far away from the object, and the object is small—this is the case when we take telescopic pictures of a planet or an artificial satellite from the earth), the LSI model is a reasonable approximation.

The impulse responses $h_i(x, y)$ are random in nature and can be considered as noise in (42). This noise, rather than added to the signal f, is convolved with it. However, we can change the situation to the more familiar additive one, by taking the Fourier transform of both sides of (42) and then taking the logarithm [165]. We get

$$\log P_i(u, v) = \log F(u, v) + \log H_i(u, v), \qquad i = 1, 2, \cdots, M \qquad (43)$$

where P_i, F, and H_i are the Fourier transforms of p_i, f, and h_i, respectively.

Now we can apply to (43) any techniques of statistical estimation which are appropriate for additive noise. In particular, we can sum both sides of (43) over i,

$$\sum_{i=1}^{M} \log P_i(u, v) = M \log F(u, v) + \sum_{i=1}^{M} \log H_i(u, v). \qquad (44)$$

We expect that the summation at the right-hand side of (44) is almost a constant (K, say) for a reasonably large M. Therefore,

$$F(u, v) \simeq \left[\prod_{i=1}^{M} P_i(u, v) \right]^{1/M} e^{-K/M}. \qquad (45)$$

Therefore, except for a multiplicative constant, we can estimate $F(u, v)$ by

$$\hat{F}(u, v) = \left[\prod_{i=1}^{M} P_i(u, v) \right]^{1/M} \qquad (46)$$

or

$$|\hat{F}(u, v)| = \left[\prod_{i=1}^{M} |P_i(u, v)| \right]^{1/M} \qquad (47a)$$

and

$$\angle \hat{F}(u, v) = \frac{1}{M} \sum_{i=1}^{M} \angle P_i(u, v) \qquad (47b)$$

where we have used $\angle Z$ to denote the phase angle of the complex number Z.

In a slightly different approach, Harris [89] argued that atmo-spheric turbulence could only decrease the magnitude of each spatial frequency component of the object. Therefore, for each pair of values $u = u_0$ and $v = v_0$, he used the estimation

$$|\hat{F}(u_0, v_0)| = \max_i |P_i(u_0, v_0)|. \qquad (48)$$

For the phase angle, (47b) was used. Laboratory simulation indicated that Harris' method worked quite well.

A more elaborate discussion on statistical estimation was given by Kennedy [131]. Also Moldon [159] suggested a method of estimating $F(u, v)$ by taking a large number of independent measurements of the short-term mutual coherence function at the entrance pupil of the imaging system and then averaging the results appropriately.

D. Determining the Characteristics of LSI Degrading Systems

In Section II-C, we discussed the restoration of images degraded by LSI systems, assuming that we know the impulse response $h(x, y)$, of the degrading system. We now ask the question: How do we determine $h(x, y)$? Some comments on terminology are in order. The impulse response $h(x, y)$ of an optical system is usually referred to as its point spread function (PSF); the Fourier transform $H(u, v)$ its optical transfer function (OTF). The magnitude of the OTF is called the modulation transfer function (MTF). The response of an optical system to a sharp line (i.e., an impulse sheet) is called its line spread function (LSF). When the system is linear shift-varying (LSV), the PSF still makes sense, but the OTF does not. The shape of the PSF of an LSV system will, of course, vary with the position of the input point.

1) Measurement of Degrading System: In some cases, the degrading system is available to us. For example, we may have the camera-film system which we used to get our pictures. Then, we can simply measure either the PSF or the OTF of the lens and film [68], [227], [209], It should be mentioned that some of the degrading effects of lens and film are LSV and nonlinear. However, if we have the degrading system available to us, we can try to measure the LSV and nonlinear characteristics as well. One prominent example was the work carried out at the Jet Propulsion Laboratory in connection with the Ranger and Mariner pictures of the moon and Mars [161]. Extensive measurements were made on the vidicon camera system before the satellite was launched. Later, the received pictures were enhanced superbly using these measured characteristics.

In many other cases, however, either the degrading system is not available to us or it is time-varying (e.g., atmospheric turbulence). Then we have to think of other ways of estimating its characteristics.

2) Theoretical Analysis: By postulating a reasonal model for an LSI degrading system, we can often calculate theoretically its PSF or OTF. For example, a defocused lens, from a geometrical-optics point of view, can be thought of as having a PSF which is constant and nonzero in a circular disk and zero elsewhere. A more accurate calculation would involve the effect of diffraction [73], [74]. It can be shown that [101], [102], [211] when the defocusing is large, the geometrical OTF agrees well with the diffraction OTF for low spatial frequencies.

The PSF due to lens aberration can also be calculated theoretically [158], [42], [33], [177]. However, except for spherical aberrations (which can be approximated by an LSI system) the other abberrations are definitely LSV. For third-order spherical aberration, the PSF is approximately

$$h(x, y) = \begin{cases} \dfrac{1}{12\pi B^{2/3} d^2} (x^2 + y^2)^{-2/3}, & \text{for } \sqrt{x^2 + y^2} \le BR^3 \\ 0, & \text{for } \sqrt{x^2 + y^2} > BR^3 \end{cases} \qquad (49)$$

where d is the distance between the object and the exit pupil, R the radius of the exit pupil, and B the spherical aberration coefficient. We have adopted the convention here that the spatial coordinates in the image plane are scaled by a factor M (the lateral magnification) so that the imaging system can be considered as an LSI system.

The calculation of the PSF due to a relative translational motion between the object and the camera during exposure has been done by many researchers [177], [190], [166], [207b]. Let the motion be described by

$$x = a(t)$$
$$y = b(t) \tag{50}$$

where $a(t)$ and $b(t)$ are functions of the time variable t. Then the PSF is

$$h(x, y) = \int_{-T/2}^{+T/2} \delta(x - a(t), y - b(t))\, dt \tag{51a}$$

where we have assumed $(-T/2, T/2)$ to be the exposure time interval. The corresponding OTF is

$$H(u, v) = \int_{-T/2}^{T/2} \exp\left(-j[ua(t) + vb(t)]\right) dt. \tag{51b}$$

For example, if the motion is linear and uniform (along the x direction, say)

$$x = kt$$
$$y = 0 \tag{52}$$

where k is a constant, we have

$$H(u, v) = T\, \frac{\sin (kuT/2)}{kuT/2}. \tag{53}$$

If the motion is simple harmonic (along the x direction, say) with a period equal to T,

$$x = A \cos \frac{2\pi}{T}\, t$$
$$y = 0 \tag{54}$$

where A is a constant, the OTF is

$$H(u, v) = J_0(Au) \tag{55}$$

where J_0 is the Bessel function of the zeroth order.

Several researchers have considered the effects on motion OTF by camera shutter operation [167], [98], [191] and by the exponentially-decaying response of some detectors [145].

The OTF due to atmospheric turbulence was calculated by Hufnagel and Stanley, and Fried [117], [116], [64], [65], [150]. For long exposure time (~ 100 ms), the OTF of the optical system together with atmospheric turbulence is

$$H(u, v) = H_{\text{op}}(u, v) \exp\left\{-K(u^2 + v^2)^{5/6}\right\} \tag{56}$$

where $H_{\text{op}}(u, v)$ is the OTF of the optical system in the absence of atmospheric turbulence, and K a constant. For short exposure time (~ 1 ms), the PSF and the OTF of atmospheric turbulence look random. The ensemble average of the OTF (after elimination of linear phase factors) is

$$\overline{H(u, v)} = H_{\text{op}}(u, v) \exp\left\{-K(u^2 + v^2)^{5/6}\left[1 - \left(\frac{u^2 + v^2}{f^2}\right)^{1/6}\right]\right\} \tag{57}$$

under near field conditions $(D \gg (L\lambda)^{\frac{1}{2}}$, where D is the diameter of the entrance pupil of the optical system, L the length of propagation path through the turbulent medium, and λ the wavelength of Light), where f is the cutoff frequency of the optical system. Under far-field conditions $(D \ll (L\lambda)^{\frac{1}{2}})$, the ensemble average becomes

$$\overline{H(u, v)} = H_{\text{op}}(u, v) \exp\left\{-K(u^2 + v^2)^{5/6}\left[1 - \frac{1}{2}\left(\frac{u^2 + v^2}{f^2}\right)^{1/6}\right]\right\}. \tag{58}$$

We note from (56)–(58) that at spatial frequencies close to the cutoff frequency of the optical system, the long exposure OTF is considerably smaller than the short-exposure average. Therefore, short-exposure pictures are preferred to a long-exposure one.

We mention in passing that the atmosphere, in addition to being turbulent, also scatters and absorbs light. These latter effects cause a decrease in image contrast [86], [43], [123].

3) Edge Analysis: If we have reason to believe that the original scene contains a sharp point, then the image of that point gives us the PSF or impulse response of the imaging system. For example, in a picture of Jupiter and its satellites, we can consider the image of one of the satellites as the degrading impulse response and devise a corresponding inverse filter to improve the quality of the Jupiter image.

Usually, the original scene will probably not contain any sharp points. However, it is quite likely that it contains sharp edges. If the degrading system is circularly symmetric, then it is well known that we can derive the impulse response from an edge response [41]. It is less well known but nonetheless true that if the degrading system is not circularly symmetric, we can still estimate the impulse response, if we know the responses of edges in many different directions. This latter problem turns out to be mathematically equivalent to the problem of reconstructing three-dimensional structures from two-dimensional projections [58], [220].

Let $h(x, y)$ be the PSF or impulse response of the degrading system, and let $g(y)$ be the response of the system due to an input $\delta(y)$ which is an impulse sheet on the x axis representing a line input. We have used $\delta(\cdot)$ to denote the Dirac delta function. Then it is readily shown that the OTF, which is the two-dimensional Fourier transform of $h(x, y)$, and the one-dimensional Fourier transform of $g(y)$ are related by

$$H(0, v) = G(v). \tag{59}$$

Since the choice of the directions of the x and y axes is really arbitrary, we conclude that the one-dimensional Fourier transform of the response of the system due to an input line at an angle θ from the x axis is equal to the OTF evaluated along a line passing through the origin and at an angle θ from the v axis. Therefore, we can get the OTF of a system, if we know the responses of the system due to input lines at all directions. We note finally that the line response is the derivation of the edge response.

One major obstacle in this method of estimating the impulse response is the film grain noise in the degraded image. The effects of noise on the determination of the line spread function (and its one-dimensional Fourier transform) from measured edge traces, and various methods of smoothing the noise have been studied by numerous researchers [125]–[127], [35], [230], [38], [39], [159], [180], [87].

4) Image Segmentation: The method of estimating the OTF of LSI degrading systems which we are going to describe now was inspired by the very interesting work done by Prof. Stockham, Jr., Computer Science Department, University of Utah, on the restoration of old Caruso recordings. The mathematics is quite similar to the multiframe processing scheme we discussed in Section II-C4-1).

Suppose we divide the original into M regions (all identical in size) and denote the light intensity distribution in region i by $f_i(x, y)$; $i = 1, 2, \cdots, M$; where (x, y) are spatial coordinates. Let $p_i(x, y)$; $i = 1, 2, \cdots, M$; be the light intensity distributions of the corresponding regions in the degraded image. Assuming the extent of the de-

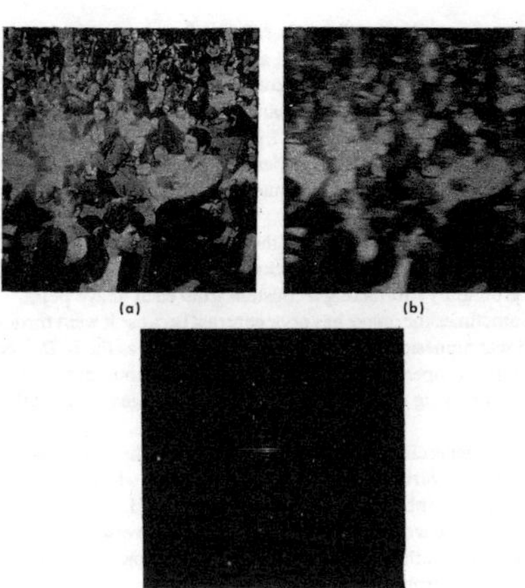

Fig. 3. (a) Original scene, digitized to 256 × 256 samples, with 256 brightness levels per sample. (b) Degraded image, obtained from the original scene by smearing (16-point average) in the horizontal direction. (c) Estimated impulse response of the degrading system. The intensity of the display is proportional to the magnitude of the impulse response.

grading impulse response $h(x, y)$ is small compared to that of each region of the image, we have, except for edge effects,

$$p_i(x, y) = f_i(x, y) \otimes h(x, y), \qquad i = 1, 2, \cdots, M \tag{60}$$

where $\otimes$ denotes convolution. Taking the Fourier transform of both sides of (60), we get

$$P_i(u, v) = F_i(u, v) \, H(u, v), \qquad i = 1, 2, \cdots, M \tag{61}$$

where we have used capital letters to denote the Fourier transforms. Taking the product over i, we get

$$\prod_{i=1}^{M} P_i(u, v) = \left[\prod_{i=1}^{M} F_i(u, v) \right] H^M(u, v)$$

or

$$H(u, v) = \left[\prod_{i=1}^{M} P_i(u, v) \right]^{1/M} \Big/ \left[\prod_{i=1}^{M} F_i(u, v) \right]^{1/M}. \tag{62}$$

If the light distributions in the M regions of the original scene vary sufficiently fast and are sufficiently different from one another, then we expect that the denominator at the right-hand side of (62) is approximately a constant (i.e., independent of u and v). Therefore, we can estimate $H(u, v)$ and hence $h(x, y)$ from $P_i(u, v)$ which we can calculate from the degraded image.

In most cases we shall encounter, it is probably reasonable to assume that the phase angle of $(\prod_{i=1}^{M} F_i)^{1/M}$ is approximately constant. However, in most images, the magnitude of $(\prod_{i=1}^{M} F_i)^{1/M}$ will not be constant. Therefore, we have to guess at the form of $|(\prod_{i=1}^{M} F_i)^{1/M}|$ in order to obtain an estimate of H.

We have done some preliminary investigations on this method of estimating impulse responses on a digital computer [62]. A fast-varying picture [Fig. 3(a)] was taken as the original. We degraded this picture in the computer by smearing it in the horizontal direction. Each point of the degraded image [Fig. 3(b)] was the average of 16 points in the original. The impulse response of the degrading

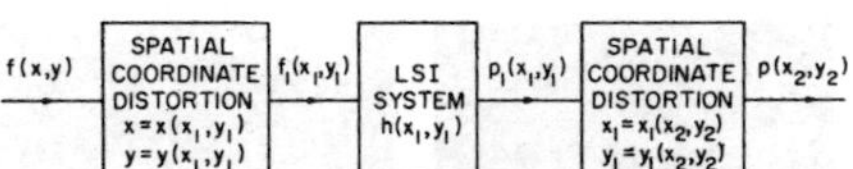

Fig. 4. A special class of LSV systems.

system was then estimated from the degraded image by using (62), assuming that the denominator was a constant. The image was divided into 16 regions, each containing 64 × 64 points. The result is shown in Fig. 3(c), which is rather close to the actual impulse response.

We are currently looking into ways of improving this method of estimating impulse responses, in particular, by being more careful in handling the phase angles of P_i and by applying results of statistical estimation theory.

E. Linear Shift-Varying (LSV) Degrading Systems

As mentioned earlier, some degrading systems (e.g., lens aberrations) can be modeled by the block diagram in Fig. 2 with the linear system shift-varying. Some aspects of shift-varying image formation were discussed by Cutrona [55], and Lohmann and Paris [148]. The output $p(x, y)$ and the input $f(x, y)$ of an LSV system are related by a superposition integral

$$p(x, y) = \int \int_{-\infty}^{\infty} k(x, y; \alpha, \beta) f(\alpha, \beta) \, d\alpha \, d\beta \tag{63}$$

where $k(x, y; \alpha, \beta)$ equals the output at (x, y) due to an input impulse at (α, β). The restoration problem is: Find $f(x, y)$ from given $p(x, y)$ and $k(x, y; \alpha, \beta)$. That is we want to solve the linear integral equation (63).

Equation (63) can be solved if we can find a complete set of eigenfunctions for the kernel $k(x, y; \alpha, \beta)$. Unfortunately, in most cases of interest, we simply do not know how to find the eigenfunctions; we do not even know whether they exist. In theory, we can always find an approximate solution to (63) by brute force.

We digitize the equation to get a set of linear algebraic equations which we then solve for the samples of $f(x, y)$. However, in practice, the number of samples we have to take in an image is so large that the roundoff errors in calculation and the inherent noise (due to detector) in the degraded image (which we neglected in (63)) will swamp the numerical process.

1) *Piecewise—LSI Approach*: If the impulse response $k(x, y; \alpha, \beta)$ of an LSV system varies relatively slowly with the position (α, β) of the input impulse, then we can divide the input image into pieces and in each of these pieces approximate the LSV system by an LSI system. Then, in each piece we can use LSI inversion techniques. The question of how many pieces we shall cut the image into was discussed by Granger [79]. The mathematical theory behind the inversion of piecewise LSI systems (which involves Wiener-Hopf techniques) was studied by Robbins [178].

2) *A Special Class of LSV Systems*: In several cases of practical interest, the LSV systems belong to a special class depicted in Fig. 4. First, the input spatial coordinates are distorted according to

$$\begin{cases} x = x(x_1, y_1) \\ y = y(x_1, y_1) \end{cases} \tag{64}$$

so that the ideal image $f(x, y)$ becomes

$$f_1(x_1, y_1) = f(x(x_1, y_1), y(x_1, y_1)). \tag{65}$$

Then $f_1(x_1, y_1)$ is degraded by an LSI system with impulse response $h(x_1, y_1)$, yielding $p_1(x_1, y_1)$. Finally, the output spatial coordinates

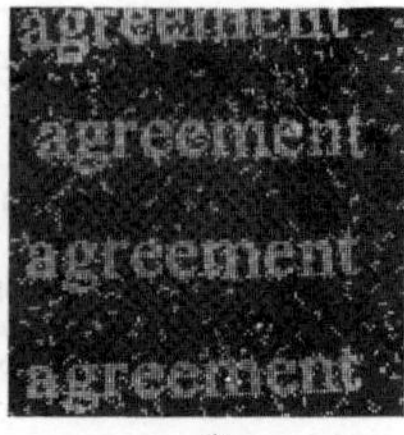

(a) (b)

Fig. 5. Nonlinear noise reduction. (a) Noisy image. (b) Noise reduced.

are distorted according to

$$\begin{cases} x_1 = x_1(x_2, y_2) \\ y_1 = y_1(x_2, y_2) \end{cases} \tag{66}$$

yielding the final degraded image

$$p(x_2, y_2) = p_1(x_1(x_2, y_2), y_1(x_2, y_2)). \tag{67}$$

It should be obvious that if (64) and (66) have unique inverses, then the inversion of the special class of LSV systems depicted in Fig. 4 can be reduced to that of LSI systems.

One prominent example of an LSV degrading system that falls in this special class is the third-order coma aberration of a spherical lens [178]. Details on inverting the coma aberration are contained in a paper by Robbins and Huang in a forthcoming issue of the PROCEEDINGS on digital picture processing (July, 1972).

We note in passing that geometrical distortion [161], [36] can be considered as a special case of the class of LSV system depicted in Fig. 4—the case when only the first block is operating.

F. Nonlinear Processing

We have discussed so far mainly *linear* techniques of restoring linearly degraded images. It goes without saying that when the degrading system is nonlinear, it is natural to use nonlinear inverse filters. However, even when the degrading system is linear, nonlinear techniques are potentially more powerful. A general discussion on the use of optimum nonlinear filters in image restoration was given by Frieden [67].

1) Elimination of Interference: If we know the exact form of the interference, we can subtract it out from the image (on a digital computer, for instance). The most common type of interference in electrooptical imaging is sine-wave interference. In order to subtract a sine-wave interference out, we have to know both its amplitude and its phase. If the phase is not known, we can use a notch filter to eliminate the particular frequency component corresponding to the interfering sinewave [161]. It is important that this notch filter should have a linear phase so that it will not distort the image.

2) Noise Reduction: We give several examples of the use of nonlinear techniques in reducing noise in an image. Fig. 5(a) shows a noisy image which arose from a particular digital coding scheme for efficient picture transmission [113]. The image here has only two levels of intensity—each point is either white or black. The noise consists of white points spreading randomly over the image. We can reduce the noise by eliminating (i.e., changing to black) isolated small groups of white points. For example, when we eliminate in Fig. 5(a) all isolated white-point groups of size less than 3 points, the picture in Fig. 5(b) was obtained.

Graham [78] devised a nonlinear scheme for reducing random noise in continuous-tone images. Essentially, he considered any

image point which is sufficiently different from its neighbors a noise point, and replaced it by a local average. The scheme was tried on television pictures with some success.

The optimum least-mean square LSI filter for noise reduction can be obtained by setting $H(u, v) = 1$ in (9). Bose [40] developed a procedure for obtaining optimum (least mean-square) nonlinear shift-invariant filters. However, because of its complexity, one is yet to see it applied to images.

3) Contrast Enhancement: If the contrast of an image is poor because of an excessive uniform background, we can remove part of the background by subtracting a constant from each image point.

Sometimes the image has poor contrast because it went through a nonlinear amnesic shift-invariant operator, such as the *H-D* curve of a film. If this operator has an inverse, then we can improve the contrast by applying the inverse operator to the image on a digital computer.

More generally, the image may have gone through a nonlinear amnesic shift-variant operator. Such is the case when we use a television camera tube which has a nonuniform field. Then each image point has to be treated with its own particular inverse operator. This was done by Nathan [161] on Moon and Mars pictures transmitted back to earth from satellites.

4) Crispening: Oftentimes we want to make an image appear sharper. One way to do this is to pass the image through a two-dimensional high-pass filter and thereby emphasize the high-frequency components of the image. Since noise is always present in an image, we have to be careful not to emphasize in the frequency range where the noise is larger than the signal.

Stockham [165] has shown experimentally that one can crispen much better if one compresses the dynamic range of the image logarithmically before the high-pass filter and then expands it exponentially afterwards. This can be explained heuristically by noting that the brightness of an image is approximately the product of the illumination $I(x, y)$ and the reflectance of the object $R(x, y)$. Taking the logarithm makes the two factors additive.

$$\log IR = \log I + \log R. \tag{68}$$

Therefore, the details of the object can be crispened more or less independently of the illumination.

An example of crispening using this technique is shown in Fig. 6. For computational convenience, we replaced the logarithm by the square root function (which has similar characteristics). The square root of the original image in Fig. 6(a) is shown in Fig. 6(b) which has a Fourier transform whose magnitude is displayed in Fig. 6(c). A high-pass filter was applied to the image in Fig. 6(b) to get the image shown in Fig. 6(e), the magnitude of whose Fourier transform is displayed in Fig. 6(d). Finally, the image in Fig. 6(e) was squared to get the enhanced image shown in Fig. 6(f).

III. Efficient Picture Coding

A. The Problem

The transmission of images finds applications in many diverse fields, such as picturephone, computer–computer and man–computer communications, and remote sensing (in space exploration, reconnaisance, biomedical engineering, and other areas). In still other cases, although image transmission to a remote location is not required, one does need to store the images for future retrieval and analysis. Some examples are the filing and storage of engineering drawings, finger prints, and library books and journals.

The trend in image transmission and storage is to use digital instead of analog techniques. This is because of the many inherent advantages of digital communication systems [144] in the case of transmission, and the flexibility and ubiquity of digital computers in

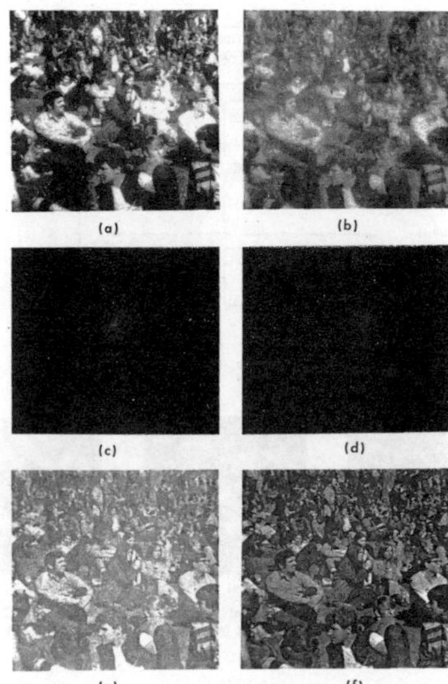

Fig. 6. Image crispening. (a) Original image $f(x, y)$. (b) $\sqrt{f(x, y)}$. (c) Magnitude of the Fourier transform of $\sqrt{f(x, y)}$. (d) Magnitude of the Fourier transform of $\sqrt{f}$ multiplied by the frequency response of a high-pass filter. (e) $\sqrt{f(x, y)}$ high-passed. (f) Square of the high-passed $\sqrt{f}$.

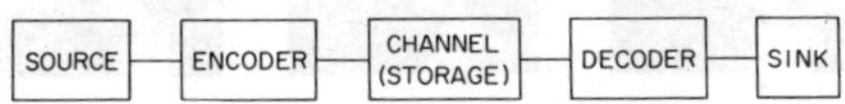

Fig. 7.   A general block diagram for a transmission (storage) system.

the case of storage. In both cases, one major advantage of digital over analog techniques is that the errors are much easier to control for the former.

Since images generally contain a large amount of information, a common problem one encounters in the digital transmission and storage of images is that the required channel or storage capacity is often excessive. It is desirable and sometimes mandatory to find ways to reduce this capacity requirement. The reason that this capacity reduction is possible is twofold. First, there is statistical redundancy in images: image points which are spatially close to each other tend to have nearly equal brightness levels. Secondly, there is psychovisual redundancy in images: one can intentionally destroy some of the information contained in an image without causing a loss in its subjective quality. Many schemes have been devised in which some of the statistical and psychovisual redundancies of images are removed to reduce the channel (storage) capacity requirement [226].

1) *Rate-Distortion Theory:* A general block diagram for a signal transmission (storage) system is shown in Fig. 7. The source puts out signals, which in our case are images. The signals are transferred to the sink, in our case a human observer, via the channel or storage. The encoder transforms the source images into a form suitable for the channel or storage, and the decoder transforms the output from the channel or storage into a form suitable for the human observer. The problem a system engineer has at his hands is to optimize this system: Given a source, a sink, and a fidelity criterion or distortion

measure for picture quality, how do we design the encoder and decoder so that the channel (storage) capacity requirement is a minimum? Alternately: Given a source, a sink, and a channel (storage), how do we design the encoder and decoder so that the quality of the image reaching the sink is maximized?

The ideal mathematical framework for our optimization problem is Shannon's rate-distortion theory [196], [27]. The main result of this theory states that: For a given source and a given fidelity criterion or distortion measure D, there exists a function $R(D)$, called the rate of the source, such that we can transfer our signal to the sink with a distortion as close to D as we wish as long as the channel (storage) capacity C is larger than $R(D)$, and this is impossible if $C < R$.

There are, however, considerable difficulties in trying to apply the rate-distortion theory to practical problems. First, in order to calculate the rate R, we need to have a realistic mathematical model (in statistical terms) of the source and a mathematical expression of the distortion measure D which agrees reasonably well with subjective judgment. Both of these are yet to be found. Second, even if we should find a realistic source model and a good distortion measure, they would probably be so complicated that we would have great difficulty in calculating the rate R analytically. Third, the rate-distortion theory tells us only what is the best we can do; it does not tell us in detail how to do it.

If mean-squared error is used as a fidelity measure, and if the image is modeled as a Gaussian random process, then one can compute the rate-distortion function in a fairly simple way [133]. This result has been extended to the weighted squared error criterion [183] and to contain classes of non-Gaussian processes [184]. A similar calculation can be made if the coding is done on a single scanning line [185].

It is interesting to note that the performance of realizable systems, such as feedback encoders and transformational coding comes very close to this bound [57], [215].

2) *A Practical System Layout:* In practice, instead of the general block diagram of Fig. 7, we prefer to work with a more detailed layout as shown in Fig. 8. A two-dimensional image is first spatially filtered, and then sampled in space and quantized in brightness. The psychovisual and statistical encoders remove, respectively, some of the psychovisual and statistical redundancies in the digitized image. The error-detection-and-correction encoder adds redundancy into the binary sequence representing the coded image to protect it from channel (storage) noise. The output binary sequence of this encoder is transformed by the modulator into waveforms suitable for transmission through the channel (or putting into storage). On the other side of the channel (storage), the demodulator and the decoders try to recover the best they can the output of the quantizer. Finally, the two-dimensional (spatial) post-filter smoothes out the recovered digital image into a continuous image for viewing by human observers.

The operations of the filters, the sampler, the quantizer, and the psychovisual and statistical coders are based on the properties of the source: they are called source coding. The operations of the error-detection and-correction coders and the modem (modulator and demodulator) are based on the properties of the channel (or storage): they are called channel coding. In the remainder of this chapter, we shall phrase our discussions in terms of image transmission, although most of the results apply to image storage as well.

Since all the blocks in Fig. 8 interact with each other, it is an impossible task to optimize the total system. One can only hope to design a good system instead of an optimum one, and to do so is as much an art as a science.

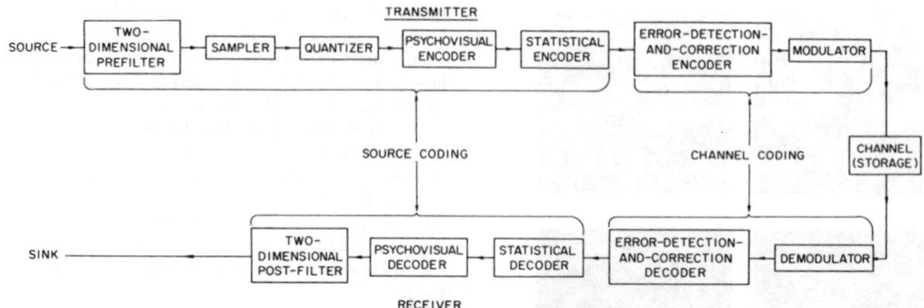

Fig. 8. A practical block diagram for an image transmission (storage) system.

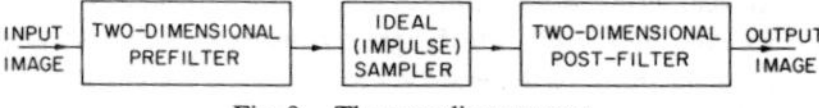

Fig. 9. The sampling process.

B. Image Digitization

1) *Sampling:* To concentrate on the sampling process, let us consider the simplified subsystem depicted in Fig. 9. With respect to this system, the basic question is: For a fixed number of samples per image frame, how should we choose the pre-filter and post-filter to optimize the output image quality?

Let the picture be sampled at a square array of points. Peterson and Middleton [169] showed that, for a fixed number of samples per frame pre- and post-filtering with two-dimensional ideal low-pass filters (whose cutoff frequencies are chosen to avoid aliasing) gives the least mean-square difference between the output of the post-filter and the input to the pre-filter. Subjective tests [112] indicated that these same filters also give reconstructed pictures with the best subjective quality in the case of very low resolution (64×64 samples per frame) systems.

For higher resolution systems (256×256 samples per frame), high-spatial-frequency accentuation at the post-filter seems to improve the output image quality; however, no extensive subjective tests have been done to verify this. Note that to obtain a received image with resolution comparable to that of present-day U. S. commerical television pictures, about 500×500 samples per frame are required.

2) *Quantization:* To each input sample (with a continuous brightness range) the quantizer assigns a discrete level. The quantization can be either uniform or nonuniform. If uniform quantization is used, about 5 to 8 bits per sample or 32 to 256 brightness levels (depending on the S/N of the original, the viewing conditions, etc.) are required to eliminate artificial contours (the so-called quantization noise). One can save about 1 bit per sample by using logarithmic quantization to take advantage of the properties of human vision (Weber-Fechner law).

Some examples of uniformly and logarithmically quantized images are shown in Figs. 10 and 11. The original image used in these examples contains a cameraman as the central object with grass and sky as background, and has a S/N (peak signal to rms noise ratio) of about 40 dB before quantization and a resolution of 256×256 sample points.

C. Redundancy Reduction

1) *Statistical Coding:* To transmit a digitized image by direct PCM requires $N = L \times L \times B$ bits per frame, where $L \times L$ is the num-

Fig. 10. Images uniformly quantized to various numbers of levels (256×256 samples per frame). (a) 2 bits or 4 levels. (b) 3 bits or 8 levels. (c) 5 bits or 32 levels.

Fig. 11. Image logarithmically quantized to various numbers of levels (256×256 samples per frame). (a) 2 bits or 4 levels. (b) 3 bits or 8 levels. (c) 5 bits or 32 levels.

ber of samples per frame and B the number of bits per sample (2^B being the number of discrete levels used for the brightness of each sample). Since the channel capacity requirement increases with an increase in the number of bits used to represent the image, it is the purpose of the psychovisual and the statistical encoders (Fig. 8) to reduce the number of bits needed to characterize the digitized image. We shall first take up statistical coding.

We can characterize a digitized image by a sequence of messages. The messages can be, for example, the brightness levels of each individual sample. Or, each message may contain the brightness levels of a pair of neighboring samples. Still a third example is that the messages may be first differences of adjacent samples along each horizontal line. There are many ways to choose our messages, the only requirement being that we should be able to reconstruct the digitized image from the sequence of messages.

For a particular choice, let the possible messages by $m_1, m_2, \cdots, m_n$; and let the probability distribution of these messages (over the class of digitized images we are interested in) be $p_1, p_2, \cdots, p_n$. The main idea in statistical coding is to use variable-length binary codewords for the messages, using short codewords for the more probable messages and longer codewords for the less probable ones so that on the average we will have a small number of bits per message. Shannon's theory [196] tells us that we can always find a code such that

PROCEEDINGS OF THE IEEE, NOVEMBER 1971

the average number of bits per message r satisfies the inequality

$$H \leq r \leq H + 1 \qquad (69)$$

where the entropy H is by definition

$$H \equiv - \sum_{i=1}^{n} p_i \log_2 p_i. \qquad (70)$$

The simple and elegant procedure of Huffman [115] guarantees that we will get a code with the minimum r.

The entropy H for a probability distribution is maximum when all p_i are equal, and is minimum when all p_i but one are zero. Generally speaking, the more nonuniform or peaky a probability distribution, the smaller its entropy. Therefore, in order to do effective statistical coding, we should choose a message set which has a peaky probability distribution.

2) *Psychovisual Coding:* If the received picture is to be viewed by humans, then one can take advantage of the properties of human vision. Here, the purpose is to distort the picture in such a way that it can be described by a smaller number of bits; however, the distortion is not great enough to be noticeable or objectionable to the human viewer. Psychovisual encoding, then, can be considered as an operation to derive a sequence of messages from the digitized image such that these messages require less channel capacity to transmit than the original digital image and that from these messages we can reconstruct a reasonable replica of the original digital image. Statistical encoding can, of course, be applied to the output messages of a psychovisual encoder to reduce their statistical redundancy.

We shall see that it is in psychovisual coding that we can hope for large amounts of redundancy reduction. Indeed, without taking advantage of the psychovisual properties of human vision, we would have had neither movies nor black-and-white and color television. The discrete-frame approach of movies and television (around 30 frames/s) is satisfactory because of the limited resolution of the temporal response of the human vision. Color television is possible because we can synthesize any subjective color by using a finite (3 or 4) number of color components. In both cases, a continuum is reduced to a finite discrete set: the bandwidth compression or redundancy reduction ratio is infinite.

Many redundancy reduction schemes have been developed and studied by various research groups, especially at the Bell Telephone Laboratories. One of the most simple and practical schemes is perhaps differential PCM. However, since our paper concerns image processing, in the remainder of this section we shall describe only two schemes which make use of truly two-dimensional processing techniques.

D. Contour Coding

1) *The Contours of Images:* If a drawing consists of a relatively small number of thin black lines on a white background the important points are obviously the black ones since the entire image may be constructed only from the black points and there are relatively few of them. In the more general case of a continuous-tone picture, the significant points must be selected in a more complicated manner. They are usually points of sharp brightness change. From the statistical point of view, these points are significant because they are highly correlated and thus can be efficiently coded. From the perceptual point of view, points of sharp brightness change are significant because they are usually associated with the outlines of objects.

In the reconstruction of images from outlines it is obvious that in the case of graphical, i.e., two-level data, the image may be re-created exactly from the outline information since all that is necessary is to fill in the spaces between the outlines with black. It turns out that continuous-tone images may also be recreated exactly from the outlines provided that they also contain information about the

spatial gradients of the image. Just as a function of single variable can be reproduced to within an additive constant from its derivative, a function of two variables, i.e., an image, can be recovered from its gradient [187]. The outlines are generally found to consist of connected series of points having gradients significantly different from zero. Thus if all the significant outlines are transmitted all the significant gradient information will be available for picture reproduction.

An alternate and less efficient way of characterizing continuous-tone pictures in terms of outlines or contours may also be mentioned here. Assume that the picture has been sampled in space and quantized in brightness. Then the picture can be considered as consisting of areas, each area containing a connected group of points with the same brightness level. We can characterize the picture completely by specifying the boundary points and the brightness levels of all the areas. This and related methods of picture coding, such as bit-plane encoding [208], suffer from the fact that many of the area boundaries do not correspond to the outlines of natural objects, but are merely artifacts of the quantization process. We might mention in this connection that Baer [31] looked into the efficient coding of the medial axis transforms of picture areas, with rather disappointing results.

2) *Transmission of Contour Information:* The information which needs to be transmitted about the outlines or contours in an image consists simply of the location of the contour points in the case of graphical data or the location plus gradient information or area brightness levels in the case of continuous-tone images.

Several coding techniques are available for transmitting contours [189], the most natural among which is perhaps to trace the contours directly. We first transmit the coordinates of an initial contour point. Then we trace the contour. In a digitized picture, each picture point has only 7 neighboring points. Therefore, once we are on a contour, it takes at most 3 bits to indicate the next contour point. In the case of continuous-tone images where gradient information must also be transmitted, one may also transmit the value of the gradient at the initial contour point and incremental information permitting the calculation of the gradient at the rest of the points.

3) *Coding of Typewritten English:* We give an example of the contour coding of typewritten English characters.

Based on a standard table of frequencies of the English letters, it was calculated that the average number of contours per letter is 1.5. At a resolution of 300 points/in, the number of contour points of the lower case elite type letters were counted, and the average number of contour points per letter was calculated to be 120 points/letter. On a standard single-space typewritten page, each letter occupies 1/12 by 1/6 in or, at 300 points/in, $25 \times 50 = 1250$ points.

We now estimate the compression ratios for the contour coding schemes on a single-letter basis. The compression ratios for an ordinary typewritten page, which contains margins and spaces, would be considerably higher. For direct contour tracing using 3 bits per contour point and 11 bits for the initial contour point, the compression ratio is:

$$\frac{1250}{11 \times 1.5 + 3 \times 120} \approx 3.$$

We should point out that the compression ratios of most coding schemes depend critically on image resolution [189], [108]. For instance, in the above numerical example, we have assumed a resolution of 300 points/in. If the resolution is increased to 1000 points/in, the compression ratio becomes 10.

4) *Continuous-Tone Pictures—Gradient Approach:* The contour coding of continuous-tone pictures using gradient information will now be described in some detail. This scheme takes advantage of the

fact that the human eye tends to emphasize edges (abrupt changes in brightness) in a picture but is relatively insensitive to the amount of changes in the brightness over edges; on the other hand, in areas where the brightness changes slowly, quantization noise is easily discernable. Therefore, edges and slowly varying part of a picture were treated differently.

The original image $s(x, y)$ is passed through a two-dimensional low-pass filter. If the bandwidth of the low-pass filter is $1/100$ of that of the original image $s(x, y)$, then the output $a(x, y)$ needs to be sampled only $1/100$ as often as $s(x, y)$; each sample of $a(x, y)$ still has to have 6 bits to avoid quantization noise. The image $s(x, y)$ is also passed through a gradient operator, since $|\nabla s|$ is large at the edges in the image this signal contains mainly edge information. It can be shown readily that if the low-frequency part $a(x, y)$ and the gradient components $\partial s/\partial y$ and $\partial s/\partial x$ are sent exactly (and if the channel is noiseless), then one can synthesize the high-frequency part, viz., $s(x, y) - a(x, y)$, exactly, by passing the gradient components through appropriate two-dimensional linear filters, and the original picture will be reproduced exactly [187a]. Graham worked on the problem of how to approximate the gradient so that we can achieve a large amount of reduction and also at the same time obtain good received pictures [77]. He considered as edge points all points whose gradients had magnitudes greater than a certain threshold. The gradients of these edge points then were transmitted by contour tracing. For each continuing contour point, he transmitted the changes in contour direction, gradient direction, and gradient magnitude using a Huffman code [115]. From the probability distributions of these quantities, he estimated the compression ratios of 4 to 23 (depending on picture complexity) could be achieved on 256×256-point 6-bit (64-brightness level) pictures.

Fig. 12 illustrates this scheme. Note that a tremendous amount of redundancy reduction was possible using this scheme. However, the reconstructed image suffered from a loss of textures. This was because the textures are often high-frequency low-amplitude signals. They are on the one hand not included in the low-frequency part of the image, and, on the other hand, not large enough to pass the gradient threshold.

5) An Operational Definition of Texture: The shortcoming of Graham's contour coding schemes suggests the following operational definition of texture. We consider an image as the sum of three components: the low-frequency part, the edges, and the textures. The low-frequency part and the edges correspond, respectively, to the low-frequency part and the synthesized high-frequency part (from approximate gradient information) in Graham's scheme. The texture component is then by definition what is left over in the original image after we subtract from it the low-frequency part and the edges. We should mention that much work on texture has been done recently by Rosenfeld and his colleages at the University of Maryland [11].

E. Transformational Coding

1) Linear Transformation and Block Quantization: The results of the rate-distortion theory strongly suggest that the use of linear transformation and block quantization might be quite efficient in coding data. Such an approach was analyzed by Kramer and Mathews [136] and Huang and Schultheiss [105]. The basic scheme is as follows. A block of N data samples x_i are linearly transformed into y_i by an $N \times N$ matrix A. The y_i are quantized and transmitted. At the receiver, the quantized y_i are transformed by another $N \times N$ matrix B into z_i. For a given bit rate, the matrices A and B are chosen to minimize the mean-square error between z_i and x_i. It turns out that the optimum matrix A consists of the eigenvectors of the correlation matrix of the samples x_i, and the optimum matrix B is the inverse of A. It appears, however, that a much simpler type of matrices, the so-called Hadamard matrices work almost as well as

Fig. 12. The contour coding scheme of Schreiber and Graham. (a) Original (256×256 samples, 6 bits/sample). (b) Low-frequency part of the picture. (c) Gradients. (d) Synthetic highs. (e) Reconstruction (0.3 bit/sample).

the optimum [174], [85]. A Hadamard matrix contains only $+1$ and -1 as its elements, and is orthogonal. Except for a scalar factor, it is its own inverse.

2) Hadamard Transform Coding: The application of Hadamard matrices to block quantizing images was studied by Huang and Woods [114], [229]. Let us assume, for simplicity, that the sampled image is divided into 2×2 blocks. Call the intensities of the 4 samples in a block x_1, x_2, x_3, and x_4. These intensities are transformed into y_i by a 4×4 Hadamard matrix:

$$\begin{pmatrix} y_1 \\ y_2 \\ y_3 \\ y_4 \end{pmatrix} = \begin{pmatrix} 1 & 1 & 1 & 1 \\ 1 & -1 & 1 & -1 \\ 1 & 1 & -1 & -1 \\ 1 & -1 & -1 & 1 \end{pmatrix} \begin{pmatrix} x_1 \\ x_2 \\ x_3 \\ x_4 \end{pmatrix}. \tag{71}$$

Since in a typical image neighboring samples tend to have equal intensities, $y_i\,(i \neq 1)$ tend to be very small. Therefore, in quantizing the y_i, we use more bits for y_1 and fewer bits for y_2, y_3, and y_4, hoping that we may end up with a small average number of bits per sample and yet get a good quality reconstructed image.

This scheme was applied to several images, and various block sizes were tried. It was found that for a given average bit rate, the use of a large block size tended to make the degradation in the reconstructed image appear as random noise, while the use of a small block size made the degradation appear in the form of discon-

Fig. 13.   Hadamard block quantization (block size = 8 × 8).
Average number of bits per sample. (a) 1. (b) 2. (c) 3.

Fig. 14.   Hadamard block quantization (block size = 16 × 16).
Average number of bits per sample. (a) 1. (b) 2. (c) 3.

Fig. 15.   Hadamard block quantization (block size = 1 × 256).
Average number of bits per sample. (a) 1. (b) 2. (c) 3.

tinuities at block boundaries. Some results (using square blocks) are shown in Figs. 13 and 14 (all pictures contain 256 × 256 samples). Note that with 3 bits per sample, the picture quality becomes as good as that of 6-bit originals.

In implementing image coding schemes in real time, it is easier to work along a scan line rather than in two dimensions. Therefore, the Hadamard block quantization scheme was also tried with one-dimensional blocks. Some results are shown in Fig. 15 (all pictures contain 256 × 256 samples). Note that the 3-bit picture is as good as the 3-bit picture using 16 × 16 blocks, but the 2-bit and 1-bit pictures have inferior quality when compared to the corresponding pictures using 16 × 16 blocks.

We mention in passing that similar results of Hadamard image coding have been obtained independently by other researchers [140], [85]. Pratt, Kane, and Andrews [172] studied the coding of the Hadamard transform of the entire image. The results thus obtained appeared not as good as those obtained from coding small pieces of the image.

3) Other Schemes: In the preceding section, we described a scheme of block quantizing images using Hadamard transforms. It turns out that we can also achieve good results using Fourier instead

of Hadamard transforms. Furthermore, we can encode the transformed variables in many different ways other than dividing them into groups and use a fixed number of quantization levels for each group. In short, a variety of transformational coding schemes exist. We might mention that a piecewise Fourier-transform coding scheme of Anderson and Huang [26] gives good quality pictures at about 1 bit per point on the average.

IV. OPTICAL IMAGE PROCESSING TECHNIQUES

A. Preliminaries

In Sections II and III, we have discussed some of the important mathematical operations we often want to perform in image processing. Some of these operations are linear; e.g., Fourier and Hadamard transformation, linear filtering, and correlation. Others are nonlinear; e.g., contour tracing. In Sections IV–VI, we shall describe the implementation of these mathematical operations using optics, digital computers, and special electrooptical devices.

B. Fourier Transformation

The main uses of coherent optical systems in image processing have been Fourier transformation and linear filtering. These operations are possible because of the Fourier-transforming property of a lens [56], [74], [199]. If a film transparency with amplitude transmission $g(x, y)$ is placed in the front focal plane of a lens, where x and y are the spatial coordinates of the front focal plane, and is illuminated with collimated monochromatic light, then the amplitude of the light at the back focal plane of the lens will be

$$G(2\pi\xi/\lambda f, 2\pi\eta/\lambda f) = G(u, v)$$

the Fourier transform of $g(x, y)$, where u and v are frequency variables, ξ and η the spatial coordinates of the back focal plane, λ the wavelength of the light, and f the focal length of the lens.

It is to be noted that if we put a detector (e.g., film) at the back focal plane of the lens, we will detect $|G|^2$—the phase information is lost.

C. Linear Filtering and Correlation

Linear filtering can be performed by first obtaining the Fourier transform of the input image $g(x, y)$ using a lens as described in the preceding subsection, and then putting a transparency, with amplitude transmission $H(u, v)$ in the back focal plane of the lens, and using a second lens whose front focal plane coincides with the back focal plane of the first lens. Then at the back focal plane of this second lens, the light amplitude will be $p(\alpha, \beta) = g(\alpha, \beta) \otimes h(\alpha, \beta)$ where α and β are the spatial co-ordinates, $\otimes$ denotes convolution, and $h(\alpha, \beta)$ is the inverse Fourier transform of $H(u, v)$.

The cross-correlation function $R_{gk}(x, y)$ of two real functions $g(x, y)$ and $k(x, y)$ can be expressed in terms of a convolution

$$R_{gk}(x, y) = g(x, y) \otimes k(-x, -y). \tag{72}$$

Therefore, we can do the cross correlation by performing a linear filtering with $g(x, y)$ as the input and $k(-x, -y)$ as the impulse response of the filter.

We mention in passing that several alternative ways of performing linear filtering and correlation using coherent optics were described by Weaver *et al.* [224].

D. Making the Spatial Filter

In doing general linear (shift-invariant) filtering using the setup described in subsection C, the filter $H(u, v)$ can be complex. We can generate a complex filter by controlling both the density and the thickness of a film transparency. However, the control of film thickness is difficult. Fortunately, there are methods by which one can perform complex filtering using film transparencies which have density variation only. We shall describe three such methods.

The first method, due to Vander Lugt [222], employs a phase modulation technique to embed the phase information of the filter in the density variation. Instead of using $H(u, v)$, which is complex, we use as our filter the real and positive function

$$H_1(u, v) = |H(u, v) + A \exp(jau)|^2 \tag{73}$$

where A and a are constants. Then, in the output plane, we get $g(x, y) \otimes h_1(x, y)$ where $h_1(x, y)$ is the inverse Fourier transform of H_1. It is readily shown that $g \otimes h_1$ contains a term $g \otimes h$, which is the desired output, shifted a distance a away from the optical axis.

The second method due to Lohmann [45], [149], and the third method due to Lee [142]–[144] both produce sampled filters. Brown and Lohmann essentially generate on a digital computer a halftone image of the desired filter $H(u, v)$. The trick lies in the shifting of the position of the halftone dot to control the phase information. The computer-generated filter can be plotted on a Calcomp plotter and then photoreduced to produce a filter transparency of the appropriate size.

Lee uses a digital computer and a precision CRT scanner to generate a sampled filter on which each group of four samples represent one point of the desired complex filter; the intensities of the four samples being proportional to the positive real part, the negative real part, the positive imaginary part, and the negative imaginary part, respectively, of the complex value of the filter point.

Just as in the case of the Vander Lugt filter, when we use either the Lohmann filter or the Lee filter, the desired output will appear off the optical axis. Two examples of the use of Lee filters are shown in Fig. 16 (differentiation) and Fig. 17 (matched filtering).

E. Real-Time Operations

In a coherent optical Fourier transforming or filtering system, the input image and the filter are usually recorded on photographic (silver-halide) film transparencies. The development of photographic film is messy and time-consuming. Therefore, in order to operate the optical system in "real-time," i.e., to have the capability of changing the input and the filter very quickly, one has to search for a better medium than the photographic film. One needs a medium which can be modulated quickly by some form of energy (light, electron beam, sound, etc.), read at a visible wavelength, and be quickly erasable. One also requires that this medium be very sensitive, have high resolution and large dynamic range, and be fatigueless.

Such a medium has not yet been found. However, encouraging preliminary experiments have been done by various researchers with KDP crystals [171], photochromics [99], ultrasonic light-modulators [29], [157], photopolymers [182], and magnetooptical devices [51].

F. Other Optical Filtering and Correlation Schemes

It is possible to do linear filtering and correlation with noncoherent optics [155], [186], [221], [80] and partially coherent optics [52b]. However, they are much less flexible than the coherent case; in particular, the form of the filter function is rather restricted and cannot be specified arbitrarily.

Using polarized light and Polaroid Vectorgraph film, Marathay [152] developed a method of doing complex spatial filtering that yields filtered images on axis.

G. Matrix Multiplication

The basic concepts of doing matrix multiplication by coherent optics were discussed by Cutrona [55]. A more detailed analysis was carried out by Heinz, Artman, and Lee [96].

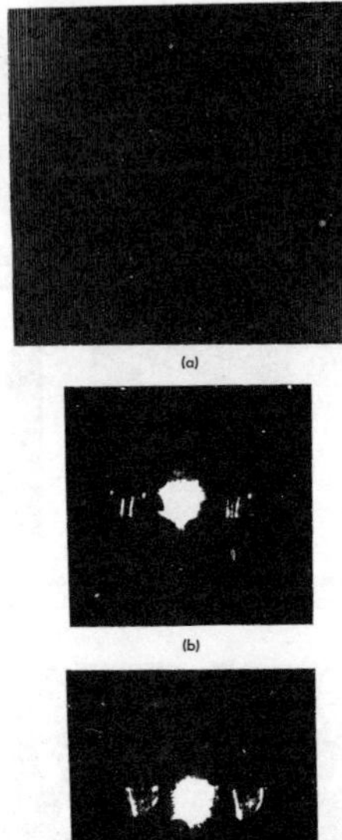

Fig. 16. Differentiation using a Lee filter. (a) Derivative filter. (b) Output pattern obtained using the letter "T" as input pattern. (c) Output pattern obtained using a sector of a circular disk as the input pattern.

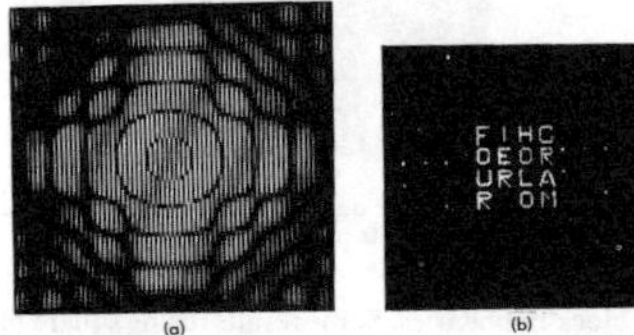

Fig. 17. Matched filtering using a Lee filter. (a) Matched filter for the letter "O." (b) Output pattern. Note that the input pattern appears in the center, while the desired output is off axis.

H. Holographic Subtraction

Bromley, Monahan, Bryant, and Thompson [44] developed a holographic technique by which two dissimilar optical fields can be subtracted to yield only their difference. The principle underlying this technique is that of optical interference between a holographically reconstructed field and a direct real-time one. One application of this technique is to detect changes between photographic transparencies of some scene taken at different times.

V. Digital Computer Image Processing Techniques

A. Fourier Transformation

To do any operation on a digital computer, the input image has to be sampled. If the input image contains N uniformly spaced samples, then it can be easily shown that one needs N samples for the Fourier transform. For the sake of simplicity, let us consider the one-dimensional case. Let the values of the samples of the input, $g(x)$, be $g_0, g_1, g_2, \cdots, g_{N-1}$ and those of the Fourier transform be $G_0, G_1, G_2, \cdots, G_{N-1}$. Then

$$G_k = \sum_{j=0}^{N-1} g_j w^{-jk} \tag{74}$$

where

$$w = \exp\left[i(2\pi/N)\right]. \tag{75}$$

Equation (74) is a discrete approximation of the continuous Fourier integral, and can be written in matrix form:

$$G] = Wg] \tag{76}$$

where

$$G] = \begin{bmatrix} G_0 \\ G_1 \\ \cdot \\ \cdot \\ G_{N-1} \end{bmatrix} \tag{77}$$

$$g] = \begin{bmatrix} g_0 \\ g_1 \\ \cdot \\ \cdot \\ g_{N-1} \end{bmatrix} \tag{78}$$

and

$$W = \begin{bmatrix} 1 & 1 & 1 & \cdots & 1 \\ 1 & w^{-1} & w^{-2} & \cdots & w^{-(N-1)} \\ 1 & w^{-2} & w^{-4} & \cdots & w^{-2(N-1)} \\ \cdot & \cdot & \cdot & \cdots & \cdot \\ \cdot & \cdot & \cdot & \cdots & \cdot \\ 1 & w^{-(N-1)} & w^{-2(N-1)} & \cdots & w^{-(N-1)^2} \end{bmatrix}. \tag{79}$$

The samples of the Fourier transform can be obtained by carrying out the matrix multiplication of (76). To do this matrix multiplication directly, we need N^2 basic operations, a basic operation being defined as a complex multiplication plus a complex addition. To get each of the N output samples, we need N basic operations on the input samples. Therefore, the computer time required for the direct method is

$$T_d = kN^2 \tag{80}$$

where k is a constant, depending on the particular computer and the particular program.

An efficient method of digital Fourier analysis, which had been suggested by Good [71], was recently developed by Cooley and Tukey [53]. This method is based on the following theorem.

Let $N = r_1 \times r_2 \times \cdots \times r_n$, where $r_1, r_2, \cdots, r_n$ are positive integers. Then the $N \times N$ matrix W of (79) can be factored into n matrices:

$$W = W_1 W_2 \cdots W_n \tag{81}$$

where the $N \times N$ matrix W_i has only $r_i N$ nonzero elements.

It follows from this theorem that (76) can be written as

$$G] = W_1 W_2 \cdots W_n g]. \tag{82}$$

If we do the matrix multiplication step by step, multiplying W_n and $g]$ first, then multiplying W_{n-1} and the product $W_n g]$, etc., then the computer time required will be

$$T_c = k(r_1 + r_2 + \cdots + r_n)N. \tag{83}$$

The case $r_1 = r_2 = \cdots = r_n = 2$ offers important advantages for computers with binary arithmetic, both in addressing and in multiplication economy. In particular, the entire calculation can be performed within the array of $2N$ storage locations used for the input. (The input samples are in general complex, hence, each sample takes 2 storage locations.) For this special case the computer time required is, according to (83),

$$T_c = k2N \log_2 N. \tag{84}$$

We note that while in the direct method the computer time T_d is proportional to N^2, in the Cooley-Tukey method, the computer time T_c is proportional to $N \log_2 N$. Therefore, for large values of N, considerable savings in computer time can be achieved by using the Cooley-Tukey algorithm.

For a typical computer, such as the IBM 7094, $k \approx 30 \ \mu s$. Using this figure we have

for $N = 64 \times 64, \ T_d = 8$ min, $T_c = 30$ s
for $N = 256 \times 256, \ T_d = 30$ h, $T_c = 1$ min
for $N = 512 \times 512, \ T_d = 20$ days, $T_c = 5$ min
for $N = 1024 \times 1024, \ T_d = 1$ year, $T_c = 20$ min.

The preceding estimates were made based on the assumption that the computer memory is large enough to store all the input samples. Also, the estimates do not include the input/output time.

In two dimensions, the discrete Fourier transform relation can be written as

$$G_{qk} = \sum_{p=0}^{M-1} \sum_{j=0}^{M-1} g_{pj} w^{-(pq+jk)} \qquad (q, k = 0, 1, 2, \cdots, M-1) \tag{84a}$$

or in matrix form

$$[G] = W[g]W \tag{84b}$$

where

$$[G] = \begin{bmatrix} G_{00} \cdots\cdots G_{0,M-1} \\ \cdot \\ \cdot \\ G_{M-1,0} \cdots G_{M-1,M-1} \end{bmatrix} \tag{84c}$$

$$[g] = \begin{bmatrix} g_{00} \cdots\cdots g_{0,M-1} \\ \cdot \\ \cdot \\ g_{M-1,0} \cdots g_{M-1,M-1} \end{bmatrix} \tag{84d}$$

and W is as defined in (79) except that N is replaced by M. Equation (84b) suggests that we can calculate the two-dimensional Fourier transform of $[g]$ by first calculating the one-dimensional transform of each row in $[g]$ and then in the resulting array calculating the one-dimensional transform of each column. It is easy to see that if we use the Cooley-Tukey algorithm to do the one-dimensional transforms in this procedure, then the time requirement of doing a two-dimensional transform is again given by (84), where $N = M^2$ is the total number of input samples.

The Cooley-Tukey algorithm is now commonly known as the Fast Fourier Transform or FFT [110]. A similar fast algorithm is available for the Hadamard transform [172], [1], [72].

B. Linear Filtering

Again, let us consider the one-dimensional case. Let g_i be the values of the input samples, and p_j those of the output. There are two types of digital filters: 1) Nonrecursive filters—each output sample is a weighted sum of the input samples, viz.,

$$p_k = \sum_{j=0}^{M-1} A_j g_{k-j} \tag{85}$$

where A_j are constants. 2) Recursive filters—each output sample is a weighted sum of the input samples and the previously calculated output samples, viz.,

$$p_k = \sum_{j=0}^{M-1} b_j g_{k-j} + \sum_{i=1}^{q} c_i p_{k-i} \tag{86}$$

where b_j and c_i are constants. Equation (85) can be considered as a discrete approximation of the convolution integral; while (86), a difference equation corresponding to the differential equation describing the continuous linear filter.

There are various methods of designing both types of filters [37], [129], [70], which we will not go into here. It suffices to say that for a given continuous filter, approximating it by a recursive filter usually requires a smaller number of terms. On the other hand, error analysis is easier for nonrecursive filters.

We shall estimate the computer time requirement for digital filtering using a two-dimensional nonrecursive filter, the case of recursive filter being completely similar. Consider the filter operation:

$$p_{jk} = \sum_{a=0}^{m-1} \sum_{b=0}^{m-1} \{g_{j-a,k-b} h_{ab}\} \qquad (j, k = 0, 1, \cdots, n + m - 1). \tag{87}$$

Assume the filter has $M = m \times m$ samples. Let the number of samples of the input image be $N = n \times n$. Assume that $M \ll N$, as usually is the case. Then the computer time required for calculating all the output samples is approximately

$$T_1 = Kn^2 m^2 = kNM. \tag{88}$$

For $k \approx 30$ μs, $N = 200 \times 200$, and $M = 20 \times 20$, we have $T_1 = 8$ min, which is a long time, considering the moderate sizes of input and filter samples.

The computer time can be cut down considerably, if the filter is separable, i.e., if

$$h_{ab} = h'_a h''_b. \tag{89}$$

Then (87) can be written as

$$p_{jk} = \sum_{a=0}^{m-1} \left\{ \sum_{b=0}^{m-1} g_{j-a,k-b} h''_b \right\} h'_a. \tag{90}$$

The inner summations can be evaluated first resulting in a computer time of

$$T'_1 = kn^2 2m = kn^2 2\sqrt{M}. \tag{91}$$

Observe that

$$T_1/T'_1 = m/2. \tag{92}$$

For $k \approx 30$ μs, $N = 200 \times 200$, and $M = 20 \times 20$, $T'_1 = T_1/10 \approx 0.8$ min. Therefore, whenever situations permit, one should use a separable filter or a sum of a small number of them instead of a nonseparable filter.

An alternative way to do linear filtering is to work in the frequency domain [210]. We first take the Fourier transform of the input, and multiply it by the filter frequency response, and finally take the inverse transform of this product to obtain the desired output. Assuming either $M \ll N$, or that the filter characteristic is given in the frequency domain, we observe that the computer time required in this method is approximately:

$$T_2 = k4N \log_2 N. \tag{93}$$

Comparison of (91), (94), and (96) yields:

$$T_2 < T_1, \qquad \text{if } M > 4 \log_2 N \tag{94}$$

$$T_2 < T'_1, \qquad \text{if } M > 4(\log_2 N)^2. \tag{95}$$

For example, for $N = 200 \times 200$: $T_2 < T_1$, if $M > 7 \times 7$; and $T_2 < T'_1$, if $M > 30 \times 30$.

Our discussions of nonrecursive filtering can be applied equally well to the calculation of correlation functions. We might mention in this respect that an improved algorithm for autocorrelation was recently proposed by Rader [173].

C. Two-Dimensional Nonrecursive Filters

Although a considerable amount of work has been done in the design of digital filters in one dimension, only very recently did researchers start to turn their attention to two-dimensional digital filters. In Subsections C and D, we shall discuss briefly some of the similarities and differences between one- and two-dimensional digital filters.

1) Sampling and Truncation: We are given an analog impulse response $h(x, y)$ where x and y are spatial variables. We would like to design a nonrecursive digital filter which approximates $h(x, y)$. Just like in the case of one dimension, there are two issues involved here, viz.: 1) How often do we have to sample? and 2) How shall we truncate $h(x, y)$? Both of these issues are resolved in the same way as in the one-dimensional case.

Let the Fourier transform of $h(x, y)$ be $H(u, v)$, and the Fourier transform of the input $f(x, y)$ be $F(u, v)$, where u and v are spatial frequencies. Assume

$$F(u, v) = 0 = H(u, v), \qquad \text{for } (u^2 + v^2) > R^2 \tag{96}$$

where R is a constant. Then we should sample h and f with a period less than $1/2R$ in both the x and the y direction. It is assumed that we use a square sampling grid.

To truncate $h(x, y)$, we multiply it by a window function $w(x, y)$:

$$w(x, y) = 0, \qquad \text{for } |x| > X \text{ and } |y| > Y \tag{97}$$

where X and Y are positive constants. To reduce ringing in the frequency response, we should choose $w(x, y)$ such that its Fourier transform $W(u, v)$ has small sidelobes. Since many good windows have been discovered in one dimension [129], [37] we can use

$$w(x, y) = w_1(x) w_1(y) \tag{98}$$

where $w_1(x)$ is a good one-dimensional window. In some cases, we may want our two-dimensional window to be circularly symmetrical. Then, we can use [109]:

$$w(x, y) = w_1(\sqrt{x^2 + y^2}). \tag{99}$$

To actually carry out the nonrecursive filtering, we can either do a direct convolution, or use the FFT, just like in the one-dimensional case.

2) Circularly Symmetrical Filters: Suppose the given analog impulse response is circularly symmetrical, and we wish to approximate it by a nonrecursive digital filter which is as nearly circularly symmetrical as possible. The obvious thing to do would be to sample

$h(x, y)$ by a polar raster, i.e., to sample at the points with polar coordinates $(m\Delta\gamma, n\Delta\theta)$ where $\Delta\gamma$ and $\Delta\theta = 2\pi/N$ are constants, and $m = 0, 1, 2, \cdots$; $n = 0, 1, 2, \cdots, N-1$. However, we can do neither direct discrete convolution nor FFT conveniently with polar samples. Therefore, if we insist on a sampling raster which is more nearly circularly symmetrical than a square one, we should use a triangular raster. To do direct convolution and FFT on a triangular raster is completely analogous to doing them on a square raster.

D. Two-Dimensional Recursive Filters

1) A Fundamental Curse: A fundamental curse in two-dimensional recursive filtering is that the fundamental theorem of algebra in one dimension does not extend to two dimensions. In one dimension, any polynomial $P(Z)$ of degree n can be factored into n first-degree factors:

$$P(Z) = K(Z - Z_1)(Z - Z_2)\cdots(Z - Z_n) \tag{100}$$

where K and Z_i are constants. There is no corresponding factorization for a polynomial in two variables $P(Z_1, Z_2)$.

One implication of this curse is that we cannot realize our two-dimensional recursive filters in parallel or cascade form to reduce the effect of digitization errors.

Another implication of this curse is that the test of the stability of two-dimensional recursive filters is almost impossible except for very simple filters.

2) Stability: A basic stability theorem for two-dimensional recursive filters, due to Shanks [194], states that: A recursive filter with Z transform $H(Z_1, Z_2) = A(Z_1, Z_2)/B(Z_1, Z_2)$, where A and B are polynomials in Z_1 and Z_2, is stable if and only if there are no values of Z_1 and Z_2 such that $|Z_1| \leq 1, |Z_2| \leq 1$, and $B(Z_1, Z_2) = 0$. By definition

$$\begin{cases} Z_1 = e^{-s_1 a} & \text{(101a)} \\ Z_2 = e^{-s_2 b} & \text{(101b)} \end{cases}$$

where s_1 and s_2 are, respectively, the horizontal and the vertical complex spatial frequencies, and a and b are constants (sampling periods in the horizontal and the vertical directions, respectively). It is not hard to convince oneself that to test stability using Shanks' theorem is hard work.

It can be shown [111] that after a suitable change of variables, Shanks' theorem becomes equivalent to a result in circuit theory due to Ansell [28], [225]. For filters with numerical coefficients, Ansell's stability-test procedure is often less tedious to use.

3) Design Techniques: The impulse-invariant technique [70] cannot be extended to two dimensions, since we cannot do partial-fraction expansion in two variables (thanks to our fundamental curse).

The method of moments [37] can be extended to two dimensions. So can a spatial-domain approximation technique of Shanks [193], [194], [50]. However, the filters designed according to these two methods may be unstable.

There is a class of one-dimensional methods, which we shall call transform methods, in which the analog transfer function $H_A(s)$ of a stable filter is given and an approximate digital filter $H_D(Z)$, is obtained by replacing s in H_A by $g(Z)$. The function g is suitably chosen so that stability is preserved. The transform method can be readily extended to two dimensions. Given $H_A(s_1, s_2)$, we get $H_D(Z_1, Z_2)$ by

$$H_D(Z_1, Z_2) = H_A(g(Z_1), g(Z_2)). \tag{102}$$

However, here the relation between $H_D(e^{-ju a}, e^{-jv b})$ and $H_A(ju, jv)$ is much harder to visualize than in the one-dimensional case. Also,

the specification of the filter is often given in the form of the magnitude of the frequency response. To obtain a stable $H_A(s_1, s_2)$ with $H_A(ju, jv)$ approximating the given magnitude response is much harder to do in two dimensions than in one dimension.

4) Some Open Questions: With respect to two-dimensional recursive filters, the most important practical questions we want to ask are as follows: 1) How do we design filters that are guaranteed to be stable? 2) If a given filter is unstable, how do we stabilize it without changing its frequency response?

One approach to attacking question 1) is to study what types of frequency responses we can get from classes of simple filters whose stability we know how to control.

With respect to question 2), we might mention a conjecture of Shanks [195]. Let $H(Z_1, Z_2) = 1/B(Z_1, Z_2)$ be an unstable filter. We first determine a least mean-square inverse of $B(Z_1, Z_2)$ which we call $G(Z_1 Z_2)$. We next determine a least mean-square inverse of $G(Z_1, Z_2)$, which we call $\hat{B}(Z_1, Z_2)$. Then Shanks' conjecture states that the filter $\hat{H}(Z_1, Z_2) = 1/\hat{B}(Z_1, Z_2)$ is stable and that the magnitude of the frequency response of $\hat{H}$ is approximately equal to that of H. It was proven by Robinson [179] that a one-dimensional version of Shanks' procedure does yield stable (one-dimensional) filters. However, whether the procedure yields stable filters in two dimensions is still an open question. Also, no analysis is available on how close the magnitude of the frequency response of $\hat{H}$ is to that of H.

We have yet another open question with respect to 2). In the one-dimensional case, if we are doing nonreal-time filtering, then we can always decompose an unstable filter with no poles on the unit circle into two stable ones recursing in opposite directions. We associate the poles of the original filter outside the unit circle with a filter recursing in the positive direction, and the poles inside the unit circle with a filter recursing in the negative direction. Is there an analogous procedure in two dimensions?

E. Separable-Sum Approximations

1) The Main Result: In this section, we present a result which finds applications in the design of both nonrecursive and recursive filters in two dimensions.

We shall solve the problem of representing arbitrary $h(i, j)$; $i = 1, 2, \cdots, l$; $j = 1, 2, \cdots, m$ by a separable sum

$$h_a(i, j) = \sum_{k=1}^{n} f_k(i) \cdot g_k(j).$$

The approximation is such that the error, defined by

$$\varepsilon = \sum_{i,j} |h_a(i, j) - h(i, j)|^2 \tag{103}$$

is as small as possible. The solution is as follows. Consider $h(i, j)$ as an l by m matrix H, and assume that $l < m$. Then H may be written as [137]:

$$H = \sum_{k=1}^{l} u_k v_{k_T}. \tag{104}$$

(u_k and v_k are column matrices. v_{k_T} being the transpose of v_k is a row matrix.) The vector v_k is a normalized eigenvector of

$$H_T H v_k = \mu_k v_k \tag{105}$$

and $\mu_k \geq 0$. The vectors u_k are defined by

$$u_k = H v_k. \tag{106}$$

We order the vectors by the rule

$$k_1 \geq k_2 \rightarrow \mu_{k_1} \geq \mu_{k_2}.$$

The best approximation is obtained by

$$H_a = \sum_{k=1}^{n} u_k v_{k_T} \tag{107}$$

and the error associated with this approximation is

$$\varepsilon = \sum_{k=n+1}^{l} \mu_k. \tag{108}$$

This is proven by Tretiak [219]. A similar result was obtained by Treitel and Shanks [218].

2) Application to Nonrecursive Filters: We have now a procedure for approximating an arbitrary two-dimensional filter by a sum of separable filters. Equation (108) shows that the sum of separable filters can be made to be identical to the desired filter by including all the terms with nonzero eigenvalues.

Let us consider the computational effort required in the approximation. The direct evaluation requires $(l \times m)$ multiplications and additions for each output point. The approximation, however, requires $(l+m) \times n$ operations. In general, if all the terms must be included, this is equal to $(l^2 + l \times m)$ and it will be less efficient than the direct method. If, however, the required filter is approximated closely by only a few terms, a substantial saving may be achieved. Whether or not this is practical can easily be seen by examining the spectrum of eigenvalues of (105).

The procedure was applied to the filter given in Table I. The following are the eigenvalues for this matrix.

$$66.47 \quad 6.27 \quad 2.07 \quad 1.19.$$

Since only those four of the eigenvalues are nonzero, this matrix can be represented exactly by a sum of four separable filters. The magnitude of these eigenvalues are such that an approximation with error of 4.5 percent can be obtained if a two-term approximation is used.

3) Application to Recursive Filters: Equation (104) can be considered as a (very poor) substitute for a fundamental theorem of algebra in two dimensions. Given an analog two-dimensional impulse response $h(x, y)$, we can first sample and truncate it, and then expand in a separable sum, (104), or an approximation thereof, (107). Then we can design one-dimensional recursive filters for the components $f_k(i)$ and $g_k(j)$, using all the one-dimensional techniques we have in store. However, unless the number of terms n in (107) is small, the resulting recursive filter will probably not be very efficient, i.e., it will contain a large number of terms.

F. Numerical Solution of Linear Integral Equations

As we mentioned in Section II-E, the problem of restoring an image degraded by an LSV system is that of solving the linear integral equation (63). The brute-force way of doing it is to digitize both sides of (63), yielding a set of linear algebraic equations.

$$\begin{bmatrix} p_1 \\ p_2 \\ \cdot \\ \cdot \\ \cdot \\ p_m \end{bmatrix} = \begin{bmatrix} k_{11} & k_{12} & \cdots & k_{1n} \\ k_{21} & k_{22} & \cdots & k_{2n} \\ \cdot & \cdot & \cdot & \cdot \\ \cdot & \cdot & \cdot & \cdot \\ \cdot & \cdot & \cdot & \cdot \\ k_{m1} & k_{m2} & \cdots & k_{mn} \end{bmatrix} \begin{bmatrix} f_1 \\ f_2 \\ \cdot \\ \cdot \\ \cdot \\ f_n \end{bmatrix} \tag{109}$$

where p_i and f_i are samples of $p(x, y)$ and $f(\alpha, \beta)$ respectively, and k_{ij} are, except for a positive scale factor, samples of $k(x, y; \alpha, \beta)$. If we make $m=n$, and if the determinant of $[k_{ij}]$ is nonzero, then in principle, we can solve (109) for the f_i's.

The number of samples we have to take in digitizing (63) was discussed by Huang [107] and Granger [79]. In almost all practical

TABLE I
A Sampled Filter Array

0	0	0	1	1	1	1	0	0	0
0	0	1	1	1	1	1	1	0	0
0	1	1	1	1	1	1	1	1	0
1	1	1	1	1	1	1	1	1	1
1	1	1	1	1	1	1	1	1	1
1	1	1	1	1	1	1	1	1	1
1	1	1	1	1	1	1	1	1	1
0	1	1	1	1	1	1	1	1	0
0	0	1	1	1	1	1	1	0	0
0	0	0	1	1	1	1	0	0	0

cases, the number will be so large that the solution of (109) is simply out of the question. Even in the case when the number of equations $(m=n)$ is small enough (a few hundreds, say), their solution is still very tricky because of the noise contained in the degraded image. Instead of solving the equations directly, iterative methods are often much more preferred [137]. Also, we might want to oversample p to obtain more equations than unknowns (i.e., to make $m>n$), and then try to find a least-square solution for the f_i's [137].

G. Geometrical Operations

Geometrical operations are useful when we want to correct for geometrical distortions in images and when we want to perform rotation or scale change on images.

The general problem is as follows. The relation between the desired image $g(x, y)$ and the original image $f(x, y)$ is first specified:

$$g(x, \ y) = f(a(x, y), b(x, y)) \tag{110}$$

where a and b are functions of x and y. Then, we are given the samples $f(i\Delta x, j\Delta y)$; $i, j = 1, 2, \cdots, N$ from $f(x, y)$, and asked to determine the samples $g(i\Delta x, j\Delta y)$; $i, j = 1, 2, \cdots, N$ (where Δx and Δy are constants).

One approach to solving this problem is to use interpolation. From (110) we have

$$g(i\Delta x, j\Delta y) = f(a(i\Delta x, j\Delta y), b(i\Delta x, j\Delta y)). \tag{111}$$

Let I and J be two fixed integers, and let (a_0, b_0), where $a_0 = a(I\Delta x, J\Delta y)$, $b_0 = b(I\Delta x, J\Delta y)$, lie in the rectangle with vertices $p_1 = (K\Delta x, L\Delta y)$, $p_2 = (K\Delta x, (L+1)\Delta y)$, $p_3 = ((K+1)\Delta x, L\Delta y)$ and $p_4 = ((K+1)\Delta x, (L+1)\Delta y)$. Let $a_0 = (K+\alpha)\Delta x$, and $b_0 = (L+\beta)\Delta y$. Then, using bilinear interpolation, we have

$$\begin{aligned} g(I\Delta x, J\Delta y) &= f(a_0, b_0) \\ &= f(p_1)(1 - \alpha)(1 - \beta) + f(p_2)(1 - \alpha)\beta \\ &\quad + f(p_3)\alpha(1 - \beta) + f(p_4)\alpha\beta. \end{aligned} \tag{112}$$

More elaborate procedures may be developed by using higher order polynomials for interpolating functions. For rotation and scale change, several simpler methods have been studied [124].

H. Some Nonlinear Operations

The flexibility of a digital computer permits it to perform many nonlinear operations required in image processing.

1) Edge Extraction: The gradient and the Laplacian operators are often used in extracting edges in an image. In the computer, these operators must be approximated by finite differences. Operators built of finite differences cannot be invariant under rotation, though they can be approximated arbitrarily closely. The squared gradient operator may be approximated by

$$|\nabla f|^2 \approx (f(i+1,j+1) - f(i,j))^2 + (f(i+1,j) - f(i,j+1))^2 \quad (113)$$

and the Laplacian by

$$\nabla^2 f \approx f(i+1,j) + f(i,j+1) + f(i-1,j) + f(i,j-1) - 4f(i,j). \quad (114)$$

These forms have a high degree of symmetry.

It is possible to transform differential operators to discrete operators by starting with the definition of a derivative given by

$$f_x \equiv f(i+1,j) - f(i,j) \quad (115a)$$

$$f_y \equiv f(i,j+1) - f(i,j) \quad (115b)$$

and to obtain higher order derivatives by applying this definition recursively. The operators obtained in this way tend to be not as symmetric as those defined earlier.

To extract edges, we set a threshold and call any point an edge point if the squared gradient (or the absolute value of the Laplacian) at that point exceeds the threshold.

2) Contour Tracing: In some efficient picture coding schemes, we want to trace contours in sampled two-level images. There are several ways of doing it. One of the simplest is due to Mason and Clemens [153]. Assume we have black objects in a white background. Then, the tracer simply turns right after a white point is encountered and left after a black point.

3) Smoothing: A sampled two-level image can be represented by a matrix of values f_{ij}; $i,j=1, 2, \cdots$, where each f_{ij} is either 1 (black) or 0 (white). In such an image, we often have noise in the form of scattered black points in the white background and missing black points in the objects—the so-called pepper and salt noise. A popular way to reduce the noise is due to Dinneen [59].

The improved image g_{ij} is obtained from f_{ij} as follows. Let

$$S_{ij} = \sum_{p=-m}^{m} \sum_{q=-n}^{n} f_{i+p,j+q} \quad (116)$$

where m and n are fixed integers. Then

$$g_{ij} = \begin{cases} 1, & \text{if } S_{ij} \geq \theta \\ 0, & \text{if } S_{ij} < \theta \end{cases} \quad (117)$$

where θ is a fixed threshold.

4) Thinning: In transmitting line drawings, the thickness of the lines often contains little information. We might therefore want to "thin" each line to a one-sample wide line. To accomplish this, Sherman [198] proposed that we change a black point to white if in doing so we will neither create a gap nor shorten any one-sample wide line.

I. Comparison Between Coherent Optics and Digital Computer

1) Flexibility: Coherent optical systems are essentially limited to linear operations on the amplitude transmission variations of a film transparency. On the other hand, digital computers can be used to do linear operations on either the amplitude transmission, or the intensity transmission, or the density. More importantly, digital computers can also be used to do nonlinear operations.

2) Capacity and Speed: In a coherent optical system, the film is used as the storage, resulting in an enormous capacity. More importantly, the data on the film can be operated on in parallel, so that the speed is limited, in principle, only by the speed of light. Although a digital computer usually has a limited memory, any amount of auxiliary memory can be attached to it. If the computer has a film scanner, then films can also serve as its storage. However, present-day digital computers operate essentially sequentially on the data. Therefore, if a large number of data points need to be operated on, it takes a long time to bring the data into the central processor, and still a longer time to process them.

Let us consider an example. A giant coherent optical system [135] at the Institute of Science and Technology, University of Michigan, is capable of processing 70-mm films with a resolution of 100 cycles/mm. It can therefore do a Fourier transformation on approximately 2×10^8 data points essentially instantaneously.

Now suppose we do the same thing on a digital computer. It would take more than an hour just to read in the data points, if the computer film reader reads at 30 μs/point. Assume that the Cooley and Tukey algorithm is used, and assume that the computer had a core memory of more than 4×10^8 words, it still would take about 100 h to perform the Fourier transform. (We assumed as before that it takes the computer 30 μs to do a basic operation.)

We might mention that several researchers have been developing computers which perform some parallel processing [69], [206]. These computers could be several orders of magnitude faster than the more conventional ones.

3) Accuracy: In digital processing, there are inherent errors due to sampling and amplitude quantization. These errors, however, can be made arbitrarily small by increasing the sampling rate and the number of quantization levels. In practice the accuracy of digital computer image processing is limited by the film scanner. It is probably difficult at present to build a film scanner with an accuracy better than 0.01 percent.

In a coherent optical system, there are various sources of errors, such as: imperfect optical components, film grain noise and nonlinearity, spurious thickness variations of film emulsions, errors in spatial filters, nonuniformity of light beam across the input aperture, and imperfect alignment of the optical system. These errors are not easy to control. One can probably expect an accuracy of only 3 to 5 percent in a coherent optical system. We might also mention the speckle effect [162] due to the coherence of the light which tends to obscure details in an image.

4) Cost: Coherent optical systems are usually cheaper than digital computers. However, large-aperture diffraction-limited coherent optical systems can be rather expensive. The giant system at the University of Michigan which we mentioned earlier cost about 500 000 dollars.

In summary, the main advantages of a coherent optical system are its information storage capacity and processing speed, and the main advantages of a digital computer are its flexibility and accuracy. Coherent optical systems are suitable for doing linear operations, such as Fourier transformation and linear filtering, on large-volume data; but when nonlinear operations or accurate linear operations on a limited amount of data are required, digital computers can be used to advantage. In some cases, although the filtering is best done by a coherent optical system, the spatial filter is most conveniently made on a digital computer.

VI. ELECTROOPTICAL DEVICES

A coherent optical system does linear operations in parallel, obtaining all output points at once, while most present-day digital computers do things serially. There are a number of special electrooptical devices which work partly in parallel and partly serially.

A. Linear Filtering by Analog Scanning

One can perform convolution by passing through the input transparency $f(\alpha, \beta)$ a light beam having an aperture function $h(x_0 - \alpha, y_0 - \beta)$, where x_0 and y_0 are constants. The output electrical signal of a phototube, which integrates the light beam after it has passed through the input transparency, will be the value of the desired output $g(x, y)$, at the point (x_0, y_0). We can get as many output points as we like by scanning the beam across the input transparency.

The above scheme is of course limited to the case where $h(\alpha, \beta)$ is everywhere nonnegative. However, it can easily be modified to handle the more general case where $h(\alpha, \beta)$ can be negative as well as positive. For example, we can superimpose two light beams orthogonally polarized with respect to each other, the first one having an aperture function

$$h_1(\alpha, \beta) = \begin{cases} h(\alpha, \beta), & \text{when } h(\alpha, \beta) \geq 0 \\ 0, & \text{elsewhere} \end{cases} \tag{118a}$$

and the second one having an aperture function

$$h_2(\alpha, \beta) = \begin{cases} |h(\alpha, \beta)|, & \text{when } h(\alpha, \beta) < 0 \\ 0, & \text{elsewhere.} \end{cases} \tag{118b}$$

After the two beams have passed through the input transparency $f(\alpha, \beta)$ they can be picked up by two separate phototubes by using a beam splitter and two polarizers. The difference between the outputs of the two phototubes is the desired output $g(x, y)$.

Since noncoherent light can be used in this scheme we do not have the speckle and other noise problems associated with the case of the coherent light, where every little speck of dirt counts. The speed of this scheme is limited by the scanning speed.

A scanner along the lines discussed previously has been constructed by Shack [192], [213]. The same idea was used by Schreiber [188] in sharpening wire-photo pictures. Schreiber has also built a digital image recording-display CRT scanner which can be used to do some linear filtering. An example of using this scanner to do high-pass filtering on an X-ray picture is shown in Fig. 18. The reader will also be interested in the work of Craig [54] and Burnham [49].

B. Linear Filtering and Correlation by Image Tubes

Hawkins [95], [94] used a modified image storage tube to do linear filtering. The input light image $f(x, y)$ is first converted to an electron image, then by controlling the electric circuits associated with the tube, this image is deflected, amplified (or attenuated), and stored electrostatically on a mesh as $h_{ij}f(x-\alpha_i, y-\beta_j)$, where α_i, β_j, and h_{ij} are constants which can be either positive and negative. By superimposing many such images on the mesh, one can store

$$g_1(x, y) = \sum_{i,j} h_{ij}f(x - \alpha_j, y - \beta_j). \tag{119}$$

By choosing appropriate h_{ij}, α_j, and β_j, one can approximate $g(x, y)$, the desired output by $g_1(x, y)$ of (119). This image $g_1(x, y)$, which has been stored on the mesh, can be either converted to a proportional light image, or quantized electrically to yield a two-level display. The resolution of the tube is around 10 to 20 cycles (line pairs)/mm, and the total number of points is around 4×10^5. A typical filtering operation takes a few milliseconds.

A slightly different type of image tube is available from ITT [118], [119] which can perform cross correlation between two consecutive input images. The first image f_1 is again stored electrostatically on a mesh. The operating potentials of the tube are then shifted electronically so that the photoelectrons from the photocathode, generated by the second input optical image f_2, no longer strike the mesh but are allowed to partially penetrate or reflect from the mesh holes, depending on the stored charge pattern. The electron image passing through the mesh is then $f_1(\alpha, \beta)f_2(\alpha+x, \beta+y)$, where x and y are constants depending on the amount of deflection of the second image with respect to the first one. This electron image is integrated by an electron multiplier to give

$$R_{12}(x, y) = \int_{-\infty}^{\infty}\!\!\int f_1(\alpha, \beta)f_2(\alpha + x, \beta + y)d\alpha d\beta \tag{120}$$

which is the cross-correlation function between f_1 and f_2.

A different approach was taken by Abram *et al.* [24]. They modified an image dissector tube by replacing the conventional signal aperture by a 3×3 array of channeltron electron multipliers.

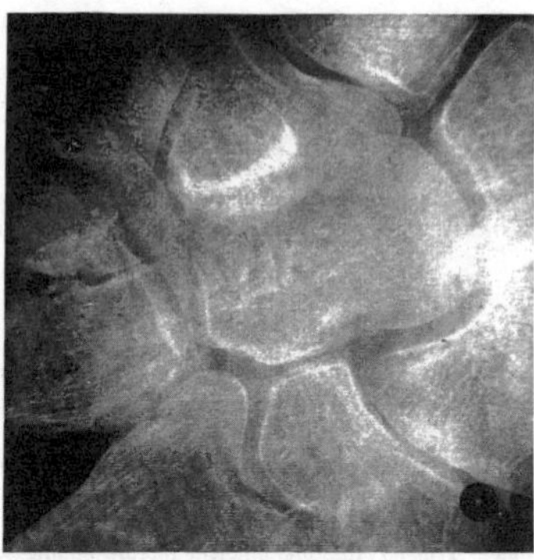

(a)

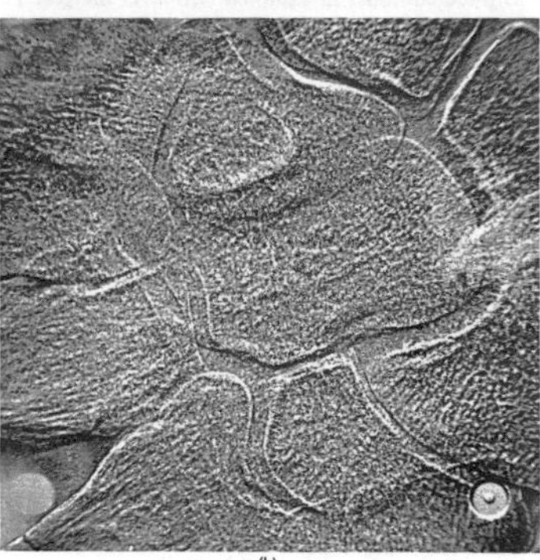

(b)

Fig. 18.   X-ray picture. (a) Original. (b) High-pass filtered.

One then has access to nine points on the input image simultaneously and can operate on them electrically in parallel. In particular, we can take a weighted sum of the points to approximate linear filtering. Of course, for a good approximation, we need more points, i.e., a larger array of channeltron electron multipliers.

VII. Image Description

In order to process an image on a digital computer, we have first to describe the image to the computer. In most cases, we feed the image into the computer in the form of a matrix, each element of which represents the brightness of an image sample point. This form of representation is quite appropriate for image enhancement work, since there we manipulate with a group of input sample values (e.g., doing linear filtering) to produce an output sample value. However, in pattern recognition and efficient picture coding, the matrix representation of an image is rather unnatural. Indeed, the goal of both pattern recognition and efficient picture coding is to find suitable ways of describing images. In pattern recognition, we want the description to be such that classification will be simplified. In the efficient coding of pictures, we want on the one hand to have a description of the image that is efficient and on the other hand to be able to reconstruct a good replica of the original image from the description.

The various methods of feature extraction in pattern recognition and the several schemes of redundancy reduction in Section III can all be considered as ad hoc attempts of finding suitable ways of describing images. A fruitful direction of a unified study of image description seems to lie in the linguistic approach [19], [132], [100], [156], [82], [83], [130]. In this approach, we consider our images as generated from a set of basic elements according to a certain grammar. Although, up to the present, the linguistic approach has been applied successfully only to simple classes of images, such as line drawings, we have already seen its practical application to pattern recognition problems [60], [160], [141], [88].

We will not go into a detailed discussion of the linguistic approach to image description here. Rather, we would just like to mention in passing that one way of describing a continuous-tone image is to first decompose it into three components—edges, low-frequency part, and texture, as we proposed in Section III-D 5) and then use the linguistic approach to describe the edges and possibly Fourier spectra to describe the low-frequency part and the texture.

VIII. IMAGE QUALITY

The effects of various parameters on picture quality have been discussed by Schreiber [187b]. In most applications, picture quality is defined in subjective terms, and can only be measured in terms of observer response [168]. There is no good reason to suppose that subjective quality is a one-dimensional quantity, and if it is multi-dimensional, it cannot be ranked. In practice, it is treated as a scalar, and is defined in terms of the protocol used to measure it. It is usually specified in terms of a four-to-six step scale running from "excellent" to "unacceptable." A more attractive scale is graded in just-noticeable difference in image quality, so that subjective measurement of relevant system parameters is quite a difficult and tedious procedure. Measurement of subjective image quality is very difficult: one can see this by reflecting on the fact that a 30-percent increase in bandwidth produces a just-noticeable difference increment in appearance [32].

The practical problems in the measurement of subjective quality and the desire to design systems analytically brought forth several objective measures of subjective image quality. The most popular measures proposed to date are the mean-square error and its variants, such as the weighted mean-square error. These measures have the distinct advantage that they are mathematically tractable. They also appear to agree reasonably well with subjective evaluation in many cases.

A. Mean-Square Error Criteria

Let $f(x, y)$ be the input image, and $g(x, y)$ the output image where (x, y) are the spatial coordinates and f and g are brightness. We define the error as

$$\varepsilon(x, y) = f(x, y) - g(x, y) \tag{121}$$

and denote its Fourier transform by $E(u, v)$ where (u, v) are spatial frequencies. Then the mean-square error is

$$D_1(f, g) = \int_{-\infty}^{\infty} \int dx dy \varepsilon^2(x, y) = \int_{-\infty}^{\infty} \int du dv |E(u, v)|^2 \tag{122}$$

and the weighted mean-square error

$$D_2(f, g) = \int_{-\infty}^{\infty} \int du dv W(u, v) |E(u, v)|^2 \tag{123}$$

where $W(u, v)$ is called the weighting function. The weighting function reflects the sensitivity of the eye to various spatial frequency components in the image.

The mean-square error criteria have at least two defects. First, the subjective quality of a degraded image $g(x, y)$ depends not only on the error $\varepsilon(x, y)$ but also on the original image $f(x, y)$. Second, some image degradations are geometrical in nature—for example, block quantization using Hadamard transform (Section III-E) sometimes yields pictures containing "staircases" along the edges. The mean-square error criteria do not seem appropriate for geometrical distortions. A more satisfactory criterion should be based on some kind of edge error.

B. A Proposed Distortion Measure

We propose the distortion measure

$$D(f, g) = AD_a(f, g) + BD_b(f, g) \tag{124}$$

where A and B are positive constants, D_a is a weighted mean-square error modified to take care of the dependence on the original image, and D_b is a measure of edge error. One possible choice for D_a is

$$D_a(f, g) = \int_{-\infty}^{\infty} \int du dv |E(u, v)|^2 W_1(u, v) W_2(u, v) \tag{125}$$

where W_1 reflects the eye sensitivity, and W_2 reflects the dependence on the original image (and is a function of f). Much experimentation needs to be done to determine suitable forms for D_b and W_2.

IX. CONCLUDING REMARKS

We have discussed in this paper some of the common problems underlying the three major areas of image processing, viz., image enhancement, efficient picture coding, and pattern recognition (with emphasis on the first two areas). In particular, we have described in some detail the mathematical operations we are most likely to encounter in image processing and ways of implementing these operations by optics and on digital computers. We have also sketched very briefly the problems of image description and image quality evaluation. These two latter topics are probably the most important among all image processing problems. The brevity of our description of them reflects the fact that much more work needs to be done.

BIBLIOGRAPHY

[1] H. Andrews, *Computer Techniques in Image Processing*. New York: Academic Press, 1970.
[2] *Appl Opt. (Special Issue on Optical Processing of Information)*, Apr. 1965.
[3] G. Cheng *et al.*, Eds., *Pictorial Pattern Recognition*. Washington, D. C.: Thompson, 1968.
[4] M. Faimen *et al.*, Eds., *Pertinent Concepts in Computer Graphics*. Urban, Ill.: Univ. Illinois Press, 1969.
[5] G. L. Fisher *et al.*, Eds., *Optical Character Recognition*. Washington, D. C.: Spartan, 1962.
[6] A. Grasselli, Ed., *Automatic Interpretation and Classification of Images*. New York: Academic Press, 1969.
[7] T. S. Huang and O. J. Tretiak, Eds., *Picture Bandwidth Compression*. New York: Gordon & Breach, to be published in 1971.
[8] *Proc. IEEE (Special Issue on Redundancy Reduction)*, vol. 55, Mar. 1967.
[9] L. N. Kanal, Ed., *Pattern Recognition*. Washington, D. C.: Thompson, 1968.
[10] P. A. Kolers and M. Eden, Eds., *Recognizing Patterns*. Cambridge, Mass.: M.I.T. Press, 1968.
[11] B. Lipkin and A. Rosenfeld, Eds., *Picture Processing and Psychopictorics*. New York: Academic Press, 1970.
[12] S. Morgan, Ed., "Restoration of atmospherically-degraded images," NSF Summer Study Rep., Woods Hole, Mass., 1966.
[13] M. Nagel, Ed., "Evaluation of motion-degraded images," in *Proc. NASA/ERC Seminar* (Cambridge, Mass., Dec. 1968).
[14] G. Nagy, "State of the art in pattern recognition," *Proc. IEEE*, vol. 56, May 1968, pp. 836–862.
[15] N. Y. Acad. Sci., *Proc. Conf. Data Extraction and Processing of Optical Images in the Medical and Biological Sciences* (New York, June 1967).
[16] *Pattern Recognition J. (Special Issue on Image Enhancement)*, May 1970.

[17] a) *Pattern Recognition J.* (*Special Issue on Character Recognition*), Aug. 1970.
b) *Pattern Recognition J.* (*Special Issue on Feature Extraction*), Apr. 1971.
[18] D. K. Pollock *et al.*, Eds., *Optical Processing of Information.* Washington, D. C.: Spartan, 1963.
[19] A. Rosenfeld, *Picture Processing by Computer.* New York: Academic Press, 1969.
[20] *Proc. SPIE Seminar on Filmed Data and Computers* (Boston, Mass., June 1966).
[21] *Proc. SPIE Seminar on Computerized Imaging Techniques* (Washington, D. C., June 1967).
[22] J. T. Tippett *et al.*, Eds., *Optical and Electro-Optical Information Processing.* Cambridge, Mass.: M.I.T. Press, 1965.
[23] J. Tou, Ed., *Advances in Information Systems Science*, vol. 3. New York: Plenum, 1970.

REFERENCES

[24] J. M. Abram, C. E. Catchpole, and G. W. Goodrich, "Image processing with a multiaperture image dissector," *SPIE J.*, vol. 6, 1968, pp. 93–96.
[25] N. G. Altman, "Use of electro-optical image correlation for measuring and providing compensation for image motion," *op. cit.* [13].
[26] G. B. Anderson and T. S. Huang, "Picture bandwidth compression by piecewise Fourier transformation," in *Proc. Purdue Centennial Symp. Information Processing* (Purdue Univ., Lafayette, Ind., Apr. 1969); also (revised version), "Piecewise Fourier transformation for picture bandwidth compression," *IEEE Trans. Commun. Technol.*, vol. COM-19, Apr. 1971, pp. 133–140.
[27] H. C. Andrews, "Bibliography on rate distortion theory," *IEEE Trans. Inform. Theory* (Corresp.), vol. IT-17, Mar. 1971, pp. 198–199.
[28] H. G. Ansell, "On certain two-variable generalizations of circuit theory, with applications to networks of transmission lines and lumped reactances," *IEEE Trans. Circuit Theory*, vol. CT-11, June 1964, pp. 214–223.
[29] M. Arm, M. King, A. Aimette, and B. Lambert, *Proc. Symp. Modern Optics.* Brooklyn, N. Y.: Polytechnic Press, 1967.
[30] A. E. Attard and D. E. Brown, "Photoelectroplating light modulator," *Appl. Opt.*, vol. 7, Mar. 1968, pp. 511–515.
[31] T. Baer, "Picture coding using the medial axis transform," S.M. thesis, Dep. Elec. Eng., Mass. Inst. Tech., Cambridge, May 1969.
[32] M. W. Baldwin, Jr., "The subjective sharpness of simulated television images," *Bell Syst. Tech. J.*, vol. 19, Oct. 1940, pp. 563–568.
[33] R. Barakat, "Numerical results concerning the transfer functions and total illuminance for optimum balances 5th-order spherical aberration," *J. Opt. Soc. Amer.*, vol. 54, Jan. 1964, pp. 38–44.
[34] C. W. Barnes, "Object restoration in a diffraction-limited imaging system," *J. Opt. Soc. Amer.*, vol. 56, May 1966, pp. 575–578.
[35] M. A. Berkovitz, "Edge gradient analysis OTF accuracy study," in *Proc. SPIE Seminar on Modulation Transfer Function* (Boston, Mass., Mar. 1968).
[36] F. C. Billingsley, "Applications of digital image processing," *Appl. Opt.*, vol. 9, Feb. 1970, pp. 289–299.
[37] R. B. Blackman, *Linear Data-Smoothing and Prediction in Theory and Practice.* Reading, Mass.: Addison-Wesley, 1965.
[38] E. S. Blackman, "Effects of noise on the determination of photographic system modulation transfer function," *Photogr. Sci. Eng.*, vol. 12, Sept.–Oct. 1968, pp. 244–250.
[39] ——, "Recovery of system transfer functions from noisy photographic records," in *Proc. SPIE Seminar on Image Information Recovery* (Philadelphia, Pa., 1969).
[40] A. G. Bose, "A theory of nonlinear systems," MIT/RLE, Tech. Rep. 309, May 1956.
[41] R. N. Bracewell, *The Fourier Transform and its Applications.* New York: McGraw-Hill, 1965.
[42] C. P. C. Bray, "Comparative analysis of geometric vs diffraction heterochromatic lens evaluations using optical transfer function theory," *J. Opt. Soc. Amer.*, vol. 55, Sept. 1965, pp. 1136–1138.
[43] G. C. Brock, *Physical Aspects of Aerial Photography.* New York: Dover, 1967.
[44] K. Bromley, M. A. Monahan, J. F. Bryant, and B. J. Thompson, "Holographic subtraction," *Appl. Opt.*, vol. 10, Jan. 1971, pp. 174–180.
[45] B. R. Brown and A. W. Lohmann, "Complex spatial filter with binary mask," *Appl. Opt.*, vol. 4, 1966, p. 967.
[46] E. B. Brown, "Prediction and compensation of linear image motions in aerial cameras," *op. cit.* [13].
[47] O. Bryngdahl and A. Lohmann, "Holographic penetration of turbulence," *op cit.* [13].
[48] G. J. Buck and J. J. Gustincic, "Resolution limitations of a finite aperture," *IEEE Trans. Antennas Propagat.*, vol. AP-15, May 1967, pp. 376–381.
[49] D. C. Burnham, "Electronic averaging of one-dimensional television pictures," *Appl. Opt.*, vol. 9, Nov. 1970, pp. 2565–2568.
[50] C. S. Burrus and T. W. Parks, "Time domain design of recursive digital filters," *IEEE Trans. Audio Electroacoust.*, vol. AU-18, June 1970, pp. 137–141.
[51] J. C. Cassidy, "Magneto-optically generated inputs in optical data processing," *J. Opt. Soc. Amer.*, vol. 61, Mar. 1971, pp. 378–385.
[52] a) D. A. Chesler, "Resolution enhancement by variable filtering," Phys. Res. Lab., Massachusetts General Hospital, Boston, Internal Rep., Jan. 1969.
b) P. S. Considine, R. H. Dumais, and R. A. Profio, "Interactive optical enhancement devices," presented at the SPIE Seminar on Recent Advances in the Evaluation of the Photographic Image, Boston, Mass., July 1971.
[53] J. W. Cooley and J. W. Tukey, "An algorithm for the machine calculation of complex Fourier series," *Math. Comput.*, vol. 19, 1965, pp. 297–301.
[54] D. R. Craig, in *Proc. SPIE Seminar on Image Enhancement* (St. Louis, Mo., Mar. 1963).
[55] L. J. Cutrona, "Recent developments in coherent optical technology," *op. cit.* [22].
[56] L. J. Cutrona, E. N. Leith, C. J. Palermo, and L. J. Porcello, "Optical data processing and filtering systems," *IRE Trans. Inform. Theory*, vol. IT-6, June 1960, pp. 386–400.
[57] L. D. Davisson, "Data compression: Theory and application," in *Proc. Kelly Communications Conf.* (Univ. Missouri, Rolla, Oct. 1970).
[58] D. J. De Rosier and A. Klug, "Reconstruction of three-dimensional structures from electron micrographs," *Nature*, vol. 217, Jan. 13, 1968, pp. 130–134.
[59] G. P. Dinneen, "Programming pattern recognition" in *1955 Proc. Western Joint Computer Conf.* (Los Angeles, Calif.), vol. 7, pp. 91–100.
[60] M. Eden, "Handwriting generation and recognition," *IRE Trans. Inform. Theory*, vol. IT-8, Feb. 1962, pp. 160–166.
[61] D. G. Falconer, "Image enhancement and film-grain noise," *Opt. Acta*, vol. 17, Sept. 1970, pp. 693–705.
[62] A. E. Filip, "Estimation of the impulse response of image-degrading systems," MIT/RLE Quart. Progr. Rep. 99, Oct. 15, 1970, pp. 135–140.
[63] C. Flammer, *Spheroidal Wave Functions.* Stanford, Calif.: Stanford Univ. Press, 1957.
[64] D. L. Fried, "Optical resolution through a randomly inhomogeneous medium for very long and very short exposures," *J. Opt. Soc. Amer.*, vol. 56, Oct. 1966, pp. 1372–1379.
[65] ——, "Limiting resolution looking down through the atmosphere," *J. Opt. Soc. Amer.*, vol. 56, Oct. 1966, pp. 1380–1384.
[66] B. R. Frieden, "Bandlimited reconstruction of optical objects and spectra," *J. Opt. Soc. Amer.*, vol. 57, Aug. 1967, pp. 1013–1019.
[67] ——, "Optimum nonlinear processing of noisy images," *J. Opt. Soc. Amer.*, vol. 58, Sept. 1968.
[68] H. Frieser, *Photogr. Sci. Eng.*, vol. 4, 1960, p. 324.
[69] B. Gold, I. L. Lebow, P. G. McHugh, and C. M. Rader, "The FDP, a fast programmable signal processor," *IEEE Trans. Comput.*, vol. C-20, Jan. 1971, pp. 33–38.
[70] B. Gold and C. M. Rader, *Digital Processing of Signals.* New York: McGraw-Hill, 1969.
[71] I. J. Good, *J. Roy. Statist. Soc.*, vol. B20, 1958, pp. 361–372; also, Addendum, vol. B22, 1960, pp. 372–375.
[72] ——, "The relationship between two fast Fourier transforms," *IEEE Trans. Comput.* (Short Notes), vol. C-20, Mar. 1971, pp. 310–317.
[73] J. W. Goodman, "Use of a large-aperture optical system as a triple interferometer for removal of atmospheric image degradations," *op. cit.* [13].
[74] ——, *Introduction to Fourier Optics.* New York: McGraw-Hill, 1968.
[75] J. W. Goodman, D. W. Jackson, M. Lehmann, and J. W. Knotts, "Holographic imagery through atmospheric inhomogeneities," *op. cit.* [13].
[76] J. W. Goodman and W. T. Rhodes, "An optical system designed for image processing," *op. cit.* [16].
[77] D. N. Graham, "Image transmission by two-dimensional contour coding," *Proc. IEEE*, vol. 55, Mar. 1967, pp. 336–346.
[78] R. E. Graham, "Snow removal—A noise-stripping process for picture signals," *IRE Trans. Inform. Theory*, vol. IT-8, Feb. 1962, pp. 129–144.
[79] E. M. Granger, "Restoration of images degraded by spatially-varying smear," *op. cit.* [13].
[80] R. L. Green, "Diffraction in lensless correlation," *Appl. Opt.*, vol. 7, 1968, pp. 1237–1239.
[81] R. L. Gregory, "A technique for minimizing the effects of atmospheric disturbance on photographic telescopes," *Nature*, vol. 203, July 18, 1964, pp. 274–275.
[82] U. Grenander, "Foundations of pattern analysis," *Quart. Appl. Math.*, vol. 27, Apr. 1969, pp. 1–55.
[83] ——, "A unified theory of patterns," in *Advances in Computers.* New York: Academic Press, 1969.
[84] E. A. Guillemin, *Synthesis of Passive Networks.* New York: Wiley, 1957.
[85] A. Habibi and P. A. Wintz, "Image coding by linear transformations and block quantization," *IEEE Trans. Commun. Technol.*, vol. COM-19, Feb. 1971, pp. 50–62.

[86] H. J. Hall and H. K. Howell, Eds., *Photographic Considerations for Aerospace.* Lexington, Mass.: Itek Corp., 1965.

[87] H. B. Hammill and C. Holladay, "The effects of certain approximations in image quality evaluation from edge traces," *SPIE J.*, vol. 8, Aug.–Sept. 1970, pp. 223–228.

[88] W. J. Hankley and J. T. Tou, "Automatic fingerprint interpretation and classification via contextual analysis and topological coding," *op. cit.* [3].

[89] J. Harris, "Restoration of atmospherically distorted images," Scripps Inst. Oceanography, Univ. California, San Diego, SIO Ref. 63-10, Mar. 1963.

[90] J. L. Harris, "Diffraction and resolving power," *J. Opt. Soc. Amer.*, vol. 54, July 1964, pp. 931–936.

[91] ——, "Image evaluation and restoration," *J. Opt. Soc. Amer.*, vol. 56, May 1966, pp. 569–574.

[92] ——, "Potential and limitations of techniques for processing linear motion-degraded imagery," *op. cit.* [13].

[93] ——, "Information extraction from diffraction limited imagery," *Pattern Recognition J.*, vol. 2, May 1970, pp. 69–77.

[94] J. K. Hawkins, "Parallel electro-optical picture processing," *op. cit.* [3].

[95] J. K. Hawkins and C. J. Munsey, "Image processing by electron-optical techniques," *J. Opt. Soc. Amer.*, vol. 57, July 1967, pp. 914–918.

[96] R. A. Heinz, J. O. Artman, and S. H. Lee, "Matrix multiplication by optical methods," *Appl. Opt.*, vol. 9, Sept. 1970, pp. 2161–2168.

[97] C. W. Helstrom, "Image restoration by the method of least squares," *J. Opt. Soc. Amer.*, vol. 57, Mar. 1967, pp. 297–303.

[98] L. O. Hendeberg and W. E. Welander, "Experimental transfer characteristics of image motion and air conditions in aerial photography," *Appl. Opt.*, vol. 2, 1963, pp. 379–386.

[99] S. Herman, *Proc. Symp. Modern Optics.* Brooklyn, N. Y.: Polytechnic Press, 1967.

[100] Y. C. Ho and A. K. Agrawala, "On pattern classification algorithms: Introduction and survey," *Proc. IEEE*, vol. 56, Dec. 1968, pp. 2101–2114.

[101] H. H. Hopkins, "The frequency response of a defocused optical system," *Proc. Roy. Soc., Ser. A*, vol. 231, 1955, pp. 91–103.

[102] ——, "Interferometric methods for the study of diffraction images," *Opt. Acta*, vol. 2, Apr. 1955, pp. 23–29.

[103] J. L. Horner, "Optical spatial filtering with the least mean-square-error filter," *J. Opt. Soc. Amer.*, vol. 59, May 1969, pp. 553–558.

[104] ——, "Optical restoration of images blurred by atmospheric turbulence using optimum filter theory," *Appl. Opt.*, vol. 9, Jan. 1970, pp. 167–171.

[105] J. J. Y. Huang and P. M. Schultheiss, "Block quantization of correlated Gaussian random variables," *IEEE Trans. Commun. Syst.*, vol. CS-11, Sept. 1963, pp. 289–296.

[106] T. S. Huang, "Some notes on film grain noise," *op. cit.* [12].

[107] ——, "Digital analysis of linear shift-variant systems," *op. cit.* [13].

[108] ——, "Coding of graphical data," EG&G Tech. Rep. B-3742, Mar. 1968.

[109] ——, "Two-dimensional windows," M.I.T. Lincoln Lab. Tech. Note 1970-41, Dec. 31, 1970.

[110] ——, "How the fast Fourier transform got its name," *Comput.*, May 1971.

[111] ——, "Stability of two-dimensional recursive filters," M.I.T. Lincoln Lab. Tech. Note 1971-20, May 19, 1971.

[112] T. S. Huang and O. J. Tretiak, "Research in picture processing," *op. cit.* [22].

[113] ——, "A pseudorandom multiplex system for facsimile transmission," *IEEE Trans. Commun. Technol.*, vol. COM-16, June 1968, pp. 436–438.

[114] T. S. Huang and J. W. Woods, "Picture bandwidth compression by block quantization," presented at the Int. Symp. Information Theory, Ellenville, N. Y., Jan. 1969; abstract in *IEEE Trans. Inform. Theory*, vol. IT-16, Jan. 1970, p. 119.

[115] D. A. Huffman, "A method for the construction of minimum-redundancy codes," *Proc. IRE*, vol. 40, Sept. 1952, pp. 1098–1101.

[116] R. E. Hufnagel, "An improved model turbulent atmosphere," *op. cit.* [12, vol. 2].

[117] R. E. Hufnagel and N. R. Stanley, "Modulation transfer function associated with image transmission through turbulent media," *J. Opt. Soc. Amer.*, vol. 54, Jan. 1964, pp. 52–61.

[118] ITT Industrial Laboratories, "Pattern recognition image tubes," Application Note E13, Feb. 1967.

[119] ——, "Seesaw image correlation tubes," *News Lett.*, June 1967.

[120] P. A. Jansson, "Method for determining the response function of a high-resolution infrared spectrometer," *J. Opt. Soc. Amer.*, vol. 60, Feb. 1970, pp. 184–191.

[121] P. A. Jansson, R. H. Hunt, and E. K. Plyler, "Response function for spectral resolution enhancement," *J. Opt. Soc. Amer.*, vol. 58, Dec. 1968, pp. 1665–1666.

[122] ——, "Resolution enhancement of spectra," *J. Opt. Soc. Amer.*, vol. 60, May 1970, pp. 596–599.

[123] N. Jensen *Optical and Photographic Reconnaissance Systems.* New York: Wiley, 1968.

[124] E. G. Johnston and A. Rosenfeld, "Geometrical operations on digitized pictures," *op. cit.* [11].

[125] R. A. Jones, "An automated technique for deriving MTF's from edge traces," *Photogr. Sci. Engr.*, vol. 11, Mar.–Apr. 1967, pp. 102–106.

[126] ——, "Accuracy test procedure for image evaluation techniques," *Appl. Opt.*, vol. 7, Jan. 1968, pp. 133–136.

[127] R. A. Jones and E. C. Yeadon, "Determination of the spread function from noisy edge scans," *Photogr. Sci. Engr.*, vol. 13, July–Aug. 1969, pp. 200–204.

[128] R. J. Jones, "V/h sensor theory and performance," *op. cit.* [13].

[129] J. F. Kaiser, "Digital filters," in *System Analysis by Digital Computer*, F. F. Kuo and J. F. Kaiser, Eds. New York: Wiley, 1966, ch. 7.

[130] S. Kaneff, Ed., *Picture Language Machine.* New York: Academic Press, 1970.

[131] R. S. Kennedy, "On statistical estimation of incoherently illuminated objects," *op. cit.* [12, vol. 2].

[132] R. A. Kirsch, "Computer interpretation of English text and picture patterns," *IEEE Trans. Electron. Comput.*, vol. EC-13, Aug. 1964, pp. 363–376.

[133] A. N. Kolmogorov, "On the Shannon theory of information transmission in the case of continuous signals," *IRE Trans. Inform. Theory*, vol. IT-2, Dec. 1956, pp. 102–108.

[134] V. A. Kovalvsky, "Pattern recognition: Heuristics or science?" *op. cit.* [23].

[135] A. Kozma and N. Massay, *1964 Annual Radar Symp.* (Inst. Sci. Technol., Univ. Michigan, Ann Arbor).

[136] H. P. Kramer and M. W. Mathews, "A linear coding for transmitting a set of correlated signals," *IRE Trans. Inform. Theory*, vol. IT-2, Sept. 1956, pp. 41–46.

[137] C. Lanczos, *Linear Differential Operators.* Princeton, N. J.: Van Nostrand, 1961, pp. 115–118.

[138] H. J. Landau and H. O. Pollak, "Prolate spheroidal wave functions, Fourier analysis, and uncertainty—II," *Bell Syst. Tech. J.*, vol. 40, 1961, pp. 65–84.

[139] ——, "Prolate spheroidal wave functions, Fourier analysis and uncertainty—IV: The dimension of the space of essentially time- and band-limited signals," *Bell Syst. Tech. J.*, July 1962.

[140] H. J. Landau and D. Slepian, "Some computer experiments in picture processing for bandwidth reduction," *Bell Syst. Tech. J.*, 1970.

[141] R. S. Ledley, L. S. Rotolo, J. B. Wilson, M. Belson, T. J. Golab, and J. Jacobsen, "Pattern recognition studies in the biomedical sciences," in *1966 Spring Joint Computer Conf., AFIPS Conf. Proc.* (Boston, Mass.).

[142] W. H. Lee, "Computer generation of holograms and spatial filters," Sc.D. dissertation, Dep. Elec. Eng., Mass. Inst. Tech., Cambridge, Sept. 1969.

[143] ——, "Sampled Fourier transform hologram generated by computer," *Appl. Opt.*, vol. 9, Mar. 1970, pp. 639–643.

[144] ——, "Filter design for optical data processors," *op. cit.* [16].

[145] L. Levi, "Motion blurring with decaying defector response," *Appl. Opt.*, vol. 10, Jan. 1971, pp. 38–41.

[146] M. D. Levine, "Feature extraction: A survey," *Proc. IEEE*, vol. 57, Aug. 1969, pp. 1391–1407.

[147] A. Lohmann, "Aktive Kontrastübertragungstheorie," *Opt. Acta*, vol. 6, Oct. 1959, pp. 319–338.

[148] A. W. Lohmann and D. P. Paris, "Space-variant image formation," *J. Opt. Soc. Amer.*, vol. 55, Aug. 1965, pp. 1007–1013.

[149] ——, "Frannhofer hologram generated by computer," *Appl. Opt.*, vol. 6, 1968, p. 1739.

[150] R. F. Lutomirski and H. T. Yura, "Modulation-transfer function and phase-structure function of an optical wave in a turbulent medium—I," *J. Opt. Soc. Amer.*, vol. 59, Aug. 1969, pp. 999–1000.

[151] D. P. MacAdam, "Digital image restoration by constrained deconvolution," *J. Opt. Soc. Amer.*, vol. 60, Dec. 1970, pp. 1617–1627.

[152] A. S. Marathay, "Realization of complex spatial filters with polarized light," *J. Opt. Soc. Amer.*, vol. 59, June 1969, pp. 748–752.

[153] S. J. Mason and J. K. Clemens, "Character recognition in an experimental reading machine for the blind," *op. cit.* [10].

[154] M. J. Mazurowski and R. E. Kinzly, "The precision of edge analysis applied to the evaluation of motion-degraded images," *op. cit.* [13].

[155] W. Meyer-Eppler and G. Darius, *Proc. 3rd London Symp. Information Theory*, C. Cherry, Ed. New York: Academic Press, 1956.

[156] W. F. Miller and A. C. Shaw, "Linguistic methods in picture processing—A survey," in *1968 Fall Joint Computer Conf., AFIPS Conf. Proc.*, pp. 279–290.

[157] J. Minkoff, W. R. Bennett, L. B. Lambert, M. Arm, and S. Berstein, *Proc. Symp. Modern Optics.* Brooklyn, N. Y.: Polytechnic Press, 1967.

[158] L. Miyamoto, "Wave optics and geometrical optics in optical design," in *Progress in Optics*, vol. 1, E. Wolf, Ed. Amsterdam, The Netherlands: North-Holland, 1961.

[159] J. C. Moldon, "High resolution image estimation in a turbulent environment," *op. cit.* [16].

[160] R. Narasimhan, "Labelling schemata and syntactic description of pictures," *Inform. Contr.*, vol. 7, 1964.

[161] R. Nathan, "Picture enhancement for the moon, Mars, and man," *op. cit.* [3].

[162] B. M. Oliver, "Sparkling spots and random diffraction," *Proc. IEEE*

(Corresp.), vol. 51, Jan. 1963, pp. 220–221.

[163] B. M. Oliver, J. R. Pierce, and C. E. Shannon, "The philosophy of PCM," *Proc. IRE*, vol. 36, Nov. 1948, pp. 1324–1331.

[164] E. L. O'Neill, *Introduction to Statistical Optics.* Reading, Mass.: Addison-Wesley, 1963.

[165] A. V. Oppenheim, R. W. Schafer, and T. G. Stockham, Jr., "Nonlinear filtering of multiplied and convolved signals," *Proc. IEEE*, vol. 56, Aug. 1968, pp. 1264–1291.

[166] D. P. Paris, "Influence of image motion on the resolution of a photographic system—I," *Photogr. Sci. Eng.*, vol. 6, 1962, pp. 55–59.

[167] ——, "Influence of image motion on the resolution of a photographic system—II," *Photogr. Sci. Eng.*, vol. 7, 1963, pp. 233–236.

[168] D. E. Pearson, "Techniques for scaling television picture quality," *op. cit.* [7].

[169] D. P. Peterson and D. Middleton, "Sampling and reconstruction of wave-number-limited functions in n-dimensional Euclidean spaces," *Inform. Contr.*, vol. 5, 1962, pp. 279–323.

[170] S. M. Pizer and H. G. Vetter, "Processing quantum limited images," *op. cit.* [11].

[171] W. J. Popplebaum, "Adaptive on-line Fourier transform," *op. cit* [3].

[172] W. K. Pratt, J. Kane, and H. G. Andrews, "Hadamard transform image coding," *Proc. IEEE*, vol. 57, Jan. 1969, pp. 58–68.

[173] C. M. Rader, "An improved algorithm for high speed autocorrelation with applications to spectral estimation," *IEEE Trans. Audio Electroacoust.*, vol. AU-18, Oct. 1970, pp. 439–441.

[174] W. R. Crowther and C. M. Rader, "Efficient coding of vocoder channel signals using linear transformation," *Proc. IEEE* (Lett.), vol. 54, Nov. 1966, pp. 1594–1595.

[175] C. L. Rino, "Bandlimited image restoration by linear mean-square estimation," *J. Opt. Soc. Amer.*, vol. 59, May 1969, pp. 547–553.

[176] ——, "The application of prolate spheroidal wave functions to the detection and estimation of band-limited signals," *Proc. IEEE* (Lett.), vol. 58, Feb. 1970, pp. 248–249.

[177] G. M. Robbins, "Impulse response of a lens with Seidel aberrations," MIT/RLE Quart. Progr. Rep. 93, Apr. 5, 1969, pp. 243–250.

[178] ——, "The inversion of linear shift-variant imaging systems," Sc.D. dissertation, Dep. Elec. Eng., Mass. Inst. Tech., Cambridge, Aug. 1970.

[179] E. A. Robinson, *Statistical Communication and Detection.* New York: Hafner, 1967.

[180] P. G. Roetling, R. C. Haas, and R. E. Kinzly, "Some practical aspects of measurement and restoration of motion-degraded images," *op. cit.* [13].

[181] C. K. Rushforth and R. W. Harris, "Restoration resolution, and noise," *J. Opt. Soc. Amer.*, vol. 58, Apr. 1968, pp. 539–545.

[182] J. B. Rust, *Opt. Spectra*, vol. 2, 1968, p. 41.

[183] D. Sakrison, "The rate distortion function of a Gaussian process with a weighted square error criterion," *IEEE Trans. Inform. Theory*, vol. IT-14, May 1968, pp. 506–508.

[184] ——, "The rate distortion function for a class of sources," *Inform. Contr.*, vol. 15, Aug. 1969, pp. 165–195.

[185] ——, "Factors involved in applying rate-distortion theory to image transmission," in *Proc. Kelly Communications Conf.* (Univ. Missouri, Rolla, Oct. 1970).

[186] K. Sayanagi, *J. Appl. Phys.* (Japan), vol. 27, no. 10, 1958, pp. 623, 632.

[187] a) W. F. Schreiber, "The mathematical foundation of the synthetic highs system," MIT/RLE Quart. Progr. Rep. 68, Jan. 1963, p. 149.
b) ——, "Picture coding," *op. cit.* [8, pp. 320–330].

[188] ——, "Wirephoto quality improvement by unsharp masking," *op. cit.* [16].

[189] W. F. Schreiber, T. S. Huang, and O. J. Tretiak, "Contour coding of images," *WESCON Conv. Rec.*, Aug. 1968.

[190] R. M. Scott, *Photogr. Sci. Eng.*, vol. 3, 1959, p. 201.

[191] R. V. Shack, "The influence of image motion and shutter operation on the photographic transfer function," *Appl. Opt.*, vol. 3, Oct. 1964, pp. 1171–1181.

[192] ——, "Image processing by an optical analog device," *op. cit.* [16].

[193] J. L. Shanks, "Recursion filters for digital processing," *Geophys.*, vol. 33, Feb. 1967, pp. 33–51.

[194] ——, "Two-dimensional recursive filters," *SWIEECO Rec.*, 1969, pp. 19E1–19E8.

[195] ——, "The design of stable two-dimensional recursive filters," in *Proc. Kelly Communications Conf.* (Univ. Missouri, Rolla, Oct. 1970).

[196] C. E. Shannon and W. Weaver, *The Mathematical Theory of Communications.* Urbana, Ill.: Univ. Illinois Press, 1949.

[197] C. B. Shaw, "Improvement of the resolution of an instrument by numerical solution of an integral equation," Autonetics, Anaheim, Calif., Autonetics Rep. X70-510/501, Mar. 27, 1970.

[198] H. Sherman, "A quasi-topological method for the recognition of line patterns," in *Proc. Int. Conf. Information Processing* (Paris, UNESCO, June 1959), pp. 232–238.

[199] A. R. Shulman, *Optical Data Processing.* New York: Wiley, 1970.

[200] D. Slepian, "Prolate spheroidal wave functions, Fourier analysis, and uncertainty—IV: Extensions to many dimensions; generalized prolate spheroidal functions," *Bell Syst. Tech. J.*, Nov. 1964.

[201] ——, "Some asymptotic expansions for prolate spheroidal wave functions," *J. Math. Phys.*, vol. 44, June 1965, pp. 99–140.

[202] ——, "Linear least-squares filtering of distorted images," *J. Opt. Soc. Amer.*, vol. 57, July 1967, pp. 918–922.

[203] ——, "Restoration of photographs blurred by image motion," *Bell Syst. Tech. J.*, vol. 46, Dec. 1967, pp. 2353–2362.

[204] D. Slepian and H. O. Pollak, "Prolate spheroidal wave functions, Fourier analysis and uncertainty—I," *Bell Syst. Tech. J.*, vol. 40, 1961, pp. 43–46.

[205] D. Slepian and E. Sonnenblick, "Eigenvalues associated with prolate spheroidal wave functions of zero order," *Bell Syst. Tech. J.*, Oct. 1965.

[206] D. L. Slotnick, "The fastest computer," *Sci. Amer.*, vol. 224, Feb. 1971, pp. 76–87.

[207] a) H. A. Smith, "Improvement of the resolution of a linear scanning device," *SIAM J. Appl. Math.*, vol. 14, Jan. 1966, pp. 23–40.
b) S. C. Som, "Analysis of the effect of linear smear on photographic images," *J. Opt. Soc. Amer.*, vol. 61, July 1971, pp. 859–864.

[208] D. R. Spencer and T. S. Huang, "Bit-plane encoding of continuous-tone pictures," in *Proc. Symp. Computer Processing in Communications.* Brooklyn, N. Y.: Polytechnic Press, 1969.

[209] *Proc. SPIE Seminar on Modulation Transfer Function* (Boston, Mass., Mar. 1968).

[210] T. G. Stockham, Jr., in *1966 Spring Joint Computer Conf., AFIPS Conf. Proc.*, vol. 28.

[211] P. A. Stokseth, "Properties of a defocused optical system," *J. Opt. Soc. Amer.*, vol. 59, Oct. 1969, pp. 1314–1321.

[212] J. Stratton *et al.*, *Spheroidal Wave Functions.* Cambridge, Mass.: M.I.T. Press, 1956.

[213] W. Swindell, "A noncoherent optical analog image processor," *Appl. Opt.*, vol. 9, Nov. 1970, pp. 2459–2469.

[214] C. W. Swonger and F. Y. Chao, "Computing techniques for correction of blurred objects in photographs," *op. cit.* [13].

[215] M. Tasto and P. Wintz, "Adaptive block quantization," Dep. Elec. Eng., Purdue Univ., Lafayette, Ind., Rep. TR-EE 70-14, July 1970.

[216] G. Toraldo di Francia, "Degrees of freedom of an image," *J. Opt. Soc. Amer.*, vol. 59, July 1969, pp. 799–804.

[217] J. T. Tou, "Engineering principles of pattern recognition," in *Advances in Information Systems Science*, vol. 1, J. T. Tou, Ed. New York: Plenum, 1969.

[218] S. Treitel and J. L. Shanks, "The design of multistage separable planar filters," presented at the Arden House Workshop on Digital Filtering, Harriman, N. Y., Jan. 1970; also in *IEEE Trans. Geosci. Electron.*, vol. GE-9, Jan. 1971, pp. 10–27.

[219] O. J. Tretiak, "Approximating a matrix by a sum of products," MIT/RLE Quart. Progr. Rep. 98, July 1970.

[220] O. J. Tretiak, E. Eden, and W. Simon, "Internal structure from X-ray images," in *Proc. 8th ICMBE* (Chicago, Ill., July 1969).

[221] J. Tsujinchi, "Corrections of optical images by compensation of aberrations and by spatial frequency filtering," in *Progress in Optics*, vol. 2, E. Wold, Ed. Amsterdam, The Netherlands: North-Holland, 1963.

[222] A. Vander Lugt, "Signal detection by complex spatial filtering," *IEEE Trans. Inform. Theory*, vol. IT-10, Apr. 1964, pp. 139–145.

[223] S. Watanabe, "Feature compression," *op. cit.* [23].

[224] C. S. Weaver, S. D. Ramsy, J. W. K. Goodman, and A. M. Rosie, "The optical convolution of time functions," *Appl. Opt.*, vol. 9, July 1970, pp. 1672–1682.

[225] L. Weinberg, "Approximation and stability-test procedures suitable for digital filters," presented at the Arden House Workshop on Digital Filtering, Harriman, N. Y., Jan. 1970.

[226] L. C. Wilkins and P. A. Wintz, "Bibliography on data compression, picture properties, and picture coding," *IEEE Trans. Inform. Theory*, vol. IT-17, Mar. 1971, pp. 180–197.

[227] R. N. Wolfe, E. W. Marchand, and J. J. DePalma, "Determination of the MTF of photographic emulsions from physical measurements," *J. Opt. Soc. Amer.*, vol. 58, Sept. 1969, pp. 1245–1256.

[228] H. Wolter, in *Progress in Optics*, vol. 1, E. Wolf, Ed. Amsterdam, The Netherlands: North-Holland, 1961, pp. 156–210.

[229] J. W. Woods and T. S. Huang, "Picture bandwidth compression by linear transformation and block quantization," presented at the M.I.T. Symp. Picture Bandwidth Compression, Cambridge, Mass., Apr. 1969; also to appear in *op. cit.* [7].

[230] E. C. Yeadon, R. A. Jones, and J. T. Kelly, "Confidence limits for individual modulation transfer function measurements based upon the phase transfer function," *Photogr. Sci. Eng.*, vol. 14, Mar.–Apr. 1970, pp. 153–156.

Reprinted from the PROCEEDINGS OF THE IEEE
VOL. 59, NO. 11, NOVEMBER, 1971
pp. 1586-1609